TCP/IP Bible

TCP/IP Bible

Rob Scrimger, Paul LaSalle, Clay Leitzke,
Mridula Parihar, NITT, Meeta Gupta, NITT

WILEY

Wiley Publishing, Inc.

TCP/IP Bible

Published by
Wiley Publishing, Inc.
111 River Street
Hoboken, NJ 07030
www.wiley.com

Copyright ©2002 by Wiley Publishing, Inc.,
Indianapolis, Indiana

Published simultaneously in Canada

For general information on our other products and
services or to obtain technical support, please
contact our Customer Care Department within the
U.S. at 800-762-2974, outside the U.S. at 317-572-3993,
or fax 317-572-4002.

Wiley also publishes its books in a variety of
electronic formats. Some content that appears in
print may not be available in electronic books.

***Library of Congress Cataloging-in-Publication
Data:***

Library of Congress Control Number: 2001092915
ISBN: 0-7645-4842-5

1B/RW/RQ/QR/IN

Credits

Acquisitions Editors
Katie Feltman
Nancy Maragioglio

Project Editor
Amanda Munz Peterson

Technical Editor
Tim Crothers

Copy Editor
Gabrielle Chosney

Editorial Manager
Ami Frank Sullivan

Senior Vice President, Technical Publishing
Richard Swadley

Vice President and Publisher
Mary Bednarek

Project Coordinator
Ryan Steffen

Graphics and Production Specialists
Amy Adrian
Barry Offringa
Jacque Schneider
Betty Schulte
Brian Torwelle
Jeremey Unger
Erin Zeltner

Quality Control Technicians
Laura Albert
John Greenough
Andy Hollandbeck
Carl Pierce
Marianne Santy

Illustrator
Kate Shaw

Proofreading and Indexing
TECHBOOKS Production Services

Cover Image
Kate Shaw

About the Authors

Rob Scrimger has worked as a computer operator, a programmer, a trainer, a network administrator, and a network manager for various companies. Rob has gained a solid understanding of the TCP/IP protocol and helped write several other TCP/IP books, including *Networking with Microsoft TCP/IP: Certified Administrator's Resource Edition* and *MCSE Training Guide: TCP/IP 2nd Edition*. Rob has three MCSEs to his credit: NT 3.5, NT 4.0, and Windows 2000 (Charter Member). In addition, he is an MCT, MCDBA, MCSE+I, MCP+SB, CTT, A+ Certified Technician, and Network + Certified.

Paul LaSalle is a Microsoft Certified Systems Engineer (MCSE) and president of Enchanted Forest Systems, a network consulting and training firm that runs out of Rockland, Ontario Canada. When Paul isn't writing, consulting, or training, he can be found enjoying his other passions, which include spending time with his family, woodworking, fishing, camping, gardening, and music. He can be reached at paul@efs.ca.

In her professional life, **Mridula Parihar** has seen both sides of the training coin with India's leading IT training and education company, NIIT Ltd. She has both taught and developed instructor-led material. Mridula is also a Microsoft Certified Solution Developer (MCSD). With her training background, she has experience conducting sessions on networking concepts and administrating local area networks.

Meeta Gupta has spent three years as a trainer with NIIT Ltd. She holds a Master's degree in Computer Engineering. Meeta is a qualified CNE. Her core competency is in the areas of networks and troubleshooting network problems.

Clay Leitzke is President and CEO of Northwest Computer Training in Coeur d' Alene, Idaho and spends most of his time teaching Windows 2000 Bootcamps around the country. His company has certified more than 2000 MCSEs. Clay is certified as an MCSE and MCT since NT 3.5 and specializes in Exchange. He also holds certifications in Cisco, CompTIA, and Novell. Clay can be contacted at www.nwcomputertraining.com.

As always, I would like to thank my family for supporting me and putting up with me during the writing process. I'd also like to thank WWOZ New Orleans for being on the Internet and for providing me with excellent accompaniment music to my typing. Keep up the good work. ~Rob Scrimger

For Karen, who taught me how to love and learn again, and my guys Ryan and Shawn, who in addition to being my inspiration, allowed me the space to work on this project for what must have seemed like forever. ~Paul LaSalle

This book is dedicated to my mother, who was a source of tremendous support and inspiration while I was writing this book. As always, she has been by my side. Without her, it would have been impossible for me to write this book. ~Mridula Parihar

This book is for my family. Thank you, Ma' and Daddy, for being there all the time and never complaining in spite of my long working hours. Vikas, my dear brother, I couldn't have continued this task without your sparkling sense of humor and brotherly support. ~Meeta

Many thanks to Ron Gilster and Diane McMichael for showing me the ropes, and to Katie Feltman for the opportunity to write this book. Thank you my three angels, Kayla, Lauren, and Mitchell, for giving me the reason to smile every day. ~Clay Leitzke

Preface

About the Book

Many books have been written about TCP/IP—how to implement it, how to secure it, and how to calculate subnet masks. However, the *TCP/IP Bible* provides one-shot coverage of all the important topics related to TCP/IP, starting with the TCP/IP model all the way through to how to *really* implement it. As much as possible, the material in the book has been kept generic so that the information can be used with Solaris, Linux, or even Windows 2000.

Treat this text as a starting point—a primer if you will—on the TCP/IP protocol. It is not the "everything book" for every platform—you won't need a forklift to bring it home. However, if you have already started to work with TCP/IP, this book will be an invaluable reference. It gives you the tools you need to explore more aspects of the TCP/IP protocol suite *and* serves as a starting point for setting up a Web server, implementing IPSEC, or choosing an enterprise directory system. As you continue to face new challenges, you can return to this text time and again.

How the Book is Organized

Essentially, there are four parts to successfully implementing TCP/IP. First and foremost, you need to understand the basics of how the protocols in the TCP/IP suite work, the processes and theory. Then you need to know how to actually work with TCP/IP, how to install it, how to configure it and how to find other computers. Once you have a TCP/IP network and the systems are running, you need to do something with it. This means that you need to set up servers that will provide functionality to the users that are part of the network. Once you have mastered the art and function of TCP/IP and have an understanding of what TCP/IP can do, you need to know how to plan a TCP/IP implementation. This book is broken down into four sections to reflect the four areas you need to master.

Part I—Understanding TCP/IP Communications

In Part I, the basics of the TCP/IP protocol are discussed: how the protocol stack works and what you can do with it. First, it provides an overview of the TCP/IP stack and then examines each of the layers in detail, starting with the Physical layer. From there, we will look at the other layers—Network Interface, Internet, Transport, and Application—as we move up the stack. This information may seem somewhat esoteric; however, understanding the function of the layers and how they interact is the key to troubleshooting thorny issues.

Part II — Working with TCP/IP

In this part, we start by looking at installing and configuring TCP/IP. We then examine the topics of naming and name resolution. Because names are easier to remember than numbers — after all, we don't normally memorize IP addresses, either on the Internet or within an Intranet — you need a method to ensure that users will be able to find and connect to other systems on the network. This is where naming becomes important. Understanding naming and name resolution will also help you troubleshoot problems with connectivity.

Part III — Common TCP/IP Applications

Part III takes you through a whirlwind tour of the various uses of TCP/IP and provides an overview of most of the current applications that run on it, such as NFS and HTTP. Thus, you will have a better idea about the services that will fit the particular needs of your network.

Part IV — Building and Maintaining TCP/IP Networks

Part IV presents information that will help you take the basics and implement them. Here, our discussion focuses on guidelines rather than facts, such as how to determine the number of hosts to put on a segment. We finish by talking about some of the technologies that will affect you in the near future, such as the wireless Internet and smart appliances.

Icons Used in This Book

This book contains a few icons to help point out important information to you.

 This icon gives you information that could cause planning, implementation, or functionality problems.

 This icon points the way to useful information found in other chapters in the book.

 This icon gives you additional information about a subject at hand.

 This icon provides a piece of friendly advice.

Acknowledgments

I'd like to thank Gabrielle for all her hard work, making what I write look like English. As I am both dyslexic and a bad typist, she has certainly had a challenge. I'd also like to thank Amanda for her patience; perhaps someday I will finish a book on time. I'd like to thank Nancy, Ami, and Katie for making the project a reality. And finally, I'd like to thank Tim for keeping me honest throughout the process. ~Rob Scrimger

Huge thanks go to Killer Katie, Amanda, Nancy the Long Island Enforcer, and Scrim for sage advice when I needed it. ~Paul LaSalle

I would like to thank Anita Sastry for her cooperation and guidance. I would also like to thank my friend and co-author Meeta Gupta for her companionship during the writing of this book. ~Mridula Parihar

Thank you to Suchi, Namrata, Sunil, Anghsuman, Anita, Ashok, Rashim, and Kurien for all the invaluable support and help that each of you gave me during the writing of this book. ~Meeta Gupta

I would like to thank Ron Gilster and Diane McMichael Gilster for showing me the ropes, and Katie Feltman for the opportunity to write. Most importantly, I would like to thank my children, Kayla, Lauren, and Mitchell, for their constant love and support and for always showing me that life is supposed to be fun. ~Clay Leitzke

Hungry Minds would like to acknowledge our summer intern, Leslie Kersey, for her hard work on this project.

Contents at a Glance

Contents

Part III: Common TCP/IP Applications   225

Chapter 11: Providing Internet Access 227

Chapter 12: File Utilities 259

Understanding TCP/IP Communications

In Part 1, we examine the basics of TCP/IP communications. We discuss the TCP/IP protocol stack and how the layers work with each other to move data between two hosts.

Chapter 1 discusses the basics of networking and provides a quick review of the OSI model. This model is compared to the smaller TCP/IP model in Chapter 2, where the layers are defined and the purpose of each layer is explained. In Chapters 3 through 7, we examine each layer in detail.

This part provides a fundamental understanding of TCP/IP— the protocol required to design, implement, and troubleshoot almost all of today's networks.

Understanding Network Fundamentals

Almost every facet of our lives is touched by computers. The goal throughout this book is to help you better understand how the computers that touch our lives communicate through the use of the Transmission Control Protocol and Internet Protocol (TCP/IP).

Over the last decade, our society has been deemed the "Internet generation." Our daily lives continue to be impacted by new advances in the Internet. It is now possible to pay bills, search for a job, make travel reservations, and do more than a million other things over the Internet. But before we can divulge the secrets of TCP/IP, an understanding of the fundamentals of networking is required.

The components that make network communication possible are covered briefly in this chapter. It covers the basics of networking, including the OSI model, topologies, and TCP/IP addressing.

What Is a Network?

In the most basic sense, a *network* is two or more computers that share information. However, networks can be very diverse—ranging in size from just a few clients to millions of clients. A *client* is a requestor on the network—a computer that solicits network traffic. For example, checking e-mail may be one of the client's functions. The client will request information from an e-mail server. The e-mail server in turn will request information from the client, which also makes the e-mail server a client.

In first grade, we learned that all sharks are fish, but not all fish are sharks. The same principle can be applied to clients and nodes. All clients are nodes, but not all nodes are clients. Even so, the terms *client* and *node* are often used interchangeably. A *node* is used to reference any device on your network with a network card that is active on your network. When a node is active on the network, it will place traffic on the network in the form of a request or a reply. Some devices, such as printers, routers, and switches, typically do not place requests on the network. These devices respond to requests from other clients when something—such as a connection or a file—is needed. Devices like routers and switches typically do not have anything to ask for from clients. This is not to say these devices do not initiate traffic; it just means these devices do not request services from other clients.

The first requirement of a network is that the clients/nodes speak the same language, or *protocol*. A multitude of protocols are available for network communication; however, this book will focus on TCP/IP.

Components of a Network

Any communication—whether oral, written, or electronic—requires some kind of mechanism. Network communication is no exception. In a basic network, the only required mechanism is a Network Interface Card (NIC). Networks can have two clients that connect using a crossover cable. A *crossover cable* allows clients to send to and receive directly from one another without the use of other connection devices, such as hubs, switches, or routers.

Network cards are available for all types of networks. In a basic sense, the *topology* of a network is a mapping of network cables—in other words, how these cables are arranged. Later in this chapter, we will discuss different types of network topologies and the type of network cards that can be used in each.

Types of Network Configurations

The two main network configurations are peer-to-peer networks and client-server networks. However, it has been debated whether a pure peer-to-peer or client-server environment really exists. Thus, the terms *centralized* and *decentralized* were introduced.

Decentralized networks

Peer-to-peer (or decentralized) networks were once defined as networks that had no servers, only clients. In other words, all clients on the network were able to request and provide information. There was no a central server from which all clients would request information. Eventually, the tendency was for one client on the network to store files for all other clients. As a result, the client storing the information came to be thought of as the *server*. This is still the case in many small office environments.

As network needs changed and programs grew in size from a few megabytes to several hundred megabytes, dedicated *servers* (network computers that function solely as servers) became widespread. The dedicated servers offered centralized storage. Clients would request information from the server and not from one another; however, network administration was still a tedious task. No server contained all the user accounts — rather, these user accounts were maintained on each client.

When a user logs on to a network, a user name and a password will be entered. If the user accounts and passwords are stored throughout the network, it is decentralized, or peer-to-peer.

A decentralized network has many network resources available to it, such as e-mail servers, databases servers, file storage, printing, and graphics programs, but these resources do not make it centralized, nor do they make it a client-server network configuration. Decentralized networks are typically characterized by the following:

✦ Small in size, with an approximate limit of 20 clients on the network.

✦ Security is not an issue.

✦ Network-level administration is not required.

✦ Client-level administration is required.

Figure 1-1 shows a decentralized network environment. This type of network is also referred to as a peer-to-peer, or workgroup, network.

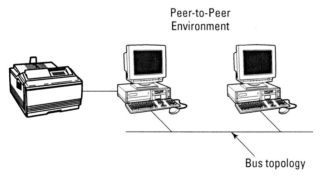

Figure 1-1: A decentralized network

Centralized networks

A centralized (or client-server) network is a network that dedicates at least one computer as a server. This server provides services to clients, such as file storage and e-mail. It will also provide information when requested by the clients.

Centralized networks provide a server, or a group of servers, that hold all user account information. Microsoft has Windows NT and 2000, and Novell has NetWare eDirectory Services (NDS). When a network stores user accounts in a single database, it becomes known as a centralized network. Windows NT and 2000 domains and Novell Networks store user accounts in a centralized database. The administrative overhead to manage a centralized network is lower than that of a decentralized network because the administrator in a decentralized network has to go to each client to administer it. In a centralized network, administration can be performed on any client on the network. Centralized networks are typically characterized by the following:

✦ Network-level administration is required.

✦ Client-level administration is minimal.

✦ There is no limit on the number of clients that can be used.

Some centralized networks have fewer than ten clients, while other networks, such as the one for the U.S. Postal Service, have more than 1,000,000. Figure 1-2 depicts a centralized network. The servers can be used to store resources and user accounts so that all clients can have access.

Client Server Network Environment

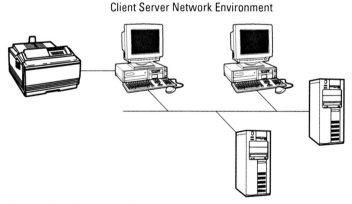

Figure 1-2: A centralized network

No standard defines the terminology for the different types of networks, such as peer-to-peer or centralized, but there are standards that define how communication takes place on a network.

The OSI Reference Model

Network traffic is generated when a request is made across the network. The request has to be changed from what the user sees to a format that can be used on the network. This transformation is made possible through the Open Systems Interconnection (OSI) reference model, developed by the International Organization for Standardization (ISO).

Network traffic is sent in the form of data packets. A *data packet* is user information transformed to a format understood by the network. Every transformation is a derivative of the seven-layer OSI model, which is used as a guideline for developers of network programs. Although many manufacturers manipulate the model, it is still the foundation used in development.

The seven layers of the OSI model, shown in Figure 1-3, operate as building blocks for the data packet. Each layer will add information to the data packet, but the data packet is not changed. The information added to a packet is called a *header*. Each layer's header is simply information that details the formatting of the data packet. This header is received at the corresponding layer on the receiving client and is used to understand the packet format. Every layer communicates with the layers that are adjacent to it. This means that any layer can communicate with the layer directly above or below it. Figure 1-3 shows the seven-layer OSI model.

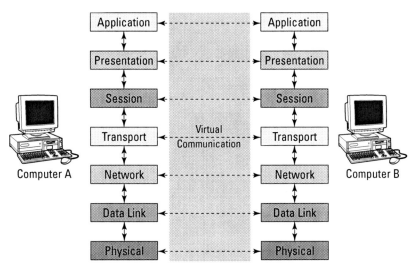

Figure 1-3: The OSI model

Communication through the seven-layer OSI model does not have a definitive path, but communication is always in a vertical direction. Data packets do not have to start at Layer 7, which is the top or Application layer. It is possible, for example, for communication to start at Layer 3, but Layers 2 and 1 will have to be used so that headers can be added.

Suppose that Client 1 uses a utility that starts at Layer 3. Layer 3 adds a header and passes it to Layer 2, which also adds a header and passes it to Layer 1. Layer 1 adds a header and places it on the network. Client 2 receives the packet and processes it, starting at Layer 1. Layer 1 removes the header that was added by Layer 1 at Client 1 and passes the remaining information to Layer 2. This layer then removes the header that was added by Layer 2 at Client 1 and passes the remaining information to the Layer 3. Layer 3 removes the header that was added by Layer 3 at Client 1 and processes the request.

All seven layers are used *only* if a user makes a request. Regardless of which layer initiates the communication, headers are added at each level and removed by the corresponding layer on the receiving client, as indicated in Figure 1-4. The data packet is traced from the sender on the left to the receiver on the right. As the packet is passed down from Layer 7 to Layer 1, each layer adds a header. When the packet is received by the receiver, each header is subtracted, and the remaining data is passed to the next higher layer.

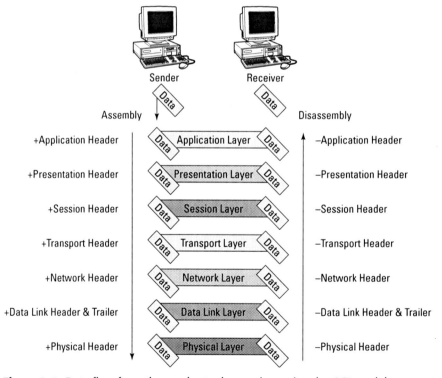

Figure 1-4: Data flow from the sender to the receiver using the OSI model

The Application layer

The highest layer (Layer 7) in the OSI model is the Application layer. This layer is responsible for interacting with the user application; it accepts the application data from the software application and provides the network application service that is responsible for the user request. A few examples of data transformation at the Application layer include the following:

✦ When a user sends an e-mail, the Application layer will provide access to the Simple Mail Transfer Protocol (SMTP) service.

✦ A file transfer can be accomplished by using the File Transfer Protocol (FTP). The FTP service is a responsibility of the Application layer.

✦ Requesting a Web sites such as `www.nwcomputertraining.com`, from your browser will place a request to the Application layer for name resolution through DNS and also a protocol request for HTTP.

Applications do exist at the Application layer, but these applications are transparent to the user. The Application layer is the *only* layer that interacts with the user software application.

The Presentation layer

The sixth layer of the OSI model is the Presentation layer, which accepts data from the Application layer. The primary function of the Presentation Layer is conversion, namely language conversion. Recall that the language spoken on a network is a protocol. If two clients do not use the same protocol, a protocol conversion is necessary. This conversion is the responsibility of the Presentation Layer.

The Presentation layer is also responsible for all data management. It provides character set conversion, data encryption, and data compression. The Presentation layer is responsible for the redirection of input and output requests.

The redirection of data is a function of the *network redirector,* which operates at the Presentation layer. Although the concept of a *network redirector* may seem intimidating, it is simple to understand. The Presentation layer accepts the data packet from the Application layer and is required to select the correct network service. If a client is requesting information, the workstation service is used. If a client is providing information, the server service is used. If a request is being made to a different type of client, a network protocol translator is used. For example, if you are using a Microsoft client to access information on a UNIX machine, the protocol translator being used is SAMBA. SAMBA converts Microsoft client requests to a format that can be understood by UNIX.

Both the Application layer and Presentation layer provide network services, but each provides a different type of service; consequently, the usage of the term *network services* can be confusing. Remember the following to help remove the confusion:

✦ Network application services are user-invoked and talk directly with the Application layer. An e-mail from a user will use the SMTP application service at the Application layer.

✦ Network services are not invoked directly by users but are required for network communication. These services are transparent to users. When the Application layer receives the request from the user to send an e-mail, the Application layer uses an SMTP header to describe the user request and passes this to the Presentation layer. The Presentation layer will use the workstation service to request services from the e-mail server.

✦ Network application services are user-invoked and operate at the Application layer. Network services are transparent to the user and operate at the Presentation layer. Once the correct network service is selected, a session has to be established.

The Session layer

The fifth layer of the OSI model is the Session layer — although a better name might be the "application connection layer." The Session layer allows identical applications operating on two different clients to communicate. It does this by establishing a virtual connection, based on a user name, computer name, or client's network credentials.

The Session layer manages this *virtual connection* by issuing checkpoints in the data it receives. A *checkpoint* tells the application which data has been received. If a connection failure occurs, the Session layer will evaluate the checkpoints and begin the transfer at the point of the last checkpoint. Suppose, for example, that Computer 1 is transferring 10MB of data from Computer 2, and the connection is lost at the 8MB point. Instead of having to retransmit all the data, the Session layer will look for the last checkpoint and begin the retransmission at the location of the checkpoint (in this case, 8MB). Because the Session layer manages the communication, the data transfer resumes instead of restarting.

Because the connection used at the Session layer is a virtual connection, it does not provide the assurance of packet delivery.

The Transport layer

The fourth layer, the Transport layer, is responsible for error checking and dataflow control. At this layer, two protocols are used for data transmission: the Transmission Control Protocol (TCP) and the User Datagram Protocol (UDP).

At this layer, an additional connection level is provided if TCP is used as the transport protocol. This additional connection level is a result of a three-way handshake and assures data packet delivery through acknowledgment packets. The three-way handshake is a set of greetings used to ascertain that both the sender and receiver are ready for data transfer.

The flow control provided by the Transport layer is a result of the TCP/IP Window size. The Window size specifies how much data a sender will send to the receiver without receiving an acknowledgement packet. A typical Window size is 4096 bytes. The Transport layer is responsible for dividing large data packets into smaller packets, usually 1500 bytes, but this value can be changed. With the typical Window size of 4096 bytes, there can be a total of four unacknowledged packets on the network. Typically, once the receiving client receives a packet, an acknowledgement packet will be sent to the sender. Once the sender receives this packet, additional data packets can be sent to the receiver. In the event that some data packets are not acknowledged, a retransmission may occur, but that is dependent on the protocol being used. The primary difference between the two protocols of the Transport layer, TCP and UDP, is the acknowledgement packet.

TCP

TCP is reliable packet delivery because of the acknowledgement packets, although it is slower than UDP. An example of an application that uses TCP is the FTP service.

UDP

UDP does not offer assurance of packet delivery, but it does offer packet integrity. Both TCP and UDP will perform error checking on data packets received. If a packet is found to be in error, the packet will be discarded. UDP is usually faster than TCP because UDP has a lower overhead for data transmission. An example of an application that uses UDP is the TFTP service.

Once the sender has determined how the data needs to be packaged, it must know where to send the data.

The Network layer

The third layer of the OSI model is the Network layer, which is responsible for network addressing and routing. The Internet Protocol is used for addressing packets and will specify the source (sender) address and destination (receiver) address of the data packets. The specified address is a unique 32-bit address, known as the *TCP/IP address*. IP addresses will be discussed later in the chapter.

The Internet Protocol will also fragment packets and identify each one with a unique ID. Once the packet is received at the receiving client's Network layer, the Internet Protocol will reassemble the fragmented packets and pass the data to the Transport layer.

Routing is performed at the Network layer to determine the best path or route to the destination. Common routing protocols that operate at the Network layer include the Routing Information Protocol (RIP), Open Shortest Path First (OSPF), and Border Gateway Protocol (BGP).

It is easy to refer to the Network layer as the "traffic cop" on the network. It specifies the sending and receiving of IP addresses and determines the best route to the destination. Once the IP addresses are specified, a physical address has to be determined.

The Data Link layer

The second layer of the OSI model is the Data Link layer. The Data Link layer is divided into two sub-layers: Logical Link Control and Media Access Control (Center).

The Logical Link Control sub-layer is responsible for placing a header and a trailer. All layers add header information to the data packet, but the Data Link layer (through the Logical Link Control sub-layer) adds a trailer to the data packet. The trailer is a cyclical redundancy check (CRC) that performs a parity calculation of the data packet and places the result in the trailer. When the receiving client receives the data packet, a CRC is performed, and the result is compared with the CRC of the sender. If the results match, the data is considered valid and is passed to the next layer. If the two results do not match, the data is considered invalid and is discarded.

The MAC (Media Access Control) sub-layer places the physical address of the NIC into the header that is added to the data packet. A MAC address is a unique 12-digit hexadecimal number that is on every NIC. An example of a MAC address is: 00-80-C7-4D-B8-26.

Note   The 802 Project Model is referenced through the Data Link layer. The 802 Model was developed by the Institute of Electrical and Electronic Engineers (IEEE) to specify how data is physically placed on the network. Network topologies are defined by the 802 Project Model and are discussed later in this chapter.

Once the CRC, MAC, and topology are defined, the data has to be converted and placed on the network.

The Physical layer

The first layer of the OSI model is the Physical layer, which is primarily responsible for placing raw data on the network. Raw data is represented in binary format, or sets of 1s and 0s.

Referred to as the "Hardware Layer," the Physical layer establishes and maintains connections between the sender and receiver. Because the data can exist in different formats (such as electrical pulses, radio frequencies, and light pulses), the Physical layer determines the duration of each pulse.

In a nutshell, the Physical layer defines how a network cable is attached to the NIC and how the data should be formatted for transmission.

Types of Area Networks

Networks come in different shapes and sizes, but they usually fall into one of two categories: local area networks (LANs) and wide area networks (WANs). Derivatives of LANs and WANs include personal area networks (PANs), metropolitan area networks (MANs), and campus area networks (CANs).

Local area networks

When you divide any task into smaller parts, it is often easier to manage. It follows that if a large network is divided into pieces, network administrators can manage the network more easily. A network is divided into *segments*. A LAN can have many segments, all connected by a network device called a *router*. A router is responsible for connecting segments of a network and is discussed in more detail in a later section.

When different segments of a network are connected by means of permanent connection media, the result is a LAN. A LAN does not have any connection that relies on dial-up lines, or leased lines. All cables for a LAN are part of the network and do not have a signal from anywhere other than the router or clients. Think of the network as a building with ten floors, where each floor is a segment of the network. There are routers on every two floors to provide connectivity between the floors. The routers are connected by cables from the network, not by an outside communication company. There is no need to purchase a dedicated line or leased line for the routers to communicate, because all connectivity is local to the building. Because there are no leased lines, this is considered to be a LAN. When communication between two areas of a network is dependent on communication through leased lines, that connection is called a wide area network connection.

Wide area networks

WANs exist in almost every network environment. Nearly every Internet connection is made through a WAN connection. A WAN connection is a connection media that is not part of your LAN, which means that external vendor services are required for communication. Often, the connection type is a serial connection that is obtained from a local telephone carrier.

Many types of WAN connections are available. For example, a company may choose to purchase a low bandwidth line. *Bandwidth* is the amount of data that can be passed over the line at one time. Bandwidth is similar to a water pipe. Only a finite amount of water can pass through the pipe at any one time, and if more water is needed, a larger pipe is required. The same is true for bandwidth. A typical WAN connection is a factor of 64 Kbs (Kilobits per second), with the most common types of WAN connections being the following values: 128 Kbs, 256 Kbs, 512 Kbs, and a T-1 at 1.544 Mbs (Megabits per second.)

One differentiating factor in the connection media for LANs and WANs is that the WAN connection is not permanent. If the local carrier accidentally flips the wrong switch, your WAN link no longer exists, and you are restricted to local communication. On the other hand, the only way to lose connectivity on a LAN is through cable breakage or a power outage.

Suppose that a company (Company B) needs to purchase a WAN link. Local Carrier B leases Company B a T-1 for $900 per month. Company B has two locations that operate independently of each other, but they are able to share information through the WAN link. If Company B forgets to pay Local Carrier B, the WAN link will not operate, and Company B will be restricted to local communication at the two locations.

LANs have no outside fees for communication lines and are not dependent on a local carrier. WANs are communication lines that usually have a monthly fee and are dependent on local carriers.

Project Model IEEE 802

The IEEE (Institute of Electrical and Electronic Engineers) developed standards for network communication that enhanced the Data Link layer and Physical layer of the OSI model. The result was the two sub-layer breakdown of the Data Link layer, and the focus of the breakdown was on the NIC (network interface card) and how the data was to be formatted for network transmission. Earlier, it was mentioned that clients need to have the same network protocol if communication is going to be successful. However, this is not the only requirement of successful communication. Clients must also have the same data format, defined by the IEEE 802 Project Model.

The IEEE 802 Project Model is divided into categories. The categories define data transfer to the different layers of the OSI model. The most common categories are:

- ◆ **802.1** — Defines the OSI model and network management.

- ◆ **802.2** — Defines the Data Link layer and divides it into the LLC (Logical Link Control) and MAC sub-layers.

- ◆ **802.3** — Defines the MAC layer for Ethernet networks that use the Carrier Sense Multiple Access/Collision Detection (CSMA/CD). This category is generally referred to as the *Ethernet category.* Prior to data transmission, the NIC senses the network and waits for the line to be clear before transmitting. If two clients transmit at the same time, it is referred to as *collision.* 802.3 is then responsible for retransmitting the data.

- ◆ **802.4** — Defines the MAC layer for Token Bus networks. Clients receive a token before transmitting data, and when transmitted, the data follows the path of a straight line.

✦ **802.5**—Defines the MAC layer for Token Ring networks. Clients receive a token before transmitting data, and when transmitted, the data follows the path of a logical ring, or circle.

✦ **802.12**—Defines Demand Priority. When 802.12 is used in data transfer, a priority bit is specified. This bit tells the rest of the network to always accept this packet. When this bit is set, the receiver of the packet that has the demand priority bit set will have to accept the packet regardless of the configuration the receiving client currently has. The demand priority bit led to many vicious network attacks and is generally not used in data transfer.

Once the category has been defined, the topology of the network is also defined.

Network Topologies

The design of the network will dictate the network topology. The topology of the network refers to the data path of the network. How will data get from Client 1 to Client 2? It is difficult to find a topology that works for all networks, but the most basic types of topologies are discussed in the following sections.

Bus topology

The *Bus topology* (shown in Figure 1-5) is a topology where all clients are attached to one wire, typically using coaxial cable as the link. At one time, the Bus topology was the most prevalent topology found on networks. It is very easy to install and troubleshoot, which made it a win-win situation; however, the Bus topology is limited by distance and the number of clients it can support. Its prevalence was short-lived.

The Bus topology normally uses coaxial cable—like what you see in your home—and was categorized by the IEEE as 802.3 10b2 (10 base 2). 10b2 networks typically transmit data at a rate of 4 Mbs over distances not exceeding 185 meters. All clients are attached to one wire that carries all the data, which is how the term "bus" originated. A Bus network has a starting point and an ending point, terminated with 50-ohm resistors.

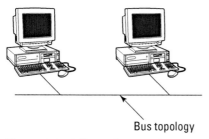

Bus topology

Figure 1-5: A linear Bus topology

The Bus topology can also be used as a backbone for network traffic. The backbone is categorized by the IEEE as 802.3 10b5 (10 base 5). Data transmission is increased to 10 Mbs, and the maximum distance is increased to 500 meters. The primary difference between 10b2 and 10b5 is the size of the coaxial cable that is used.

Some advantages and disadvantages of the Bus topology include:

✦ Ease of installation and troubleshooting.

✦ Distance restrictions and bandwidth.

✦ Potential loss of the Bus. If the cable is broken, no client has the ability to communicate.

Note   Although distance is a disadvantage, it can be increased through the use of repeaters.

Star topology

The need for more clients and faster networks led to the development of the *Star topology*. In this design, all clients connect to a central device that accepts input from clients and redirects the data to the receiver. The central device is usually a hub or a switch. The Star topology is shown in Figure 1-6.

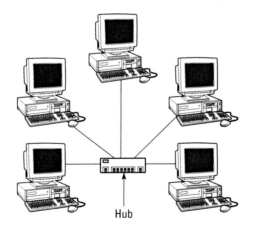

Hub

Figure 1-6: A Star topology can be identified by a hub, the central connection point for the network.

The Star topology is able to transfer data at speeds up to 1 Gbs. The Star topology is categorized by the IEEE as 802.3 10bT. The distance limitation has been reduced to 100 meters but can be lengthened with a repeater. The Bus and Star topologies both use CSMA/CD for network access.

Ring topology

IBM was the primary designer of the Token Ring technology, which forced clients to be courteous on the network. Before a client can place data on the network, it must possess a network access token. This token is passed along a logical ring or circle. There is only one token on the network at any given time; thus, only one client can use the token at a time. This may appear to slow network traffic down, but a Token Ring network can pass a token around a 2,000 meter ring 10,000 times per second. Figure 1-7 shows a Ring topology.

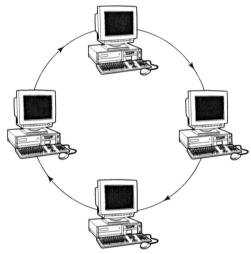

Figure 1-7: In a logical Ring topology, network traffic circles the ring and passes a single token for all clients to share.

Large network environments use a fault-tolerant ring design. In the event that one of the rings goes to down state, the secondary ring will allow the network to continue to operate. Clients typically connect through a special hub called a Multi Station Access Unit (MSAU). The most common form of ring topology today is the Fiber-Optic Ring, typically used as a backbone.

Mesh topology

The ultimate in fault-tolerant network design is the Mesh topology, shown in Figure 1-8. In a Mesh topology, the only point of failure is a natural disaster. All clients are connected to each other. A Mesh topology is generally a very small network because of the hardware requirements. After installation, overhead for the Mesh topology is minimal. It is possible to have several failed components in a Mesh topology because of the redundancy on each client.

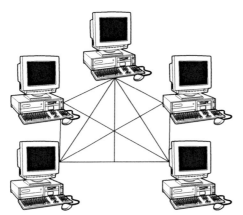

Figure 1-8: In a Mesh topology, all clients are connected to each other.

Hybrid topology

It is a rare environment that uses only a single topology. Often, the needs of an organization require the use several different topologies. A hybrid topology often allows areas of a network to continue operation if the backbone suffers a failure. The following section discusses two types of hybrid topologies: Star-Bus and Star-Ring.

Star-Bus

A collection of Star networks connected by a Bus network results in a Star-Bus hybrid topology. Although fault-tolerance is not provided, this topology has no single point of failure. Figure 1-9 shows a Star-Bus hybrid topology.

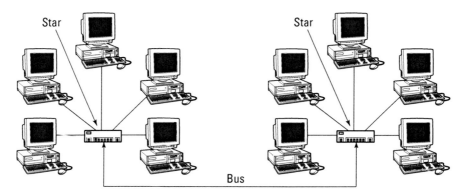

Figure 1-9: A Star-Bus topology has two separate star segments connected by a bus.

As you can see, a Bus network connects two Star networks. If the Bus network fails, the Star networks can operate independently. If either of the Star network hubs fail, the other Star network will continue to operate. Simple design and simple trouble-shooting are the main advantages of the Star-Bus topology.

Star-Ring

A collection of Star networks connected by a Ring network results in the Star-Ring hybrid topology, which is one of the most common hybrids in use. The Star-Ring offers one distinct advantage over the Star-Bus: fault tolerance.

A Ring topology is designed with a primary ring and a secondary ring. If a Ring is in a failure state, the network will continue to operate. If a Star network fails, the rest of the network will continue to operate.

A typical Star-Ring hybrid topology will have Ethernet networks for the Star networks, and a Fiber Ring for the Ring network. This design increases the data transfer speeds between the Star networks.

Figure 1-10 shows a Star-Ring hybrid topology.

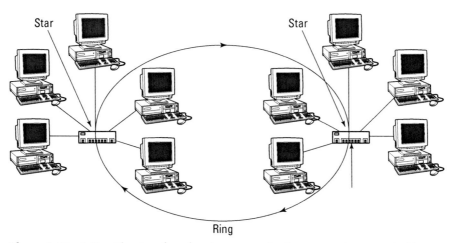

Figure 1-10: A Star-Ring topology has two separate star segments connected by a ring.

Network Infrastructure

Network communication has now been defined and theoretical principles have been explained. This section will explore the network infrastructure and the hardware components needed for network connectivity. These components are presented in the order of their OSI operational level, starting with Layer 1.

Repeaters

All network topologies are limited to a finite distance. Some networks use a 10bT topology that has a limit of 100 meters, while other networks use 10bF (Fiber Optics), which has a theoretical limit of 2000 meters.

The distance limitation often hinders network operations and must be overcome. A repeater, which operates at the Physical layer of the OSI model, offers the solution to this distance limitation. A repeater is used to strengthen the signal and reduce cable attenuation. *Cable attenuation* is the weakening of the signal on the cable and can result in data corruption and packet loss. A repeater is used only to strengthen the signal on the cable. The unwritten rule for a repeater is that its location should be within 15 meters of the maximum cable distance for the given topology. If a network is using 10b2, the repeater should be placed around the 170-meter point on the cable.

Network Interface Card

The Network Interface Card, or NIC, operates at both the Physical and Data Link layers of the OSI model. The NIC uses the MAC address from the Data Link layer and uses the topology of the Physical layer.

Hub

In a Star network, a hub is the central connection point for all clients. A hub operates at the Data Link layer of the OSI model and is concerned only with the MAC address. A hub is not used to create additional network segments. A hub only provides a connection point.

The network can be expanded by joining hubs with a crossover cable. When joining hubs, a repeater is often used to extend the distance between the two hubs. A hub has a collective bandwidth. If a hub is rated as 100 Mbs, a total of 100 Mbs can be present on the hub at one time.

Switch

A switch is also present at the Data Link layer. A switch is similar to a hub in that it joins clients together at a central point. The operation of a switch is based on MAC addresses. However, a switch uses a table of MAC addresses to help segment a network. The segments created with a switch are called *Virtual LANs*. In addition to being able to virtually segment a network, a switch distributes the bandwidth to each port.

If a switch is rated at 100 Mbs, every client can potentially communicate at 100 Mbs. The primary difference between a hub and a good switch is approximately $1200.

Bridge

A network bridge is similar in function to a bridge that connects different sections of land. The network bridge simply connects different types of networks. A bridge operates at the Data Link layer of the OSI model and is used to translate topologies.

As mentioned earlier in this chapter, clients must use the same protocol and operate with the same topology to communicate. If clients have different topologies but are using the same protocol, a bridge can be used to join the two. A bridge understands both topologies and translates between the two.

A bridge may also be used to help reduce the propagation of *broadcast traffic.* Broadcast traffic is network traffic that is sent to all clients on the network and is also the archenemy of every network administrator.

A bridge does not look at or care about the network address. The network address is considered to be above the reading level of the bridge. A bridge that has graduated from a network address school is a router.

Router

Nestled inside the Network layer is the router. A router serves as a traffic cop to all clients. Because it knows where other networks are located, it can direct traffic to the appropriate location.

Every segment of the network must be able to communicate with other segments, and this communication is made possible through the use of a router. A router routes; it does not translate. It lives and operates only at Layer 3. The router is not concerned with the MAC addresses of clients — that's the job of Layer 2 devices.

Brouter

The brouter, which can both route and translate, offers the best of both worlds.

A brouter operates at Layer 2 and Layer 3 of the OSI model. A brouter would typically be used in an environment that has segments of varying topologies and different network addresses (defined later in this chapter). The brouter can translate the topologies and route the packet to the destination request.

Most brouters today can operate as bridges.

Gateway

A network gateway does not perform the same operations as that of the default gateway. A default gateway address is the address of the router. A network gateway is used to translate protocols, and it can also be used to translate addresses from one protocol to another.

Gateways can use all seven layers, but it is most common to see gateways operating at Layer 4 and higher. At these levels, a network gateway can accept data from a client using TCP/IP and a client using IPX/SPX (Internet Packet Exchange/Sequence Packet Exchange, a protocol used by Novell) and translate the protocols so that the clients can communicate.

Introduction to TCP/IP

The Internet originated over 40 years ago with the Department of Defense/ Advanced Research Project Agency (DOD/ARPA), which wanted to build a national communication system so that computers around the country and the world could send and receive information. Technically, the government didn't intend to build what we now know as the Internet; they simply wanted to create a communication system for defense. It took nearly 30 years to develop a governing board to oversee the development of the Internet.

The Internet Architecture Board (IAB) is the governing body for Internet standards. The IAB contains two major groups: the Internet Research Task Force (IRTF) and the Internet Engineering Task Force (IETF):

✦ **IETF**—Focuses primarily on short-term engineering problems. The IETF is divided into approximately ten groups that collectively form the Internet Engineering Steering Group (IESG).

✦ **IRTF**—Focuses on long-term engineering strategies of the Internet. As the IETF's counterpart, the IRTF is divided into groups that collectively form the Internet Research Steering Group (IRSG).

Request for Comments

The DOD/ARPA project started small, but in just a few years, there were several agencies working on the project. The Request for Comments (RFC) process was established early on, serving first to develop standards for TCP/IP and now serving to develop standards for the Internet. The RFC process is simply a review and file process. New RFCs are proposed to the IETF and are reviewed by a group of RFC editors. Once the proposed RFC has been reviewed, the IETF will file the RFC in a category that defines how the RFC should be used.

RFCs are numbered and can be submitted by anyone. The rules for proposing an RFC are covered in RFC 1543. The biggest misconception about RFCs concerns their content. RFCs cover the entire TCP/IP suite of communication, not just protocols. Protocols, topologies, utilities, and standards are just a few of the areas that are covered in the RFC process.

Tip   You will never see any modifications made to an existing RFC once an RFC has been published. All revisions and replacements are published as new RFCs. A new RFC that revises or replaces an existing RFC is said to "update" or "obsolete" that RFC.

Some RFCs are described as information documents, while others describe Internet protocols. The IAB maintains a list of the RFCs that describe the protocol suite. Each of these is assigned a status.

An Internet protocol can have one of the following statuses:

✦ **Standard** — When the IAB receives a document for a possible new standard or modification to an RFC, it is reviewed by technical experts, a task force, or the RFC Editor. The IAB then issues a classification to help determine whether the document is being considered as a standard.

✦ **Required** — All systems must implement the required protocols.

✦ **Recommended** — All systems should implement the recommended protocols.

✦ **Elective** — All systems may or may not implement an elective protocol. This is usually a sign that it received limited demand during its maturity level.

✦ **Limited use** — These protocols are for use in limited circumstances — perhaps due to their specialized nature, limited functionality, or experimental or historic state.

✦ **Not recommended** — These protocols are not recommended for general use — perhaps due to their limited functionality, specialized nature, or experimental or historic state. If and when the IAB establishes that the protocol has the potential to become a standard, it goes through different stages of development, testing, and acceptance.

✦ **Proposed standard** — These protocol proposals *may* be considered by the IAB for standardization in the future. This rating usually indicates that the specification is generally stable and well understood. Implementations and testing by several groups are desirable.

✦ **Draft standard** — The IAB is actively considering this protocol as a possible standard protocol. Substantial and widespread testing and comments are desired. Comments and test results should be submitted to the IAB. There is a possibility that changes will be made in a draft protocol before the protocol becomes a standard.

✦ **Internet standard** — The Internet standard means that the proposed RFC has received approval to proceed as an active standard to be adopted by the Internet community. This rating indicates that the protocol has gone through rigorous testing and a high degree of technical maturity.

Once the RFC has been classified as Standard, it will be assigned a unique number. A complete list of RFCs can be downloaded from the following site: www.rfc-editor.org.

TCP/IP reference model

TCP/IP is not a single protocol; it is a suite of protocols. Because of the diversity of TCP/IP, it does not directly use the OSI model. Instead, it uses a four-layer model for communication, as shown in Figure 1-11.

OSI Model	TCP/IP Protocol Suite
Application	Application:
Presentation	Telnet
Session	FTP and Others
Transport	Transport : TCP
Network	Internet : IP, ARP,
Data Link	ICMP
Physical	Physical

Figure 1-11: There is no one-to-one correspondence between the OSI and TCP/IP models. Each layer of the OSI model maps to one or more layers of the TCP/IP model.

Application layer

The fourth layer of the TCP/IP reference model is the Application layer. This layer is responsible for TCP/IP applications. There are two types of applications at this layer: socket-based applications and Network Basic Input Output System (NetBIOS) applications.

Socket-based applications exist on all clients that use TCP/IP. Three elements are required for socket-based applications: an IP address, a port, and a service type. As previously mentioned, each client that uses TCP/IP will have a unique 32-bit address. Each address has 65,536 entry points, called *ports*. TCP/IP applications operate on particular ports. (Common TCP/IP applications will be defined later in this section, along with the port each application uses for communication).

NetBIOS applications are commonly seen on Microsoft operating systems. NetBIOS is one of the least understood aspects of Microsoft networking. The most common misconception is that a NetBIOS name is the same as a computer name. A computer name plus a service indicator produces a NetBIOS name. In addition to ridiculous amounts of network traffic, NetBIOS-based networks have a tremendous amount of administrative overhead. Another misconception about NetBIOS is that it is a protocol. NetBIOS is a Session layer transport that provides virtual communication to applications on different clients. What this means is that applications appear to be able to communicate based solely on computer names. The service indicator for a NetBIOS name is represented in a hexadecimal format. The most common NetBIOS service indicators on a Microsoft network are listed below:

  ✦ Computername[00h] indicates the Workstation Service.

  ✦ Computername[03h] indicates the Messenger Service.

  ✦ Computername[20h] indicates the Server Service.

The primary disadvantage to NetBIOS applications is the number of broadcasts placed on the network for service advertising and browsing.

Transport layer

The third layer of the TCP/IP model is the Transport layer. Put simply, the purpose of the Transport layer is to connect or not to connect. Two protocols are used in the Transport layer: Transmission Control Protocol (TCP) and User Datagram Protocol (UDP). TCP is a connection-oriented reliable communication that is slower in transmission. UDP is a connectionless non-guaranteed communication that is faster in transmission.

When an application uses TCP for communication, a three-way handshake is established, ensuring that packets are delivered error-free, in sequence, and without data loss or duplication. The TCP/IP window size is defined at the Transport layer using TCP. TCP assures packet delivery but is slower in transfer.

An application that uses UDP does not establish a three-way handshake and does not offer a guarantee of packet delivery. Essentially, UDP sends the data to the receiving client and hopes that it is received. There is no follow-up communication for data retransmission. UDP is much faster than TCP but DOES NOT guarantee delivery.

The client does not have the option to select UDP or TCP. The application developer makes this decision during the development of the application.

Internet layer

The second layer of the TCP/IP model is the Internet layer. The Internet layer functions much like the Network layer of the OSI model. The Internet layer is primarily responsible for network addressing and routing. In addition, this layer is responsible for packet fragmentation. Data packets are assembled and disassembled for transmission at this layer.

Several protocols operate at the Internet layer, but the most common are:

✦ **Internet Protocol (IP)** — A connectionless protocol that provides addressing and route selection. The header information added to the data packet contains source and destination addresses, and the route selection is made based on these addresses. IP also performs packet assembly and disassembly, sometimes called *fragmentation,* for the Network Interface layer. IP also helps control traffic through routers by adjusting the Time to Live (TTL) value of packets as they are passed through routers. The TTL specifies how long a packet can be on a network. As a packet passes through a router, the TTL is decremented by 1 second, and when a TTL of 0 is reached, the packet is discarded.

✦ **Internet Control Message Protocol (ICMP)** — Used most often with the utility Packet Internet Groper (PING). PING is used most often to troubleshoot connectivity problems. ICMP is also used to send router source quench packets that inform clients that too much traffic is coming too fast, and packets are in danger of being dropped. A more advanced use of ICMP is router solicitation. Clients can use ICMP Router Discovery Protocol to locate routers on a network.

✦ **Address Resolution Protocol (ARP)** — Used to resolve IP addresses to MAC addresses. Once the MAC address is known, the packet can be sent from the client directly to the receiving client if the clients are on the same segment. If the clients are on different segments, the packet is sent to the router.

✦ **Internet Group Management Protocol (IGMP)** — Sometimes referred to as the Internet Group Messaging/Membership Protocol, this protocol is used to identify members in a group that receive multicast data packets. A *multicast packet* is sent to a group of clients, rather than to all clients (as with a broadcast). A *unicast* is sent to only one client. IGMP has many uses in a network, but some of the most common include video conferencing, Internet chat, and dynamic router updates.

Network Interface layer

The first layer of the TCP/IP model — the Network Interface layer — corresponds to the Data Link and Physical layers of the OSI model and is responsible for network access. The Network Interface layer communicates directly with the network. It is the liaison between the network topology and the Internet layer.

IP addressing overview

Every node on a TCP/IP network must have a unique 32-bit address. The IP address is very similar to the address of a home or office. A home address specifies a country, state, city, street, and location on the street. An IP address identifies a node by specifying the network address, the subnet address, and the node address.

The network is referenced with a network address. A segment of the network is referred to as a subnet and is referenced with a subnet address. Each piece of the segment is referred to as a node and is referenced with a node address.

Communication through TCP/IP requires two parameters: an IP address and a subnet mask. The subnet mask is discussed in more depth in later chapters; however, a general understanding is required to complete this chapter. The large network can be segmented with subnets by manipulating the subnet mask. Changing the subnet mask changes the number of subnets on the network and the number of nodes on each subnet.

IP addresses have four parts, and each part is called an octet because each has eight bits. Four parts with eight bits provides you with a 32-bit address. The first part of the IP address always identifies the network class. There are five classes of address (three are shown in Table 1-1), and each class has a different number of addresses that can be assigned:

✦ Class A networks have a range of 1–126 in the first octet. Class A networks use the first octet only to identify the network address. The U.S. Postal Service has been allotted the 56 network. The network address is referenced as 56.0.0.0. Class A networks use a default subnet mask of 255.0.0.0.

✦ Class B networks have a range of 128–191 in the first octet. Class B networks use the first two octets to identify the network address. For example, Delta Air Lines uses an internal network address of 172.16.0.0. The default subnet mask for a class B network is 255.255.0.0.

✦ Class C networks have a range of 192–223 in the first octet. Class C networks use the first three octets to identify the network address. For example, Northwest Computer Training has been allotted the 216.18.17.0 network. The default subnet mask for a class C network is 255.255.255.0.

✦ Class D networks have a range of 224–239 in the first octet. Class D networks are used only for multicasting and use a default subnet mask of 255.255.255.255.

✦ Class E networks have a range of 240–255 in the first octet. Class E networks are reserved for future use.

When a network is using the default subnet mask for its corresponding network class, the network is not being subnetted. Table 1-1 describes the default characteristics of routable address classes.

Table 1-1
Default Characteristics of Routable Address Classes

Class	Range of First Octet	Default Subnet Mask	# of Nodes
A	1–126	255.0.0.0	16,777,214
B	128–191	255.255.0.0	65,534
C	192–223	255.255.255.0	254

TCP/IP applications

The Application layer of the TCP/IP model offers many applications for network communication, and it would be almost impossible to list each one. Some of the most common applications include:

✦ **Domain Name System (DNS)** — Used to provide name resolution to an IP address. DNS operates over port 53. Before accessing a Web site, the Web address must be resolved to an IP address. DNS provides this resolution.

✦ **File Transfer Protocol (FTP)** — Used to download and upload files on remote machines. FTP operates over port 21 for the server and port 20 for the client.

✦ **Dynamic Host Configuration Protocol (DHCP)** — Used to dynamically assign IP addresses to clients from a central server. DHCP operates over port 67 for the server and port 68 for the client.

✦ **Simple Mail Transport Protocol (SMTP)** — Used for the transmission of e-mail. SMTP operates over port 25.

✦ **Post Office Protocol (POP3)** — Used for the receipt of e-mail. POP operates over port 110.

✦ **Telnet** — Terminal Emulation is used to run commands on remote machines and operates over port 23.

✦ **Hyper Text Transfer Protocol (HTTP)** — Used to request services running on port 80. HTTP is used to access Web sites.

✦ **Secure Sockets Layer (SSL)** — Used to provide secure data transactions between clients and servers. SSL operates over port 443.

✦ **Network Basic Input Output System (NetBIOS)** — Used for name resolution. Primarily computer names on a Microsoft Network. NetBIOS operates over ports 137/138/139.

Summary

We explored the core networking concepts as a basis for understanding TCP/IP. First, networking fundamentals — including a basic overview of network functions — were covered, followed by an explanation of the primary network component, the NIC card. Next, peer-to-peer (decentralized) and client-server (centralized) network configurations were defined, followed by a detailed description of the role and importance of the OSI model. Each layer's header is the information that details the formatting of the data packet. This header is received at the corresponding layer on the receiving client and is used to understand the packet format.

The IEEE standards were covered in detail, focusing on the NIC card and enhancement of the Data Link layer and Physical layer of the OSI model and how the data was to be formatted for network transmission.

Other topics this chapter covered include WANs and LANs; network topologies; and network infrastructure components and their functions (including repeaters, NICs, hubs, switches, bridges, routers, brouters, and gateways).

Finally, an introduction to TCP/IP was provided, covering TCP/IP's evolution, the RFC process, and the TCP/IP reference model. The chapter closed with sections on IP addressing and TCP/IP applications.

✦   ✦   ✦

Architecture of the TCP/IP Protocol

✦ ✦ ✦ ✦

In This Chapter

The five-layer TCP/IP
architecture

Communication
between layers

✦ ✦ ✦ ✦

What we know today as "the Internet" came into existence in 1968 as a project funded by the U.S. government's Department of Defense (DoD). This project attempted to connect various research centers supported by the DoD through a network known as ARPANET (Advanced Research Projects Agency NETwork). Initially, Network Control Protocol (NCP) was used as the standard interconnection protocol. However, NCP failed to keep up ARPANET, which was growing at a tremendous rate. Therefore, in 1974, TCP/IP was developed. The term *TCP/IP (Transmission Control Protocol and Internet Protocol)* actually refers to two protocols that are not stand-alone protocols. Rather, they belong to the *TCP/IP protocol suite.* A protocol suite is a hierarchical collection of related protocols. Because of the revolutionary role that TCP and IP have played in the advancement of networking, the entire suite is referred to as the TCP/IP protocol suite.

For more information on the history of TCP/IP, refer to Chapter 1.

In this chapter, you learn about the five layers that are part of the TCP/IP architecture: the Physical layer, Network Interface layer, Internet layer, Transport layer, and Application layer. You learn about the role these five layers play in the successful transmission of data from one computer to another. You also learn about the communication process between the layers.

The Five-Layer TCP/IP Architecture

In the past decade, many hardware and software vendors have jumped onto the networking bandwagon. To avoid incompatibility amongst the wide range of networking products that were introduced into the market, open computing standards were developed. The development of TCP/IP was always carried out in an open environment; thus, TCP/IP is still considered the real open system interconnection protocol, despite the U.S. government's attempts to popularize the Open Systems Interconnection (OSI) protocols. Over the years, a contemporary five-layer TCP/IP architecture model has evolved as an answer to the existing seven-layer OSI reference model. The basic purpose of the model is to define a set of open standards for any current or future developments in the field of TCP/IP. A comparative overview of the OSI and the TCP/IP reference models is shown in Figure 2-1.

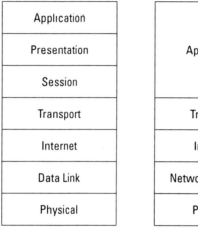

OSI Reference Model   TCP/IP Model

Figure 2-1: The OSI reference model versus the TCP/IP model

> **Note**   At times, you may come across a four-layer TCP/IP architecture model instead of a five-layer model. In the four-layer model, the first two layers — Physical layer and Network Interface layer — have been combined into one layer, called the *Network Access layer*, or simply the *Physical layer*.
>
> You may also come across instances where the Internet layer is referred to as the Network layer.

A reference model plays a very important role by serving as a functional guideline for dividing network communication processes and tasks in the following ways:

✦ Allows vendors to develop compatible products

✦ Makes it easy to understand complex operations

✦ Categorizes networking technologies and their protocol implementations, which allows specialized design development of modular functions

Like the OSI reference model, the TCP/IP architecture model is a set of layers, where each layer represents a group of specific tasks and facets of communication. Since the TCP/IP model is theoretical, these layers neither exist physically, nor do they actually perform any function(s). The protocol implementations, which are a combination of hardware and software, actually perform the functions associated with the corresponding layers. The TCP/IP model consists of the following five layers:

✦ **Physical layer**—This layer provides the physical medium (such as cables) to transmit data from one computer to another.

✦ **Network Interface layer**—This layer is responsible for identifying devices on a network on the basis of their hardware addresses, for controlling the data-flow, and for organizing the Physical layer bits into frames.

✦ **Internet layer**—This layer is responsible for transmitting (or routing) data across different networks.

✦ **Transport layer**—This layer is responsible for organizing messages received from higher layers into segments, for controlling errors, and for end-to-end flow control.

✦ **Application layer**—This layer provides the network-user interface in the form of applications and network services.

The Physical layer

The Physical layer is the lowest layer in the TCP/IP model and is responsible for the physical transmission of the data over the *transmission media*. The physical path (such as electric cables, fiber optic cables, radio waves, and so on) over which the data travels in the form of electrical or electromagnetic waves is known as the *transmission medium*. The Physical layer receives the data that has been passed from the upper layers and converts the data into a series of *bits* that can be transferred over the physical media successfully. A bit, shown in Figure 2-2, is the basic unit of communication between computers and network devices, which can have only two valid values: 0 or 1. 0 represents the absence of the signal on the physical medium, whereas 1 represents the presence of the signal on the medium.

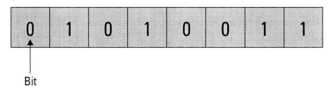

Bit

Figure 2-2: A signaling bit

Signaling

In a network, data travels from one computer to another in the form of *signals*. Depending on the transmission medium being used, signals fall into two categories:

✦ **Analog signals** — Signals that resemble a series of sine waves, where the state of the wave changes continuously and all the values in the range are included. Figure 2-3 depicts an analog signal.

Note   The analog signals are measured in terms of *amplitude, frequency,* and *phase.* Amplitude represents the strength of the current and is measured in volts (if amplitude is measured as electrical potential) and watts (if amplitude is measured as electrical power) and decibels (if amplitude is measured as the ratio of the power of two signals). Frequency represents the time taken by a signal to complete a cycle and is measured in hertz or cycles per second. Phase represents the relative state of the signal at the time of measurement and is measured in degrees.

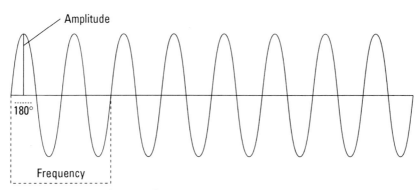

Figure 2-3: An analog signal

✦ **Digital signals** — Signals that represent only two states — the presence of data (1) and the absence of data (0). 1 is commonly referred to as the ON state, and 0 represents the OFF state. Figure 2-4 depicts a digital signal.

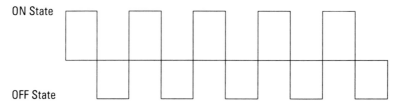

Figure 2-4: A digital signal

Cross-Reference   For detailed information on transmission media and how signals traverse them, refer to Chapter 3.

Physical connection types

The transmission medium connects the computers on a network in the following two ways:

✦ **Point-to-point connection** — In this type of connection, one transmission medium provides a direct link between two communicating devices (see Figure 2-5). This connection type is faster and more expensive than a multipoint connection. An example of a point-to-point connection is a leased line connecting an organization directly to its ISP (Internet Service Provider).

Figure 2-5: Point-to-point connection

For more information on ISPs, refer to Chapter 11.

✦ **Multipoint connection** — In this type of connection, one transmission medium is shared between three or more network devices (see Figure 2-6). As a result, the connection is comparatively slower and cheaper than point-to-point connections. For example, you can have many network devices connected to a server through one cable.

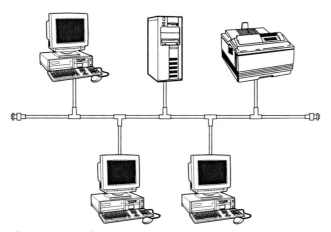

Figure 2-6: Multipoint connection

Physical topologies

In a network, the physical arrangement of transmission media is known as a *network topology*. The most common topologies in today's local area networks (LANs) are:

✦ **Bus topology** — In this topology (shown in Figure 2-7), all the network devices are connected to a main cable, called a *backbone*, either through short cables known as *drop cables* or directly through T-connectors. To prevent a signal from infinitely traversing the network, the backbone must be terminated at both ends. Of all the topologies, the bus topology is considered the easiest and cheapest to implement. However, the bus topology is slower than the others, and it is difficult to troubleshoot network problems in this topology.

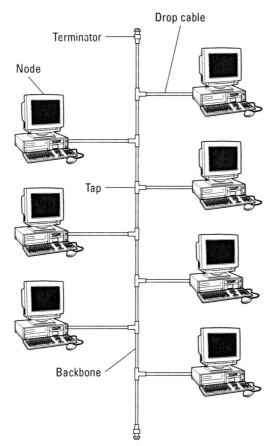

Figure 2-7: Bus topology

✦ **Star topology** — In this topology (shown in Figure 2-8), all the network devices are connected to a central device, called a *hub*, through drop cables. As a result, each device has a point-to-point connection to the hub. This topology is easy to manage, expand, and troubleshoot. However, the entire network goes down if the hub fails.

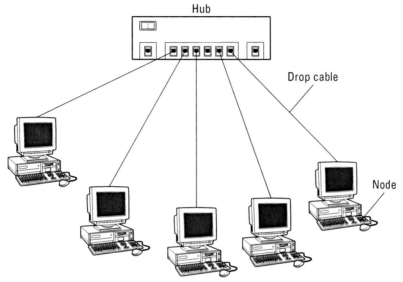

Figure 2-8: Star topology

✦ **Ring topology** — In this topology (shown in Figure 2-9), each network device is connected to the next device to form a closed loop or ring. This topology is easy to manage and troubleshoot. However, it is very expensive to implement and difficult to reconfigure.

✦ **Mesh topology** — In this topology (shown in Figure 2-10), each node is directly connected to every other node on the network through a point-to-point connection. This topology is extremely resistant to faults. However, it is extremely expensive to implement.

Cross-Reference

For more information on various topologies, refer to Chapter 3.

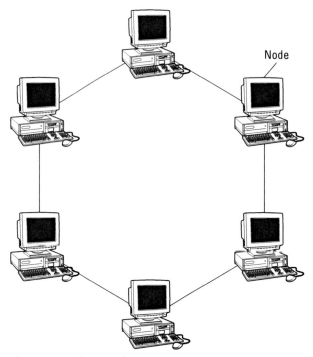

Figure 2-9: Ring topology

Physical layer network devices

A number of hardware networking devices are required to build a network and connect each computer on the network to the transmission medium. The network devices that are normally associated with the Physical layer of the TCP/IP model include:

✦ **Media connectors** — The transmission media connectors provide the point of connectivity between the network devices and the transmission medium. Every medium has one or more connectors that you can use to attach a device to it. The most commonly used physical connectors, shown in Figure 2-11, include:

- T-connectors and BNC connectors

- RJ-45

- DB-25 (also known as RS-232)

- DB-15

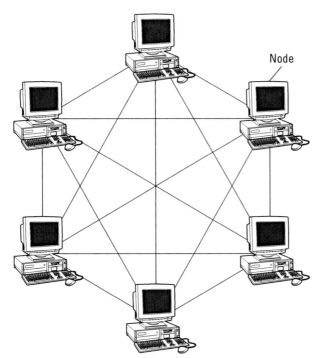

Node

Figure 2-10: Mesh topology

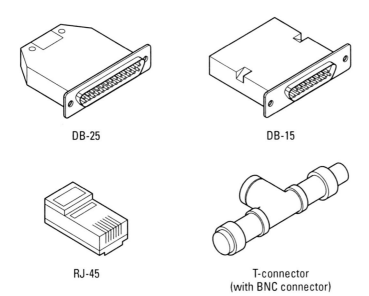

DB-25   DB-15

RJ-45   T-connector
                         (with BNC connector)

Figure 2-11: Common connectors

◆ **Repeaters** — The longer the distance a signal travels, the more it attenuates. Therefore, every transmission medium can only be used up to a certain distance. A transmission medium can, however, be extended by the use of repeaters. A *repeater* simply amplifies signals to their original strength. Figure 2-12 depicts a repeater.

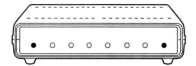

Figure 2-12: A repeater

◆ **Hubs** — Hubs act as central points for connecting multiple network devices. Figure 2-13 depicts a typical hub. Two types of hubs belong to the Physical layer:

- **Active hubs** — Hubs that regenerate a signal, in addition to acting as the central connection point.

- **Passive hubs** — Hubs that simply broadcast a signal received from a connected device. Passive hubs do not perform any signal-regeneration.

Note   There is a third category of hubs known as *intelligent hubs.* However, these hubs function at the Network Interface layer.

Figure 2-13: A hub

◆ **Modems** — If a computer (which uses digital signals) was to be directly connected to an analog telephone line (which carries only analog signals), no communication would be possible. A modem (MOdulator/DEModulator) (as shown in Figure 2-14) converts digital signals received from a computer to analog signals that can be transmitted over an analog telephone line. On receiving a signal from an analog telephone line, the modem converts the signal to digital so that the computer can process it.

Figure 2-14: A modem

The Network Interface layer

The primary responsibilities of the Network Interface layer include:

✦ Uniquely identifying the devices on a local area network (LAN) with the help of Media Access Control (MAC) addresses

✦ Organizing the bits received from the Physical layer into *frames*

✦ Converting IP addresses to LAN addresses and vice versa

✦ Detecting and notifying errors to the upper layers

✦ Controlling data flow

Network Interface layer devices

The network devices commonly associated with the Network Interface layer include:

✦ **NICs (Network Interface Cards)** — NICs are hardware expansion cards that, when installed, provide network connectivity to computers by connecting them to the transmission medium.

✦ **Bridges** — In a large network (especially if the physical topology is bus), all devices connected to the backbone receive signals that are kept on the backbone. This generates unnecessary network traffic. However, a bridge can be used to break a large network into smaller segments, thus effectively reducing the unnecessary network traffic. When a bridge receives a signal, it checks to see if the recipient device is in a local segment. If so, the bridge broadcasts the received signal in the segment and does not forward the signal to other segments. If the recipient does not belong to the local segment, the bridge forwards the signal only to that segment where the recipient device is located, thus effectively reducing the network traffic. Figure 2-15 depicts the typical bridge operation.

✦ **Intelligent hubs** — In addition to acting as the center point for network communication and regenerating signals, an intelligent hub forwards signals only to the recipient device, instead of broadcasting the signal to all the devices that are connected to it.

Media access control standards

To ensure that networks function properly, the possibility of two or more signals being placed on the transmission medium simultaneously should be either minimized or completely eliminated. Networks use rules that control when a network device can transmit data packets. These rules are known as *media access control standards*.

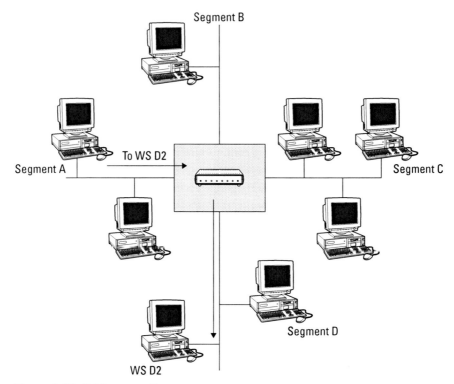

Figure 2-15: Bridge operation

Depending on the physical topology in use, there are different media access standards, such as:

✦ **Contention** — In this method, every device on the network contends to place its signal first on the transmission medium. When two or more devices place their signals on the medium simultaneously, the signals collide and are destroyed. This access method is commonly used in bus topologies.

✦ **Token passing** — In this method, a special frame, called a *token*, continuously circulates the network. Any device that wants to transmit data captures the token and places the data in the token frame. After the transmission is complete, the device releases the token. This access method is used in ring topologies.

✦ **Polling** — In this method, a master device polls the network devices at regular intervals. When a device needs to transmit data, the master device sends a request packet to the device. The device places the data in the request frame and returns the packet to the master device, which then forwards the frame to the intended recipient. Intelligent hubs in the star topology commonly use this access method.

For detailed information on media access methods, refer to Chapter 4.

Flow control

A network is made up of devices that support different transmission speeds. For example, switches are much faster than hubs. As a rule, printers are one of the slowest network devices. If the sender transmits frames faster than the receiver can handle them, the sender would keep sending frames until the receiver is swamped. Even if the transmission were error free, there would come a point when the receiver would not be able to handle the frames as they arrived and would start losing them. As a result, the amount of data that can be sent at one time when two network entities communicate is a very important issue.

Predefined rules, called *flow control* rules, make sure that the faster devices do not flood the slower ones during a transaction. The flow control throttles the transmission speed of the sender into sending no faster than the receiver can handle the traffic. The flow control uses a feedback mechanism so that the receiver can tell the sender whether or not the receiver is able to keep up with the speed of transmission. For example, when a connection is set up, the receiver might tell the sender to send n number of frames and stop until the receiver explicitly or implicitly grants permission to continue.

Note   The flow control is generally built into the various protocols as well-defined rules and regulates both end devices (such as workstations) and intermediary devices (such as routers).

The Network Interface layer flow control implements two strategies:

✦ **Guaranteed rate flow control** — In this flow control strategy, the sender and the receiver entities negotiate an acceptable transmission rate for the entire session, even before the transmission starts. This rate is guaranteed to remain constant for the entire session.

✦ **Window flow control** — This flow control allows the two communicating devices to negotiate for the size of a buffer or window into which a set number of frames can be placed. There are two types of window flow controls:

  • **Static window flow control** — When the connection is set up, the end entities agree on a window size and use this window size throughout the current session, until the connection is closed. Suppose that in the beginning of the connection, the sender and receiver agree upon a window size of eight frames. The sender then collects eight data frames, assigns a temporary number to each frame, and sets the frames on the transmission medium. In this case, the window number will vary from one to eight. Upon receiving a frame, the receiver needs to send an acknowledgement. If the sender has sent all eight frames, the sender must wait until it gets acknowledgement of at least one of the assigned numbers. The sender then restarts the whole process for the next eight frames. This process ensures that never more than eight frames are outstanding.

Caution   This strategy results in wasted available network bandwidth, since every frame that is sent needs to be acknowledged.

- **Dynamic window flow control** — When the connection is set up, a window size is agreed upon. However, this type of flow control allows the network devices to adjust the window size as and when needed, according to the current status of the receiver. At the onset of connection, the maximum size of the window is established. If at any time during the transmission the receiver's buffer starts overflowing, it immediately sends out a *choke packet.* The choke packet is a signal for the sender to slow down. After some time, the sender slowly starts increasing the transmission rate until it receives another choke packet. In this way, the window size is constantly adjusted during the transmission itself. Dynamic window flow control is also known as *floating* or *sliding window flow control.*

The Internet layer

The Network Interface layer identifies a device uniquely in a LAN with the help of *physical addresses* or the *Media Access Control (MAC) addresses* that are hard-coded into the Network Interface Cards (NICs). However, this method of identifying devices uniquely is not effective when the communication occurs between two devices that are located in different networks. The Internet layer uses *IP addresses* to transmit packets across networks.

An IP address is a 32-bit binary addressing convention that was developed to facilitate global communication. To remember them easily, IP addresses are denoted as four decimal-based integers that are separated by decimal points. This representation is known as *dotted decimal notation.* For example, 23.33.71.11 represents an IP address.

Depending on the number of hosts and networks that an address range can support, there are five IP address classes:

- ✦ Class A, which can support IP addresses from 0.1.0.0 to 126.0.0.0
- ✦ Class B, which can support IP addresses from 128.0.0.0 to 191.255.0.0
- ✦ Class C, which can support IP addresses from 192.0.1.0 to 223.255.255.0
- ✦ Class D, which can support IP addresses from 224.0.0.0 to 239.255.255.255
- ✦ Class E, which can support IP addresses from 240.0.0.0 to 247.255.255.255

Cross-Reference   For detailed information on IP addressing and IP address classes, refer to Chapter 5.

Switching

There might be more than one path that links two devices communicating across networks. To ensure a speedy delivery, a signal can switch these paths as and when required, using the following three switching techniques:

✦ **Circuit switching** — In this switching method, a dedicated communication channel (circuit) is required between the two communicating devices.

✦ **Message switching** — In this switching method, no dedicated physical connection needs to be established between the communication points. The message is divided into small parts that are each assigned a number. Each part is treated as an independent entity, and each carries the address information of the destination. The messages are stored at each switch before being forwarded to the next switch in the route.

✦ **Packet switching** — In this switching method, messages are broken into segments called *packets*, which are routed individually through the network. Each packet contains the address information of the source and the destination, along with the actual data.

Note There is one basic difference between packet switching and message switching. In message switching, there is no upper limit for the message block, but in packet switching, packets are restricted to a specific size.

Route discovery and selection

Routers are the network devices associated with the Internet layer functions. To ensure the fastest delivery of data from one device to another, the router must discover the shortest and fastest path. This method of determining routes to a destination network is known as *route discovery*. There are two types of route discovery:

✦ **Distance vector method** — In this method, each router maintains a routing table that it broadcasts at regular intervals. As a result, each router keeps updating information about any new routes that it received from other broadcasts. Though this method ensures that every neighboring router has the latest routing table, it generates a very high amount of network traffic.

✦ **Link-state method** — In this method, broadcasts are generated only when any change occurs in the existing routing table of a router. The other routers that receive the broadcast update their routing tables accordingly. As a result, this method generates considerably less network traffic.

Cross-Reference For more information on routing, refer to Chapter 5.

After a router builds its routing table by discovering routes to the destination networks, it can select an appropriate path to the destination network device by calculating the best path during a transmission. This selection can either be *dynamic* or *static:*

✦ **Dynamic route selection** — If, at any point in time, there are multiple paths available to the destination device, the router determines the best path. This selection happens at each router along the way to the destination device. In other words, the routing table is maintained automatically, without any interference from the network administrator.

✦ **Static route selection** — Even if there are multiple paths available to the destination device, only the path designated by the network administrator is used to route packets across the networks. The routers in the way to the destination device cannot make routing decisions. In other words, the routing table is created and maintained by the network administrator.

Cross-
Reference

For detailed information on static and dynamic routing, refer to Chapter 19.

The Transport layer

The fourth layer of the TCP/IP model, the Transport layer, is primarily responsible for:

✦ Providing an interface between the lower layers (Internet, Network Interface, and Physical layers) and the Application layer

✦ Delivering data from the sender to the recipient

The lower layers can locate the intended recipient (in the same network or across different networks) and transmit the data to it. However, these layers cannot ensure reliable connection services. The Transport layer fulfills both of these requirements. It uses two protocols for communication purposes — TCP and User Datagram Protocol (UDP). TCP provides connection-oriented services, whereas UDP provides connectionless services.

Note

Reliable connection services do not imply that data will be transferred no matter what. The term *reliable* means that the Transport layer protocols can acknowledge or deny the successful reception of data. If the data did not reach the recipient or was corrupted during transmission, the Transport layer can initiate retransmission. The Application layer is also informed about the failure, which can either initiate the corrective actions or inform the user.

Connection services

The Transport layer provides connection services of two types:

✦ **Connection oriented** — When data is transferred from one network device to another, each successfully transferred batch of uncorrupted data is acknowledged by the recipient. The sender does not send any data until it receives a positive acknowledgement for the last batch that it sent. If data is lost or corrupted during transmission, the sender does not receive the corresponding acknowledgement from the recipient. The sender will either have to resend the corrupted packet or send the entire batch, depending on the protocol implementations. Connection-oriented services also provide flow control and error control.

✦ **Connectionless** — The sender device transmits data to the recipient and is not responsible for retransmission of any data that was corrupted or lost while traversing to the recipient. There are two types of connectionless services:

- **Acknowledged connectionless services** — Acknowledgement messages are exchanged if the transmission is point-to-point. These services also provide error and flow control if the transmission is point-to-point.

- **Unacknowledged connectionless services** — Transmissions are not acknowledged, nor is any flow control, error control, or packet sequence control provided.

For detailed information on connection-oriented and connectionless services, refer to Chapter 6.

Segment handling

In addition to the reliable connection services, the Transport layer is also responsible for breaking large Application layer messages into segments that can be transferred over the transmission medium. This is known as *fragmentation*. When a network device receives the message in the form of several segments, the Transport layer is responsible for correctly assembling these segments into the original message, a process known as *defragmentation*.

Transport layer flow control

Transport layer flow control is also known as *end-to-end flow control* because Transport layer flow control deals with connections between the sender and receiver nodes. The Transport layer performs flow control by using the following types of acknowledgements:

✦ **Positive and negative acknowledgements** — If the transmitted data was received without any loss or corruption, the recipient sends a positive acknowledgement to the sender. If the data was corrupted, however, the recipient sends a negative acknowledgement. In this case, corrective actions are taken either by the Transport layer or by the Application layer that originated the transaction.

✦ **Go back *n* acknowledgement** — The "go back *n*" acknowledgement signifies that the sender must resend a part of the message, starting from the packet numbered *n* in the last transaction.

✦ **Selective repeat acknowledgement** — The "selective repeat" acknowledgement signifies that a string of packets was received correctly, but a few embedded packets were lost or damaged during the transmission. It tells the sender to resend only the missing or damaged packets, rather than the entire string.

Error control

At times, the loss of data is inevitable during transmission. Furthermore, it is possible that data would reach the correct destination but would become corrupted during the transmission process. The Transport layer controls these errors in the following manner:

✦ During a transmission, segments are assigned unique numbers to avoid duplication in segment numbers and therefore loss of any packets.

✦ Packets that have exceeded their existence interval (determined on the basis of TTL used by the Internet layer) are dropped, because the longer a data packet travels, the higher the probability of its corruption.

✦ During a session, only one virtual path is used to minimize the probability of loss of data packets.

For detailed information on the Transport layer, refer to Chapter 6.

The Application layer

The Application layer is the highest layer in the TCP/IP architecture model. It is also the most important layer, since it interacts with the user directly. The Application layer supports all the protocols necessary to provide network services, such as file services, message services, database services, and print services. As a result, all the transactions are initiated at this layer. Actually, the other layers of the model exist to support this layer.

Software packages, such as Microsoft Word, Excel, and so on, are *not* a part of the Application layer. Only applications that initiate a request that can be fulfilled by other network devices — such as e-mail — are considered a part of the Application layer.

The most commonly used Application layer protocols include:

✦ **File Transfer Protocol (FTP)** — A secure and reliable protocol for transferring files from a remote system to the local machine. The user needs to establish a connection with the remote computer before the file transfer is possible.

✦ **Trivial File Transfer Protocol (TFTP)** — A protocol that uses UDP as the transport protocol. As a result, the user need not establish a connection with the other device or log in to the remote system to transfer files.

For more information on FTP and TFTP, refer to Chapter 12.

✦ **TELecommunication NETwork (Telnet)** — A protocol that allows users to interact with a remote system as if they were working with the local system. This happens because Telnet overrides the local interpretation of all keystrokes.

For more information on Telnet, refer to Chapter 13.

✦ **Simple Mail Transfer Protocol (SMTP)** — A protocol that, when used with an e-mail application, allows users to send and receive electronic mail (e-mails) over the network.

For more information on SMTP, refer to Chapter 16.

✦ **Simple Network Management Protocol (SNMP)** — A network management protocol. SNMP primarily collects, analyzes, and reports data related to the performance of the various network components to network management applications.

Communication Between Layers

According to the TCP/IP architecture model, a layer in a stack can communicate with its peer layer. However, in order to do so, the layer needs to send the data or messages through the lower layers of the same stack to which it belongs. A layer can take advantage of the services of the layer immediately below it. At the same time, each layer needs to provide services to the layer immediately above it.

When a layer passes data to its lower layer, it adds its own *header* to the data. The header contains the layer's control information. Only the peer layer in the other stack can process this control information. Generally, the requests for network services originate at the Application layer. In this case, the message is passed down to the Transport layer, which breaks the message into smaller segments that can be transferred over the transmission medium. The Transport layer, like its predecessor layer, also adds its own header to each segment and passes the segments along to the Internet layer. This process of breaking down large messages into segments is known as *fragmentation*. The Internet layer, in turn, adds its header to each segment and passes the packet to the Network Interface layer. Like all the upper layers, the Network Interface layer adds its own header to the datagrams that it received from the Internet layer and sends these frames to the Physical layer. The Physical layer breaks each frame into a sequence of bits and places these signals on the transmission medium.

Note   The data at the Application layer is referred to as a *message*. At the Transport layer, the data is known as *segments* or *datagrams*. At the Internet layer, the segments are referred to as *packets*. When passed to the Network Interface layer, the packets are known as *frames,* and when passed to the Physical layer, as *bits* or *signals*.

After the signals are routed to the intended recipient by using the control information provided by the Internet layer headers and the Network Interface layer headers, the way these signals are processed at the recipient side is exactly opposite to that at the sender side. The Physical layer of the recipient takes the signals off the transmission medium and passes them to the Network Interface layer. The Network Interface layer, using the control information provided by its peer layer, converts the bits into frames and passes the frames to the Internet layer. The Internet layer, in turn, strips off the corresponding header and passes the packets to the Transport layer. The Transport layer, using the control information provided by the Transport layer header, reassembles these segments into a message. This process of reassembling segments into a message is known as *defragmentation*. Then the Transport layer passes the message to the Application layer, which processes it and, if required, displays the information to the user. The entire process of encapsulation and de-encapsulation is shown in Figure 2-16.

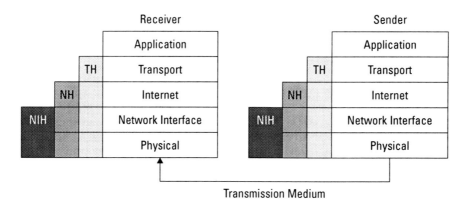

Figure 2-16: Encapsulation and de-encapsulation

Transport layer header format

Depending on the type of communication — reliable or unreliable — the Transport layer headers can be of the following two types: TCP header or UDP header.

TCP header format

The TCP header format, as shown in Figure 2-17, consists of the following fields:

✦ **Source port address** — Contains the address of the TCP port of the application at the sender side that originated the request. The length of the field is two bytes.

✦ **Destination port address** — Contains the address of the TCP port of the application at the recipient side that must answer the request. The length of the field is two bytes.

✦ **Sequence number** — Contains the sequence number of the segment when the message was broken into segments. The length of the field is four bytes.

✦ **Acknowledgement number** — Contains the number of the next segment that the recipient should receive. The length of the field is four bytes.

✦ **HLEN** — Contains the length of the segment header. The length of the field is four bits.

✦ **Reserved** — The value of the field must be zero, because the field is reserved for future use. The length of the field is six bits.

✦ **Control bits** — Contains the following six 1-bit fields, which indicate how the other fields in the header should be interpreted.

  • **URG** — If the value of the field is 0, the Urgent Pointer field should be ignored. However, if the value is 1, the Urgent Pointer field is valid.

  • **ACK** — If the value of the field is 0, the Acknowledgement number field should be ignored. However, if the value is 1, the Acknowledgement number field is valid.

  • **PSH** — If the value of the field is 0, the field should be ignored. However, if the value is 1, the segment initiates the push function.

  • **RST** — If the value of the field is 0, the field should be ignored. However, if the value is 1, the connection is reset.

  • **SYN** — If the value of the field is 1, the segment requests a new connection.

  • **FIN** — If the value of the field is 1, it signifies that the sender has no more data to send, and the connection must be closed after the current segment.

✦ **Window** — Contains the size of the sender's buffer and specifies the number of bytes the sender of the segment can currently accept. The length of the field is two bytes.

✦ **Checksum** — Contains the checksum to verify the integrity of the data received. The field also contains a *pseudoheader,* which helps the recipient device verify that the field has reached the correct destination. The length of the Checksum field is two bytes.

✦ **Urgent pointer**—Contains the information to identify the position in the segment where the urgent data ends. This field is processed only if the URG field of the Control bits is set to 1. The length of the field is two bytes.

✦ **Options**—Contains the information about several functions, such as Maximum Segment Size (MSS) that the connection ends can receive, end of options, and so on. The length of the field is variable.

✦ **Padding**—Contains a set of zeros that need to be appended to the header to ensure that the header is 32 bytes long. The length of the field is variable.

SOURCE PORT			DESTINATION PORT	
SEQUENCE NUMBER				
ACKNOWLEDGEMENT NUMBER				
HLEN	RESERVED	CONTROL BITS	WINDOW	
CHECKSUM			URGENT POINTER	
OPTIONS (IF ANY)				PADDING

Figure 2-17: TCP header format

UDP header format

The UDP header format, as shown in Figure 2-18, consists of the following fields:

✦ **Source port address**—Contains the address of the UDP port of the application at the sender side that originated the request. The length of the field is two bytes.

✦ **Destination port address**—Contains the address of the UDP port of the application at the recipient side that must answer the request. The length of the field is two bytes.

✦ **Length**—Contains the length of the segment header. The length of the field is two bytes.

✦ **Checksum**—Contains a *pseudoheader,* which helps the recipient device verify that the field has reached the correct destination. The use of the field is optional. The length of the field is two bytes.

0	16	31
UDP SOURCE PORT	UDP DESTINATION PORT	
UDP MESSAGE LENGTH	UDP CHECKSUM	

Figure 2-18: UDP header format

Internet layer header format

The Internet layer header format, as shown in Figure 2-19, consists of the following fields:

✦ **Version** — Represents the version of the IP protocol. The current version of the IP protocol is 4 (IPv4). The length of the field is four bits.

✦ **Length** — Contains the length of the Internet layer header. The length of the field is four bits.

✦ **Service type** — Contains the information on how to process the datagram and Quality of Service (QoS) desired. The length of the field is one byte.

Note The Service type field is also referred to as *Type Of Service (TOS)*.

✦ **Total length** — Contains the total length of the datagram, including the length of the header and the data contained. The length of the field is two bytes.

Note The length of the field, 16 bits, indicates that the maximum size of the IP datagram (or packet) can be up to 65,535 bytes (2^{16}). The minimum size of the IP packet is 576 bytes.

✦ **Identification** — Contains information for reassembly of the fragments of a datagram. The length of the field is two bytes.

✦ **Flags** — Contains the following three control flags:

• **Bit 0** — This is a reserved bit that must always contain a zero.

• **Bit 1** — If the value of the field is 0, the datagram may be fragmented. However, if the value of the field is 1, the datagram cannot be fragmented.

• **Bit 2** — If the value of the field is 0, the fragment is the last in the data stream, and no more are to follow. However, if the value of the field is 1, it indicates that more fragments are to follow.

✦ **Fragment offset** — Contains the position of the fragment in the datagram, if the datagram is fragmented. The length of the field is thirteen bits.

✦ **Time to Live (TTL)** — Contains the maximum time (in seconds) a datagram can exist. Each router that the datagram passes to reach the destination reduces this value by 1. If the value of this field decrements to zero, the datagram is discarded. The length of the field is one byte.

✦ **Protocol** — Contains the information about the Application layer protocol that originated the request. The length of the field is one byte.

Note   Refer to RFC 1700 for values assigned for the various protocols.

✦ **Header checksum**—Contains the checksum meant for the IP header only. Each time the header is modified, this value needs to be calculated. The length of the field is two bytes.

✦ **Source IP address**—Contains the IP address of the sender device. The length of the field is two bytes.

✦ **Destination IP address**—Contains the IP address of the recipient device. The length of the field is two bytes.

✦ **IP options**—Contains the information about several IP functions. The length of the field is variable.

✦ **Padding**—Contains a set of zeros that need to be appended to the header to ensure that the header is 32 bytes long. The use of the field is optional. The length of the field is variable.

VERS	HLEN	SERVICE TYPE	TOTAL LENGTH	
IDENTIFICATION			FLAGS	FRAGMENT OFFSET
TIME TO LIVE		PROTOCOL	HEADER CHECKSUM	
SOURCE IP ADDRESS				
DESTINATION IP ADDRESS				
IP OPTIONS			PADDING	

Figure 2-19: Internet layer header format

Cross-
Reference   For information on Network Interface layer header format, refer to Chapter 4.

Summary

In this chapter, you learned about the five-layer TCP/IP architecture model. These layers include:

✦ The Physical layer, which is responsible for transferring data (in the form of bits) over the transmission medium. It also defines the topology and the type of connection between network devices.

✦ The Network Interface layer, which is responsible for identifying network devices over a LAN, frame formation, and error control.

✦ The Internet layer, which is responsible for discovering routes to the destination device, selecting the appropriate path, and routing packets across different networks on the basis of IP addresses of the communicating devices.

✦ The Transport layer, which, in addition to acting as an interface between the highest layer (the Application layer) and the lower layers, is responsible for delivering data from the source device to the destination device. The Transport layer also plays an active role in error control.

✦ The Application layer, which acts as an interface between the user and the network.

Besides learning about their functions, you also learned about the process of communication between the layers.

✦   ✦   ✦

Physical Layer

◆ ◆ ◆ ◆

In This Chapter

Transmitting data
over a wire

Examining common
topologies

◆ ◆ ◆ ◆

Every layer in a communication system plays a crucial
role in successful communication over the network.
Failure at one single layer leads to failure of the entire communication system. Therefore, each communication layer must
work properly for the entire communication system over a
network to work properly. The Physical layer, which is the
lowest layer in the five-layer TCP/IP architecture, handles the
physical transmission of data in a computer network. The
Physical layer receives the data that is passed down to it from
the upper layers and formats it so that it can be sent over the
transmission media, such as cable, fiber optics, microwave,
and radio waves. This chapter explores the characteristics of
the Physical layer, the different media that can be used for
data transmission, and the common topologies for communication over the media.

How Signals Traverse a Wire

The Physical layer's main responsibility is to send and receive
bits. The Physical layer formats the messages received from
the upper layer and sends them (in the form of bits: 1s and 0s)
over the media. Different types of media represent these bit
values in different ways, such as distinct audio tones and different voltages. The Physical layer defines the specifications
for implementing a particular transmission medium. Some of
the Physical layer implementations are Ethernet, Token Ring,
ARCnet, FDDI, and wireless. For implementing a particular
medium, the Physical layer includes a set of protocols that
describe the bit patterns used, the way the data is encoded
into media signals, and the attachment interface of the physical medium.

The layered architecture of a communication system gives
you the advantage of changing one layer without affecting the
other layers. As technology advances in the field of physical
media, you might need to change the Physical layer accordingly. Because TCP/IP follows a layered architecture, you can
change the Physical layer to implement the new technology
without affecting the operation of the other communication
layers.

Transmission/signaling methods

Signaling methods are the methods by which data is transmitted over a medium. Signals use electric energy to communicate. Depending on the transmission media used, either analog or digital signals can be transmitted.

Analog transmission

Analog transmission involves the exchange of data between computers in the form of audio or video signals. These signals are referred to as *analog signals.* Analog signals change constantly and represent all values in the range between the two values.

Analog signals are usually represented as a series of sine waves, as shown in Figure 3-1. Each wave consists of crests (upper peaks) and troughs (lower peaks). One trough and one crest together constitute a cycle. Each wave is characterized by certain parameters, such as amplitude, frequency, and phase. *Amplitude* refers to the magnitude of a trough or a crest that is identified by the highest point of a crest or the lowest point of a trought. *Frequency* refers to the number of cycles that are formed per unit time. *Phase* refers to the angle of the wave from the point of origin. Each signal is identified by these wave parameters, which represent the actual data.

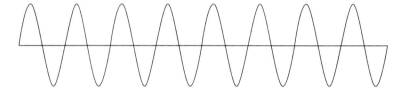

Figure 3-1: Analog signal

The Physical layer sends the binary data over the analog transmission medium. This binary data is converted into signals of varying frequency and amplitude, which are then added to electromagnetic carrier waves. *Electromagnetic (EM) carrier waves* are the analog waves that carry the signals from one end of communication to the other. During the transmission, these added signals vary one or more parameters, such as amplitude, frequency, or phase, of the carrier waves. This process of varying the parameters of EM carrier waves is called *modulation,* or *shift keying.* There are three types of shift keying:

◆ **Amplitude Shift Keying (ASK)** — The amplitude of the carrier wave is varied between discrete values to represent the digital data. For the binary data, two different voltage levels are used to represent 0 and 1, respectively. Figure 3-2 shows the Amplitude Shift Keying.

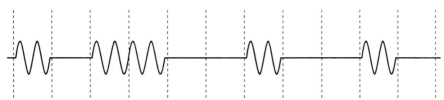

Figure 3-2: Amplitude Shift Keying

✦ **Frequency Shift Keying (FSK)** — The frequency of the carrier wave is varied between discrete values to represent the digital data. For the binary data, two different tones are used to represent 0 and 1, respectively. Figure 3-3 shows the Frequency Shift Keying.

Figure 3-3: Frequency Shift Keying

✦ **Phase Shift Keying (PSK)** — The phase of the carrier wave at the beginning of the pulse is changed between discrete values. For binary data, the carrier wave is systematically shifted 45, 135, 225, and 315 degrees at uniformly spaced intervals. Each phase shift transmits 2 bits of information. Figure 3-4 shows Phase Shift Keying.

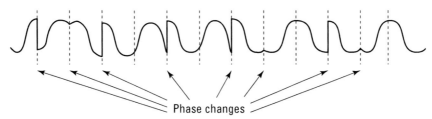

Figure 3-4: Phase Shift Keying

Digital transmission

Digital transmission involves the exchange of data between computers in the form of discrete units, that is, ON or OFF, 1 or 0. The signals that represent the discrete states are referred to as *digital signals,* and they are shown in Figure 3-5. These discrete state changes are instantaneous.

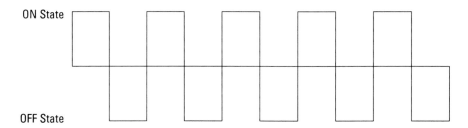

Figure 3-5: Digital signals

In digital transmission, when two computers need to communicate, they must agree upon the format of the data to be used. The way binary data is formatted is called *Pulse Code Modulation (PCM)*. Some of the different PCM formats used are NRZ-L, NRZ-M, NRZ-S, Bi-Phase-L, Bi-Phase-M, Bi-Phase-S, DBi-Phase-M, and DDi-Phase S.

Errors during the PCM transmission process can be checked by using the *parity checksum* method. In this method, a *checksum* is added to each piece of transmitted data. Parity checksum can be even or odd. In an *even parity checksum,* a 0 or 1 is added to make the overall number of ones even. In an *odd parity checksum,* a 0 or 1 is added to make the overall number of ones odd.

Transmission technologies and mechanisms

Communication over a network can use different transmission technologies and mechanisms. The two techniques used for the transmission of both analog and digital signals are:

✦ **Baseband transmission** — This type of transmission uses digital signaling over a single frequency. It uses the entire media bandwidth for a single channel. Each device in a baseband network transmits signals bidirectionally. A baseband system uses *repeaters* that regenerate a digital signal to its original strength at regular intervals.

✦ **Broadband transmission** — This type of transmission uses analog signaling and provides the functionality to divide the entire bandwidth into multiple channels. Since each channel can carry a different analog signal, a broadband network supports multiple simultaneous transmissions over a single transmission medium. In a broadband transmission, signal flow is unidirectional. A broadband system uses *amplifiers* that regenerate an analog signal to its original strength at regular intervals. Since the signal flow is unidirectional, two paths need to be provided for data flow so that the signal can reach all devices. Two common ways to provide two paths for data flow are:

- **Mid-split broadband** — The bandwidth is divided into two channels, each using a different frequency or range of frequencies. One channel is used to transmit, and the other is used to receive the signals.

- **Dual-cable broadband** — Each device is attached to two cables. One cable is used to send signals, and the other is used to receive signals.

Circuit-switching

The *circuit-switching,* or *connection-oriented,* mechanism requires a dedicated connection (or circuit) between the two communication points. The analog signal transmission, such as with the telephone system, follows the circuit-switching communication mechanism. In this system, when a call is made from the sender's telephone, a circuit is established between the sender's telephone through the local switching office, across trunk lines, to the remote switching office, and ultimately to the receiver's telephone. The same mechanism is also followed across some computer networks that use telephone lines as the communication medium.

Message-switching

In *message-switching,* no dedicated physical connection needs to be established between the communication points. The message is divided into small parts; each part is an independent entity and carries the address information of the destination. The messages are stored at each switch before being forwarded to the next switch in the route. *Switches* are specialized devices that are used to connect two or more transmission lines. At each switch, messages are received in buffers, checked for errors, and then retransmitted. To store the messages in buffers until forwarding is possible, the switches must be equipped with sufficient storage. The networks that use the message-switching technique are also called *store-and-forward* networks.

In message-switching, there is no upper limit on the size of the message block. Therefore, the messages might get delayed if a single message block obstructs the communication line. Hence, this mechanism cannot be used for real-time applications, including data communication, audio, and video. It can, however (due to its low cost), be used for applications where a certain amount of delay is admissible, such as workflow, calendaring, and groupware.

Packet-switching

In the *packet-switching* mechanism, messages are broken into segments called *packets,* which are routed individually through the network. Each packet contains the address information of the source and the destination along with the actual data.

Although packet-switching seems similar to message-switching, the two mechanisms differ in one way. In message-switching, there is no upper limit for the message block, but in packet-switching, packets are restricted to a specific size and can thus be routed more rapidly and efficiently than with message-switching. The packet-switching mechanism also lets the switching devices manage the packet data entirely in memory, eliminating the need to have switching devices store data temporarily on disk.

Packet-switching is useful when there is a need to transfer data through more than a single channel between two computers. In packet-switching, this can be accomplished without using separate lines for different channels, because the same communication channel can be used to transmit packets from several messages — a technique called *multiplexing*. Multiplexing can be of two types: Frequency Division Multiplexing (FDM) and Time Division Multiplexing (TDM). In *Frequency Division Multiplexing*, the frequency spectrum is divided into logical channels. Each user is allocated a frequency channel exclusively. In *Time Division Multiplexing*, on the other hand, each user gets the entire bandwidth periodically.

Two other variations of the packet-switching mechanism are frame relay and cell-switching.

✦ The *frame relay* mechanism is a high-speed version of packet-switching and is well suited for high-speed applications. In this mechanism, data is chunked into frames. The length of these frames can vary, depending on the type of network.

✦ The *cell-switching* mechanism operates under the same principles as the packet-switching mechanism, overcoming the limitation of Time Division Multiplexing (TDM). In TDM, the sending and receiving devices are synchronized to recognize the same time slots. Therefore, certain time slots can be unused. In cell-switching, the time slots are allocated when needed. Therefore, the use of time slots is optimized.

Analog transmission versus digital transmission

Analog transmission has been used for communication for the past 100 years. However, with the advent of digital transmission in 1962, digital transmission has become more popular compared to analog transmission. There are many ways in which the digital signals transmission is superior to the analog signals transmission, some of which are discussed below:

✦ **Error rate** — As signals travel along the network medium, they gradually decrease in strength and can become distorted. This distortion of signals is called *attenuation*. Digital signal transmission has a very low error rate. Analog signals suffer from attenuation. Although analog circuits use amplifiers to compensate for the attenuation, the signals can never be fully compensated. And if many amplifiers are used over a long distance, the errors cumulate, and the signals suffer considerable distortion. On the other hand, digital signals represent only two values: 0 and 1. Therefore, the weak digital signals over long distances can be restored to the exact original value, averting any cumulative distortion.

✦ **Multiplexing** — Voice, data, music, or images (such as television, facsimile, or video telephone) can be multiplexed together.

✦ **Data rates** — Refers to the amount of data that can be transmitted per second. With digital signal transmission, higher data rates are possible.

Public communication systems, such as telephone systems, were originally designed for analog signal transmission. However, as the advantages of digital transmission were recognized, public communication systems began to use digital transmission. The decreasing cost of computers and integrated circuit chips also promotes the use of digital transmission. Therefore, to meet the growing demand of data transmission, facsimile, and video, a major portion of the worldwide telephone system has been replaced with an advanced digital system called *Integrated Services Digital Network (ISDN)*.

Physical media

The Physical layer can use any of the following physical media:

✦ Electrical

✦ Mechanical

✦ Optical

In this section, you learn about different physical media that are used for communication.

Coaxial cable

Coaxial cable is the most common type of network cable, primarily because it is inexpensive, light, flexible, and easy to work with. A coaxial cable contains two conductors that share a common axis, as shown in Figure 3-6. There is a central conductor wire (a copper wire) surrounded by an outer conductor, or *shield*, which serves as a ground and protects the inner conductor from Electromagnetic Interference (EMI). An insulator layer between the inner and the outer conductor keeps the outer conductor evenly spaced from the inner conductor. Finally, an outer plastic jacket protects the cable. These cables enable data transmission speeds between 10 and100 Mbps. There are two types of coaxial cables: thin and thick.

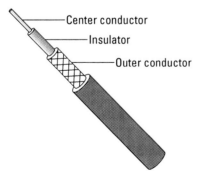

Figure 3-6: Coaxial cable

Thin coaxial cable

Thin coaxial cable, or *thinnet*, is a flexible cable about 0.25 inches thick. Thinnet can transmit a signal at a distance of about 185 meters (607 feet) without any loss in strength. It also has an impedance of 50 ohms, which means that it offers a resistance of 50 ohms to an alternating current that passes through it. Thinnet belongs to a family of cables called the RG-58 family. Cables that are included in this family use a stranded or solid copper core. Table 3-1 lists the types of coaxial cables commonly used in networks.

Table 3-1
Specifications for Coaxial Cable

Cable	Description
RG-58 /U	Solid copper wire
RG-58 A/U	Stranded wire core
RG-58 C/U	Military specification of RG-58 A/U
RG-59	Used for cable television; has an impedance of 75 ohms
RG-62	Used for ARCnet

Thick coaxial cable

Thick coaxial cable, also called *thicknet* or *standard Ethernet*, is a rigid cable about 0.5 inches thick. Thicknet can support data transfer over large distances (approximately 500 meters). However, it is more expensive than thinnet.

Note   Thinnet coaxial cable can be connected to thicknet coaxial cable with a device called a *transceiver* or *Media Attachment Unit (MAU)*.

Coaxial connection hardware

A coaxial cable requires connection components to make connections between the cable and the computer. These are known as *British Naval Connectors (BNCs)*. Several BNC components are available, such as:

- ✦ A BNC cable connector, which is either soldered to or plugged into the end of the cable

- ✦ A BNC T-connector, which joins the network interface card in the computer to the network cable

- ✦ A BNC barrel connector, which joins two separate thinnet cables to make one long cable

- ✦ A BNC terminator, which terminates each end of the bus cable

Twisted-pair cable

A twisted-pair cable contains a pair of insulated copper wires twisted around each other, as shown in Figure 3-7. This twisting reduces:

✦ The tendency of the cable to radiate radio frequency noise, which might interfere with nearby cables and electronic components. This tendency of the cable to radiate radio frequency noise is because the radiations from the twisted wires cancel each other.

✦ The tendency of wires to cause EMI.

✦ Crosstalk. (*Crosstalk* is defined as a situation where signals from one transmission channel get mixed with signals from another transmission channel.)

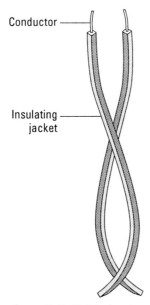

Conductor

Insulating jacket

Figure 3-7: Twisted-pair cable

There are two types of twisted-pair cables:

✦ **Unshielded Twisted Pair (UTP)** — UTP cable contains pairs of insulated copper wires twisted around each other to cancel the electromagnetic interference. UTP is becoming popular in LAN cabling. One of the main reasons for its popularity is that it is commonly used for existing telephone systems and is already installed in many office buildings. These cables are not expensive and have a connection length of approximately 100 meters (328 feet). Transmission speed ranges between 10 and 100 Mbps. One of the main disadvantages of UTP is that it is very susceptible to crosstalk. Nevertheless, this crosstalk can be considerably reduced if the UTP is shielded.

✦ **Shielded Twisted Pair (STP)** — STP cable is medium- to large-sized cable that has a metal sheath enclosing the twisted pairs of wire. The outer metal sheath protects against outer electrostatic interference. Therefore, STP is less susceptible than UTP to crosstalk *and* supports higher transmission rates. STP cables are more expensive than thin coaxial or UTP, but STP cables are less expensive than thick coaxial or fiber-optic. These cables have a connection length of approximately 100 meters, and their transmission speed ranges between 10 and 100 Mbps.

Twisted-pair cabling components

Twisted-pair cables use *RJ connectors,* which are connectors that resemble plugs, to connect to a computer. The RJ connectors are built to different specifications for different types of twisted-pair cables. The most familiar type, called RJ-11, is used for telephones. The RJ connector is simply inserted into a corresponding socket on the network adapter card.

Fiber-optic cable

A fiber-optic cable uses pulses of light instead of electrical signals to transmit data. Therefore, data signals must be converted to light signals. This conversion is performed by the light source that emits light pulses when electrical current is applied. These sources could be *LED (Light Emitting Diode)* or *laser diode.* A light pulse represents a 1 bit, while the absence of a light pulse represents a 0 bit. The detector *(photodiode)* at the end of the cable receives the light signals and converts them back to electrical signals.

As shown in Figure 3-8, the fiber-optic cable contains a highly refined glass (or fused silica) in the center that can transmit light signals. A glass cladding encases the central strand. This glass cladding has a lower density than the central strand, which ensures that the light signals are kept within the central strand by total internal reflection. Strengthening wires and a plastic outer sheath surround the glass cladding. Fiber-optic cables are more expensive than electrical cables, but they have higher bandwidths and can transmit over longer distances.

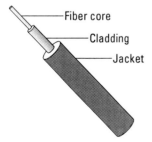

Figure 3-8: Fiber-optic cable

Fiber-optic cables possess three advantages over electrical cables:

✦ **Bandwidth capacity** — Fiber-optic cables provide extremely high bandwidth. Because fiber-optic cables use light instead of electrical signals (and light travels faster than electricity), the amount of data sent per unit time is much higher than what is possible with electric cables. Current technologies enable data transmission rates between 100 Mbps and 2 Gbps.

✦ **Attenuation** — Fiber-optic cables have lower attenuation than copper wire. Because the light rays are radiated in fiber-optic cables, the electricity radiated from copper wires is not lost. Fiber-optic cable segments can carry signals over distances measured in kilometers.

✦ **Electromagnetic Interference (EMI)** — Fiber-optic cables are immune to EMI. Since these cables do not leak signals, they do not allow crosstalk. Also, fiber-optic cables cannot be easily tapped and are, therefore, very secure.

Modems

Modem is an acronym for MOdulator/DEModulator and is used for communication between different networks that use an analog signal transmission medium, such as a telephone line. The Physical layer sends binary data, while the analog medium can transmit only analog signals. To enable communication in such a situation, the digital signals must be converted to analog signals; likewise, at the receiving end, the analog signals must be converted back to digital signals. At the sending end, modems convert the binary data signals into analog signals to be transmitted over the analog medium. This process is called *modulation*. At the receiving end, a modem converts analog signals back to digital data signals. This process is called *demodulation*. Figure 3-9 shows the functioning of a modem.

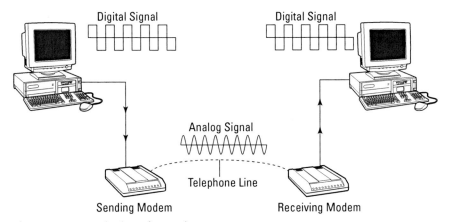

Figure 3-9: Functioning of a modem

Modems can be installed internally or externally on a computer. Internal installation involves inserting the modem into one of the expansion slots on the computer's motherboard. On the other hand, an external modem is a small box-like device that is connected to the computer. All modems require the following hardware for communication:

✦ A serial RS-232 communication interface

✦ An RJ-11 telephone line interface

Depending on the transmission method used, modems fall into two separate categories:

✦ **Asynchronous** — These modems employ asynchronous transmission for communication. In other words, the data is broken into a serial stream of bytes, and each byte is separated from the others by a start bit and a stop bit. There is no coordination between the sending computer and the receiving computer; thus, the communication is asynchronous.

✦ **Synchronous** — These modems coordinate transmissions between the sending computer and the receiving computer. In this method, the data is transmitted in the form of frames that do not use start and stop bits. Special characters facilitate synchronization and ensure the accuracy of transmission.

Error correction is a method that modems can use to verify the accuracy of data during transmission. Modems that support this feature break up data into small chunks called *frames*. The modem sending the data determines a value summary for each data frame. This value summary is called *checksum* and is attached to each data frame that is sent. The modem at the receiving end also determines the value summary for each data frame and verifies it against the checksum attached to the data frame. If the two checksums do not match, the entire frame is resent.

Wireless media

Wireless media, as the name suggests, does *not* employ any cable or wiring for transmission of data. In most cases, wireless media relies on the earth's atmosphere to act as the transmission medium. However, a network that uses wireless media is not completely free of wiring. In a mixed component network, wireless components communicate with a network that uses cables.

Because it does not require any physical media for communication, wireless media technology is expanding rapidly. It is especially useful in situations where it may not be feasible to connect network components by using cables. Usually, a computer network within a single building uses physical media, such as an electric cable or a fiber-optic cable. However, connecting two different computer networks in separate buildings within a factory complex would entail digging under the streets for cabling—an expensive undertaking. In this case, wireless media would be the best choice.

Wireless networks fall into three categories, based on the transmission techniques they employ:

✦ **Local area networks (LANs).** Wireless LANs use four transmission techniques:

  • Infrared

  • Laser

  • Narrow-band (single-frequency) radio

  • Spread-spectrum radio

✦ **Extended local area networks.** The range of wireless networks can be extended by using specialized wireless components, such as a wireless bridge. A *bridge* uses a wireless technology, such as spread-spectrum radio, to provide a path for data transfer between two networks. Both voice and data can be transferred using this method.

✦ **Mobile computing.** This technology enables travelers to remain connected to a computer network. Mobile computing employs telephone carriers and public carriers for the exchange of signals. This technology uses one of the following services:

  • **Packet-radio communication**—The data is broken up into units called packets, which are then uplinked to a satellite and broadcast in a particular area. Computers will receive those data packets that are addressed to them.

  • **Cellular networks**—A cellular network is an extended wireless LAN. It uses the services provided by cellular telephone service companies. It is also called *Cellular Digital Packet Data (CDPD)* and is fast enough to provide real-time transmissions.

  • **Microwave systems**—A microwave system consists of two radio transceivers, which are required to receive and transmit broadcasts. It also contains two bidirectional antennas, which point at each other to establish communication of the signals broadcast by transceivers.

Infrared and radio techniques are the most commonly used techniques. The following sections describe these techniques in detail.

Infrared

Infrared communication technology is most commonly used in television remote controls. Every time you press a button on the remote control, it emits pulses of infrared light. These pulses carry coded information to a receiver on the television set.

Infrared transmissions are limited to within 100 feet. The high bandwidth of infrared supports data transfer speeds up to 10 Mbps. There are four types of infrared communication technology:

✦ **Broadband optical telepoint** — Uses broadband technology and can handle high-quality multimedia requirements.

✦ **Line-of-sight infrared** — Requires a clear line of sight for communication between the transmitter and the receiver.

✦ **Reflective infrared** — Computers direct all transmissions to a common location. The transmissions are then redirected to the appropriate computers.

✦ **Scatter infrared** — Transmitters broadcast signals that eventually hit the receiver after being reflected off floors, walls, and ceiling. Because of this scattered path, the data transfer rates are slow.

Radio

In radio transmission, the transmitter need not be placed along a direct line of sight. Also, since radio waves are reflected by the earth's ionosphere, they can travel long distances. There are two types of radio transmission:

✦ **Narrow-band radio transmission** — This type of radio transmission is also called *single-frequency radio transmission*, as transmissions occur at a single frequency. This transmission does not require the transmitter to be placed along a direct line of sight. The range of narrow-band radio is also greater that that of infrared transmission.

✦ **Spread-spectrum radio transmission** — In this technique, transmissions occur at multiple frequencies. Spread-spectrum radio is commonly used for WAN transmissions and can use one of the following methods:

• **Frequency hopping** — The transmission occurs by switching between several available frequencies. Frequency hopping can only work if the transmitter and receiver are synchronized. This method supports bandwidths from 250 Kbps to as high as 2 Mbps.

• **Direct sequence modulation** — The original message is broken into parts called *chips*, which are then transmitted on separate frequencies. This method supports bandwidths from 2 Mbps to 6 Mbps.

Common Topologies

A network topology defines the structure of the network. Topologies are categorized in two ways:

✦ **Physical** — Defines the blueprint of the connected network and the actual layout of wire or media.

✦ **Logical** — Defines the way the hosts (computers, printers, or scanners) access the media (wire and cable) and communicate over a medium.

Thus, the topology of the network not only determines the type of equipment used, but also provides the guidelines for its implementation. The topology also determines how computers communicate on the network. Computers access the transmission medium by using an *access method*, or a set of rules that govern the sharing of the transmission medium.

Selecting one topology over another can impact the hardware and software requirements, management, and growth of the network. Consider the following factors when you decide what type of topology you want for your network:

✦ Network budget

✦ Network size

✦ Level of security required

✦ Physical layout of the network

✦ Type of business

✦ Amount of network traffic

Some common topologies include broadcast bus, token bus, token ring, fiber distributed data interface, and asynchronous transfer mode. The following sections take a closer look at these topologies.

Bus

In a bus topology, all computers on the network share a single communication channel, called the *backbone* or *trunk line*. The backbone can be linear or tree-shaped. Figure 3-10 shows a bus topology.

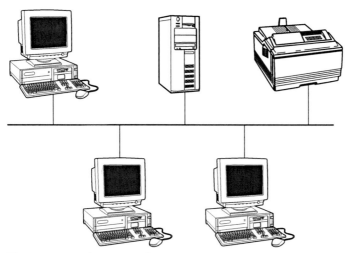

Figure 3-10: A bus network

Networks using the bus topology can broadcast messages in both the directions or only in a specific direction. The bus networks must have a special connector, called a terminator, at the end of the trunk line to prevent signals from reflecting back on the cable and causing interference. For a unidirectional bus, which can only transmit signals in a single direction, the cable should be terminated in such a way that the signals can traverse down the cable but not reflect back and cause disruption.

A bus topology is advantageous because it:

✦ Is simple, reliable in very small networks, easy to use, and easy to understand

✦ Requires the least amount of cable to connect the computers together

✦ Is easily extended

✦ Is the least expensive (as compared to other topologies)

A bus topology has the following disadvantages because:

✦ It does not work efficiently under heavy network traffic. The random transmission of data by computers in a bus network may lead to interruptions caused by simultaneous transmission in case of heavy traffic.

✦ Too many extensions on a bus can weaken the electric signal.

✦ Troubleshooting a bus network can be difficult.

Depending on the mechanism used for communication over the network, the bus topology can be a broadcast bus topology or a token bus topology.

Broadcast bus

In the broadcast bus topology, not only do all computers share a single communication channel, but all transceivers receive all transmissions on the network. A *transceiver* is a device that senses and sends the signals over the media. A host interface or host adapter is required to control the operations of a transceiver. A *host interface* plugs into the computer's bus (on the motherboard) and connects to the transceiver.

When a computer transmits, the packets are broadcast to all the transceivers. Each transceiver, in turn, passes all the packets to the host interface. The host interface chooses all the packets that are addressed to the destination computer and filters out all the others. In this mechanism, the hardware does not provide any information to the sender about the delivery of the packets. If packets are transmitted to a computer that is powered off, the packets will be lost, and the sender will not be notified.

The broadcast bus topology follows the *Carrier Sense Multiple Access/Collision Detection (CSMA/CD)* access method for communication. In this method, when a computer transmits the data and a collision occurs, the data is retransmitted after a random period of time.

Token bus

This topology follows the *token passing* access method for communication. In this method, each computer on the network knows the address of the computer to its left and right. A single frame, called a *token,* is circulated over the network in a logical ring, as shown in Figure 3-11. Only the computer that has the token is permitted to transmit. After transmission, the computer passes the token to the next computer on the network.

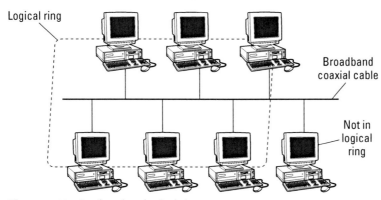

Figure 3-11: A token bus logical ring

Token Ring

The token ring topology uses the token passing access method for communication. In a ring topology, computers are connected on a single circle of cable. Unlike the bus topology, the token ring topology does not have terminated ends. Each computer in the network is connected to its neighbors on either side, as shown in Figure 3-12. The signals travel around the loop in one direction only, passing through each computer. Each computer incorporates a receiver and a transmitter, and each serves as a repeater to boost the signal that passes on to the next computer. Since the signal is regenerated at each computer, the signal degeneration is low. However, because failure of one computer in a ring topology can result in the failure of the entire network, the physical ring topology is very rarely used. The ring topology is mostly used as a logical topology.

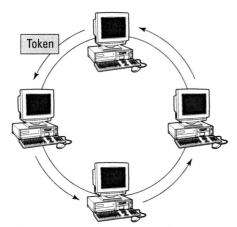

Figure 3-12: A token ring topology

A token ring network has the following advantages:

✦ Network efficiency can approach 100 percent under heavy network traffic conditions.

✦ The network enables equal access to all computers.

A token ring network has the following disadvantages:

✦ Failure of one computer on the ring can affect the entire network.

✦ Troubleshooting a token ring network is difficult.

✦ Adding or removing computers disrupts the network.

Star

In the star topology, shown in Figure 3-13, individual computers are attached to a single central computer, called a *concentrator*. This central concentrator can be a hub, a switch, or another machine. A unique number identifies each cable that connects individual computers to the concentrator. When data is transmitted from an individual computer to a target computer, the data proceeds from the individual computer to the concentrator and then to the target computer.

The star topology has one major advantage over the bus or ring topology. If one computer is disconnected from the concentrator, the rest of the network continues to work without being affected. However, since each computer must have a cable connected to the concentrator, a star network requires a lot of cable.

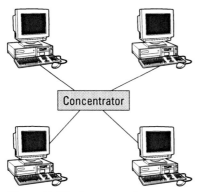

Figure 3-13: A star topology

Fiber Distributed Data Interface

Fiber Distributed Data Interface (FDDI) is similar to the token ring topology. Like token ring networks, FDDI forms a cycle that starts at one computer, passes through all other computers, and ends back at the source. Also, like token ring networks, FDDI uses the token passing access method for communication. This access method gives equal opportunity for transmission to all the computers on the network.

FDDI network differs from the token ring in two ways. First, unlike a token ring, which uses electrical cables, FDDI uses glass fibers and transfers data by encoding it in pulses of light. Second, an FDDI network is self-healing because of its ability to detect and correct errors. Therefore, the hardware can automatically accommodate a failure.

An FDDI network uses two independent rings, and both rings connect to each computer, as shown in Figure 3-14. The two independent rings are used to provide automatic recovery from failures. The traffic passes in opposite directions on each ring.

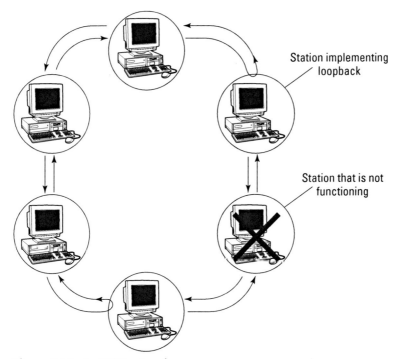

Figure 3-14: An FDDI network

While there is no hardware error on the network, FDDI functions exactly like a token ring network using only one of the two rings. However, in the case of malfunction, such as when the host interface of a computer in the network fails, the second ring (called the backup ring) is used to bypass the failure. Thus, whenever a hardware failure occurs, FDDI automatically loops data across the backup ring, where traffic passes in opposite directions, to permit communication between remaining computers. Figure 3-15 shows an FDDI network in which a host interface has failed and demonstrates the resulting implementation of loopback.

Asynchronous Transfer Mode

Asynchronous Transfer Mode (ATM) is a high-speed connection-oriented network technology. ATM networks, shown in Figure 3-16, use physical mesh topology, in which each computer is linked to all or most of the other computers. High-speed networks have a data transfer rate of 100 Mbps or higher. The ATM networks can switch data at gigabit speeds. To implement such a high speed, ATM networks require complex equipment. Thus, ATM networks are more expensive compared to other network technologies.

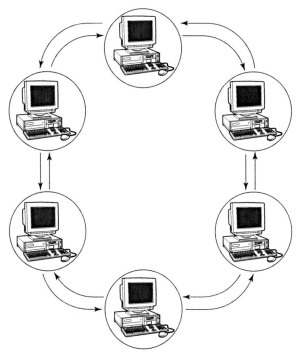

Figure 3-15: An FDDI network after a failure

An ATM network achieves high transfer speeds by using special-purpose hardware and software techniques, such as:

✦ High-speed switches that connect to host computers and to other ATM switches

✦ Optical fibers for connection, which includes the connection between host computers and ATM switch

✦ Fixed size frames, called *cells* (53 bytes long: 5 bytes header and 48 bytes of data), which ATM switches can process quickly

ATM uses connection-oriented technology instead of packet-switching networks. A host computer that needs to send cells to a remote host computer needs to interact with the ATM switch to specify the destination address. This interaction is analogous to a telephone call. The host computer waits for the ATM switch to contact the remote system and establish a path. If the connection cannot be made for some reason (for example, if the remote computer rejects the request or does not respond, or the ATM switch cannot currently reach the remote computer), the communication request by the host computer cannot be fulfilled.

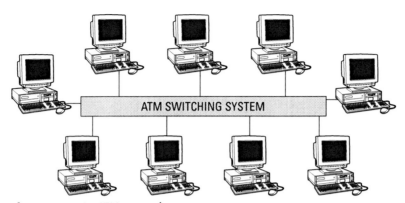

Figure 3-16: An ATM network

On the other hand, if the connection is successful, the ATM switch sends a connection identifier to the host computer along with a message informing the host that the connection is successful. The host computer then uses this connection identifier while sending and receiving cells. This type of connection path is called *virtual circuit*.

When the host computer does not need the connection any more, it requests that the ATM switch break the connection. Finally, the switch disconnects the two computers on the network.

Summary

This chapter explored the Physical layer of TCP/IP architecture in detail. First, you learned the methods that are used for data transmissions in computer networks. The two transmission technologies are baseband and broadband. The transmission can follow one of these mechanisms: circuit switching, message switching, or packet switching. Each transmission mechanism possesses its own set of advantages and disadvantages and is used, depending on the requirement of transmission. Second, you learned the characteristics, advantages, and disadvantages of different physical media, such as coaxial cable, twisted-pair cable, and fiber-optic cable. You also learned the characteristics, advantages, and disadvantages of the LAN wireless technologies, including infrared and radio. Finally, you learned the common topologies that computer networks follow — broadcast bus, token bus, token ring, star, FDDI, and ATM.

✦　　✦　　✦

Network Interface Layer

CHAPTER

4

♦   ♦   ♦   ♦

In This Chapter

Reviewing the
Network Interface
layer

Examining media
access control
standards

Mapping the
physical address to
the IP address

♦   ♦   ♦   ♦

TCP/IP maps to the conceptual four-layer Defense
Advanced Research Project Agency (DARPA) model. This
model was developed by the U.S. government agency,
DARPA — an agency that also played a major role in develop-
ing TCP/IP. The Network Interface layer, also known as the
Network Access layer, is the second layer of this model. It cor-
responds to a part of the Physical layer and the complete
Data Link layer of the OSI reference model.

This chapter introduces you to the Network Interface layer
and the role it plays in data transmissions. Data is transmitted
in the form of small blocks that are referred to by specific
names at each layer. For example, the blocks are called *frames*
at the Network Interface layer, but the general term applied to
the blocks across all layers is *packets*. This chapter touches on
such topics as the contents of a packet and the most common
frame (Ethernet); various media access control standards;
polling used in ATM and ARCnet; and token passing used in
Token Ring. It also discusses how the physical addresses of
computers are mapped to their corresponding IP addresses
by using ARP during a transmission. In the fast-emerging ATM
networks, the IP addresses of the network hosts are mapped to
their physical addresses by using ATMARP.

Overview of the Network Interface Layer

The MAC addresses, network card drivers, and specific interfaces for a network card function at the Network Interface
layer. Though the Network Interface layer focuses on communication with network cards and other networking hardware,
IP functions do not exist at this layer. This means that the
Internet layer cannot take advantage of any acknowledgment

or sequencing services that might exist at the Network Interface layer. Communication might be unreliable. As a result, the layers above the Network Interface layer ensure the reliability of communication.

Note   Although the Network Interface layer corresponds to a part of the Physical layer of the OSI reference model, it does not take part in actual data transmissions.

The network devices associated with the Network Interface layer are:

✦ NICs (Network Interface Cards)

✦ Bridges

✦ Intelligent hubs

The primary responsibilities of this layer are:

✦ Identifying the nodes (or computers) on the network

✦ Organizing the bits received from the network medium into logical groups, known as *frames,* and controlling the size of the frames

✦ Converting IP addresses to LAN addresses

✦ Controlling the data flow

✦ Encapsulating and transmitting the outgoing data

✦ Detecting errors but not correcting them

✦ Providing services (such as Quality of Service) and addressing capabilities (unicast, multicast, or broadcast) to the Internet (sometimes also referred to as the Internetwork) layer

TCP/IP was designed to be independent of the various network access methods, frame formats, and transmission media. Thus, TCP/IP can be used to connect heterogeneous network types — technologies that include LAN (such as Ethernet and Token Ring) and WAN (such as X.25 and Frame Relay). Independence from any specific network technology allows new technologies, such as Asynchronous Transfer Mode (ATM), to readily adapt TCP/IP.

Of the aforementioned technologies, Ethernet is the most widely used. Computers attached to an Ethernet network use a high-level protocol, such as TCP/IP, to send data to one another. These high-level protocol packets are transacted between computers in the form of Ethernet frames.

Contents of an Ethernet frame

As mentioned earlier, data packets at the Network Interface layer are known as frames. In the Ethernet system, the devices communicate with each other by using *Ethernet frames.* An Ethernet frame consists of a set of bits that are organized into fields. These fields include various address fields, a data field, and an error-control field that controls the integrity of the data encapsulated in the frame. The data field can vary from 46 to 1500 bytes. Figure 4-1 depicts one of the more popular Ethernet IEEE 802.3 frame formats.

		6		2	1	1	1	Variable	4
Destination Address		Source Address		Length	DSAP	SSAP	Control	Data	FCS

Figure 4-1: The IEEE 802.3 Ethernet frame format

Note Many versions of Ethernet frames are currently available, including IEEE 802.3 (also known as the standard Ethernet), DIX (DEC/Intel/Xerox) Ethernet (sometimes referred to as Version II Ethernet or Ethernet_II), IEEE 802.3 SNAP (or Ethernet_SNAP), and so on. It should be noted that these versions are not necessarily compatible with one another.

The IEEE 802.3 specification consists of a 14-byte Data Link header followed by a 3-byte Logical Link Control (LLC) header. The *Data Link header* specifies the address of the destination and the sender node, along with the length of the data field of the frame. The *Logical Link Control (LLC) header* points to the memory buffer of the receiving node where the data frame would be stored, which allows the upper layers to easily locate the data. The fields containing the user data and Frame Check Sequence (FCS) follow these headers.

Tip Ethernet_II and Ethernet_802.3 (or Novell Proprietary) lack the LLC header. Ethernet_SNAP, like the IEEE 802.3 implementation, consists of the LLC header. In addition, it also consists of a 5-byte-long Sub-Network Access Protocol (SNAP) header, from byte number 18 to byte number 22.

The various fields of Ethernet IEEE 802.3 frame are:

✦ **Preamble**—Regardless of the frame type that is used, signals in all Ethernet networks are encoded the same way, by a method known as *Manchester Encoding*. The efficacy of this method is based on two requirements: that the internal clocks of each computer in the Ethernet network are synchronized, and that the length of each bit time is agreed upon during the transmission itself. Both of these requirements are facilitated by the *preamble*—a sequence of ones and zeros that precedes the actual Ethernet frame. The preamble consists of eight bytes of alternating ones and zeros, ending with "11." When a computer on the Ethernet network transmits, other computers use the preamble to lock on (or synchronize) to the sender's internal clock. Because it takes some time to establish synchronization, initial preamble bits are generally lost. After the synchronization between the sender and the receiver is established, the receiver waits for the "11" sequence that signals the following Ethernet frame. Since the preamble is just used to establish synchronization between the stations, no preamble bit enters the network card adapter's memory buffer.

✦ **Destination address** — The first six bytes of the frame, numbered 0–5, constitute the address of the destination node (or computer). Regardless of the
Ethernet frame type, the destination address format remains the same for all
implementations.

Tip

When all the bits of the destination address have a value of one, the message is a
broadcast message and will be received by all nodes on the local segment.

✦ **Source address** — The next six bytes of the frame, numbered 6 through 11,
specify the address of the sender node. Like the destination address, the
source address format remains the same for all implementations of Ethernet.

✦ **Length** — The next two bytes, numbered 12 and 13, specify the length of the
data frame excluding the preamble, 32-bit CRC, DLC addresses, or the Length
field itself.

Tip

The minimum length of an Ethernet frame is 64 bytes, and the maximum is 1518
bytes.

✦ **Destination Service Access Point (DSAP)** — The next byte, numbered 15,
points to the address of the memory buffer where the recipient node should
store the received data. This field plays an important role where nodes have
multiple protocol stacks.

✦ **Source Service Access Point (SSAP)** — The next byte, numbered 16, points to
the address of the sending process.

✦ **Control Byte** — The next byte, numbered 17, specifies the type of LLC frame.

✦ **Data** — The next 43 to 1497 bytes constitute the user data. The length of this
field is variable.

✦ **Frame Check Sequence (FCS)** — The last four bytes are also known as *Cyclic
Redundancy Check (CRC)* bytes. When the recipient node receives a packet, it
generates a checksum using a complex polynomial. It then cross checks the
data with the checksum received in the last four bytes of the frame. If the two
checksums do not match, the frame is assumed to be corrupt and is subse-
quently discarded. This ensures that transmission errors are detected and
that the integrity of the received frames is maintained.

Typical parts of a network packet

A *packet* is a block of data sent over the network. At different layers, it is known by
different names:

✦ At the Physical layer, a packet is known as *bits*.

✦ At the Network Interface layer, a packet is known as a *frame*.

✦ At the Internet layer, a packet is referred to as a *datagram*.

✦ At the Transport layer, a packet is referred to as a *segment*.

✦ At the Application layer, a packet is known as a *message*.

During a transmission, each layer adds its own content to the packet that originates at the Application layer. But regardless of the layer, every packet contains similar parts, such as:

✦ **Header** — The header contains the source address, destination address, and frame type. The *source address* refers to the address of the node where the packet originated. The *destination address* contains the address of the node that will process the information encapsulated in the packet. The header also contains a two-byte-long *frame type* field that makes the packet self-identifying. This means that when a packet reaches the destination node, the node's operating system uses the frame type field to identify the protocol software that will process the packet. The frame type field allows a single node to support and use many protocols at the same time.

✦ **Data (or Information)** — This field contains the user-defined data that needs to be transmitted from one node to another over the network. The length of this field varies according to the protocol being used.

✦ **CRC (or FCS)** — This field is four bytes in length and helps detect transmission errors, if any. The sender computes Cyclic Redundancy Check (CRC) as a function of the data enclosed in the packet. When the receiver gets the packet, it recomputes the CRC. If the results match, the data is error free. Otherwise, the packet is discarded.

Media Access Control Standards

If a network has a large number of devices capable of transmitting data whenever the network is ready, it is highly probable that multiple devices will transmit simultaneously. In such cases, there will be more than one signal on the transmission medium (such as cable), resulting in damage to all the signals on the transmission medium and loss of the data they carry. This is known as *collision,* which destroys effective communication.

Tip   The transmission medium is popularly referred to as *channel.*

Collisions should be either minimized or eliminated in order for networks to operate effectively. Networks use specific rules, known as *media access control standards,* that control when a device can transmit data packets.

Different topologies support different media access control standards. For example, Ethernet supports *contention,* ARCnet supports *polling,* and Token Ring supports *token passing.*

Ethernet

Ethernet uses the contention access method, shown in Figure 4-2, to control the occurrence of collisions. According to this method, media access is allowed on a first-come, first-served basis, which means that each network device has to compete to access the transmission medium. Whenever a device wants to transmit data, it keeps its signal on the transmission medium. When this method is used, there is a high probability that two or more devices will put their signals on the medium at the same time, thus leading to collision.

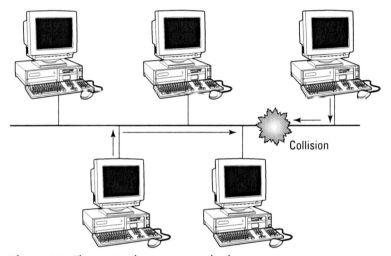

Collision

Figure 4-2: The contention access method

Caution   The larger the number of network devices, the greater the probability of collisions.

To reduce the number of collisions in an Ethernet network, contention protocols known as *Carrier Sense Multiple Access* (*CSMA*) were developed. Examples of CSMA protocols are *Carrier Sense Multiple Access with Collision Detection* (*CSMA/CD*) and *Carrier Sense Multiple Access with Collision Avoidance* (*CSMA/CA*). These protocols cause a device to "listen" to the transmission medium before transmitting. If they find the medium free of any signal, they place their signals on the medium for transmission. Otherwise, CSMA waits until the medium is free. Although CSMA protocols reduce the possibility of collisions, they do not eliminate it completely. Collisions *can* still occur when two devices sense that the medium is free and keep their signals on the medium simultaneously.

CSMA/CD

The CSMA/CD protocol makes the network devices "listen" to the transmission medium before transmitting a signal. In addition, it helps the devices detect a collision. When a collision is sensed, all the network devices refrain from transmitting data for a stipulated amount of time. After the waiting period is over, the devices start contending for the medium. Ethernet_II and IEEE 802.3 are examples of CSMA/CD protocols.

CSMA/CA

The CSMA/CA protocol greatly reduces the possibility of collisions in one of two ways: Either each device has a specified time slot for transmission, or a device sends a request to gain access to the transmission medium before keeping the data on it. In the former method, every device has a specified time slot and has to wait for its slot to be able to transmit. No device can use the other device's time slot for transmission. Thus, the CSMA/CA protocol helps avoid the occurrence of collisions. Apple's LocalTalk is one example of the CSMA/CA protocol.

ARCnet

ARCnet uses an "interconnected star" cabling topology that uses the *polling* access method to control a device's accessibility to the transmission medium. In the polling method, the protocol software designates a device as the *master* (or *primary* or *controller*) and the other devices as *secondary* devices. The master device polls (or queries) each of the secondary devices in a predetermined manner to check if they have information to transmit. If a device has to transmit data, the master device sends a request packet to the secondary device. In answer to the request packet, the secondary device sends the data to the master device, which then forwards the data packet to the intended segment where the recipient device is located. The amount of data that a secondary device can transmit after a poll is limited by the protocols. Figure 4-3 shows the polling method used in ARCnet.

Tip   The master device is also referred to as a *channel access administrator.*

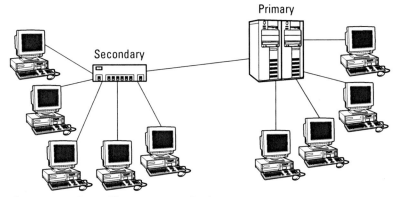

Figure 4-3: The polling access method

The polling method might cause delays for some applications while other devices are being polled. However, setting priorities can ensure faster access. Also, the polling method enables the complete use of the transmission medium's capacity by completely eliminating the probability of collision.

Tip   Networks using polling systems are best suited for time-sensitive networking devices, such as automation equipment.

Token Ring

The networks based on the Token Ring setup use the token-passing access method to control a device's access to the transmission medium. According to this access method, a special data frame called a *token* circulates over the entire network. Each device knows from which device it received the token and to which device the token should be passed. The device that wants to transmit data "captures" the token, thus gaining temporary control over the transmission medium. The transmitting device uses the token frame to encapsulate the data it wants to transmit and places the token over the medium. Each intermediate device that receives the frame checks if it is the intended recipient. If it is, it accepts the data and sends the token back to the sender. Otherwise, the token is passed to the next device. The token remains in a captured state until the sender device finishes transmission, after which the token is "released." Figure 4-4 depicts the token-passing access method used in Token Rings.

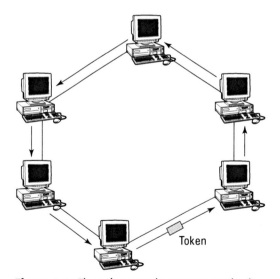

Token

Figure 4-4: The token-passing access method

Passing the token around distributes access control among the network devices. The interval for which a device can control the token is limited by corresponding protocols. Each device, in its turn, gets control of the token frame, transmits data, and releases the token to the next device to use.

Tip   The token-passing access method is ideal for networks where the traffic — such as voice and video signals — is time-sensitive and of set priority.

Asynchronous Transfer Mode

Asynchronous Transfer Mode (ATM) has been heralded as the rising star in the network technology because it provides extremely high-speed and reliable data transport over short and long distances. ATM supports a wide range of applications, including conventional data and real-time audio and video communications.

ATM provides many advantages over conventional LANs — most notably, its flexibility to be used over a variety of physical media at various speeds. ATM supports coaxial, twisted pair, and fiber-optic mediums at speeds ranging from 25 Mbps to 2.5 Gbps. The standard speed is 155 Mbps over the fiber-optic medium. The aggregate bandwidth increases as more hosts are added to the network.

ATM is based on a network of interconnected switches and hosts. These switches and hosts are arranged to form an interconnected star. Since the ATM networks are based on star topology, the polling access method is used. An ATM switch acts as the central hub of the star as well as the channel access administrator or the master device.

To communicate with another computer successfully, every device needs to be properly and uniquely identified. This isn't a problem in a LAN, since the number of devices in the network is not extremely high, and the physical addresses of the devices can be used to identify them. The physical address, or *Media Access Control Address* (*MAC address*), is hard-coded into the device's Network Interface Card (NIC). However, using hard-coded addresses for identifying network devices is impossible in a large, heterogeneous, and global network system, such as the Internet. To make the communication possible, any computer from any network must be able to communicate with any other computer, no matter how it is named.

To facilitate global communication, a naming system was developed, in which each computer is assigned a unique binary 32-bit *Internet address,* or *IP address.* Following is an example of an IP address:

```
10000000 00001000 00000111 00011111
```

Virtual Channels

ATM is based on the connection-oriented model that uses virtual channels to enable fast synchronous or asynchronous data transfer. In other words, ATM requires that a virtual end-to-end connection be established before data transfer can begin. Virtual end-to-end connections are referred to as *virtual channels*.

A virtual channel transports fixed-length 53-byte cells between two endpoints. Each virtual channel consists of a *VCI (Virtual Channel Identifier)* and a *VPI (Virtual Path Identifier)* that is included in the 5-byte header of the ATM cell to provide identification for proper switching from an input port to an output port within an ATM switch. As the Virtual Channel (VC) spans multiple links, the VCI can potentially change for each link. When a virtual channel is created, the ATM switch creates and maintains a table entry that maps inbound VCIs on an inbound port to outbound VCIs on the outbound port. Due to its simplicity, the ATM algorithm is easily implemented in hardware. Software is only required to manage the connections and maintain the switching table.

Although the preceding representation is unique, it is difficult for human beings to remember. Therefore, an IP address is denoted as four decimal-based integers that are separated by decimal points. Each integer represents a byte (or octet). This type of representation is known as *dotted decimal notation*. When the preceding IP address is converted from the binary format to decimal notation, it looks like this:

```
128.8.7.31
```

Cross-Reference   For more information on IP addressing, refer to Chapter 5.

The IP address is divided into two parts: the *network address* and the *host address*. The network address represents the address of the network that the computer (or host) belongs to. The host address, as the name suggests, represents the address of a host in a network. Using an IP address, how does a sender host locate the correct destination host, especially when it is located in a different network? In other words, how does the sender computer map the IP address of the destination host to its physical address?

Mapping the Physical Address to the IP Address

When a computer communicates with another computer that is located in a different network, the address mapping must be done twice:

   1. The sender must map the address(es) of intermediate router(s) that exist in the way to the destination network so that the transmitted data reaches the correct destination network.

2. The sender must also map the IP address of the destination computer to its physical address so that data reaches the correct destination host.

The mapping of high-level addresses (IP addresses) to low-level physical addresses is known as *address resolution*. Addresses can be resolved in several ways. For example, each computer on a network can maintain tables that map high-level addresses to corresponding physical addresses. Also, physical addresses can be encoded into the high-level addresses. However, both of these methods create a large overhead and need to be manually maintained.

To solve the problem of address resolution without creating large overheads or manual maintenance at each computer, ARP and RARP protocols were developed. Today, ARP and RARP are some of the most commonly used techniques for resolving addresses. With the advent of the ATM technology, Asynchronous Transfer Mode Address Resolution Protocol (ATMARP) is a new, but a fast-growing, technology.

ARP and RARP

When a network card fails and is replaced, the computer's physical address also changes. This causes problems if each computer maintains a table that maps IP addresses to their corresponding physical addresses. In this case, the table maintained at each computer needs to be manually changed. *Address Resolution Protocol (ARP)* facilitates replacements and addition of new devices to the existing network without having to manually change the tables maintained by each computer. ARP is a low-level protocol that dynamically binds the IP addresses of devices on a network to their physical addresses by using the broadcast capability of a network.

Tip   When a protocol directly works with the hardware, it is known as a *low-level protocol.*

Using ARP, when a computer needs to find out the physical address of a computer, it broadcasts a special packet. This packet contains the requests for the host with a given IP address to respond to with its physical address. Since the packet is a broadcast message, all the devices receive the packet. However, only the host for which the request was issued recognizes its IP address and responds with its IP and physical addresses.

Broadcasts use up much of the transmission medium's capacity, which is why computers using ARP maintain an *address resolution cache* that contains the recently received IP-to-physical address bindings. Whenever a computer needs to transmit data, it first tries to access the required address in its cache. If it is successful, it doesn't need to broadcast the address resolution request. This reduces the number of broadcasts considerably, thus bringing down the communication cost as well as the network traffic.

Functionally, ARP can be divided into two parts. One part maps an IP address to the corresponding physical address, and the other part is responsible for answering address-resolution requests received from other computers. Mapping IP addresses to corresponding physical addresses and answering address resolution requests might seem simple, but the following minor details may cause problems:

✦ **The target computer is down or too busy to accept the ARP request.** In this case, the sender might not receive a reply, or the reply might be delayed. This can cause some application programs on the sender computer to go into a state of hang until the ARP request is processed.

✦ **The sender recently received the mapping for another computer.** In the meantime, the target computer failed and was replaced. As a result, its physical address was also changed. Though the target computer's physical address has changed, the entry in the sender's cache didn't. Next time the sender sends data to the target, transmission will be impossible between the two.

ARP maintains a cache of IP address-to-media access control address mappings for future use. This also helps in considerably reducing the number of broadcasts over the network. The ARP cache can contain following two types of entries:

✦ **Dynamic entries** — The dynamic entries are added and removed automatically from the ARP cache over a specific time interval.

✦ **Static entries** — The static entries remain in the ARP cache until the computer is rebooted.

The dynamic entries can remain in the ARP cache for a maximum interval of ten minutes. When new entries are added to the cache, they are timestamped. If an entry is not reused within two minutes of being added to the ARP cache, it is removed from the cache. If an entry is used, two more minutes are added to its lifetime. If an entry is used constantly, it receives an additional two minutes of lifetime up to a maximum lifetime of ten minutes, after which it is removed.

The ARP cache has a specific size and cannot exceed the defined size limit. If it is allowed to grow without check over time, the cache might be filled with entries that are either incomplete or obsolete. To prevent this from happening, the ARP cache is periodically flushed of all entries. This deletes unused entries and frees space in the cache for newer and more useful entries. It also reduces the probability of contacting computers that are currently down.

RARP

Usually, a computer's IP address is stored on its hard disk and retrieved when the machine boots. However, the determination of the IP address becomes a critical problem for computers that lack a hard disk, since they need a valid IP address to successfully retrieve their initial boot image.

A diskless computer uses *Reverse Address Resolution Protocol* (*RARP*) to obtain its IP address from a server. RARP belongs to the TCP/IP protocol suite. Unlike ARP, RARP also allows devices to issue requests to inquire about the IP address of a computer other than the target computer (that is, a third computer) and multiple physical network types.

 Caution   Like ARP requests, RARP requests can be lost or corrupted during transmission.

ARP/RARP protocol frame format

ARP and RARP request-packets have the same frame format. The format of an ARP/RARP message (or frame) is shown in Figure 4-5.

0	8	16	24	31

HARDWARE TYPE		PROTOCOL TYPE	
HLEN	PLEN	OPERATION	
SENDER HA (octets 0-3)			
SENDER HA (octets 4-5)		SENDER IP (octets 0-1)	
SENDER IP (octets 2-3)		SENDER HA (octets 0-1)	
TARGET HA (octets 2-5)			
TARGET IP (octets 0-3)			

Figure 4-5: ARP/RARP protocol frame format

The fields in an ARP/RARP frame are:

✦ **Hardware Type** — Specifies the hardware interface type that is being used by the sending device. Ethernet interface is represented by the value of 1.

✦ **Protocol Type** — Specifies the address of the high-level protocol that originated the request. IP addresses are represented by the value of 0800_{16}.

✦ **HLEN** — Specifies the length of the hardware address contained in the Hardware Type field.

✦ **PLEN** — Specifies the length of the high-level protocol address contained in the Protocol Type field.

✦ **Operation** — Specifies whether the frame is an ARP request/response or RARP request/response. If the value contained in the field is 1, it represents an ARP request. The value 2 represents an ARP response. Similarly, 3 represents a RARP request, and the value 4 represents a RARP response.

✦ **Sender HA (Hardware Address)** — Specifies the hardware address of the sender device.

✦ **Sender IP** — Specifies the IP address of the sender device.

✦ **Target HA** — Specifies the hardware address of the target (or destination) device, if known by the sender.

✦ **Target IP** — Specifies the IP address of the target device.

After receiving the frame, the destination device fills in the missing addresses, if any, changes the operation field to a response, and swaps the sender and target fields. As a result, the reply frame carries the physical and IP addresses of the original sender and the receiver device for which the address resolution was sought.

ATMARP

In an ATM network, when a host needs to transmit data to another computer, it needs to specify the hardware address of the destination host. Mapping a host address to the corresponding ATM hardware address in ATM networks is a problem because ATM networks, unlike broadcast-based technologies, such as Ethernet and Token Ring, do not support hardware broadcasts. To resolve an IP address to its corresponding hardware address, the ATM host in question must contact a server that contains the mapping. The Asynchronous Transfer Mode Address Resolution Protocol (ATMARP) frames facilitate this communication between a host and server.

ATMARP resembles ARP used in Ethernet and Token Ring networks in many ways. When an ATM host needs to map the physical address of another machine on the basis of its IP address, it frames a request that contains the destination host's IP address. The request is then sent to the ATMARP server. If the server has the required hardware address in its cache, it forwards the *ATMARP reply.* Otherwise, a *negative ATMARP reply* is returned.

The format of the ATMARP packet is slightly different from the traditional ARP frame format. Additional address length fields have been incorporated to accommodate the multiple address formats that introduce the two-level address hierarchy in ATM.

Tip   ATM supports multiple address formats because the telephone companies offering ATM network and services use an 8-byte address format. On the other hand, according to the ATM Forum, each computer attached to the ATM network can be assigned a 20-byte address known as *Network Service Access Point (NSAP).* This gives rise to a two-level address hierarchy, according to which the 8-byte address is used for the remote access, whereas NSAP is used for local access.

Figure 4-6 shows the format of an ATMARP packet. The hardware type, the protocol type, and the operation fields are the same as in an ARP frame.

0	8	16	24	31
HARDWARE TYPE		PROTOCOL TYPE		
SEND. HLEN	SEND. HLEN2	OPERATION		
SEND. PLEN	TAR. HLEN	TAR. HLEN2	TAR. PLEN	
SENDER'S ATM ADDRESS (octets 0-3)				
SENDER'S ATM ADDRESS (octets 4-7)				
SENDER'S ATM ADDRESS (octets 8-11)				
SENDER'S ATM ADDRESS (octets 12-15)				
SENDER'S ATM ADDRESS (octets 16-19)				
SENDER'S PROTOCOL ADDRESS				
TARGET'S ATM ADDRESS (octets 0-3)				
TARGET'S ATM ADDRESS (octets 4-7)				
TARGET'S ATM ADDRESS (octets 8-11)				
TARGET'S ATM ADDRESS (octets 12-15)				
TARGET'S ATM ADDRESS (octets 16-19)				
TARGET'S PROTOCOL ADDRESS				

Figure 4-6: ATMARP packet format

The fields in an ATMARP packet are:

✦ **Hardware Type** — Specifies the hardware interface type that is being used by the sender. The value 0x0013 represents ATM interface.

✦ **Protocol Type** — Specifies the protocol that is being used by the sender. The value 0x0800 represents IP.

✦ **Send HLEN** — Specifies the length of the sender's ATM address.

✦ **Send HLEN2** — Specifies the length of the sender's ATM subaddress.

✦ **Operation** — Specifies whether the frame is a request/response frame. If the value contained by the field is 1, it represents ATMARP request. Similarly, the value 2 represents ATMARP reply, 8 represents inverse ATMARP request, 9 represents inverse ATMARP reply, and 10 represents ATMARP negative acknowledgement.

✦ **Send PLEN** — Specifies the length of the sender's protocol address.

✦ **Tar HLEN** — Specifies the length of the target's (destination's) ATM address.

✦ **Tar HLEN2**—Specifies the length of the target's ATM subaddress.

✦ **Tar PLEN**—Specifies the length of the target's protocol address.

✦ **Sender's ATM Address**—Specifies the sender's ATM address. This field can be 20 bytes long.

✦ **Sender's Protocol Address**—Specifies the protocol address that originated the request at the sender.

✦ **Target's ATM Address**—Specifies the target's ATM address.

✦ **Target's Protocol Address**—Specifies the address of the protocol at the target host that will process the request.

Summary

This chapter covered many concepts related to the Network Interface layer and the role it plays in data transmissions. Data is sent in small blocks, known as packets, which are given different names at different layers. This chapter discussed the typical parts of a packet and the format of the Ethernet frame. It also discussed how devices in different topologies use different methods (access methods) to access the transmission medium. For example, Ethernet uses contention, ARCnet and ATM use polling, and Token Ring uses token passing. Finally, this chapter outlined the role ARP and RARP play in mapping the IP addresses of devices to their physical addresses in Ethernet and other such networks. In the ATM networks, this mapping is done by ATMARP.

✦   ✦   ✦

Internet Layer

Much of the work that takes place at the Internet layer of TCP/IP is hidden from users the way an engine is hidden under the hood of a car. In fact, the Internet layer can be thought of as the TCP/IP engine. This chapter will take you "under the hood of the car," so to speak, focusing on packet addressing and delivery. By the time you have finished this chapter, you will better understand how packets are addressed and routed. You will also have a basic knowledge of many of the topics covered in later chapters, such as planning your addressing scheme (see Chapter 18) and subnetting (see Chapter 19).

The Purpose of the Internet Layer

If your data needs to pass over an IP router network that uses different frame sizes, then you have seen the Internet layer at work. If your computer tries to communicate with a nonexistent host across the network, the Internet layer ICMP protocol is responsible for the message, which lets you know that "nobody is home" on the far side. If you use collaborative tools, which allow you to hold virtual meetings over the Internet with a select group of attendees, you've used the Internet layer to address the meeting content to only those recipients. All of these functions are provided by a relatively small group of protocols operating at the Internet layer. In short, the Internet layer of TCP/IP is responsible for packaging addressing and routing datagrams across networks.

Three protocols work together to provide Internet layer services.

✦ The Internet Protocol (IP) provides the packaging and addressing service. IP identifies local or remote hosts. If the path to the destination network uses a different packet size, IP fragments the packet, allowing it to be transmitted without error. IP then reassembles or packages the packet at the destination host. In addition, IP discards outdated packets. Finally, IP sends designated packets up to higher-layer protocols. IP addressing is documented in RFC 791.

Tip   RFCs can be referenced by number at www.ietf.org.

✦ The Internet Control Messaging Protocol (ICMP) is used to report on or diagnose problems during transmission. You have probably seen certain ICMP messages, such as "destination host unreachable." ICMP is documented in RFC 792.

✦ The Internet Group Management Protocol (IGMP) is responsible for managing the use of multicasting or selective delivery without broadcasting. IGMP is documented in RFCs 1112 and 2236.

Note   The terms *Ethernet address*, *MAC address*, and *Physical address* are interchangeable, as are the terms *subnet* and *segment*.

Determining whether the destination is local or remote

Each packet on the network is addressed at the Internet layer by two IP addresses: one for the source and one for the destination of the packet. These fields can be seen and used by other hosts who process IP packets. IP determines whether the destination of each packet is local or remote by comparing the destination address field in the packet to the local host's own IP address. The difference between local and remote traffic is quite significant because the local host can deliver local traffic, whereas remote traffic needs to be forwarded to a router for delivery.

Address Resolution Protocol

The Address Resolution Protocol (ARP) is depicted as an Internet layer protocol. In fact, ARP straddles the boundary between the Data Link layer and the Internet layer. As mentioned in the previous chapter, the function of ARP is to resolve IP addresses to physical or MAC addresses so that packets can be delivered to the appropriate network adapter on the local segment. ARP uses broadcasts to find the destination host, so its functionality is limited to the local network since most routers do not forward broadcast traffic. ARP, which is documented in RFC 826, is typically used in one of two ways:

✦ The host uses ARP to exchange IP addresses and MAC addresses with a local destination host so that IP datagrams might be delivered to the destination host.

✦ The host uses ARP to exchange IP addresses and MAC addresses with its configured default gateway or router so that IP datagrams can be delivered to the router network.

Overview of routing

Does your organization conduct business from multiple locations? If so, you may have a wide area network (WAN) link, such as ISDN or T1 service, between locations. WAN is quite expensive to use and limited in speed. Do you quickly move your data from one place of business to another by e-mail, file transfer, or an intranet? Are groups in your organization regularly decreasing network performance by moving large blocks of data? Routing addresses these business issues by selectively allowing data to pass between networks.

A routed environment allows for redundant communication links between locations, such as Montreal and Tokyo, in Figure 5-1. Traffic can be routed to the fastest link if available, but it can also use the slower link in the event the faster link is unavailable. Furthermore, only directed traffic will use up bandwidth on the WAN. Routing can also keep the graphics group's data from slowing the network for anyone else by creating a personal link for that group.

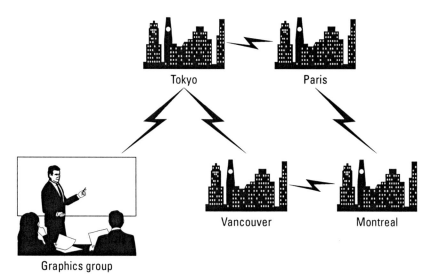

Figure 5-1: A routed network

Internet Protocol Addresses

For some, an Internet Protocol address is just a 12-digit number separated into four 3-digit parts by periods. However, IP addresses are more than just a number. They are used to uniquely describe each device on the network. Computers, routers, network-ready printers, and even Web sites each have unique IP addresses.

For a device to function on an IP inter network, it must be configured properly. IP hosts can be automatically or manually configured. Each device needs an IP address, a subnet mask, and a default gateway. Figure 5-2 shows an IP configuation screen from Windows NT computer. Other operating systems may have different methods for manual IP configuration, but the effect is the same.

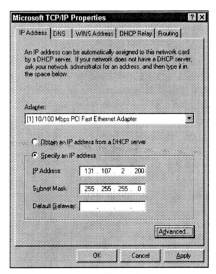

Figure 5-2: IP configuration on Windows NT

Manual configuration involves *correctly* entering the IP address, subnet mask, and default gateway parameters. This task is the single most frequent point of failure on an IP network.

Automatic configuration of IP parameters requires that a Dynamic Host Configuration Protocol (DHCP) server is present and functioning on the network. If a DHCP is available, then the client need only select the "Obtain an IP address from a DHCP server" check box to receive automatic IP configuration.

Cross-Reference

See Chapter 9 for more information on Dynamic Host Configuration Protocol (DHCP).

IP addresses are optimized for use by computers. If you understood binary as well as you read English, you could read IP addresses like phone numbers and a router table as easily as a road map. However, this is probably not the case. You really need to know how to convert IP addresses between binary and decimal to understand how the Internet Protocol works. So, before diving into the details of IP, you'll be presented with a brief binary math lesson. For those of you who are already binary gurus, feel free to skip to the "Network IDs and host IDs" section.

Binary and decimal notation

Consider a very common IP address: 192.168.0.1. An IP address has four numbers separated by dots. This type of notation system is called *dotted decimal notation.* Each of these four numbers is termed an *octet,* since it actually represents an 8-bit binary number. Consequently, the maximum decimal value of each of the four numbers in an IP address is 255, not 999.

Binary to decimal conversion

Table 5-1 presents a binary-to-decimal conversion table. The *binary bit value (BBV)* of an octet has been laid out across the top row of this table. A bit-by-bit comparison of an octet to this BBV chart allows us to easily convert the binary bits to human readable decimal without having to memorize the bit values first. The top row (BBV) shows the decimal value of a binary one (1) if it should occur in that bit of the octet. We sum all the BBVs with a 1 underneath to achieve the decimal conversion, so if the value is a zero (0), we do not add that BBV to our total.

In Row A, all the bits are ones. To convert the binary number in Row A to decimal, you add up the BBV of all the ones and ignore the zeros. Therefore, the maximum value of an 8-bit binary number is 255. In other words: 128 + 64 + 32 + 16 + 8 + 4 + 2 + 1 = 255.

In Row B, only three binary bits are set to 1s. Once again, you only need to add the BBVs with 1s underneath to do the decimal conversion. In this case, 128, 64, and 4 are summed for a total of 196.

				Table 5-1					
			Binary-to-Decimal Conversion Table						
BBV	**128s**	**64s**	**32s**	**16s**	**8s**	**4s**	**2s**	**1s**	**Decimal**
Row A	1	1	1	1	1	1	1	1	255
Row B	1	1	0	0	0	1	0	0	196
Row C									

This same process can be applied to each octet of an IP address to convert the binary notation to dotted decimal. 11000000 10101000 00000000 00000001 is the IP address 192.168.0.1 expressed as a binary number. If you compare each octet to the BBVs using Row C, you will eventually end up with 192.168.0.1.

Decimal-to-binary conversion

How do you convert a dotted decimal IP address into binary notation? One octet at a time. Simply subtract the largest BBV possible from the decimal value and keep track of which ones you have used until you run out of remainder. You can use Table 5-1, Row C to convert the decimal value, 168, to binary with the following steps:

1. Start by subtracting 128 from 168, since 128 is the largest BBV that will fit into 168.

2. 168 − 128 = 40, which will give you a binary 1 under the 128s column.

3. 64 is larger than 40. Clearly, there are no 64s in 40, so you can skip the 64 BBV and move on to 32.

4. 40 − 32 = 8, which will give you a binary 1 under the 32s column.

5. You can skip 16, too, since 16 cannot be subtracted from 8.

6. 8 − 8 = 0, which will give you a binary 1 in the 8s column.

7. Once you pad zeros in the places where you skipped BBVs, you end up with 10101000.

8. One octet has been converted. Apply the same process to each decimal in the dotted decimal notation.

Tip

Use the Windows calculator in scientific view. F6 and F8 will do the binary-to-decimal conversions for you. You may need to pad zeros on the left side to end up with eight bits.

Each decimal number in an IP address represents a binary number. Understanding the binary notation of IP addresses will help elucidate concepts — such as routing and subnetting — discussed later in the chapter.

Network IDs and host IDs

IP addresses are made up of two identifiers: the host ID and the network ID. Distinguishing the host ID from the network ID is the key to understanding IP addressing.

The network ID

Each IP network must have a unique network ID, which is common to all hosts on that segment. Since networks that are exposed to the Internet are identified by their network ID, that ID must be unique worldwide. No two networks can possess the same ID. You can reserve a network ID by contacting your ISP or the Internet Assigned Numbering Authority (IANA) (www.iana.org). Standard network IDs can be 8, 16, or 24 binary bits in length.

Cross-Reference

See Chapter 18 for more information about obtaining IP addresses and connectivity.

The host ID

The host ID is used to describe each device on a network. Host IDs must be unique to the network. No two hosts can have the same host ID on the same network. Two special addresses are reserved on each network. The first is a subnet broadcast address, identified by a host ID of all ones in binary. This address can be used to send traffic to every host on the network at once. The second is a local-only address that is not routed but is identified by a host ID of all zeros — also in binary. So, host IDs can be any combination of binary values, except all ones and all zeros. The length of standard host IDs ranges from 8 to 24 bits.

Caution If two hosts have the same host ID on the same subnet, one of these hosts will not be able to communicate on the network, and both will probably receive repeated error messages.

Guidelines for network and host IDs

These guidelines are widely followed for network and host IDs:

✦ Network IDs must be unique to the Planet and registered if exposed to the Internet.

✦ Network IDs must not be 127, the reserved local loopback address.

✦ Host and network IDs must not be set to all ones binary. All ones are reserved for broadcasts.

✦ Neither the host ID nor the network IDs can be set to all zeros binary. This special address is reserved for "local-only" packets, which are not forwarded by routers.

✦ Host IDs must not be duplicated in the same network.

Note The Internet Assigned Numbers Authority (IANA) has reserved the following three blocks of IP address space for addressing of private networks:

IP 10.0.0.0 – 10.255.255.255, with a Subnet Mask 255.0.0.0

IP 172.16.0.0 – 172.31.255.255, with a Subnet Mask 255.240.0.0

IP 192.168.0.0 – 192.168.255.255, with a Subnet Mask 255.255.255.0

More information can be found on private IP addressing in RFC 1918.

Classes of IPv4 Addresses

IP addressing allows TCP/IP to scale from very small networks to huge multi-million-dollar host enterprises by using a single addressing scheme. Currently, the Internet Protocol version 4 (IPv4) is in widespread use. Organizations that wish to have IP connectivity over the Internet will generally reserve a range of addresses for their own use by contacting their ISP or the IP address-issuing authority in their country.

IPv4 consists of five classes of addresses, labeled by the letters A through E. A, B, and C class addresses are available for reservation. Class D addresses are set aside for special applications that use multicasting (a concept that will be discussed later in this chapter), and class E addresses are experimental. Classes A through C will be focused on for now.

Table 5-2 shows that IP classes can be distinguished by examining the decimal value of the first octet in the IP address. IP classes are separated to distinguish small, medium, and large networks. If they have millions of hosts, very large organizations may need a Class A address. However, very few Class A addresses are available. Medium-sized organizations may use a Class B address. Class B address ranges can still host over 65,000 devices per network, and many more Class B ranges are available for use than Class A ranges. Most commonly, you will see Class C addresses in use. Even though Class C addresses cannot address more than 254 hosts per network, over 2 million Class C ranges are available.

	Table 5-2		
	IP Address Ranges and Capacities		
Address Class	*First Octet Range*	*# of Networks*	*# of Hosts per Network*
A	1–126	126	16,777,214
B	128–191	16,384	65,534
C	192–223	2,097,152	254
D	224–239	N/A	N/A
E	240–254	N/A	N/A

Note   Class D and E addresses do not support host addressing in the usual sense. Class D is used for multicasting, and Class E addresses are reserved for experimental use.

Table 5-3 displays a binary depiction of Class A through C addresses, where N stands for network ID bits and H stands for a host ID bit. Class A addresses only use the first octet for the network ID. This leaves 3 octets, or 24 bits, for the host ID. Class B addresses use the first two octets for the network ID and the last two octets for the host ID. They have 16 bits binary for each ID. Class C addresses use the first three octets for the network ID and the last octet for the host ID. They have 24 bits for the network ID and 8 bits for the host ID.

		Table 5-3		
	Standard Network and Host ID Lengths			
Address Class	*Octet 1*	*Octet 2*	*Octet 3*	*Octet 4*
A	NNNNNNNN	HHHHHHHH	HHHHHHHH	HHHHHHHH
B	NNNNNNNN	NNNNNNNN	HHHHHHHH	HHHHHHHH
C	NNNNNNNN	NNNNNNNN	NNNNNNNN	HHHHHHHH

If you take into account the reserved "local only" and "subnet broadcast" addresses that we cannot use for host IDs by subtraction, you could express the maximum number of host IDs on a network by the formula: $(2^x) - 2$, where x equals the number of bits in the host ID.

The maximum number of host IDs by IP address class would be as follows:

Class A example: host ID length = 24 bits, so 2^{24} = 16,777,216 − 2 = 16,777,214

Class B example: host ID length = 16 bits, so 2^{16} = 65,536 − 2 = 65,534

Class C example: host ID length = 8 bits, so 2^8 = 256 − 2 = 254

What the address represents

An IP address is similar to the address you use to send mail through the postal system. The address *must* represent the complete set of information required to effect delivery. Otherwise, the letter will not arrive at the proper destination. An incomplete or incorrect address affects IP addressing the same way it affects the delivery of mail. For example, using a street number alone (the number 100 to indicate a residence) is not an efficient or complete addressing method, since each city or town could have many residences identified as "100." Neither is it sufficient to simply use a street name, such as Oak Road, as an address. In all likelihood, there is more than one house on Oak Road.

An IP address is a combination of the host ID and the network ID. There can be no doubt about the location of host 47.0.0.18. It is the 18th host on the 47.0.0 network. The combined network and host IDs in an IP address provide complete and unambiguous information about how to reach the destination host, the way a street address, such as 100 Oak Road, provides unambiguous instructions for mail delivery.

How the subnet mask is used

A *subnet mask* is a continuous string of binary ones that identifies or *masks* out the network ID portion of the IP address. The purpose of the subnet mask is to identify the length and value of the network ID. IP uses the local subnet mask in combination with the local IP address to identify the local network. Table 5-4 shows the standard subnet masks of 8, 16, and 24 bits in length. Note that the first octet in the Class A IP address shown in the table is masked out by the subnet mask below it. The network ID of the Class A address is 11. Also note that the first two octets in the Class B IP address are masked out by the subnet mask. The network ID of the Class B address is 131.107. The Class C IP address has all but the last octet masked out by the subnet mask. The Class C network ID is 192.168.0.

Note   The purpose of the subnet mask is to identify the value of the network ID.

Table 5-4 Standard Subnet Masks		
Address Class	**IP Address or Subnet Mask in Binary**	**IP or Subnet Mask in Dotted Decimal**
A	00001011.00000000.00000001.00010010	11.0.1.18
	11111111.00000000.00000000.00000000	**255**.0.0.0
B	10000011.01101011.00000010.11001000	131.107.2.200
	11111111.11111111.00000000.00000000	**255.255**.0.0
C	11000000.10101000.00000000.00001111	192.168.0.15
	11111111.11111111.11111111.00000000	**255.255.255**.0

The default gateway

In a routed environment, each host is normally configured with the address of the router on that segment. The IP address of the router on each subnet is referred to as the default gateway. Hosts on Network A are configured with 192.168.1.1 as their default gateway. Hosts on Network B are configured to use 10.0.0.1 as their default gateway. From the client's point of view, the default gateway is used to deliver *all* remote traffic. Remote IP datagrams on Network A will be delivered to the default gateway at 192.168.1.1. Remote IP datagrams on Network B will be delivered to the Network B default gateway at 10.0.0.1.

Classless and Classful Routing

We have discussed using the subnet mask in Class A, B, and C networks to highlight the need for comparison of the IP address and subnet mask to achieve proper datagram delivery over a routed network. Use of these standard subnet masks is referred to as *classful routing*. While a grasp of classful routing is key to understanding packet delivery, very few networks actually use it, due to wasted IP addresses. Internet routers commonly use *Classless Inter-Domain Routing (CIDR)* as a method of recovering wasted IP address space. Rather than dividing the subnet mask into octets, CIDR divides the subnet mask by bits into 32 sections. This allows for better sizing of networks and fewer wasted IP addresses. Imagine a network with 2,000 hosts using a Class B address range and wasting over 60,000 IP addresses. Using CIDR would allow that same Class B network to be subnetted into a 2,046-host network, wasting only about 50 addresses instead of 60,000. The remaining addresses could be assigned to other networks. CIDR notation follows the IP address by the number of subnet mask bits used. A 10.0.0.0 network with a 12-bit subnet mask would be written as 10.0.0.0/12 in CIDR notation. Classless and classful routing will be discussed further in Chapter 19.

Determining whether the destination is local or remote

IP uses the local subnet mask, together with the local and remote host's IP address, to determine what network the local host is on. Datagrams destined for networks other than the local network are considered to be remote, and they are handled appropriately. IP uses a Boolean AND function to compare the local and destination host's IP addresses to the local subnet mask. This comparison results in a network ID for both the local and destination hosts. If the network IDs have the same value, then the destination host is local. If not, then the destination host is remote.

The actual determination is quite simple, now that all the parts of the puzzle have been discussed. The network ID of the local host and the destination host are compared. If they are the same value, the traffic is considered to be "local."

Note

A Boolean AND function compares binary values bit-wise and only results in a 1 (or "true") condition if both input values are 1 to start with. In other words, 1 AND 1 = 1.

In Figure 5-3, only two of the three hosts are able to communicate locally because only two of their network IDs are the same. Host A's network ID is 192.168.0, and Hosts B and C have a Network ID of 192.168.1. Hosts B and C are local with respect to one another, but A is not. Host A does not have the same network ID as the other two, so it is remote. It is the combination of the IP address and the subnet mask that allows IP to make the local/remote determination.

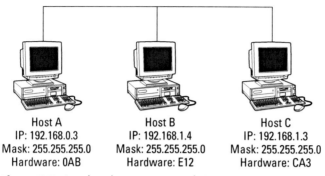

Host A
IP: 192.168.0.3
Mask: 255.255.255.0
Hardware: 0AB

Host B
IP: 192.168.1.4
Mask: 255.255.255.0
Hardware: E12

Host C
IP: 192.168.1.3
Mask: 255.255.255.0
Hardware: CA3

Figure 5-3: Local and remote network IDs

> **Note**
>
> IP logic at a host follows these rules:
>
> If the destination host is local, deliver the packet with the help of ARP.
>
> If the destination host is remote, deliver the packet to the default gateway with the help of ARP.
>
> If the packet is destined for a remote host *and* no default gateway is configured, discard the packet.

The following steps are taken at an IP host to deliver a packet to a local destination host:

1. A packet is passed down to IP from a higher layer protocol with a destination IP address specified in the packet. IP compares the destination host's network ID to the local host's network ID and determines that they are the same value.

2. Since the destination network ID is the same as the local host's network ID, the packet is bound for a host on the local network.

3. ARP broadcasting is used to exchange IP and Ethernet address information with the destination host.

4. The packet is passed to the Data Link layer for delivery to the destination host.

The following steps are taken at an IP host to deliver a packet to a remote destination host:

1. A packet is passed down to IP from a higher layer protocol with a destination IP address specified in the packet. IP compares the destination network ID to the local host's network ID and determines that they are a different value.

2. Since the destination host's network ID is not the same as the local host's network ID, the packet is bound for a remote host.

3. IP checks the route table for a route to the destination network. It does not find one, so the default route is used.

4. ARP broadcasting is used to exchange IP and Ethernet address information with the local host's default gateway, which is found in the default route.

5. Data Link layer protocols are used to deliver the packet to the default gateway where it enters the router network.

6. The router network completes the packet delivery. The last router has a local route to the destination host and can deliver the packet using ARP for the destination host.

Basics of Routing

Routing is a function of the IP protocol that allows packets to be passed between IP networks. Each IP datagram contains embedded addressing information that can be used by routers to help the packet reach its destination. Depending on the size of the inter network, many routers may need to handle a packet to ensure its delivery. IP routing can be a process of successive approximation, where each router that processes a packet moves it a little closer to its destination. You could think of a router as the keeper of the network map.

Hardware and software routers

Routers are not limited to desktop computers. In fact, using a server as a router in a large environment can pose serious performance problems. A PC-based router is commonly referred to as a *software router*. Certain manufacturers of hardware routers, such as Cisco and Nortel Networks, provide the high-speed communications required to handle the aggregate traffic of many busy subnets, as well as rich feature sets suited to specific environments.

Types of routes

The Internet is an example of a very complex routed network. Packets are sent and received across this network from destinations around the globe by a huge mesh of interconnected routers. Each of these routers needs frequent updates on the state of the network. The network state is contained in a route table housed on each router. A *route table* is comprised of a list of routes, which describe the best way to a destination. The method used to update those routes to each router defines the type of route used. There are three types of routes: default, static, and dynamic.

Dynamic routes and protocols are covered in detail in Chapter 19.

Default routes

Routing is a function of IP. Each host has a table of routes that it knows. Default routes are created in a table on every IP host as a result of the IP configuration. They are used to help deliver packets to a number of locations. The following is an example of a default route table captured from a single-homed Windows 95 computer with an IP address of 131.107.2.252 and a default gateway of 131.107.2.169. Here is the result of typing `route print` at a command prompt:

```
Network Address      Netmask      Gateway Address   Interface Metric
        0.0.0.0          0.0.0.0   131.107.2.169   131.107.2.252    1
      127.0.0.0        255.0.0.0        127.0.0.1       127.0.0.1    1
    131.107.2.0    255.255.255.0   131.107.2.252   131.107.2.252    1
  131.107.2.252  255.255.255.255       127.0.0.1       127.0.0.1    1
  131.107.255.255 255.255.255.255   131.107.2.252   131.107.2.252
  1
      224.0.0.0        224.0.0.0   131.107.2.252   131.107.2.252    1
  255.255.255.255 255.255.255.255   131.107.2.252   131.107.2.252
  1
```

The following list describes the seven default routes as output from the `route print` command.

1. 0.0.0.0 is the default entry, which is used when no other route fits.

2. 127.0.0.0 is the local loopback address used to send packets to the local host.

3. 131.107.2.0 is the local subnet route.

4. 131.107.2.252 is the local host route.

5. 131.107.255.255 is the subnet broadcast route.

6. 224.0.0.0 is the multicast route used by hosts to register in multicast groups.

7. 255.255.255.255 is the limited broadcast address.

The following list describes the five columns in the route table:

✦ **Network Address** — The *network address* in the route table is the destination address, which can be a host, subnet, or default route.

✦ **Netmask** — The *Netmask* defines the criteria for route use. If the network ID of the destination IP address matches the portion of the Network address that the Netmask covers, then the route can be used.

✦ **Gateway Address** — The *gateway address* is the address to which the packet must be sent.

✦ **Interface** — The *interface* is the address of the network adapter through which the packet must be sent.

✦ **Metric** — The *Metric* is the cost of the route. A lower metric value indicates a preferred route.

Routing need not be complicated — it can be as simple as a multi-homed computer spanning two networks. The computer can be configured to pass packets between networks by enabling IP forwarding. Figure 5-4 shows a multi-homed computer acting as a router. Packets can be passed from the 10.0.0.2 interface to the 192.168.1.12 interface, or in the other direction. All the routes required to pass datagrams between these two networks are default routes.

Note A multi-homed computer has two or more network interfaces, which are normally connected to different subnets.

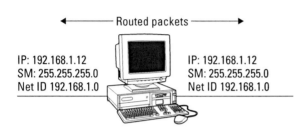

IP: 192.168.1.12
SM: 255.255.255.0
Net ID 192.168.1.0

IP: 192.168.1.12
SM: 255.255.255.0
Net ID 192.168.1.0

Figure 5-4: A multi-homed computer

No other configuration is required to move packets between the networks connected by the multi-homed computer. However, packets destined for any network other than the two listed in the default routing table would be discarded, because IP only knows how to find the two local subnets.

If we expand the router network a bit to include three networks connected by two routers, things get a bit more interesting. As discussed earlier in the chapter, network IDs are used by IP to describe local and remote destinations. Routers use network IDs to identify destination networks. As shown in Figure 5-5, there are three networks. While hosts on the 192.168.1.0 network and the 172.16.0.0 network each can forward packets to the 10.0.0.0 network, neither can reach each other. Hosts on the 192.168.1.0 network cannot forward packets to the 172.16.0.0 network, and vice versa.

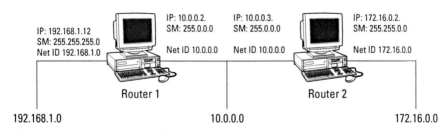

IP: 192.168.1.12
SM: 255.255.255.0
Net ID 192.168.1.0

IP: 10.0.0.2.
SM: 255.0.0.0

Net ID 10.0.0.0

IP: 10.0.0.3.
SM: 255.0.0.0

Net ID 10.0.0.0

IP: 172.16.0.2.
SM: 255.255.0.0

Net ID 172.16.0.0

Router 1

Router 2

192.168.1.0

10.0.0.0

172.16.0.0

Figure 5-5: Two routers on three networks

Note Multi-homed computers can only forward IP packets to segments to which they have a local interface. If they need to route to remote subnets, a default gateway or a route table entry will be required to find each remote network.

You can solve the problem of routing to remote subnets by using the default gateway, as shown in Figure 5-6. If you configure the 10.0.0.3 network card to use 10.0.0.2 as its default gateway, and 10.0.0.2 to use 10.0.0.3, you will effectively crisscross the default gateways. The routing problem is solved, because traffic that is remote to each router will now be sent to the other. Since there are only three networks, using the default gateway may not be a bad idea. However, keep in mind that as the LAN expands to five and six networks, the default gateway solution will become ineffective.

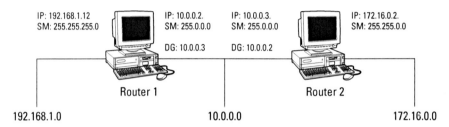

IP: 192.168.1.12	IP: 10.0.0.2.	IP: 10.0.0.3.	IP: 172.16.0.2.
SM: 255.255.255.0	SM: 255.0.0.0	SM: 255.0.0.0	SM: 255.255.0.0
	DG: 10.0.0.3	DG: 10.0.0.2	

Router 1   Router 2

192.168.1.0   10.0.0.0   172.16.0.0

Figure 5-6: Routing by using default gateways

Caution   Default gateways are not normally configured on routers. They have been used here to show the effect of the default (0.0.0.0) route.

Assume that a host at 192.168.1.14 network needs to communicate with a host at 172.16.0.72. The process works as follows:

1. On the 192.168.14 host, packets are passed down from a higher layer protocol with 172.16.0.72 as the destination.

2. IP at the host compares the destination network ID to the local network ID and determines that the traffic is bound for a remote host.

3. ARP is used to find the default gateway (in this case, 192.168.0.12), and the packet is sent to Router 1.

4. IP at Router 1 examines the incoming packet for the destination network ID. The destination address (172.16.0.72) does not match either of the local network IDs and is therefore considered remote to Router 1.

5. Router 1 has a default gateway configured, so ARP is used to resolve the default gateway. IP at Router 1 decrements the packets TTL and passes the packet on to 10.0.0.3.

6. IP at Router 2 examines the destination IP of the incoming packet for network ID and finds that the packet is addressed to one of its local networks, the 172.16.0.0 network.

7. ARP is used to find the hardware address of the destination host.

8. The packet is delivered to 172.16.0.72.

As you can see, each router will pass remote bound packets to its configured default gateway. While the simplicity of this configuration is desirable, it does not scale well. This configuration is only suitable for small networks with very few segments.

Static routes

Another way of routing to all three networks is to use a route table entry at each router. Each route table entry is used to identify a remote network and to point out the IP address of the next router on the way to the remote network. Figure 5-7 shows the required route table entries for this three-segment network.

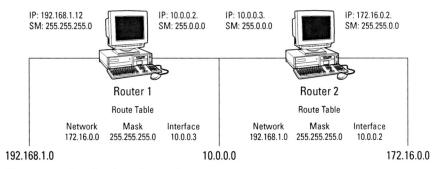

Figure 5-7: Routing by using static routes

Once again, assume that a host at 192.168.1.14 needs to communicate with a host at IP address 172.16.0.72. Here is how the process works, using route table entries instead of a default gateway:

1. On the 192.168.1.14 host, packets are passed down from a higher layer protocol, with 172.16.0.72 as the destination.

2. IP at the host compares the destination network ID to the local network ID and determines that the traffic is bound for a remote host.

3. ARP is used to find the host's default gateway. In this case, the default gateway is 192.168.0.12, and the packet is forwarded to Router 1.

4. IP at Router 1 examines the incoming packet for the destination network ID. The destination address (172.16.0.72) does not match either of the local network IDs, and is therefore considered remote to Router 1.

5. IP at Router 1 checks its router table for a route to the 172.16.0.0 network and finds one. The route specifies interface 10.0.0.3.

6. ARP is used to resolve 10.0.0.3 and to exchange hardware addresses between Routers 1 and 2. The packet is forwarded on to 10.0.0.3.

7. IP at Router 2 examines the destination IP of the incoming packet for network ID and finds that the packet is addressed to one of its local networks, the 172.16.0.0 network. The packet TTL is decremented, and a new checksum is computed.

8. ARP is used to find the hardware address of the destination host.

9. The packet is delivered to 172.16.0.72.

Dynamic routes

Dynamic routes are not a function of IP but of specific routing protocols, such as the Routing Information Protocol (RIP) or the Open Shortest Path First (OSPF). All dynamic routing protocols have some method of sharing routing information over the network by means of advertising their route tables in whole or in part to nearby routers. Since the router can learn of its surrounding area by listening to the broadcasts of its neighbors, implementation of routers that use dynamic routes is greatly simplified.

While dynamic routers can use manually entered routes (such as static routes), the *major* advantage of implementing dynamic routing lies in the ability of the router network to react to changing conditions by modifying the content of route table entries and metrics.

Cross-Reference Chapter 19 will discuss Open Shortest Path First (OSPF) and Routing Information Protocol (RIP) — two dynamic routing protocols.

Fragmentation and reassembly

Regardless of whether static, dynamic, or default routing is used, there must be a mechanism to adjust the size of packets so they will fit onto the destination network without causing problems or losing data. This mechanism is the Internet Protocol fragmentation and reassembly function.

As a router inspects an incoming packet, the total length is compared to the Maximum Transmission Unit (MTU) of the next network. If the packet size exceeds the MTU of the next network, the packet is divided up into fragments small enough to fit into packets on the next segment. Each fragmented packet shares the same identify field information (indicating that they are part of the same original packet) and a unique offset, which is used to reassemble the packet fragments in the proper order at the destination.

Examining an IP Datagram

An IP datagram consists of two distinct parts: a header and a payload. The header is used to control behavior at the IP layer, such as routing, fragmentation, and so on. Higher layer headers and data are encapsulated in the IP payload, or data area. The following section examines the structure of an IP packet.

IP header

The first 20 bytes or so of an IP packet contain essential information about how the packet is to be handled. This information is referred to collectively as the IP header. The fields that make up an IP header are depicted in Table 5-5.

Table 5-5 IP Header Fields							
4 bits	4 bits	4 bits	4 bits	4 bits	4 bits	4bits	4 bits
Ver.	IHL	Type of Service		Total Length			
Identifier				Flags		Fragment Offset	
Time to Live		Protocol		Header Checksum			
Source Address							
Destination Address							
Options and Padding							

The following is a listing of these fields and a brief functional explanation where appropriate:

✦ **The Version (Ver.)** — The version of IP in use — currently version 4.

✦ **IP Header Length (IHL)** — The length of the IP header in 32-bit words.

✦ **Type of Service** — This field allows for precedence of traffic and for the insertion of delays if required.

✦ **Total Length** — The total length of the packet in octets, including the header and data. The minimum value is 576 octets, and the maximum is 65,535 octets, or 64K bytes.

✦ **Identification** — This field provides a unique 8-bit identity for each packet.

✦ **Flags** — This 3-bit field allows for the control of fragmentation by specifying whether or not a packet may be fragmented or more fragmented.

✦ **Fragment Offset** — In the case of a fragmented packet, this field is used to measure where, starting from the front of the datagram, this particular fragment fits. Offset is measured in 64-bit units.

✦ **Time to Live (TTL)** — Time to live is measured in router hops or seconds. A TTL zero packet is discarded.

✦ **Protocol** — This field indicates the next protocol header to follow the IP header. If the protocol field value contained a 6, then the packet would be passed up to the TCP protocol.

Some common examples of IP protocol field values are listed in Table 5-6.

Table 5-6
IP Protocol Field Values

Value	Protocol	Description
1	ICMP	Internet Control Message Protocol
2	IGMP	Internet Group Management Protocol
6	TCP	Transmission Control Protocol
8	EGP	Exterior Gateway Protocol
17	UDP	User Datagram Protocol

✦ **Header Checksum** — A mathematical checksum that is recomputed at each router as the header information changes.

✦ **Source Address** — The IP address of the originating host in 32-bit binary notation.

✦ **Destination Address** — The IP address of the destination host in 32-bit binary notation.

✦ **Options and Padding** — This field can be used to include options from the sender, such a route the packet should take to the destination. The padding field is used to ensure that the IP header ends on a 32-bit boundary.

IP payload

The IP payload is a variable length field from 8 bits to 64K bytes in length, including the IP header plus higher layer data. Payload at the IP layer consists of headers from higher layer protocols, such as TCP or UDP, and data from applications that use those protocols.

Internet Control Messaging Protocol

Networks should work properly all the time, but they don't. When things go wrong at the Internet layer, Internet Control Messaging Protocol (ICMP) acts as a trouble-shooter. ICMP is a maintenance protocol that reports on host-to-host errors. ICMP is documented in RFC 792.

Purpose of ICMP

Datagrams are delivered on a "best effort" or connectionless basis at the Internet layer. The ICMP protocol is a set of messages that ride in IP datagrams and can report errors in the delivery of other IP datagrams. The following list describes some of the reasons gateways or hosts might send ICMP messages:

✦ If a router or host becomes too congested to buffer any more datagrams, ICMP messages are used to slow the flow of datagrams to that router.

✦ If a router or host finds a better route to a destination, it could send an ICMP message to the source host, informing him of the shorter route.

✦ If a destination host is unreachable, the last gateway would send an ICMP message back to the source host, informing him of the unreachable destination host.

✦ If a host or gateway processes a packet with a Time to Live of 0 hops, it will discard that packet, perhaps sending an ICMP message to the source host.

ICMP messages are the "built-in" Internet layer diagnostic tools. If two hosts cannot communicate, ICMP messages can usually help diagnose the problem.

Since there could be a flood of messages in a fast-changing environment, there are no ICMP messages generated as a result of non-delivery of ICMP messages. Specifically, if an ICMP destination host unreachable message does not arrive at the source host, it will not generate another ICMP message.

ICMP packets

An ICMP packet is contained in the IP datagram itself and identified by the fact that the IP protocol field is set to 1. An ICMP packet will have 8-bit Type and Code fields and a 16-bit Checksum field, as shown in Table 5-7.

Table 5-7
ICMP Packet Fields

8 bits	8 bits	16 bits
Type	Code	Checksum

The Type field in the ICMP packet is used to identify the ICMP message type, as listed in Table 5-8.

Table 5-8
Common ICMP Messages

Type	ICMP Message
0	Echo Reply
3	Destination Unreachable
4	Source Quench
5	Redirect
8	Echo
11	Time Exceeded

ICMP types and codes

The Code field contains further information about that message type if needed:

✦ **Echo Request** — The Echo Request is used to check connectivity between two hosts. The PING utility sends ICMP echo requests.

✦ **Echo Reply** — The Echo Reply is the response to an Echo Request.

✦ **Source Quench** — If a router is overwhelmed by traffic from a host, it can send a Source Quench message to that host. The Source Quench message indicates imminent data loss due to congestion at the router.

✦ **Redirect** — If a router knows of a better route to a destination, it can inform sending hosts of that route through a Redirect message.

✦ **Time Exceeded** — If a router receives a packet with a TTL of 0, it may send a Time Exceeded message to the original host.

✦ **Destination Unreachable** — For various reasons, packets may not be deliverable. The Destination Unreachable message type has codes that indicate some of the reasons a packet might not reach its destination. These codes are listed in Table 5-9.

Table 5-9
Destination Unreachable Codes

Code	Description
0	Network unreachable
1	Host unreachable
2	Protocol unreachable

Code	Description
3	Port unreachable at destination host
4	Fragmentation needed and don't fragment field was set
5	Source routing information supplied and failed

Common ICMP utilities

PING and Tracert are two of the most common, convenient ICMP utilities currently being used.

PING

The Packet InterNet Groper utility (PING) is the most widely known and universally used Internet-layer troubleshooting tool. PING uses an ICMP echo and echo reply to verify connectivity between two IP hosts. In fact, PING repeatedly transmits part of the alphabet from the source host to the destination host. At the destination host, ICMP replies to the echo by sending back the same data in an Echo Reply packet. As the data arrives back at the source host, various types of information, such as how long it took the data to go round trip, are displayed at the source host. The following code shows a ping to the destination host at IP address 131.107.2.169 and the reply indicating the response time and TTL of the packet.

```
C:\>ping 131.107.2.169

Pinging 131.107.2.169 with 32 bytes of data:

Reply from 131.107.2.169: bytes=32 time<10ms TTL=128
Reply from 131.107.2.169: bytes=32 time<10ms TTL=128
Reply from 131.107.2.169: bytes=32 time<10ms TTL=128
Reply from 131.107.2.169: bytes=32 time<10ms TTL=128

Ping statistics for 131.107.2.169:
    Packets: Sent = 4, Received = 4, Lost = 0 (0% loss),
Approximate round trip times in milli-seconds:
    Minimum = 0ms, Maximum =  0ms, Average =  0ms
```

Tracert

The Tracert utility takes advantage of the Type 11 Time Exceeded ICMP message to map the route to a destination network. When a Tracert command specifies a destination host, ICMP echos are sent to that host with an increasing TTL starting at 1. Since each gateway that processes that packet must decrement the TTL, each TTL reaches 0 on the next gateway to the destination. The route trace is formed by examining the Time Exceeded messages from each of the gateways between the two hosts. The following code shows a Tracert to a popular Web site. Notice how each gateway identifies itself with the Time Exceeded message.

```
C:\>tracert www.yahoo.com

Tracing route to www.yahoo.akadns.net [216.32.74.52]
over a maximum of 30 hops:

  1    200 ms    200 ms    180 ms  tnt6.ottawa.on.da.uu.net [142.77.230.80]
  2    200 ms    201 ms    200 ms  dr.t4.tnt6.ottawa.on.da.uu.net [142.77.230.221]
  3    201 ms    200 ms    200 ms  209.47.71.101
  4    201 ms    200 ms    200 ms  207.ATM2-0.XR1.TOR2.ALTER.NET [152.63.129.89]
  5    200 ms    200 ms    201 ms  295.ATM3-0.TR1.TOR2.ALTER.NET [152.63.128.46]
  6    221 ms    220 ms    220 ms  137.at-7-3-0.TR1.DCA8.ALTER.NET
[146.188.141.209]
  7    220 ms    220 ms    221 ms  0.so-5-0-0.XR1.DCA8.ALTER.NET [152.63.25.38]
  8    200 ms    221 ms    220 ms  POS6-0.GW2.DCA8.ALTER.NET [146.188.162.197]
  9    220 ms    220 ms    221 ms  exodus-OC12.DCA8.customer.alter.net
[157.130.42.58]
 10    221 ms    220 ms    220 ms  dcr03-g9-0.stng01.exodus.net [216.33.96.145]
 11    221 ms    220 ms    220 ms  csr22-ve242.stng01.exodus.net [216.33.98.19]
 12    220 ms    221 ms    220 ms  216.35.210.126
 13    241 ms    220 ms    220 ms  www3.dcx.yahoo.com [216.32.74.52]

Trace complete.
```

Internet Group Management Protocol

If your network card were a TV and the content was delivered by multicasted transmissions over the Internet, then the Internet Group Management Protocol (IGMP) would be the television tuner, permitting selective access to the right channel.

IGMP is an Internet Layer Protocol that allows a host (application) to join or leave a multicast group, and in some cases, it specifies the source of the multicast information. At a router, IGMP helps keep track of the networks that need to have multicasts sent to them based on the existence of host group memberships. IGMP is documented in RFC 1112. The terms *host* and *host application* are used interchangeably in the context of IGMP client communications.

Overview of multicasting

Most of the network traffic on your LAN is probably unicast, or directed, traffic. *Unicast traffic* is "one-to-one" traffic. In other words, each packet is transmitted once, addressed to a specific destination host. Some of the traffic on your network is broadcast-based. *Broadcast traffic* is "one-to-many" traffic, which means that each broadcast packet is transmitted once but sent to all hosts. Each host processes the broadcast packet — just in case the data is intended for it. Network designers try to limit the use of broadcast traffic wherever possible, because it slows network performance.

There is an ever-increasing number of multimedia applications coming into widespread use and a corresponding decrease in the available bandwidth on traditional file and print networks. In these applications some, but not all, of the hosts on a network may need to see information from a common source. If that information were transmitted by broadcast, then all routers and hosts everywhere would have to process that traffic, even if they were not members of the group that wanted to see the transmission. If unicast transmission were used by the application, then the information would need to be sent once for each member host. As you can see, neither broadcast nor unicast traffic suits the "one-to-selective group" communication requirement. Each method of transmission uses far too much bandwidth, either by retransmitting data or by flooding the network with data that only a few host applications currently need.

Multicasting suits the above application examples by allowing all the clients who need the information to register in a group. This multicast group would be identified to the local routers as needing the specific traffic for that application. As long as the router has group members on its networks, it would forward the multicast traffic to them. The source server would only send out the traffic once. Only the hosts in the group would receive the multicast traffic. Multicasting provides a much more effective solution for "one-to-selective group" traffic scenarios than either broadcast or unicast transmission.

How IGMP works with clients

IGMP packets are contained inside IP datagrams in much the same way as ICMP packets. Multicasting uses Class D IP addresses in the range of 224.0.0.0 to 239.255.255.255, so IGMP packets can be identified at the IP layer by IP address. The multicast address used is also directly mapped to shared Ethernet addresses to facilitate Data Link layer delivery.

Hosts that need to join multicast groups should inform immediately neighboring routers which multicast host group they wish to join and also if they wish to leave.

Note IGMP Explicit Leave messages are a function of later enhancements to the IGMP protocol. The original IGMP version 1 simply allowed the host multicast group to "time out," whereupon the router would stop sending content.

Joining a host to a multicast group involves two processes at the client:

1. The host notifies the router that he wants to join the appropriate multicast group.

2. The host dynamically binds IP to the multicast address reserved for that application and binds that IP address to a reserved Ethernet address.

Joining a multicast group is achieved through transmission of an IGMP Host Membership Report packet. This packet contains the IP address of the desired multicast group.

How IGMP works with routers

Periodically, each router will poll its networks to ascertain the continued need for multicasted content delivery. This is achieved through a "host membership query," which is directed to the "all hosts" reserved IP address of 224.0.0.1 and carries a TTL of 1. Hosts with multicast memberships will reply to this message with a report whose destination address equals the multicast group address they require.

Note   IGMP Host Membership queries carry a TTL of 1 to ensure they are not forwarded on to any other networks.

Because the routers can see which groups are needed from the results of this periodic host report, they will discard all multicast packets that are not required.

IGMP is the last step in multicast packet delivery. In a large environment (such as the Internet), multicasted traffic may need to be forwarded through many gateways (whose local hosts are not members) to reach a gateway whose hosts *are* multicast members. Refer to Figure 8-8. This router-to-router communication and delivery is the function of Multicast Router Protocols, not IGMP.

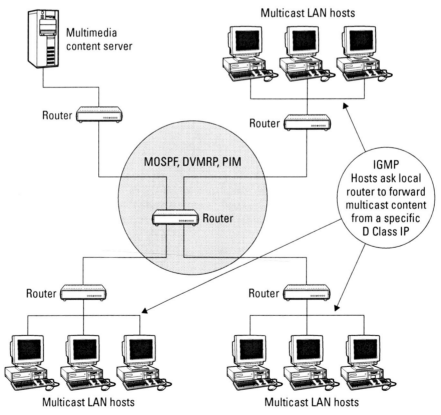

Figure 5-8: Multicasting and IGMP

Router-to-router delivery of multicasted content is the result of protocols like Multicast Extensions to OSPF (MOSPF) and Distance Vector Multicast Routing Protocol (DVMRP) — not IGMP. These router-to-router multicasting protocols have been developed with different algorithms that control how the tree of routers that carry multicasted communications is built, maintained, and pruned.

The following RFCs describe three common router-to-router multicasting protocols:

✦ **RFC 2117** — Protocol Independent Multicast protocol (PIM)

✦ **RFC 1584** — The Multicast Extensions to OSPF (MOSPF)

✦ **RFC 1075** — Distance Vector Multicast Routing Protocol (DVMRP)

What multicasting is used for

Multicasting is used to deliver content selectively to only those hosts that have indicated that they need it. Hosts can register in multicast groups at any time to receive the content addressed to that group. Hosts can also leave the group at any time, which ends the multicast reception. Typically, Web sites announce the date and time of special events that client applications can "tune" into by using multicasting.

IGMP packets

There are only two packet types of interest to IGMP clients. Table 5-10 shows the structure of an IGMP packet, including a 32-bit group address field, a 16-bit checksum, and two 4-bit fields for version and type.

<table>
<tr><td colspan="4" align="center">Table 5-10
IGMP Packet Structure</td></tr>
<tr><td>*Version*</td><td>*Type*</td><td>*Unused*</td><td>*Checksum*</td></tr>
<tr><td colspan="4">Multicast Group Address</td></tr>
</table>

The following is a description of each field of an IGMP packet and its possible values.

✦ **Version** — Denotes the version of IGMP that is used. Possible values are 1, 2, or 3.

✦ **Type** — Indicates the two possible messages of interest to multicast hosts:

   • 1 = Host Membership Query

   • 2 = Host Membership Report

✦ **Checksum** — Mathematical computation designed to ensure packet integrity.

✦ **Group Address** — In a host membership query, the Group address is left blank. In a host membership report message, the group address field holds the IP address of the reported multicast group.

Summary

This chapter provided you with a "look under the hood" at the Internet layer — the "engine" of the TCP/IP protocol suite. It discussed the purpose and operation of the three main protocols (IP, ICMP, and IGMP) that operate at the Internet layer. It also examined such topics as IP addressing, IP classes, and routing. ICMP was shown to be the problem detection and reporting mechanism of the Internet layer. In addition, multicasting was discussed from the client's and router's point of view. An understanding of these protocols can help you troubleshoot your own network problems. It also provides a springboard from which you can jump into the next chapter on the Transport layer.

✦   ✦   ✦

Transport Layer

The Transport layer, which resides between the
Application layer and the Internet layer, is the core of the
layered network architecture. The Transport layer breaks the
data that arrives from the Application layer into segments and
passes it with destination address to the next layer for transmission. It also provides a *logical communication* between
application processes running on different hosts. In this type
of logical communication, although the application processes
on the source and destination computers are not physically
connected, they communicate as if they were.

This chapter explores different types of data transfer that the
Transport layer supports, the connectionless data transfer
protocol (User Datagram Protocol): and the connection-based
data transfer protocol (Transmission Control Protocol).

Types of Data Transfer

One primary task that the Transport layer performs is the
passing of data streams from the Application layer to the
Internet layer in the form of segments. On the sending side,
the Transport layer converts the messages received from a
sending application process into *segments*. These segments
contain the data to be transmitted, along with a *header* that
contains specific information, such as source and destination
address. On the receiving side, the Transport layer receives
the segments from the Internet layer, reassembles the messages, and passes them to a receiving application process.
The application processes use the logical communication provided by the Transport layer to send messages to each other,
without worrying about the details of the physical infrastructure that is used to transmit these messages. Figure 6-1 shows
this logical communication.

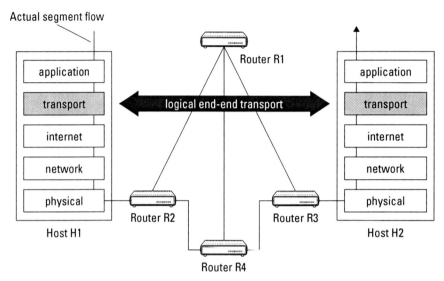

Figure 6-1: Logical communication provided by the Transport layer

The logical communication provided by the Transport layer can be connectionless or connection-oriented. In a connection-oriented data transfer, a connection needs to be established between the application processes on the source and destination hosts before data is actually sent. In a connectionless data transfer, no formal connection needs to be established before the data is transferred.

Data transfer can also be categorized as reliable or non-reliable, stateful or stateless. *Reliable* data transfer ensures that the segments are transferred to their destinations in the sequence in which they were sent. On the other hand, *unreliable* data transfer completely relies on the lower layer for data transfer and, therefore, does not ensure the delivery of segments to their destination.

Stateful data transfer means that the information included in one request sent from the source to the destination can be used to modify future requests. *Stateless* data transfer means that information in one request *cannot* be tied to any other request and thus cannot be used further.

There are certain fundamental networking issues that need to be addressed at the Transport layer for successful and efficient data transfer. These issues are:

✦ **Addressing**—For communication between hosts, the address of the destination must be known. The addresses of all processes on a host are known to common services, such as word processing and time sharing. Furthermore, the addresses of these common services are known to the operating system on a host. Thus, when the destination is a specific process, the initiating user can send a process request to a service whose address is known. The user at the address can then return the process address to the initiating user.

✦ **Reset/Restart problem** — Network failures can cause network connections to restart or reset, which may result in loss of segments. Most of the transport protocols address this problem in one of two ways:

- Whenever a connection reset occurs, the network services communicate this to the affected transport entities by sending signals. The receiver transport entity acknowledges the reset condition and provides the last segment number received to the sender. On the other hand, the sender transport entity refrains from sending any new segment until the corresponding information regarding reset is received from the other end.

- Whenever the underlying network connection is lost, the side that first initiated the connection needs to issue a request to the network services for a new network connection. Then it needs to issue the communication request to the host at the other end.

✦ **Communication over an unreliable channel** — The Transport layer uses the underlying Internet layer, which in turn uses the Network layer, for physical transmission of data between the sender and the receiver. Since the Internet layer uses Internet Protocol (IP) that uses the connectionless unreliable data transfer mechanism, the transport protocol should reliably deliver data between the applications.

✦ **Multiplexing/Demultiplexing** — Transport protocols must provide multiplexing/demultiplexing services for communication between two processes residing on different hosts. Otherwise, the communication won't be possible at all.

Note

You will see the terms multiplexing and demultiplexing used in many facets of networking. In the most general sense, *multiplexing* means combining multiple components into a single component, and *demultiplexing* means separating the multiple individual components.

The process of gathering data at the source host from different application processes, creating segments, and passing the segments to the network layer is called *multiplexing*. The process of delivering the data in a Transport layer segment to the correct application process is called *demultiplexing*.

✦ **Sequencing** — The Transport layer breaks the data stream that is passed onto it from the Application layer into small chunks called *segments*. These segments must be numbered so that they can be reassembled at the receiving end. If the segments are not numbered and the packet that was sent first reaches the destination after the second packet (due to certain network delays), the data at the receiving end cannot be reassembled and is damaged.

✦ **Flow control and buffering** — The Transport layer residing in the hosts at the two ends of communication maintains a specific amount of storage space, called *buffer*, that identifies the amount of data that can be stored. The application can then read from this buffer. If the sender continues sending the data irrespective of the buffer size, overflow might occur — resulting in data loss. Therefore, the rate at which the receiving application is reading must match the rate at which the sender is sending. This matching of the speeds at the two ends is called *flow control*, and it ensures complete and efficient data delivery without any loss of data.

✦ **Congestion control** — *Congestion* occurs when there are too many packets present in the network, resulting in poor performance. This situation may be due to several factors, such as slow routers on the network or no free buffers at the routers. The Transport layer must address this issue during transmission.

✦ **Duplication** — When two or more copies of the same segment are sent to the receiver during a Transport layer connection, *duplication* occurs. This situation can arise when multiple acknowledgements are received for the same segment or when retransmission occurs due to delayed data delivery or lost acknowledgements. To avoid transmission errors, the Transport layer must detect duplication.

✦ **Crash recovery** — The protocol must handle a situation where one of the systems crashes during segment transmission. The situation becomes even worse when the active (sending) side of the connection continues to send segments and waits for acknowledgement from the receiver, which has crashed.

✦ **Retransmission strategy** — The underlying Internet Protocol is unreliable. Therefore, the Transport layer requires a strategy for retransmission of segments in case a segment:

- Fails to arrive at its destination.

- Arrives at its destination, but in a damaged state. The Transport layer at the receiving end should detect the error and discard the segment.

The Transport layer provides transport services through the transport protocols. The transport protocols include User Datagram Protocol (UDP) and Transmission Control Protocol (TCP). These protocols address many fundamental networking issues.

Reliable versus unreliable delivery

Reliable data delivery ensures the delivery of segments to their destination in proper sequence, without any damage or loss. A reliable protocol like TCP takes care of all the fundamental networking problems, such as congestion, data flow, and duplication.

Unreliable data delivery does not promise the delivery of segments to their destination. In the process of unreliable data delivery, segments might get corrupted or lost. An unreliable protocol, such as UDP, assumes that the underlying network is completely reliable. Therefore, unreliable protocols do not take care of certain fundamental networking problems, such as congestion, data flow, and duplication. Table 6-1 compares the two types of data delivery.

Table 6-1
Reliable versus Unreliable Delivery

Features	Reliable Delivery	Unreliable Delivery
Functionality	Ensures data delivery to the destination without any damage or loss.	Does not ensure data delivery to the destination.
Sequencing	On the sending side, the packets are numbered sequentially, and thus reliable protocols ensure that the packets reach their destination in order.	The packets are not numbered. Therefore, data at the receiving end might be jumbled.
Acknowledgement	The receiver sends an acknowledgement after receiving a segment from the sender and thus ensures reliability without data loss.	The sender continues to send segments without receiving an acknowledgement from the receiver.
Retransmission	If a packet does not reach the destination or reaches the destination in a damaged state, the sender retransmits the lost or damaged packets.	If the segments are lost or errors are detected, there is no retransmission.
Duplicate detection	Reliable protocols can detect duplication that might occur due to retransmission.	Unreliable delivery does not use the concept of acknowledgements and retransmission. Therefore, duplication does not arise.
Flow control	Reliable protocols provide flow control, preventing any data loss.	Unreliable protocols do not provide flow control, resulting in data loss.
Congestion control	Reliable data delivery addresses the congestion problem and ensures congestion control.	Unreliable data delivery does not ensure congestion control.

Note   Reliability can also be achieved with an unreliable transport if the underlying layers used by the Transport layer are reliable. A prime example to mention here is Trivial File Transfer Protocol (TFTP).

Stateful versus stateless delivery

Stateful data delivery uses the concept of a "session," in which a batch of requests is sent and the responses received. Thus, information divulged in one request can be used to modify future requests. Consider a situation where searches over large databases are required. If the stateful protocol is used, the server can return the first segment of the results to users, allowing them to start using the information while it continues to search the rest of the data. Stateful delivery is thus more efficient because such servers provide high performance. However, the stateful servers are more complex because they need to implement state maintenance. Figure 6-2 shows a stateful delivery. In case of failure, inconsistent states might result. When inconsistent states result, stateful servers must rebuild the stored state by interacting with clients in the event of a crash. Alternatively, client connections can be aborted.

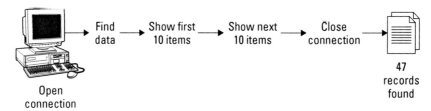

Figure 6-2: Stateful data delivery

In stateless data delivery, each request is self-contained, without any other information being tied to any other request. Therefore, the client needs to provide the server with complete information on each request in order to obtain a proper response, because the data in a response is based only on the information the client sends in the request. Figure 6-3 shows a stateless delivery. The stateless servers are simple and robust — the probability of anything going wrong during data delivery is low because each request is self-contained. Also, since the information in one request cannot be used for future requests, stateless servers do not provide high performance. However, in case of a failure, stateless servers have more graceful failure semantics and can be replicated or replaced.

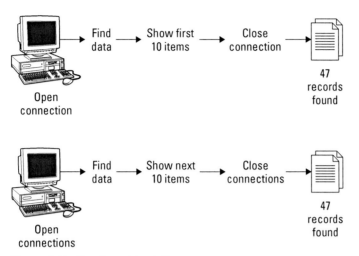

Figure 6-3: Stateless data delivery

Table 6-2 compares the two types of data transfer.

Table 6-2	
Stateful versus Stateless Data Delivery	
Stateful Delivery	*Stateless Delivery*
Uses the concept of a "session," in which requests are sent and received in batches.	No session is initiated in this delivery. Each request is self-contained.
Stateful servers are complex.	Stateless servers are simple.
In case of a failure, inconsistent states might result. Therefore, the states must be restored. Moreover, client communications can be aborted.	In case of a failure, stateless servers can be replicated or replaced.

Connectionless Data Transfer

User Datagram Protocol (UDP) provides connectionless, stateless, and unreliable data delivery between processes running on different hosts. To ensure communication between processes running on different hosts, the addresses of the processes must be known. A unique process ID identifies each process on a host. However, addressing a process on a host can be problematic for several reasons:

✦ Processes are created and destroyed dynamically.

✦ Other processes might replace the processes that receive data without informing the sender. For example, when the computer at the other end is rebooted, all the process IDs are changed.

✦ The sender needs to identify the destination from the functions that they implement without knowing the process that implements the functions.

UDP does not consider a process as the ultimate destination. Instead, it uses a set of abstract destination points called *protocol ports.* The processes running on a host access a specific port. To do so, they use an interface mechanism provided by the local operating system. These ports are buffered, indicating that before a process is ready to accept the data, the protocol software located inside the operating system keeps segments that arrive for a particular port in a queue until the process extracts it. Therefore, to communicate with a foreign port, the sender should know the IP address of the destination computer and the protocol port number of the destination process within that computer.

UDP uses the underlying Internet Protocol (IP) of the Internet layer to transport messages between computers. However, unlike IP, UDP adds the ability to distinguish between multiple destinations within a given host computer. Also, it provides for error checking (not correcting). Thus, when UDP is used instead of TCP, the application is almost directly talking with IP.

Why should you select UDP over TCP when TCP provides reliable data transfer? Certain applications, such as DNS, SNMP, and RIP use UDP by default, These applications prefer UDP to TCP for several reasons:

✦ **No connection establishment** — Since there is no connection establishment, the UDP transfers data faster. Therefore, DNS would have been much slower if it had used a connection-oriented protocol instead of UDP.

✦ **No connection state** — UDP does not maintain a connection state and does not track any of the parameters, such as receive and send buffers, congestion control parameters, and sequence and acknowledgement number parameters. Therefore, a server that is devoted to a particular application can support more active clients when UDP is used.

✦ **Small header size** — Every segment contains 8 bytes of header, which is a small size compared to that of TCP. Thus, there are fewer overheads, and communication is fast and efficient.

In general, UDP is selected when speed and efficiency are more important than reliability. However, it is also possible for an application to have reliable data transfer with UDP. Application programs should take full responsibility for implementing reliability with UDP, including message loss, duplication, delay, out-of-order delivery, and loss of connectivity. Keep in mind, however, that this approach may not be practical, because it puts more responsibility on the application developer. Moreover, since network software is often tested by using reliable, low-delivery LANs, testing might not explore potential failures. Thus, UDP is used in situations when the load on network reliability is not a major concern, and the speed of transfer is of prime importance.

The UDP protocol of the Transport layer breaks the data stream into segments called *user datagrams.* Figure 6-4 shows the format of a UDP datagram.

```
0                        16                       31
 ┌─────────────────────┬─────────────────────────┐
 │  UDP SOURCE PORT    │  UDP DESTINATION PORT    │
 ├─────────────────────┼─────────────────────────┤
 │ UDP MESSAGE LENGTH  │     UDP CHECKSUM         │
 ├─────────────────────┴─────────────────────────┤
 │                   DATA                         │
 ├────────────────────────────────────────────────┤
 │                    ...                         │
 └────────────────────────────────────────────────┘
```

Figure 6-4: The UDP datagram format

Conceptually, a UDP datagram consists of a UDP header and a UDP data area. The application data occupies the data field. The header contains four fields, each consisting of 16 bits. The four fields of the header are:

✦ **Source port** — This field contains the port number of the process that is running on the source.

✦ **Destination port** — This field contains the port number of the process running on the destination. The source and destination port numbers are required by UDP to perform multiplexing and demultiplexing and thus transfer data.

✦ **Length** — This contains the total length of the datagram.

✦ **UDP checksum** — UDP checksum provides for error detection. This field contains the 1's complement of the sum of all the 16-bit words in the segment. The 1's complement is obtained by converting all the 0s to 1s and converting all the 1s to 0s. For example, if the sum of all 16-bit words is 1100101011001010, the checksum is 0011010100110101. At the receiving end, all 16-bit words are added together, including the checksum. If there are no errors, then the sum at the receiving end is 1111111111111111. However, if one of the bits is 0, an error is indicated.

Connection-Oriented Data Transfer

The TCP protocol of the Transport layer is a connection-oriented, reliable, and stateful protocol. TCP establishes a connection between the process on the source and the process on the destination host before sending the actual data segments. Once the connection is established, data can be transferred in both directions between two hosts — a process called *full duplex data transfer*. For example, if a TCP connection has been established between process A on the source host and process B on the destination host, data can flow from A to B as well as from B to A simultaneously. To establish a connection between two processes on different hosts, the following identification sources are required:

✦ **TCP port numbers** — These uniquely identify a process on a host. This port number need not be same on the two hosts.

✦ **TCP sockets** — A TCP socket is a combination of the IP address of the machine and the TCP port number of the process on that machine. To establish a TCP connection, an application must request a unique TCP socket from the TCP protocol. This is called *opening a socket*. Therefore, for successful communication, the application must know the TCP socket on the source, as well as the TCP socket on the destination.

Because TCP is a reliable protocol, it addresses all the fundamental networking problems, such as congestion control, sequencing, and flow control. A TCP connection is always between a single sender and a single receiver — called a *point-to-point* connection. The following section describes TCP in detail.

Initiating a session

An application on a computer that needs to send data to another application on a different computer sends data to the Transport layer. The TCP protocol of the Transport layer receives data from the application and breaks it into small segments called *TCP segments*. TCP encapsulates these segments within IP datagrams, which are then routed over the network. However, before they start to send the data, the two processes on both hosts must first "handshake" with each other. During the connection establishment, certain quality parameters must be agreed upon between the source and destination. These parameters are called *Quality Of Service (QOS) parameters,* and the process of QOS agreement between the source and destination is called *option negotiation*. QOS parameters ensure a certain level of quality standard for data transmission. The different QOS parameters are:

✦ **Connection establishment delay** — The time elapsed between a request for a transport connection and the receipt of the transport confirmation. The shorter the delay, the better the service.

✦ **Connection establishment failure probability** — The probability of a connection not being established within the maximum establishment delay time.

✦ **Throughput** — The number of bytes of data transfer per second. The throughput is measured separately for each direction, from source to destination and from destination to source.

✦ **Transit delay** — The duration between the time the message is sent from the source and the time the message is received by the destination. Like throughput, this parameter is also handled separately for each direction.

✦ **Residual error rate** — The number of lost or garbled messages as a fraction of the total messages being sent over a specific time interval. Ideally, the residual error rate should be zero, but practically, a finite residual error rate is permitted and is agreed upon.

✦ **Transfer failure probability** — During the establishment of a connection, a given level of throughput, transit delay, and residual error rate are agreed upon. The transfer failure probability is the fraction of times that the agreed-upon goals were not met over an observation time period.

✦ **Connection release delay** — The time duration between the initiation of a connection release and the actual release of the connection.

✦ **Connection release failure probability** — The probability of a connection not being released within the maximum release delay time.

✦ **Protection** — This parameter is specified to provide protection against unauthorized third parties (wiretappers) reading or modifying the transmitted data.

✦ **Priority** — This parameter ensures that the high-priority connections get serviced before the low-priority ones.

✦ **Resilience** — This parameter indicates the probability that the Transport layer will terminate a connection itself due to internal problems or congestion.

TCP resides within the hosts and is implemented at the two ends of the logical Transport layer connection. While the TCP connection is being established, both sides of the connection initialize many TCP state variables. Some of the TCP state variables include the number of permissible unacknowledged segments and the maximum traffic that a host can send in a connection associated with the TCP connection. The following discussion describes how a TCP connection is established between the two hosts.

The host that initiates the connection is called the *client host*, and the host that addresses the client requests is called the *server host*. The client application process first informs the client TCP that it wants to establish a connection with a process on the server. The client TCP then proceeds to establish a TCP connection with the server TCP. There are several steps, shown in Figure 6-5, involved in connection establishment:

1. The client TCP first sends a special TCP segment to the server TCP by encapsulating it within an IP datagram. This special TCP segment contains the client's initial sequence number (*client_isn*) and a bit, called SYN bit, set to 1. The SYN bit refers to the synchronization status; the value 1 indicates that the two hosts are not synchronized, and a connection is requested. This special TCP segment is called *SYN segment* and does not contain any application data, because the connection needs to be established before sending the application data. Also, the client sends the *window size* that indicates the client buffer size to store incoming segments from the server.

2. When the IP datagram arrives at the server host, the server extracts the TCP SYN segment, allocates TCP buffers and state variables for connection, and acknowledges its receipt by sending a connection-granted segment (also called *SYNACK segment*) to the client TCP. To acknowledge, the server puts a value, *isn + 1,* in the connection-granted segment. The connection-granted segment also has the SYN bit set to 1 and contains the server's initial sequence number (*server_isn*). The segment encapsulates the message, indicating to the client that the server TCP has received the client SYN packet with the client's initial sequence number (*client_isn)* and that the server TCP agrees to establish this connection with the initial server sequence number (*server_isn).* Also, the server sends the window size that indicates the server buffer size to store incoming segments from the client.

3. When the client receives the SYNACK segment from the server, it also allocates client buffers and state variables for the connection. The client host then sends another segment to the server with SYN bit set to 0, as the connection is established. This last segment acknowledges the server's connection-granted segment by putting the value *server_isn + 1* in the segment.

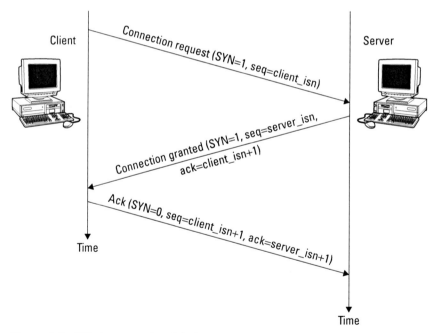

Figure 6-5: TCP three-way handshake

The connection establishment procedure requires that a total of three segments is sent between the client and the server hosts. Therefore, the process is called a *three-way handshake.* After the connection is established, the client and server can send segments containing data to each other. However, TCP running on the client and the server makes transition through various states during the life of a TCP connection. These states are called *TCP states.* As shown in Figure 6-6, a client TCP passes through a sequence of TCP states in the following order:

1. **CLOSED** — When an application process on one host wants to initiate a connection with an application process on another host, the client side initiates a new TCP connection.

2. **SYN_SENT** — The client TCP sends a SYN segment to the server TCP, after which the client enters the SYN_SENT state. While in this state, the client TCP waits for the acknowledgement from the server and the SYN bit set to 1.

3. **ESTABLISHED** — After the client receives the segment from the server, the client enters the ESTABLISHED state. While in this state, a TCP client can send and receive TCP segments containing application-generated data.

4. **FIN_WAIT_1** — If the client application decides to close the connection, the client TCP sends a segment with a bit called FIN set to 1 to the server. This state is called FIN_WAIT_1 state. While in this state, the client TCP waits for the acknowledgement from the server.

5. **FIN_WAIT_2** — When the client TCP receives the acknowledgement, it enters the FIN_WAIT_2 state. In this state, the client does not send anything to the server and waits for the FIN bit set to 1 from the server.

6. **TIME_WAIT** — When the client receives the FIN bit set to 1 from the server, it sends the acknowledgement to the server and enters the TIME_WAIT state. After waiting for approximately 30 seconds, the connection is formally closed, all resources on the client side are released, and the client enters the CLOSED state.

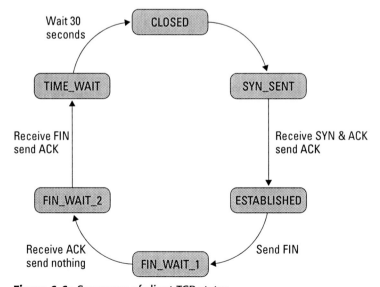

Figure 6-6: Sequence of client TCP states

As with the client, the server TCP also passes through various TCP states. As shown in Figure 6-7, a server TCP visits a series of TCP states in the following order:

1. **CLOSED** — There is no connection between the client and the server host application processes.

2. **LISTEN** — The server application creates a listen socket and listens at a specific port number.

3. **SYN_RCVD** — When the server host receives the SYN segment from the client, it enters the SYN_RCVD state. While in this state, the server sends the connection-granted segment, also called a SYNACK segment, to the client.

4. **ESTABLISHED** — When the server receives the acknowledgement for the SYNACK segment, it enters the ESTABLISHED state.

5. **CLOSE_WAIT** — When the server receives the segment from the client with the FIN bit set to 1, the server enters the CLOSE_WAIT state. While in this state, it acknowledges the client.

6. **LAST_ACK** — The server enters the LAST_ACK state when it sends the FIN bit to the client. When the server receives the last acknowledgement, the connection is closed formally.

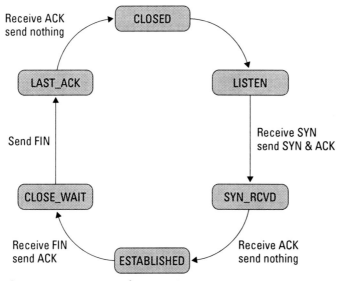

Figure 6-7: Sequence of server TCP states

Maximum Segment Size

After the connection is established between the application processes, the actual data transfer can take place. As mentioned earlier, the data received from the application is divided into small segments. At the receiving end, the segments must be reassembled. However, because there is a maximum limit to the data that can be reassembled, the data chunks must be limited by some specific size. The upper limit of the data chunk is called *Maximum Segment Size (MSS)*. The default TCP MSS is 536 bytes. Therefore, when TCP receives data from the application, it divides it into chunks no larger than 536 bytes.

During the connection establishment, TCP provides options that can be used to indicate the MSS that can be accepted over the connection. This MSS is sent from the receiver to the sender, indicating the maximum size (X) that the receiver can accept. This size X can be larger or smaller than the default MSS.

TCP sends and receives windows

TCP implements flow control by transmitting segments according to the buffer size at the receiver. This ensures that the buffer at the receiving side does not overflow and that the segments are not lost. As mentioned earlier, the buffer size (also called the *window size* or *receive window*) is agreed upon at the time of connection establishment between the client and the server. Figure 6-8 shows the buffering at the sending and receiving side.

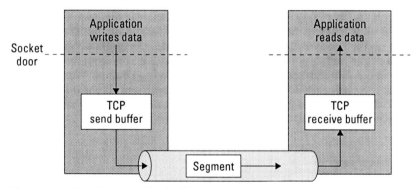

Figure 6-8: Send and receive buffers

For reliable data delivery, the client must receive an acknowledgment from the receiver for every segment that it sends. Since the client must wait for an acknowledgement from the server before transmitting another segment, this process might lead to a slow data transfer. Moreover, the network resources are not fully utilized. To minimize the network idle time and provide efficient and reliable data transfer, TCP uses the concept of sliding windows. In a *sliding window,* multiple segments are transmitted before waiting for an acknowledgement. The number of segments that a sender can send on a particular connection before it gets an acknowledgement from the receiver indicating that it has received at least some of the data segments is called a *send window.*

Note   Several segments can be acknowledged in the same acknowledgment message.

Figure 6-9 shows a TCP send window. This window has a fixed size, and all the segments that lie inside this window can be transmitted without waiting for the acknowledgement. For example, if the window size is 8, the sender is permitted to transmit 8 segments before it receives an acknowledgement.

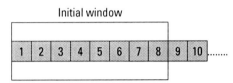

Figure 6-9: TCP send window

When the sender receives an acknowledgement for the first segment inside the send window, the window slides along and the next segment is transmitted, as shown in Figure 6-10. If an acknowledgement is received for more than one segment (three segments, for example), the window slides accordingly, and the next three segments are transmitted. However, the number of segments that can be sent varies depending on the receive window. At the server side, the application process reads the data from the buffer at a specific rate. Therefore, the receive window size varies according to the rate at which the data is read from the window. When the server sends an acknowledgement for data segments to the client, the window size is advertised with it. The client then sends the segments in the send window so that it does not overflow the receive window on the server side.

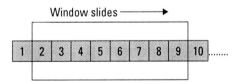

Figure 6-10: A sliding window

The TCP protocol at the sending side always remembers which segments have been acknowledged and keeps a separate timer for each unacknowledged segment. In case a segment is lost and the timer expires, the sender retransmits the segment.

The TCP protocol at the receiving side maintains an analogous window to accept and acknowledge segments as they arrive. Thus, the segments are partitioned into three sets:

✦ Segments to the left of the window that have been successfully transmitted received, and acknowledged.

✦ Segments to the right of the window that have not yet been transmitted.

✦ Segments that lie within the window that are being transmitted

Congestion window

Congestion causes delay in data delivery. The situation becomes even worse when TCP uses timeout and retransmission in case of lost segments. To avoid congestion, the client TCP must remember the size of the receive window. Also, depending on the amount of congestion, the send window size is reduced. This reduced send window is called the *congestion window limit* or the *congestion window*. The congestion window is a flow control mechanism imposed by the sender and is based on the sender's assessment of the network congestion. On the other hand, the receive window is a flow control mechanism imposed by the receiver and is based on the amount of available buffer space. At any time, the allowed window size is:

```
Allowed_window = Min (receiver_advertisement, congestion_window)
```

In a steady state when there is no congestion, the size of the congestion window is the same as that of the receiver window. However, in case of congestion, the window size is reduced. To estimate the congestion window size, TCP uses the following strategy:

1. Reduces the congestion window by half for every segment loss

2. Reduces the congestion window exponentially if the loss continues

3. Eventually, limits transmission to a single segment and continues to double timeout values before retransmitting

Slow start algorithm

TCP controls congestion by reducing the size of the congestion window exponentially. After the congestion ends, if TCP tries to recover by reversing this multiplicative decrease in the congestion window, an unstable situation that oscillates between no traffic and congestion might result. Therefore, when congestion ends, TCP recovers by using an algorithm called the slow start algorithm. In *slow start*, TCP starts the congestion window at the size of a single segment and increases the congestion window by one segment each time an acknowledgement arrives. TCP always follows the slow start algorithm while starting traffic in a connection. The connection might be a new connection or the one that is recovering from congestion.

Transmission Control Protocol header

The TCP segment consists of header fields and a data field. The application data is broken into small chunks and is put in the data field of the TCP segment. The size of the chunk is limited by the Maximum Segment Size (MSS). Therefore, several TCP segments make up the complete application data. The header fields contain information for connection management and error checking. Figure 6-11 shows the structure of a TCP segment.

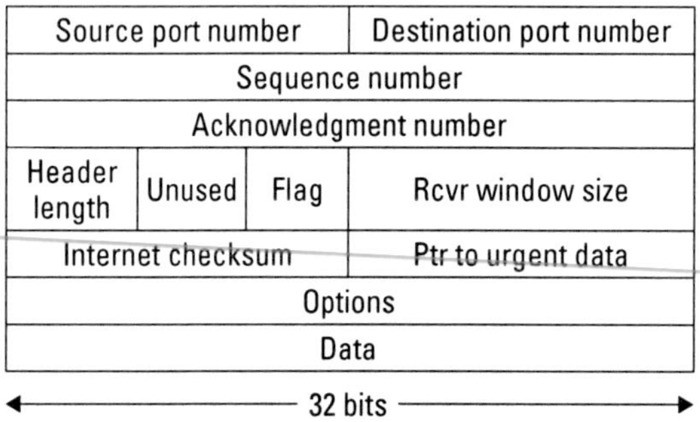

Source port number			Destination port number	
Sequence number				
Acknowledgment number				
Header length	Unused	Flag	Rcvr window size	
Internet checksum			Ptr to urgent data	
Options				
Data				

◄─────────── 32 bits ───────────►

Figure 6-11: TCP segment structure

As compared to the UDP header size (8 bytes), the TCP header size is large (20 bytes). Like the UDP header, the TCP header contains the source and destination port numbers, which are used for multiplexing and demultiplexing. Also like the UDP header, the TCP header contains a checksum field for error detection (not correcting). In addition to the mentioned fields, the header contains the following fields:

✦ **Sequence number** — A 32-bit field that contains the sequence number of the segment. The byte-stream number of the first byte in the sequence is the *sequence number of the segment.* For example, if the data stream consists of a file of size 100,000 bytes, the MSS being 1000 bytes, TCP creates 100 segments. As shown in Figure 6-12, the first segment is assigned sequence number 0 if the first byte of the data stream is numbered 0, the second segment is numbered 100, and so on.

✦ **Acknowledgment number** — A 32-bit field that contains the acknowledgment number of the segment. The *acknowledgment number* is the next byte that the server is expecting from the client. Consider a TCP connection that has been established between host A and host B. Since TCP provides full duplex transfer, the traffic can flow in both directions — from host A to host B and vice versa. Suppose host A wants to send a segment that contains bytes numbered from 0 to 535 to host B. Since the next byte that host B is expecting is 536, host A puts 536 in the acknowledgment number field of the next segment that it is about to send. The sequence number and acknowledgment number fields are very critical because they implement reliable data transfer service.

✦ **Header length** — A 4-bit field that contains the length of the TCP header in 32-bit words. The header length can vary due to the Options field (discussed later in the list).

✦ **Flag** — A 6-bit field that contains certain flag bits:

- **URG** — Indicates that the data in the segment has been marked as "urgent" by the sending side Application layer.

- **ACK** — Indicates that the value in the acknowledgment number field of the segment is valid.

- **PSH** — Indicates that the receiver should pass the data in the segment to the upper layer immediately.

- **RST** — Indicates the reset status of the connection.

- **SYN** — Indicates that the connection needs to be established.

- **FIN** — Indicates that the connection needs to be closed.

✦ **RCVR Window size** — A 16-bit field that is used to implement the flow control service of the TCP. As mentioned earlier, TCP is full duplex, and both sides of the connection maintain a buffer. Therefore, the buffer size at each receiving end should not be less than the data sent, so as to avoid data overflow. This field contains the receive window size, which varies throughout the connection lifetime. If the receive window size is 0, the receiving buffer is full. Then, the new segment is not sent until there is enough buffer available at the receiving end for the segment.

✦ **PTR to urgent data** — A 16-bit field that contains the location of the last byte of the urgent data, if the URG bit of the flag field is set indicating that the segment has been marked as urgent.

✦ **Options** — An optional field that has a variable length. This field is used when the sender and receiver negotiate the MSS.

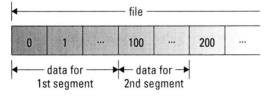

Figure 6-12: TCP segments division

Summary

This chapter explored the features and functionality of the Transport layer in detail. First, you learned the different types of data transfer, such as reliable, unreliable and stateful, stateless. Then, you learned the features of the connectionless transport protocol — that is, the User Datagram Protocol (UDP). The UDP datagram structure, which gives you an essential understanding of the basic features of UDP, was discussed. Finally, you learned the features of connection-oriented transport protocol — for example, the Transmission Control Protocol (TCP). You also learned the following concepts: how a session is initiated, Maximum Segment Size (MSS), how data transfer takes place, and the definitions of a congestion window, slow start algorithm, and the TCP segment format.

✦   ✦   ✦

Application Layer

◆ ◆ ◆ ◆

In This Chapter

Overview of ports

Understanding sockets

◆ ◆ ◆ ◆

he Internet is a heterogeneous network that comprises various computers running on different platforms, such as Macintosh, Windows, UNIX, OS/2, and so on. These platforms support different filenaming conventions, text representations, data encoding methods, and terminal types. The Application layer, which is the fifth and last layer of the TCP/IP model, is responsible for ensuring successful communication and compatibility among these heterogeneous platforms. It contains a variety of protocols, such as SMTP (for e-mails), Telnet (for virtual terminals), and FTP (for file transfers) to carry out its functions. In addition, the Application layer contains user-defined applications (or programs).

In this chapter, you learn how applications running on separate nodes communicate with one another. You learn about ports and sockets and the role they play in peer-application communication. You also learn about the popular socket APIs, such as Berkeley (BSD) sockets, Transport Layer Interface (TLI), Transport Independent Remote Procedure Calls (TI-RPCs), and Windows Sockets (WinSock). Finally, you learn about the role of Remote Procedure Call (RPC) in globally distributed networks.

Overview of Ports

During a communication, sending a message to the recipient is not enough. Not only does the sender need to ensure that the message reaches the intended recipient, but — that of all the processes running on the recipient end — the message is delivered to the specified process that originally initiated the communication at the sender end. Networking protocols facilitate this end-to-end communication between a user and an application and between applications by using ports and sockets.

Note   The recipient of the message can be another node or a service running on the same node.

A *port* provides the interface between an application and the network on which the application is running. In other words, a *port* is a communication end-point that enables an application, end user, or another node on the network to obtain a connection to an application. On a TCP/IP-based network, every application that needs to communicate with its peer application running on another node has to use a *port number*.

Tip   Port numbers are similar to telephone extension numbers. You dial one number to reach the main office building, and then you dial an extension number to reach a particular person in the office. Per this analogy, the IP address of a node is like a main office number. Each service running on the node has a fixed port number — like an extension number — through which the service can be accessed.

A port number is a 16-bit number whose value can vary from 0 to 65535. Generally, port numbers below 1024 are used for popular communication services. Values above 1024 are reserved solely for a node's use. Most server ports use port numbers less than 1024. This practice has been carried forward from the days of UNIX, which allows only root processes to bind to ports less than 1024.

If a server port is already in use, a temporary port number is assigned to the subsequent requests. For example, a node receives multiple FTP requests. In this case, only one requesting node can access the FTP service at port number 21, which is the FTP port number. Other nodes that request simultaneously are temporarily assigned an available port number above 1024. In this way, many requestors can access the FTP service at the same time. System and network programmers can also use the port numbers above 1024 for programming purposes.

Note   Most operating systems maintain a file that contains the port numbers and their corresponding services. However, the port number values can vary, depending on the hardware and software platform on which the TCP software is running.

Most TCP/IP applications use the client/server model for communication. At the user site, a client sends requests to a particular service through its server port, and then the server responds. When a connection is established via a port that is assigned to a particular protocol, the corresponding services are invoked faster; thus, port numbers effect faster TCP-based communications.

Well-known port numbers

The port numbers are popularly categorized in three categories. These include:

✦ **Well-known port numbers** — Port numbers 0 to 1023 are referred to as well-known port numbers. Internet Assigned Numbers Authority (IANA) has published a list of frequently used port numbers and their corresponding services. For example, FTP is associated with port number 21, Telnet with 23, SMTP (e-mail protocol) with 25, Web servers with 80, and POP3 with 110. Table 7-1 provides a list of well-known port numbers.

Note Port numbers assigned by IANA are unique. Another service (or protocol) *cannot* use the port numbers that have been assigned to a service (or its corresponding protocol).

✦ **Registered port numbers** — Port numbers ranging from 1024 to 49151 are known as registered port numbers.

✦ **Private port numbers** — Port numbers 49152 through 65535 are known as private port numbers (and sometimes as dynamic port numbers).

Table 7-1
Well-Known TCP/IP Ports and their Numbers

Port Number	Service	Description
1	TCPMUX	TCP Port Service Multiplexer
7	ECHO	Echo
11	USERS	Active Users
13	DAYTIME	Time of the Day
15	NETSTAT	Network Statistics
17	QUOTE	Quote of the Day
18	MSP	Message Send Protocol
19	CHARGEN	Character Generator
20	FTP-DATA	File Transfer Protocol-Data
21	FTP	File Transfer Protocol-Control
22	SSH	SSH Remote Login Protocol
23	TELNET	Telnet
25	SMTP	Simple Mail Transfer Protocol
31	MSG-AUTH	Message Authentication
37	TIME	Time
41	GRAPHICS	Graphics Support
42	NAMESERV	Host Name Server
43	WHOIS	Nickname Location
49	LOGIN	Login Host Protocol
53	DOMAIN	Domain Name Server
67	BOOTPS	Bootstrap Protocol Server

Continued

Table 7-1 *(continued)*

Port Number	Service	Description
68	BOOTPC	Bootstrap Protocol Client
69	TFTP	Trivial File Transfer Protocol
70	GOPHER	Internet Gopher
79	FINGER	Finger
80	WWW	HTTP
101	HOSTNAME	NIC Host Name Server
103	X400	X.400
107	RTELNET	Remote Telnet
109	POP-2	Post Office Protocol Version 2
110	POP3	Post Office Protocol Version 3
111	RPC	Remote Procedure Call
119	NNTP	Network News Transfer Protocol
123	NTP	Network Time Protocol
137	NETBIOS-NS	NetBIOS Name Service
138	NETBIOS-DGM	NetBIOS Datagram Service
139	NETBIOS-SSN	NetBIOS Session Service
143	IMAP2	Internet Message Access Protocol Version 2
161	SNMP	Simple Network Management Protocol
162	SNMP-TRAP	Simple Network Management Protocol-TRAP Service
163	CMIP-MAN	CMIP-Manager
164	CMIP-AGENT	CMIP-Agent
165	XNS-COURIER	Xerox
179	BGP	Border Gateway Protocol
194	IRC	Internet Relay Chat
199	SMUX	SNMP UNIX Multiplexer
201	AT-RTMP	AppleTalk-Routing Management Protocol
202	AT-NBP	AppleTalk-Name Binding Protocol
209	QMTP	Quick Mail Transfer Protocol
213	IPX	Internetwork Packet Exchange

Port Number	Service	Description
372	ULISTSERV	UNIX List Server
444	SNPP	Simple Network Paging Protocol
465	SSMTP	SMTP over SSL
487	SAFT	Simple Asynchronous File Transfer
512	EXEC	Execute
513	LOGIN	Login
515	PRINTER	Spooler
517	TALK	Talk
526	TEMPO	New Date
531	CONFERENCE	Chat
533	NETWALL	Emergency Broadcasts
765	WEBSTER	Network Dictionary
873	RSYNC	Remote Synchronization
1080	SOCKS	SOCKS Proxy Server

Note For a complete list of port numbers, refer to the site `www.iana.org/assignments/port-numbers`.

For more information on ports, refer to RFCs 1700 and 793.

Understanding Sockets

A *socket* is an interprocess communication mechanism that serves as an end-point of communication. A *socket* is a combination of a node's IP address and the TCP port number. The socket serves as the basic entity for communication in a TCP/IP network and provides a communication framework between processes executing either on the same host or on nodes across a network. The use of sockets makes each client/server connection unique and eliminates the necessity of writing the data to the recipient's hard drive during every transaction. Instead, the data is temporarily stored in the recipient's memory buffer cache.

Tip Since both the port number for a given service and a node's IP address are unique, socket numbers are also unique.

Sockets exist within the *communication domain* (or simply *domains*). Addressing structure and the set of protocols that implement the various types of sockets constitute the communication domain. Sockets generally support three domains —

Internet domain, UNIX domain, and *NS domain.* Although the TCP/IP protocol suite can support all three domains, the Internet domain is most commonly used. In the Internet domain, sockets can be of two types — *stream sockets* and *datagram sockets.* Because stream sockets are TCP-based, they provide connection-oriented, bidirectional, reliable, sequential, and unduplicated data transmission. In contrast, datagram sockets support connectionless, bidirectional, unreliable data exchange, which might not be sequenced, reliable, or unduplicated.

Bidirectional socket-based communications

In a TCP/IP-based network, when a node sends a connection request to another node, it also sends a socket number. If the receiver node is free to set up the connection, it returns a socket number that contains the receiver's IP address and port number of the service that will handle the request. This is known as *binding.*

Tip   Telephone communication is a good analogy to socket-based communication. As with a telephone, a socket serves as an end-point in a two-way communication. When you make a phone call, you connect your telephone with someone else's, enabling communication between yourself and the person on the other end. Similarly, when you connect two sockets, data can be passed between two processes that might be running on different nodes (or computers).

When a connection is established between two ends, the identity of each end-point is exchanged before any data is exchanged. Also, this information is maintained at each end so that it can be referred to at any time during the transmission. This helps prevent the large overhead (in the form of excess network traffic) that might be generated by transmitting the identity of the sending socket with each data packet.

Note   A node can request more than one connection from a destination node. In this case, the sender node has to use different port numbers to create different sockets. This prevents the requesting processes from waiting until the recipient serves the earlier requests.

When a client application accesses a service that is available on the server, it uses a port on the client host. To access a service on the server, the client needs to follow a standard process called *bind-listen-connect-accept.* This process involves the following steps:

1. The server process binds itself to a particular port.

2. After the server port binds itself to a port, it starts listening to the client requests on that port.

3. When a service is required from the server, the client process binds itself to an available port on the client host.

4. The client uses the port to send a request to connect to the server process via the corresponding server port.

5. The server process accepts the connection and informs the client to begin the transaction.

This bidirectional communication process is shown in Figure 7-1.

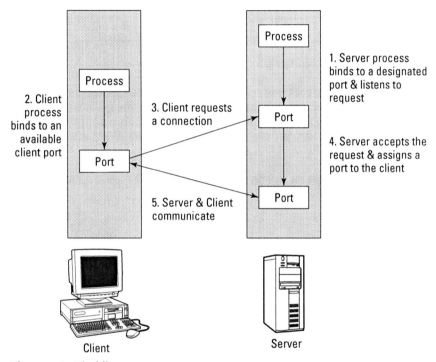

Figure 7-1: Bind-listen-connect-accept process

Sockets are highly system-dependent and programmable. They are implemented on the network interface as *Application Programming Interfaces (APIs)*. APIs provide a link between the Network layer protocols and the Application layer programs to implement network functionality. They also enable a systems programmer to use computer resources, such as a windowing system, file system, database system, and, of course, networking system.

Note Since sockets are implemented at the hardware level, they are system dependent.

Although sockets are system dependent, the socket APIs should support three basic features: *Network-layer protocol transparency, asynchronous operations,* and *data transfer rate.* Network-layer protocol transparency means that sockets should be independent of the underlying Network-layer protocols. Asynchronous operations mean that the API function calls should be event driven, rather than follow a sequence of network actions. In addition, the socket APIs should support sufficient data transfer rates that do not cause delays. The data transfer rate is the speed with which the data is exchanged between the two communicating ends. The popular socket APIs are:

✦ Berkeley sockets

✦ Transport Layer Interface (TLI)

✦ Transport Independent Remote Procedure Calls (TI-RPCs)

✦ Windows Sockets (WinSock)

Sockets and TLI provide pretty much the same functionality (access to TCP and UDP) and are mutually exclusive, though it is possible for a systems programmer to write conditionally compiled code to support both. RPC APIs support network subroutines by using Sun's RPC protocol. Microsoft Windows offers a Sockets-like API called WinSock.

Note   For more information on sockets, refer to RFCs 204, 1323, and 2292.

Berkeley sockets

The Berkeley sockets interface was developed at the University of California, Berkeley, for the 4.1c release of Berkeley Software Distribution (BSD). It was a simple interface that was initially used in various versions of UNIX, such as SCO, Linux, and SunOS. Eventually, it was incorporated in Windows 9x, Windows NT, NetWare, and other operating systems. Berkeley sockets provide moderate rates of data transfer as they do not support overlapped I/O functions. As a result, the Berkeley sockets network interface is best suited for multiprocessor-based network operating systems.

Tip   Berkeley sockets are also popularly known as BSD sockets.

Berkeley sockets provide an interface that is easy to use and implement. With the Berkeley sockets, there are two ways in which applications can access network transport services:

✦ **Connection-oriented access** — A virtual channel is maintained between the sender and the receiver. The data delivery is confirmed or denied with the help of acknowledgements or negative acknowledgements. If the data is not delivered to the recipient, either retransmission of the lost data is initiated, or upper layers are informed of the failure. The upper layers can then take the necessary corrective actions. Connection-oriented services are maintained by TCP.

✦ **Connectionless access**—The data is sent to the recipient without waiting for acknowledgements. If all or part of the data is lost during transmission, the sender will not know about it. User Datagram Protocol (UDP) provides connectionless services.

Tip

Protocols such as Simple Mail Transfer Protocol (SMTP) are TCP-based, while protocols such as Echo can use both TCP and UDP. However, protocols such as Simple Network Management Protocol (SNMP) are completely UDP-based.

Programmatically, Berkeley sockets are created by the `socket()` function, which takes two key arguments—*domain* and *type*. In TCP/IP networks, the most commonly used domain is PF_NET (though other domains also exist). The two primary types of Internet sockets are STREAM (for TCP) and DGRAM (for UDP). The STREAM sockets cannot send or receive data until a connection has been established. On the other hand, the DGRAM sockets can immediately transmit data.

In a connection-oriented TCP communication, the sender uses the `send()` function to specify the IP address and the port number of the recipient to create an active socket. This initiates the TCP connection. The recipient uses the `listen()` and `bind()` functions to wait for the incoming connection. After detecting the incoming request, the recipient uses the `accept()` function to accept the connection and create an active socket.

In the connectionless UDP communication, the sender creates the DGRAM sockets and sends the UDP packets by using the `sendto()` function. To receive the packet, the recipient attaches the socket to a local port number by using the `bind()` function. After attaching the packet to the UDP port, the socket can be used to transmit packets (using the `sendto()` function) or receive them (using the `rcvfrom()` function).

Note

For more information on Berkeley sockets, refer to RFCs 793 and 1122.

Transport Layer Interface

The *Transport Layer Interface (TLI)* API provides a protocol-independent interface to the Transport layer for accessing network resources. The Bell Labs introduced TLI in the late 1980s with the release of AT&T UNIX System V Release 3 (UNIX SVR3). It was developed to support distributed applications that run on different platforms. The Bell Labs used the OSI Transport layer as a model for developing TLI. Therefore, it fully conforms to the OSI Transport services, which is also TLI's main claim to superiority over sockets that do not operate in the OSI environment. It can support TCP, UDP, IPX/SPX, and other Transport-layer protocols.

Although TLI is a Transport-layer API, it provides nearly the same functionality as Berkeley sockets and can interact with sockets- and IP-based services. Unlike Berkeley sockets, however, a TLI-based service cannot directly access the data sent or received during the transmission. It has to use the backend, such as databases or files, to communicate with the network connection. As a result, TLI is not as widely accepted as Berkeley sockets.

Note   TLI is slowly starting to gain popularity. Most operating systems, especially UNIX, support both sockets and TLI. However, many vendors prefer the TLI interface due to its fast, reliable transactions and compatibility with OSI protocols. For example, UNIX SVR4 and Sun's Solaris 2.*x* consider TLI the preferred transport interface. TLI has always been the favored interface in all versions of Novell NetWare. For more information on TLI, refer to RFC 1122.

During transactions, TLI creates transport end-points that can be easily manipulated by functions, which are analogous to the socket functions. TLI and Berkeley sockets differ only in their syntaxes.

Tip   Recently, *X/OPEN Transport Interface (XTI)* has evolved as an extension of TLI. XTI was developed by the X/Open Company Ltd. in 1996 as a refinement of the existing TLI interface. In addition to the traditional TCP/IP and IPX/SPX data packets, XTI also allows access to the NetBIOS packets. For more information on XTI, refer to the site `www.tru64unix.compaq.com/faqs/publications/base_doc/ DOCUMENTATION/HTML/AA-PS2WD-TET1_html/netprog4.html`.

Transport Independent Remote Procedure Call

Transport Independent Remote Procedure Call (TI-RPC) is the latest development in the field of Remote Procedure Call (RPC). It provides seamless transition from one protocol to another by abstracting the underlying protocol used at the Network layer. This capability makes the RPC specification transport-independent.

TI-RPC introduced a layered concept of RPC, in which RPC APIs were grouped into various levels:

✦ **Simplified level** — All the API calls are combined into one procedure. Although customization of clients or services is not allowed, an RPC service and corresponding client application can be developed.

✦ **Top level** — Client and services can be easily customized. Parameters are quite similar to those at the Simplified level.

✦ **Intermediate level** — Differentiation between layers begins at this level, which also allows a greater degree of customization and control over the transport.

✦ **Expert level** — The lowest level of the available TI-RPC APIs. The customization of the client and the service is much greater at the Expert level, allowing control over the transport, the buffer sizes, and other minute details of the application.

Tip The Expert level of TI-RPC uses name-to-address-translation APIs that provide an interface similar to the socket calls.

Other APIs can be used, primarily in conjunction with all layers except the Simplified layer. They provide methods for sending back errors from the service to the client, freeing space allocated to the clients and services, and enhanced error detection and reporting.

Note For more information on TI-RPC, refer to RFCs 1057, 1058, and 2292.

WinSock

In the Windows environment, the *Windows Socket (WinSock)* specification is used, which is a variant of Berkeley sockets. Microsoft first introduced the *WinSock API (WSA)* in January 1993 as an interface for creating TCP/IP-based universal applications in the Windows environment. Originally, it focused on TCP/IP only, although it could support other protocol suites. The second and improved version of WinSock, WinSock Version 2, was released in mid 1995. This version supports many more protocol suites, such as IPX/SPX, ATM. DECnet, and so on. It also provides complete backward-compatibility with the earlier version of WinSock (Version 1.1) and allows you to create network protocol-independent applications.

Tip WinSock is a library of procedures, function calls, and data structures that provide a standard interface for Windows-based applications. A WinSock 2 application can select a protocol based on its service requirements. Using the mechanisms provided by WinSock 2, the application can also adapt to differences in network naming and addressing schemes.

Since WinSock was based on the original Berkeley sockets, WinSock communication resembles the Berkeley socket communication. As in the Berkeley sockets, the WinSock sockets are created by using the `socket()` function, which takes domain and type as arguments. On the Internet (or TCP/IP-based networks), the most prevalent domain is AF_NET. The type argument can take two values — SOCK_STREAM (for TCP-based communication) and SOCK_DGRAM (for UDP-based communication).

Note For more information on WinSock, refer to RFC 1122.

With more and more organizations creating a global presence, the scope of networks is also expanding. Now, a company's network might not be limited to a city or even a country. Networks are being stretched all over the globe. These networks are called *distributed systems,* or *intranets.* In addition, the entire intranet need not use the same platform, machines, and applications. The platforms — software and hardware — can be as diverse as possible. To accommodate the distributed physical nature of the networks, distributed software (such as network directory services and distributed databases), have come into existence. The need for distributed software running on heterogeneous processors and operating systems has led to the development of *Remote Procedure Call (RPC).*

Remote Procedure Call

Developed at the Center for Nuclear Research (CERN), Remote Procedure Call (RPC) is a method for building distributed client/server-based applications and systems. It enables an application running on one computer to call a subroutine, which may be executing on a remote computer. However, the caller application doesn't realize that the subroutine is remote. In other words, RPC is a method of using existing communication features in a transparent manner.

Note   A subroutine is part of a program that performs a specific task or an ordered set of tasks.

RPC does not contain any communication code. As a result, it is independent of the following:

✦ Communication platforms and hardware

✦ Communication protocols

✦ Operating systems

✦ Calling sequences that would need to use the underlying communication software

The interface independence isolates the distributed RPC-based applications from the physical and logical elements of data communication and allows the applications to use various modes of data transport. It also helps distributed-application programmers ignore the details of the interface while programming. Therefore, RPC makes the client/server-computing model more powerful and easily programmable.

A wide range of applications has successfully incorporated the concept of RPC. Remote files and databases were some of the earliest applications to use RPC. Sun Microsystems's Sun Network File System uses Sun XDR RPC. Remote monitoring applications, such as GKS, and remote software task management applications used on VAX machines also use RPC.

When a remote call to a subroutine is generated, the calling program is referred to as the client, and the called subroutine acts as the server to produce stub modules. The client, as well as the server, requires the names of the procedures that will be involved in the transactions, number of parameters that will be passed, and the data type of each parameter. When a client calls the server, RPC ensures the following:

✦ All the parameters that are to be passed to the server are transferred to the remote computer, where the subroutine is executing.

✦ The subroutine executes on the remote computer.

✦ The results and parameters that are generated as the result of the execution of the subroutine are transferred back to the client (or the calling program).

RPC uses *stub modules* to facilitate communication between the server and the client. The stub is a subroutine, which resembles the remote subroutines. The stubs do not contain any information related to the physical addresses of the computers involved in the transaction. Therefore, they use RPC Run-Time System to track the target computer. As the RPC RTS handles all the communication, the stub contains only the code related to the application that initiated the remote call. The entire communication process proceeds through the following steps:

1. The client program is bound to a client stub module. The client stub module is a subroutine that accepts the data from the caller process and encapsulates the data as a message. This process is called *marshalling*.

2. The client stub sends the message to the server (process) by using a routine in RPC RTS. The client stub immediately goes into wait mode, where it starts waiting for the reply message from the server stub, which is located on the remote computer.

3. The RPC RTS notifies the server stub when the computer receives the message from the client. The server stub disassembles, or *unmarshals,* the parameters received in the message, calls the target subroutine, and waits for the results from the server (process).

4. When the server completes the execution, it returns the resulting parameters to the server stub. The server stub now marshals the return parameters as a message and sends the message to the client stub.

5. On receiving the reply, the client stub unmarshals the return parameters, calls the client process as a normal routine, and substitutes the values into the variables of the calling program.

On the client side, the caller remains dormant until it receives the result from the called subroutine. On receiving the awaited parameters, the client process resumes execution. However, after sending the results, the server subroutine becomes dormant. Figure 7-2 shows the entire communication process.

Tip   Although the client process is dormant while the client waits for the parameters from the server side, the client is not. The client can perform other tasks while it waits. This makes the RPC calls asynchronous.

A shell command called *rpcinfo* can be used to determine all the RPC services registered on a specific host and to report their addresses. It can also be used to determine the current RPC registration information. Administrators can use the registration information to delete any services or registrations that might be redundant, obsolete, or useless. The rpcinfo command can also be used to ping a program running on a computer and to find out if a response was received or not. This helps determine whether a remote machine is in a hang or not. The result of the rpcinfo command is shown in Figure 7-3.

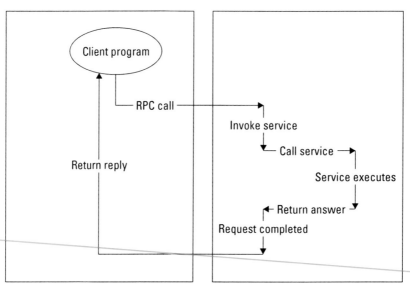

Figure 7-2: Network communication with RPC

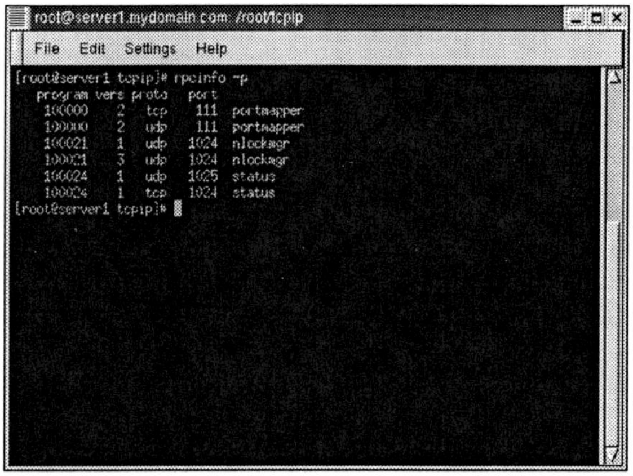

Figure 7-3: rpcinfo command window

RPC facilitates communication between the topmost OSI layer, the Application layer, and lower layers that deal with the distributive aspect of a global intranet. It can serve as a pivotal point for the upper layers the way the transport service does for lower layers. Work is in progress to make RPC a standard.

Note   For more information on RPC, refer to RFCs 1050, 1057, 1700, and 1831.

Summary

In this chapter, you learned how applications running on the same node or separate nodes communicate with each other by using ports and sockets. You learned about the most commonly used ports and their numbers. You also learned about the popular socket APIs, such as Berkeley (BSD) sockets, Transport Layer Interface (TLI), Transport Independent Remote Procedure Calls (TI-RPCs), and Windows Sockets (WinSock). Finally, you learned the role of Remote Procedure Call (RPC) in globally distributed networks.

✦   ✦   ✦

Working with TCP/IP

Once the basics of the protocol stack are understood, it
is time to install and work with the protocol. Part II
examines some of the key areas of working with TCP/IP, such
as installation on both Microsoft and UNIX platforms, and the
configuration of the protocol once it is installed. Simple manual configuration of the TCP/IP protocol is discussed, as well
as automatic configuration using BOOTP and DHCP.

Name resolution is addressed in Chapter 10. Name resolution
enables you to find hosts both on intranets and on the
Internet with user-friendly names rather than IP addresses.
One of the most common problems when using TCP/IP is an
error in name resolution, so a good understanding of this concept is important as we move into the last two parts of the
book.

Installing and Configuring TCP/IP

Previous chapters discussed the TCP/IP protocol layers and the TCP/IP communication process. Before you implement TCP/IP in networks, you should know how to install and configure it. Although the basic approach to installing and configuring TCP/IP on different operating systems is the same, variations do exist. This chapter explores the installation and configuration of TCP/IP in the worlds of Linux and Microsoft.

Configuring TCP/IP

The same, basic approach is used to configure TCP/IP on different operating systems. Therefore, before you start configuring TCP/IP on any operating system, obtain the necessary information for every computer on the network. All of this information isn't necessarily needed when you set up the system. Much will be asked for and determined automatically. This section has categorized the information according to its priority. The information has been categorized as "Always needed information" or "Sometimes needed information."

Always needed information

Irrespective of the operating system on which you are configuring TCP/IP, you'll always need the following information:

✦ The machine name or host name that represents the symbolic name of a computer on the network. Host names can be assigned in two ways — nickname and Fully Qualified Domain Name (FQDN). Nicknames are aliases to IP addresses and can be assigned and used by individual users. On the other hand, a FQDN such as server1.domain1.com is a hierarchical name. Host names must be unique on a local network. However, different networks can have computers that have the same host name. Host names are more familiar than IP addresses and can therefore be used in place of IP addresses.

Cross-Reference   For more information on host names, refer to Chapter 10.

✦ The device driver that represents the network interface card driver. Device drivers instruct the operating systems on how to communicate with the network interfaces.

Note   The latest device drivers can be obtained from the vendor. Even if the operating system includes certain device drivers, you should obtain them from the vendor to ensure that the drivers are latest.

✦ The hardware network card configuration information that identifies the frame format of the network adapter. If the adapter is a token ring card, the frame format is 802.n; otherwise, it is Ethernet II. The token ring frame types are either 802.5 or 802.2.

✦ The IP address, a 32-bit number that represents the full address of a computer on the network. The IP address must be unique and can be assigned by a system administrator.

Cross-Reference   For more information on IP addresses, refer to Chapter 5.

✦ The network mask that represents the IP address with the network ID stripped off, leaving only the host ID. A network mask is a series of bits designed to mask certain portions of an IP address. For example, in the standard network mask address of a class C network (255.255.255.0), the last octet (0) means, "look here for the machine name"; the remaining part of the address is the network number. The network mask uniquely identifies the local network and is primarily used for subnetting.

✦ The *broadcast address* that represents an IP network address consisting of all 1s, such as 255.255.255.255. The broadcast address is required when a message needs to be broadcast to all computers on the network, because a network card ignores the packets that do not contain its specific IP address.

Note   If the DHCP client is configured on the machine, and the DHCP server is available in the network, the DHCP server assigns the IP address, network mask, and broadcast address automatically.

Sometimes needed information

Sometimes while configuring TCP/IP, you might be prompted by your system for the following information:

✦ The domain name that identifies the entire network. A domain name is necessary when a network needs to connect to computers outside the network. A system administrator can provide the domain name. However, when the network needs to interface with the Internet, the domain name must be approved by the Internet Network Information Center (InterNIC).

✦ TCP/IP connections that represent the maximum number of TCP/IP connections allowed at a time.

✦ The gateway status that indicates whether or not the computer works in a gateway mode. The *gateway mode* indicates that the packets will be forwarded and redirected between the different networks. When a network interface (adapter or serial lines) is configured, the default gateway status that is assigned is "non-gateway mode." However, when you configure a second network interface, you are prompted to choose between a gateway mode and a non-gateway mode.

✦ The address of the name server that translates the host names to their IP addresses. The TCP/IP hosts use IP addresses for communication, whereas individuals employ host names because they are convenient to use. Therefore, the host names must be resolved to the respective IP addresses to enable communication between hosts. This process is called *name resolution*. If you are using only the loopback mode, you do not need a name server. Configuring TCP/IP in a *loopback mode* enables TCP/IP connections only to your computer.

 For more information on name resolution, refer to Chapter 10.

As mentioned earlier, certain basic steps must be followed when configuring TCP/IP, although variations may exist on different operating systems:

1. Enable TCP/IP by linking it to the operating system's kernel, or load it during the boot stage.

2. Add the names of all computers on the network for name resolution.

3. Create *routing tables* that control where and how the packets will be routed from source to destination. Also, routing tables identify the routing path of the packets.

4. Configure the name domain server if a distributed database system, such as the Berkeley Internet Name Domain Server (BIND), is used. In a *distributed database system*, the name domain server enables clients to name resources and objects and share this information with other objects on the network.

5. Tune the computer to optimize performance.

Configuring TCP/IP in the Linux World

Configuring TCP/IP in the UNIX world requires you to modify the content of several files so that the necessary configuration information can be added. For different types of UNIX servers (such as SCO UNIX, BSD UNIX, or Linux) the names of the files can be different. However, the configuration information stored in these files is consistent across the different operating systems. The configuration files that need to be modified when configuring TCP/IP on Linux include:

✦ **/etc/hosts**—Contains a list of names and the network addresses of all the computers on the network. If any computer is added to the network, an entry for the computer needs to be added in the HOSTS file, in case the name server is not configured and the HOSTS file is being used for name resolution. The following code represents a sample line from the HOSTS file.

```
127.0.0.1      localhost.localdomain    localhost
172.17.55.51   server1.mydomain.com     server1
```

✦ **/etc/networks**—Contains a list of network names and their addresses. These network names are required only when the users in the local network need to connect to other networks. Use of this file is optional, depending on the user's needs. You can add the domain name and the network address as shown in the following code.

```
xserver. xdomain.com    145.205.15.1
```

✦ **/etc/services**—Contains information about all the TCP and UDP services that are supported by the system. The following code displays some of the services contained in this file.

```
echo        7/tcp
tftp        69/udp
```

✦ **/etc/protocols**—Contains a list of all the transport protocols and their respective protocol numbers. This file is updated automatically as part of the TCP/IP software installation. It contains the protocol name, protocol number, and any alias for the protocol. The following code represents a sample from this file.

```
ip        0        IP
tcp       6        TCP
udp       17       UDP
```

✦ **/etc/hosts.equiv**—Contains a list of machine names, and is used to control access from other computers. The machines whose names are listed in the file are called *trusted hosts*. Any valid user (except root) is allowed to log in to the machine remotely with the same account information without entering a password. This is called *user equivalence*. In this file, the entry for an allowed user is represented by a "+" symbol. On the other hand, the "-" symbol indicates that a specific user is not allowed the access. The content of this file uses the following format.

```
[+|-] [hostname] [username]
```

✦ **/etc/ftpusers**—Contains a list of FTP users who must be prevented from accessing the computer. Whenever one of these unauthorized users tries to log in, the connection is disconnected immediately. The following code represents a sample list of ftp users included in this file.

```
root
mail
news
```

✦ **/etc/inetd.conf**—Contains the list of all the processes that are started by the inetd daemon during the system boot. The processes that run continuously in the background are called *daemon processes*. The inetd daemon provides certain Internet services internally and starts any other daemon only if needed, thereby reducing load on the system. The following code displays some sample lines from this file.

```
log_on_success = HOST PID
log_on_failure = HOST RECORD
```

✦ **/etc/sysconfig/network-scripts/ifcfg-interfacename**—Contains the device information. A device is represented by interfacename. For example, if the device name is eth0, the file name is ifcfg-eth0. Depending on the type of interface, the contents of this file can vary. The following code represents some sample lines from this file.

```
DEVICE="eth0"
ONBOOT="yes"
```

✦ **/etc/sysconfig/network**—Contains information about the desired network configuration on the server.

```
NETWORKING=yes
HOSTNAME=server1.mydomain.com
GATEWAY="172.17.55.1"
GATEWAYDEV=""
FORWARD_IPV4="yes"
```

Some of the network configuration parameters included are described below.

- **NETWORKING**—Can take either a "yes" or a "no" value, indicating whether to enable networking

- **HOSTNAME**—Indicates the host name of your computer

- **GATEWAY**—The IP address of a remote gateway, if available

- **GATEWAYDEV**—The device name that is used to access the remote gateway

- **FORWARD_IPV4**—Can take either a "yes" or a "no" value, indicating whether to forward the IP packets

The rest of this section covers the configuration of TCP/IP for Linux. However, remember that the basic procedure to configure TCP/IP is the same on all UNIX operating systems. Linux is also available in various versions from different vendors, such as SlackWare and RedHat. This section presents a general configuration procedure for the Linux operating system.

Before configuring TCP/IP on the Linux operating system, the */proc file system* should have been created and mounted. A *file system* refers to the method of organizing files on a storage device, such as diskettes and hard disks. *Mounting* a file system involves specifying the device that contains the file system, the type of the device, and the directory hierarchy to mount the file system. With Linux, you can choose a file system from a number of available file systems, such as ext2. In addition to these file systems, certain file systems, such as /proc, have been built into the operating system kernel. The kernel uses the /proc file system to obtain network information.

In most of the Linux versions, the /proc file system is automatically created when the operating system is installed. However, in some cases, you need to modify the /etc/fstab file to add the following statement:

```
none /proc proc defaults
```

This statement is used to force the mounting of the /proc file system automatically. After you ensure that the /proc file system has been created on the Linux system, you must set the host name (nickname) for the Linux computer. To do so, use the `hostname` command:

```
hostname name
```

In this command, `name` refers to the system name for your computer. You can also specify the FQDN for your computer. For example, in the following command, the computer name is set as `server1` on the domain called `domain1`:

```
hostname server1.domain1.com
```

You can also create an entry for the host name in the /etc/hosts file. You can open this file and verify that your computer's name appears there. To open this file from the root directory, use the following command:

```
vi /etc/hosts
```

This command opens the file in a text editor called *vi editor*. A sample output is shown in Figure 8-1. To quit this editor, press Esc, type `:q`, and press Enter.

Figure 8-1: A sample HOSTS file

The next step involves configuring the network interface by using the `ifconfig` command. This command makes the Network layer of the operating system's kernel work with the network interface by giving it an IP address. After the interface has been configured and activated, the kernel can send and receive data through the interface. The `ifconfig` command can be used to configure several interfaces, such as the loopback driver and the Ethernet interface driver. To display the status of the currently active interfaces, as shown in Figure 8-2, use the `ifconfig` command without any argument:

```
ifconfig
```

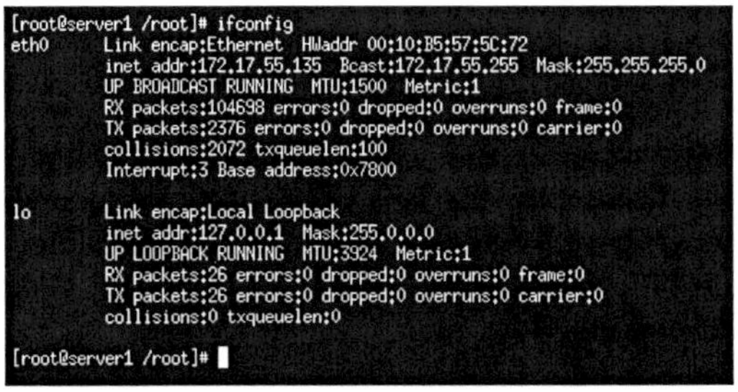

```
[root@server1 /root]# ifconfig
eth0      Link encap:Ethernet  HWaddr 00:10:B5:57:5C:72
          inet addr:172.17.55.135  Bcast:172.17.55.255  Mask:255.255.255.0
          UP BROADCAST RUNNING  MTU:1500  Metric:1
          RX packets:104698 errors:0 dropped:0 overruns:0 frame:0
          TX packets:2376 errors:0 dropped:0 overruns:0 carrier:0
          collisions:2072 txqueuelen:100
          Interrupt:3 Base address:0x7800

lo        Link encap:Local Loopback
          inet addr:127.0.0.1  Mask:255.0.0.0
          UP LOOPBACK RUNNING  MTU:3924  Metric:1
          RX packets:26 errors:0 dropped:0 overruns:0 frame:0
          TX packets:26 errors:0 dropped:0 overruns:0 carrier:0
          collisions:0 txqueuelen:0

[root@server1 /root]# 
```

Figure 8-2: A sample output of the ifconfig command

You can display the status of a specific interface with the following command:

```
ifconfig interface_name
```

In the above command, the argument `interface_name` is the name of the interface whose status needs to be displayed. The interface name is usually a driver name followed by a unit number. For example, eth0 is the interface name for Ethernet. When you need to display the status of all the interfaces, whether or not they are active, use the following command:

```
ifconfig -a
```

The general format of the `ifconfig` command is:

```
ifconfig interface option | address
```

Some of the options used with the `ifconfig` command are:

✦ **up** — Activates the interface

✦ **down** — Causes the interface driver to shut down

✦ **netmask addr** — Specifies IP netmask for the interface

✦ **irq addr**—Sets the IRQ used by the interface; needs to be used when the device cannot change the IRQ dynamically

✦ **mem-start address**—Sets the start address of the shared memory that is used by the interface

✦ **address**—Sets the IP address for the interface

When you've activated the network interfaces, you need to add or remove routes in the kernel's routing table to enable your computer to find other computers on the network. To modify the routing table, the `route` command is used. To add or remove a route from the kernel's routing table, the `route` command can be formatted like this:

```
route add|del IP_Address
```

The `add` option is used to add a route, whereas the `del` option is used to remove a route from the kernel's routing table. To display the kernel's routing table, use the `route` command without any option. Figure 8-3 shows a sample routing table.

Cross-Reference   For information on routing, refer to Chapter 5.

```
[root@server1 /root]# route
Kernel IP routing table
Destination     Gateway        Genmask         Flags Metric Ref    Use Iface
172.17.55.0     *              255.255.255.0   U     0      0        0 eth0
127.0.0.0       *              255.0.0.0       U     0      0        0 lo
default         172.17.55.1    0.0.0.0         UG    0      0        0 eth0
[root@server1 /root]#
```

Figure 8-3: A sample output of the route command

You can force the operating system to display only the IP addresses in a routing table by using the `-n` option:

```
route -n
```

After you've added routes to the routing table, you should identify the path the packets take between the source and the destination hosts. To do so, use the `traceroute` command:

```
traceroute destination_address
```

In this command, `destination_address` is the IP address or the domain name of the destination host.

Configuring TCP/IP on a Linux platform involves the configuration of a couple of interfaces. First, the loopback interface needs to be installed. Then, you need to add the Ethernet driver for the network.

The loopback driver is usually installed during the installation of the operating system. The IP address of the loopback interface is always 127.0.0.1. To check whether or not the loopback driver exists on your computer, you can view the /etc/hosts file. The /etc/hosts file should have the following line if the loopback driver exists:

```
localhost 127.0.0.1
```

You can also use the ifconfig command to check whether the loopback driver exists. Figure 8-4 shows a sample output of the command.

```
ifconfig lo
```

Figure 8-4: A sample output of the ifconfig lo command

If this command results in an error message, the loopback driver does not exist. To create the loopback interface, use the ifconfig command:

```
ifconfig lo 127.0.0.1
```

The above command creates an entry for the loopback driver in the /etc/hosts file.

After creating the loopback interface, you need to add it to the kernel's routing table. To do so, use the route command as follows:

```
route add 127.0.0.1
```

You can also use the following command to add the loopback driver to the routing table:

```
route add localhost
```

Next, check the routing by using the ping command. The ping command sends some data packets to network hosts and is used to check the destination host's response. To check the response from the localhost, use the following command:

```
ping 127.0.0.1
```

You can also check the routing by using:

```
ping localhost
```

Both of the above commands give the same output. Figure 8-5 shows a sample output of the `ping localhost` command. If the command did not result in any replies, you need to recheck the configuration files and the routing entries because the address and the name of the loopback interface might not have been recognized. However, if the configuration files and the routing tables contain the correct entry, the problem could be more serious. There could be a mismatch in the versions of kernel drivers and network utilities, or the network kernel may not be properly configured. Thus, the entire process may need to be repeated.

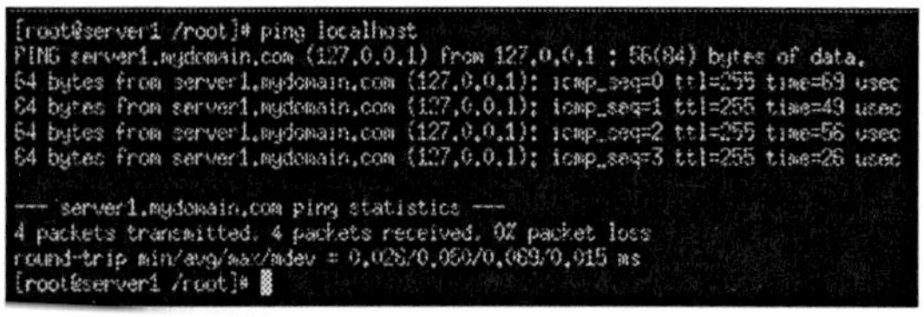

```
[root@server1 /root]# ping localhost
PING server1.mydomain.com (127.0.0.1) from 127.0.0.1 : 56(84) bytes of data.
64 bytes from server1.mydomain.com (127.0.0.1): icmp_seq=0 ttl=255 time=69 usec
64 bytes from server1.mydomain.com (127.0.0.1): icmp_seq=1 ttl=255 time=49 usec
64 bytes from server1.mydomain.com (127.0.0.1): icmp_seq=2 ttl=255 time=56 usec
64 bytes from server1.mydomain.com (127.0.0.1): icmp_seq=3 ttl=255 time=26 usec

--- server1.mydomain.com ping statistics ---
4 packets transmitted, 4 packets received, 0% packet loss
round-trip min/avg/max/mdev = 0.026/0.050/0.069/0.015 ms
[root@server1 /root]#
```

Figure 8-5: A sample output of the ping localhost command

After you've added the loopback interface and checked the routing, you need to add the Ethernet driver to the kernel. You will follow the same procedure to add the Ethernet driver that you used to add the loopback driver. First, you need to set up and activate the Ethernet interface by using the `ifconfig` command:

```
ifconfig eth0 IP_address
```

In the above command, `eth0` is the Ethernet interface. To check the interface, use the following command:

```
ifconfig eth0
```

The next step in configuring the Ethernet driver is to add its entry in the kernel's routing table so the kernel comes to know about the local machine's network address. You can also set the network address for the entire local area network by using the `-net` option of the `route` command as follows:

```
route add -net IP_address
```

Alternatively, you can use the /etc/networks file, which contains a list of network names and their IP addresses. For example, if the /etc/networks file contains an entry for a network called tcp_net, you can add this network to the routing table as follows:

```
route add tcp_net
```

After adding a route entry for the Ethernet interface, you can check the routing by using the `ping` command, as you did earlier for the loopback interface.

Note Some of the latest Linux versions provide a program/command called `netconf`. This command provides a graphical interface that displays options you can use to configure TCP/IP.

Installing and Configuring in the Microsoft World

The Microsoft world of operating systems is quite large. It includes such operating systems as Windows 95, Windows 98, Windows NT, and most recently, the Windows 2000 and Windows Me operating systems. In this section, you'll learn about installing and configuring TCP/IP on different Microsoft operating systems.

Installing TCP/IP on Microsoft operating systems

Usually, TCP/IP is installed when the operating system is installed. However, with Microsoft operating systems, you can install TCP/IP at a later time.

Microsoft Windows 98

Use the following steps to install TCP/IP on a Windows 98 computer:

1. Select Start ➪ Settings ➪ Control Panel to open the Control Panel window.

2. Double-click the Network icon to open the Network dialog box, shown in Figure 8-6. By default, the Configuration tab is active.

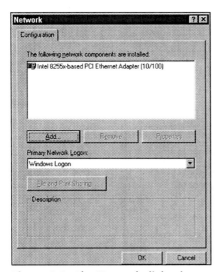

Figure 8-6: The Network dialog box

Tip   You can also open the Network dialog box by right-clicking the Network Neighborhood icon on the desktop and selecting Properties from the short-cut menu.

3. Click Add to open the Select Network Component Type dialog box, shown in Figure 8-7.

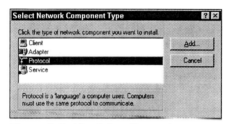

Figure 8-7: The Select Network Component Type dialog box

4. Select Protocol, and then click Add to open the Select Network Protocol dialog box, as shown in Figure 8-8.

5. From the Manufacturer's list, select Microsoft. The Network Protocols list to the right displays all the Microsoft protocols.

6. From the Network Protocols list, select TCP/IP and click OK.

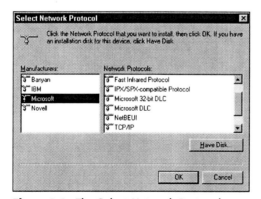

Figure 8-8: The Select Network Protocol dialog box

After TCP/IP is installed, the list of installed components displays an entry for it.

Microsoft Windows NT Server

Before beginning the installation of TCP/IP, ensure that you are logged on as an Administrator or as a member of the Administrators group.

1. Select Start ➪ Settings ➪ Control Panel to open the Control Panel window.

2. Double-click the Network icon to open the Network dialog box, shown in Figure 8-9. By default, the Identification tab is active.

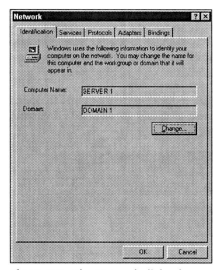

Figure 8-9: The Network dialog box

3. Activate the Protocols tab and click the Add button to open the Select Network Protocol dialog box.

4. From the Network Protocols list, select TCP/IP Protocol and click OK.

5. If a DHCP server is configured, a message box appears, asking you whether or not to use the DHCP server. Select No for manual configuration.

Note

DHCP is an acronym for *Dynamic Host Configuration Protocol* and is used to support automatic configuration and addressing for computers using TCP/IP. For more information on DHCP, refer to Chapter 10.

6. In the Windows NT Setup dialog box, enter the full path of the Windows NT distribution files and click the Continue button to copy all the necessary files to your hard disk.

Note   If you select the options for installing SNMP and FTP, you are directed to the automatic configuration of these services.

After the files are copied and the installation is complete, you need to reboot the computer. The TCP/IP protocol is now displayed in the Network settings dialog box.

Microsoft Windows 2000 Server

TCP/IP is installed by default when the network card adapter is detected automatically during the installation and setup of Windows 2000 Server. However, if TCP/IP has been overridden during the installation of the operating system, you'll need to install it.

Before you start installing TCP/IP on Windows 2000 Server, you must ensure that you are logged on as an Administrator or as a member of the Administrators group. To install TCP/IP:

1. Select Start ➪ Settings ➪ Network and Dial-Up Connections to open the Network and Dial-Up Connections dialog box, as shown in Figure 8-10.

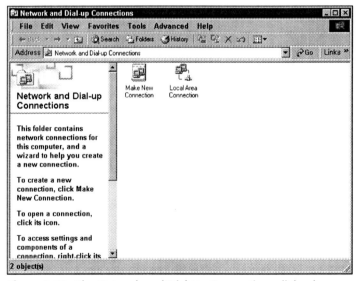

Figure 8-10: The Network and Dial-Up Connections dialog box

2. Right-click the connection for which you want to install TCP/IP and select Properties from the shortcut menu. If you want to configure the local area network, right-click "local area connection" and select Properties from the shortcut menu to open the Local Area Connection Properties window.

3. Activate the General tab.

4. If the list of installed components does not display Internet Protocol (TCP/IP), click Install to start the installation process.

5. Click Protocol and then click Add to open the Select Network Protocol dialog box.

6. Click Internet Protocol (TCP/IP) and click OK.

Enter the full path of the distribution files when prompted. After the files are copied, you have to restart the computer. Internet Protocol (TCP/IP) is now displayed in the list of installed components.

Configuring TCP/IP manually

Now that you've learned how to install TCP/IP on different Microsoft operating systems, you need to know how to activate the different TCP/IP services to configure it. You can configure TCP/IP with one of the following methods:

✦ **Automatic configuration** — This configuration automatically provides default IP addresses in the reserved range from 169.254.0.1 to 169.254.255.254 and a subnet mask of 255.255.0.0. However, gateway, WINS, and DNS servers are not automatically configured. The automatic configuration feature is designed for those networks that consist of single segments and are not connected to the Internet. Such networks do not require gateway, WINS, or DNS servers.

✦ **Dynamic configuration** — This configuration requires the network to have a DHCP server. In this configuration method, hosts obtain IP addresses, subnet mask, gateway, DNS, and WINS server configuration information dynamically from the DHCP server.

✦ **Manual configuration** — When a network has multiple segments and there is no DHCP server, TCP/IP needs to be configured manually. In manual configuration, you need to assign the information, such as IP address, subnet mask, gateway, WINS, and DNS configuration, manually.

To configure TCP/IP for the Microsoft operating systems, you need to configure the following items:

✦ **IP address** — Each network interface on each host must have a unique IP address. This item is not optional.

✦ **Subnet mask** — Each network interface on each host must have a subnet mask so that the IP address and the subnet mask together yield the network ID. The network ID should be the same for all the network interfaces in a network segment. Thus, the subnet mask for all the interfaces on the same network segment must be the same. This item is not optional.

✦ **Default gateway** — A *gateway* is a local router that forwards packets to other networks. At least one of the network interfaces should be configured with the IP address of a default gateway so that the TCP/IP host can communicate to other networks. This item need not be configured if the network consists of a single network segment.

✦ **DNS (Domain Name System) server** — You can configure a TCP/IP host with the IP address of a DNS server on your network. A *DNS server* maps the Fully Qualified Domain Names to their respective IP addresses. This name resolution is essential for communicating between TCP/IP hosts.

For information on DNS, refer to Chapter 10.

✦ **WINS server** — You can configure a TCP/IP host with the IP address of a WINS server on your network. A WINS server maps the NetBIOS names to their respective IP addresses. *NetBIOS* is a protocol that allows application programs to communicate to the network. Network programs and services, such as the File and Printer sharing service in Microsoft Windows 2000, use NetBIOS names.

For more information on NetBIOS, refer to Chapter 10.

Microsoft Windows 98

If your network has a DHCP server, TCP/IP can be configured dynamically. Otherwise, you need to configure TCP/IP manually with the following steps:

1. In the Network dialog box, select TCP/IP and click Properties to open the TCP/IP Properties dialog box, shown in Figure 8-11.

2. In the IP address tab, select "Specify an IP address" and enter the IP address and the subnet mask.

3. Configure the gateway, WINS, and DNS servers if required by using the Gateway, WINS Configuration, and DNS Configuration tabs respectively.

After the configuration is complete, you need to restart the computer so that the settings take effect.

Microsoft Windows NT

When installing TCP/IP, if you select the Enable Automatic DHCP Configuration option in the TCP/IP Properties dialog box and a DHCP server is available on the network, the TCP/IP configuration settings are completed automatically. Otherwise, you need to configure TCP/IP manually as follows:

1. In the Network Settings dialog box (in the Network Software box), select the TCP/IP protocol. Then, click the Properties button to open the Microsoft TCP/IP Properties dialog box, shown in Figure 8-12.

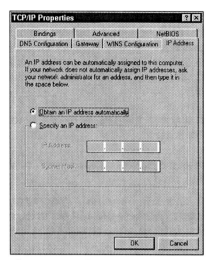

Figure 8-11: The TCP/IP Properties dialog box

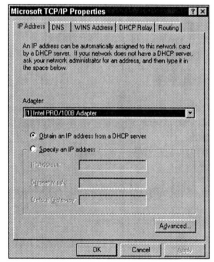

Figure 8-12: The Microsoft TCP/IP Properties dialog box

2. From the Adapter list, select the network adapter that you want to configure. The Adapter list contains all the adapters that are installed on the computer.

3. Select "Specify an IP address." In the IP Address box, enter the IP address that identifies the IP address of the local computer. In the Subnet Mask box, enter the subnet mask address that allows the computer to separate the IP address into host ID and network ID. In the Default Gateway box, enter the IP address, which is the address of the default gateway (IP router) used to forward packets to other networks and subnets.

Note   If the default gateway address is not specified, the packets cannot be routed outside the subnet unless the route utility is used.

4. If you want to use a DNS server for name resolution, you can click the DNS tab and add the DNS server information.

5. If you need to use WINS server for name resolution, and your network has a WINS server, you can activate the WINS Address tab and enter its address. However, if WINS server is not specified, the name resolution is limited to the local network.

6. To enable packet routing, click the Routing tab and select the "Enable IP forwarding" check box.

Note   The Routing Information Protocol (RIP) allows routes to be determined statically as well as dynamically. The RIP service, which enables RIP functioning, can be installed by using the Services tab of the Network dialog box.

7. Click the OK button to close the TCP/IP Properties dialog box.

8. Click OK to close the Network dialog box.

If you are installing TCP/IP for the first time, you need to restart the computer for the configuration settings to take effect. However, if you are modifying the settings, you do not need to restart the computer.

Microsoft Windows 2000 Server

Follow these steps to configure TCP/IP manually on a Windows 2000 server:

1. Open the Network and Dial-up Connections window.

2. Right-click the network connection that you want to configure, and then select Properties from the shortcut menu.

3. Activate the General tab.

4. Select Internet Protocol (TCP/IP) and click Properties to open the Internet Protocol (TCP/IP) Properties dialog box, shown in Figure 8-13.

5. Click the check box next to "Use the following IP address." If you selected local area connection, enter the IP address, subnet mask, and default gateway (if necessary). For other connections, enter the IP address.

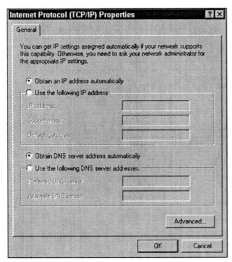

Figure 8-13: The Internet Protocol (TCP/IP) Properties dialog box

Note   You can configure the DNS server by clicking the check box next to "Use the following DNS server addresses."

In Windows 2000 Server, you need to restart the computer for the configuration settings to take effect if you are installing TCP/IP for the first time. However, if you are modifying the settings, you do not need to restart the computer.

Viewing the IP Configuration

Whenever network problems arise, the first step in troubleshooting is to view the IP configuration information, which includes IP address, subnet mask, and default gateway. You can view this configuration information by using the ipconfig utility, (a command-line utility). Figure 8-14 shows a sample output of the ipconfig command.

Note   Use the winipcfg utility to view the IP configuration for Windows 95 and Windows 98.

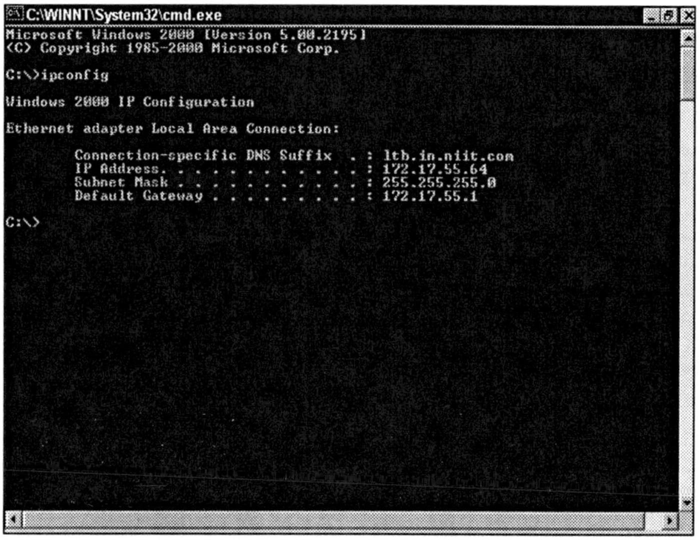

Figure 8-14: A sample output of the ipconfig command

You can view a detailed configuration report by using the `/all` switch with the `ipconfig` command. The `ipconfig /all` command displays a detailed configuration report for all the interfaces.

Summary

In this chapter, you learned the basic steps involved in the installation and configuration of TCP/IP on any operating system; you also learned that these steps may vary depending on the particular operating system used. Then, you identified the different configuration files that need to be modified to configure TCP/IP in the Linux world. You learned the procedure that is followed to install and configure TCP/IP on Microsoft operating systems, including Windows 98, Windows NT Server, and Windows 2000 Server. Finally, you learned how to use the `ipconfig` command to view the IP configuration.

✦   ✦   ✦

Automatic Configuration

Most of us have discovered that properly installing and configuring TCP/IP to provide network connectivity and functionality is an uphill task. One needs considerable expertise to make the installation work. At some point, you probably even wondered if there was a way to automate the entire process, much like the widely available plug-and-play utilities that allow users to start using software without having to manually configure it. BOOTstrap Protocol (BOOTP) and its successor, Dynamic Host Configuration Protocol (DHCP), play a major role in automating the configuration of TCP/IP in a network.

In this chapter, you learn about automatically configuring the TCP/IP protocol, and the role that BOOTP and DHCP play in this process. You learn about the bootstrap process, the BOOTP data packet format, the shortcomings of BOOTP, and the BOOTP-enabled routers. You also learn about the DHCP process, DHCP lease policies, scope and DHCP server options, DHCP data packet format, and DHCP routing.

Overview of Automatic Configuration

To install and configure the TCP/IP software, you need the following information:

+ IP addresses to the TCP/IP devices
+ Network addresses
+ Subnet masks
+ The name of the domain to which the device belongs
+ The address of the default gateway or router
+ The address of the name server

Automatic configuration of the TCP/IP software denotes the ability to automate the installation and configuration process of the TCP/IP software. Rather than having to manually specify information, users can start using their computers immediately when they connect to the network.

Note   Automatic configuration is also commonly referred to as *autoconfiguration*.

Benefits of automatic configuration

Automatic configuration of TCP/IP has many benefits over the traditional method of manually configuring TCP/IP. These benefits are best understood if you compare the two methods, as shown in Table 9-1.

Table 9-1 Manual Configuration versus Automatic Configuration	
Benefits of Manual Configuration	*Benefits of Automatic Configuration*
The network administrator needs to assign a unique IP address for each network device. If the number of devices in the network is large, this can be a cumbersome task.	Each network device is automatically assigned a unique IP address. As a result, the administrator's work is considerably easier.
Incorrect or duplicate IP addresses can cause a lot of trouble, as the administrator would need to manually trace the devices with incorrect or duplicate addresses.	Since addresses are assigned automatically, the possibility of incorrect or duplicate IP addresses is practically nil.
In addition to IP addresses, the administrator needs to specify the subnet masks and address of the default router or gateway.	In general, information regarding the address of the default router, as well as the address of the default gateway and subnet mask, is configured automatically.
Additional information, such as time offset from GMT, IP address of the time server, IP address of the boot server, and name of the boot file, needs to be manually configured on each device.	Additional information is automatically configured.
Administrators may face problems while moving devices from one subnet to another.	Moving devices from one subnet to another is not a large problem, since the relocated devices would automatically configure themselves accordingly.

Benefits of Manual Configuration	Benefits of Automatic Configuration
The administrator needs to manually manage the devices in the network.	Automatic configuration allows for centralized management of the network, thus saving the administrator the trouble of running from device to device.
Manual configuration is highly administrator dependent.	Automatic configuration reduces a considerable amount of responsibility from the administrators, and users need not be solely dependent on administrators.

Note   The address of the domain and the name server cannot be automatically configured. You need to specify these addresses manually.

Considerations for multisegment networks

In the current environment of big conglomerates, the focus of networking has shifted from local networks to global *multisegment networks*. A multisegment network consists of small, medium, or large local networks that are interconnected by routers. However, this shift has resulted in a couple of problems related to automatic configuration of TCP/IP:

✦ To automatically configure itself while booting, a network device (or host) requires information that is generally obtained from an external source, known as a *boot server*. (Any computer that stores the required boot information is referred to as a boot server.) If the boot server is located in the local subnet, obtaining the configuration information may not be difficult. However, if the boot server is located in a different subnet, the request for configuration information needs to be sent across a router. Normally, this information is not routed via the routers.

✦ If the boot server is down or unreachable for some reason, the entire network may shut down, as hosts cannot obtain the start-up information from the server.

Manually configuring information on network devices is a tedious task, especially if the network is large. Moreover, the router's inability to transmit configuration requests and responses has led to the subsequent development of two protocols — BOOTP and DHCP. These protocols provide the necessary framework for transferring the configuration information to the hosts in a TCP/IP network, to preclude the necessity of manually configuring the individual devices in the network. In other words, these protocols allow the network devices to automatically configure the required information and successfully connect to the network and start working, thus easing the ever-increasing burden on the network administrators.

Bootstrap Protocol

Every device needs system information at the time of start-up. This start-up information, or *boot information*, is generally located in the boot sector of the hard disk of the computer. In the case of diskless computers, however, this information is not available. In a networked environment, these diskless computers also need to have a unique IP address. As a result, these computers must obtain the required information from an external source. For the same reason, such diskless computers, also known as "dumb terminals," use Reverse Address Resolution Protocol (RARP) to obtain a valid IP address and retrieve the boot information from the boot server. RARP, however, is associated with the following shortcomings, which make it unsuitable for obtaining the configuration information at start-up:

✦ The packet exchanged between the server and the client contains only the 4-byte IP address of the client. The client also needs the start-up information to boot, which is not supplied by the RARP packet.

✦ RARP uses a host's MAC address for its identification. As a result, it cannot be used in networks where the hardware addresses are assigned dynamically.

Cross-Reference   For more information on RARP, refer to Chapter 4.

The BOOTstrap Protocol (BOOTP) was developed as a means of overcoming the drawbacks posed by RARP. Apart from containing the IP address, the BOOTP messages (or packets) contain the start-up information required by a diskless computer to boot up successfully. The same message also contains the address of the BOOTP server and the default router or gateway on the network. Also, you can effectively use BOOTP in networks where the hardware addresses are assigned dynamically.

The BOOTP bootstrap process

The BOOTP bootstrap process consists of two phases. The first phase is known as the *address determination and boot file selection* phase. After the client obtains its IP address and the required boot file is selected, control is passed to the next phase, which is known as the *boot file transfer* phase. In this phase, the client uses a transfer protocol to copy the boot file from the boot server. These phases are described below:

✦ **The address determination and boot file selection phase**—When a diskless machine starts up, it sends a request for an IP address and boot image file to the BOOTP server using port 68. The boot server listens to the BOOTP (and DHCP) requests on port 67. After the server identifies the client workstation by using the MAC-layer address, which is sent along with the client request, it selects the boot image file that has been preconfigured for the specific client.

Note A boot server does not have to run on the same computer that stores the boot image files. Generally, the server operates as a simple database, where the boot image files are mapped to names or aliases. The boot image files, in this case, are stored on a separate machine, which is contacted by the server to extract the corresponding image file, when required.

✦ **The boot file transfer phase** — After the BOOTP server identifies the client and selects the corresponding image file, the client uses a transfer protocol, such as Trivial File Transfer Protocol (TFTP) or File Transfer Protocol (FTP), to transfer (or copy) the boot file to its memory.

Looking at the BOOTP packet

A BOOTP packet consists of 15 fields, which are of fixed length to keep the BOOTP implementation simple and small enough to fit in the client's memory. For the same reason, the BOOTP replies have the same format as the BOOTP requests. Figure 9-1 shows the BOOTP packet format.

0	8	16	24	31

OP	HTYPE	HLEN	HOPS
TRANSACTION ID			
SECONDS		UNUSED	
CLIENT IP ADDRESS			
YOUR IP ADDRESS			
SERVER IP ADDRESS			
ROUTER IP ADDRESS			
CLIENT HARDWARE ADDRESS ⋮			
SERVER HOST NAME ⋮			
BOOT FILE NAME ⋮			
VENDOR-SPECIFIC AREA ⋮			

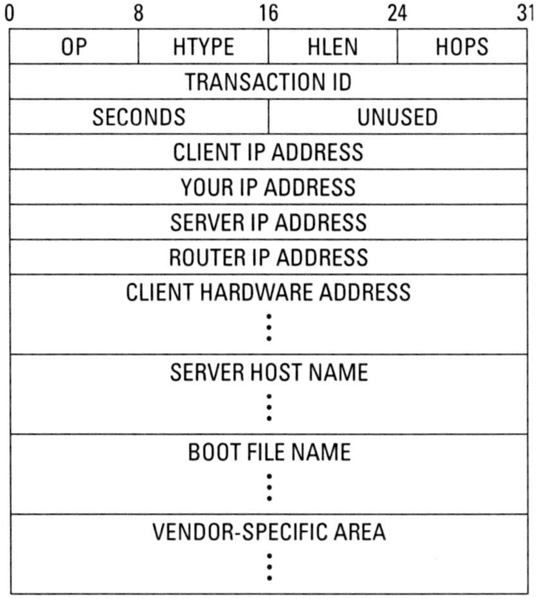

Figure 9-1: The BOOTP packet format

The fields in the BOOTP packet include:

✦ **Op** — specifies the message type. If the message is a request from the client, the field value is 1. If the message is a reply from the boot server, the field value is 2. The length of the field is 1 byte.

✦ **Htype (Hardware Type)** — specifies the hardware interface type, which is being used by the sending device. For example, the Ethernet interface is represented by the value 1. The length of the field is 1 byte.

✦ **Hlen (Hardware Length)** — specifies the length of the hardware address contained in the Hardware Type field. For example, if the value of the field is 6, it represents an Ethernet interface address. The length of the field is 1 byte.

✦ **Hops** — represents the number of servers the message was passed across. The client sets the value of this field to 0. If a server passes the message to another server, it increments the hop count. The length of the field is 1 byte.

✦ **Xid (Transaction ID)** — contains a randomly generated integer that is used by the client to match a boot request with the responses that it generates. The length of this field is 4 bytes.

✦ **Seconds** — represents the number of seconds elapsed since the client's booting process started. The length of the field is 2 bytes.

✦ **(Unused)** — is not used. The length of the field is 2 bytes.

✦ **CIAddr (Client IP Address)** — contains the client address in the boot request message, if the client knows its IP address. Otherwise, the field value is 0. The length of the field is 4 bytes.

✦ **YIAddr (Your IP Address)** — contains the client IP address filled in by the server, if the Claddr field that was received in the boot request message was empty. In other words, the server fills in this field if the client doesn't know its IP address. Otherwise, the field is ignored. The length of the field is 4 bytes.

✦ **SIAddr (Server IP Address)** — contains the server's IP address, which can either be filled in by the server in the boot reply message or by the client itself in the boot request message. If the client knows the IP address of the server from which it can obtain its boot information, the client fills in this field. However, if the client doesn't know the IP address of the server, the field is set to 0. Any boot server that can answer the request replies to the message and inserts its IP address in this field. The length of the field is 4 bytes.

✦ **GIAddr/RIAddr (Gateway/Router IP Address)** — contains the IP address of the default router or gateway. This field is optional and is required only if the boot server is located in a separate subnet. The length of this field is 4 bytes.

✦ **CHAddr (Client Hardware Address)** — contains the hardware address (or the MAC address) of the client. The client fills in this field. The length of the field is 16 bytes.

✦ **Server Name** — contains the server host name, which can either be filled in by the server in the boot reply message or by the client itself in the boot request message. If the client knows the host name of the server from which it can obtain its boot information, the client fills in this field. However, if the client doesn't know the host name of the server, the field is set to 0. Any boot server that can answer the request replies to the message and puts its host name in this field. The use of this field is optional. The length of the field is 64 bytes.

✦ **Boot File Name** — contains the generic name of the boot file required by the client to boot successfully. This field can be filled in by the client, if it knows the name of the boot file, or it can be filled in by the server in the boot reply message as a fully qualified directory path. The length of the field is 128 bytes.

✦ **Vendor-specific** — contains the optional information specified by the vendors that must be passed from the server to the client. This information might include the client's hardware type or serial number in the boot request and remote file system handle in the boot reply. The subnet mask for the local network, IP address of the time server, IP address of the domain server, and size of the boot file are also a part of this field. The length of the field is 64 bytes.

BOOTP-enabled routers

Routers are used in TCP/IP networks to connect devices and exchange information across different physical network segments that are known as *subnets*. It is quite possible, especially in environments where portable computers are used, that the client and the boot server are located in different subnets. To support this cross-router booting, the BOOTP requests must pass through one or more routers.

Cross-Reference

For more information on routers and subnets, refer to Chapter 5.

If the BOOTP packets were not passed through the routers, the network administrator would need to set up a separate server in each subnet — a costly and time-consuming exercise. However, you can find routers on the market that recognize the BOOTP packets and allow these packets to be transferred across to the destination. These routers are referred to as *BOOTP-enabled routers*, or *DHCP/BOOTP-enabled routers*. The DHCP/BOOTP-enabled routers comply with the *BOOTP relay agent* capabilities. As the name suggests, BOOTP relay agents transmit BOOTP messages between clients and boot servers that are located in separate networks.

Tip

As a network administrator, you may come across a situation in which cross-router booting is necessary, but the existing router does not allow the BOOTP messages to pass through it. Furthermore, your budget does not allow you to invest in a new BOOTP-enabled router. In this situation, you can set up a proxy or other server and configure it to act as the relay agent by installing a Network Operating System (NOS), such as Windows NT 4.0 or Windows 2000, that has built-in BOOTP/DHCP relay agents.

Shortcomings of BOOTP

As portable PCs and mobile computing become more popular, the nature of the networking environment has changed from static to dynamic. In a static environment, each device is permanently connected to the network and the network configuration doesn't change for weeks or even months. However, in the dynamic environment, the configuration can change on a day-to-day basis as devices, such as laptops, palmtops, and notebooks, are moved from one place to another with ease.

BOOTP was developed for a static networking environment, where a once-created BOOTP configuration file could be used to specify the BOOTP parameters for each device that needed the information. This file contained the mapping of all the hosts in a network with the parameters of the hosts. The larger the number of hosts in the network that needed boot information from an external source, the larger the size of the BOOTP configuration file.

Because of the static nature of the network, the BOOTP configuration file does not need to be frequently updated. However, managing the BOOTP file becomes a full-time responsibility in the case of dynamic networks. Whenever a device is moved from one location to another, the network administrator needs to make the following changes to the current settings:

✦ Re-enter the BOOTP parameters for the device — a cumbersome task if a large number of devices are frequently changing location.

✦ Assign a unique IP address to the hosts if they have moved to another domain or subnet.

For the above reasons, BOOTP has failed to keep up with the rapidly growing dynamic networking environment. As a result, Internet Engineering Task Force (IETF) developed an advanced version of BOOTP, called Dynamic Host Configuration Protocol (DHCP). DHCP was designed to address most of the drawbacks of BOOTP.

Dynamic Host Configuration Protocol

Like BOOTP, DHCP allows a network device to obtain the complete configuration information at start-up. However, it is superior to BOOTP because it also allows a device to obtain its IP address dynamically. As a result, a DHCP client can be relocated without the necessity of being manually reconfigured. This capability of automatic reconfiguration makes more sense in case of temporary movements, where a client is moved to another location for a very short period of time (such as a few hours or a day). In addition to dynamic allocation of IP addresses, DHCP has a built-in mechanism for managing the local clients on a TCP/IP network, for logging traffic, and for providing basic security. Last but not least, DHCP is easy to install, configure, and maintain. All these features make the job of administering a TCP/IP network relatively simple and efficient with DHCP.

In addition to solving the problem of dynamic allocation of IP addresses to clients in a TCP/IP network, DHCP solves another problem: fast-dwindling unique IP addresses. In the static networking environment, when a new device is added to the network, the network administrator assigns a unique IP address. Even if the device is rarely used (or used temporarily), no other device can use its IP address, however badly the address may be needed. In the case of DHCP, which allocates the IP addresses dynamically, the IP addresses are assigned when needed and are released when not in use, thus saving the precious IP addresses.

DHCP leasing

A DHCP server maintains a pool of valid IP addresses that can be assigned to clients. This pool of IP addresses is known as *scope*. When a client boots, it broadcasts a request for an IP address. All the DHCP servers that receive the request reply with an IP address and corresponding configuration information. Thus, the client receives many replies to its request. The client then selects an appropriate IP address for use and leases it from the DHCP server. A *lease* specifies the amount of time granted by the DHCP server to the client to use the specified IP address. After the lease is confirmed, the client becomes a part of the network operations. After the specified time elapses, the lease is revoked by the DHCP server.

In the dynamic network environment, leasing is important because it prevents a client from monopolizing an IP address for a long period of time. When a lease expires, it is returned to the server's address pool (or scope), from which the address can be leased to other clients that require the address. However, if the lease reaches its expiration limit and the client is still using it, the server can renew the lease and allow the client to continue using the same address. In some cases, unused leases can be automatically returned to the address pool.

The duration of a lease depends on the network and the requirements of the client. For example, the lease in a corporate network may need to last a day or even a week, depending on the type of work that is done. On the other hand, the leases in an Internet cafe might last for only an hour. For this reason, DHCP specifications do not recommend a specific time period. The clients can negotiate for a specific lease period as per their requirements. On the other hand, the DHCP servers can be configured to restrict the lease period. The length of the average lease period depends on the network administrator. DHCP also allows leases an infinite amount of time (for example, the time value of the Lease Duration field is 0xffffffff). Allocating infinite leases resembles the static IP address allocation.

DHCP lease process

The DHCP lease process, shown in Figure 9-2, includes the following steps:

1. The client boots and broadcasts the *discover message (DHCPDISCOVER)* in the local subnet. This is known as the *initialization state.*

Note

In the case of cross-booting, the broadcast message can be transmitted to other subnets. To broadcast messages to other subnets, you need BOOTP-enabled routers.

2. All the DHCP servers that receive the discover message and can lease an IP address reply with an *offer message (DHCPOFFER)*. This offer message contains an IP address and related configuration information.

3. The client can receive multiple lease offers, depending on the number of DHCP servers that responded to the discover message. The client now enters the *selection state.* In this state, the client examines the offer messages and selects an offer.

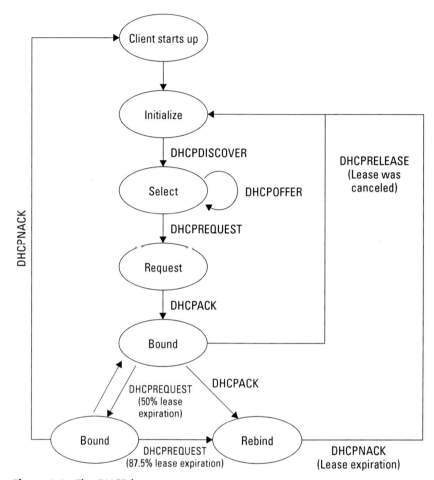

Figure 9-2: The DHCP lease process

4. The client enters the *request state.* It sends a *request message (DHCPREQUEST)* to the corresponding server, requesting the configuration that was offered by the server.

5. The server sends a *positive acknowledgement message (DHCPACK)* to the request message sent by the client. In addition to the IP address and the configuration information, this message contains the lease information.

6. When the client receives the acknowledgement, it enters the *bound state.* In this state, the leased IP address is bound to the client and the client becomes a part of the network. In the bound state, the client uses three timers that control the expiration, renewal, and rebinding of the lease.

7. Depending on the expiration timer setting, when 50 percent of the lease time elapses — or when the lease expires — the client tries to renew the lease by issuing the DHCPREQUEST message to the server that leased the address. However, the client can also attempt to terminate a lease early by issuing the *release message (DHCPRELEASE)*.

8. After sending the DHCPREQUEST message to the server, the client enters the *renew state*. In this state, the client awaits the response from the server. The server can respond to the renewal request either by accepting the request *(DHCPACK)* or by rejecting the request *(DHCPNACK)*. If the request is rejected, the client releases the address and returns to the initialization state.

9. If the client does not receive a response from the server within the specified time limit, the server is assumed to be down or unreachable. In this case, when 87.5 percent of the lease time elapses, the client enters the *rebind state*. In this state, the client restarts broadcasting the DHCPREQUEST message to all the available DHCP servers.

10. If the client receives even one positive response, it returns to the bound state. On the other hand, if all the DHCP servers respond negatively, the client returns to the initialization state.

Lease policy

The lease policy determines how long an average lease will last and if renewal of leases is allowed or not. However, the lease policy can differ for specific clients or groups of clients, as per their requirements. Network administrators set the lease policy for the entire network during the initial configuration of the DHCP server.

While setting the lease policy, the lease time value specified by the administrator should be small enough so that one client cannot monopolize an IP address for long and the IP addresses can be returned to the address pool. At the same time, the value of the lease period should be large enough so that the clients need not regularly broadcast requests for renewal of the IP addresses, thus increasing the network traffic unnecessarily. Also, if the corresponding DHCP server is down or unreachable, the clients can continue to function normally until the DHCP server becomes available again.

Tip   The rule of thumb for calculating the lease period is that the lease period should be twice the average downtime of the DHCP servers in a given subnet.

The administrator can specify the lease time as number of weeks, days, or hours for which the client can continue using the allocated IP address. When a client receives an IP address from the address pool, its lease expiry time is calculated by adding the lease period of the request to the time stamp on the client's request message, DHCPREQUEST. For example, if a client is allocated an IP address for one hour (that is, if the lease period is one hour) and the time stamp on its DHCPREQUEST message is June 20, 2001, 10:43 a.m., the client's lease would expire at June 20, 2001, 11:43 a.m.

Note   The lease expiration information for a client can be viewed using the DHCP Manager in the Windows NT 4.0 environment. Each Operating System (OS) has its own corresponding DHCP utility.

The lease policy also dictates whether or not clients can request for renewal of lease. The lease negotiation option is used to set this feature. If lease renegotiation is allowed in the lease policy, the clients can send a lease renewal request to the server when the 50 percent lease time period elapses. However, the network administrators should consider one important fact while planning the lease policy. If the number of devices in the network exceeds the total number of IP addresses in the address pool, the lease period should be such that devices do not have to wait a long time to obtain an IP address. If there is no dearth of IP addresses in the network, the lease periods should be long enough to prevent the clients from unnecessarily interrupting the current session to renegotiate the lease.

Caution   Hosts that provide network services — such as file servers, mail servers, and print servers — should be allocated IP addresses manually, rather than being leased for a time period. If required, these hosts should be given permanent leases so that they can continue to provide uninterrupted services to the other devices.

Scope and server options

The *DHCP scope* represents the complete range of valid IP addresses that are available to all the DHCP clients in a physical subnet. All the DHCP scopes have the following properties:

✦ Scope name

✦ The complete range of IP addresses

✦ Subnet mask

✦ Lease duration

✦ Reservations

✦ Options

Cross-Reference   For more information on options, refer to the section "DHCP server options" later in this chapter.

Network administrators use scopes to divide physical subnets into a number of logical subnets. A DHCP server provides DHCP services to each of these logical subnets. This server also identifies and stores the configuration information for all the clients in the given subnet. A client in one logical subnet can request configuration information from servers in other logical subnets also.

Note   DHCP offered by Microsoft allows network administrators to group a number of scopes into a *superscope,* which allows policies that are common to all the scopes to be applied in one transaction. The superscopes can also be used to solve common DHCP server issues, thus further easing the burden on the network administrators.

Sometimes, a range of IP addresses within the scope is not offered to the clients of the DHCP server. This type of range is known as an *exclusion range.* To use the IP addresses in the exclusion range, the administrator needs to manually configure these addresses on the network devices, such as printers, that cannot use DHCP. The remaining addresses in the scope form the *address pool* of the scope. Only the addresses from the scope's address pool are dynamically offered to the clients. When a host on the network permanently leases an address, the address is *reserved* for the client. Only the specified host can lease the address reserved for it.

To enable clients to use the services offered by the DHCP server, a scope needs to be defined and configured. The process of setting up DHCP scopes includes the following steps:

1. Create the scope using the corresponding DHCP utility offered by the operating system you are using. For example, you can use the Microsoft DHCP Manager in Windows NT 4.0 and later versions.

Note   For the detailed procedure of creating DHCP scopes, refer to the documentation provided with the OS you are using.

2. Set the exclusion range, if required, by creating an exclusion for the specified addresses. The exclusion range IP addresses should only be used for network devices, such as modems and printers, that cannot obtain IP addresses dynamically.

3. Create the reservations for devices that would need to permanently lease an IP address from the address pool. These devices include various servers that are available on the network. Routers also need to be assigned reserved IP addresses.

Note   Reservations should only be made for network devices that can obtain an IP address dynamically — for example, devices that are DHCP-enabled.

4. Specify the lease duration. The default duration is three days, which is generally acceptable in most cases. The administrator can modify the value as necessary.

5. Define the necessary options as per requirements.

6. After a scope has been successfully created and configured, it needs to be activated so that the DHCP servers can process the lease requests and allocate IP addresses to the clients dynamically.

The DHCP packet

Since DHCP and BOOTP closely resemble one another, the DHCP packet format is quite similar to the BOOTP packet format. However, one of the fields in the DHCP packet is treated differently and another differs content-wise from its BOOTP counterpart. Figure 9-3 shows the format of a DHCP packet.

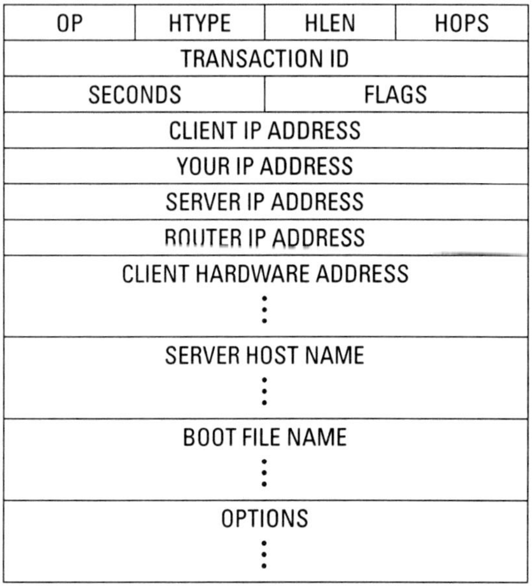

OP	HTYPE	HLEN	HOPS
TRANSACTION ID			
SECONDS		FLAGS	
CLIENT IP ADDRESS			
YOUR IP ADDRESS			
SERVER IP ADDRESS			
ROUTER IP ADDRESS			
CLIENT HARDWARE ADDRESS ⋮			
SERVER HOST NAME ⋮			
BOOT FILE NAME ⋮			
OPTIONS ⋮			

Figure 9-3: DHCP packet format

Only two fields in the DHCP packet are different from the fields in the BOOTP packet. These fields are:

✦ **Flags** — This field is equivalent to the "Unused" field in the BOOTP packet. In a BOOTP packet, all the bits of the "Unused" field are set to zero. In a DHCP packet, all the other bits are set to zero except for the leftmost bit. The value of the leftmost (or the high-order) bit is interpreted as a broadcast message. This means that the DHCP client can request the DHCP server to send responses using IP broadcast messages. The length of the field is 2 bytes.

✦ **Options** — This field is equivalent to the "Vendor-specific" field in the BOOTP messages. As in BOOTP packets, this field contains the extra configuration information provided by the vendor. This information includes the lease duration, subnet mask for the local network, IP address of the time server, IP address of the domain server, and size of the boot file as part of this field. The length of the field is 64 bytes.

Cross-Reference For details on the rest of the fields, refer to the section "Looking at the BOOTP packet" earlier in the chapter.

DHCP server options

When a DHCP server leases IP addresses to the DHCP clients, it can also assign other configuration parameters required by the client, which are known as *DHCP options* or *DHCP server options*. These DHCP options include the address of the default router or the gateway or the address of the name server. The basic options available for configuring DHCP clients are listed below:

✦ **Pad (Option code-0)** — Aligns the following fields to word boundaries.

✦ **Subnet Mask (Option code-1)** — Represents the subnet mask for the given physical subnetwork.

✦ **Time offset (Option code-2)** — Represents the Universal Coordinated Time (UCT) in seconds.

✦ **Router (Option code-3)** — Lists the IP addresses of all the routers available in the subnet.

✦ **Time server (Option code-4)** — Lists the IP addresses of all the time servers that are available to the client.

✦ **Name servers (Option code-5)** — Lists the IP addresses of all the name servers that are available to the client.

✦ **DNS servers (Option code-6)** — Lists the IP addresses of all the Domain Name Servers (DNSs) that are available to the client.

✦ **Log servers (Option code-7)** — Lists the IP addresses of all the log servers that are available to the client.

✦ **Cookie servers (Option code-8)** — Lists the IP addresses of all the cookie servers that are available to the client.

✦ **LPR servers (Option code-9)** — Lists the IP addresses of all the Line PRinter (LPR) servers that are available to the client.

✦ **Impress servers (Option code-10)** — Lists the IP addresses of all the Impress servers that are available to the client.

✦ **Resource location servers (Option code-11)** — Lists the IP addresses of all the resource location servers that are available to the client.

✦ **Host name (Option code-12)** — Represents the name of the client, which can be up to 63 characters long.

✦ **Boot file size (Option code-13)** — Represents the size of the client's default boot file.

✦ **Merit dump file (Option code-14)** — Represents the path of the backup boot file of the client. This file is accessed if the client's default boot file becomes unreachable because of the server crash.

✦ **Domain name (Option code-15)** — Represents the DNS domain name that should be used by the client to resolve DNS host name.

✦ **Swap server (Option code-16)** — Represents the IP addresses of the swap server available to the client.

✦ **Root path (Option code-17)** — Represents the path to the root disk of the client.

✦ **Extensions path (Option code-18)** — Represents the file that contains the information, like the vendor-extension field of BOOTP reply messages. This file can be retrieved through TFTP.

Routing DHCP

Typically, a BOOTP-enabled router can also route DHCP requests and responses across the subnets. To do so, the router must support the DHCP/BOOTP relay service. Any hardware or software that can route configuration information from one subnet to another subnet is known as a *relay agent*. Therefore, a BOOTP enabled router can also be referred to as a *DHCP/BOOTP relay agent*. The process of routing these requests is as follows:

1. A DHCP client originates a request for configuration parameters via TCP port 68.

2. The relay agent intercepts the request and interprets the subnet to which the request needs to be forwarded.

3. In the destination subnet, one or more DHCP servers may hear the broadcast and reply to the client with an available IP address.

4. The DHCP/BOOTP agent routes the reply to the client, which then selects one of the responses, sends the request message to the corresponding server, and obtains a lease, which is again relayed through the relay agent.

Summary

In this chapter, you learned about protocols such as BOOTP and DHCP that allow automatic configuration of TCP/IP, thus reducing the onus of manually configuring the TCP/IP software on network hosts. You learned the role of BOOTP and DHCP in automating the installation and operation of TCP/IP. You also learned about the two-step bootstrap process, the format of the BOOTP data packet, and the BOOTP-enabled routers. You also learned about the shortcomings of the BOOTP protocol that led to the development of DHCP, the DHCP process, DHCP lease policy, scope and DHCP server options, DHCP data packet format, and DHCP routing.

✦   ✦   ✦

Finding Hosts on an IP Network

Names are a large part of one's identity, and much easier to remember than numbers. This chapter will detail the processes that convert the user-friendly names we use in applications to computer-friendly numbers, such as IP addresses. We need our names. Imagine what would happen if you could not use names in your Web browser — you would have to know the IP address of every Web site you wanted to visit. Your Favorites list would look quite different, too. This chapter delves into the details of name resolution, or the process that makes the Internet user-friendly. It examines host names and NetBIOS names and how they are used to aid communication to a specific computer. Many applications, such as e-mail, FTP, Telnet, Web browsers, and newsreaders, rely on names to function. Thus, understanding name resolution provides a solid base from which to troubleshoot all sorts of applications.

Overview of Host Names

A host name is simply a label or an alias for an IP address. Every device on an IP network has a host name. Using host names is beneficial because:

✦ Host names are easier to remember than IP addresses.

✦ They provide stability in a mobile computing environment. While a client may be moved from one subnet to another using a different IP address on each network, the host name will stay the same on each network.

✦ A single computer can have multiple host names, none of which need to match the computer's NetBIOS name.

✦ Host names can be stored locally in a HOSTS file or in a DNS server database for global access.

Someone once said that host names are a "guy" thing. In the very early days of IP networking, there were a group of individuals (guys) who wanted to use labels for IP addresses, since IP addresses were difficult to remember. They used a local file to store the lookup table that matched the names to IP addresses. They used different colors for the host names — blue, green, red, black, white, brown, and orange. However, they quickly realized the error of their ways when they ran out of colors. You see, there were no entries with dusty rose, no frosted midnight indigo, no balmy bahama beige. These were *real* guys: They only recognized seven colors, two of which were black and white.

While this is a cute story, the truth is that Peggy Karp, a researcher for the MITRE Corp., Washington D.C., first suggested using host names in RFC 226 on September 20, 1971. Peggy suggested assigning a four-letter code to popular Telnet servers in order to simplify access procedures. Thus, the name resolution process was born.

While host names have undergone significant change since 1971, the initial concept has persevered. People remember names better than they remember IP addresses. Almost everyone knows how to find Microsoft's Web site, searching by Web address, but how many people actually know the site's IP address? (If you do, you have far too much time on your hands.)

Host names were originally implemented on a Host Name Server at SRI-NIC in a file named hosts.txt. The file would be downloaded to each client daily via FTP. As time went on, the process of distributing the hosts.txt file became problematic for a number of reasons:

✦ The download process used far too much bandwidth.

✦ Daily downloads of the hosts.txt file were not frequent enough to provide up-to-date information.

✦ The explosive growth of the Internet dramatically increased the work involved in maintaining the hosts.txt file.

✦ The growth of the hosts.txt file itself exacerbated the download time and bandwidth problems.

✦ The nature of the client base was changing. Rather than time-sharing a large-scale computer, organizations were grouping workstations into local area networks. These organizations managed their own name space, but constantly needed to wait for SRI-NIC to update the hosts.txt file.

The concept of using a method to qualify host names was suggested in numerous RFCs, beginning with RFCs 799, 819, and 830. While the method for implementing "name space" was different with each RFC, the need for a hierarchical database was a common thread in all three. In November 1987, the Domain Name System was defined in RFCs 1034 and 1035. Since then, over 20 RFCs have clarified, redefined, or referenced the Domain Name System.

Basic host names

A basic host name is used to describe a computer or device on the network. An example of a basic host name might be: slowpoke, ou812, or the ever-popular "sparky." Applications that use the Sockets interface or the Winsock API use host names as end points for communication. In order to use a host name, the host name must exist in a hosts file on the local client, or on a DNS server to which the client has access.

Host names can contain up to 256 characters and may or may not be case-sensitive (depending on the operating system implemented). Most recent Windows operating systems use case-insensitive host names, but some UNIX systems may still be case-sensitive.

Cross-Reference

For detailed information on the Sockets interface and Winsock applications, see Chapter 7.

Fully Qualified Domain Names

If your organization has a registered Domain Name System (DNS) domain name, then that name could be used to qualify a basic host name. A DNS domain name appended to your host name creates a Fully Qualified Domain Name (FQDN).

Just for a moment, pretend that your computer's host name is "goofy" and your registered domain is cartoons.com. Your FQDN would then be goofy.cartoons.com. There may be many goofys, but only one goofy.cartoons.com. The domain name is used to further qualify the host name, which makes it unique even if other goofys existed. Using FQDNs can extend the host name's usefulness to the global level.

Figure 10-1 shows an NT host name and DNS domain name configuration screen where the host name is goofy and the DNS domain name is cartoon.com.

Tip

Append your DNS domain name to your host name to create a Fully Qualified Domain Name (FQDN).

Canonical names and aliases

There are times when it is useful to refer to a host by a name other than its DNS host name. The de facto standard on the Internet is to refer to Web servers using the host name www. The www name is normally not a host name at all. It is an *alias*, or label, for a host name, which points to the same host using a different name.

One of the benefits of using aliases is the ability to hide the host name of the server from the client. If a server needed to be replaced, the use of aliases would hide the change from the clients it serviced. Aliases allow for redundancy, in that multiple servers can "answer to the same name."

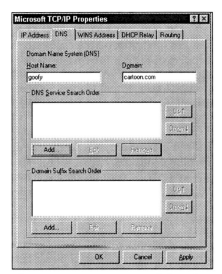

Figure 10-1: Host name and domain configuration

For example, we have a great Web server that hosts the `www.tcpipbible.bk` Web site. The Web server's host name is really `barney.tcpipbible.bk`, but we use a DNS canonical name (CNAME) resource record to point all requests for `www.tcpipbible.bk` to barney. Once in a while, we take barney down for maintenance, but we put wilma up in his place. Wilma is aliased to `www`, just like barney. Nobody knows. When the Web site is busy, we leave them both up.

Note   An *alias* is just a nickname for a host name.

Aliases can be implemented in a host file or on a DNS, but the method of implementation for each is different.

Webster's Encyclopedic Dictionary defines *canonical* as "conforming with, or ordered by, canon law." There is confusion about the definition of a canonical name. A canonical name conforms to the rules. It is a Fully Qualified Domain Name. The Canonical Name (CNAME) resource record in DNS is the culprit of this confusion. Some people think that a CNAME record denotes a canonical name, while it actually points to the canonical name. It seems odd that the CNAME record is the only non-canonical record in DNS.

In the following excerpt from a DNS zone file, the last two records are CNAME records. The owner of the record is the alias and is located on the left side of the record. This is the part the user would see and type into his or her browser. An alias can be thought of as a nickname. The canonical name is on the right side of the record; it points to the FQDN of the target host.

A Few Words on the www Standard

There is really no compelling technical reason to use the "www" standard for Web sites except that it is easy to remember (and the obvious World Wide Web). In hindsight, things might have been different if the Internet Engineering Task Force had imagined TV and radio announcers painfully trying to pronounce URLs. "www" is nothing less than a 9-syllable acronym! Compared to the words "FTP," "Telnet," and "NNTP," which roll right off your tongue, "www" is a pronunciation challenge. There is only one letter in the English alphabet whose pronunciation has more than one syllable, and we now use it three times in front of each of the millions of Web sites on the planet. Don't you just love committee decisions?

```
happy        IN     A      192.168.0.4
dopey        IN     A      192.168.0.3
sleepy       IN     A      192.168.0.2
grumpy       IN     A      192.168.0.1
dp           IN     CNAME      dopey.efs.ca
www          IN     CNAME      happy.efs.ca
```

A canonical name record refers a nickname to a FQDN.

The Local HOSTS File

Prior to DNS, there was only one way to resolve other hosts by name—the HOSTS file. Many UNIX operating systems refer to this file as the hosts.txt file. Microsoft operating systems refer to it as the HOSTS file, without an extension. Both Microsoft and UNIX operating systems store the host file in the drivers\etc folder. The HOSTS file is a lookup table for host name to IP address mappings maintained locally at each individual computer.

Format of the HOSTS file

Each line of the local HOSTS file contains mappings of IP addresses to host names. A typical HOSTS file content might appear like this:

```
172.16.23.91 bugs.cartoon.com        # development server
192.168.2.123 goofy.cartoon.com       # web server
192.168.2.33 tweety.cartoon.com tweetie   # mail server
#192.168.2.22 sylvester.cartoon.com # old mail server
172.16.23.42 bugs.cartoon.com        # development server
127.0.0.1 localhost
```

The first line maps bugs.cartoon.com to 172.16.23.91. The second line maps goofy.cartoon.com to 192.168.2.123. The pound (#) symbol indicates that what comes next is considered a comment. Consequently, goofy is a Web server. In the third line, the mail server, tweety.cartoon.com, also has the alias tweetie entered on the same line. Whole lines of code can be commented out using the # symbol. Such is the case with the fourth line, where Sylvester is the old mail server and is no longer in service. The final entry in the file is the default entry for the local host.

Caution　Care should be taken when editing a HOSTS file in a Windows environment. If Notepad is used as the editor, be sure that the file is saved as "hosts," with no extension in the drivers\etc folder for Windows 2000 and NT systems, or the Windows root folder for Windows 95 and 98. Saving the HOSTS file with the wrong name or in the wrong place will cause name resolution to ignore the HOSTS file.

Name resolution

Name resolution using a HOSTS file involves parsing the file line-by-line from top to bottom. In the HOSTS file code sample, there is a problem. The second entry for bugs.cartoon.com (fifth line) will never get used because the parsing happens from top to bottom and stops at the first matching entry. If the second "bugs" entry was correct, this host would direct the application traffic intended for bugs.cartoon.com to whomever was using 172.16.23.91, regardless of their host name.

Tip　Always ping the host names of the entries you have just made to your HOSTS file to ensure that each works properly.

The following steps are taken to resolve a host name using a host file.

1. Host name data is entered into an application or at a command prompt, such as a Web site URL in a browser or an FTP site in an FTP client.

2. The operating system checks to see if the destination host name matches the locally configured host name. If there is a match, the local host IP address is used to facilitate communications at the Internet layer.

3. If there is no match to the local host name, the local HOSTS file is parsed from top to bottom. If there is a match in the host file, it is used to facilitate communications at the Internet layer.

4. If there is no match in the HOSTS file, then the user receives an error message and no further processing occurs.

Tip　If you are unsure whether host names are case-sensitive in your target environment, include various versions of the host name on the same line of your HOSTS file.

Using DNS to Resolve Host Names

The Domain Name System is a three-element system that was developed to extend the application of host name resolution, while minimizing and distributing the workload of those responsible for performing the day-to-day maintenance of the name space itself. DNS has the following components:

✦ Name Server

✦ Resolver (a client)

✦ Name Space

DNS is a distributed database that is used by TCP/IP to resolve host names to IP addresses (and vice versa) of every computer on the planet, without the need to have a locally maintained HOSTS file at all. If a client is configured with the IP address of a DNS server, then it can send name query requests to that server, rather than using its local HOSTS file. DNS clients are usually capable of repeating a query to a busy name server at specified intervals of five seconds or so.

Figure 10-2 shows the DNS configuration of a typical Microsoft client. It is configured to use a specific IP address to reach a DNS server.

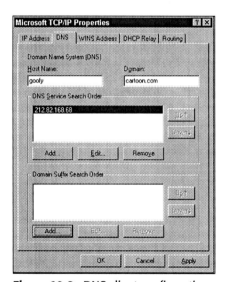

Figure 10-2: DNS client configuration

The following steps are taken to resolve a host name using a DNS server:

1. Host name data is entered into a sockets application or at a command prompt, such as a Web site URL in a browser or an FTP site in an FTP client.

2. The operating system checks to see if the destination host name matches the locally configured host name. If there is a match, then the local host IP address is used to facilitate communications at the Internet layer.

3. If there is no match to the local host name, then the local host sends a name query request for the destination host to its configured DNS server. The resolver may repeat the request at intervals of 5, 10, 20, and 40 seconds. If the DNS server responds with an answer to the request, the answer (normally an IP address) is used to facilitate communications at the Internet layer.

4. If there is no answer from the DNS server, the user receives an error message, and no further processing occurs.

Cross-Reference Once TCP/IP has an IP address for the destination host, the application data is passed down the protocol stack to facilitate routing to the destination. This process is the same regardless of what happens at the higher layers. Successful name resolution requests eventually end up being routed to the destination by the TCP/IP Internet layer. For more information on routing, see Chapter 5.

What is a domain?

A DNS domain is simply a node in name space. A DNS domain consists of the original name and all domains under it. Another way to think of a DNS domain is as a corporate identity. Each organization on the Internet needs to be unique — registered domain names achieve this uniqueness. The proliferation of Windows operating systems in use has coined another domain: the Windows NT domain. There is *no* relationship between an NT domain and a DNS domain; however, the same cannot be said for Windows 2000. DNS domains and Windows 2000 domains will probably have the same name. Windows 2000 needs DNS to operate, whereas NT did not.

Name servers

A DNS name server is a computer that runs a DNS server application. That server can store zone file information locally or in memory. A DNS server responds to client requests for name resolution by trying to find those names (and associated IP addresses) in name space. A name server also performs database management tasks on the zone files, such as resource record updates and zone transfers.

Resolvers

A resolver is a DNS client. Resolvers can be TCP/IP workstations or servers, but *must* be configured to send name resolution requests to the IP address of at least one DNS server. Most desktop computers in a DNS environment are resolvers. Figure 10-2 shows the required resolver configuration.

Understanding name space

The DNS name space is comprised of an unnamed root, and branches off that root are called domains. DNS uses a hierarchical organization to keep track of where the domains belong. The root domain is the parent to all other domains, and is signified by a period (.). Both the root domain and the top-level domains are managed by the Internet Corporation for Assigned Names and Numbers (ICANN) in the U.S. Other top-level domains are managed internationally. Top-level domains are arranged under the root organizationally, functionally, and geographically as shown in Figure 10-3.

DNS name space works much like a group of separately managed databases housed on different systems, all of which are able to find and use one another's entries. Name space consists of a large number of name servers, called *systems*, that are logically connected in parent-child fashion. While each system may only be responsible for a small area of name space, host names from other systems can be referenced in response to client requests.

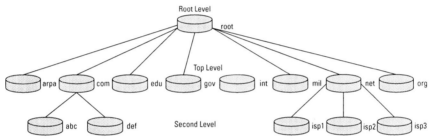

Figure 10-3: DNS domain name space

Root servers

The root domain name servers contain entries for the name servers in each of the top-level domains. The function of the root server is to find name servers in top-level domains and resolve their addresses for other name servers. Other name servers always use a root server as a starting point for DNS searches. The root server represents a "worst-case" condition for name resolution, in that name servers from different domains only query the root if they can't find the answer anywhere else. Every name server on the public Internet has a "root hints," or cache file, that points to a list of root servers. The U.S. government manages the root servers through a private contractor (ICANN). The root servers are updated daily.

Top-level domains

Top-level domains (TLDs) are used to group organizations by type or function. Organizations normally do not register TLDs. TLDs are used to classify types of organizations such as educational, for profit commercial, and non-profit.

The eight common DNS TLDs can be classified as generic or special-purpose. The generic top-level domains are:

✦ **.com** — For commercial enterprises

✦ **.net** — For networks

✦ **.org** — For nonprofit organizations

The special-purpose top-level domains are:

✦ **.edu** — For educational institutions

✦ **.gov** — For government organizations

✦ **.mil** — For military service

✦ **.int** — For organizations established by international treaty

✦ **.arpa** — For reverse lookups (resolving IP addresses to host names)

In addition to the eight TLDs, each country has a two-letter country code top-level domain (for example, .ca for Canada, .tw for Taiwan, and so on), which brings the total number of TLDs in use to over two hundred! In Canada, the Canadian Internet Registration Authority (CIRA) manages the .ca top-level domain name space.

 Cross-Reference The appendix contains a list of top-level domains currently in use.

The function of common top-level domains is to point to second-level domains. For example, the ".com" top-level domain name server can find a name server for every .com second-level domain. Each .com top-level server has a database, which contains entries for second-level name servers, and any hosts that might exist at the top-level domain itself. In Figure 10-3, the .com name server has entries for the name servers in abc.com and def.com, so the .com name server could refer other name servers to those entries in his zone.

 Note A definitive list of TLDs can be found at `www.alldomains.com/alltlds.html`.

Ongoing development is underway in the form of the New TLD Program at ICANN, the nonprofit regulatory authority for DNS name space. The project details a proposal for seven additional top-level domains. In fact, on November 16, 2000, ICANN announced the new TLDs, but they were not set to go live until October 2001. Some registrars were already accepting pre-registrations of domains under the new TLDs at the time this book was written. The seven new TLDs are:

✦ **.aero** — For the air-transport industry

✦ **.biz** — For businesses

✦ **.coop** — For cooperatives

✦ **.info** — For unrestricted use

✦ **.museum** — For museums

✦ **.name** — For individuals

✦ **.pro** — For professionals, doctors, lawyers, and accountants

Most top-level domains are managed and administered by ICANN, with the exception of country code domains, which are managed locally.

Second-level domains

It is at the second-level domain when the distributed nature of DNS name space starts to make a difference. Second-level domains are not managed by ICANN. With second-level domains, organizations can manage their own name space. Second-level domains can contain name servers, hosts, and lower-level domains called *sub-domains*. Every second-level domain contains information about the hosts, name servers, mail servers, and ftp sites in that domain.

Note

One of the requirements for registering a second-level domain is the need for two DNS servers to be exposed to the Internet. Complete requirements can be found by contacting your ICANN accredited registrar or your Internet service provider.

Zones within the name space

A *zone* is a contiguous area of name space that a name server is responsible for. A zone can be a small corner of a DNS domain, or it can span multiple domains. A zone can also be used to define the amount of DNS name space that an administrator is required to manage. Until recently, managing a DNS server required administrators to manually enter and maintain each record in the zone, so effective division of responsibility was the key to a well-managed DNS domain. DNS administrators with oversized zones are often error prone and slow to update the zone, based on the volume of work in the zone. DNS zones can be primary or secondary, forward or reverse.

Tip

RFC 2136 defines the Dynamic DNS update protocol, which allows supported clients to automatically update DNS information in the zone file. BIND 8.2.3 and Windows 2000 DNS servers support this new feature.

Primary zones

A primary zone consists of resource records and configuration information, which are entered and maintained in a locally stored file on a DNS Name Server. DNS servers containing a primary zone file require trained staff to manage the ongoing changes and additions to the zone database. Only one DNS server can be primary for a given zone.

Secondary zones

A secondary zone consists of resource records and configuration information that are normally not transferred at power up and at regular intervals from another DNS name server, which is referred to as the *master*. Figure 10-4 shows that a DNS master need not be primary for the zone to be transferred. Secondary zones are very useful for remote locations that need a DNS server, but do not want the responsibility of managing it.

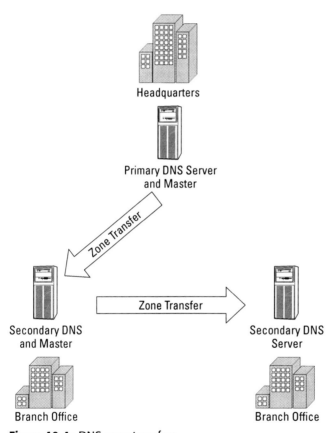

Figure 10-4: DNS zone transfers

Typically, organizations need more name servers than zones. A company may have three offices, but only one DNS domain and one DNS administrator. To add a DNS server at each office would require a trained body to administer it, but to point all clients from all offices to a single DNS server in one location would overload that server. Using primary and secondary DNS zones can alleviate this problem.

Figure 10-4 shows that one of the three offices will set up a primary zone and staff an administrator to manage it. The other two offices will each set up a secondary zone. Since transferring data from a master populates the secondary zone, no staff is needed for day-to-day management. Using this simple DNS implementation, each office will have local DNS services available with the minimum amount of management.

One of the strengths of DNS *is* its versatility. There are myriad configuration possibilities for a DNS structure.

Forward lookup zones

Forward lookup zones are used to resolve IP addresses from FQDNs. With a forward lookup zone, a DNS client can find the IP address for a given host name. This is the most common form of DNS query. If a URL is typed into a Web browser application, the TCP/IP protocol on that computer will formulate a forward lookup query in an effort to resolve the URL to an IP address. If that request is successful, the Web site appears in the browser; if not, an error appears.

Certain UNIX-based DNS forward lookup files use the form db.zone. Most Windows-based DNS forward lookup zones use the zone.dns file name. Accordingly, if you had the cartoon.com domain and you implemented a UNIX DNS forward lookup zone, you could expect the zone file to be called "db.cartoon.com". If you used the same domain and zone with a Windows DNS, the zone file would be called "carton.com.dns". Forward lookup zones can be primary or secondary.

Reverse lookup zones

If a DNS client already has an IP address for the destination computer, but wants to convert that IP to a FQDN, the client needs to send a query to a DNS server that has a reverse lookup zone. Reverse lookup zones provide host name responses to IP address requests. The top-level domain ".arpa" is reserved for reverse or "inverse" address resolution lookups. UNIX reverse lookup zones use the file name "db.address," where the address is the network ID portion of the IP address. Windows reverse lookup zones use the form "address.in-addr.arpa.dns," where "address" is the network ID, only flipped backwards. So, if you had the B class 142.204.0.0 IP address registered and you wanted to build a UNIX reverse lookup zone, the file name would be " db.142.204." The Windows version of the same file would be named "204.142.in-addr.arpa." Notice that the 204.142 is reversed from the actual IP of 142.204.

A Web server that logs the IP address of all visitors could use reverse lookup queries to populate the log file with FQDNs instead.

Most DNS servers in use today have both forward and reverse lookup zones, which are either primary or secondary.

DNS Servers without Zones

Some DNS servers have no zones at all. They are called *caching-only servers*. They forward all client requests to other servers, but remember or cache the answers in case another client asks the same question later. Typically, caching-only servers hold on to cached entries for at least an hour. Caching-only servers are used in situations where DNS name resolution is required, but zone transfer traffic is intolerable. Imagine a situation where 20 clients from a 10,000-user network exist at a remote location, which is connected to the main campus by a limited bandwidth WAN link. In this scenario, regular DNS zone transfers of all 10,000+ records would saturate the WAN link. The load of those 20 users' name queries through a caching-only server could provide acceptable name resolution performance, while eliminating the zone transfer completely.

Building a zone file

A zone file consists of header information and resource records. The header information controls the behavior of the zone, and the resource records comprise the DNS database. The following listing is an example of a typical zone file. Line numbers have been added for your convenience. You will note that remarks follow semicolons. Also, zone file entries that span multiple lines are encased in brackets. Such is the case with Lines 1 through 6.

```
1   @   IN  SOA     tweety.cartoon.com. dnsadmin.cartoon.com. (
2                            20010420           ; serial number
3                            36000              ; refresh   [1h]
4                            600                ; retry     [10m]
5                            86400              ; expire    [1d]
6                            3600 )             ; min TTL   [1h]
```

Every zone file starts with the same type of record: the Start Of Authority (SOA) record. Line 1 shows the SOA record type and the host name of the authoritative server (in this case, tweety.cartoon.com), followed by the e-mail address of the administrator responsible for tweety. Note that the e-mail address uses a period in place of the @ symbol common today. This administrator could be reached by e-mail at dnsadmin@cartoon.com. What follows on Lines 2 through 5 is the zone configuration information.

Line 2 shows the version of the DNS file. This number must be updated each time the file is modified. Secondary name servers use the version field to figure out if they are up-to-date or not. I have set the initial version to today's date; however, other DNS administrators may choose to index by another method.

Line 3 is the refresh interval, in seconds. Because of this setting, secondary name servers for this zone will request a zone transfer every hour.

Line 4 is the retry interval. In case of a failed zone transfer request, the secondary server will wait for the specified amount of time before retrying the transfer request. In this case, the interval is set to 10 minutes.

Line 5 lists the expiry interval, during which a secondary server will keep trying to transfer the zone from its master, while using the current zone file. After the expiry period has lapsed, the secondary server will dump the zone and act as a caching-only server until new zone information can be transferred in.

Line 6 is the minimum Time to Live (Min TTL) interval. Queries that are resolved through communication with other name servers are held in memory in case other resolvers need them, but only for an hour. If another resolver asks for the same host name, in five minutes the name server can use the cached entry rather than consulting other name severs to find the answer.

```
 7  @            IN  NS      tweety.cartoon.com.
 8  @            IN  NS      sylvester.cartoon.com.
 9  tweety       IN  A       192.168.1.7
10  sylvester    IN  A       192.168.1.8
```

Lines 7 and 8 identify tweety and sylvester as name servers for this zone. Notice the NS record type for name server.

Lines 9 and 10 are host or address records that tie or glue tweety and sylvester's host names to their respective IP addresses. These are sometimes referred to as *glue records*.

```
11  localhost    IN  A       127.0.0.1
```

Line 11 allows a DNS query to the local host to work in DNS, even though there is no HOSTS file on the client.

```
12  @            IN  MX      10      tom
13  @            IN  MX      15      jerry
14  tom          IN  A       192.168.1.17
15  gerry        IN  A       192.168.1.18
```

Lines 12 through 15 identify tom and jerry as mail servers. Note that tom is the preferred mail exchanger because of his smaller preference number of 10. Jerry will only get used if tom is unavailable. Lines 14 and 15 glue tom and jerry to their IP addresses.

```
16  bugs         IN  A       192.168.1.135
17  elmer        IN  A       192.168.1.11
```

Lines 16 and 17 are host records for bugs and elmer, which glue them to their respective IP addresses. Since there is no period (.) after these host names, the default domain suffix is implicitly applied, so bugs becomes bugs.cartoon.com, and elmer becomes elmer.cartoon.com, as do the other host entries above for tweety, sylvester, tom, and jerry. If you wanted to place an entry in the zone file for a host from another domain, you could use its FQDN, followed by a period in an A type or host record.

```
18 ftp          IN  CNAME   bugs
19 www          IN  CNAME   elmer
```

Lines 18 and 19 are canonical name (CNAME) records, which allow bugs and elmer to be referenced by nicknames. The nickname for bugs is ftp.cartoon.com, and the nickname for elmer is www.cartoon.com. Since bugs and elmer are already glued to IP addresses in Lines 16 and 17, nothing else is required to make them answer to their nicknames.

If a resolver queried tweety for www.cartoon.com, tweety would look for www in the zone file and find that it points to elmer. Tweety would then look for elmer in the zone file and find that it pointed to 192.168.1.11 (from Line 17). Tweety would then return the answer 192.168.11 to the resolver.

If there were multiple servers hosting our Web site, each of them could have a CNAME record with an alias of www. DNS would balance the load between all the www aliases. This common technique is called DNS "round robin."

If the above sample were a reverse lookup zone file, the header would be just the same, but the records would be different. A reverse lookup zone uses an FQDN as a leaf object. Pointer records (PTR) are used to find the host name for a given IP address.

Our discussion on building a zone file has been basic, but it demonstrates the process of manually creating a zone file, which is still commonplace in many UNIX environments. Many applications — such as Windows DNS servers — have a GUI, which convert graphical input to zone file entries so the administrator need not deal with creating and directly maintaining the zone files themselves.

Iterative and recursive queries

Resolvers send recursive queries to name servers. The term *recursive* probably refers to the fact that the query can cause the name server to recurse the global name space. This is sometimes referred to as "walking the tree." The relationship between the resolver and the name server requires that one of two responses be sent to a name query request: 1) the answer, or 2) an error stating that the host doesn't exist. The name server cannot refer the resolver to another name server. It has to either obtain the answer or find out that there is no answer.

When a name server receives a name query request from a resolver, it checks its name cache, and then its zone file. If neither has an entry for the desired host name or IP address, then the name server uses its cache or root hints file, together with iterative queries, to walk the tree in an effort to find the answer for the resolver. If the answer exists in name space, then walking the tree will find it; however, this process may take some time. Figure 10-5 shows how iterative and recursive queries work:

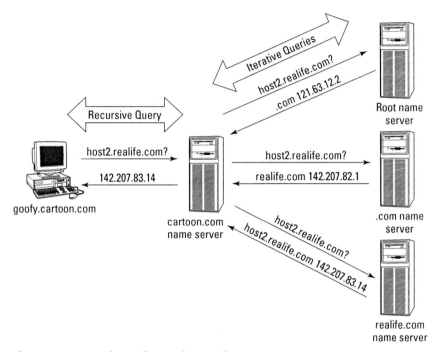

Figure 10-5: Iterative and recursive queries

1. Goofy.cartoon.com queries his name server for the IP address of host2. realife.com.

2. The cartoon.com name server checks to see if it has authority (a zone file) for realife.com. It does not. The name is not in cache either, so the cartoon.com formulates an iterative query, and sends it to one of the root servers listed in its cache file.

3. The root server answers with the best information it has. Since the only part of the host2.realife.com name the root server knows about is the .com part, it answers the query with the IP address for a .com name server, which it finds in its root zone file.

4. The cartoon.com name server once again forwards goofy's request for host2.realife.com, but this time to the .com name server.

5. The .com name server answers with the best information it has. The .com server zone file only has an entry for the realife.com name server; thus, it can only send this information back to the cartoon.com name server.

6. Once again, the cartoon.com name server sends out goofy's request, this time to the realife.com name server, which is authoritative for that domain.

7. The realife.com name server answers with the IP address for host2.realife.com.

8. The cartoon.com name server answers goofy.cartoon.com with the IP address for host2.realife.com.

From the resolver's point of view, his name server knows all the IP addresses and host names in the global name space. The resolver asks the question and gets the answer using a recursive query.

Name servers, on the other hand, have the ability to refer each other based on the best information available. This iterative querying can result in the need to communicate with many name servers to complete a single resolver request.

Configuring DNS using the Berkeley Internet Name Daemon

The Berkeley Internet Name Daemon (BIND) method of DNS configuration is based on the existence of a boot file, which contains the initial startup parameters for the DNS server. Windows DNS servers do not need to use a boot file, since DNS configuration information is kept in the Registry. However, if the existing BIND DNS configuration needs to be ported to a Windows DNS, a boot file can easily be used.

The boot file must be called "boot," and must contain certain commands and arguments. These commands control how DNS starts. There are different styles of boot files for BIND version 4 and version 8. This section will deal with a BIND 4 boot file.

The following is a simple DNS boot file. The line numbers have been inserted only for your convenience. Boot file commands start at the beginning of a line, preceded by no spaces.

```
1. cache      c:\winnt\system32\dns\cache.dns
2. primary    cartoon.com    cartoon.com.dns
3. secondary realife.com    192.168.1.22      db.realife.com
4. forwarder 192.168.1.47   192.168.1.48
5. option     no recursion
```

Line 1 uses the cache command to specify the name of the cache file and the location of the cache file. The cache or root hints file is used to help find a name server for the root domain. Line 2 specifies that the server is authoritative for a primary zone, cartoon.com, whose data is stored in a zone file called cartoon.com.dns. Line 3 specifies that the name server is also authoritative for a secondary zone realife.com, and the local name for caching that zone information. Line 4 specifies a list of name servers, which are willing to try to resolve recursive queries on behalf of this name server. Line 5 uses the option command to specify that the name server should send non-recursive queries to other name servers.

BIND name servers have no choice but to use a boot file for configuration. Windows name servers can be configured from the Registry or boot file. Different versions of Windows DNS servers have varying methods of configuration to allow them to start using a boot file. One method is to use a DNS Registry entry for BootMethod. A value of 1 selects the file method, and a value of 2 selects the Registry method.

Configuring Windows 2000

Windows 2000 DNS has some added features, such as Dynamic DNS, Service Incremental zone transfer, and Active Directory Integrated zones, that need to be configured correctly for proper DNS operation.

Dynamic DNS

The most labor-intensive and error-prone aspect of managing a DNS server is manually entering each resource record. Dynamic DNS (DDNS) solves this problem by allowing the client computer to enter its own resource records in the DNS zones upon power up. Windows 2000 clients have DDNS. Other clients still need to be manually entered; however, if you have implemented a Windows 2000 DHCP server, it can provide DDNS capabilities for non-DDNS clients. DDNS is documented in RFC 2136. Dynamic DNS can be set on a per zone basis. Figure 10-6 shows that cartoon.com is set to use DDNS.

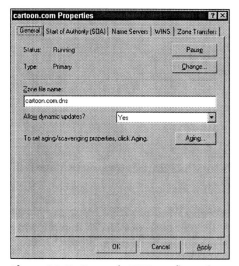

Figure 10-6: Dynamic DNS configuration

Incremental zone transfer

Each Zone file has a serial number field in its Start of Authority record that is used for version control. Since there is only one serial number for the whole file, it is impossible to track changes to individual records with a single value. In the past, a zone transfer included the complete set of records for that zone (regardless of how few or many had changed) with each transfer. This is referred to as an AXFR zone transfer.

RFC 1995 details a new type of zone transfer that only sends the resource records that have changed during each zone transfer. Windows 2000 DNS supports RFS 1995 type zone transfers, as does BIND version 8.

Active Directory Integrated zones

Windows 2000 also supports Active Directory Integrated zones, as well as the Standard Primary and Standard Secondary zones. While Windows 2000 DNS will operate on any Windows 2000 server, Active Directory Integrated zones are only available on Windows 2000 domain controllers. The zone file is not stored in the usual %systemroot%\system32\dns location; rather, it is stored in the Active Directory.

Zones can be changed from Primary to Secondary to AD Integrated and back again. Figure 10-7 shows how to change zone types in Windows 2000 DNS.

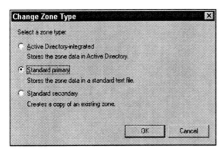

Figure 10-7: Windows 2000 DNS zone types

There are two advantages to Active Directory Integrated zones over Standard zones:

1. The need for DNS zone transfers between Windows 2000 computers is eliminated, since the Active Directory is already replicated to all domain controllers in the domain. Active Directory Integrated zones support zone transfers to BIND secondary servers.

2. DNS dynamic updates can be secured. Each resource record in an AD Integrated zone can be protected by an Access Control List (ACL), which can control who can update or remove that record.

NetBIOS Name Resolution

In addition to the plethora of applications written to the Sockets interface for use on the Internet, there are NetBIOS applications. The word processor and spreadsheet applications in any Windows operating system are probably NetBIOS applications. As a matter of fact, once upon a time, Windows operating systems only had a NetBIOS application interface. To use an Internet application such as a Web browser, a Sockets interface had to be added on. We remember using Trumpet Winsock to supplement the TCP/IP protocol suite we *purchased* for Windows 3.1 for Internet access.

Although NetBIOS was originally developed for IBM in 1983, every Microsoft operating system we ever worked with has used NetBIOS. NetBIOS was responsible for putting the workgroups in Windows for Workgroups. It is generally implemented both as a session layer protocol and as an Application Programming Interface (API).

NetBIOS applications are written to use friendly names as end points for communication, instead of using IP addresses. TPC/IP is then responsible for converting the user-friendly NetBIOS name to network-friendly IP addresses similar to DNS. NetBIOS Name Resolution is detailed in RFC 1001 and RFC 1002, which were written in March 1987 to detail recommendations for implementing NetBIOS in a TCP/IP environment.

What is a NetBIOS name?

NetBIOS names can represent many things: users, computers, workgroups, NT services, and even domains. All of these objects have one thing in common — they can be end points for communication. NetBIOS applications use NetBIOS names to communicate.

A Windows computer has a computer name, and when that computer shares folders over the network, the NetBIOS computer name is used to find the list of shared folders available on that Windows computer. Network printers are identified on the network by NetBIOS names. Windows NT domains are NetBIOS names, as are workgroups. All of the "net" utilities from the Server Message Block protocol (SMB), Explorer, and File Manager use NetBIOS names to communicate.

Figure 10-8 demonstrates that almost everything on a Windows network has a NetBIOS name. UNIX hosts do not use NetBIOS names, because they do not communicate using the Server Message Block protocol. However, many UNIX operating systems will support an add-on application called SAMBA, which enables them to communicate using NetBIOS names and the SMB protocol.

NetBIOS names are:

- ✦ not case-sensitive
- ✦ less than 15 characters in length

✦ padded to 15 characters and followed by a hexadecimal number when used to describe an NT service

✦ alphanumeric, with no spaces, periods, or symbols

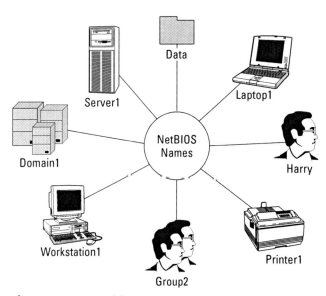

Figure 10-8: NetBIOS names

Microsoft's networking components

Most operating systems have clearly defined roles for communication between the various elements that make up the network structure. Servers listen for calls from requestors, but don't make calls for resources themselves. Clients request the use of server resources, but don't advertise their own capabilities. In UNIX and NetWare operating systems, a server is only a server and a client is only a client, but that is not so for Microsoft operating systems.

With the development of Windows for Workgroups, Microsoft introduced a different communication model: the workgroup. All members of a workgroup could have both a server and a requestor component active on the same computer. This communication model continues to be popular. Even though domains have by and large replaced workgroups, the communication model has persevered: each computer on the network is capable of acting as a server or a requestor.

The most basic Microsoft networking components include a server and a workstation (other components include messaging and browsing components). These components are implemented as services or individual files, depending on the operating system used. Some Windows NT networking components are exposed to the operating system as file systems and to the network as services. These services use the NetBIOS names of the user, computer, workgroup, or domain, with special numeric identifiers to communicate and be identified on the network. So, while a NetBIOS computer only has one computer name (unlike a UNIX system, which may have many host names), the NetBIOS computer will probably use upwards of six different NetBIOS names to identify its components to the network. Refer to Table 10-1 for common NetBIOS Services.

Table 10-1
Common NetBIOS Services

Service Name	NetBIOS Name	Numeric Suffix	Type
Workstation	Computer name	00	Unique
Server	Computer name	20	Unique
Master Browser	Domain name	1B	Unique
Force Election	Workgroup or domain	1E	Unique
Domain Controller	Domain	1C	Group
Messaging	User, computer, or domain	03	Unique

Upon system power up, NetBIOS names are registered with the local NetBIOS name service and, optionally, with a configured NetBIOS name server. The local NetBIOS name service or configured name server makes sure that there are no duplicate unique NetBIOS names. The service can issue error messages and deny registration if duplicate name registration attempts occur.

Resolving NetBIOS names — Pre-Windows 2000

Prior to Windows 2000, Microsoft Networking used NetBIOS. To effect communication over the network, the destination NetBIOS name needs to be converted to an IP address. The following methods are commonly used for NetBIOS name to IP address resolution.

Broadcast

The most basic NetBIOS name resolution method is to broadcast the NetBIOS name of the desired destination host, and hope that the host responds with its IP address. This method is commonly used in very small (one segment) environments, because routers generally discard NetBIOS broadcasts.

WINS

RFC 1002 defines a NetBIOS Name Server (NBNS), an application that can accept NetBIOS registrations from numerous segments by allowing clients to use directed traffic to register instead of broadcasts. The Windows Internet Name Server is Microsoft's NBNS. WINS clients register their NetBIOS names at power up. They can also query the WINS database for name resolution of other registered names.

LMHOSTS

The LMHOSTS file is a simple text file located in the drivers\etc folder on a NetBIOS client that contains IP addresses to NetBIOS name mappings of computers on remote segments. The LMHOSTS file acts much the same way as a HOSTS file, except that the LMHOSTS file is only used for remote names. During name resolution, the LMHOSTS file is parsed from top to bottom. If a duplicate entry exists, only the uppermost entry in the LMHOSTS file will be used. Thus, it is important to test each new entry by using a "net use" command.

HOSTS

If the system is configured to do so, the locally stored HOSTS file can be used for NetBIOS name resolution. It is located in the drivers\etc folder and is parsed once from top to bottom.

DNS

If the client is properly configured, a DNS server can be used for NetBIOS name resolution. Figure 10-9 shows the required NetBIOS configuration controls for an NT client.

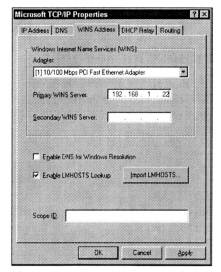

Figure 10-9: NetBIOS name resolution controls

The Primary and Secondary WINS Servers dialog boxes will contain the IP address of at least one WINS server to enable WINS registrations and queries. Towards the bottom, the Enable LMHOSTS Lookup check box allows you to control whether or not the LMHOSTS file is parsed during name resolution. Finally, the Enable DNS for Windows resolution check box allows HOSTS files and DNS to be used to resolve NetBIOS names with the same spelling.

Since there are numerous tools available for NetBIOS name resolution (for effective troubleshooting), make sure you are clear on the order in which they are used. NetBIOS applications use NetBIOS name resolution. Winsock applications use HOSTS files and DNS. Thus, to examine the order of name resolution, you need to start a NetBIOS application. Explorer, File Manager, or even a "net use" command will do; however, don't use ping ftp or telnet, as they are Sockets applications.

Using Figure 10-10 as a reference, take a look at how COMPUTER2 attempts to resolve the NetBIOS name COMPUTER3.

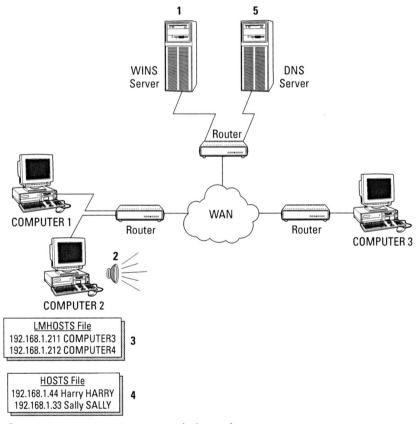

Figure 10-10: NetBIOS name resolution order

The user at COMPUTER2 has just issued the command `net use x: \\COMPUTER3\ APPLICATIONS` in an attempt to map x: to the applications share on COMPUTER3. If COMPUTER2 had connected to COMPUTER3 in the last few minutes, the NetBIOS name mapping would be retained in COMPUTER2's NetBIOS name cache; however, this is not the case.

1. Since there is no locally cached entry for COMPUTER3 and COMPUTER2 is configured as a WINS client, COMPUTER2 formulates a NetBIOS name query request and sends the query to its WINS server. The WINS server is available. If the server has an entry in its WINS database for the server service at COMPUTER3, the associated IP address will be sent back to COMPUTER2 in a name query response, and communication will commence. The WINS server has no entry for COMPUTER3.

2. COMPUTER2 formulates a broadcast for the local NetBIOS name service, which contains the name COMPUTER3. If COMPUTER3 is on the local segment, it will answer this broadcast with its IP address, and communications will commence. Clearly, COMPUTER3 is not on the same segment as COMPUTER2.

3. COMPUTER2 parses the locally stored LMHOSTS file once from top to bottom. There is a COMPUTER3 entry in the LMHOSTS file. The IP address next to that entry will be used to set up communications with COMPUTER3. However, if there were no entry for COMPUTER3, the process would continue.

4. If COMPUTER2 is configured to use DNS for Windows Networking, then COMPUTER2 will parse the locally stored HOSTS file in the hopes that it will contain a host name that matches COMPUTER3. If there is a match, then the IP address next to COMPUTER3 will be used to set up a session.

5. If parsing the HOSTS file fails to produce a match and COMPUTER2 is configured as a resolver, then COMPUTER2 will send a query to its configured DNS server for COMPUTER3. If the DNS server responds with an answer, then the IP address in the answer will be used to set up communications with COMPUTER3.

If all these methods fail to resolve COMPUTER3's IP address, then COMPUTER2 will display an error, and no further action will take place.

NetBIOS node types

The order of name resolution methods for WINS and broadcast can be switched by modifying the client NetBIOS node type.

RFC 1002 specifies four NetBIOS node types: B for Broadcast only, P for NBNS only, H for NBNS then Broadcast, and M for Broadcast then NBNS. NetBIOS node type is configurable through DHCP options or manually.

Microsoft enhances the four RFC-compliant node types by adding capabilities to use the LMHOSTS file, WINS proxies, and Windows Socket calls, which allow DNS and HOSTS files to be used for NetBIOS name resolution.

We have shown that a client running a NetBIOS application uses name resolution methods in a specified order. That name resolution order can be modified to suit the surrounding network conditions by manipulation of the NetBIOS node type. Node types are really only used to control the order in which clients use WINS or broadcasting.

Table 10-2 shows the effect on name resolution of the four NetBIOS node types.

Table 10-2 NetBIOS Node Types	
Node Type	*Name Resolution Order*
B-Node	Broadcast only
P-Node	NBNS only
H-Node	NBNS, then broadcast
M-Node	Broadcast, then NBNS

If your network does not use a NBNS, then it is most likely to use broadcast node types, which is the Windows default.

Imagine that we are about to implement WINS in a 600-user, single location, three-subnet LAN. We are unsure of the load that will be placed on our WINS server, so implementing WINS on all clients at once is undesirable. How would we go about the implementation?

One way of implementing WINS is to manually configure all clients. While this approach allows for an incremental implementation, it is unrealistic for a 600-client network.

A better approach might be to use the DHCP servers on each subnet to configure all the clients for WINS, one subnet at a time. This is still a staggered implementation, but much less labor-intensive. The DHCP approach can also be used to modify the client node type. Based on the requirement of staggered client implementation, M-node type might be the best initial setting.

With M-node type set at the client only, name resolution requests that fail broadcast will be sent to the WINS server. This could significantly reduce the load on the server. As the implementation goes on and all subnets are WINS-enabled, the choice to switch to H-node type can be made based on the load on the WINS server.

Administrators of some networks have declared war on broadcast traffic. They may choose to implement the P-node type, which will cause the clients to use WINS only — not broadcast at all.

Resolving NetBIOS names in Windows 2000

NetBIOS is optional in Windows 2000, but DNS is mandatory. In a pure Windows 2000 environment, NetBIOS is unnecessary. The primary object identification tool changed in Windows 2000 from WINS to DNS.

The methods used to resolve NetBIOS names in Windows 2000 are similar to the standard methods described above, with a few differences.

First, NetBIOS can be turned off or controlled by dynamic configuration information received from DHCP. Figure 10-11 shows the configuration screen that controls NetBIOS functionality on a Windows 2000 professional client. The LMHOSTS lookup is controlled from this screen.

 Cross-Reference   For more information on the Dynamic Host Configuration Protocol (DHCP), see Chapter 9.

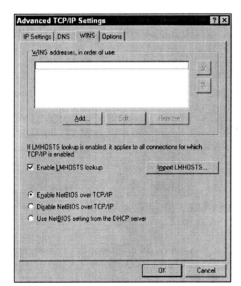

Figure 10-11: NetBIOS configuration on Windows 2000

If NetBIOS is turned on, then all four of the RFC-compliant node types apply; however, the Enable DNS for Windows Resolution dialog box is missing in Windows 2000. If you want to use DNS or a HOSTS file for Windows resolution in Windows 2000, then you will need to edit the local registry for Netbt\parameters to include an EnableDns entry, and a value of 1.

Even when NetBIOS is not turned on, the SMB protocol still functions, due to a new interface in Windows 2000 called the SMB device. This interface allows Windows

Networking connections without NetBIOS. It works like a Sockets application, in that it uses DNS and HOSTS files natively, and runs on TCP port 445 instead of the standard NetBIOS TCP port 139.

Finally, Windows 2000 NetBIOS over TCP/IP checks the NetBIOS name for the presence of a period (.) or more than 15 characters. If either condition is present, DNS is used first to resolve the name, and NetBIOS after.

The following steps demonstrate how NetBIOS name resolution works on a Windows 2000 computer. (We will assume that NetBIOS is turned on, that the application being used is a NetBIOS application, and that a name has been entered in the application.)

1. The NetBIOS node type of the local computer is checked.

2. The incoming name is checked for length and content. The usual NetBIOS name resolution methods are used, starting with the NetBIOS name cache, then WINS and/or Broadcast — depending on the NetBIOS node type. If the name is over 15 characters in length or contains a period, then a standard DNS query is sent out because the name is assumed to be a host name.

3. If the DNS query fails, then the usual NetBIOS name resolution methods are used, starting with the NetBIOS name cache, then WINS and/or Broadcast — depending on the NetBIOS node type.

4. If all the other methods fail, then the LMHOSTS file will be parsed if LMHOSTS lookup is enabled (refer to Figure 10-11).

5. If the EnableDns registry setting is entered and enabled on the local computer, then the HOSTS file will be parsed to resolve the NetBIOS name.

6. Finally, if the HOSTS file lookup fails, then DNS will be tried again.

If all these methods fail to resolve the NetBIOS name to an IP address, then an error message will be sent to the local computer and resolution will fail.

Summary

This chapter took you on a tour of the Domain Name System (DNS). First, we examined the traditional method of resolving names with HOSTS and LMHOSTS files. Then, we discussed NetBIOS names and resolution methods, and it was shown that NetBIOS uses everything but the kitchen sink to resolve an IP address. Finally, it's important to view the changes that Windows 2000 brought to name resolution methods.

An experienced network troubleshooter knows what type of application he is dealing with and what order it uses for name resolution. The ability to distinguish application types is one of the most valuable network troubleshooting skills that you can develop.

✦   ✦   ✦

Common TCP/IP Applications

Now that TCP/IP is installed and running, it is time to examine some of the ways it can be used. Part III discusses the various applications that you can use with the TCP/IP protocol to provide functionality on the network.

Chapter 11 shows you how to connect your network to the Internet and how to build your own network using point-to-point technologies. From there, the discussion shifts to moving data across your network and to the Internet, which includes moving files (Chapter 12), print jobs (Chapter 14), Web pages (Chapter 15), and other media over the network both directly and using multicasting.

Chapter 13 discusses how to use a system remotely, examining simple protocols, such as Telnet, and more complicated solutions, like terminal servers. Chapter 17 focuses on enterprise information systems, including NIS, STDS, NDS, and AD, all of which are based on X.500.

Providing Internet Access

The Internet has become a ubiquitous presence, invading every aspect of modern life from learning to entertainment. Since most products and services are now available online, it has even revolutionized the way we conduct business. In fact, Internet access is becoming less of a privilege and more of a necessity. As a result, more and more individuals and corporations (big and small) are connecting to the Internet.

The best feature of the Internet is that it has an "open culture," which causes some people to refer to it as "Utopia" or "true democracy." However, this very availability and accessibility can be detrimental, since certain people take advantage of the Internet for their own selfish or malicious reasons. For example, the Internet has emerged as the most popular medium for spreading viruses that can bring down an entire corporate network. As a result, more and more networks belonging to companies and corporations are under the constant threat of having their sensitive data stolen, damaged, or tampered with.

In this chapter, you will learn about the private networks belonging to companies and organizations. You'll learn the addressing scheme used in private networks and the limitations imposed by the current IPv4 addressing scheme. You'll learn to connect to the Internet using the account and gateway facility provided by Internet Service Providers (ISPs) that allow a company or an individual to connect to the most famous network of all, the Internet. You'll also learn about the fast emerging Application Service Providers (ASPs) that lease various softwares, ranging from Windows to highly complex and expensive Enterprise Resource Planning (ERP) to organizations. Connecting to the Internet can pose a major security risk to a network. You'll learn about firewalls that secure a company's network from unauthorized access and hackers.

Next, you'll learn about Network Address Translation (NAT) and how it helps network administrators combat the ever-threatening problems of rapidly depleting IP addresses and increasing vulnerability of a network to malicious attacks. You'll also learn about Proxy servers and Microsoft's Internet Connection sharing. Finally, you'll learn about fast-emerging and highly secure Virtual Private Networks (VPNs), which allow globally distributed corporate networks to exchange sensitive data securely and economically.

Overview of Private and Public Internetworks

With the worldwide acceptance of TCP/IP as a networking standard, an extremely large number of networks have been using TCP/IP and its addressing capabilities for internetwork, as well as intranet, communications. In a TCP/IP network, hosts can be divided into three categories:

✦ Those that do not need to access remote resources and services provided by hosts in another network or on the Internet itself.

✦ Those that need to access limited resources or services provided by "trusted" networks or hosts outside their own network. These services might include e-mail, FTP, remote login, and so on.

✦ Those that need constant and unlimited access to resources and services provided by other networks or hosts outside their native network.

The hosts in the first and second categories belong to a *private network*. A good example of a private network is the network found in a banking organization, where branch offices may be located in different cities all over the world. For successful operation, the networks of all the branches need to be interconnected. However, to ensure the sanctity and security of transactions and data, "outsiders" should not be allowed access to the network. Hosts belonging to the third category constitute the *public network*. The Internet, which can be accessed by anyone from anywhere, is one of the best-known examples of a public network.

Each device on a TCP/IP-based network is assigned a unique IP address for the purpose of identification and proper operation. All the computers in a public network use the globally unique IP addresses assigned by an Internet registry. They can communicate with all the computers that belong to the network, as well as with computers belonging to other public networks. However, they do not have connectivity to computers in a private network.

 Note Several authorized entities, such as InterNIC, are responsible for the distribution of IP addresses to Internet Service Providers (ISPs) and companies to ensure that addresses assigned over the Internet and other public networks are unique.

For the sake of convenience, complete control, and cost reduction, many companies implement their own IP addressing scheme within their private network. This addressing scheme is effective until the independently addressed network needs to communicate with other networks. Moving a computer from a private domain to a public domain, or vice versa, involves a change in its IP address, changes to DNS entries, and changes to other files on other computers that reference the given computer by IP address.

Cross-Reference For more information on DNS, refer to Chapter 10.

Private network addressing

A private network uses *non-routable addresses*, also known as *private IP addresses*. As the name suggests, routers do not pass traffic to these IP addresses. These addresses cannot be routed on the Internet and other public networks. In a sense, a private network is "cut off" from other networks and the Internet.

The Internet Assigned Numbers Authority (IANA) has reserved three blocks of non-routable addresses for the use of private networks:

   ✦ 10.0.0.0 to 10.255.255.255

   ✦ 172.16.0.0 to 172.31.255.255

   ✦ 192.168.0.0 to 192.168.255.255

Note For more information on private network addresses, refer to RFC 1918.

The addresses in the first block belong to a single class A network, while the addresses in the second block are a set of 16 contiguous class B network numbers. The addresses in the third block are a set of 256 contiguous class C network numbers. Any private network can use these three address-blocks for addressing purposes. That is, addresses within this private address space are unique only within the private network or set of networks that need to communicate with each other in their own private internetwork. Private addresses have no global meaning outside the network. As a result, routing information related to private networks is not propagated on internetwork links, and data packets with private source or destination addresses are not forwarded to routers. Generally, routers of public networks, especially those of ISPs, are configured to reject the routing information about private networks.

Note According to RFC 1918, if a router of a public network receives information regarding private networks, the rejection of such information is not treated as a routing protocol error.

Computers in a private network can communicate with all other computers within the private network. Although they can't access computers outside their network or a trusted network, they still have access to external services through gateways. In contrast, in the case of public networks, a globally unique address space is required, which can be obtained from an Internet registry. IP addresses requested for external connectivity are never assigned addresses from the block of non-routable addresses.

For more information on IP addressing and IP address classes (A, B, and C), see Chapter 5.

Guidelines for designing a private network

Several points should be kept in mind when designing a private network:

✦ In today's scenario, more than one computer may need to be connected to the Internet or other public networks on a full-time basis, even if it is a part of a private network. With this in mind, the best strategy would be to first design the private part of the network, and then the public subnet.

The private network design should not be permanent, as one or more computers may need to change their status from private to public, or vice versa. Hence, it is advisable to group hosts with similar connectivity requirements in a separate subnet. This helps a network administrator avoid major network disruptions.

✦ Placement of hosts with public and private addresses on the same physical medium should be avoided.

✦ Routers that connect a private network to other networks, especially public networks, should be configured with appropriate packet and routing filters at both ends. This helps prevent packet and routing information leakage.

✦ If two private networks communicate with each other via an untrusted public network, they should implement data encapsulation, thereby minimizing the risk of unauthorized access.

An untrusted network is an external network whose data cannot be considered trustworthy and secure.

✦ To prevent address clashes when two private networks communicate with each other, an organization should choose randomly from the pool of reserved private addresses.

For more information on subnets, see Chapter 5.

Advantages and disadvantages of private network addressing

There are several advantages of using the private address space:

✦ It helps conserve fast-dwindling globally unique addresses because it only uses them when required.

✦ It enables creation of operationally and administratively convenient addressing schemes and easier growth paths due to the fact that network administrators have more address space at their disposal than what is available in the globally unique pool.

✦ It provides security by preventing unauthorized access, because the network is not "visible" to outsiders.

Using the private address space has some major disadvantages:

✦ Address-related problems can arise when connecting to other networks or the Internet. Suppose a private network uses IP addresses that weren't assigned by IANA or any other Internet registry. It's possible that the address space it uses was legally assigned to other network(s). So, this private network later connects to the Internet and address clashes may occur, resulting in serious routing problems.

✦ If a private network connects to the Internet and other public networks, it would need to re-address some or all computers that belong to it, creating extra expenditure to the company. The cost of re-addressing is directly proportional to the number of hosts that need to undergo the transition from private to public.

Tip   The problem of re-addressing can be alleviated by the use of the Network Address Translation (NAT) mechanism.

✦ In the case of a merger of two or more private networks, some addresses in the resulting network may not be unique. Once again, the necessity to re-address computers with clashing addresses arises.

✦ Administrative responsibilities increase in a private network, because all the computers need to be assigned a unique IP address from the private address space. The larger the number of hosts that need to be addressed, the greater the overhead on the network administrator(s).

In the past few years, especially in the last decade, Internet usage has exploded. Companies that wanted to maintain the privacy of their intranet have now turned towards the Internet for global connectivity. However, the Internet's tremendous growth has posed a few scaling problems and exposed a few loopholes in the current IP addressing scheme.

The limitations of IPv4

IP version 4 (IPv4), popularly known as IP, was designed in the late 1970s and has served as the basic communication mechanism of the TCP/IP protocol suite. In fact, it is the most popular communication mechanism over the Internet. Its design is so stable, powerful, and flexible that it has remained virtually unchanged until now.

Note   Although different versions of IP had been developed before IPv4, they were never formally named.

In the past decade, IT technology has advanced in leaps and bounds. Processor speed has increased. Computers are available with RAM in gigabytes. Faster LAN technologies, such as ATM and FDDI, have been taking over older and slower technologies, such as the Ethernet. And most importantly, the number of hosts (or computers) on the Internet has crossed the 100 million mark. Recent research estimates that the Internet is doubling in size every nine months. As a result of this technological growth, IPv4 — in spite of its sound design — has experienced two major scaling issues as it simultaneously struggles to keep up with the fast advancing technology and provide continuous and uninterrupted growth:

✦ **The eventual exhaustion of the address space.** IPv4 was designed to provide a 32-bit address space. This means there are *only* 4,294,967,296 (2^{32}) IP addresses available. Initially, when only a few organizations used LANs, and still fewer had access to corporate WANs, this seemed like a huge address space. However, with the projected growth of the Internet, this finite number of IP addresses will eventually be exhausted. In addition, portions of the IP address space have not been efficiently allocated. If current allocation policies are not changed soon, new users may be unable to connect to the Internet at all.

✦ **The growth in the size of the Internet routing tables.** Routers on the Internet need to maintain complete routing information. In recent years, the size of these routing tables has grown exponentially, as more and more individuals and organizations keep connecting to the Internet. Factors (such as the CPU's capability to process route-related changes, the dynamic nature of internetwork connections, the effect of the dynamic nature of routes on the cache, and the sheer volume of information that needs to be manually and mechanically managed) also add to the problem. This growth cannot be dealt with simply by installing more router memory or by increasing the size of the routing table. If the number of entries in the global routing tables is allowed to increase without any restrictions, Internet backbone routers will be forced to drop routes, making portions of the Internet unreachable.

Internet organizations, especially the Internet Engineering Task Force (IETF) and the Internet Architecture Board (IAB), have been working on IPv4-related problems for some years. As a result of their efforts, the limitations of IPv4 have been worked out in a new version of IP known as *IP version 6 (IPv6)* or *IP Next Generation (IPng)*.

IPv6 addresses all the problems posed by IPv4. It supports 128-bit addresses, flexible header format, support for resource allocation, and provision for further extension of protocol. However, it will take a few years before the existing network infrastructure migrates to IPv6.

A network using private addresses is called a private network, whereas a network using non-private IP addresses is called a public network. The difference between private and public networks is depicted in Table 11-1.

Table 11-1 Public versus Private Networks	
Private Networks	**Public Networks**
A private network is information owned, operated, and managed by a single organization and operates autonomously from the other networks.	A public network is owned by the intermediary carrier, such as a Public Services Telephone Network (PSTN).
The connectivity to external networks and public networks such as the Internet is limited and closely controlled.	The connectivity to other networks is unlimited.
A private network is highly secure from malicious attacks, such as virus attacks and hackers.	A public network is extremely vulnerable to virus attacks and hackers.

Today, you can easily access the Internet either from home or work. In the case of large companies, accessibility is provided via private gateway(s). Small companies usually take advantage of the services of *Internet Service Providers (ISPs)*, commercial companies that provide Internet connectivity to its clients. If you connect from home, you will also use the services of an ISP — all you need is a telephone line, modem, and an active account with an ISP.

Connecting to the Internet

Generally, you connect to the Internet for services such as e-mail, FTP, Telnet, World Wide Web (WWW), chat, and Usenet newsgroups. Depending on your amount of Internet usage and the types of services you need to access, you should carefully choose the way you want to get connected — there is an overwhelming number of companies and entities in the market.

Caution Although every ISP promises to provide all services and types of access, this is not always the case. Therefore, carefully select the provider that meets your requirements.

To access various services, you can connect to the Internet in a variety of ways:

✦ **Directly with a dedicated computer** — Though expensive, this method provides full access to all the services on the Internet. This method is recommended for large corporations.

✦ **Via remote gateway** — A very economical method, using someone else's direct connection to the Internet backbone. It allows full access to all the Internet services. This method is recommended for students who can use a university's gateway or for company employees who can use the organization's gateway to access the Internet.

✦ **Through an ISP or an online service provider** — This method allows access to the Internet after paying for the monthly connection and usage costs to an individual or commercial setup. Depending on the ISP or the online service provider, you can have full access to the Internet services, or access to some services might be restricted. This method is recommended for people who connect to the Internet from their homes.

✦ **Free Internet access** — This method is an alternative when deciding on a method of connecting to the Internet. The ISPs and online service providers generally offer this method to attract customers. The only expense for the user is that telephone charges are incurred while working on the Internet. Access is paid for by advertisers. The disadvantage of free access is that online time is highly limited, and the user doesn't have a choice of services.

Only large companies and corporations can bear the cost of setting up the infrastructure to connect permanently to the Internet. Therefore, if you are looking for a way to connect to the Internet as an individual user, finding an ISP, online service provider, or permission to use a remote gateway might be your best choice. However, to use someone's infrastructure, you must either be a student or an employee of the company that provides you the Internet connectivity.

For users who access the Internet from home for personal reasons, an ISP or an online service provider is the best solution. Both types of provider allow users to work on the Internet at their own pace. However, keep these points in mind:

✦ Some ISPs and online service providers do not provide full access to all the services.

✦ Connection and usage charges can be very high. Make sure you examine these charges carefully before signing up.

✦ Check the access speed that the ISP or online service provider is offering. If the offered access speed is 9600 baud or less, you should probably look for a different ISP.

Caution

If you frequently access the Internet from your home, you may end up paying huge fees to your ISP or online service provider.

After you have got the required infrastructure in place and connectivity to the Internet, you need to configure the connectivity software provided by your ISP for login name and the dial-up telephone number. After this, you need to follow the steps given below to connect to the Internet:

1. If you are using a dial-up connection, run the software provided by the ISP to establish the connection.

2. If the connection to the ISP's gateway is established successfully, you will be prompted for the password to your Internet account. If the password you supplied is correct, you are connected to the Internet.

You may not be prompted for a password if you have already configured the connection software with the password.

3. Now, you can run the applications that let you use various services provided by the ISP. You can run an Internet browser (Internet Explorer, Netscape Navigator, and so on) to browse various sites available on the Internet, run a chat program to chat with people, or access your mail.

If you are accessing the Internet through your company's or university's gateway (or leased line), you may not need to perform these steps.

Internet Service Providers

Internet Service Providers (ISPs) are the companies that provide *metered Internet access* to small commercial setups and individual users generally accessing the Internet from home. ISPs provide connectivity to the Internet by sharing their Internet gateways or routers with their clients. However, because the user needs to sign up with the ISP and is required to pay for the monthly connection and usage, the access is considered *metered.*

If you need to stay logged in to the Internet for long periods of time, metered access is not recommended, since it can be expensive. Metered access is best for users who want to access the Internet from home for entertainment, personal amusement, or occasional use.

When you contact an ISP for an Internet account, make sure you obtain the following information to be able to successfully connect to the Internet:

✦ User name or login ID

✦ Password

✦ Dial-up phone number

✦ Host and domain names

✦ Address of the DNS server

✦ IP address and subnet mask, if any

✦ Gateway address

✦ Authentication process

Tip   You should use Point-to-Point Protocol (PPP) accounts, if your ISP offers them. They are much faster than Serial Line Interface Protocol (SLIP) accounts.

Various ISPs offer different service packages according to the requirements of the users. Some ISPs provide all the services, while some do not. You should choose a package that best suits your needs. Keep in mind that the connection speed is highly dependent on the connection lines provided by the ISP. Also, be wary of any policies that may seem arbitrary. If you don't understand a policy, be sure to clarify it to your satisfaction, or you might end up paying more money than you want to.

An end user can connect to an ISP with any type of computer (PC, Macintosh, or UNIX-based). All that is required is telephone connectivity, a modem, a valid ISP account, and software that supports the connection protocols. Users generally connect to an ISP with a *dial-up connection*, which means that the user needs to dial a number provided by the ISP using the modem. After users are connected to the ISP, they are connected to the Internet, most commonly with the *Point-to-Point Protocol (PPP)* or *Serial Line Interface Protocol (SLIP)*. Since many users just need e-mail service, some ISPs also support *Unix-to-Unix Copy Protocol (UUCP)*.

Note   A large selection of software packages is available that helps a user connect to an ISP. You should choose the package that is preconfigured for the operating system you use. MKS's Internet Anywhere and Microsoft's Dialup Networking are popular dial-up software. However, Microsoft's Dialup Networking is available only with Windows operating systems.

Most of us think of connecting to the Internet as a "one-way" process. We forget that while our computer is connected to the Internet, anyone with access to the Internet can also access our computer and its resources (files, e-mails, and so on). Most computers are vulnerable, since the basic computer architecture does not provide support against outside attacks. Moreover, software technologies such as Java and ActiveX actually bring down the level of security, because they tend to take control of the computer's environment and resources while they execute on it. Most of the time, it is not even possible to detect such controls, especially Java applets, while they are executing on a computer. You may just visit a site and the applets get automatically loaded and start executing. This situation can lead to serious security hazards, as sensitive information — related to individuals as well as the company — can be stolen.

A firewall is an effective means of protecting a network from most Internet security threats. It prevents unauthorized access to a network or a computer. When a system is under attack, firewalls keep damage on one part of the network (e.g., eavesdropping, a worm program, file damage) from spreading to the rest of the network. Without firewalls, network security problems can rage out of control, dragging more and more systems down.

Using a Firewall

Connecting a company's private network to the Internet and other public networks poses a high security risk because of the possibility of unauthorized access, such as hacker attacks. Such untrustworthy access can lead to network crashes, which may take a day or more to be rectified. As a result, a company may face huge losses, not to mention the compromise of confidentiality, if it fails to properly secure its network. The solution to the detrimental effects of security breaches is provided by *firewalls*.

Note   According to a survey conducted by Warroom Research, Inc., 58 percent of companies polled (236 total) reported hacker attacks on their networks in a twelve-month period. 57 percent of the companies were attacked at least 11 times in the specified time period. One-third of these attacks cost the companies at least one million dollars in damage repair.

Role of firewalls

Firewalls are the access-control mechanisms that produce a secure network by screening the network or organization from unwanted access. A firewall is basically a router or set of routers that is installed at the point where the private network is connected to the public network. The placement of the firewall system is depicted in Figure 11-1. The computers on the private network are not directly exposed to the "outer" world. Any malicious attempt to access them would require getting through the firewall. Thus, a firewall acts as a buffer between a private network and a public network, such as the Internet. In other words, a firewall protects a network from untrustworthy access.

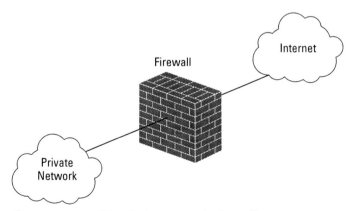

Figure 11-1: Traditional placement of a firewall system

Usually, the firewall routers use an *access control policy* (or simply, *access lists*) to secure a network. This access control policy is based on a pair of mechanisms — one that is responsible for blocking unwanted traffic, and the other for permitting the rest of the "harmless" traffic into the network. If the access control policy is not clear (in other words, if the network administrators do not have a clear idea about what traffic to allow and what to deny), a firewall will not be very useful.

Tip   In addition to acting as a security blanket for an organization's intranet, a firewall can also be used to separate sensitive portions of a network from its users, even if they are trusted. For example, the part of the network used by the Human Resources Department can be placed behind a firewall to protect sensitive payroll and personnel information from the rest of the organization. This type of firewall is often referred to as the *intranet firewall*.

A packet-filtering router or set of routers, along with *bastion hosts*, can be used to set up a firewall system. A bastion host is a highly secure host (or server) that allows limited access to outsiders. Any outsider can access specific data or applications on the host, but with limited rights so that they would not be able to harm the system. Web servers, anonymous FTP servers, Domain Naming Servers (DNSs), and Terminal Access Controller Access Control System (TACACS) nodes are a few examples of bastion hosts.

Besides controlling and logging traffic between networks, a firewall may perform other functions, such as:

✦ Creating Virtual Private Networks (VPNs)

✦ Supporting e-mail virus scanning

✦ Uniform Resource Locator (URL) filtering, by denying access to unauthorized sites

✦ Application filtering, by blocking unauthorized access to remote applications that may be unsafe for the network

Although firewalls are a powerful mechanism for preventing private networks from malicious "outside" accesses and attacks, they cannot protect an organization's resources from all attacks and break-ins.

✦ Firewalls do not offer any protection against attacks that were initiated from within the network they are protecting. They can only offer perimeter security.

✦ Firewalls cannot handle malicious codes, Trojan horses, or viruses since there are too many ways of encoding binary files for transfers over networks. Also, the sheer number of viruses is overwhelming. However, these threats can be reduced to some extent by installing powerful anti-virus software on the firewall, as well as on each network computer, which is susceptible to *data-driven attacks*. In data-driven attacks, viruses and other malicious codes are mailed or copied to an internal host.

✦ Firewalls may not be configured correctly. After a firewall is configured, the testing and verification of the rules is often ignored. Configuration changes must be applied to a running firewall, and logs should be carefully and constantly monitored to confirm that rules are being applied correctly.

Types of firewalls

Conceptually, three types of firewalls function at various levels of the OSI reference model: *packet filter firewalls, stateful packet inspection firewalls,* and *application proxy firewalls.* The packet filter firewalls function at Layer 3 of the OSI model, whereas stateful packet inspection and application proxy firewalls function at Layers 5 to 7. Many commercially available firewalls are striving to use a combination of two or more of these types. An administrator must carefully determine the organization's security requirements and choose a firewall accordingly.

Tip
One rule of thumb is that the lower the OSI layer at which the firewall functions, the less capable the firewall is, since it can perform only limited examination of the incoming traffic.

Future firewalls are being designed that combine the best features of existing firewalls. The goal is to create fast packet-screening firewalls that log and audit the traffic passing through them. Also, firewalls are increasingly incorporating end-to-end encryption to protect traffic passing through them over the Internet. Such firewalls are referred to as *hybrid firewalls* since they combine the features of all the existing firewalls. Though more expensive than the rest, they are extremely effective and are recommended by the experts.

Packet filter firewalls

Whether it's trying to reach another computer two feet away or two continents apart, every IP packet must contain a destination address and port number. Every packet must also contain the IP address and port number of the originating machine, so the receiving computer knows who sent the packet. In other words, any packet traveling the Internet contains—first and foremost—its complete source and destination addresses.

Cross-Reference
For more information on IP packets, see Chapter 5.

The packet filter firewalls decide whether to "deny" or "permit" a packet based on the following information carried by the packet:

✦ Source address

✦ Destination address

✦ Port (source as well as destination)

A router belongs to the traditional packet filter firewall category, since it operates on the above information. The distinguishing feature of the packet filter firewalls is that they route traffic directly through them. Thus, in order to successfully cross a firewall, a packet needs to belong to the block of IP addresses that the firewall is configured to allow, or it should use the IP address of the private network that the firewall is protecting. Figure 11-2 shows the typical packet filter firewall setup.

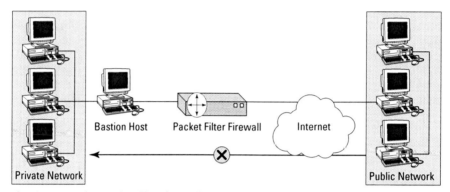

Figure 11-2: The packet filter firewall setup

There are several advantages to using packet filter firewalls:

✦ They are fast because they operate on IP addresses and TCP port numbers only, ignoring the data content of the packets.

✦ They are application-independent because they ignore the data content of the packets.

✦ They are the least expensive of all the types of firewalls.

✦ They do not require any configuration-related changes to be made on the computers they protect.

There are also some disadvantages of using the packet filter firewalls:

✦ They are least secure out of the three types of firewalls, since they can perform only limited examination of the incoming traffic.

✦ They ignore the data content of the packets, making it impossible to block users from accessing unauthorized Web sites.

✦ They cannot implement a complex firewall.

Stateful packet inspection firewalls

Most firewalls base their "permit" or "deny" decisions on the source and destination addresses carried by an IP packet. However, they don't attempt to "understand" the data in the packets they're admitting or blocking. The stateful packet inspection firewalls, as the name suggests, intercept the incoming packets to determine the state of connection. Only if the incoming packets fulfill all the conditions set on the firewall are they allowed in the network. The stateful packet inspection firewalls gradually build dynamic state tables that they use to track the connections through them. Only packets belonging to valid and established connections are allowed into the network.

Note   The mechanism used by stateful packet inspection firewalls is applicable to all protocols.

In addition to considering the IP addresses and data content of the packets, these firewalls also take the state of the connections into account. Consequently, an inbound packet can be matched with an outbound request before it is allowed into the network. This prevents an incoming packet, masquerading as a response to a nonexistent outbound request, from gaining entry into the network. A stateful packet inspection firewall also uses the *session filtering* mechanism to gather information about a session from beginning to end. Along with the IP packet information and data content analysis, this information is used in filtering decisions.

There are several advantages of using stateful packet inspection firewalls:

✦ They provide better security than basic firewalls, as they match incoming replies to outgoing requests.

✦ They provide elaborate logging of transactions that will help network administrators easily locate the root of the problem in the case of network disruptions.

✦ They reduce administrative overhead, as any configuration changes to the computers within the private network are not required.

There are also several disadvantages of using stateful packet inspection firewalls:

✦ Configuring them is complicated.

✦ They do not provide user authentication.

✦ They are slower than packet filter firewalls. This is because they need to remember the state of connections. As a result, they are resource-intensive.

✦ They are more expensive than packet filter firewalls.

Application proxy firewalls

Application proxy firewalls allow traffic in from one side and send it out the other, after the traffic passes through the *application proxy software*. The proxy application scans all the data passing through it and drops the unauthorized and unsafe data packets. When a computer outside a protected network communicates with an internal host, the proxy mimics the internal host. Similarly, when an internal host communicates with an external client, the proxy masks the origin of the computer that initiates the connection. As a result, an internal host is never exposed to the "outside" world. Figure 11-3 depicts the setup of an application proxy firewall.

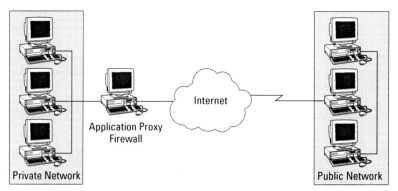

Figure 11-3: The application proxy firewall setup

There are several advantages of using application proxy firewalls:

✦ They offer the highest degree of security, since they do not let the end points directly communicate with each other.

✦ They offer the best content filtering capability.

✦ They authenticate users and log activities comprehensively, thus ensuring a high degree of security.

✦ They are policy-based. Policies can be configured easily. Thus, it is easier to configure application proxy firewalls than stateful packet filtering firewalls, which operate on packet filtering rules.

There are several disadvantages of using application proxy firewalls:

✦ They are the slowest of the three firewall types.

✦ They require a separate proxy software for each protocol.

✦ They are TCP-based and may not support UDP.

✦ They require configuration changes to all the internal hosts.

✦ They are the most expensive of the three types of firewalls.

The lines between different firewall devices are largely non-existent. For instance, you can purchase a software "firewall" add-on for Cisco routers that runs in the router, allowing the router to act as a firewall.

Common network configurations using firewalls

There are two common network configurations using firewalls: a *simple firewall system* that uses routers, and a *three-part firewall system,* which consists of three layers (or parts).

Simple firewall system

Figure 11-4 shows a simple firewall topology implemented using routers.

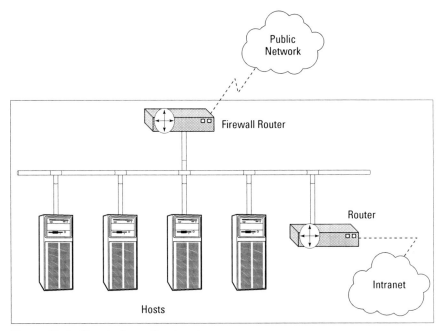

Figure 11-4: Simple firewall network

In this setup, a firewall router is placed at the exit point of the private network that connects to the outside world. Every inbound and outbound data packet has to traverse through this firewall router. Security must be implemented at every point where the network needs to connect to the other public networks and the Internet.

Three-part firewall system

Figure 11-5 shows the setup of the classic three-part firewall system. This firewall system consists of the following three specialized layers:

✦ **Isolation LAN** — This layer acts as the buffer between the corporate internetwork and the untrustworthy networks. The isolation LAN is given a unique network number, which is different from the corporate internetwork. Only the isolation LAN is visible to the outside network.

> **Note** Isolation LANs are also known as Demilitarized Zones (DMZs).

✦ **Inside packet filter** — This layer is a router (or set of routers) that filters the packets traveling between the isolation LAN and the corporate internetwork.

✦ **Outside packet filter** — This layer is a router (or set of routers) that filters the packets traveling between the isolation LAN and the outside world.

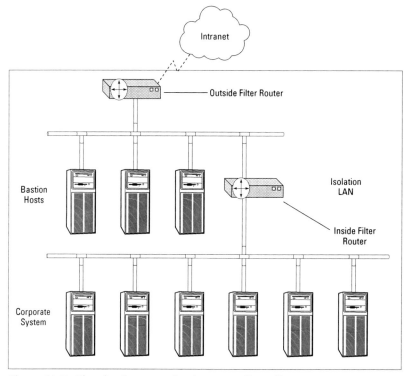

Figure 11-5: The classic setup of a three-part firewall system

If users of the corporate internetwork need access to Internet services, allow the TCP outbound traffic — but only on the condition that the TCP packets are a response to a valid request issued earlier. Block all new inbound TCP traffic, since it might be initiated by hackers trying to establish a session with one of the corporate network hosts.

When setting up a three-part firewall system, follow these rules:

✦ The outside and inside packet filters should allow inbound packets only if they belong to a pre-established session.

✦ The outside packet filter should allow packets bound to the bastion host(s).

✦ The outside packet filter should not have unnecessary services and connections.

✦ The following recommendations should be implemented on the outside packet filter router, if possible:

- Use static routing only

- Strictly prohibit TFTP services

- Disable the Finger, proxy ARP, IP redirection, IP route caching, and Telnet services

- Use password encryption

- Avoid making the outside packet filter a MacIP server, which provides IP connectivity over AppleTalk

✦ The traffic from the firewall routers to the corporate internetwork should be blocked, since these firewall routers might be overtaken by a hacker attack. If you block any traffic from the firewall into the network, the chances that your network will go down are low.

✦ The firewall routers and bastion hosts should have as few programs as possible. Furthermore, these programs should not be complex, since complex applications are prone to more bugs, which create security holes.

Firewalls are an effective — but expensive — solution. Moreover, they need to be handled by experts, as they are difficult to implement and maintain. For these reasons, firewalls are often out of the reach of small companies and users accessing the Internet from home. On the other hand, *Network Address Translation* (*NAT*) provides a cost-effective protection that doesn't require an elaborate setup. NAT is a powerful mechanism for conserving already-depleted registered IP addresses in large networks and for simplifying IP addressing management tasks.

Using Network Address Translation

To connect to the Internet, every computer requires a unique IP address. However, the number of hosts connected to the Internet continues to grow exponentially, which means that the eventual scarcity of IP addresses is imminent. IPv6 is the solution to this problem, but because it requires modifications to the entire existing infrastructure of the Internet, it will take several years to implement. In the meantime, a "stopgap" solution is required.

NAT was originally developed by Cisco as a routing mechanism for conserving registered IP addresses in large networks. Over time, it has also emerged as an effective method for protecting private networks from unauthorized external access. NAT allows a private network, using addresses that are not registered with InterNIC or other registry agencies, to connect to the Internet and other public networks by translating these addresses into globally registered IP addresses.

Caution

NAT is a good solution for the address depletion and scaling problem because it requires very few changes and can be installed incrementally. However, it has many negative features that make it inappropriate as a long-term solution.

NAT needs to be installed at the exit point between a private network and the rest of the world. Generally, this exit point is the router. Every device supporting NAT has a translating table, which is used to translate private IP addresses to globally unique IP addresses. If there is more than one exit point in the network, it is very important that each router supporting NAT has the same translation table. Figure 11-6 shows the configuration of NAT.

Note   In general, the NAT mechanism is used by routers, though it can also be used by firewalls. Routers using NAT are sometimes called *NAT routers,* or simply *Network Address Translators.*

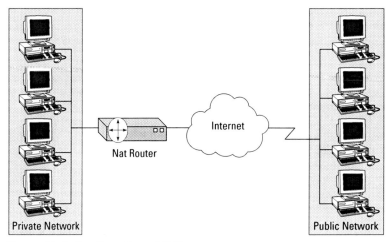

Figure 11-6: Configuration of NAT

Implementing NAT automatically creates a firewall between a private network and the outside world. A device using the NAT mechanism acts as an agent between a private network and the rest of the world. In other words, a single IP address can be used to represent an entire network, which provides an added measure of network security by hiding the internal IP addresses from the outside world.

With NAT, only those connections that originated inside the network are allowed to pass through. Thus, an internal computer can successfully connect to a computer located outside its network. However, an external computer would not be able to connect to an internal computer, as it would need to originate the connection (something that NAT doesn't allow). As a result, users belonging to the network can browse the Internet, connect to computers belonging to other public networks, and even download files, but it is impossible for someone to access internal hosts by using their IP addresses.

Note   NAT can be compared to a receptionist, who forwards only those calls that you want and rejects the undesired calls.

If required, the administrator of a private network could allow external clients to access services, such as FTP and Web services on some internal hosts, in a controlled manner. This is done by mapping some well-known TCP ports to an internal address — a process known as *inbound mapping*.

There are two forms of NAT: *static* and *dynamic*. Furthermore, there are two types of dynamic NAT: *overloaded* and *overlapped*.

✦ **Static NAT** — An unregistered IP address is mapped to a registered IP address on a one-to-one basis, as shown in Figure 11-7. For example, 160.111.7.8 will always translate to 192.1.1.5. This NAT is used when an internal host needs to be accessed from outside the network.

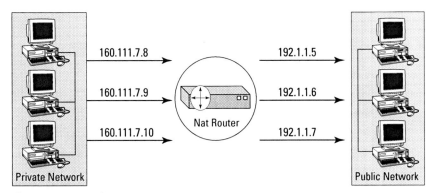

Figure 11-7: Static NAT

✦ **Dynamic NAT** — An unregistered IP address can be mapped to any first-available address in a block of registered IP addresses, as shown in Figure 11-8. For example, 160.111.7.8 will be translated to the first available address in the block of 192.1.1.1 to 192.1.1.120. This NAT is used when an internal host needs to access an external host.

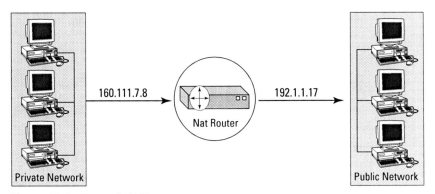

Figure 11-8: Dynamic NAT

- **Overloaded dynamic NAT** — Multiple unregistered IP addresses are mapped to a single registered IP address by using different ports, as shown in Figure 11-9. For example, 160.111.7.8 will be translated to 192.1.1.5:209, and 160.111.7.10 will be translated to 192.1.1.5:210. Overloaded dynamic NAT is also known as *Port Address Translation (PAT), port-level multiplexed NAT,* or *single address NAT.*

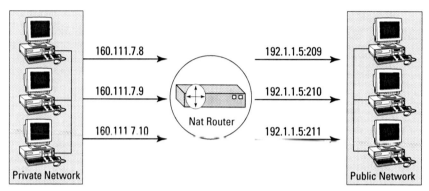

Figure 11-9: Overloaded dynamic NAT

- **Overlapped dynamic NAT** — If an IP address block is used in a private network, which is legally registered to another network, NAT router(s) must intercept it and replace it with a unique registered address. If not, the data packets might be lost because two or more hosts on the Internet may have the same IP address. Suppose, for example, that a private network uses the 162.111.xx.xx-address block. However, the same block has been assigned to another network by an Internet registry agency. To avoid any potential address clashes, the NAT router should translate an unregistered IP address to a registered IP address, when an internal host needs to communicate with a host belonging to the other network. Similarly, the NAT router must also translate the registered global IP address to an unregistered IP address used within the private network, when an external host sends information to an internal host. The overlapped dynamic NAT is shown in Figure 11-10.

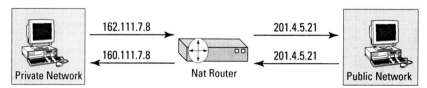

Figure 11-10: Overlapped dynamic NAT

Benefits of using NAT

NAT significantly simplifies the IP addressing management tasks. On a TCP/IP network, each computer needs to be separately configured for a correct IP address, subnet mask, domain name, default router, and DNS address. The larger the network, the harder it is to coordinate the distribution of addresses. Moreover, failure in configuring even a single computer can lead to part of the network going down. NAT can reduce administrative overhead significantly. It is also beneficial for the following reasons:

✦ NAT can be used to divide a large network into many smaller networks. Computers can be added, removed, or their addresses changed without affecting other units.

✦ NAT is a router function. Therefore, only the routers located at the end-points of the network would need modifications.

✦ NAT can support Dynamic Host Configuration Protocol (DHCP), which allows TCP/IP-related information to be updated on all the computers automatically. Thus, the administrator doesn't need to change this information manually on each and every computer on the network.

✦ NAT allows administrators to prohibit access to sites that might be unsafe or contain questionable content.

✦ NAT provides traffic-logging facilities that can help an administrator trace users, sites, or network connections that cause problems.

✦ Mostly, NAT does not use a host machine protocol stack. Therefore, they are less susceptible to low-level protocol attacks, such as "SYN FLOOD", and so on.

✦ NAT supports packet-level filtering and routing, thus providing a high level of security to the internal hosts.

In spite of all the benefits that NAT provides, there are some negative aspects to it:

✦ In the case of global corporate networks, it is not desirable to use NAT because a large number of hosts may want to communicate with each other, which increases the size of the translation tables.

✦ Any application data packet carrying IP addresses will not work through NAT unless NAT is aware of such instances and has the mechanism to do the appropriate translations.

✦ Although NAT supports application-level encryption, it does not support TCP-header checksum encryption, thereby reducing the security options.

✦ NAT can make the detection of security violations difficult. For example, if an internal or external host attacks another host or sends a large number of junk information, it may be difficult to pinpoint the source of trouble because the IP address of the host is hidden.

In contrast to NAT, which is generally implemented on the routers, a *proxy server* does not require routing. In other words, it does not require any specific hardware. It can be installed on any computer that meets its requirements. A proxy server gives network administrators the ability to "hide" their network from the rest of the world, thereby protecting the valuable data traveling over the network.

Note   For more information on NAT, refer to RFCs 1631 and 2663.

Transparent versus non-transparent

Since the working of NAT closely resembles the working of application proxies, the two are often confused. However, there are differences:

✦ NAT is transparent to the two communicating ends (internal as well as external). This means that during a transaction, neither the internal nor the external hosts realize that a third party exists in between. On the other hand, a proxy server is not transparent to the internal hosts. Though the internal hosts know about the existence of the proxy software, the external hosts do not know about it, as the proxy software mimics the internal host.

✦ If the NAT mechanism exists on the border router or the firewall, the internal hosts do not need to be separately configured for it. On the other hand, all the internal hosts need to be configured for the information related to the proxy.

✦ NAT operates at Layer 3 of the OSI reference model, whereas proxy servers usually work at Layer 4 (and higher) of the OSI reference model.

✦ NAT, being a low-level protocol, is much faster than some proxy servers.

Caution   Do not confuse NAT with proxy servers.

Using a proxy server

A proxy server acts as a gateway between a private network and other public networks, including the Internet. A *gateway* is a software (application), or a computer running the special software, that acts as a barrier between two networks and at the same time facilitates the communication between the two networks.

A *proxy server* is a network application that is configured to act on behalf of the assigned network. When an application running on an internal host issues a request for data from outside the network, the proxy server intercepts the request, translates it and passes it to the target network. When an external host needs to communicate with an internal host, the proxy server once again intercepts the request, verifies that the data is safe, and then passes the data packet to the target internal host. To the external hosts, it would always seem that the requests and responses originate at the proxy server. In this manner, the internal host is always hidden from the outside world.

Note   Proxy services may or may not perform Network Address Translation (NAT).

The proxy server also maintains a cache of the latest requests. If a host — external as well as internal — requests information that was requested recently, the proxy server fulfills the request from its cache, instead of renewing the request to the target host. This helps to further protect the network and speed up the transactions.

One disadvantage of the proxy server is that it is non-transparent to the users, and every internal host needs to be configured to use it. This increases administrative overhead considerably. On the other hand, a proxy server provides several advantages:

✦ By configuring internal hosts to utilize the proxy server, Internet applications can be extended to every computer in the network.

✦ By utilizing the caching capability of the proxy server, the performance and security level of the private network can be improved significantly.

✦ By configuring the proxy server to permit or deny outbound access by internal users, ports, or domains, secure access can be provided to the internal users. Certain "unsafe" sites can be completely blocked with ease.

Note   For more information on proxy servers, refer to RFCs 1445, 1906, 2607, 2616, and 2843.

To gain a competitive edge in today's economy, a business must be connected to the Internet. But for many small businesses and individuals, maintaining multiple Internet connections can be an expensive enterprise. The solution is to share a single Internet connection across your home, home office, or small office network.

Microsoft's Internet Connection Sharing

Microsoft released the *Internet Connection Sharing (ICS)* service with the second edition of Windows 98. It enables multiple users to share one Internet connection across a home or small office network. When ICS is installed on a computer, the machine is referred to as an *Internet Connection Sharing (ICS) computer*. This computer must have an Internet connection. After ICS is installed, the computer is capable of providing private IP addresses and name resolution services for the rest of the computers on the network. Figure 11-11 shows the connectivity provided by the ICS computer to the rest of the computers in a small network.

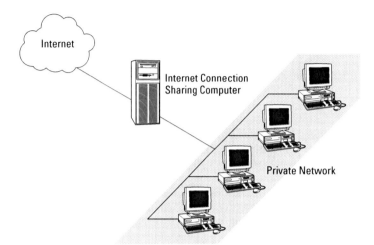

Figure 11-11: The typical ICS setup

When a computer on the network accesses the Internet, its IP address is passed on to the ICS computer. The ICS computer then translates the received private IP address into its own globally unique IP address. The request is then forwarded to the Internet. When the ICS computer receives a response to the sent request, it translates the IP address back to the private address of the original requestor and routes the information to the computer.

In addition to providing multiple Internet connectivity, ICS hides the rest of the network from the Internet and other public networks. The only computer visible to the outside world is the ICS computer. None of the other computers on the network have a direct link to the outside world. In other words, ICS is an effective and inexpensive security measure for small networks.

Although many third-party products are available in today's market for sharing an Internet connection, Microsoft's ICS has a definite edge for a couple of reasons:

✦ From Windows 98 and up, Microsoft's ICS is built into the operating system. Therefore, you don't have to buy separate software to connect to the Internet.

✦ ICS is user-friendly. In other words, you don't need an expert to get the connection up and running.

The risks associated with connecting to the Internet have given rise to various security methods and mechanisms, such as firewalls, proxies, and NAT. *Virtual Private Network* (*VPN*) is the latest development in network security technology.

Virtual Private Networks

Private networks use dedicated leased lines to provide secure interconnectivity between distributed sites of a corporate network. In contrast, the VPN technology provides secure connection between distributed units of a corporate network over public networks, including the Internet, without being dependent on expensive leased lines or Permanent Virtual Circuits (PVCs). Rather, VPNs use the open and distributed infrastructure of the Internet to their own advantage. VPNs are IP-based networks that use encryption and tunneling to provide:

✦ **Secure remote access** across a corporate network.

✦ **Intranet access** by linking the networks of branch offices to an enterprise network.

✦ **Extranet access** by extending a corporation's intranet resources to partners, customers, and suppliers.

In other words, VPNs behave like a private network in terms of security and performance. However, they extend the reach of the private network by using trust relationships without putting the security of the network on the line. Figure 11-12 shows the typical setup of a VPN.

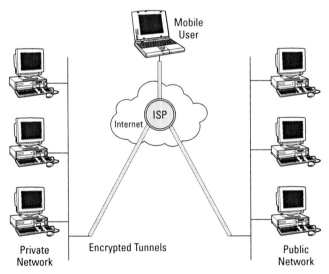

Figure 11-12: A Virtual Private Network

To set up a VPN, a corporation needs to connect to local connection points, called *Points-of-Presence (POPs)*, at their ISP's network. Connectivity details and the transmission of data to appropriate destinations across the Internet are the responsibility of the ISP. Since the data needs to travel across the Internet to reach its destination, a VPN's administrator must implement adequate measures to encrypt data that is passed between two networks. This will protect the data from eavesdropping and from being tampered with by unauthorized users.

Since VPNs do not use dedicated leased lines or WAN links and the corporate data needs to traverse the Internet, VPNs provide four critical functions to ensure the security of the data:

✦ **Authentication** — On receiving a packet, a VPN verifies that the data originated from a trusted source.

✦ **Confidentiality** — VPNs use various encryption methods, such as *public* and *private key cryptography*, to prevent the data from being read and copied during transmission. In private key cryptography, the sender encrypts the message with its private key and the recipient's public key. On receiving the encrypted message, the receiver then decrypts the message using its own private key and the public key of the sender.

✦ **Integrity** — VPN also ensures that the data is not altered during a transmission. It uses *hash functions, Message Authentication Codes (MACs),* and *digital signatures* to do so.

  • **Hash functions** — A hash function generates a hash value of a file before sending it. This hash value makes it difficult to generate a file that will correspond to the hash value supplied with the incoming packets. On receiving the data packets of the file, the receiver calculates the hash value and compares it with the value sent by the sender. If the two values do not match, the data is corrupt and is discarded. MD5, RIPE-MD-160, and SHA-1 are examples of the hash algorithms.

  • **Message Authentication Codes (MACs)** — MACs add a key to the hash functions. After generating the hash value, the MAC is calculated and appended to the data. The receiver calculates its own MAC and compares it with the value sent. If the two values do not match, the packet is discarded.

  • **Digital signatures** — The sender "signs" the packet with its own private key. On receiving the packet, the receiver verifies the signature using the sender's public key that was sent by the sender along with the message.

✦ **Access control** — A VPN necessitates a logging process to prevent unauthorized users from accessing the network. It can use Challenge Handshake Authentication Protocol (CHAP), Remote Authentication Dial-In User Service (RADIUS), and hardware-based tokens to authenticate users and control access to the network resources.

Implementing VPNs can provide many benefits to an organization. The main benefits include:

✦ **Cost savings** — Third-party network products can be used with VPNs. As a result, corporations need not use expensive leased lines, modem banks, or frame relay technology to connect remote parts of the intranet to the main corporate network. This reduces the in-house demand for technical support resources and personnel, ultimately bringing down network cost.

✦ **Maximum bandwidth use** — VPNs do not maintain permanent links between communicating end-points. A connection is created when an authentic request is issued, which is why these networks are called *Virtual* Private Networks. After the transaction is over, the connection is destroyed. As a result, the network resources are free for other connections and the network bandwidth is used to its maximum.

✦ **Security** — Every VPN uses advanced encryption methods, such as public key and private key cryptography, to protect the data in transit from being tampered with. Other methods, like hash functions, Message Authentication Codes (MACs), and digital signatures, are used to ensure the integrity of data sent and received across public networks. VPNs also use authentication protocols to protect a network from unauthorized access.

✦ **Scalability** — Corporations work closely with the ISPs. Therefore, they can add a huge amount of computer space without having to invest in infrastructure, thereby reducing WAN connection setup and administrative overheads.

✦ **Support to mobile users** — Instead of depending on expensive and not-so-dependable resources, such as modem-banks and remote access servers that lead to enormous sums spent on phone charges, mobile sales people and telecommuters can connect to the corporate intranet via high-speed broadband connectivity provided by DSL and cables. This helps increase the flexibility and efficiency of the network.

 Note For more information on VPNs, refer to RFCs 2547, 2637, and 2684.

In addition to advanced encryption methods to protect packets from being snooped by outsiders, VPNs use *tunneling* to establish secure, end-to-end intranet connections over the Internet and extranets. Tunneling enables a sender to encapsulate the data packets in such a manner that the underlying routing and switching information is hidden from the receiver. The most famous tunneling protocols used to create VPNs are *Point-to-Point Tunneling Protocol (PPTP)* by Microsoft and Cisco's *Layer-2 Tunneling Protocol (L2TP)*.

 Note Other famous VPN protocols are *Layer-2 Forwarding (L2F)* and *IP Security (IPSec)*. Both are protocols by Cisco.

Point-to-Point Tunneling Protocol

Microsoft's PPTP was one of the earliest protocols used for dial-in VPNs to provide remote access that can be tunneled across the Internet to a destination site. PPTP is implemented in the RAS systems. Therefore, the RAS can provide the call-control and management capability, when necessary. This allows control of remote dial-in calls. These calls can originate either from a Public Service Telephone Network (PSTN) or from Integrated Services Digital Network (ISDN). PPTP can also initiate outbound calls.

PPTP was built using the Point-to-Point Protocol (PPP) as its base. PPP is the most commonly used protocol for remote access. Rather than changing the entire structure of PPP, a few changes and additions were introduced in its basic design to accommodate VPNs.

PPTP has two components: *control connection* and an *IP tunnel* between the VPN and the call originator:

> ✦ **Control connection** — A control connection is a standard TCP session that must be established between the target host in the VPN and the computer originating the call before tunneling can be established between them. PPTP call control and management information is passed in this session.

> ✦ **IP tunnel** — After the connection is established successfully, a *tunnel* (or virtual channel) is established between the sender and the receiver. The establishment of the tunnel is required to ensure the success of the data exchange session, as the tunnel would eventually carry the PPP packets.

Since PPTP builds on the functionality of PPP for secure remote access, it uses the same authentication methods as PPP. These include CHAP, MS-CHAP, and Password Authentication Protocol (PAP). However, a more powerful encryption method, called Microsoft Point-to-Point Encryption (MPPE), has recently been incorporated for use with PPTP.

PPTP packets resemble PPP packets. However, they are encapsulated using the modified version of the Generic Routing Encapsulation (GRE) protocol. The use of GRE provides PPTP the capability of functioning at Layer 2 (the Data Link layer) of the OSI reference model. Thus, it is capable of handling protocols other than IP, such as Internet Packet eXchange (IPX), AppleTalk, and Network Basic input/output system Extended User Interface (NetBEUI). GRE also provides a flow- and congestion-control encapsulated datagram service for carrying PPP packets. This makes PPTP more flexible than its predecessor — PPP.

There are several advantages of PPTP:

✦ It provides flexible IP address management.

✦ It supports non-IP protocols, such as AppleTalk, IPX and so on.

There are several disadvantages of PPTP:

✦ It does not provide strong encryption methods for protecting data.

✦ It does not support token-based methods of user authentication, which are more powerful than PAP and CHAP.

While Microsoft presented PPTP, Cisco (the leader in the market of networking products), developed Layer-2 Tunneling Protocol (L2TP), which was released in the market as an enhancement of Cisco's Layer-2 Forwarding (L2F) protocol to address the shortcomings of PPTP. It was accepted as a standard protocol by the Internet Engineering Task Force (IETF) and is undergoing further modifications as the heir of PPTP.

 Note   For more information on PPTP, refer to RFC 2637.

Layer-2 Tunneling Protocol

L2TP is a standards-based VPN protocol that combines the functionality of PPTP with L2F. Like PPTP, L2TP uses PPP as a base to provide remote dial-in access that can be tunneled through the Internet to a target network. However, L2TP uses its own tunneling protocol. As L2TP tunneling is IP-independent, it can work with various media, such as frame relay, Asynchronous Transfer Mode (ATM), X.25, and so on.

Like PPTP, L2TP uses PPP for dial-up connections. Therefore, it uses the PPP-authentication methods — PAP and CHAP. It also uses the extensible authentication methods provided by PPP, such as RADIUS. However, there are two levels of user-authentication. First, a user is authenticated by the ISP before the tunnel is set. Then the user is again authenticated when the connection is set up at the corporate gateway.

Encapsulating an L2TP frame within a UDP packet creates an L2TP tunnel. This UDP packet in turn is encapsulated inside an IP packet. As per Cisco recommendations, if L2TP is used in conjunction with IPSec, strong encryption and security is available by using the cryptographic keys in the IP environment. This provides strong protection to the data that flows within the L2TP tunnel. The basic difference between L2TP and PPTP is that L2TP defines connections in a tunnel, allowing a tunnel to support more than one connection at a time.

The disadvantage of using L2TP is that it does not support a strong encapsulation mechanism on its own. Another protocol, called IPSec, is required. Together, they provide a strong security base. In contrast, the advantages of using L2TP are numerous because:

✦ It is a standard protocol. As a result, ISPs, customers, and network managers do not have to depend on the products offered by a single vendor. They can use a wide range of services available from multiple vendors.

✦ It provides more security compared to PPTP, since a user is authenticated at two levels.

✦ It can operate successfully in non-IP environments, including AppleTalk, NetBEUI, IPX, and so on.

Note   IPSec is a Cisco protocol that was later adopted by IETF as a standard. IPSec provides a high degree of security to the VPNs when they transact data over public networks because they support key cryptography and token-based authentication. However, IPSec was designed to handle IP packets only. As a result, it is unsuitable for non-IP environments. RFCs 2407 and 2409 provide more information on IPSec.

For more information on L2TP, refer to RFC 2261

Summary

In this chapter, you learned about the addressing scheme used in private networks. Next, you learned about the various limitations imposed by the current IPv4 addressing scheme that necessitated the emergence of IPv6. Additional topics that were covered include: the role of Internet Service Providers (ISPs) in connecting to the Internet; and the fast-emerging Application Service Providers (ASPs) that lease various softwares to corporations and organizations, ranging from Windows to highly complex and expensive Enterprise Resource Planning (ERP).

This chapter discussed the security risks that are incurred when a network connects to the Internet, and the various measures — such as firewalls — that help combat this problem. This chapter also addressed the concept of Network Address Translation (NAT), which helps network administrators combat the ever-threatening problems of rapidly depleting IP addresses and securing a network. Proxy servers and Microsoft's Internet Connection Sharing were examined. Finally, you learned about fast-emerging and highly secure Virtual Private Networks (VPNs), which allow globally distributed corporate networks to exchange sensitive data securely and economically.

✦   ✦   ✦

File Utilities

T he basic aim of having computers on a network is to share resources — especially files. TCP/IP provides various file utilities that can be used over the network to manage files, such as Network File System (NFS), Distributed File System (DFS), and file transfer utilities like File Transfer Protocol (FTP), Trivial File Transfer Protocol (TFTP), and Remote Copy Protocol (rcp). Besides discussing these utilities, this chapter also looks at configuring an NFS server and DFS on Windows 2000.

Network File System

Network File System (NFS) is a protocol that provides users transparent access to shared file resources across a network by using the TCP/IP protocol. Transparent access to file resources means that users can access remote files and directories as if they were located on the local system *without* having to log in to the remote system.

NFS overview

NFS is about connecting file systems on different computers across a network to provide transparent file access to users. To understand transparent file access, consider a company that owns a computer named stock1. This computer stores the stock reports for all the products in the /stocks/reports folder. The Sales department owns a computer named sale1, which it uses while selling. The Sales department needs to access the stock reports from the sale1 computer on a fairly frequent basis to check product availability. If the network uses TCP/IP and the computers have NFS installed and running, the users in the sales department can access stock reports without having to log in to the stock1 computer or copying the stock files to the sale1 computer.

However, before users can access the stock reports, certain steps need to be performed on both computers (stock1 and sale1):

✦ On the stock1 computer, the /stocks/reports folder that contains the stock reports needs to be shared. While sharing the directory, the administrator can restrict access to certain computers and allow read and write or read-only access. The stock1 computer acts as an NFS server. A *server* is a computer that provides services and resources.

✦ On the sale1 computer, a connection needs to be made between the shared /stock/reports directory on the stock1 computer to a directory, such as /all_reports/stocks, on the local sale1 computer. (In the UNIX environment, this process is called *mounting*). The sale1 computer acts as an NFS client. A *client* is a computer that needs access to the services or resources of another process on another computer in the network. The directory that is connected to the directory on the NFS server is called the *mounted directory*.

After the directory is mounted, the users of the Sales department can access the stock reports from their sale1 computer. To do so, users simply need to change the working directory to the mounted /all_reports/stocks directory on the local sale1 computer. Then, they can access the stock reports files as if the files were located on their local computer.

NFS servers are *stateless* — they do not maintain any protocol state information about any of the NFS clients. This feature of NFS server offers an advantage in the event of server failure. The client does not know that the server has crashed. It only retries the request until the server responds. Therefore, no recovery issues need to be addressed at the client side.

NFS implements the transparent file access by using the Remote Procedure Call (RPC) protocol over the eXternal Data Representation (XDR) standard.

Remote Procedure Call

Remote Procedure Call (RPC) is a protocol used for communication between processes on different computers in a network by providing a logical client-to-server communication system. RPC uses remote procedures, which are programs specified by a host address, program number, and procedure number for communication.

The RPC model is similar to the model used for communication between different processes on the same computer. An RPC process on the client computer requests a particular service from another computer on the network. This request message is called the *call message*. The server authenticates the request, and then provides the service itself or starts another process to do the same. Finally, the server replies back to the client. This reply from the server is called the *reply message*. Each call message is matched to a reply message.

For more information on RPC, refer to Chapter 7.

RPC provides a logical client-to-server communication by using a transport protocol, such as TCP or UDP, to carry the message data between the communicating programs. However, RPC is independent of the transport protocols — the method in which messages are transmitted from one process to another makes no difference to RPC. Therefore, RPC does not attach any specific semantics to the remote procedures while implementing the logical communication between the processes. The semantics are inferred from the underlying transport protocols. Also, RPC does not provide any kind of reliability. Instead, it depends on the underlying transport protocols. Therefore, the applications must be aware of the type of transport protocol that is being used underneath the RPC protocol. The applications need to implement reliability if the underlying transport protocol is unreliable, as in the case of UDP.

EXternal Data Representation

In the NFS implementation, the file resources need to be accessed across a network. The data representation on each machine depends on the machine model and the operating system that is being used (these can vary). For example, American Standard Code for Information Interchange (ASCII) uses 7-bit code to represent characters. On the other hand, Extended Binary Coded Decimal Interchange Code (EBCDIC) uses 8-bit code. In each data representation, a character is represented by a character code. For example, the character "A" is represented by the character code "65"in ASCII, and by the character code "193" in EBCDIC. These data representations are machine-specific. Consequently, for successful communication, there must be a standard way to represent data that is independent of the machine architecture and the operating system. EXternal Data Representation (XDR) is a standard way to represent data on a network. XDR uses a data description language to encode data formats so that data can be transferred to any machine irrespective of the machine model and the operating system over the network. The XDR standard thus makes communication possible across different operating systems and machine architectures.

NFS services

For NFS to work, certain NFS services *must be* running on the NFS server. These services are provided by certain daemons:

✦ **nfsd** — Handles the file creation, searching, and reading or writing. Every time a client requests a communication, a separate nfsd daemon is started to handle the communication. The client then uses the services provided by this daemon.

✦ **mountd** — Checks for the list of file systems that are being shared from the server's local system and listens to the computers for any mount request for files and directories. If the requested files or directories are available, the mountd daemon enables the client to mount them. The daemon also keeps track of the resources that are mounted by remote systems.

✦ **pcnfsd** — Used by the clients to get the authentication information from the server for further transactions. When a client initiates a communication, it sends the username and password that gets checked on the server.

✦ **portmapper** — Provides port numbers that the clients can bind to. Therefore, before sending packets to a server, all clients must query the portmapper to identify the port to which the packets must be sent.

✦ **statd** — Monitors the status of both the server and client computers, such as a reboot of the computers on the network to recover from NFS locks.

✦ **lockd** — Manages the locked systems to avoid data modifications by several clients at the same time. The statd and lockd daemons work together to recover the locked systems. In the event of a system lockup, the statd daemon waits for a system to retry for the locked files. However, if any of the locked systems do not respond, the statd daemon sends alert messages to the systems administrator. On the other hand, the lockd daemon processes the lock requests.

Security issues in NFS

NFS provides easy access to shared files on a network. However, several security issues make the NFS system insecure, as described below:

✦ In NFS, only computers whose names or IP addresses are listed in a special file on the server are allowed to mount the resources. However, a person can take over the trusted address and then access the mounted resources.

✦ After the mount procedure, the user's access to files is controlled by the file system. Now consider a situation where a user with a specific user ID accesses a file that needs to be accessible only to this user and marked as read-only for others. If a person maps to the specific user ID, the person is able to access the file that was marked as read-only by its user.

The security issues associated with NFS can be taken care of if you install the most current NFS security patches. Also, you should export file systems as read-only. However, if this is not possible, you should export file systems only to a restricted number of hosts.

Cross-Reference   For more information on NFS security issues, visit the Webopaedia Web site at www.pcwebopaedia.com or the Sun Microsystems Web site at www.sun.com.

NFS versions

NFS allows users to manage files on several computers in a network as if they were located on the local hard disk. NFS was developed by Sun Microsystems in the mid-1980s. However, the first version of NFS was never released. The revised second version of NFS was released and implemented with the SunOS 2.0. Since then, Sun Microsystems has included NFS in the SunOS. Because NFS is independent of machine architecture, operating system, network, and transport protocol, NFS has been implemented on different platforms, such as UNIX, MS-Windows, NetWare, and OS/2. However, NFS Version 2 has several limitations, and at least eight new NFS versions have been suggested since Version 2 to fix the problems. (Not all of the suggested versions have been implemented).

NFS Version 3 continues to be stateless. As in Version 2, each request is complete and sufficient and does not depend on other requests for processing. The server does not need to maintain any state information. Also, the server crash recovery is simple. The client only needs to retry the request until the server responds. Version 2 uses UDP for network transport, but Version 3 uses TCP. (TCP is more reliable, but provides low performance.) The differences between Version 2 and Version 3 include:

✦ **File handle size** — A *file handle* is a pointer to the shared file on an NFS server. Version 2 used a file handle of fixed size (32 bytes). In Version 3, the size of the file handle has been increased to a variable length of 64 bytes maximum.

✦ **Maximum data size** — Version 2 imposed an 8K data size limitation on the READ and WRITE procedures affecting the performance of clients. The READ procedure is used for all the read requests from the client. Version 3 does not impose this data size limit.

✦ **Reliable asynchronous file writes** — In Version 2, a server writes data to a stable storage, such as hard disks synchronously, before acknowledging to a client's WRITE request. This affects performance. In Version 3, a server acknowledges to the client immediately after receiving an asynchronous WRITE request. Then, to check whether or not the data has been saved to a stable storage, the client sends a COMMIT request to the server. The server replies to this COMMIT request only after the data has been safely stored.

✦ **Cache consistency** — In Version 2, clients maintain files and directories in the cache to improve performance. To check the validity of the cache data, clients match the file or directory modification time from the server and the client's cache. If the two modification times match, the client concludes that the cache data is up-to-date. However, when the client itself modifies the cache data, the time factor cannot be used to check the validity of the data. As you can see, the method fails. However, in Version 3, the cache consistency is being maintained by using the two versions of the file attributes, the pre-operation attributes, and the post-operation attributes on the server. If the modification times in the two operations match, the cache is valid.

Although NFS Version 3 addresses most of the Version 2 problems, a new NFS Version 4, released in mid-2000, provides improved

✦ Data and cache consistency

✦ Security features

✦ Cross-platform interoperability

Configuring an NFS server

You need to configure an NFS server to implement the NFS protocol for transparent access to shared files in a network. The NFS server can be configured on different operating systems, both Windows and UNIX. This section describes the NFS server configuration on Linux and Windows 2000.

Configuring an NFS server in Linux

Configuring an NFS server in Linux involves editing some configuration files. However, before you begin, you should ensure that TCP/IP is configured and working properly. Also, ensure that an appropriate nfs-utils package is installed. The nfs-utils package consists of a collection of daemons required for NFS functionality and is stored either in the /sbin or /usr/sbin directory. The three configuration files that need to be edited to set up an NFS server are: /etc/exports, /etc/hosts.allow, and /etc/hosts.deny.

The /etc/exports file contains entries for all those directories that are shared on the network. The entries also represent the access details for the shared directories. For example, certain directories can only be read, whereas certain directories can be read and modified. You need to edit this file to add entries for all shared directories. A typical entry looks like this:

```
directory computer1(option11,option12) computer2(option21,option22)
```

In this syntax,

- ✦ **directory** represents the directory to be shared. If a directory is shared, all the directories under it will be shared as well.

- ✦ **computer1** and **computer2** represent the computers that can have access to the shared directory. The computers can be listed either by their IP addresses or by their DNS names. However, it is more secure to use IP addresses.

- ✦ **option** represents the type of access that each computer will have for the shared directory. These options include:
  - **ro** — Indicates a read-only access to the shared directory. This is the default option.
  - **rw** — Indicates a read and write access to the shared directory.
  - **no_root_squash** — Indicates that a root user on the client computer will have the same level of access to the files that a root user has on the server. This option is usually not specified due to security reasons. However, if you need to perform some administrative task on a client computer, you might need to use this option.
  - **no_subtree_check** — Indicates that whenever a client requests for a file, the server (with a routine called subtree checking) verifies that the file is located in the appropriate part of the partition if only a part of the partition is exported. However, if the entire partition is exported, this option need not be used to speed up transfers.

Consider a situation where two directories on the server, /usr/sales and /usr/reports, need to be shared to the computers USER1 and USER2 on the network. The IP addresses of the two computers are 192.17.0.1 and 192.17.0.2, respectively. If the computers need to have only read access, the /etc/exports file should have the following entries:

```
/usr/sales 192.17.0.1(ro) 192.17.0.2(ro)
/usr/reports 192.17.0.1(ro) 192.17.0.2(ro)
```

If the number of computers that require access to the server is large, you can use the range of computers, instead of individual computer names. In this case, you can specify the network and netmask address to specify the computers in a subnet.

The /etc/hosts.allow and /etc/hosts.deny files contain entries for all the services on the server that other computers on the network can use. Entries in these files list the services and the set of computers as follows:

```
service: computer1, computer2
```

In this example, you can use either computer names or IP addresses.

Whenever a client sends a request to the server, the server performs the following:

✦ The server checks the hosts.allow file to see if the computer that sent the request has an entry for the requested service. If yes, the server allows the access.

✦ If the computer does not have an entry for the requested service in the hosts.allow file, the server checks the hosts.deny file for the same. If the computer's entry for the requested service is found, the access is denied.

✦ If the server does not find the computer's entry for the requested service in any of the two files, the server allows the access.

After editing the three configuration files, you simply need to reboot the server to get NFS up and running. When you reboot the server, the startup scripts automatically detect the /etc/exports settings and start NFS. Use the *rpcinfo -p* command to verify that NFS is running. Sometimes, you may need to add the entries in the start-up file to start the NFS services or daemons. For example, to start the mountd and nfsd daemons, you should add the following lines in the start-up scripts:

```
rpc.mountd
rpc.nfsd
```

Configuring an NFS server in Windows NT Server

When you install the Windows NT Server 4.0 operating system, the NFS server software does not get installed automatically. To install NFS, you need the Microsoft Windows NT Services for UNIX (SFU) add-on pack. The SFU pack allows for sharing of network resources among Windows NT, Windows 2000, and UNIX-based operating systems. After you install SFU, you can configure the NFS server. Configuring

NFS server in Windows 2000 server is similar to that in Windows NT Server. To configure NFS on Windows NT Server 4.0, you need to create the folder to be shared, add NFS client groups, share the folder that needs to be accessed by clients, and assign permissions to users. The following steps will help you do this:

1. Right-click the folder to be shared and select Properties from the shortcut menu.

2. Activate the Security tab, click Permissions, and then select the Replace Permissions on Subdirectories check box.

3. Select the Replace Permissions on Existing Files check box.

4. Under the Name area, select one individual permission at a time and click Remove to delete it.

5. Click Add, and then click Show Users.

6. Select Everyone, the administrators group, and the user named administrator. Click Add.

7. Change the type of access to FULL CONTROL and close the dialog box.

8. Select Start, Programs, Windows NT Services for Unix, Server for NFS.

9. Activate the NFS Client Groups tab. Press Alt + G, enter a group name, and click OK to add a client group. Press Alt + M, enter the hostname or IP address of the NFS client, click OK and then click Apply to add a member to the client group.

Note   A client group is a group of computers that can access the NFS shared folders.

10. Activate the Share Options tab. Enter the full path of the folder to be shared and change the type of access to No Access. Press Alt + A, select the client group that you created, and click Add.

    Assign the root privilege as either Root or Anonymous. To grant root privilege as Root, press Alt + A, and set the type of access to Root. To grant root privilege as Anonymous, press Alt + A, and set the type of access to Read-Write. Press Alt + Y and click Apply to apply the share option settings.

11. Configure user/group mappings to map the Windows users/groups to UNIX users/groups. Press Alt + O, and then Alt + E to edit the password file to enter the new user name, user ID, and group ID.

    Press Alt + A and then press Alt + O. Select users under NFS Users and Windows Users, and then press Alt + D to add the mapping.

    Press Alt + A to apply the changes.

After the NFS server is configured, UNIX NFS clients can access the shared files by simply mounting the NFS Server share.

Distributed File System

File systems that are available with different operating systems — such as FAT and NTFS — only manage data organization on local physical media. However, users often need to locate information on the network, which is usually scattered on different servers. Therefore, users face problems when they need to search for the information by looking at the shared folders on different machines across the network. Network administrators can avoid this problem by using the Distributed File System (DFS). DFS saves you the hassle of searching manually through the entire network for a file.

DFS overview

In the race to be Internet-ready, Microsoft provided DFS, which evolved from NetBIOS — a component in the TCP/IP protocol suite. The *Distributed File System (DFS)* enables users to access the shared files and directories that are physically distributed across a network without actually specifying their physical location. DFS can be configured on any of the Windows 2000 network servers. DFS puts together all the shared files and directories that are physically located across the network and makes them available to users as if they were located on a single server in which DFS is configured. For example, if sales data is scattered across multiple servers in a network, you can use DFS to access the data in a manner as though it were located on a single server.

Note In Windows 2000 network servers, you can also configure DFS server on Windows NT 4.0 server.

A DFS consists of a DFS root, one or more DFS links, and one or more DFS shared folders to which each DFS link points. The DFS root, DFS links, and DFS shared folders together constitute *DFS topology*. The server on which the DFS root resides is called a *host server*. A *DFS root* refers to a shared directory on a host server that acts as a starting point and host to other shares. Within the DFS root, you can create DFS shared folders with DFS links that link to the actual physical path of the shared folder on a computer on the network. Thus, DFS provides a logical path to all the shared files and directories/folders on the network. Users can access the shared network files and directories by simply mounting the DFS. Since users do not need to know the name of a server or the share, they can access files and directories from the same DFS shared folders, even if their physical locations are changed. A DFS server provides many different benefits:

✦ A single hierarchical structure to view all the shared folders on the network, which behaves as a single high-capacity hard disk. This structure makes it easy for users to access shared network resources.

✦ Users do not need to know the physical location of files and folders. Administrators can move shared folders without affecting the users' access to data. Therefore, DFS provides flexible data management.

✦ Multiple DFS shared folders that are physically distributed across a network can reside within a single DFS root. Thus, if a file on a single server is heavily accessed, users do not need to access the files from the same server, reducing load on the server. Instead, the user access to files is distributed to multiple servers. However, for users, the file seems to reside only in one location on the network.

✦ DFS is interoperable with other network operating systems, such as Microsoft Windows 95, Windows 98, and Windows NT 4.0.

✦ DFS allows clients to cache the information about shared folders on the host server. The local cache on the clients minimizes network traffic and improves user response time.

✦ DFS ensures security integration without any additional overhead for implementing security. A user who accesses a DFS root can access only those files for which he or she has appropriate permissions.

Stand-alone versus domain DFS roots

A DFS can be implemented by creating a stand-alone DFS root or by creating a domain DFS root. In a stand-alone DFS, there is only one host server in a domain — DFS root resides only on one domain server. In a domain DFS, on the other hand, there are multiple host servers. Since a stand-alone DFS implementation has only one host server, users cannot access their files if the host server is unavailable, due to a variety of reasons (such as server maintenance). However, since domain DFS implementation has multiple host servers, it ensures high availability of files to users. It does this in two ways:

✦ Windows 2000 automatically publishes the DFS topology to the Active Directory. *Active Directory* is a service included with Windows 2000 Server that stores the network object information and makes it available to users and network administrators. Therefore, a domain DFS ensures that the DFS topology is visible to users on all servers in the domain.

✦ Domain DFS implementation allows automatic replication of DFS roots and DFS shared folders on multiple servers. *Replication* means duplicating DFS roots and shared folders on multiple servers in a domain. Therefore, if one of the physical servers becomes unavailable, users can still access their files.

Configuring DFS on Windows 2000

DFS can be configured over either a FAT or NTFS partition. However, since NTFS provides more security features than FAT, it is advisable to configure DFS over an NTFS partition. Configuring DFS involves creating a DFS root, DFS links, and DFS shared folders.

Creating a DFS root

Follow these steps to create a DFS root:

1. Select Start ➪ Programs ➪ Administrative Tools ➪ Distributed File System.

2. Select New DFS Root from the Action menu to start the wizard.

3. Click Next to open the Select the DFS Root Type window. By default, the Create a domain DFS root option is selected. If you want to create a stand-alone DFS root, select Create a stand-alone DFS root. Click Next to go to the next step of the wizard.

4. If you have opted to create a domain-based DFS root, you are prompted to enter the name of the domain where you want to create the DFS root. Enter the domain name and click Next.

5. Enter the name of the host server for DFS root and click Next to open the Specify the DFS Root Share window.

Tip   You can click Browse to select a server name instead of entering the server name.

6. In the Specify the DFS Root Share window, you can specify a shared folder. Specify the path of an existing shared folder or a new shared folder to create. Click Next.

7. A default name for the DFS root is displayed. You can also specify a new Dfs root and click Next.

8. Click Finish. The new DFS root is created.

After the DFS root is created, you need to restart the server for the new DFS implementation to take effect.

Creating a DFS link or shared folders

A DFS link can contain multiple shared folders. However, when you create a DFS link, the first shared folder is automatically added. Follow these steps to create a DFS link:

1. Select Start ➪ Programs, Administrative Tools ➪ Distributed File System.

2. Right-click the DFS root to which you need to assign the shared folder, and click New DFS Link from the shortcut menu.

3. Enter the name of the folder in the Link Name box.

4. Provide the link for the shared folder by entering the path of the shared folder in the Send the user to this shared folder box.

Note   The folder name that you enter into the Link Name box will be visible to users on the network.

File Transfer Utilities

There are times when you may want to share or transfer files from one computer to another. File transfer is the process of moving a file from one computer to another. You can transfer files over the Net by using the file transfer utilities. One of the major usage areas of TCP/IP protocols is in file transfer. TCP/IP provides protocols, such as File Transfer Protocol (FTP), Trivial File Transfer Protocol (TFTP), and Remote Copy (rcp), that help you transfer and manage files over the network. In this section, we discuss these file transfer utilities in detail.

File Transfer Protocol

One of the most widely used applications of TCP/IP is file transferring.

Note   Transferring files means that the files are copied from one machine to another without affecting the original copy.

FTP is one of the protocols in the TCP/IP suite. FTP is a set of rules that handles the transfer of files from one computer to another. It also ensures that the data is transferred in a reliable and efficient manner. FTP has various commands that help transfer files and create and manage directories. FTP is different from other protocols in the TCP/IP suite because it uses two TCP/IP ports — port 20 and port 21. These two ports are known as Data Transfer Process (DTP) and Protocol Interpreter (PI), respectively. Port 20 is used to transfer directory and file listings, whereas port 21 is used to transfer commands.

FTP works on a client/server architecture. The client connects to the server at port 21 while the server uses its port 20 to connect back to the client to transfer data. The client starts a session by sending a request at port 21 to connect to the FTP server. This is known as Control Channel connection. The client sends the PORT command that carries the port number to which the server needs to connect for port-to-port exchange of data. The FTP server then transfers the data from its port 20 to the port that was specified by the client in the PORT command. Because this transfer of data is initiated by the server and is not controlled by the client, the firewall at the client end is not able to detect the source of the data. This can lead to security problems, since unwanted data can pose as FTP data transfer and reach the client. The problem can be solved with passive FTP, in which the client sends the PASV command rather than the PORT command. The PASV command asks the server to specify the client port that it would be using for data transfer. The server sends the port number, which is then used by the client to initiate data exchange. As, in this case, the server responds to the client-initiated request, the firewall is able to detect the source from which the data is coming. Most of the FTP clients use passive FTP.

When you use FTP to transfer files, the FTP program on your machine or local host computer communicates with the FTP program on the remote computer. However, the remote and host computer need not have the same operating system. A series of commands are exchanged to transfer the files. When the files are transferred, the connection can be terminated from the local host machine.

A variety of FTP programs is available. These programs have either a character user interface or a graphical user interface. The character user interface or command line programs are available for character-based operating systems, such as DOS and UNIX, while graphical user interface programs are available for operating systems such as Windows. In case of command line programs, the user needs to type commands to transfer or manage files. However, if the FTP program has a graphical interface, using the buttons and icons carries out the file transfer and management actions.

FTP transfers files in two formats: binary and ASCII. Binary format is used to transfer binary data files and executable files. ASCII format is used to transfer text files. By default, the files are transferred in the ASCII format. This is because Unix and Windows use different line endings in the text files. While Unix uses linefeed character as a line ending in a text file, Windows uses carriage return/linefeed as the line ending. Using ASCII format ensures proper translation of these line endings when file transfer takes place between different host environments.

Note   It is important that you specify the correct format to transfer the files. If you specify a binary file as ASCII, the file that would reach the remote computer would be corrupted. However, if you specify an ASCII file as binary, the file would be transferred without any changes.

So how does FTP work? Though there are slight differences in the working of different FTP programs, the basic mechanism remains the same. The basic steps involved in the working of an FTP program are:

1. The host computer establishes a connection with the remote computer.

2. The user on the host computer logs on to the remote host.

3. The user creates or locates the directory on the remote computer. This directory is the one which contains the needed file, or in which a file needs to be put.

4. The user uses the appropriate command or menu/buttons to transfer the files, depending on the type of FTP program that is being used.

5. When all the files have been transferred, the user quits the ftp session by logging out of the remote computer.

Usually, the character-based FTP programs need a username and password at startup. The GUI-based FTP programs, on the other hand, usually display a window from which you need to select the name or the IP address of the remote system from the list. After the connection is established, you need to provide a username and password to log on to the remote computer.

Over the Internet, you can use FTP to download freeware and files from the public libraries hosted on *anonymous FTP servers*. These sites allow you to connect to the server anonymously. Hence, you need to log in as Anonymous. If you are prompted for a password, you can enter your e-mail ID. These sites provide only read permissions to the anonymous users so no change can be made to the archives.

Trivial File Transfer Protocol

Trivial File Transfer Protocol (TFTP) is a TCP/IP protocol used to transfer files (text or binary) from one computer to another. TFTP uses port 69 of UDP for file transfers. It is designed to be simple and easy. So, unlike FTP, TFTP cannot be used to perform file and directory operations, such as directory listings and file management. It also does not ensure user authentication. TFTP is implemented on User Datagram Protocol (UDP). It is primarily used to boot routers and diskless workstations. Because TFTP does not check for authentication, the host computer does not need to provide the username and password, which is why this protocol is used only for trusted clients.

The TFTP works as follows:

1. The host computer sends the request for file transfer to the remote computer.

2. When the remote computer accepts the request, the requested file is sent in the form of fixed-length packets of 512 bytes. Each packet that is sent is numbered.

3. The recipient computer then acknowledges the receipt of the packet by sending an acknowledgement containing the block number of the packet received.

4. If a packet of less than 512 bytes is sent, the transfer of packets between the recipient and the sender is terminated.

If the data packet or acknowledgement is lost during transmission, it needs to be resent. When TFTP is used to transfer files over the network, both computers act as senders and receivers. The host computer receives the data and sends the acknowledgement. The remote machine sends the packets and receives the acknowledgement.

Remote Copy Protocol

Remote Copy Protocol (rcp) is a TCP/IP protocol that belongs to the category of r-utilities. It is used to transfer files to or from a remote computer. This protocol is implemented in the form of an *rcp* command. Before you use the rcp command, you need to create a .rhosts file on the remote computer. This .rhosts file contains the names of the systems that the remote computer can trust. However, if different user names are to be used to access the remote computer, you also need to specify the user names after the system names in the .rhosts file. When using remote call protocol, the user needs to provide the system name. This system name is then compared with the system name that is stored in the .rhosts file. The files can be copied only when the system name provided as an argument with the rcp command matches the one in the .rhosts file. If the user names on the remote and local computers are different, you need to specify the user name before the system name in the rcp command. You do not need to specify the password while using the rcp command. Consider a situation where there are two computers, machine 1 and machine 2, and machine 1 is the remote computer. For machine 2 to be able to access files on machine 1, you need to add the following statement to the .rhosts file on machine 1.

```
machine 2.<domain name>
```

The rcp command to copy a file called file1 from machine 1 to machine 2 would be

```
machine 1$ rcp machine 2: file1 file1
```

If you have the username as user 1 on machine 1 and as user 2 on machine 2, you need to specify the username after the system name in the .rhosts file as shown below.

```
machine 2.<domain name> user2
```

In this case, the rcp command to copy a file called file1 from machine 1 to machine 2 would be

```
machine 1$ rcp user2@machine 2: file1 file1
```

The rcp command takes various arguments. Table 12-1 describes the arguments:

Table 12-1 rcp Command Arguments	
Argument	**Explanation**
-a	Used to specify the ASCII transfer mode – the default transfer mode for rcp.
-b	Used to specify the binary transfer mode. This mode should be used to transfer the executable and binary files.
-h	Used to transfer the hidden files along with the other files.
-r	Used to copy the contents of subdirectories.
Host	Used to specify the local or remote host.
.user	Used to specify the username. This should be used when the user is not the current user.
Source	Used to specify the files that need to be copied.
Path\destination	Used to specify the relative path to the logon directory on the remote computer.

Summary

In this chapter, you learned about the TCP/IP file utilities that are used to transfer and manage files over the network. You also learned about the Network File System (NFS) and its versions; how to configure NFS server on Linux and Windows NT Server; the features of Distributed File System (DFS); and the difference between the stand-alone and the domain Dfs root.

This chapter ended with a discussion of the way in which files are transferred over the network by using FTP. The concepts of Trivial File Transfer Protocol (TFTP) and Remote Copy Protocol (rcp) were also touched upon.

✦   ✦   ✦

Remote Command Utilities

This is the age when enterprise knows no international barriers: Company networks may be spread across the globe. The last decade has also witnessed a tremendous rise in the mobile workforce, which means that new methods must be developed to help remote workers access resources beyond their physical reach. How, for example, can a traveling businessman work on a computer located in a home office? How can a network administrator troubleshoot a workstation remotely?

The answer to these questions is *remote access* — the process of accessing resources and services that are physically remote. Various utilities are available that can help you access remote resources; these utilities provide interactive connection to a remote computer and issue commands in an interactive mode. While you work with the remote computer, the local system becomes transparent. The commands you type at the local computer are directly transmitted to the remote machine and the response(s) from the remote machine are displayed on the user's monitor.

In this chapter, you will learn about popular remote command utilities — such as Telnet, Remote login (rlogin), Remote shell (rsh), Secure shell (ssh), and Remote execute (rexec) — that enable you to access remote resources and services. You'll also learn how terminal servers such as Sun Ray, Microsoft Terminal Server, and Citrix help you access remote resources and services.

Remote Command Utilities Overview

Most remote command utilities were developed at the University of California at Berkeley (UCB) as a part of their development work on TCP/IP. Because the names of most of these utilities start with the letter "r," they are popularly known as *r-utilities*. The "r" stands for "remote." Originally, r-utilities were part of the UNIX operating system. As a result, they are highly UNIX system-dependent. However, with time, the r-utilities have been ported to other platforms and environments, such as Windows. Some of the popular r-utilities are rlogin, rsh, and rexec. Although ssh provides some services that are similar to r-utilities, it is not an r-utility. It is a separate protocol that is much closer to Telnet.

Note   Sometimes, you may find that the r-utilities are also referred to as *Berkeley r-utilities.*

Although the r-utilities are still popular with UNIX and Linux operating systems, they are rapidly being replaced by the standard TCP/IP services, such as Telnet and File Transfer Protocol (FTP) for the following reasons:

✦ The r-utilities are meant for internal use over a *trusted network*. A network behind a firewall is known as a trusted network.

✦ Most of the r-utilities provide Character User Interface (CUI), which is not so easy to use since the user has to remember the related commands.

These days, the r-utilities are rarely implemented in the commercial TCP/IP packages. Telnet provides a familiar and easy-to-use interface, which makes it one of the most popular services offered by TCP/IP.

Cross-Reference   For more information on firewalls, refer to Chapter 11.

Telnet

Initially, accessing a remote computer was a cumbersome process, which required modifications in the requesting computer's operating system. Also, due to the possible heterogeneity of a network, it wasn't determined how the keystrokes would be interpreted at the other side. For example, using Ctrl + D to end a session on a local computer would not necessarily end the current session on the remote system.

Gradually, system programmers succeeded in developing a utility that enabled users to interact with the remote system as if they were working with the local system. This utility was called *TELecommunication NETwork,* or *Telnet.* Telnet overrides the local interpretation of all keystrokes. In other words, Telnet was developed as a service to allow users to log in and execute commands on remote computers as if they were sitting at the console of the remote machine.

Note Telnet as a protocol actually precedes the rest of the TCP/IP protocols. It was the original protocol and TCP/IP was built around it. Telnet is also considered the "universal" protocol, since it can be used to "hand-connect" to almost all of the other protocols. The Telnet service is connection-oriented. Therefore, it is TCP-based. TCP port number 23 supports the Telnet Service.

Telnet was based on three principles: *Network Virtual Terminal (NVT)*, the *principle of negotiation*, and a *symmetric view of terminals and processes*.

✦ **Network Virtual Terminal (NVT)** — To support heterogeneity (interoperability with different platforms and systems), Telnet uses NVT, which is the standard representation of data and command sequences. NVT is an implementation of the client-server architecture, which treats each end of the connection as a virtual terminal (logical I/O device). The logical input device (or the keyboard of the user) produces the outgoing data and the logical output device (or the monitor) responds to the incoming data and other output from the remote system. When instructions are issued at any of the virtual terminals, they are translated to the corresponding physical device instructions. In other words, the Telnet program at the client-end (user-end that initiated the Telnet request) maps the NVT codes sent by the server to the codes that can be understood by the client-end. At the same time, the codes generated by the client-end are mapped to the NVT codes that can be understood and processed by the server-end. Figure 13-1 shows the working of Telnet using NVT.

Tip NVT is a half-duplex mechanism, which allows one end to issue commands at a time.

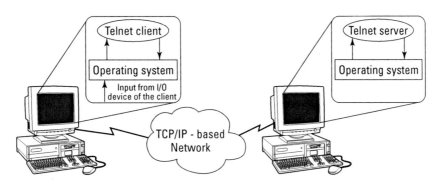

Figure 13-1: Telnet communication using NVT

✦ **Principle of negotiation** — Some systems may provide services in addition to those available within an NVT. As a result, the systems using minimal services are not able to communicate properly with the other end. Thus, when two computers communicate through Telnet, communication and terminal parameters are set during the connection process, and services or processes that cannot be handled by either of the two computers are ignored. This eliminates the need for interpreting exchanged information from the operating systems at both ends. For example, a user may negotiate the Echo option and specify if the echoing is to be done locally or remotely.

Note Either side can initiate a negotiation during the session, if required, in addition to the negotiation that occurs at the beginning of a session.

✦ **Symmetric view of terminals and processes** — This signifies the symmetry in the negotiation syntax, which allows either the client or the server to request for a specific option. This symmetric view of terminals and processes optimizes the services provided by the other end. Telnet not only allows a terminal to interact with remote applications, but also allows process-process and terminal-terminal interactions.

Users can perform the following tasks using Telnet:

✦ Connect to an online database to access information.

✦ Connect to online knowledge bases, such as libraries, to search for information.

✦ Connect to a remote system to use applications, such as e-mail.

Telnet connection process

The Telnet connection is established between the user and server ports. Both the server and the client listen to and issue any Telnet-related requests on port 23.

Note The server can have more than one simultaneous connection.

1. To invoke a Telnet session, the user needs to specify the IP address of the target computer (132.45.78.44 in the following command) or the name that is mapped to this specific IP address (lperry in the following command). Formats of the command are given below.

   ```
   Telnet 132.45.78.44
   Telnet lperry
   ```

   Since Telnet can accept IP addresses, it can be used even if the name-to-address mapping is not successful. However, if the IP address or the computer name is not specified, Telnet goes into the command mode and waits for further instructions.

2. Next, a user ID and password are requested. To log in to the remote system, the user needs a valid user ID. However, if the computer from which the user is accessing the remote computer is a trusted host, a password is not

required. The Telnet login screen is shown in Figure 13-2.

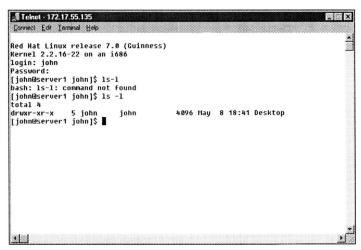

```
Red Hat Linux release 7.0 (Guinness)
Kernel 2.2.16-22 on an i686
login: john
Password:
[john@server1 john]$ ls-l
bash: ls-l: command not found
[john@server1 john]$ ls -l
total 4
drwxr-xr-x   5 john     john         4096 May  8 18:41 Desktop
[john@server1 john]$ ▮
```

Figure 13-2: Telnet login screen

3. If the user ID and the password are successfully validated, the Telnet connection is established and the local computer (where the user is working) starts behaving like the remote computer.

Tip

To exit a Telnet session, the command used at the recipient end (usually Ctrl+D) should be used. In a Windows-based system, closing the Telnet window ends the session.

Common Telnet commands

Telnet supports various commands that control the process of server-client interaction and details related to the process. These commands are sent as a part of the data that is exchanged between the two ends. Nearly all the Telnet commands are made of at least two bytes. The first byte consists of an escape character called Interpret As Command (IAC), which is used to introduce the following command. The next byte contains the code of the command that needs to be processed. Common Telnet command codes are shown in Table 13-1. The format of the Telnet commands is specified below:

```
IAC <command_code>
```

Table 13-1
Telnet Command Codes

Command Value	Command	Description
240	SE	Sub-negotiation End — Signifies the end of the sub-negotiation phase.
241	NOP	No Operation.
242	Data Mark	Data Portion of a Sync.
243	BRK	BReaK Instruction.
244	IP	Interrupt Process — Interrupts, aborts, or ends a process.
245	AO	Abort Output — Completes the process, but does not send the output to the client.
246	AYT	Are You There — Queries the other end of the connection to ensure that the process is functioning.
247	EC	Erase Character — Erases a character from the output stream.
248	EL	Erase Line — Erases a line from the output stream.
249	GA	Go Ahead — Permission to proceed in a half-duplex communication.
250	SB	Sub-negotiation — Initiates a client-requested sub-negotiation.
251	Will	Signal to the other end to emulate the opposite end.
252	Won't	Rejection of emulation.
253	Do	Acknowledgement to perform an action.
254	Don't	Negative acknowledgement of an action.
255	IAC	Interpret As Command — Following string would be interpreted as a command.

Caution   The above command codes have meaning only if preceded by the IAC escape character.

In addition to the above commands that control the interaction between the server and the client-end, there are various options that can be negotiated between the two ends at any time during the connection. These options ensure that both ends understand the extra capabilities affecting the data-exchange. The commands that deal with option negotiation consist of three bytes. The first two bytes are the same as general commands. The third byte represents the code of the option that is being referenced. Table 13-2 lists the options and their command codes. The format of the option negotiation commands is as follows:

```
IAC <command_code> <option_code>
```

Table 13-2
Option Negotiation Command Codes

Option Value	Option	Description
1	Echo	Echoes the data characters received from the other end.
5	Status	Initiates the exchange of the current status of the Telnet options.
24	Terminal type	Initiates the exchange of the possible terminal types and selects the most appropriate.
31	Window size	Initiates the negotiation of the window size of data stream.
32	Terminal speed	Initiates the negotiation of the data-exchange speed.
33	Remote flow control	Initiates the negotiation over whether to allow or disallow flow control during data exchange.
34	Line mode	Initiates the negotiation that terminal characters will be interpreted at the client side rather than the server side.

Installing Telnet

Being one of the most popular utilities of the TCP/IP stack, Telnet is generally pre-installed with the operating system. You may not need to install Telnet if you are a Windows 9x, Windows NT, or Windows 2000 user. Also, Telnet is installed with the UNIX operating system.

Note If Telnet is not installed on your computer, you can download the Telnet programs from the Internet for free. One of the famous sites for downloading Telnet programs from the Internet is win3x.tucows.com/softterm.html.

Installing Telnet on the Windows platform

Although Telnet is already installed in the Windows operating systems, you may want to install a more robust Telnet application that provides better services than the default Telnet application. Some of the popular Telnet programs used on

Windows platforms include EWAN and QVTTerm. The steps for installing the Telnet program in this case are as follows:

1. Extract the installation file, if it is compressed.

2. Double-click the installation file to start the installation process. Complete the process as specified in the README file provided with the Telnet application.

3. When the installation is complete, the installation process would create a Start Group menu. Run the application.

Tip   During installation, if you are prompted for the location where the installation process will create the application folder, accept the default installation path.

Installing Telnet on the Macintosh platform

To install Telnet on a Macintosh system, you need to follow the steps given below:

1. Copy the Telnet installation file to the desired folder.

Note   One of the most widely used Telnet programs is NCSA's Mac Telnet 2.6. Other popular Telnet programs include NiftyTelnet, DataComet, and BetterTelnet.

2. Double-click the file to self-extract it.

3. Load the application and select File ➪ Open Connection to display the Open Connection dialog box. You can use this dialog box to establish a session with the intended host.

Note   To install the Telnet application on your Macintosh system, you'll need to have the corresponding TCP software installed on your machine. If you are using version 8.0 or higher, you'll need to have Open Transport PPP installed. If you are using versions lower than 8.0, the corresponding TCP software is MAC TCP.

Installing Telnet on the UNIX platform

Like other popular operating systems such as Windows, Telnet is also pre-installed in the UNIX system. However, the steps to install a more robust Telnet program are listed below:

1. Download the required file from the Internet. You can also get the required file from CDs.

2. Unpack the file, if you obtained it in compressed format, using the corresponding utility. This step is optional, if the file is not compressed.

3. Copy the installation file to a directory of your choice.

4. Read the instruction file (README or INSTALL) carefully and follow the instructions.

Note   Since Telnet is one of the most popular utilities, many RFCs are dedicated to it. For more information on the various aspects of the Telnet protocol, refer to Request For Comment (RFC) 854, 855, 856, 857, 858, 859, 860, 861, 927, 933, 1041, 1073, 1079, 1091, 1096, 1097, 1116, 1143, 1184, 1205, 1372, 1408, 1571, 1411, 1416, 1572, 2066, and 2217. Though obsolete, RFC 854 provides comprehensive information about the Telnet protocol.

Remote login

Remote login (*rlogin*) is a UNIX command that allows a user to connect and log on to a remote computer. The rlogin service provides similar functionality as Telnet. Most of the time, any difference between the user interfaces of the rlogin and Telnet services is transparent to the user. However, the difference lies in the way end-to-end communications are held and session characteristics set.

At the sender end, the rlogin service is invoked by the rlogin command. Just like Telnet, the `rlogin` command takes either the IP address or the name of the target computer as a parameter to identify the recipient. A daemon (or server thread) called *rlogind* controls the rlogin service at the recipient end. When the connection is successfully established, the user is not prompted for the user name, but only for the password. The rlogin service does *not* allow the user to log in to the remote computer with a different user name. Only the registered user name used by the recipient computer is allowed. This is the basic difference between rlogin and Telnet, which allows logging in to the system by using any valid user name. Figure 13-3 shows the rlogin screen.

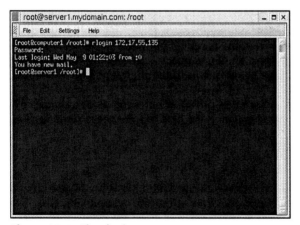

Figure 13-3: The rlogin screen

The target computer provides access to the recipient only if the following conditions are met:

✦ The /etc/hosts.equiv file at the remote end contains an entry for the recipient computer.

✦ The $HOME/.rhosts file at the remote end contains an entry for the computer and the user name that has initiated the request for the connection.

Tip   To prevent outside attack, only the owner should have the read/write permission in $HOME/.rhosts.

rlogin connection process

To connect using rlogin:

1. The rlogin connection request is invoked at the sender end by using the `rlogin` command, followed by the IP address (`132.45.78.44`) or the name of the recipient (`lperry`). Formats of the command are:

   ```
   rlogin lperry
   rlogin 132.45.78.44
   ```

   Three character strings separated by zeros are sent to the recipient (or the server). The first string contains the login ID used at the sender end. The second string contains the user ID that will be used to log in to the remote system. This ID is the same as the user ID used on the recipient end. The last string contains the additional sender's identification, if any, and the transmission rate to be used by the sender.

2. The recipient, on receiving the strings, converts them into environmental variables that control the method and various details of the interaction between the client and the server. When the received parameters (especially the transmission rate) are agreed upon, the login process is over. After this, every character typed at the requestor's end is sent to the recipient, and vice versa.

Tip   To exit the rlogin session, either press Ctrl+D or enter the escape character on a new line. The default escape character is the tilde (~). However, some versions of rlogin use "~!".

Installing rlogin

The rlogin utility is built into the UNIX operating system. It is installed automatically when you install UNIX. However, in other operating systems, such as Windows and Macintosh, where the utility is rarely used, you need third-party utilities. Samba and PCNFS are some of these utilities. To install the third-party utilities, download them. However, note that these files may not be freeware. Uncompress the downloaded file(s), if required, and follow the instructions specified in the accompanying instruction file to finish the installation process.

Note For more information on rlogin, refer to RFC 1258.

Remote shell

The *rsh* utility is used to execute commands on a remote system. (The user doesn't need to log in to the remote system to execute these commands). As one parameter, the `rsh` command takes the IP address or the computer name of the remote computer. The other parameter is the command that needs to be executed on the remote machine. A background process at the recipient (or the server) end, called *rshd*, executes the commands issued at the client end.

Caution The rsh utility should *not* be confused with the UNIX shells, such as C shell and Bourne shell.

`rsh` and the computer name should precede the commands that are issued at the client end. Examples of the `rsh` command are:

```
rsh lperry ls
rsh 132.45.78.44 ls
```

In this example, `lperry` is the remote computer name where the `ls` command is to be executed. The `rsh` command fails if the corresponding entries do not exist either in the *hosts.equiv* or *.rhosts* files, or if these files are corrupt or missing. These files contain the login information needed by the computers that will execute commands remotely.

You don't need to install rlogin in the UNIX environment, as it is built into the system. To install rsh in the Windows environment to enable Windows-UNIX inter connectivity, you need to follow the steps given below:

1. Copy rshsetup.exe, rshsvc.dll, and rshsvc.exe to the System32 folder. The folder is located in the Windows folder if you are using Windows 9*x*. In the case of Windows NT 4.0, the folder is located in the WinNT/%SystemRoot% folder.

2. Double-click rshsetup.exe to execute it. A message should appear to the effect that the "Remote Shell Service was successfully installed."

3. At the command prompt, type `net start rshsvc` to start the command. If you get the message that the remote shell service started successfully, rlogin was successfully installed. After starting the service, you need to configure the .rhosts file to provide access to the UNIX clients.

Note For more information on rsh, refer to RFC 1282 and 1258.

Secure shell

The rsh utility is not considered secure. Anyone who has root access to the computers on the network or access to the communication channel can gain unauthorized access to the system. This person can also log all the traffic to and from the system, including passwords. This poses grave danger to the integrity of the confidential data traveling across the network.

Secure shell (ssh) was originally developed by Tatu Ylonen of Finland to address the security loopholes posed by rsh and other r-utilities. The utility quickly gained popularity and has slowly evolved into a utility that is being used by over 2 million users all over the world. Although, it was originally meant for the UNIX platform, its popularity ensured that it was ported to other platforms. Today, various implementations of ssh exist. These include:

✦ **SSH1** — This was the first implementation of ssh and was meant for the UNIX platform. It was one of the first protocols that was available to users for free.

✦ **SSH2** — This version introduced many changes to the previous version and could be supported by UNIX and Macintosh, as well as Windows. SSH1 and SSH2 encrypt a packet differently. Moreover, SSH1 uses server and host keys for authentication purposes. On the other hand, SSH2 uses the host key only. This version is also a freeware, though its licensing is restrictive.

Note   Further development of SSH1 was undertaken by the Internet Engineers Task Force (IETF). However, the changes that were meant to strengthen SSH2 made it incompatible with its predecessor.

✦ **LSH** — This version is being developed as a free version of SSH2.

✦ **FreeSSH** — This version doesn't trace its origins from the original ssh developed by Tatu Ylonen. This version only works on the UNIX platform. It is still under development.

✦ **sftp** — This is an FTP application that works on an SSH tunnel. This version is meant only for UNIX and Linux.

✦ **MindTerm SSH** — This is a free ssh client, written in Java, which can run with or without a Graphic User Interface (GUI).

✦ **Windows SSH clients** — There are various Windows ssh clients.

  • **TTSSH:** This Windows version is a free terminal emulation application.

  • **Putty:** This is a free Win32/ssh client.

  • **Winscp:** This Windows utility offers an extremely easy-to-use user interface.

✦ **OpenSSH** — This is the latest offering on the market. This version supports Linux, FreeBSD, UNIX, Solaris, AIX, IRIX, and HP/UX.

Note There are other Windows-based ssh utilities, such as iXplorer, FiSSH, and Cygnus, that are available to the users as freeware. However F-secure SSH and VanDyke SSH are commercial Windows ssh utilities.

ssh allows a user to log in to a remote computer over a network, execute commands on it, and move files from one computer to another. Compared to the r-utilities, ssh provides strong authentication and secure communication over unsecured channels and vulnerable operating systems, such as X Windows. ssh can tunnel traffic effectively for the X Windows clients. This means that an X Windows client can connect to the X Windows host and, after authenticating itself, can directly access X Windows applications. With ssh, secure remote sessions can be established that are transparent to the user. In addition, accessing remote clients by using ssh is more convenient for the users, as they can continue to use the old .rhosts and /etc/hosts.equiv files used for rsh.

Tip If a remote site does not support ssh, a fallback mechanism to rsh is included.

In ssh-based transactions, sensitive data such as passwords are sent in an encrypted format. This prevents a person with malicious intent from gaining an unauthorized entry into the system. Also, ssh is very effective against *spoofing* because it implements elaborate authentication methods and uses secure communication to transfer data across networks. In spoofing, a remote host, which is not an authorized member of the given network, sends packets that pretend to come from a trusted host into a network. Once these packets gain entry into the network, they can be used to tap confidential information or hack the network. Spoofing can be local as well as remote.

Note When used over TCP/IP, ssh is associated with port number 22.

ssh connection

The steps in the ssh connection process are as follows:

✦ Normally, a computer listens for ssh requests issued by other nodes at port 22. The formats of the `ssh` command are

```
ssh lperry who
ssh 132.45.78.44 who
```

✦ When a request is intercepted, both ends exchange an identification string followed by a newline character (/n). The string's maximum length (including the newline character) is 255 characters. Normally, without waiting for the identifier from the other side, key exchange begins immediately.

Tip When ssh is installed, no encryption is in effect, no compression is used, and no MAC is in use. During key exchange, an encryption method, a compression method, and a MAC method are selected dynamically.

✦ Data is compressed during transmission. However, if data compression was not agreed upon, *key exchange* begins. Key exchange is the technique used to generate random security codes (such as passwords) with the consent of the two sides that are involved in the transaction. An encryption algorithm and a key are negotiated during the key exchange. Each side has a preferred algorithm, and it is assumed that the other side also uses the same algorithm. The sender may even send an initial key exchange packet according to the algorithm. However, if the recipient does not use the same algorithm, sender and recipient ignore each other's first data, a common algorithm is agreed upon, and the initial key exchange packet is sent again.

There are two types of key exchange: *RSA* and *Diffie-Hellman*. In RSA exchange, separate keys are used to encrypt and decrypt information. The encryption key is publicly provided to network devices so that they can encrypt their data using it. However, the decryption key is private to each device. By using this private decryption key, along with the publicly available encryption key, each device can securely decrypt the message it receives during a transmission. In Diffie-Hellman exchange, the parties involved in the transmission derive a shared secret message via exchanging messages and authenticating the other end by using a signature that is unique to each network device.

✦ Next, the client sends its own host authentication message. If this message is not sent, the server will consider the client unnamed for authentication purposes. It is expected that many servers refuse to "talk" to clients that do not first authenticate themselves.

✦ After the client and the host are authenticated, a service request is issued. The format of the request is:

```
"ssh <IP_address/host_name> <command>"
```

Installing ssh

Use the following steps to install ssh:

1. Download ssh from one of many sites on the Internet. The official site for distributing ssh is `ftp://ftp.cs.hut.fi/pub/ssh`.

2. Uncompress the file, if necessary.

3. Read the instruction file (INSTALL) and execute the following commands to install the utility:

```
./configure
make
make install
```

ssh will be installed in its default configuration, which is all that is required to work. However, refer to the INSTALL file for more information, if you want to customize the configuration.

For more information on ssh, refer to RFC 793.

Remote execute

Like the rsh utility, *rexec* enables the execution of commands on a remote computer. The rexec utility first appeared in the earlier versions of UNIX. The computer where the commands will be executed uses the *rexecd* background process to run the commands. rexec works similarly to rsh, except for two points:

✦ The password that is sent with the request is encrypted. Therefore, it becomes very difficult for the intruder to tap into the passwords.

✦ A complete login process exists.

Like rsh, rexec accepts two parameters. The first parameter is the name or the IP address of the remote machine. The second parameter specifies the command that needs to be executed at the remote end. The formats of the command are

```
rexec lperry ls
rexec 132.45.78.44 ls
```

If the $HOME/.netrc file does not contain the corresponding entry for the remote computer, the user is prompted for the login ID and the password. After the requested login information is supplied, the output of the issued command is displayed on the client end.

Like other r-utilities, rexec is built into the UNIX system. However, rexec is not supported by Windows. Therefore, a third-party software needs to be installed. One of such popular utilities is the Ataman TCP Remote Logon Services (ATRLS), which provides rsh, rlogin, and Telnet services in addition to the rexec service.

The rexec utility is rarely used these days, since rsh is faster and more convenient.

In addition to r-utilities and standard services, such as ssh, FTP, and Telnet, TCP/IP supports a GUI-based service (or utility) called *Terminal server*. Terminal server provides highly secure access to remote resources over a network. It is a powerful utility because it can easily service multiple sessions simultaneously. In addition, a network setup using Terminal server can considerably bring down the cost of maintaining the entire network because the workstations require little maintenance (Terminal server being the data and application storehouse). Moreover, the deployment of Terminal server can also dramatically reduce the vulnerability of the network to outside attacks. However, if Terminal server is not properly secured, the entire network can go down if Terminal server fails or is hacked.

Terminal Servers

A terminal server is a powerful tool to deploy, manage, and support applications from a centralized location. Terminal servers provide a UNIX-like multiuser environment, which is, by definition, a *thin-client* architecture. In the thin-client architecture, all application and service processing happens centrally on the terminal server. A thin-client is a diskless "dumb terminal" that lacks processing capabilities and can may be as simple as a monitor, a keyboard, and network connectivity. A variety of terminal server software is available in today's market to provide access to different platforms, such as Macintosh, UNIX, Windows, and Solaris. The foremost competitors in the field of terminal servers are Microsoft Terminal Server, Sun's Sun Ray Terminal Server, and Citrix MetaFrame.

Note   When a computer is referred to as a terminal server, it actually means that the terminal server software is installed on it. However, there are stand-alone terminal servers that also have the terminal server software embedded in the system.

A terminal server consists of three components: the *multiuser server core,* the *terminal server client software,* and the *protocol* used for client-server communication.

- ✦ **Multiuser server core** — Provides the basic capability to host multiple simultaneous client sessions. It also includes administration tools for managing both the server and the various client sessions.

- ✦ **Terminal server client software** — Needs to be installed on all the nodes that access the terminal server for various services and applications. Using the Terminal server client software can be as simple as working with Telnet.

Note   The clients can be either "dumb" terminals or "intelligent" terminals with processing capabilities.

- ✦ **Protocol** — Used to facilitate communication between the terminal server and various clients. One of the most famous examples of the terminal server protocols is Remote Desktop Protocol (RDP), which is used by Microsoft Terminal Server.

Sun Ray

Sun's proprietary terminal server software, *Sun Ray*, provides highly centralized and secure system management and administration. This includes authentication of users, server group management, and redirection of input and output to the *Sun Ray appliances*. Administrative functions, such as managing authentication policies, are also included in the Sun Ray server software. All of the Sun Ray server software resides on the terminal servers — nothing is stored on or downloaded to the Sun Ray appliances.

Tip

SPARC server running the Solaris 2.6, Solaris 7, or Solaris 8 Operating Environment can host the Sun Ray server software.

The Sun Ray appliances are *stateless* thin-client computers. Note that devices that possess only the basic Input/Output devices (for example, keyboard, mouse, and display screen) are referred to as stateless devices. Sun Ray appliances entirely lack an operating system, but they do possess 8 MB RAM and 512K of Flash EPROM. The Sun Ray appliances support a special feature called *Hot desk,* which enables users to access their desktops from any Sun Ray appliance by either inserting a personalized smart card or by logging on with their user name.

Note

The 512K Flash memory contains the system firmware that handles Power-On Self Test (POST), communication with the shared Sun Ray server, authentication, local device drivers, and on-screen displays.

Sun Ray Server Software provides fully centralized control and security. Because the Sun Ray appliances do not support floppy drives, individual security settings, and options to open files that are considered unsafe by the system, a properly setup server is secure.

Caution

The biggest disadvantage in a server-centric setup is the considerable increase in network traffic.

Setting up the Sun Ray terminal system is quite simple. To set up the system, the Sun Ray Server software and user applications are installed on a server. (Up to 30 nodes can be connected to the terminal server via 10/100 MBPS fast Ethernet). Each node consists of a monitor, a mouse, and a keyboard connected to the node through Universal Serial Bus (USB) ports. Generally, peripheral devices (such as printers or scanners) can only be accessed from the server, not the individual nodes. Figure 13-4 displays this setup.

Sun Ray server software supports several functions that are used to maintain and manage a network of Sun Ray appliances. These functions include authentication management, session management, group management, virtual device driver support, peripheral device support, and various administrative tools.

✦ **Authentication manager** — Performs client and user identification and authentication. By default, the client's Ethernet address is used for identification and authentication purposes. Optionally, a smart card's (if available) type and ID are taken, rather than the Ethernet address. Registered users are only accepted if they have been registered with the server prior to authentication.

Note

A smart card is a small, detachable card-like chip in which a microprocessor and memory have been embedded. As an access-control device, a smart card stores the information required for logging in. It also makes personal and business data available only to the appropriate users. Smart cards function much like payment cards (for example, credit cards and ATM cards).

✦ **Session manager** — Maps a user session on a server to a physical Sun Ray appliance and binds/unbinds related services to and from specific Sun Ray appliances.

✦ **Group manager** — Keeps track of server group memberships. In addition, it performs static load distribution and facilitates server selection and redirection.

✦ **Virtual device drivers** — Handles all input and output for the connected Sun Ray appliances.

✦ **Peripheral device support** — Manages the peripherals attached directly to the Sun Ray server. These devices are remote to the Sun Ray appliances.

✦ **Administration tools** — Provides various tools for managing the users and monitoring server usage.

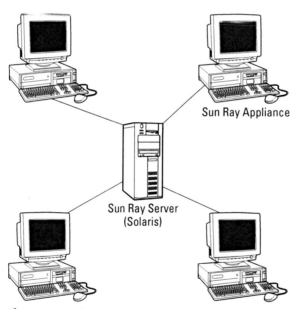

Figure 13-4: Sun Ray setup

Microsoft Terminal Server

Microsoft Terminal Server is an extension of Windows NT Server 4.0 that provides terminal support to the Windows operating systems family product line (9x and NT). It also provides a *super-thin client* environment that allows multiple clients to remotely run various 16- or 32-bit Windows-based applications on a centralized server. The term *super-thin client* is related to Microsoft Terminal Server, since it can be accessed from many different desktop and non-desktop platforms like UNIX, Macintosh, X-based Terminals, MS-DOS, networked computers, and so on.

Tip   Occasionally, Microsoft Terminal Server is referred to as Windows NT Server 4.0, Terminal Server Edition (TSE). With the advent of Windows 2000, terminal services have been integrated into Windows 2000 Server itself and new features have been incorporated. It is easier to deploy and still easier to manage. It replaces the need to buy separate terminal server software.

The Microsoft Terminal Server setup consists of a powerful machine on which the terminal server software is installed. Various user applications are also loaded on the terminal server. TSE is capable of supporting up to 250 clients. The clients can have local hard disks or can lack the hard disk entirely. Figure 13-5 displays the Microsoft Terminal Server setup.

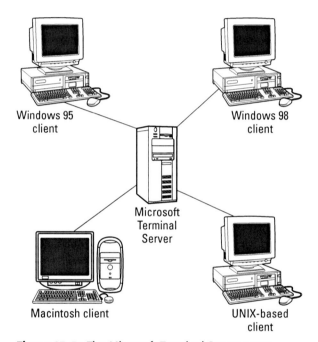

Figure 13-5: The Microsoft Terminal Server setup

Microsoft Terminal Server Edition consists of three components: *terminal server, super-thin client,* and *Remote Desktop Protocol (RDP).*

✦ **Terminal Server** — Provides the capability of simultaneously hosting compatible multiuser clients running on various Windows-based and non-Windows-based platforms (hardware as well as software). The Terminal service, termsrv.exe, is the controlling process in the Terminal server architecture. It is responsible for the initiation, management, and termination of user sessions and session event notifications.

✦ **Super-thin client** — Displays the 32-bit Windows user interface on a variety of Windows-based and non-Windows-based platforms.

✦ **Remote Desktop Protocol (RDP)** — Allows Terminal Server clients to access the Terminal server. It is the key component of the Microsoft Terminal Server. RDP is based on the International Telecommunications Union (ITU) T.120 suite of standard communications protocols. The RDP client can be installed and run on any Windows- or non-Windows-based client.

Note   The Terminal services are entirely protocol-independent. They can function using RDP or a third-party protocol.

The client connects to the terminal server and operates in the following manner:

✦ The client initiates a connection to the Terminal Server through the TCP port. At this point, before the client can log on to the server, the licensing details are negotiated between the server and the client. In the case of Windows-based clients, the license is verified on the machine that requests the connection. If the client is non-Windows-based, a connectivity license is issued to allow connection to the Terminal server.

✦ After the session details have been negotiated, the user is prompted with the Windows NT logon screen. When the user types a user name and password, account authentication is performed to ensure that the user has authority to log on. If the client is registered on the terminal server, the terminal server desktop is displayed to the user.

✦ When the user selects an application, the commands are passed to the terminal server, which launches the selected application. If a user disconnects a session by mistake (exiting the session without logging out), the session processes and memory occupied are not destroyed. When the user reconnects, the existing session is reloaded as if the session never ended. However, when a user logs off from a session, all processes associated with the session are terminated and the memory allocated to the session is released.

Tip   The logon screen will not appear if auto-logon is configured for a client. In this case, the encrypted user name and password is passed to the terminal server, and the logon proceeds.

Citrix

Citrix MetaFrame is a server-based thin-client software that provides an extension to Microsoft's Windows-based Terminal Server and remote services to UNIX clients. It delivers a complete server-based solution by extending client and server functionality. This includes support for heterogeneous environments, enterprise-scale management, and seamless integration.

Citrix uses the *Independent Computing Architecture (ICA)* protocol, which provides additional client- and server-side functionality to Microsoft's Terminal Server to support diverse clients as well as terminal-server-like remote accessibility to UNIX-based clients. It allows for cost-effective deployment, management, and access of applications over a network, regardless of the client platform or network connection.

Note The current version of Microsoft Terminal Server is a subset of the Terminal services offered by Citrix MetaFrame. Microsoft co-developed their Terminal server with Citrix (with Citrix doing the lion's share). The Citrix solution is more comprehensive as a result of the deal worked out between Microsoft and Citrix.

The ICA protocol used by Citrix MetaFrame supports a wide variety of client platforms, including DOS, Windows, OS/2, UNIX, and Linux. It also allows applications running on various hand-held devices and Internet appliances to start sessions on a MetaFrame server. ICA is capable of providing separate application-user interfaces simultaneously to all the applications executing on a server. Installing MetaFrame on a Solaris server is an effective solution — especially in the case of ever-increasing mobile clients, such as sales personnel — because it is easy to install and configure.

The additional client- and server-side capabilities that are provided by Citrix to the Microsoft Terminal Server include: *thin-client/server management, heterogeneous client, network, or protocol support,* and *seamless desktop integration for applications* that may be running remotely or locally.

✦ **Thin-client/server management** — Citrix extends the management tools included with Microsoft Terminal Server. For example, it provides additional enterprise management tools for users, systems, and applications, which can help administrators manage version control, support remote users, resolve configuration problems, and eradicate data replication across the various branches of the corporate network.

Note In case of increased user demand, Citrix MetaFrame-based terminal servers can support a huge number of clients by adding additional servers. Organizations that are building large enterprise networks with the Windows-based Terminal Server can view, administer, and scale their "server farms" from a single point, thereby reducing total cost of ownership.

✦ **Heterogeneous environment support** — Provides access to a broad range of applications in a heterogeneous environment made up of various desktop devices, network types, and operating systems. It can support virtually any type of hardware (PCs, networked devices, wireless devices, and so on) and operating system (MS-DOS, Windows 3.*x*, Windows 9*x*, Windows NT, UNIX, OS/2, Mac OS, Java Virtual Machine (JVM), and so on). It can work on any network connection, such as LAN, WAN, dial-up, Internet, and intranet. Also, Citrix can support a diverse range of protocols that includes TCP/IP, IPX/SPX, SLIP, PPP, and NetBIOS.

✦ **Seamless desktop integration** — Provides seamless (or transparent) access to a wide range of applications that may be Windows-based, Java-based, or browser-based, including audio-based applications. Although the applications are executed on the terminal server, they behave as if they are executing on the user's system.

Citrix functions in much the same way as Microsoft Terminal Server. In addition to Windows-based clients, Citrix also provides terminal services for the UNIX-based client. Any computer running MetaFrame for UNIX 1.0 client can establish a session with a terminal server running the Metaframe host. As per Citrix specifications, Sun Solaris 2.6 or 2.7 with either Sparc or Intel MetaFrame must be used as the terminal server, because it provides UNIX's scalability and allows legacy applications to be easily deployed with mobile and thin clients.

 Note   Legacy applications are applications that run on the UNIX platform.

Citrix MetaFrame provides many advantages over other terminal servers, including:

✦ Support to Microsoft Terminal Server, as well as UNIX servers. In addition, it provides seamless integration of a huge range of clients.

✦ Smooth functioning with as little as 15 KBPS bandwidth in the case of UNIX backbone. This leads to quicker response times and reduction in overall traffic on the WAN link.

✦ Provision of the facility to monitor user sessions and allow the administrator to take over the session, if necessary. This is very helpful when troubleshooting problems.

✦ Easy installation. Also, maintenance does not entail a large overhead cost.

Summary

In this chapter, you learned about various remote command utilities, such as Telnet and r-utilities. You learned that Remote login (rlogin), Remote shell (rsh), and Remote execute (rexec) are the r-utilities that enable you to access remote resources. You also learned in detail about the Secure shell protocol that was developed to address the security loopholes of the r-utilities. Finally, you learned about terminal servers — such as Sun's Sun Ray, Microsoft Terminal Server, and Citrix — and how they help you access remote resources and services.

✦   ✦   ✦

Printing over the Network

T his chapter discusses printing as it relates to both the
UNIX/Linux and Microsoft worlds. The topics that are
covered include: the printing procedure for both Microsoft
and UNIX/Linux operating systems; the configuration of printers on both platforms; procedures for configuring the lpd
server; and the Microsoft Internet Printing Protocol.

One primary advantage of configuring TCP/IP is the ability to
print over the network. You can configure TCP/IP to print files
on Windows as well as UNIX/Linux machines. Thus, this chapter examines printing from both local and network printers.

Printing Overview

In the business environment, printing is one of the most common tasks performed on a day-to-day basis. Sending a job for
printing might not look difficult, but configuring a printer is. In
general, printers fall in two separate categories: local and network. A *local printer* is a printer that is connected to only one
machine. Thus, only the user of that particular machine can
issue print jobs. Local printers are useful for people who work
at home on a personal computer. In contrast, *network printers*
are commonly found in large organizations, where it is not feasible to have a separate printer for each employee. In this
case, a network printer can be configured on the server, and
all employees who are part of the network are able to use it.
Thereafter, server users can request jobs from the printer
attached to the server. Note that you can attach local or network printers to both Linux and Windows machines.

Printing in the Linux world

Printing services are available in all of the Linux software offered by different vendors, although these services may contain slight variations. In this chapter, you will learn to manage print jobs on Linux operating system, offered by one of the most popular vendors of Linux, Red Hat. Red Hat Linux offers a variety of programs, files, and directories that assist you in the printing process.

In Red Hat Linux, users can print files with the help of a centrally located printer. You can configure a Linux machine to print on a printer that is connected to a Linux server or a WindowsNT/2000 server. In Red Hat Linux, the *line printer daemon (lpd)* is responsible for spooling files on the server. The lpd accepts files from the clients and stores them on the server till the printer is ready to print.

Note that the line printer daemon should be running *anytime* you want to use your system's print services. You can check whether the lpd is running by using the lpc status command at the command prompt. If you want lpd to start at boot time, you can use the `ntsysv` command and set the lpd daemon to start at boot time.

Note   Spooling is a process in which the daemon stores the print documents on the disk and then sends them to the printer for printing.

To have a thorough understanding of the printing process, you need to understand concepts pertaining to components of Linux print services such as the printer device file, spooling, print queues, and the /etc/printcap file. These components of Linux print services are described in the following sections.

Printer device file

System hardware is represented as device files. Printer devices are character-mode devices that are located in the /dev directory. The printer device file represents the parallel line printer (in other words, the printer connected to the parallel port).

The printer file listing looks like this:

```
# ls -l /dev/lp*
crw-rw----    1 root      lp          6,   0 Aug 24  2000
/dev/lp0
crw-rw----    1 root      lp          6,   1 Aug 24  2000
/dev/lp1
crw-rw----    1 root      lp          6,   2 Aug 24  2000
/dev/lp2
```

Tip   A port is an interface by which you can connect a hardware device to a computer. A port can be internal or external. *Internal ports* are used to connect devices like hard disks and display screens. *External ports* are used to connect devices like modems, mice, and printers.

Spooling

Spool stands for *Simultaneous Peripheral Operations On Line.* Spooling is the process by which print jobs are rendered to the disk file that is understood by the printer and then sent for printing. Spooling temporarily allocates memory for the issued print job. Therefore, if the printer is busy, it can complete its current job and begin with the new print job. The process of printing is carried on by the line printer daemon.

Print queue

The print queue refers to the list of jobs that have been sent to the printer for printing, but have not yet been printed. In other words, the print queue is made up of jobs that are in the pipeline for being printed. You can view documents in the print queue by typing the lpq command.

The printcap file

All necessary information about the printers that you have configured is present in the /etc/printcap file. The line printer daemon uses these files to manage spooling. Attributes (such as fonts required for printing the output, margins, the spaces to be left on the paper, and the protocol to be used for communicating with the printer) are also specified in this file.

The following listing is a sample printcap file:

```
# /etc/printcap
#
# Please don't edit this file directly unless you know what you
are doing!
# Be warned that the control-panel printtool requires a very
strict format!
# Look at the printcap(5) man page for more info.
#
# This file can be edited with the printtool in the control-
panel.

##PRINTTOOL3## SMB
lp:\
    :sd=/var/spool/lpd/lp:\
    :mx#0:\
    :sh:\
    :af=/var/spool/lpd/lp/acct:\
    :lp=/dev/null:\
    :if=/usr/lib/rhs/rhs-printfilters//smbprint:
```

In this example, only one printer has been added. The printer is connected to the Server Message Block (SMB) service. Table 14-1 explains the entries in the printcap file.

Table 14-1
Entries in the printcap File

Entry	Description
:sd=/var/spool/lpd/lp:\	This entry specifies the spool directory.
:mx#0:\	This entry specifies the maximum file size. Zero indicates that the file size can be unlimited.
:sh:\	This entry indicates that the printer should suppress the printing of page headers.
:af=/var/spool/lpd/lp/acct:\	This entry specifies the name of the accounting file.
:lp=/dev/null:\	This entry specifies the name of the device to open for output.
:if=/usr/lib/rhs/rhs-printfilters//smbprint:	This entry specifies the name of the Input filter that is also responsible for accounting.

Print services use certain system files that are explained in Table 14-2.

Table 14-2
Files Used by the Linux Printing Utility

File Name	Description
/etc/passwd	This file is useful for personal identification to check the printer access permission.
/etc/printcap	This file maintains the Printer Capability Database.
/usr/sbin/lpd	This file is the line printer daemon.
/var/spool/lpd/*	These are the directories used for spooling.
/var/spool/lpd/*/cf*	These are daemon control files.
/var/spool/lpd/*/df*	These are the data files specified in the "cf" files.
/var/spool/lpd/*/tf*	These are temporary copies of the "cf" files.

Printing in the Microsoft world

Microsoft Windows' operating systems are widely used. Therefore, understanding how print jobs are managed by Windows operating systems is important. The print process on a Windows machine can be described in the following steps:

1. The user decides to print a document.

2. The user either submits the document from a Windows machine or one that doesn't use a Windows operating system. If the print job is running off a Windows machine, the application that the user is using is called a *Graphics Device Interface (GDI)*. The GDI communicates with the printer driver associated with the printer from which the print job is requested. The GDI and the driver then exchange data and render the print job in the language of the printer. The printer interprets the print job and the job is passed on to the client-side spooler. If the print job is running off a non-Windows machine, then another component specific to the operating system you are using replaces the GDI and performs the necessary tasks. The GDI is used only with Windows 2000 operating systems.

3. The client computer passes the print job to the print server. For Windows 2000 and Windows NT clients, the client-side spooler makes a Remote Procedure Call (RPC) to the server. The RPC uses the router to connect to the remote print provider on the client side. Then the remote print provider sends another RPC to the server spooler, which then receives the print job over the network.

4. The print server identifies the jobs sent by Windows machines as Enhanced Metafiles (EMF) data type. The jobs that are sent by most non-Windows 2000 applications are identified as ready to print, *RAW data type.* This data type doesn't allow you to change or modify the print job before printing.

5. The router on the print server is responsible for passing the print job to the local print provider on the server. Then, the local print provider spools the print job. In other words, it writes the print job to the disk.

6. The print processor receives the print job after recognizing the data type of the print job. Depending on the data type, the print processor converts the print job.

7. If specifying the name of the target printer configures the client computer, the print server service decides whether the server spooler should alter the print job or assign a different data type to the print job. The print job is then passed to the local print provider, and later on, written to the disk.

8. The control of the print job is passed to the separator page processor. This page processor adds a separator page to the front of the job, if specified.

9. The job is despooled to the print monitors. In the case of bidirectional printers, a language monitor manages the two-way communication between the sender and the printer. The job is passed on to the port monitor. In case the printer is not bidirectional, the print job travels directly to the port monitor. The port monitor sends the print job to the target printer.

10. After receiving the print job, the printer converts each page to a bitmap format and prints it.

Printing from the client

The computers in most organizations are part of an internal network that enables users to share files and resources; users can also benefit from server resources, such as the printer. In a client-server network, users that connect to the server are known as clients. In order to print documents, a connection must exist between the client and the server. This connection can be constituted in several different ways: Linux/UNIX client connecting to a Linux/UNIX server, Linux/UNIX clients connecting to a remote Windows server, Windows clients connecting to a Linux/UNIX server, and Windows clients connecting to a Windows server.

To connect a Windows client with a Windows server, you need MS proprietary SMB. Whenever we talk about TCP/IP printing, we talk about lpr/lpd printing (services used for printing in the TCP/IP environment).

Configuring an lpd Server

The Linux server can be configured with five types of printers. The type you choose to install will depend on your requirement. Your requirement would be based on the operating system you, and other users on the network are using. It would also depend on to which server operating system you plan to install the network printer.

✦ **Local printer connected to the Linux server** — This printer is connected to the parallel port of the Linux machine. Only the user of the machine to which the printer is installed can use the printer.

✦ **Remote UNIX/Linux (lpd) printer** — This printer is connected to a UNIX/Linux machine. Those who are using UNIX/Linux can request print jobs from this machine.

✦ **Windows 95/Windows NT (SMB) printer** — This printer is physically attached to a Windows 95 or Windows NT machine. If Linux users want to use the printer connected to a Windows NT server, the SMB service will have to be configured.

✦ **Novell Netware (NCP) printer** — This printer is attached to a Novell Netware server.

✦ **Direct to port printer** — This printer is not attached to a machine (server). All clients on a network can directly access it.

Remote Linux/UNIX printers

Before you begin using a printer that is connected to a remote UNIX/Linux machine, you need to enter the following information:

✦ The name of the printer connected to the remote Linux or UNIX machine

✦ The location of the spool directory

✦ The maximum size for the spool directory

✦ The remote machine's host name

✦ The name of the remote printer

✦ The Input Filter — that is, the driver for the printer

Tip   There is a spool directory on the local machine used by the lpd. It is used only when the printer is busy or offline. In such cases, the print jobs in the local machine wait in the spool area until they can be sent.

When you configure the remote Linux printer, the changes are reflected in the /etc/printcap file. The :rm and :rp entries are made in the file for the printer. The rm parameter consists of the name of the remote host, and the rp parameter defines the remote printer name, such as lp, lp1, and so on.

In order to print a file from the remote printer, the remote printer should grant you the required permission. In other words, the remote machine to which the printer is attached should accept a print request from the client machine.

The printtool utility

The printtool utility is a very handy tool used to configure printers on Linux. To invoke the printtool utility, type `printtool` at the command prompt. You can use the printtool utility to configure a local printer, remote UNIX (lpd) printer, SMB/Windows 95/NT printer, Netware printer, and direct to port printer.

Connecting to a local printer

You can use the printtool utility to configure a local printer on your machine. Before you start configuring the printer, ensure that the printer you are using is compatible with Linux. Then proceed by typing `printtool` at the command prompt, which will open the Red Hat Linux Print System Manager dialog box shown in Figure 14-1.

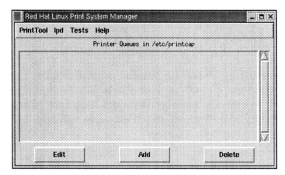

Figure 14-1: Opening screen of the printtool utility

Next, click the Add button to install a new printer. The Add a Printer Entry dialog box appears, as shown in Figure 14-2.

Figure 14-2: The Add a Printer Entry dialog box

The Add a Printer Entry dialog box lists five different options that can be used to configure printers. You have the choice of installing a local printer, a remote UNIX (lpd) queue, an SMB/Windows 95/NT printer, a Netware Printer (NCP), and a Direct to port printer. Select "Local Printer" and click OK. The Info dialog box now appears, as shown in Figure 14-3.

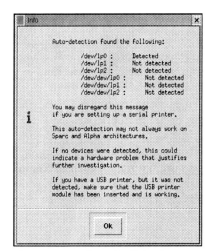

Figure 14-3: The Info dialog box

The Info dialog box provides information about the parallel printer devices that have been detected. The message in the Info dialog box also indicates that if no hardware devices were detected, a problem with the hardware may exist. Click the OK button to proceed. The Edit Local Printer Entry dialog box will appear, as shown in Figure 14-4.

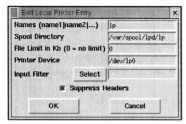

Figure 14-4: The Edit Local Printer
Entry dialog box

The Edit Local Printer Entry dialog allows you to change settings regarding the name of the printer (by default it is lp), the path of the spool directory, the maximum file size, the printer device, and the Input Filter. The Input Filter can be used to configure the driver of the printer. To view the Configure Filter dialog box (shown in Figure 14-5), click the Select button next to the Input Filter option.

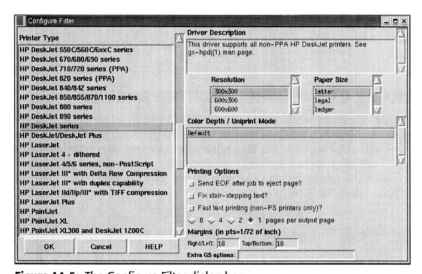

Figure 14-5: The Configure Filter dialog box

The Configure Filter dialog box allows you to set the resolution, margins, paper size, and pages per output page for a particular document. You can customize the print settings according to your requirements, as shown in Figure 14-5. You can select the make of the printer you want to install and click OK after choosing the required settings.

After making the required changes, the Input Filter box in the Edit Local Printer dialog box now contains the name of the printer that you chose to install. Click the OK button to finish installing the printer. The settings that are made using the printtool utility are automatically reflected in the /etc/printcap file. Figure 14-6 appears after you click the OK button. Notice that the entry for the printer you have added appears.

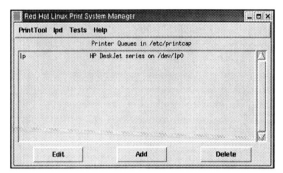

Figure 14-6: The Red Hat Linux Print System Manager dialog box

Connecting to a network interface printer

If you are part of a Linux network, you might want to configure a printer on the Linux server. If so, certain settings must be made to enable you to print files from a printer attached to a Linux server. This type of printer can be configured by using the printtool utility, as shown earlier in Figure 14-1. Start by selecting the option "Remote UNIX (lpd) Queue" from the Add a Printer Entry dialog box, as shown in Figure 14-7, and then click OK.

Figure 14-7: The Add a Printer Entry dialog box

In the Edit Remote UNIX (lpd) Queue Entry dialog box, shown in Figure 14-8, you need to specify information regarding the remote host, remote queue, and input filter. For example, in the Remote Host column, enter the name of the remote Linux server to which the printer is attached. In the Remote Queue column, enter the name of the remote queue.

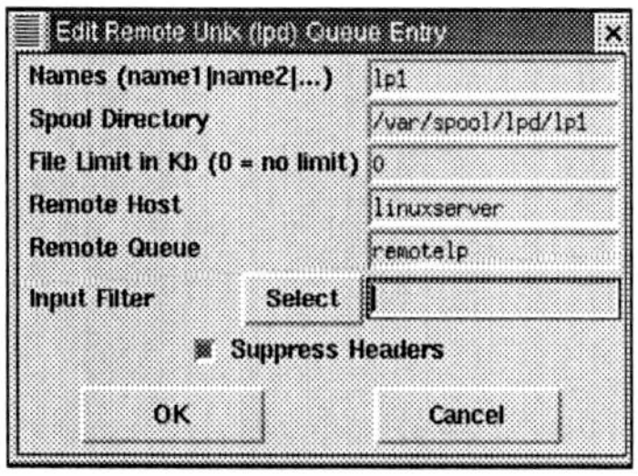

Figure 14-8: The Edit Remote UNIX
(lpd) Queue Entry dialog box

Click the Select button to open the Configure Filter dialog box, as shown in Figure 14-9.

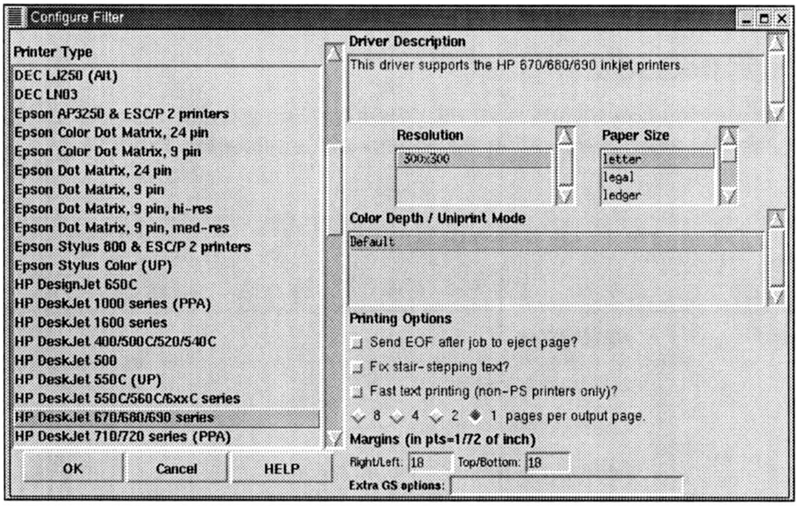

Figure 14-9: The Configure Filter dialog box

In the Configure Filter dialog box, you can select the printer make that is connected to the remote Linux/UNIX server. You can also customize your print settings. After you make the necessary changes, click OK. The `printtool` command will automatically make necessary additions in the /etc/printcap file.

To allow users to print documents successfully from the remote Linux/UNIX printer, you need to create a file named hosts.lpd in the /etc directory of the remote host computer. In this file, you need to enter a list of host names or IP addresses of the users that will be allowed to issue print jobs from the server machine. The contents of the hosts.lpd file should be as follows:

```
# vi hosts.lpd
john.home.org
172.17.55.135
172.17.55.10
renne.home.org
steve.home.org
172.17.55.255
```

You can see that host names of client machines as well as IP addresses have been specified. Only users whose IP address or host name is specified in this file are able to print files using the remote printer. For more information about remote printer entries, refer to the man page for printcap. After you have configured your printer, an entry for the remote printer appears in the printtool utility's main dialog box.

Tip   Host names can be specified in the hosts.lpd file only when DNS is configured. If DNS is not configured, you need to specify the IP address of the machines.

Print commands

You can use certain commands from the command line interface to print the files of your choice. The most frequently used commands are listed in Table 14-3.

Table 14-3	
Print Commands	

Command	Description
Lpr	Makes print requests.
Lpq	Checks the print queue.
Lprm	Removes jobs from the print queue.
Lpc	Controls the operations of the line printer system.
Lpstat	Prints the current status of the LP print service.

Now let us examine each of the print commands given in Table 14-3 in detail. We will also discuss options that are frequently used with these print commands.

The lpr command

The lpr command is used to send print jobs to the printer after you have successfully configured the printer. The syntax for the lpr command is as follows:

```
lpr [options] filename
```

Several options can be used with the lpr command. The frequently used options are listed in Table 14-4.

Table 14-4
Options Used with the lpr Command

Option	Function
–t or –T	These options can be used to assign a title to the print job.
–d	This option is used to assign a destination for the print job.
–P	This option is used to specify the printer name of the printer you want to issue the print job.
–o	This option is used to specify additional options.
–n	This option is used to specify the number of copies.

The lpq command

The lpq command is used to check the print queue. You would ideally want to check the print queue to view the status of the print job that you have issued. The syntax of the lpq command is as follows:

```
lpq [options]
```

There are several options that can be used with the lpq command. Table 14-5 lists a few of the most frequently used options.

Table 14-5
Options Used with the lpq Command

Option	Function
–a	This option is used to list the print jobs that have been issued to each of the printers that have been configured on your machine.
–P	This option, followed by the printer name, lists the print jobs issued to the specified printer.
–V	This option is used to provide information about the print version.
–s	This option is used to display a single line of information about each queue.

The lprm command

This command is used to cancel a print job and remove the print job from the queue. The syntax of the lprm command is as follows:

```
lprm [options]
```

Tip
Note that if you are an ordinary user using a network printer, you can use the lprm command to cancel only your own print jobs. You need to be a system administrator to cancel print jobs that are issued by other users.

There are several options that can be used with the lprm command to remove specific print jobs from the print queue. The lprm command used without any option removes the last print job that you issued. Table 14-6 lists some more options that are used with the lprm command.

Table 14-6
Options Used with the lprm Command

Option	Function
–a	This option is used to delete all print jobs from all print queues.
–P	This option, followed by the printer name, deletes the print job from the print queue of the specified printer.
–U	This option, followed by the user name, removes the print job of the specified user. You need to have adequate permissions to use this command if you are not the root user.

The lpc command

The lpc command is used to control the line printer system. The syntax of the lpc command is as follows:

```
lpc [options]
```

The root user of the system can only use this command. It is a powerful command and enables the system administrator to perform the following tasks:

✦ Disable all printers or a specific printer installed

✦ Enable all printers or a specific printer installed

✦ Move print jobs to the top of the print queue

✦ Move print jobs from one printer to another printer

✦ Temporarily stop any print job and resume it

✦ Reprint a print job

A few of the options that can be used with the lpc command are given in Table 14-7.

	Table 14-7
	Options Used with the lpc Command

Option	Function
–P	This option, followed by the printer name, can be used to specify the printer spool queue to operate on.
–V	This option is used to provide information about the print program version.
–U	This option, followed by the user name, is used to specify a user name for the request.

The lpstat command

This command is used to print the status of the print service. If no options are used with the lpstat command, it displays the current status of all the print jobs issued to the default printer. The syntax for this command is as follows:

```
# lpstat [options]
```

Table 14-8 lists various options that can be used with the lpstat command.

	Table 14-8
	Options Used with the lpstat Command

Option	Function
–a	This option, followed by the printer name/s, is used to check whether the destinations are accepting print requests or not.
–d	This option is used to print the system default destination for output requests.
–p	This option, followed by the printer name/s, is used to display the status of printer/s.
–t	This option is used to print all the current status information.

Note For more information on remote printing with LPR and LPD, refer to RFC 1179.

Microsoft Internet Printing Protocol

Internet Printing Protocol (IPP) is a protocol designed by Microsoft for its operating systems. It enables a user to print directly to a Uniform Resource Locator (URL) over the Internet or intranet. Another advantage of the Internet Printing Protocol is that you can install printers from the Internet or intranet by using Internet Explorer.

Tip   An error message might occur while installing a printer using IPP if the required drivers for the printer are not present.

The steps to configure IPP are described in the following sections. Note that the steps for administrators are different than those for other users. This is because the administrator configures the IPP server, whereas the users just configure their machine to use the IPP server. The administrator installs the drivers for the printer.

Administrators

Before you start using IPP, you need to install the drivers for the printer you are going to install. Follow this procedure:

1. Choose Start ➪ Settings ➪ Printers to open the Printers window.

2. Double-click Add Printer to start the Add Printer Wizard, and click Next to proceed.

3. Select Local Printer (if it is not selected by default).

4. Select "Create a new port" and ensure that in the Type box, "Local Port" is selected. Click Next. The Port Name dialog box will appear.

5. In the Enter a port name text box, type the share name (for example: \\printserver\sharename).

6. Run through the Wizard and install the necessary drivers for the device.

All other users

1. Choose Start ➪ Settings ➪ Printers to open the Printers window.

2. Double-click Add Printer to start the Add Printer Wizard, and click Next to proceed.

3. Select Local Printer (if it is not selected by default).

4. Select "Create a new port" and ensure that in the Type box, Standard Port Monitor is selected. Click Next. The Port Name dialog box will appear.

5. Type the IP address of the IPP print server.

6. Run through the Wizard and install the necessary drivers for the device.

Summary

In this chapter, you learned about printing files in the Linux/UNIX and Microsoft worlds. More specifically, you learned how to configure the lpd server, then how to install a local and network printer in Linux. Finally, you learned about the Internet Printing Protocol (IPP), as well as how to configure a Windows 2000 machine to use IPP from the server and client sides.

✦   ✦   ✦

World Wide Web Applications and Protocols

The concept of the *information superhighway* — which refers to the global network of telecommunication and information technology used for commerce, education, entertainment, and so on — has revolutionized the way people communicate with each other. The backbones of this global network are the Internet and the World Wide Web.

This chapter discusses the structure and function of the World Wide Web, the role of the World Wide Web Consortium (W3C) in the development of standards for the Web, HyperText Markup Language (HTML) as a language for creating documents for the Web, and HyperText Transfer Protocol (HTTP). This chapter also examines various World Wide Web applications.

Overview of the World Wide Web

What is the Internet? What is the World Wide Web? Are these two terms interchangeable? How did these technologies evolve? The following section discusses the answers to these questions.

Introduction to the Internet

The Internet is a collection of computers that are interconnected for the purpose of sharing information. The Internet is not a single network; rather, it is a network of other networks, all of which use TCP/IP as their communication protocol.

The Internet originated with the development of ARPANET, a network created by the United States Defense Advanced Research Project Agency (DARPA) in 1969. ARPANET provided a fault-tolerant computer-based communication system that could withstand the loss of one or more computing centers, such as a military base or a city. Initially, ARPANET consisted of four host computers, which used the Network Control Protocol (NCP) for communication. The technology used for communication was called *packet switching*. However, NCP wasn't able to handle an ever-increasing volume of network traffic. Therefore, in 1974, Transmission Control Protocol (TCP) and Internet Protocol (IP) were proposed and implemented as more robust communication protocols.

> **Note**
> Packet switching is the process of dividing data communications messages into small packets. A packet is similar to a letter, in that it contains a portion of the message as well as the recipient's address. Each packet is transmitted individually over the network. After all packets reach their destination, they are reorganized to form the complete message. The TCP/IP protocol is based on the packet-switching technology.

During the 1980s, researchers and organizations realized the benefits of the ARPANET network. As a result, it branched out, adding networks from universities, corporations, and user communities. In 1982, the ARPANET network came to be commonly known as the *Internet*. Because of its power and scope, the Internet has grown exponentially in just a few years. Different services, such as Gopher, Wide Area Information Server (WAIS), and the World Wide Web, have all been developed to help users access data on the Internet.

> **Note**
> Gopher is a software program that was developed in 1991. It divides information into logical categories and organizes these categories in a tree-like hierarchical structure. WAIS, on the other hand, is a program that searches for documents on the Internet.
>
> With the advent of the World Wide Web, Gopher and WAIS are no longer being used. Most of the Gopher databases are being converted into Web sites, which can be easily accessed using a Web search engine.

The evolution of the World Wide Web

The most popular method of sharing information on the Internet is by using a format known as the World Wide Web (WWW, or simply, the Web). The World Wide Web consists of files called Web pages that contain information and links to other Web pages. Before the introduction of the World Wide Web, data was transferred in the form of text or binary code. The World Wide Web introduced the capability of incorporating text, graphics, audio, and animation in a single file.

The World Wide Web was developed in 1991 at the European Center for Nuclear Research (CERN). The physicists at CERN wanted a quick way to share their research information with other researchers around the world. One of their physicists, Tim Berners-Lee, proposed a text-based hypertext system as a means of exchanging data between physicists involved in high-energy physics research. He used the hypertext method, in which pointing to a highlighted word or phrase took a user to a new page on the same machine or to a remote machine on the network.

In 1993, a user-friendly client program was developed at the National Center for Supercomputer Applications (NCSA) that provided a graphical interface for the World Wide Web. This program, called *Mosaic*, was the first graphical Internet browser to let users retrieve information by simply pointing and clicking. As a result, the World Wide Web grew rapidly. Today, many Mosaic-based browsers have been developed, including the popular *Netscape Navigator* and *Internet Explorer.*

Note *World Wide Web* is the name given to the body of information on the Internet characterized by colorful graphics and hypertext links. In contrast, a *browser* is the tool that allows you to view the information that contains the colorful graphics and links.

How the World Wide Web works

The World Wide Web is based on the client/server model. In this model, a client program makes a request to a server program, which usually runs on a remote machine. The client and the server communicate with each other over a network. After receiving a request from the client, the server establishes a connection with the client, processes the request, sends the results to the client, and terminates the connection. In the case of the World Wide Web, a browser such as Internet Explorer or Netscape Navigator makes requests to the server. Any computer that stores Web pages containing the information requested by the client can act as the server. Web pages are written in a language called *HyperText Markup Language (HTML)*. HTML provides the browsers with instructions regarding how the page should be displayed. The client and the server communicate through the use of an application-level protocol called *HyperText Transfer Protocol (HTTP)*.

A user who wants to access information on the Web specifies the *Uniform Resource Locator (URL)* in the browser. A URL is a unique identifier that defines the route to a file on a host computer connected to the Internet. It can also be embedded within a document and provided as a hypertext link to the user. The working of the World Wide Web is shown in Figure 15-1.

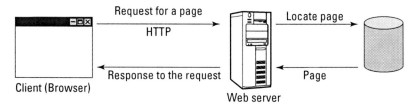

Figure 15-1: The working of the World Wide Web

The format for specifying the URL looks like this:

```
<Protocol identifier>://<server name>[:<[port]>][/<path to the HTML docu-
ment>][/<HTML file name>]
```

For example, consider the following URL:

```
http://www.webknowledgebase.com/definition/ARPANET.html
```

`http` specifies the protocol used for communication between the client and the server. The following protocols can be specified:

✦ **http** — Used to access a World Wide Web server

✦ **ftp** — Used for file transfer

✦ **wais** — Used to access a Wide Area Information Server

✦ **mailto** — Used to access e-mail

✦ **gopher** — Used for accessing a Gopher server

✦ **file** — Used to access a file on the local system

After specifying the protocol, the address of the Web server is specified (in this case, `www.webknowledgebase.com`). The suffix `com` indicates a commercial organization. Other suffixes include:

✦ **edu** — Educational institution

✦ **gov** — Government agency

✦ **org** — Non-commercial organization

✦ **mil** — Military organization

✦ **net** — Network

In the example URL given above, the port number is not specified. Therefore, the default port number for HTTP (80) will be used. `definition` is the folder on the Web server where the requested page is stored, and `ARPANET.html` is the requested page.

After the user types the URL in the browser or clicks on a hypertext link, the browser sends a request for the page to the specified Web server. The Web server retrieves the requested page and sends it to the browser, which reads the page, interprets the instructions specified in the page, and displays it to the user.

HyperText Markup Language

HyperText Markup Language (HTML), as the name suggests, is a *markup language* used for creating a Web page. A markup language uses a set of labels, called *tags,* which are embedded within the text. Tags are not visible to the reader and are not part of the content in a document, but they enhance the document by specifying its structure and display characteristics.

HTML is derived from Standard Generalized Markup Language (SGML), but HTML is much simpler to use. It serves as a *de facto* standard for describing how information is structured and displayed. Thus, it allows different vendors to develop a variety of browsers for hardware and software platforms and display the data in approximately the same way.

Note

> Introduced in 1986, SGML was the first markup language to be developed. It delivered and displayed documents regardless of the platform being used. Because SGML is a comprehensive language that is difficult to learn, Tim Berners-Lee (in 1990) developed and defined HTML as a markup language for creating Web pages.

Versions of HTML

From its inception, HTML has experienced a number of revisions. The different versions of HTML are as follows:

- ✦ **HTML 2.0** — The first definitive version of HTML. It included most of the tags that are in use today. However, it did not support tables and alignment features for the text.

- ✦ **HTML 3.2** — Incorporated support for tables, images, and alignment attributes.

- ✦ **HTML 4.0** — Incorporated some Microsoft and Netscape extensions. For example, the FRAME element (a Microsoft extension that divides a Web page into two or more parts) was introduced in HTML 4.0.

- ✦ **HTML 4.01** — The current official standard. HTML 4.01 includes a number of proprietary extensions and other features, such as forms and style sheets. It also supports internationalization.

Note

> Internationalization is the process of developing an application in such a way that it can be easily adapted to different languages and regions without any changes. Internationalization provides several advantages, such as visual consistency and support for entering and displaying characters from different languages.

Structure of an HTML document

In HTML, the text of a document is divided into logical blocks called *elements*. These elements specify the appearance of the text embedded within them. For example, HTML uses the ANCHOR element, which allows text to be displayed as hypertext. Thus, elements are the basic building blocks of an HTML document. The elements are represented in a document as tags. For example, the ANCHOR tag is represented as ⟨A⟩ in a document. More importantly, tags are usually paired. They mark the start and end of an element. For example, consider the following statement:

```
<A> Click Here </A>
```

In this example, the starting and ending points of the ANCHOR element are represented with the ⟨A⟩ and ⟨/A⟩ tag pair. The text embedded between these tags is displayed as a hypertext link.

An HTML document is divided mainly into two parts: the HEAD and the BODY. The HEAD section contains information about the document itself, such as the title to be displayed on the title bar of the browser window and the keywords included in the document. The BODY section contains the actual text that is displayed within the browser window. Take a look at the following sample HTML document:

```
<HTML>
<HEAD>
<TITLE> MY FIRST WEB PAGE </TITLE>
</HEAD>
<BODY>

    <FONT COLOR="RED">
    <H1 ALIGN="CENTER"> Introduction to  </H1>
    </FONT>
    <FONT SIZE=4>
    <P>
HTML, as the name suggests, is a markup language used for
creating a Web page. A markup language uses a set of labels
that are embedded within the text. These labels are called
tags. Tags are not visible to the reader and are not a part of
the content in a document, but they enhance the document by
specifying its structure and display characteristics. <BR>
<CNTER> <A HREF="next.html"> Next Page </A> </CENTER>
    </P>
    </FONT>
</BODY>
</HTML>
```

When you open this file in Internet Explorer, the browser will interpret the tags and display the text, as shown in Figure 15-2.

As seen in the figure, although tags are read and interpreted by the browser, they are not visible on the display screen. In this case, when the browser encounters the <P> tag, it recognizes it as the beginning of a paragraph. Similarly, when it encounters the <FONT> tag, it changes the size and color of the text as specified within the tag. Also note that the shape of the mouse cursor changes when it is moved over the text Next Page. This is a hypertext link. When you click it, the browser sends a request for another page (in this example, next.html). The file will be interpreted and displayed in a similar way by different browsers regardless of the underlying hardware and software platform.

HyperText Transfer Protocol

HyperText Transfer Protocol (HTTP) is an application-level protocol used to carry out all communications between the Web server and browsers. It specifies how messages are to be formatted and transmitted. It also specifies the action to be taken by the Web server and browsers in response to a particular command. HTTP is a stateless protocol, which means that it has no knowledge of the commands that precede the current command.

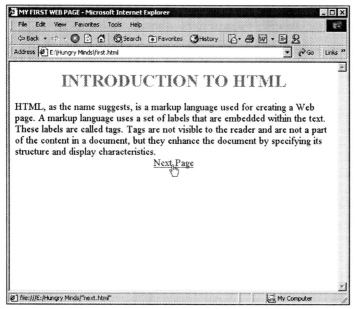

Figure 15-2: A sample HTML page

HTTP provides a feature in which the client sends a list of all the symbols that it understands to the Web server. Based on this information, the server replies in a suitable way. This feature allows the client and server to cope with the numerous graphic formats, such as GIF and JPEG.

HTTP uses the URL specified by a user in the browser to locate a resource on the Internet. The communication between the browser and the Web server takes place through various HTTP commands. Some of these commands include:

✦ **GET** — This command instructs the server to retrieve the data located at the path specified in the URL.

✦ **HEAD** — This command is similar to the GET command, except the Web server returns only the document header to the browser. It does not return the document body.

✦ **POST** — This command instructs the Web server to create a new object. Either the Web server or the browser can set the message identification field in the new object. The server assigns a URL to this new object and sends the URL to the client. The new object becomes part of the requested document.

All HTTP transactions take place over the TCP/IP protocol. An HTTP transaction goes through the following phases:

✦ **Connection** — In this phase, the browser tries to connect to the Web server. The Web server receives the request and establishes a connection.

✦ **Request** — After establishing a connection, the client sends requests to the server, specifying the protocol to be used for communication and the file to be retrieved and sent. The client also sends information about the type of information (GIFs, TIFFs, JPEGs, and so on) that it can support.

✦ **Response** — If the server succeeds in locating and processing the information requested by the client, it sends a response to the client. If it fails to locate the information, it sends an error message. The server sends a response based on the type of information supported by the client. For example, if you try to access a page that contains some Flash files and the browser does not have support for these files, a dialog box is displayed, asking whether you want to install the additional components required for displaying the files.

✦ **Close** — The connection between the client and server can be terminated either by the client or the server.

The World Wide Web Consortium

The World Wide Web Consortium, or W3C, was established by Tim Berners-Lee in 1994 to help researchers and universities around the world achieve the full potential of the World Wide Web. W3C develops common standards and protocols that promote the evolution of the World Wide Web and ensures interoperability between the various WWW-related products. Today, W3C has grown from a handful of people to a large consortium of roughly 500 member-organizations.

The long-term goals of W3C, as stated in their mission statement, include:

✦ **Universal access** — To make the Web accessible to all people, irrespective of country, culture, education, ability, limitations, and physical resources.

✦ **Web of trust** — To develop the culture of trust in the field of commerce, technology, and social issues.

✦ **Semantic Web** — To develop a software environment that allows each user to take advantage of Web resources to the best of their capability.

In the last five years, W3C has developed more than 20 technical specifications for the Web's infrastructure. These specifications, as well as the entire philosophy of W3C, are based on three design principles:

✦ **Interoperability** — The specifications of languages, protocols, and products used on the Web must be compatible with each other. As a result, third-party products should be easy to use and implement.

✦ **Evolution** — Future technologies must be accommodated easily into the Web infrastructure. The simplicity, modularity, and extensibility of the current technologies determine the ease with which future technologies can be accommodated.

✦ **Decentralization** — The aim of this principle is to decentralize the Web to scale across the entire globe, while limiting or eliminating the dependencies on central registries.

True to their mission and goals, W3C has supplied recommendations that have become building blocks for increasing the efficiency, and thus popularity, of the Web. To date, the most successful W3C recommendations include:

✦ HyperText Markup Language (HTML), which is used for creating Web pages for allowing access to information on the Web. Currently, eXtensible HyperText Markup Language (XHTML) is rigorously being developed to make current HTML pages more interactive and dynamic.

✦ Cascading Style Sheets (CSSs), which give style and color to the information available on the Web.

✦ Document Object Model (DOM), which allows access to document structure, style, events, and so on. DOM contains objects that represent different parts of a Web page, such as paragraphs, list items, images, and so on. You can access various parts of a Web page and change their appearance with the help of DOM. Thus, DOM gives Web developers more control over the documents and their appearance.

✦ Dynamic HTML, which is a combination of other technologies, such as HTML, CSS, and DOM. DHTML allows you to change the appearance of an item on a Web page on the client side. For example, you can create a dynamic Web page, which displays a list of toys available on a Web page. When a user points to a toy, you can display the image displaying the toy on the Web page by using DHTML.

✦ eXtensible Markup Language (XML), which allows the Web community to design markup languages that suit their requirements.

Although W3C has succeeded to some extent in making the Web accessible, decentralized, and interoperable, much work needs to be done. Compared to other industries, the Internet and the Web are developing at an unrivaled pace. New technologies and products are being developed so rapidly that it is difficult to keep up with them. This places even more pressure on W3C to fulfill their mission of vendor neutrality, coordination, and consensus.

World Wide Web Applications

Different user communities use the World Wide Web in a number of different ways. For example, regular users use the World Wide Web for accessing e-mails and for chatting with other users across the world. The business community uses it as a powerful medium for advertising and selling their products. In this section, you will be introduced to some of the most commonly used Web servers for hosting World Wide Web applications. You will also look at the different types of applications across the Internet.

Web servers

A Web server is any computer that stores Web pages and contains the Web server software. The Web server software accepts requests from Web clients such as Internet Explorer and Netscape and returns results to them. Some of the most widely used Web server software programs include:

✦ **Internet Information Server (IIS)** — IIS is Web server software from Microsoft that runs on Windows NT and Windows 2000. IIS is very powerful and extremely easy to set up. Besides providing support for HTTP 1.1, IIS offers additional tools, such as the Microsoft Transaction Server (MTS) for building distributed applications, Index Server for indexing and searching Web pages and Microsoft Word documents, and Site Analyst for site management and usage. IIS supports a number of features, including crash protection, support for Active Server Pages and Java, script debugging, and content management.

Note

Active Server Pages (ASP) is a server-side Web technology. For more information on ASP, refer to the "Languages" section of this chapter.

✦ **Personal Web Server (PWS)** — PWS is another Web server software from Microsoft. It is also a scaled-down version of IIS. It lacks some of IIS's advanced features, such as the Index Server. However, PWS does provide support for ASP and script debugging. It runs on Windows 9x and Windows NT Workstation. PWS facilitates the publishing of personal home pages and small Web sites, is suitable for creating intranets, and provides wizards for performing tasks such as setting up home pages and sharing files. You can use the Explorer interface or Personal Web Manager tools for starting and stopping PWS and sharing folders. PWS can also be used for testing a Web site on your Windows 9x or Windows NT Workstation before it can actually be hosted on the Internet. After testing the site for its validity of links and scripts, you can continue using Personal Web Server, or you can use Microsoft FrontPage for copying the Web site from PWS to IIS. Both PWS and IIS are packaged as part of Windows NT Option Pack 4.0, which can be freely downloaded from the Internet at:

www.microsoft.com/ntserver/nts/downloads/recommended/NT4OptPk/default.asp

Note

The Microsoft FrontPage package allows you to build complete Web sites with ease. In this package, all pages share a consistent and easily modifiable design. It also includes navigation tools that are built automatically when you add or remove pages. FrontPage's WYSIWYG editor provides dialog boxes for placing items (such as graphics, word-processing files, and ad banners) in a Web page.

✦ **Apache** — Apache is a robust Web server software that was developed by a group of 20 volunteer programmers, called the Apache Group. Apache was derived from the HTTPd Web server. Since it used the original code of HTTPd along with some patches, it was given the name *A Patchy Server*, which was later changed to *Apache Server*. It was initially developed to run under the UNIX operating system. However, the newer versions of Apache can also work on OS2 and Windows platforms.

Apache offers many advantages. For one, it can be freely downloaded. It is also easy for programmers to extend the functionality of Apache because they can download the source code of Apache. Therefore, Apache is a good choice for enterprise-level Web sites and individuals who use UNIX or a combination of UNIX and Windows NT platforms.

Note HTTP daemon (HTTPd) is Web server software from the National Center for Supercomputer Applications (NCSA). It is available for various versions of UNIX. For more information about HTTPd, refer to www.hoohoo.ncsa.uiuc.edu.

✦ **Java Web Server** — Java Web Server is Web server software developed using Java. It is the best platform for deploying Java applications and servlets. Java Web Server is extensible because you can write your own Java code and plug it into Java Web Server.

Besides the software mentioned above, other Web server software includes iPlanet Web Server (high-end enterprise-level server software from Netscape that runs under UNIX and Windows NT), and in addition, you have the Lotus Domino Web server, which provides integration with Lotus Notes and the capability of hosting Web pages. In other words, users don't need to have the Notes client installed on their computers; instead,, they can access Lotus Notes applications by using any Web browser.

Applications across the Internet

The Internet is a pool of information that is growing day by day. Although the Internet is a useful way to access information, it may sometimes be difficult to find information in such a large pool. However, various tools, called *search engines*, can make your information search simple and efficient. Search engines use a database — a collection of information about documents on the Web — to look for requested words. Some of the more popular search engines include AltaVista, Excite, WebCrawler, and Yahoo. In addition to browsing the Internet for information, there are several applications, such as Netscape Messenger and Microsoft Internet Mail, which allow you to perform the following activities:

✦ Send and receive e-mail

✦ Participate in newsgroups (discussion forums on a variety of topics)

✦ Create your own documents and publish them on the Internet

✦ Transfer and download files

✦ Connect to libraries worldwide

✦ Conduct business on the Internet

E-mail and news

E-mail, which enables users to send and receive messages, is the most widely used service on the Internet. In fact, e-mail is popular even in small networks that aren't connected to the Internet.

E-mail forums allow a group of people to participate in a group discussion. The list of people to whom mail from other people on the list is sent is called a *mailing list*. There are many e-mail programs that allow you to create an alias for a mailing list. When you have to participate in a formal discussion, you can subscribe to publicly available mailing lists. Some examples of e-mail forums are Netscape Messenger and Microsoft's Internet Mail.

Newsgroups allow thousands of people to participate in group discussions and share ideas online. A newsgroup is like a bulletin board, in that people post messages and everyone who subscribes to the group can read and respond to these messages. Newsgroups are implemented through news applications. Some examples of newsgroups are Collabra Discussions and Internet News from Microsoft.

Applications for creating Web pages

Hypertext Markup Language (HTML) is used to create Web pages. You create these Web pages with a text editor (such as the "vi" editor in UNIX) or with graphical editors (such as Microsoft Windows Notepad, MS-DOS Edit, or any word processor). Also, specialized HTML editors are available. The tools used for creating Web pages can be categorized as follows:

✦ Word processor add-ons that allow a standard word processor to be used for creating and modifying HTML pages.

✦ Stand-alone HTML editors that provide WYSIWYG (What You See Is What You Get) capability such as the FrontPage editor from Microsoft.

✦ Conversion tools that allow conversion from a specific document format into HTML.

Helper applications

A typical Web browser can display graphical images and play standard sound files. The Web server and the browser use a mechanism called Multipurpose Internet Mail Extensions (MIME) to match data sent between the browser and the server. However, other kinds of data require the use of helper applications, also called *external viewers*. If the required file is of a data type that MIME does not support, the browser hands over control to a helper application that handles the respective files.

Secure/MIME (SMIME) is a new version of the MIME protocol. Developed in response to the widespread interception and forgery of e-mail, this protocol supports encryption of messages. Although S/MIME is not widely implemented right now, people will eventually be able to use it to send secure e-mail messages.

File transfer applications

FTP servers allow you to transfer files across the Internet. The most commonly used FTP method is the anonymous FTP to download files from a public FTP server. However, to upload files to an FTP server, you need to have appropriate permissions. There are many applications that allow you to upload and download files to and from FTP servers, also called *FTP sites.* These applications are commonly called *ftp applications.* The UNIX and MS-DOS ftp applications use command-line interface. On the other hand, the ftp application for Windows, called WS_FTP, uses a point-and-click mechanism.

The Telnet application

Telnet is a very old Internet application that allows you to log on to remote computers. You can use Telnet to connect to a remote computer, log on to it, and interact with it as if it is a local computer. You can also use the Telnet application to connect to thousands of catalogs at libraries worldwide.

E-commerce applications

E-commerce applications allow users to conduct business over the Internet, facilitating trade for both the consumer and the supplier. The advantages of e-commerce applications are given below:

✦ Information can be exchanged between the customer and the supplier, including details of available products and services, customer support through technical guidance, response to customers' questions, and so on.

✦ Companies can pool their individual competencies to offer products and services.

✦ Products can be distributed physically and electronically.

Languages

Languages used for Web-based development can be broadly categorized as markup languages, programming languages, client-side scripting languages, and server-side technologies.

Markup languages

The usefulness of markup languages, such as SGML and HTML, has already been discussed. Additional markup languages that are used in Web applications include eXtensible Markup Language (XML) and eXtensible HyperText Markup Language (XHTML).

eXtensible Markup Language

Currently, XML is being used in e-commerce applications as a common data exchange format. XML is a standard for describing data on the Web. It uses tags to describe the data. The structure of an XML document is similar to that of an HTML document. However, unlike HTML, XML does not have any predefined tags. Instead, it is a meta-language that allows you to create your own markup language, or *vocabulary,* for describing the data contained in a document. For example, you could create a tag called `<CUSTOMER-NAME>` and specify the name of a customer within the tag. Thus, virtually any data items (such as product, sales rep, and amount due) can be identified, allowing Web pages to function like database records. XML describes the content in a document, whereas HTML concentrates on the presentation of the content in a Web page. Since XML is a plain text-based data format, it is platform-independent. In other words, XML documents can be displayed on any type of device, including a personal computer, laptop, or palmtop. In fact, XML has resulted in the development of a number of other markup languages. One example is WML, which is an XML application that allows you to create applications that can be accessed using a mobile phone.

Consider the following XML document:

```
<CUSTOMERS>
<CUSTOMER>
    <ID> 1001 </ID>
    <NAME> ALICIA HENLEY </NAME>
    <EMAIL> ALICIAH@HOTMAIL.COM </EMAIL>
</CUSTOMER>
<CUSTOMER>
    <ID> 1002 </ID>
    <NAME> PETER ANDREW </NAME>
    <EMAIL>PETERA@USA.NET </EMAIL>
</CUSTOMER>
</CUSTOMERS>
```

This XML document stores information about customers. Note that information about the appearance of the data is *not* provided in the XML document. It only contains data. When you open this document in Internet Explorer 5.0, it provides a default layout to the XML document. The default layout displays the XML document in a tree-view, as shown in Figure 15-3.

If you want to change the default appearance of the XML document, you need to create style sheets. You can display an XML document in a required format by using Cascading Style Sheets (CSSs) and eXtensible Style Sheet Language (XSL). For example, if you want to display the data contained in an XML document in a tabular format, you can use either CSS or XSL. Style sheets contain instructions to the browser on how to translate the structure of the source XML document into a structure that can be displayed to the user.

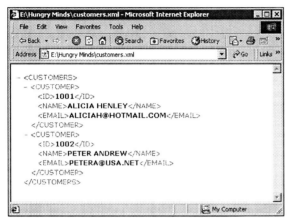

Figure 15-3: A sample XML code snippet

eXtensible HyperText Markup Language

XHTML is the reformulation of HTML 4.0 as an application of XML. It is similar to HTML 4.0, with a few minor differences. For example, XHTML makes it necessary for you to close all tags properly. Another difference is that it is necessary for you to nest all the tags properly. For example, consider the following statements:

```
<HTML>
<BODY>
    <FONT COLOR="RED">
        <P> First Para
        </FONT>
    </P>
    </BODY>
<HTML>
```

The `<P>` tag is started within the `<FONT>` tag and is closed after closing the `<FONT>` tag. This would not cause an error in HTML, but in XHTML, it would. In XHTML, it is necessary to close the innermost tag first.

Another important difference between XHTML and HTML is that HTML had its own fixed set of tags, and no variations could be made to the set of tags. XHTML, on the other hand, supports all tags of HTML and is also capable of being extended. New tags and attributes can be defined and added to those that already exist, making new ways to embed content and programming in a Web page possible. With XHTML 1.0, authors can mix known HTML 4 elements with elements from other XML applications, including those developed by W3C for multimedia. Therefore, XHTML has become a W3C recommendation for developing Web pages.

Programming languages

The most popular Web programming language is Java, which enables the building of applications that can be executed on any type of hardware and software platform without the need for any modifications. Java was developed by Sun Microsystems and was based on the C++ language. Java code is compiled, as well as interpreted. When Java program is compiled, the compiler converts the code into an intermediate language called the *bytecode*. This bytecode is independent of any specific hardware platform. The Java interpreter, also called the *Java Virtual Machine (JVM)*, interprets the bytecode into code that a specific machine can understand. Thus, programs written in Java can run on any computer that has the JVM software.

With Java, you can create either stand-alone applications or applets. When a user requests for a Java application, the application is loaded and executed on the Web server. An applet, on the other hand, is embedded within an HTML page. When a user requests the HTML page that has an applet embedded within it, the browser invokes the JVM, converts the instructions in the applet into machine-level language, and executes them.

Client-side scripting languages

A *script* is a program that contains a set of instructions for an application. It is embedded within a Web page using the `<SCRIPT>` tag. Scripting languages, unlike complete programming languages, require a host environment and are used to add functionality or enable programmatic manipulation of the host application.

Client-side scripts are executed at the client side, which means they are interpreted and executed by the browser. When a user makes a request for an HTML document that contains a client-side script embedded in it, the Web server sends the HTML document, along with the embedded script, to the browser. The browser executes the instructions within the script when a particular event, such as a mouse-click, occurs. Thus, a client-side script allows greater interactivity in a document by responding to user events. Some of the most popular client-side scripting languages include:

✦ **ECMAScript, JavaScript, and Jscript** — ECMAScript is a cross-platform, industry-standard scripting language designed to work with a wide variety of browsers. It combines features from JavaScript and JScript.

 JavaScript was developed by NetScape Communications. The European Computer Manufacturers Association (ECMA) industry standard is based on JavaScript. It is a subset of the Java programming language. It provides limited capability. In other words, it does not allow you to create any stand-alone applications.

 JScript is very similar to JavaScript and was developed by Microsoft. It is an extended implementation of ECMAScript.

✦ **VBScript** — VBScript is a lightweight version of the Microsoft Visual Basic language. It is not as widely supported as JavaScript. However, it is still preferred by a number of users because it is easy to use.

Consider the following code:

```
<HTML>
<HEAD>
    <TITLE> EXAMPLE OF A SCRIPT </TITLE>
    <SCRIPT LANGUAGE="VBSCRIPT">
    FUNCTION CHANGEFONT()
        PARA1.STYLE.COLOR="RED"
        PARA1.STYLE.FONTSIZE=28
    END FUNCTION
    </SCRIPT>
</HEAD>
<BODY>
    <P ID="PARA1" ONMOUSEOVER="CHANGEFONT"> WELCOME TO HTML
</P>
</BODY>
```

This code contains a client-side script embedded within the HTML page. When you send a request for this page, the text WELCOME TO HTML will be displayed in the browser window in black. When you move the mouse over this text, the ONMOUSEOVER event occurs. The browser executes the function associated with the event. The CHANGEFONT function changes the color and size of the text contained in the paragraph that has the ID PARA1. In a similar way, you can change images and create interactive menus and such using client-side scripts.

Server-side technologies

In contrast to a client-side script, which is executed by the browser, a server-side script is executed by the Web server. Some of the popular server-side Web technologies include:

✦ **Common Gateway Interface (CGI) script** — A CGI program is a small program written in any language, including C, C++, Java, and Perl. In addition, a CGI program is platform-independent. It can run on any operating system, including Windows NT, UNIX, Mac, and OS2. CGI is a gateway between an HTML document and other programs running on a Web server. For example, an HTML page may call a CGI script when a user clicks a button. This script can fetch data from a database, format the results as an HTML page, and send it back to the user. Initially, CGI scripts were used to make Web pages interact with databases. However, as the World Wide Web evolved, more efficient server-side scripting technologies have been developed, including Active Server Pages (ASP), Java Server Pages (JSP), and servlets.

Note Perl, or Practical Extraction Recursive Language, is one of the most popular server-side scripting languages available today. It is used in a wide variety of applications.

The working of the CGI scripts is shown in Figure 15-4.

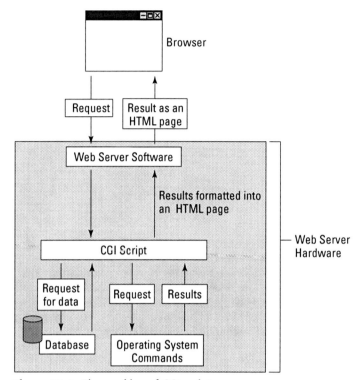

Figure 15-4: The working of CGI scripts

✦ **ASP** — ASP is a server-side technology from Microsoft. Unlike a CGI script, which is a separate program, ASP is embedded within a Web page within the <% and %> symbols. A file that has ASP embedded in it has the extension .asp. ASP code can be written either in VBScript or JScript. It uses a set of predefined objects to communicate with the browser. For example, it uses the Response object to send the output to the user. Similarly, it uses the Request object to obtain information from the user. ASP codes run on Internet Information Server (IIS) or Personal Web Server (PWS).

When a user requests a file containing ASP code, IIS passes the request to the *ASP engine*. The ASP engine is a component that runs on the Web server. It reads the file containing ASP code line-by-line and executes the code. Finally, the page containing HTML tags is returned to the browser.

ASP enables you to change the data dynamically, respond to user queries, and access databases. In addition, it is faster than CGI and Perl and also easier to learn.

✦ **Servlets** — A servlet is a Java application that runs on a Web server. It is a replacement for CGI from Sun. A servlet enables you to build Web pages on-the-fly based on the input received from a user. Servlets are more efficient than CGI. They are also more portable because they are written using the Java language.

✦ **JSP** — JSP is an alternative to ASP that was developed by Sun and Netscape. JSP is an HTML page that has Java source code embedded within it. HTML provides the layout for the page, and Java source code provides the processing capability. JSP is converted into a servlet and the servlet is compiled when it is encountered for the first time.

Security on the Web

Due to the increasing popularity of the World Wide Web over the last decade, more and more users are getting connected to the Internet. In such a situation, security should not be taken for granted. The primary motive of security over the Web is to be able to store, send, and receive sensitive data over the Internet so that unauthorized entities do not tamper with it.

If your operating system is not secure, it can be hacked. Therefore, you should take all possible measures to secure your operating system. Follow these guidelines:

✦ Run only those services that are required. Uninstall all other services that you don't require.

✦ Close open ports that you are not using. Open ports can be used by hackers to venture into your system.

✦ Install the latest service packs.

✦ Install the latest security updates and patches.

✦ Use anti-virus software to check for harmful viruses and Trojans at regular intervals.

✦ Stop accessing untrusted sites.

✦ Avoid accessing the Internet using the Administrator account (in Windows) or the root account (in Linux/UNIX). This makes your system vulnerable to fatal security attacks.

The extent to which you want to implement security depends on several factors, such as resources, technological infrastructure, and the level of requirement for storing, sending, and receiving sensitive information over the Internet. There are several third-party security tools that are available for both Windows and Linux/UNIX operating systems that can be used to ensure security over the Web.

The past decade has seen a vast improvement in Operating System Security (OSS). Certified and approved secure OSS has been introduced for operating systems such as UNIX/Linux and Windows NT/2000.

Tip Implementing security on a system with the help of security tools requires a respectable amount of processing speed and disk space. If low-end servers start implementing security, the number of users that the server can support might go down.

There are certain conventional elements of Internet security that should be used to keep the system free from security vulnerabilities. These elements include firewalls, encryption, and authentication.

Firewalls

Firewalls are an extremely popular security measure, widely used by organizations. Firewalls allow only authorized connections between computers on an internal network and those on external networks. The firewall can be configured in such a way that only authorized users are allowed to access the Internet. Firewalls can also restrict e-mail, FTP, and remote login. Firewall system providers are also concentrating on adding new facilities, such as encryption and Virtual Private Networks (VPNs).

Encryption

Encryption is a very useful way to secure data over the Internet. Encryption uses an algorithm to change the coding of data. Encrypted data cannot be interpreted or decrypted without the necessary prerequisites. Therefore, encryption is a successful method of ensuring privacy. The advantage of using encryption is that it can be used to secure data stored on the network as well as data that is communicated through the network. The most readily available encryption standard is Digital Encryption Standard (DES), which has been endorsed by the National Institute of Standards and Technology since 1975. Programs that use DES can now be used outside the U.S.

RSA

In 1978, three individuals named Ron Rivest, Adi Shamir, and Len Adleman, developed an algorithm. Later on, this algorithm was named RSA (Rivest Shamir Adleman). RSA is one of the earliest and most widely used public-key algorithms. It can be used for encryption/decryption and signing/verification to ensure data integrity.

Pretty Good Privacy

Pretty Good Privacy (PGP) is also a very useful encryption tool. PGP helps users encrypt data stored on their machines as well as send encrypted messages via e-mail. PGP generates two types of keys — *public key* and *private key.* Public key of the user is sent to the Web server and is accessible to everyone. Private key is confidential and is known only to the user. Whenever a user sends an encrypted message, he encrypts the data using the public key of the receiver. After getting the message, the receiver can decrypt the message using his private key. PGP also provides tools for creating and managing keys.

Secure Sockets Layer

Secure Sockets Layer (SSL) is a protocol that is used to ensure the security of a variety of different applications that are used for browsing the Web. These applications include e-mail, e-commerce applications, and Web-based subscription services. SSL uses a combination of secret key and public key technology to ensure the security of data that is transmitted over the network. SSL provides features such as privacy and authentication of users. It also ensures the integrity of messages that are transmitted over the network.

Authentication and integrity

A major concern of system administrators today is authentication and integrity. Authentication can be implemented in the form of passwords. But passwords are transported in an unencrypted form over the Internet and they are easy to crack. Therefore, encryption tools, such as SecureSSH, SSL, Kerberos, and LDAP, can be used.

Integrity refers to the fact that data has not been altered during transmission. With the availability of numerous hacking tools, it is difficult to maintain data integrity. But there are ways in which you can ensure the integrity of the messages you send over the Internet — by using digital signatures, for example. Digital signatures are nothing but tags attached to the end of a message ensure that the message has been sent from an authentic source. Besides digital signatures, you can also use fingerprints — a 14-character authentication medium. Digital signatures and fingerprints are rapidly increasing in popularity.

E-commerce on the Internet

In today's business environment, e-commerce is the newest catch phrase. Defined literally, *e-commerce* refers to trade conducted through any electronic medium. However, e-commerce is now used to mean business conducted over the Internet. In a very short span of time, e-commerce has opened up new markets and expanded the efficiency of traditional businesses. Today, almost 60 percent of Internet users in the U.S. are online shoppers. In general, e-commerce continues to grow in popularity because it provides several advantages over traditional business methods:

✦ **Accessibility** — Storefronts are accessible at any time and from anywhere in the world.

✦ **Reduced overhead costs** — With less paperwork to do, overhead costs are minimal compared to traditional trade.

✦ **Reduced transaction time** — Transactions are performed more quickly, compared to traditional trade.

One of the basic differences between e-commerce and traditional trade is the way in which communication takes place. In the case of e-commerce, communication takes place over the Internet, whereas communication in a traditional business environment takes place face –to face, on the telephone, or through the postal system. With e-commerce, payments are also made and handled differently. Since most transactions occur electronically, with almost no real contact between the buyer and the seller, security is of prime concern.

Business that is carried out on the Internet can be broadly categorized using two different business models: Business-to-Business and Business-to-Consumer.

The Business-to-Business model

In the Business-to-Business model, also referred to as B2B, trade is conducted between two separate businesses over the Internet. The interaction between these two businesses may take the form of placing orders, receiving invoices, or making payments. B2B is characterized by high volume and low price margins. This means that the number of products or services bought is high, but the price markup on the product is low. This business model has been on the Internet for a long time.

The Business-to-Consumer model

In the Business-to-Consumer model, also referred to as B2C, transactions take place between a business and a consumer. B2C is characterized by low volume and high price margins, which means that the number of products or services bought is low (compared to the Business-to-Business model), but the price markup is high. Today, a consumer can use the Internet to buy products ranging from books to groceries to automobiles. This is called *electronic shopping*. Electronic shopping is an ideal example of the Business-to-Consumer model.

Video and Other Advanced Data Types

In the past decade, the Internet has gradually become the primary means of data transfer. Initially, information was distributed primarily in the form of text and graphics, but with the advent of advanced multimedia technologies, images and stored audio and video emerged. Today, about 40 percent of the data downloaded from the Internet is in the form of audio and video streams. Now, downloading and playing high-quality audio and video files from the Internet is a reality. Popular Web browsers, such as Netscape Navigator and Internet Explorer, provide full support for the multimedia data types, including text, audio, still images, graphics objects, and digital video.

Streaming audio and video

Until recently, multimedia files were the most frequently downloaded files on the Internet. However, the entire file needs to be downloaded at the client's side before it can be played. Depending on the connection speed, large files can take a long time to download, which greatly increases the amount of time and bandwidth resources that are required to play the file. If the downloaded files are extremely large, they may consume much valuable hard disk space. Moreover, downloadable multimedia files are best suited for small graphics and button sounds. They are not much use when it comes to playing large audio and video files.

Audio and video *streaming* allows the clients to receive audio and video content from servers across the globe and start hearing or viewing the downloaded content as soon as the first few bytes of the stream arrive at the client site. In other words, the receiving client plays the incoming multimedia stream in real time as data is received. Although the streamed files are not stored on the client's computer, it is possible to store them on the user's hard drive for later replay. Most of the time, streaming is used for playing the archived files. This is known as *on-demand streaming*. The streaming technology also allows for the broadcasting and receiving of live events, such as video clips and music concerts, on the Internet.

Note Although audio streaming has become increasingly popular, video streaming is not as widely accepted. However, new advancements in video streaming technology are being developed, with the idea that video streaming will eventually gain the researcher's, as well as the general public's, interest.

Streaming includes compression of audio and video data, methods of stream formatting, networking protocols, and packetization of transmission. Streaming also involves client designs for display and synchronization of different media streams and the server designs for content storage and delivery. The advantages of using streaming include:

✦ Streamed files are easily downloadable.

✦ Streamed files can play immediately just seconds after a user clicks on the link.

✦ Streaming provides wider access to various users, since people are more attracted to video and audio than flat text descriptions.

Today, more and more Web sites have started using the streaming technology to attract clientele. There are two ways to implement this technology in a Web site to make it livelier and more appealing—linking and embedding:

Note Popular examples of the streaming files include RealAudio, RealVideo, VDOLive, and StreamWorks.

✦ **Linking**—In linking, the streamed audio or video file is not directly placed in the Web page. Instead, a reference (or link) is created to a *metafile*. The metafile is a reference file that contains the path to the streamed file. This reference tells the browser where to locate the file. When a visitor clicks the link represented by the metafile, the metafile directs the *streaming player* to the streamed file. The streaming player is software that is used to view the streaming files. The advantage of the linking method is that the Web page is downloaded quickly, since the streaming file is not part of the Web page. However, accessing the streaming file by clicking the link may take some time, depending on the connection speed.

✦ **Embedding**—In embedding, the streaming file is embedded in the Web page itself. As a result, the Web page may take some time to download. Embedding is also much more difficult to implement, compared to the linking method. However, it gives the Web site administrator complete control over the clip.

To include the streaming files in a Web page, you need to install a helper application or a browser plug-in, which will allow your desktop computer to play the streamed audio or video files. The following steps can be used to implement the streaming technology in a Web site:

1. **Record and edit the streaming files.** After installing the appropriate software, you need to create and edit the streaming files. Popular audio editing or recording software include SoundForge (for Windows), SoundEdit 16 plus deck II (for Macintosh), and CoolEdit. One of the most popular video streaming software products is Adobe Premiere.

2. **Encode the streaming files.** Once you have recorded and edited the clips, you need to encrypt (or encode) the digital streaming files so that they can be played by the sound/video streaming helper application or plug-in software. The most popular encoding software these days is Real Audio Encoder (for audio files) or Real Video Encoder (for video files). You may want to encode the same audio/video file in several different formats so that the clips can be played by using different helper software.

3. **Upload the files on the Web server.** To make the files available to others, you need to store the files on a Web server. It is essential that special server software, such as Real Audio, be installed and configured to run these files. All of the streamed video and some streamed audio files require this software to execute successfully. Other streamed audio files, such as Internet Wave files, can be served from a standard Web server, but will require some Web server configuration settings in order to be modified. After configuring the server software, you will need to copy your encoded files from your computer to the server by using file transfer application such as FTP.

4. **Test the files.** Although this step is sometimes overlooked, it is very important that you test your files to verify that they are playing successfully. Use the appropriate audio/video streaming helper application or plug-in software to do this.

Note   If you are using a plug-in software program to play the streamed files, you will not need to configure your Web browser software. Simply installing the plug-in will suffice. However, if you are using a helper application to play the streamed files, after installing the helper application on your computer, you will need to configure your Web browser to use the helper application.

Considerations regarding streaming

Although we are moving towards faster networking technologies, such as Integrated Services Digital Network (ISDN) and Asynchronous Transfer Mode (ATM), current network infrastructures — including the Internet — were not designed to support streaming. To transfer streaming files, data must be transferred from servers to clients at high speeds that need to be sustained at a constant rate. This introduces many considerations regarding the use of the streaming technology in the networking infrastructure used today:

✦ The streaming standards are not yet mature, which leads to a situation in which every vendor develops their own standards. As a result, third-party support is extremely limited.

✦ Browsers that support the streaming technology display the content without problems. However, other browsers that do not support streaming go into a hang forever and do nothing.

✦ Streaming is an expensive technology. Web sites that use this technology report high maintenance costs.

✦ Web sites implementing the streaming technology take more time to download.

Although streaming technology has passed the phase of infancy and — with the increased demand for audio and video data on the Internet — is rapidly moving towards maturity and stabilization, there is a lot to be done in this field. Standards and protocols for the streaming technology are still being developed.

Summary

This chapter introduced you to the World Wide Web (WWW), the difference between the Internet and the Web, and the role of the Worldwide Web Consortium (W3C) in the development of current, as well as future, Web-related standards and specifications. You learned that HyperText Markup Language (HTML) is a language for creating documents for the Web and that HyperText Transfer Protocol (HTTP) is the application-level protocol used for communication between a Web server and clients. Next, you learned about various Web-based applications, such as Web servers (IIS, Apache, and PWS), and the different languages that can be used to develop documents and applications on the Web (Java, ASP, CGI-scripts, and JSP). You also learned how to implement security on the Web and the emergence and role of e-commerce in revolutionizing the way we conduct business. Finally, this chapter discussed the streaming technology, which enables users to play audio and video files as soon as the first few bytes of downloaded data arrive at the client site.

✦   ✦   ✦

Getting News and Mail

In today's business scenario, faster access to information is of prime importance. With the advent of Internet and electronic messaging services, people can now send and receive information through e-mail in seconds. In fact, many people buy their first computer so they can have access to e-mail services.

In this chapter, we will discuss one of the most common applications of TCP/IP: sending and receiving e-mail and network news. We will discuss the entire e-mailing process, as well as the protocols (SMTP and NNTP) of the TCP/IP suite that enable the transfer of mail and news. Last but not least, we will discuss some rules of Internet etiquette.

Overview of the Mail Process

For users, who simply have to compose an e-mail and press the Send button, the e-mail process may seem relatively simple. However, the process of sending e-mail involves some complex steps. Before the technical aspects of sending and receiving e-mail messages are discussed, the general mailing process will be summarized. When a user sends a message using a mail program, such as Microsoft Outlook Express, the message first reaches the SMTP server. Based on the address for which the message is intended, the SMTP server decides how to handle the message. If the destination server of the e-mail message is the same as that of the sender, the message remains on the server and is moved to the recipient's mailbox. However, if the destination server is not the same as that of the sender, the message is sent to the appropriate server. Most users do not have a permanent connection to the Internet, and, thus, the messages need to be stored on the server until they are read. The POP server collects these messages and holds them. The client connects to the POP server by providing a user name and a password. After validating the user name, the server sends the user's messages to his or her Inbox. The mail process is shown in Figure 16-1.

In the process of sending e-mail, a Mail User Agent, a Mail Transfer Agent, and a Mail Delivery Agent are required. These components are described in detail below:

✦ **Mail User Agent (MUA)** — This is used to create and send mail. The MUA acts an interface between the user and the *Mail Transfer Agent*.

✦ **Mail Transfer Agent (MTA)** — This acts like a post office, transferring the messages received from the MUA to the appropriate destination.

✦ **Mail Delivery Agent (MDA)** — This is software that delivers e-mail to the user's mailbox.

To send and receive e-mails, the mail programs need:

✦ An Internet connection.

✦ A POP server that provides Post Office Protocol (POP). The POP manages incoming messages. You usually refer to a POP server by its version number, such as POP3.

✦ An SMTP server that provides Simple Mail Transfer Protocol (SMTP). SMTP is used by the Internet and by intranet-based e-mail servers to send messages.

Note   You can configure the same server as an SMTP and a POP server.

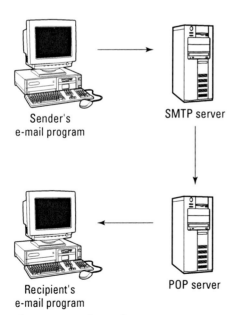

Sender's
e-mail program

SMTP server

Recipient's
e-mail program

POP server

Figure 16-1: The mail process

The actual steps involved in sending e-mail messages are more or less the same for all mail programs. Microsoft Outlook Express and Netscape Messenger, for example, send mail by using the steps given below:

1. The user composes a message and enters the ID or e-mail address of the recipient of the message in the To: field.

2. If the user wants to send a carbon copy of the message to other users, their e-mail addresses should be entered in the Cc: field. Though filling the Subject: field is not essential, it is good practice to put the topic of the mail in this field.

3. The user clicks the Send button to send the mail.

You may want to attach files to your e-mails. In Microsoft Outlook Express, use the following steps to send an attachment:

1. Compose your e-mail. From the toolbar at the top of the message window, choose Insert ➪ File Attachment.

2. The Insert Attachment dialog box opens. Select the file that you want to attach and click Attach.

3. Click Send.

If your mail program is Netscape Messenger, use the following steps to send attachments:

1. Compose your e-mail. Click the Attach button on the Messenger toolbar. From the pop-up menu that appears, choose File.

2. The Attach file dialog box opens. Select the file that you want to attach and click Open.

3. Click Send.

The Simple Mail Transfer Protocol

SMTP is a TCP/IP protocol that handles the transfer of e-mails from one mail system to another. When transferring e-mail messages, SMTP uses TCP port number 25. SMTP ensures a reliable and efficient method of mail transmission.

Note   SMTP is described in RFC 821.

When an e-mail reaches the SMTP server, it is spooled. The SMTP server checks for the messages in the queue to transfer them. To transfer messages:

1. The SMTP server first establishes a TCP connection with the destination server. If the destination server is ready, it sends a message to the SMTP server indicating that it is ready. However, if the destination server is not available, the SMTP server receives a message indicating that the destination server is not available. If the destination server is not connected to the Internet/intranet, the SMTP server attempts to connect to the destination server until the designated timeout period is over.

2. If the destination server is available, the SMTP server sends the HELO command to the destination server. As an answer to this command, the destination server sends its domain name. The SMTP server uses this domain name to verify whether it has established a connection with the right destination server.

3. The SMTP server starts the message transaction by sending the MAIL command to the destination server. If there is any error, it is reported by using the reverse-path, which is contained by the MAIL command.

4. The SMTP server then sends a DATA command to inform the destination server that the message is following.

5. The SMTP server uses the send function to transfer the message to one or more e-mail addresses. The send function takes the e-mail address and the message as its arguments. The destination server acknowledges the message by sending an OK message (or, as the case may be, an error message) to the SMTP server.

The message is stored on the SMTP server until it is transferred to the destination server. Thus, SMTP is based on *end-to-end delivery,* wherein the SMTP server connects to the destination server to transfer the message. However, if the recipient user is not available, the mail is sent back to the sender.

Post Office Protocol

Post Office Protocol (POP) is an Internet protocol that transfers e-mail messages from the POP server to the user's mailbox on a local computer. This protocol works on a client/server architecture. The POP server uses the protocol, while the local host machine with the mail program needs to be configured as the POP client. POP3 is the latest version of the Post Office Protocol. The earlier version, POP2, is now obsolete. While the POP2 required an SMTP server to send messages, POP3 works with or without an SMTP server. Also, POP3 is not compatible with POP2. POP2 used TCP port 109, while POP3 uses TCP port 110.

 Note   POP3 is described in RFC 2449.

To transfer the messages from the POP server to the local mailbox, a POP session is established. The POP session follows these steps:

1. The POP client establishes a TCP connection with the POP server.

2. When the connection is established, the POP server sends a message to the POP client. The session now enters the *authorization state*. In this state, the client needs to provide the user name and password to authenticate itself to the POP server.

3. The POP server authenticates the client if the user name and password are correct. The session enters the *transaction state*. The client then sends commands to the POP server to retrieve the e-mail message.

4. After the e-mail message is transferred to the local computer's mailbox, the client sends the `QUIT` command to terminate the session, and the session enters the *update state*.

5. The e-mail message reaches the mailbox of the local computer and can be read by the user.

Internet Mail Access Protocol

Internet Mail Access Protocol (IMAP) is an Internet protocol that is used for accessing e-mail messages that are stored on a mail server. IMAP allows accessing of messages stored on a remote server as if they are stored on the local computer. This is significant, since it allows mobile users to access their e-mail messages from home, from the workplace, or from any other place at any time. It also enables the users to modify the messages that are stored in a folder on the mail server. IMAP is compatible with the Internet standards, such as MIME. The latest version of IMAP is IMAP4, and it uses TCP port 143.

 Note IMAP4 is discussed in detail in RFC 2060.

IMAP works on a client/server architecture. At any point in time, an IMAP session exists in one of the following states:

✦ **Non-authenticated state** — The session enters this state when the connection between the client and the server starts. The client needs to provide authentication information before it can issue commands. However, if the connection is pre-authenticated, the session directly enters the authenticated state.

✦ **Authenticated state** — The session enters the authenticated state after the client is authenticated. After authentication, the user needs to select the mailbox that is to be accessed.

✦ **Selected state** — The session enters the selected state after the user has selected an appropriate mailbox.

✦ **Logout state** — The session enters the logout state when the connection is terminated by the server. The server terminates the connection as a result of a client request or a connection timeout.

Though IMAP4 is similar to POP3, there are some significant differences. While POP3 is ideal for offline access of e-mail messages on a single computer, IMAP4 enables users to access new as well as saved messages from multiple computers. Also, IMAP4 supports some additional features that are absent in POP3. For example, IMAP supports keyword search. You can search your e-mail messages for keywords while they are still on the mail server. Based on the search result, you can decide which messages need to be downloaded to your computer. Moreover, IMAP4 also supports all three modes of message access — offline, online, and disconnected mode:

✦ **Offline mode** — In this mode, the messages once downloaded from the mail server to the user's machine are deleted from the mail server.

✦ **Online mode** — In this mode, the messages remain on the mail server. The users can access, as well as manipulate, these messages by using a mail program.

✦ **Disconnected mode** — In this mode, when connected to the mail server, the mail program makes a cache copy of the selected messages before disconnecting. The users can manipulate these cached messages. Later, when the mail program connects to the mail server, these messages are resynchronized. However, the messages continue to remain on the server.

IMAP4 enables remote folder management. The users can create and manage multilevel folders on the mail server after they are authorized by the administrator. IMAP4 also allows multiple users to access a shared mailbox on the mail server from multiple locations simultaneously. One major advantage of IMAP4 is that it can separate attached files from the text message or the header of the message. This gives the users an option to download only specific parts of a message. Besides all these features, IMAP4 also enables access to non-e-mail information, such as NetNews and other documents.

Reading your mail

To read e-mail messages, you need an Internet connection and an e-mail client program. A variety of different e-mail client programs are available, the most common of which are Microsoft Outlook Express and Netscape Messenger. Although opening and reading e-mail may vary somewhat from one e-mail program to another, the basic process remains the same. In most e-mail client programs, messages are stored in a folder called the Inbox. You can open the messages in the Inbox to read them.

Microsoft Outlook Express

Microsoft Outlook Express is one of the most widely used mail client programs for Windows. It is used to create, send, and receive messages. By default, the Microsoft Outlook Express window is divided into two panes. The left pane contains a folder tree, while the right pane shows the contents of the currently selected folder, as shown in Figure 16-2. By default, all messages that you receive are placed in the

Inbox. To receive new messages, you need to click the Send and Receive button on the toolbar of the Microsoft Outlook Express window. The Outlook Express dialog box opens. It shows the status of the messages that were sent and received. When all the messages have been retrieved, the dialog box closes. To read the messages:

1. Click the Inbox icon in the Folders list in the left pane. A list of messages appears in the right pane. By default, the unread messages appear in bold.

2. To open and view a message, double-click it. A new window that displays the contents of the message opens.

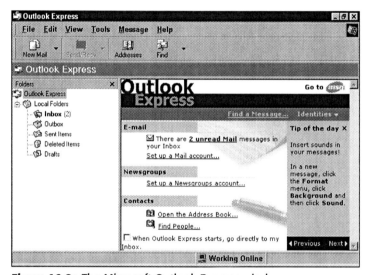

Figure 16-2: The Microsoft Outlook Express window

Netscape Messenger

Netscape Messenger is another widely used mail program that is used for creating, sending, and reading e-mail messages. By default, the Netscape Messenger window has three panes, as shown in Figure 16-3. The left pane is called the Folder list. It contains a list of all the available folders. The Message list is in the upper-right pane. It shows the list of messages stored in the currently selected folder in the left pane. The lower-right pane is called the Message body pane. It displays the body of the message that is currently selected in the message list or the upper-right pane.

To retrieve and read the e-mail messages:

1. Click the Get Msg button on the Netscape Messenger toolbar.

2. The mail program prompts you for your password. If you provide the correct password, the new e-mails are retrieved from the POP server to the inbox.

3. Click the Inbox icon in the left pane. A list of messages appears in the Message list pane. The unread messages appear in bold.

4. To open and read the contents of a message, click the message in the Message list. The body of the message appears in the Message body pane.

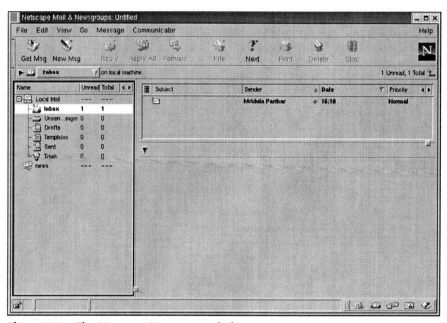

Figure 16-3: The Netscape Messenger window

MIME and S/MIME

One of the major reasons for the success of Internet mail is the standard mechanism that it provides for the exchange of messages on the 'Net. Internet standards (RFC 822) — the basis of the e-mail format — were first defined in 1982. However, these standards allowed only ASCII characters in the message body. Also, they restricted the message length to about 1000 characters. With the passage of time, there was a need for a standard that was more flexible and open to extensions.

Multipurpose Internet Mail Extensions (MIME) is a standard that was developed by the Internet Engineering Task Force Working Group in 1992. MIME defines *how* e-mails should be formatted so that they can be transferred across different e-mail systems. MIME allows e-mails to contain text, images, audio, video, application-specific files, and multimedia messages. MIME has the following features:

✦ Clearly defines a set of the *content-types* that are allowed. Content-type refers to the type of content that can be inserted in the body of the message. The content-types that can be inserted in a message are text, image, message, audio, video, multipart, and application.

✦ Provides encoding of non-ACSII data.

✦ Supports *multipart* content-type, which enables the encapsulation of more than one body part in a single message.

The MIME standard includes the following header fields, which define a specific message:

✦ **MIME-version** — This header field contains a version number to declare that the message follows the MIME standard. Using this version number, the mail processing agents can identify the messages that follow the MIME standard.

✦ **Content-type** — This header field specifies the type of data in the body. It also specifies the subtype, which defines the specific format of the type of data.

✦ **Content-transfer-encoding** — This header field indicates how the content of the message is encoded. This enables the message to move through mail transport mechanisms that have character set or data restrictions.

✦ **Content-ID and Content-Description** — These header fields further identify and describe the data in the message.

When e-mail is transferred over the Internet, security is a major concern. Secure/Multipurpose Internet Mail Extensions (S/MIME) is an Internet standard that provides security to e-mail messages in MIME format. S/MIME is an extension of MIME. S/MIME extends MIME by adding new content types (encrypted and key exchange) to enable encryption. S/MIME is used to secure MIME entities, such as MIME headers and MIME body. Any two packages that support S/MIME can communicate securely over the Internet. S/MIME ensures cryptographic security features, such as confidentiality and authenticity for e-mails. The following sections discuss how S/MIME ensures security confidentiality and authenticity.

Confidentiality

Encrypted e-mail provides confidentiality. S/MIME uses *asymmetric encryption,* in which a pair of keys is generated. This key pair contains a *public key* and a *private key.* The key pair is unique for each user. To encrypt the message, a random symmetric key is created. When the encrypted message reaches the recipient end, it needs to be decrypted. To do this, the symmetric key also needs to be sent to the recipient in an encrypted form. The public key of the recipient is used to encrypt the symmetric key. This encrypted symmetric key is transmitted before the encrypted message is sent to the recipient. The message is recovered or decrypted by using the decryption process. To decrypt messages, the symmetric key is required. The symmetric key is recovered by using the private key of the recipient. After being recovered, the symmetric key is used to decrypt the encrypted message. The information about the public key is placed in a *digital certificate* when the key pair is generated. A digital certificate is a certificate that can be attached to a document or an e-mail message and that guarantees its authenticity and provides secure encryption. The digital certificate also contains information about the owner of the public key (such as the owner's user name). When S/MIME is set for an e-mail client, a key pair and a digital certificate are generated for the user. The user needs to provide a password for gaining access to the key pair in the future.

You can obtain digital certificates from various certification authorities, such as VeriSign and Thawte Certification. To obtain a digital signature in Microsoft Outlook Express:

1. Choose Tools ➪ Options to open the Options dialog box.

2. Click the Security tab.

3. Click the "Get Digital ID" button. The browser is launched. It opens a Web page that has links to various certification authorities that provide digital certificates.

4. From the list of certificate authorities, select the appropriate vendor. The selected vendor's Web site opens. Fill in the enrollment form.

5. After you have submitted the enrollment form, a verification mail is generated and sent to the e-mail ID that you provided in the enrollment form. This verification e-mail contains the instructions to install the digital certificate, a PIN number, and the Web location for digital certificate validation and installation.

6. Navigate to the Web page specified in the verification e-mail, enter the PIN number, and install the digital certificate, as per the vendor's instructions.

After you have obtained a digital certificate, you need to associate the digital certificate to your e-mail account. To do so, proceed as follows:

1. Choose Tools ➪ Accounts to open the Internet Accounts dialog box.

2. Select the account with which you want to associate the digital certificate and click the Properties button. A Properties dialog box for the selected account opens.

3. Click the Security tab.

4. Select the "Use a digital ID when sending secure messages from" option.

5. Click Digital ID and select the default certificate for the account.

After you have associated the digital certificate with your account, you can use it for sending secure messages.

You can encrypt the messages that you send so that only the intended recipient can read it. To encrypt a message that you send in Outlook Express, you need to know the recipient's digital certificate. To add a digital certificate from a digitally signed message that you receive to your Address Book:

1. Open the digitally signed message. Choose File ➪ Properties to open the Properties dialog box.

2. Click the Security tab.

3. Click the "Add digital ID to the address book" button.

You also need to set the trust relationship. A trust relationship indicates that you are trusted to use the recipient's digital certificate. After you have obtained the recipient's digital certificate and have set the trust relationship, you can encrypt the messages that you send by using two methods. The first method is used to configure the security features in Outlook Express, so that the messages you send are automatically encrypted. The second method to encrypt messages is to click the Encrypt Message button before sending the message.

Authenticity

Authenticity is provided by using *digital signatures,* which can be used to sign messages. A digital signature is a string of bits that is generated for each message and is used to validate the identity of a sender and the integrity of the sent message. When the receiver gets the message, he also gets information about the sender and whether or not the message was modified during the process of transferring. Thus, S/MIME ensures security, authenticity, and non-repudiation when e-mail messages are transferred over the Internet — one of the main reasons S/MIME has been adopted as a standard by all major mail programs. Some e-mail products, such as Microsoft Outlook Express 4.0 and above, Microsoft Outlook 2000, and Netscape Communicator 4.03 and above, have built-in S/MIME capability.

Although e-mail is faster and more convenient than the postal mail system, it is actually less secure, since hackers can access e-mail. However, as stated earlier, you can ensure security by encrypting the e-mail messages that you send. One of the available encryption software products is Pretty Good Privacy, which is discussed in the following section.

Pretty Good Privacy

Pretty Good Privacy (PGP) is an encryption software program that you can use to secure your e-mails and attachments. PGP plug-ins are available for various mail programs, such as Microsoft Outlook Express, Eudora, and Microsoft Outlook. These plug-ins install themselves in the mail programs and then appear as a menu option or as buttons in the mail program window.

When you install PGP, a pair of keys (public and private) is generated. PGP then publishes your public key on the PGP key server. Your public key is known to all and is used to encrypt the messages that are sent to you. The process of encryption/ decryption is the same in PGP and S/MIME. The only significant difference between S/MIME and PGP is that S/MIME uses certificates to transfer the public key, while PGP uses its own storage format. Even the actual algorithms used are the same. You should not disclose your private key, which ensures that only you can decrypt and read messages that you receive. PGP also enables you to digitally sign the e-mails that you send to ensure authenticity. Digital signatures are unique for a document and user.

Note   A digital signature is unique for each document sent by a user. No two documents sent by the same user have the same digital signature.

Overview of Network News

The Internet is one of *the* major sources of information. Information can be shared broadly over the Internet in two ways: *mailing lists* and *network news.* A mailing list is made up of a group of people who are sent information through e-mail. A copy of the information is mailed to every member in the mailing list. Mailing lists enable you to communicate quickly and conveniently with a group of people by using a single address (for the group) rather than typing the addresses of all the members of the group. However, since mailing a separate copy to each member requires large network bandwidth and disk space, this method of sharing information becomes cumbersome. A better option is to use network news. Network news refers to information or news that is accessible to a large number of users over the Internet, but it does not require that a separate copy of information be sent to each user.

The concept of network news first originated in 1979, when an article was distributed between Duke and University of North Carolina. Network news is organized by topic into *newsgroups*, or discussion areas. A host of newsgroup topics exist, ranging from astrology to zoology. As a matter of fact, there is a newsgroup available on just about any topic you can think of. The articles for each newsgroup are written by newsgroup subscribers who are interested in the topic. The articles are then posted to the newsgroup, where other people can read and respond to them. In other words, a newsgroup is an online forum where users can read articles posted by other users of the newsgroup and also post messages on the topic. Although some newsgroups contain articles on current events, most of them represent discussion groups created on specific topics. For example, Usenet is a user's network that has various servers hosting thousands of newsgroups.

All newsgroups can be classified as *closed, moderated,* and *unmoderated,* depending on their accessibility. Here's a brief description of the different types of newsgroups:

✦ **Closed newsgroups** aren't open to the public. You need to send a request to the newsgroup administrator to join a closed newsgroup.

✦ **Moderated newsgroups** require all posted articles to be approved by a moderator before the articles are published.

✦ **Unmoderated newsgroups** are open to the public.

The newsgroup categories are organized in a structural hierarchy that moves from general to specific. The name of a newsgroup gives a fair idea of the theme on which the newsgroup is based. Each newsgroup name consists of a topic and subtopics that are separated by periods. For example, `sci.med.nutrition` is a newsgroup name, where `science` is the main topic, `medicine` is the subtopic under `science`, and `nutrition` is the subtopic under `medicine`, as shown in Figure 16-4.

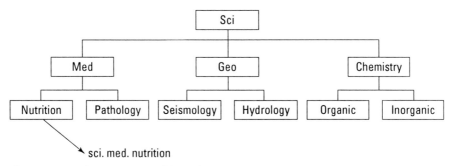

Figure 16-4: The newsgroup hierarchy

Table 16-1 describes some prefixes found in newsgroup names and the topics they are associated with:

Prefix	Associated Topic
comp	Computer-related topics
humanities	Arts and humanities-related topics
news	News network and news software-related topics
rec	Recreational activities-related topics
sci	Science and research-related topics
soc	Social issues and related topics
talk	Debatable topics
misc	Miscellaneous topics

Table 16-1
The Basic Newsgroups

You can access a newsgroup by subscribing to it. If your mail program is Microsoft Outlook Express, you can subscribe to a newsgroup while adding a news server. You might want to subscribe to a newsgroup that you are viewing but are not subscribed to. You can do this by choosing the "Subscribe to this Group" option in the Tools menu. If your mail program is Netscape Messenger, you can subscribe to a newsgroup by following these steps:

1. In the Netscape Messenger window, click the Newsgroup icon on the component bar.

2. From the File menu, choose Subscribe. A dialog box opens. Enter the appropriate information and then click the OK button. The subscribed newsgroup appears in the subscription list.

You can also request to create a new newsgroup for a specific theme. To create a new newsgroup in Usenet, follow these steps:

1. Submit a request for the new newsgroup to the newsgroup `news.groups`. This request is known as a "Request for Discussion."

2. A trial group of users is created for the proposed newsgroup, and a trial moderator monitors the readership of this group.

3. At the end of five months, the proposed newsgroup is accepted if it stands in the top 75 percent of the Usenet newsgroups. Otherwise, the proposed newsgroup is rejected.

4. The proposed newsgroup is renamed, based on the trial moderator's and trial user's suggestions, and is moved as a newsgroup of Usenet.

Servers and hubs

Network news uses a client/server architecture. The server acts as a central storage area where all the newsgroup articles are stored. This server provides information to other computers on the network. The client needs to subscribe to a newsgroup present on the server. To access newsgroups, the client needs to have a client program called a news client or newsreader, such as Microsoft Outlook Express. When configuring the newsreader, you need to designate a news server to it. The newsreader program is also required if the user wants to post or reply to an article. The transfer of the articles from the news server to the client is controlled by Network News Transfer Protocol (NNTP.)

Network News Transfer Protocol

NNTP is part of the TCP/IP suite and defines the rules for distributing, retrieving, and posting the news items over the Internet. It uses TCP port 119. It defines the standards for distribution and posting of news articles using a streaming client/server model and facilitates the user access to the news articles that are stored on a central server. NNTP also provides commands that support methods of exchanging articles between the news servers. NNTP ensures an interactive mechanism to transfer news between the servers. The server that wants to receive or send new news articles connects to the other servers by using NNTP. The news article files on the servers are compared, and any changes that need to be made are added to the news article files. Hence, only those articles that are unique are added — there is no duplication of articles on the news servers.

The news transfer process will now be looked at in detail. When a client accesses a newsgroup:

1. The newsreader on the client computer connects to the news server using the NNTP.

2. When the connection is established, the newsreader retrieves the news articles posted in the subscribed newsgroups. The client can now read the news articles.

3. If the user wishes to reply to a news article, he composes a reply and sends it.

4. The newsreader sends this reply to the news server using NNTP.

5. The news server stores this reply in the newsgroup's file. A newsgroup file is a large text file, and the reply is actually added at the end of the file.

6. The news server then connects to the other news servers using NNTP and transfers the appended newsgroup file. The news server compares this newsgroup file with its corresponding newsgroup file. If it finds changes, it adds the changes to its newsgroup file.

7. This process continues until all the newsgroups have updated information. The client's reply is now visible to all the users of the newsgroup.

The news transfer process is shown in Figure 16-5.

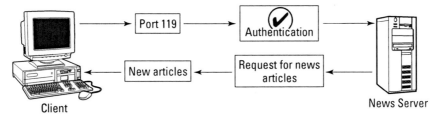

Figure 16-5: The news transfer process

Netiquette

We all follow unsaid rules of etiquette when we communicate with others. Communicating over the Internet is no exception. The word *netiquette* is a combination of two words: *net* and *etiquette.* It refers to a set of rules that one should follow when working on the Internet. Here are some netiquette rules that you should follow:

1. Do not write your entire e-mail message in caps. It gives the impression that you are shouting.

2. Before posting your messages to the newsgroup, check if it already appears in the FAQ (Frequently Asked Questions).

3. Use *emoticons* to express your emotions. Emoticons are symbols that represent expressions or emotions that cannot be conveyed in plain text. You can use various key combinations to create emoticons. For example, you can use a colon (:) and a closing parenthesis) to represent a smiley face.

4. Check the tone of your messages before sending them.

5. Keep your messages to the point.

6. Put the subject in the subject field before sending the message.

7. Do not send chain messages.

8. Remember to sign your messages.

Summary

In this chapter, you learned about the most common application of TCP/IP: sending and receiving mail. A general overview of the mailing process was provided, and the role that Simple Mail Transfer Protocol (SMTP) plays in transferring e-mail over the Internet was discussed. You learned how to use mail programs, such as Microsoft Outlook Explorer and Netscape Messenger, to read e-mail messages. You also learned the features of Multipurpose Internet Mail Extensions (MIME) and Secure/Multipurpose Internet Mail Extensions (S/MIME), which provide security by ensuring authenticity and integrity.

The last sections of the chapter dealt with network news and newsgroups. The process of transferring information from the news server to the users using the Network News Transfer Protocol (NNTP) was also covered. Finally, you learned about proper netiquette — the rules you should follow when communicating over the Internet.

✦   ✦   ✦

Enterprise Information Services

Computer networks — especially the largest one of all, the Internet — are a permanent presence in modern life. From four computers interconnected for faster communication, networks have evolved into a global base of information. As the number of users connecting to networks increases, tracking user information becomes more difficult. Moreover, network information (such as phone numbers and e-mail addresses) can be difficult to track if the information is stored in various electronic directories, because these directories may use different access protocols.

Network Directory Service Overview

Enterprise Information Service, or *Network Directory Service,* has proved to be an effective solution to this problem. Network Directory Service, a network service, is one of the most important components of an enterprise or distributed network. It keeps track of all the names, profiles, e-mail addresses, and machine addresses of every user on the network. In addition to making these resources accessible to users and applications, the Directory Service also facilitates communication on a network. Naming and locating network resources and users is the primary task of the Directory Service; however, it can also store information about network configuration. The conceptual representation of Network Directory Service is shown in Figure 17-1.

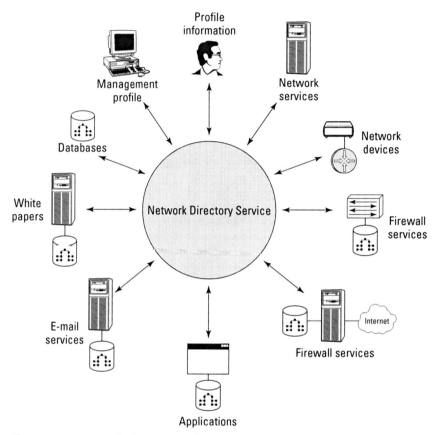

Figure 17-1: Network Directory Service

In general, a directory service maps the names of the network resources to their IP addresses. This mapping allows a user to locate a resource by specifying its name. Because the directory service makes the physical network topology and protocols transparent to users on a network, they can access any resource without knowing where or how the resource is located. Applications on a network can also use the directory services. For example, an e-mail application can use address book lookup to search for a particular user and phone number. The network directory services use highly specialized databases to provide fast lookups.

Additional advantages offered by the network directory services include:

✦ Enforcement of network security by denying access to intruders and unauthorized users.

✦ Distribution of the information across many computers in a network.

✦ Provision of information replication, which allows multiple users to access the same information simultaneously and makes the network resistant to crashes and failure(s).

✦ Provision of information partitioning, which allows the storage of a very large number of objects on various servers.

X.500 was the first step towards network directory services. It emerged as a set of standards and an information model for a directory service that could be accessed globally. Its platform independence ensured its success. But, like all the first attempts, it had few disadvantages that led to the emergence of Lightweight Directory Access Protocol (LDAP). X.500 was large, complex, and ill suited for the desktop environment that had slowly taken over from the mainframe environment. The biggest factor in popularity of LDAP was its seamless support to TCP/IP and the desktop environment.

Today a wide range of directory services are used in various networks, including Network Information Service (NIS), Network Information Service + (NIS+), Banyan StreetTalk Directory Service (STDS), Novell Directory Service (NDS), and Microsoft Active Directory (AD). Of these, NDS, and AD are most commonly used. Note that most of these directory services are based on LDAP and X.500 International Telecommunication Union (ITU) standards.

The X.500 Standard

X.500 is an International Telecommunication Union (ITU) protocol for managing the network directories of users and resources. The same standard is also published by Open System Interconnection (OSI)/IEC. The first specification of X.500 was published in 1988. In 1993, a more advanced version, compatible with the earlier edition, was released.

Note   SURFnet started the first operational X.500 Directory Service in 1992.

X.500 is a distributed directory protocol that allows hierarchies of regions, countries, organizations, and individuals to be catalogued. In other words, X.500 helps organizations all over the world create a global electronic directory of users that can be accessed through the Internet. This global electronic directory is also referred to as the *global white pages directory*, which allows a person to search for information about other people in a user-friendly manner. The search can be made by name, e-mail address, phone number, organization, and so on. By allowing its information to be a part of these white pages, an organization can make its presence felt globally.

The X.500 protocol is based on a client/server computing model. The global directory used by X.500 is known as the *Directory Information Database (DIB)*, popularly referred to as *white pages*. As per the X.500 information model, DIB is shared between *Directory System Agents (DSAs)*, or *X.500 servers*, that maintain the local information of an organization. A DSA maintains the local X.500 database and can communicate with other DSAs by using the *Directory System Protocol (DSP)*. (DSP is a protocol that belongs to the X.500 recommendation set). A *Directory User Agent (DUA)* is used to search the DSAs.

Tip   A DSA can store information for more than one organization — if the size of the organization is small. If an organization is large, its directory data can reside on more than one DSA. The distribution of information amongst the DSAs is completely transparent to the directory users.

All DSAs in the X.500 Directory Service are interconnected to form a virtual *Directory Information Tree (DIT)*, which is a hierarchical data structure. The entire structure begins with the *root*. Below the root, various *countries* are defined, which are subdivided into *organizations*. The organizations can be further subdivided into either *organizational units* or *individuals*. A simplified DIT structure is shown in Figure 17-2.

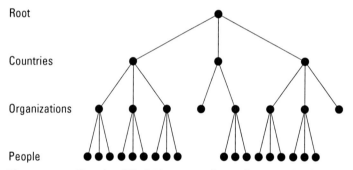

Root

Countries

Organizations

People

Figure 17-2: The simplified Directory Information Tree (DIT) structure

All the information in the X.500 Directory is stored in the form of *entries,* which belong to a *class object.* A class object can be a country, organization, organizational unit, or individual. All information related to the class objects is stored in the form of *entries.* An entry is a set of *attributes* that define the actual information. The class object to which the entry belongs defines which attributes it can have. For example, the class object "country" allows attributes, such as "name," "continent," and so on. Every entry is identified uniquely by a Distinguished Name (DN). Each component of the DN is called a *Relative Distinguished Name (RDN).* For example, `skj@nst.co.be` represents a DN entry, where the value of the name attribute is "skj," the organization is "nst," and the country name is "be." "skj," "nst," and "be" represent the RDN. The X.500 model also has *alias entries* that are used to build non-hierarchical relationships. An alias entry represents an entry in short form. The X.500 information model is shown in Figure 17-3.

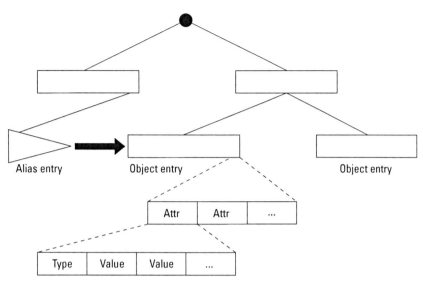

Figure 17-3: The X.500 information model

Tip

The "name" attribute, which is applicable to all the object classes, must have a unique entry at the level to which it belongs. For example, if there are two people named Andrew Lee in an organization, their entries must have a different first value for the name attribute.

The various service aspects of X.500 include replication, Directory User Agent (DUA), access control, and searching the Directory.

✦ **Replication** — While searching for information, access time can be reduced and Quality of Service (QoS) can be improved considerably if information stored on one DSA can be replicated in the other DSAs. X.500 uses *Directory Information Shadowing Protocol (DISP),* which allows replication of a portion of DIT between nodes.

✦ **Directory User Agent (DUA)** — A user accesses and retrieves the required information from the DIT by using DUA. In other words, DUA is the X.500 client that is used by the user to retrieve information from the DIT. When a user searches or browses through the DIT for information, the DUA contacts the nearest DSA for the required information. When the information is located successfully, the DUA returns the information to the user. DUA interfaces for the white pages service are available for any type of platform, including DOS, Windows, Macintosh, UNIX, and so on. Most popularly used DUAs include whois and finger.

✦ **Access control** — The user can query an X.500 server (DSA) using a DUA. A user's access to a Directory entry, or some part of it, can be permitted or denied depending on the identity of the user who is requesting the information.

✦ **Search** — A search can be carried out at any level of the DIT on the basis of the attribute type and its value provided by the user. The Directory is searched for all the entries that match the attribute's value. If a user-query cannot be answered locally, it is passed to other DSAs. After the result(s) of the query are found, the response(s) are passed back to the user. The entire process is transparent to the user, to whom it appears that the entire directory is accessible from the local DSA. However, the organizations maintaining the DSAs can restrict the search capability of users.

> **Note** The 1993 version of X.500 provides all of the above service capabilities. However, the 1988 version doesn't support access control mechanism and replication services.

Although X.500 Directory searches are fast and globally accessible, there are some drawbacks associated with it. The most important of these are:

✦ **Complexity** — Because X.500 is a complex standard to implement, vendors do not implement it completely.

✦ **Lack of support to yellow pages** — A Yellow Pages search is not supported by X.500, which means users are denied access to the complete set of information.

✦ **Lack of support of TCP/IP** — X.500 doesn't support TCP/IP. This lack of support to TCP/IP doesn't allow access to information on the Internet at the same time when one is using X.500.

Lightweight Directory Access Protocol (LDAP) was developed in 1995 to address the shortcomings in its predecessor, X.500. The idea to was to ease the burden of access from X.500 and make the directory service available to a wide variety of applications and computers. Like X.500, LDAP is used for accessing information directories. However, it is much simpler than X.500. Most importantly, it supports TCP/IP, which is necessary to access the Internet.

> **Note** For more information on X.500, refer to RFCs 2116, 1279, and 1292.

Lightweight Directory Access Protocol

Lightweight Directory Access Protocol (LDAP) was developed at the University of Michigan for accessing online X.500-based directory services on the Internet and for querying and manipulating information. In fact, the University of Michigan and many other universities still use LDAP to route e-mails and provide name lookups.

The information stored in X.500-based directories is arranged in a hierarchical treelike structure. As a client/server protocol, LDAP allows for browsing, reading, and searching information stored in the Internet-wide X.500 directory services and for performing simple management tasks.

Not just an access protocol, LDAP represents a lightweight, fast, and scalable directory service. Lightweight implies that LDAP is a simpler version of X.500. Because of its simplicity, accessing X.500 directories by using LDAP is a simple task. Therefore, LDAP is sometimes also referred to as *X.500-lite*. Although only a subset of X.500 functions have been reused in LDAP, it is capable of complete X.500 DAP functionality. At the same time, it is completely compatible with X.500. Since LDAP realizes lightweight and easy access to directory services and provides seamless support to TCP/IP, it is a better choice for the Internet environment. As a result, LDAP has now been fully accepted as the Internet standard for directory services that run over TCP/IP.

Note Scalability refers to the capability of a system — hardware, software, or network — to adapt to future growth and changes, if necessary.

The success of LDAP has been such that many directory service vendors (including Microsoft ADS, Banyan StreetTalk, and Netscape Directory Server) use LDAP as their core directory services technology. A leading network directory vendor, Novell also offers an LDAP plug-in for NDS and has integrated LDAP completely in NetWare 4.11 (IntraNetware) onwards.

Note Three versions of LDAP are already available: LDAP, LDAPv2, and LDAPv3. LDAP was released in 1993. LDAPv2 came out in 1996 and was adopted commercially. LDAPv3 is the current version and was ratified in 1997. Active Directory Service (ADS) and NDS support LDAPv3.

LDAP is an open standard. Therefore, it allows *any* application running on any platform to access stand-alone LDAP directory services or the directory services that are back-ended by X.500 and retrieve information from them. To access these services, ldap:// is prefixed in the URL of the LDAP server. (This is very similar to using File Transfer Protocol (FTP) and HyperText Transfer Protocol [HTTP].) Services supported by LDAP include e-mail address lookup facility in an e-mail client using LDAP, text, animations, audio, Uniform Resource Locator (URL), and authorized access to sensitive information (such as public keys).

Because it is based on X.500, LDAP shares many similarities with X.500, such as directory structure, data and namespace model, and the way information is accessed.

✦ LDAP, as well as X.500, uses a global directory structure. For example, information in an LDAP server is stored as entries. The type is defined by the object class to which the entries might belong. Each entry is a set of attributes that contains the actual information.

✦ The data and namespace model of LDAP resembles that of X.500. One or more LDAP servers contain the data that make up the LDAP Directory tree. In addition, LDAP uses the same hierarchy of entries as in X.500. The hierarchy starts from root of the Directory Information Tree (DIT) and continues until the individual level.

✦ The way information is organized and accessed in LDAP and X.500 is similar. An LDAP client can send a request for information or submit information for updating. On receiving a request, the LDAP server checks the client's rights to the requested information. If the client has the proper access rights, the server responds to the request or can refer the client to another LDAP server, where the information is available.

✦ Access control can be imposed on privileges to read, write, search, or compare information available on the LDAP server(s). It can be implemented for an individual as well as for a group of individuals. Access control can be done on a portion of the tree, entry, or even an attribute.

✦ Replication of information is also allowed on LDAP servers.

Although there is a strong resemblance between LDAP and X.500, there are a few differences between them:

✦ LDAP is designed to run over the TCP/IP protocol stack, which gives it the capability to access information available on the Internet. Since it doesn't support TCP/IP, X.500 lacks this capability.

✦ LDAP is much simpler in concept and easier to implement. This is why it has gained vendor acceptance quickly.

Note   Work is in progress to provide support to Yellow Pages using LDAP.

Many LDAP clients are available that will allow you to browse through LDAP-compatible directories. The most famous LDAP clients are e-mail clients, such as Outlook Express and Netscape Communicator. When integrated with LDAP, these clients can access extensive information in the form of address books. Furthermore, any client that has appropriate access permissions can access any LDAP server.

Note   For more information on LDAP refer to RFC 1777.

The most popular directory services are based on X.500 and LDAP. These directory services include NIS, NIS+, STDS, and ADS. Table 17-1 provides you with "at-a-glance" information about these directory services.

Table 17-1
Popular Directory Services

Features	NIS	NIS+	STDS	NDS	ADS
Hierarchy of Information	Flat namespace	Hierarchical namespace	Hierarchy up to three levels	Hierarchical organization of data	Hierarchical organization of data
Data Updates	Yes	Yes	Yes	Yes	Yes
Data Replication	Limited replication	Yes	Yes	Yes	Yes
Data Partition	Yes	Yes	Yes	Yes	Yes
Global Access	No	No	Limited capability	Yes	Yes
Host Lookup	Yes	Yes	Yes	Yes	Yes
Interface	Command Line Interface	Command Line Interface	Graphic User Interface	Graphic User Interface	Graphic User Interface
Security	Extremely low	Vulnerable to malicious attacks	Low security	High security	High security
Network Traffic	High	High	High	Low	Low
Interoperability	Extremely limited	Limited	Limited	Limited	High

To communicate with one another, users, computers, and applications require certain types of information, such as addresses of other computers, security settings, users' e-mail addresses, network interface-related information, services available on the network, valid groups of users, and so on. As networking technology advances, this list grows, too. In addition, a network is a dynamic environment. New computers and services are constantly being added to the network, leading to changes in current information. The changes need to be updated on every computer. In the absence of a centralized service to act as a manager, each computer would have to maintain its own copy of the information. In a small network, this task is tedious but manageable; in a medium to large UNIX- or Linux-based network, the job becomes time-consuming and unmanageable. *Network Information Service (NIS)* provides an effective solution to this problem.

Network Information Service

Network Information Service (NIS) manages the information required by users, computers, and applications to communicate with each other. It may be distributed over a local area network (LAN). The information that NIS manages is called *NIS namespace*. The information is stored over the network on various *NIS servers* and is available to any computer that requests it. The requesting computers are called *NIS clients*.

Note   NIS is historically known as *Yellow Pages* (*YP*).

There are two types of NIS servers: *master* and *slave:*

✦ **Master servers**—These maintain the master databases for a given domain, which always holds the updated information. Master servers are generally accessible only to network administrators.

✦ **Slave servers (or replica servers)**—In a large network, to prevent the master server from being overloaded, a few computers (or hosts) are designated as NIS slaves. NIS slaves can be accessed from network workstations and hence need to maintain the exact replica of databases maintained by the master server. Any changes in the network configuration are updated in the master server first and then propagated to the slave servers. Slave servers also act as a backup to the master server.

Caution   The number of slave servers in a domain should be designated in a manner such that availability is high and response time is slow without adding the expense of replicating data unnecessarily on too many hosts.

Clients and servers are grouped together in *NIS domains* (a set of servers and clients grouped together for common reasons, such as similar geographical location). Each domain has a set of characteristics associated with it. These characteristics are stored in databases called *maps* along with other system information, such as user names, passwords, and host names. The information stored in the maps is arranged in two columns: one stores the key, and the other stores information about the key. For example, the names of workstations are stored in the hosts.byname map, and their addresses are stored in the hosts.byaddress map. The information requested by a client is located by searching through these keys. A NIS domain with a master server, two slave servers, and a few clients is shown in Figure 17-4.

The use of NIS offers many advantages. These include:

✦ **Security**—Offers a high level of security, as all operations can be authenticated.

✦ **User interface**—Provides read/write access to the users.

✦ **Incremental data update**—Supports incremental data updates. As a result, only the portion of data that was affected is changed. The rest remains unaffected.

✦ **Host lookup** — Allows host Domain Name Service (DNS) type host lookups on the basis of IP addresses in a given network. DNS is a service used to locate hosts (or network devices) in TCP/IP-based networks.

✦ **Support to binary as well as ASCII data** — DNSs support only the ASCII data with restriction on packet size.

Cross-Reference   For more information on DNS, refer to Chapter 10.

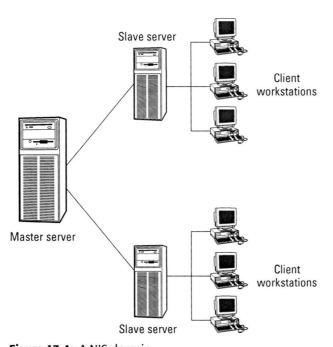

Figure 17-4: A NIS domain

There are also a few disadvantages associated with NIS. These include:

✦ **Flat namespace** — Supports flat (non-hierarchical) namespace. Therefore, NIS is only effective in a LAN.

✦ **Centralized databases** — Supports centralized non-hierarchical databases. As a result, NIS does not support partitioning of databases.

✦ **Limited replication capability** — Allows one replica to serve only one subnet, which implies that clients from other domains cannot access servers located in other domains.

✦ **Administrator-dependent** — Accessible to administrators only. As a result, only superusers (or administrators) can update and propagate information.

Note   For more information on NIS, refer to RFC 2307.

Because of the disadvantages of NIS, which make it difficult to manage (especially when the network is too large), *Network Information Service + (NIS+)* was developed.

Network Information Service +

NIS+ is an extension of NIS. It supports the *NIS+ namespace.* However, unlike the flat namespace offered by NIS, the NIS+ namespace is hierarchical. (In this respect, the NIS+ namespace is very similar to the UNIX directory structure.) Because of its hierarchical nature, the NIS+ namespace can be divided into multiple domains. Each domain can have its own administrator, instead of depending on centralized administration. If clients have appropriate permissions and rights, they can access servers located in other domains.

Note   The manner in which information is arranged in the namespace does not necessarily correspond to the physical arrangement of network resources.

The NIS+ architecture closely resembles the NIS architecture. It supports the client/server model, which is divided into domains. Each domain consists of a set of servers and clients. In a domain, one master server controls the rest of the supporting servers or replica servers. The master server also maintains the NIS+ database, which consists of multiple NIS+ tables. The NIS+ tables are duplicated on the replica servers, which are constantly updated by the master server. NIS+ uses elaborate authentication and authorization to verify whether a client has appropriate rights and permissions to access the NIS+ database.

The advantages NIS+ offers over NIS are:

✦ **Support to hierarchical namespace** — Because of its hierarchical namespace, NIS+ is closer to the organizational hierarchy.

✦ **Support to NIS+ partitioning** — The NIS+ database can be partitioned into directories that can successfully support autonomous domains.

✦ **Replication** — Each replica or backup server can serve multiple subnets.

✦ **Data updates** — Any client, even if remote, with appropriate rights can update the NIS+ database, if necessary. Updates can be automatic as well as initiated by the master server.

The disadvantages of NIS+ include:

✦ **Increased network traffic** — Supports periodic automatic updates, which increase network traffic.

✦ **Command Line Interface** — Supports only the CLI, which may not be convenient for some users.

✦ **Security** — Though NIS+ supports a sophisticated security system to protect the structure of the namespace and its information, it is more accessible than NIS. This makes it vulnerable to malicious attackers.

Note   For more information on NIS+, refer to RFC 2196 and 2065.

One of the oldest and longest-standing network directory services is *StreetTalk Directory Service (STDS)* of Banyan System, Inc. It was used in the Banyan Vines, a network operating system, long before the other vendors started incorporating the concept of network directories. In fact, STDS is so old that it is sometimes referred to as the "granddaddy" of network directory services.

StreetTalk Directory Service

STDS provides the distributed database of names and addresses that associates names with network users and resources, irrespective of the location of the resources in the intranet. The location of these resources is completely transparent to a user. StreetTalk is best suited for the enterprises that have distributed management centers across the globe. Like NIS+, STDS distributes the directory service across the corporate network on multiple servers that are distributed across multiple domains. Every server in the network supports partitions of the directory service. These partitions are synchronized automatically. To allow users to access the servers from anywhere on the network, object information is stored on the server hosting that particular object. In addition to the existing attributes of a class object, StreetTalk allows the addition of new attributes as per the company's requirements.

Note   The StreetTalk servers can automatically add themselves to the directory. Some clients can also be configured to register automatically with the directory, thereby making themselves visible to administrators.

Though some administrative tasks, such as hardware configuration, must be performed from the server console, StreetTalk servers support the *Enterprise Network Services Management Tool (ENS MT)*, which is a Graphical User Interface (GUI) tool that makes the rest of the administrative tasks easier. Because of the distributive nature of STDS, a directory-browsing tool called *StreetTalk Directory Assistant (STDA)* is available with the clients. STDA helps clients search for objects and other network resources. STDA periodically scans all the servers on the network to gather information about users, peripheral devices, and volumes.

The StreetTalk tree can support a maximum of three levels. As a result, the StreetTalk Directory Service only supports first-tier organizational units with no nesting. Users log in once to StreetTalk and thereafter have access to all servers that the administrators permit them to access.

STDS is beneficial because it:

✦ Is simple to configure and maintain.

✦ Provides a single point of management, thus making administrative tasks easier. Network administrators need not spend much time managing the directory service. They can shift their focus on managing the users instead.

✦ Creates partitions of the directory service on every StreetTalk server, thus distributing the overhead among all the servers. This makes the system more fault-tolerant by eliminating any single point of failure.

✦ Manages updates and synchronizes the distributed directory partitions itself without the administrator having to interfere.

✦ Can automatically merge two trees.

Using STDS is disadvantageous for several reasons:

✦ It does not support low-level control of the directory.

✦ Third-party support is very limited.

✦ It supports only three levels of the directory tree. As a result, it allows only first-tier organizational units and can cause naming problems in large organizations. It also doesn't support nesting.

✦ Access privileges are based on object names. Therefore, there is a possibility that access-related security problems might arise.

Note

In addition to Banyan Vines, StreetTalk is now available for other network operating systems (NOSs). It is also available for various versions of UNIX, NetWare, and Microsoft Windows NT. However, it failed in the case of Windows NT, as the solution was riddled with problems.

For more information on STDS, refer to RFCs 1006, 1537, and 1937.

Although Banyan System, Inc., has tried to make STDS compatible with the other major NOSs, it has experienced some failures as well as stiff competition in the directory service market. One of the most popular vendors of directory services is the Novell Corporation. Novell's *Network Directory Service (NDS)* has been on the market for a long time and has proved to be a stable product that has withstood the competition and emerged as a leader in the market of directory services. NDS was first introduced in NetWare 4.0 and is available in all the versions that succeeded it. It is also offered as part of its most recent version, NetWare 5.0. NDS is also available for other popular NOSs, such as Windows NT and Solaris.

Novell's Network Directory Service

Network Directory Service (NDS) is a distributed directory service that stores the information related to the Internet, intranet, and other network resources. It also ensures security and access to these resources by providing elaborate authentication and access control services. NDS is based on X.500 and is compliant with LDAP.

All the network resources, such as users and various applications, and volumes in the network file system are represented as objects in NDS. Physical devices (such as printers, fax machines, and scanners) are also considered objects. For example, individual users are represented as *user objects.* Divisions, departments, or workgroups in the organization are represented as an *organizational-unit object,* also known as a *branch object.* Each object is associated with attributes called *properties* or *fields.* For example, the fields associated with the user object can be node address, login ID (or username), password, name, address, e-mail, and telephone number. The NDS directory tree is shown in Figure 17-5.

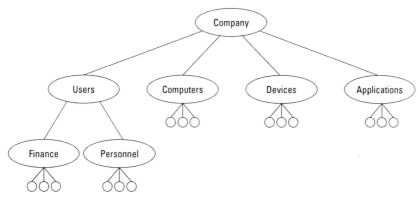

Figure 17-5: Structure of the NDS directory tree

Tip | Novell ships NDS with sample directory trees for large, as well as small, companies. This helps network administrators implement NDS without too many problems.

Accessing resources in the NDS interface resembles accessing files and directories in Microsoft Windows Explorer. The default view of NDS is the root of the directory structure. The network administrator can build the directory tree to represent the structure of the organization. Each branch of the tree represents a logical group of users. The user group can be made on the basis of department, division, or geographical location.

NDS is the strongest and most stable NOS-based hierarchical network directory service available today. Some of the advantages of using NDS are:

✦ **Centralized control** — However widely spread the enterprise network, the administrator can control the entire network from a central point. NDS also supports graphical administration utilities that make administration easier.

✦ **Global access to network resources** — The enterprise network may have multiple servers. However, this fact is transparent to the users because NDS presents a simple view of a complex infrastructure. When users log into the system, instead of viewing a collection of individual servers, they view a single information system. They can access any resource they have appropriate rights to. This system also makes administration easier and reduces administrative costs.

✦ **Replication** — Allows administrators to store entire copies or portions of copies of the NDS database on multiple servers that may be located in multiple domains. This makes the entire setup fault-tolerant and reduces the network traffic over the WAN links.

✦ **Hierarchical directory tree** — Makes access to resources easier and allows rule-based administration. Different hierarchical views in NDS also allow administrators to view the logical, as well as physical, arrangement of the directory objects.

Note   Rule-based administration enables administrators to grant rights to an entire branch of users at one go, which means that granting access permissions to all users of a company is easy and fast. The need to manage individual users and resources is also minimized.

✦ **Extensibility** — Independent software vendors can integrate new services and add new objects into the network by extending the NDS schema.

Note   The NDS schema is a set of rules that regulates the structure of the directory tree. The schema determines the definition, attributes, properties, and location of all the objects in the tree.

✦ **Scalability** — NDS can be customized to work with any type or size of network. NDS is also capable of supporting company mergers that may lead to the merger of two enterprise networks.

✦ **Flexibility** — The NDS design is very flexible. The directory tree can be modified to accommodate any changes in the company strategies or network. Objects, groups, or even entire branches of the tree can be relocated with a simple drag-and-drop.

✦ **Security** — NDS provides maximum security from intruders and unauthorized access. When users access any network resource or service, access is allowed after they are authenticated only if they have sufficient rights to the object.

Note   The whole authentication process is transparent to the users. The authentication is session-based, and the client signature is valid only for the given session.

NDS and all the other directory services (STDS, NIS+, NIS, LDAP, and X.500) have one main disadvantage — they support their own interface, which may or may not be compatible with other interfaces. Also, due to the enormous popularity of the Microsoft Windows environment, most end users prefer to work with the Windows interface. Moreover, enabling different applications to use these directory services is a cumbersome task. A number of interfaces and concepts need to be implemented at the programming level, and every directory service needs to be supported explicitly.

Note   For more information on NDS, refer to RFC 822.

Microsoft's *Active Directory Service (ADS)* was designed to provide standardized access to numerous directory services that are commonly used. ADS allows a high degree of interoperability with other directory services, thus allowing the users of ADS to access information from other directory services.

Active Directory Service

Active Directory Service (ADS) offers a standard interface to all the existing directory services with the help of an object called a *provider.* The provider implements the actual access to the data by returning an interface through which the selected directory can be accessed. The provider exists for each directory service that ADS supports. When an ADS-based client issues a request for information about a user, computer, application, or resource, the ADS interface is used to query the appropriate directory service. The directory service then invokes the specified provider, which searches for the requested information. After the query is processed, the user receives either the information or a message stating that, in effect, the target resource was not found. The whole process is transparent to the client, who doesn't need to know the details of implementation and location of the directory service.

Note   Active Directory Service (ADS) is also based on LDAP.

Since ADS is based on LDAP, the data model it uses is very similar to the LDAP data model. An entry is defined by a number of attributes called *properties.* In contrast to the concept of flat domains used in NT Directory Service (NTDS), ADS uses a hierarchical domain tree called an *NT domain tree.* All the objects (users, machines, peripheral devices, and applications) contained in a domain are treated as entries. As a result, the domain is structured as a tree. This increases the scalability of the namespace. Every domain contains a *Directory Server,* which facilitates access to all objects in a domain. Figure 17-6 shows the NT domain tree organization.

All the communications within and outside a domain are made by using LDAP. Therefore, different types of clients view the domain tree differently. For example, NT clients would view the NT domain structure, whereas other LDAP-enabled clients would view an LDAP directory interface. This LDAP directory interface can be browsed in the same way as the X.500 DIT.

A *Global Catalog (GC)* is used to facilitate fast and efficient searches of remote resources. Every object located anywhere in the domain tree needs to be registered with the GC, which is optimized for speed. When a user or application issues a request to locate an object in a remote domain, the GC is queried instead of the remote directory. This allows users to locate the remote resources with speed and ease.

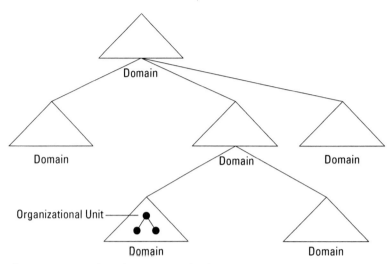

Figure 17-6: NT domain tree organization

In addition to searching and managing users and resources, ADS simplifies network management. The advantages of ADS include:

✦ **Centralized administration** — Enables administrative control of the entire network from a single point.

✦ **Single interface** — Provides a single interface from which diverse directory services, such as white pages and e-mail, can be managed. Moreover, having a single interface allows for additional interoperability between other directory services that already have varying levels of interoperability.

✦ **Integrated security** — When a user logs in, the user information is logged into the single authorization model. This helps administrators set the security parameters once for each user or object. Also, access control can be defined on objects as well as on their properties. This ensures security of sensitive information.

✦ **Extensibility** — Administrators can add new objects and their attributes to the existing domain tree. ADS also allows for the addition of new attributes to the existing object classes to customize the domain tree according to the company's requirements.

✦ **Replication of information** — Allows multi-master replication across the domain tree. The presence of many master servers enhances the network availability. This also makes the entire system more fault tolerant by eliminating one point of failure.

✦ **Flexible querying** — Users can initiate searches on the basis of a word, name, or address. Use of the Global Catalog reduces the response time and increases the performance of the network.

The primary disadvantage of using ADS is that it works *only* on the Windows platform. It is not compatible with other platforms. Therefore, to take advantage of the benefits of ADS, the user needs to implement ADS on the Windows platform only.

 Note   For more information on ADS, refer to RFCs 2251 and 2052.

Summary

In this chapter, you learned about the X.500 standard and its service aspects. You learned about its more popular successor, LDAP, and the reason it was developed. Next, you learned about the common directory services based on X.500 and LDAP, including NIS, NIS+, LDAP, STDS, NDS, and AD. You learned that NIS was developed to support the dynamic nature of modern-day networks. However, it failed to support a hierarchical format of information and fared badly in the field of security. NIS+ was developed to address these problems. However, it also had some disadvantages. It offered a command line interface and, because of frequent data updates, generated excessive network traffic. Banyan developed STDS, which was the first GUI-based network directory service. However, STDS offered limited security and global connectivity. Further, it supported only three levels of information hierarchy. Because of high security and seamless global connectivity, Novell's NDS emerged as the leader in the market of directory services. Finally, you learned about Microsoft's ADS, which, in addition to strong security and a popular interface, also provides interoperability with most of the network directory services.

✦   ✦   ✦

Building and Maintaining TCP/IP Networks

T his Part is dedicated to building a TCP/IP network. At this point, you should know how to install and configure TCP/IP and also have a good idea of the tools that are available. The challenge now is to tie all the pieces together into a network that provides functionality, security, and dependability.

Chapter 18 helps you determine your addressing needs and decide how to get the addresses that you require. Once you know this, you can decide how to break down your address space to match your topology.

Once you have determined how to break your address space down, you can identify the routing solution your network needs, a topic discussed in Chapter 19. You then determine how many routers you need and how they will update their routing information. Once you have configured routing, you can determine where servers need to be placed to best service the needs of clients on your network, which is discussed in Chapter 20.

With the physical network in place, you can start examining the remote access requirements for laptop users and users that work at home. Chapter 21 will look at remote access and at connectivity. A related topic is that of network security, specifically authentication and encryption, a topic covered in Chapter 22.

Now that you have a network plan, you can begin to implement it; in Chapter 23, we examine some strategies for troubleshooting connectivity and other problems on the network. Monitoring the network is discussed in Chapter 24.

Choosing Your Addressing Scheme

✦   ✦   ✦   ✦

In This Chapter

Determining your
addressing needs

Using Private
Network Addresses

✦   ✦   ✦   ✦

Now that you understand the workings of TCP/IP, it is time to start putting all the pieces together to build your network. To do this, you will look at the addressing requirements for your network in order to determine the best addressing scheme.

You will not normally have to build a network from scratch; more likely, you will be re-engineering an existing network. The first step in either case is to determine the addressing scheme that you will use.

Evaluating Your Addressing Needs

There are many factors that need to be evaluated before you determine what addressing scheme you will use, including:

✦ Physical network configuration

✦ Locations to be serviced

✦ Performance requirements

In the next few sections, we will look at each of these factors in greater detail.

Physical network configuration

There are several types of networks that you can use. Each network will give you different benefits. Token Ring, for example, will enable you to push the number of systems that you place on each ring much further than Ethernet. However, the speed of transmission is slower. Most of the topologies can be augmented using bridges or other network devices that will allow you to extend the number of systems that you can put on a single segment.

To effectively plan the number of stations you can put on a segment, you need to determine how much network traffic a single system will generate. Several different types of traffic could be present on your network, including:

✦ File transfers

✦ Web browser traffic

✦ Checking e-mail

✦ Network applications, such as SQL Server

✦ Multicasting

✦ Desktop applications run from a server

Each of these types of traffic must be figured into the traffic that workstations will put on your network. There might be some departments in your company that use a particular type of traffic more than others. For example, the users in your finance department may be primarily working with a network application, whereas your graphics arts department may perform more file transfers. In such a case, you will need to break down a traffic analysis by the type of workstation and determine what segments the workstations will be on.

In addition, you can count on losing 25 to over 50 percent of your network bandwidth to background traffic, such as DNS, DHCP, WINS, and/or directory service replication, depending on the type of servers that you find on your network. Figuring out these values will allow you to determine the number of hosts that you will be able to place on a segment, and therefore how many segments you will need.

As you look at breaking down your network into segments (which will later be called subnets), you need to also consider the placement of servers and the amount of traffic between different users. By understanding the traffic generated by users and by planning the correct placement of servers, you will be able to control the traffic that will be generated. Controlling the traffic provides your users with the best possible response time given the topology employed. In Chapter 20, we will look more closely at planning servers.

In addition to understanding the traffic that will be present on a segment, you will also need to know about the traffic that moves between segments. This isn't a large concern if the segments are all connected directly to the backbone; however, if your segments are spread out over a building or campus, or even across the globe, you will need to consider where the segments are.

Locations to be serviced

In small companies, you will generally be dealing with a small number of computers. Normally, all the systems will be placed in a single location and you can connect the networks together by simply hooking the various segments to a simple backbone. In this case, you won't be concerned with the different locations that you have to service.

As the size of the organization grows, though, the likelihood of having large distances to cover increases. In this case, you will need to build a larger network than the simple LAN. Networks that are larger than a LAN have different names:

✦ **Campus Area Network (CAN)** — This type of network is one in which two or more buildings that are in close proximity are connected. Typically, you can run wiring between these buildings yourself and have total control over the networks.

✦ **Metropolitan Area Network (MAN)** — This type of network is one in which the buildings are not all close together, but in the same metropolitan area. In this case, you will need to obtain the connectivity through either a local ISP or your local phone carrier. This means that some of the wiring will not be under your control.

✦ **Wide Area Network (WAN)** — This type of network is one in which you are no longer connecting systems that are located in the same city. In this case, you might be crossing the province (state), the country, or even the world. You will be working with a larger service provider that can provide you with lease lines, or you might use the Internet as your backbone. In either case, your data is more exposed, and you have much less control over the line conditions. There is also a significant cost factor that will come into play as you try to connect the office in Suva to the office in Reykjavik.

For larger networks like CANs, MANs, and WANs, you will need to use an addressing scheme that lets you keep the traffic separate on the subnets in each of the locations, but that also makes it easy to route between the different offices. In essence, you need levels of hierarchy in the addressing scheme. Another consideration will be the requirement to route packets effectively even if a link between offices goes down.

Performance requirements

Although it would be nice to provide every user across your entire enterprise network with gigabit Ethernet, it would be impractical due to the cost. Part of planning your network involves determining a realistic level of performance. When you are looking at the addressing scheme, two factors affect the performance that a user sees.

The first factor is straightforward—if you put too many hosts on a network segment, performance will suffer. This is particularly true in the case of Carrier Sense Multiple Access/Collision Detection (CSMA/CD). On this type of network, all the stations "listen" to the network for a quiet moment (a moment when no other systems are sending) and then grab the opportunity to send. As the number of systems on a network increases, there is more "noise" on the network and fewer opportunities to send. On the other hand, the more segmented your network, the more routers you will need in order to move traffic.

The second factor you need to look at is the type of traffic the hosts generate and the actual amount of time they spend communicating. If the users work locally most of the time and only require the network occasionally, then you can normally put most hosts on each segment. On the other hand, if you are running your office suite from a server, then the client will communicate constantly and you will need to restrict the number of hosts you put on the network.

There are a couple of ways that you can increase the number of systems on a network without using expensive technologies. You can use bridges and switches to reduce the traffic on each network. Keep in mind that neither of these methods is perfect, and there will still be a limited number of systems you can put on a subnet.

Using bridges

Bridges join two or more segments at the Physical layer. At the Physical layer, every packet sent on Ethernet or Token Ring is sent using broadcast—that is, every station on the bus over the ring will see the packet and evaluate the destination address. As this happens, the bridge will also see the address. If the address is known to be on a different port, the bridge will resend the packet on that port. If the address is known to be on the same port as the sender, the bridge ignores the traffic, which means that only traffic destined for the remote port will pass through the bridge.

The upside of using a bridge is that you can now have 100 systems on each side of the bridge with only the required traffic crossing to the other side. This means that you could have 200 systems in that one subnet. Of course, a bridge might have more than two ports. In that case, you could have, for example, five segments of 50 systems and push the subnet to 250 machines.

The downside is that all the systems will be dependent on the operation of the hub— in other words, if the hub goes down, many of the systems will no longer be able to communicate. The bridge also has to learn all the physical (MAC) addresses that belong to each port, which takes some time. If the segments are not well-planned, the bridge could become overloaded.

Using switches

Switches, like bridges, work at the Physical layer. But unlike bridges, which connect segments, switches normally connect individual systems. When a system sends data, the data goes to a port on the switch. This switch looks up the destination MAC address and sends the data to the port that the device is on, opening a virtual circuit between the two devices. This enables the devices to send and receive at the same time. In other words, a switch facilitates full duplex communications, doubling the amount of data that can traverse the wire.

Because each port is isolated, the stations see themselves as the *only* systems on the network. This means that they will always be able to transmit, since they are in their own collision domain. Switching technology is very common, but it also has limitations on the number of stations that are connected. In addition, switches are more expensive than normal hubs (which they replace).

In the end, network performance boils down to the number of subnets you have, the destination for the traffic (local segment or not), and the number of systems on each subnet. Switching and bridging technologies can be useful in increasing the number of systems that can be placed on a single segment. However, these technologies still have limitations. Bypassing these limitations requires routing, and therefore, the correct addressing scheme.

Private versus Public Addresses

One of the most straightforward decisions you will need to make is whether you will use private network or public (Internet) addresses. In most cases, you will use one of the private network addresses for your internal network and then use some form of network address translation to access the Internet. Doing this allows you to hide your internal addressing scheme from the Internet — reducing the risk of hacking, as well as saving you money, since you don't have to pay for the use of the addresses. The only time you would need valid Internet IP addresses is in the case of Internet Service Providers (ISPs), which need to supply a valid address to the client. In this case, a valid address would normally be used.

There are three groups of addresses that have been set aside for use as private network addresses in RFC 1918 — these addresses are never used on the Internet. The ranges are:

✦ 10.0.0.0 to 10.255.255.255

✦ 172.16.0.0 to 172.31.255.255

✦ 192.168.0.0 to 192.168.255.255

The reason these addresses are not used on the Internet is fairly simple. If, for example, the mail.ditdot.com server had the address 10.25.26.35, and you attempted to send to that address from your network (which used the 10.0.0.0 address space), the address would appear to be in your network rather than on the Internet.

Most organizations use the 10.0.0.0 address, since it provides the most flexibility. You can easily have two levels of hierarchy so you can configure routing within a location and between locations. Smaller organizations might use the 172.16.0.0 or

192.168.0.0 addresses if they either have a small number of networks or a small number of hosts per subnet. In general, the address class you choose doesn't matter, as long as you break the address down correctly.

You will most likely need to obtain some real address space. In most cases, a small number of addresses will be used for exposed servers, such as SMTP, DNS, and HTTP servers.

Obtaining Addresses and Connectivity

The address space for the Internet is under the control of the Internet Assigned Numbers Authority (IANA). This body assigns the addresses to the various ISPs and large organizations that are directly connected to the Internet. Unless you will be directly on the backbone, in essence becoming part of it, you will obtain your IP addresses from your ISP.

The number of addresses you need depends on the number of systems you will need to expose to the Internet. The good news is that normally, your ISP will be able to provide you with more valid Internet addresses. The cost of the addresses is normally part of the service provided by your ISP. However, if you need a large number of addresses, you may find yourself paying extra.

When you are choosing an ISP, there are several factors to consider. Some of the questions you might want to ask include:

✦ What is the ISP's connection to the Internet? In most cases, a business should consider a backbone provider — such as MCI, UUNET, or BellNexxia — rather than a small provider. The small providers have to purchase their bandwidth from these people as well, and you can easily cut out the middleman if you go with a backbone provider in the first place. In some cases, though, you might choose to use an ISP if they connect to multiple backbone (tier 1) providers — multiple connections provide redundancy and can provide better access to a wider group of people.

✦ How many subscribers does the ISP have? One of the most popular ways for a small provider to make money is to oversubscribe their services. Given that not all users will be online at the same time, an ISP can easily sell 110 percent or more of the bandwidth. As the number of subscribers goes up, the bandwidth available to individual subscribers decreases.

✦ What type of power backup does the ISP have? Even if there is a power failure you want access to continue. Therefore, you should ensure that the ISP has a backup power system. If your provider (and any pieces in between) doesn't have backup power, then you will be down.

✦ What are the ISP's co-location facilities like? In some cases, you might want to co-locate Web servers at your ISP's location. This will reduce the amount of bandwidth that you need to bring in-house, since the Web traffic will not have to come across the link. This is a good solution for small to mid-size companies.

✦ What can the ISP offer in terms of dial-in service? Most providers are in the dial-up business as well. Although you might not be looking at dial-in as a solution for the corporate office, the reality is that you will need to provide this type of access for home workers and laptop users. If all your clients dial in to the provider that you use to connect your office, you can reduce the number of networks that data has to pass over.

There are other questions you will want to ask when choosing an ISP, and these will depend on your exact situation. These days, most ISPs are fairly similar, and often, the question of which ISP to choose comes down to a matter of price. However, keep in mind that quality of service and the ISP's willingness to work with your organization are just as important.

Selecting the right ISP can reduce the amount of work you have to do and the number of complaints you may get. A good ISP will free you to manage your network — starting with calculating your address needs and determining what you need in the way of subnets and your routing strategy.

Calculating Your Address Needs

Now that we have dealt with the theoretical aspects of addressing and briefly discussed what you need in an ISP, it's time to get down to actual calculations. The truth is, you cannot string a single wire between all your systems and call it a network (unless you have 50 systems or less).

Although calculating your address needs is fairly simple, it is also critical. Changing your IP addressing scheme after you have already rolled out your network is a major undertaking, and since you would be taking away users' access for a period of time, you could be faced with a number of complaints.

As mentioned earlier in the chapter, an IP address is made up of two parts: the network address and the host address. In reality, however, you will need to add a subnet ID within the IP address so you can perform routing internally. If you are working strictly on a LAN, you will need to add a subnet address that can be used to determine which subnet within your network a host is on. When you are dealing with multiple locations, you will also need to add a location address. So, the 32 bits that make up the IP address may contains up to four pieces of information: network, location, subnet, and host.

To determine how much of the address to use, you will need to look at your network. How many locations do you have now, and how many locations will you likely have in the future? When you know these facts, you can establish the number of bits you will need to use for the location part of the address. If you don't have multiple locations at the moment and don't think you ever will, you can probably skip this step.

To determine the number of bits needed for the location address, follow these steps:

1. Determine the maximum number of locations you will need.

2. Convert the number to binary.

3. Count the number of bits you wrote down.

For example, if you currently have 7 locations and will possibly add another 5, you should plan for 12 locations. The number 12 in binary is 1100, or 4 bits. In this case, you will need 4 bits for the location address.

The next step is to determine the maximum number of subnets you will ever have in any location. You can use two different approaches to calculate this number. First, you can arbitrarily determine the number of subnets based on the physical layout of your network and where you feel like combining systems. Sometimes this method works and sometimes it doesn't. The second approach is to analyze your traffic (as discussed earlier) and the topology you are using to determine the maximum number of systems that you want to put on each subnet. This number can then be factored into the physical layout of subnets in your office to put users together logically on subnets.

When determining the maximum number of systems to put on a subnet, you also need to determine the amount of traffic that will be generated by the clients (as discussed earlier) and take a look at the topology.

To determine the maximum number of clients to place on a subnet, follow these steps:

1. Determine the maximum bandwidth of your topology. For 100 Mbps (megabits per second) Ethernet, that figure would simply be 100 Mbps. However, if all your stations are directly connected to a switch, you can double this amount, since the systems can run full duplex to 200 Mbps.

2. Divide the Mbps rating by 10. This gives you the approximate number of megabytes per second. Yes, there are only 7 or 8 bits in a byte, but using 10 allows for the preamble and Cyclic Redundancy Check (CRC), as well as some collisions (and it's easier).

3. Multiply the number of megabytes per second by 3,600 (number of seconds in an hour). This will give you the most data that the topology will be able to move in one hour.

4. Determine the amount of traffic a user will generate in a day. This can be done using a network monitor on your existing network, or by simply estimating the number with the calculations given in Table 18-1. Determine this number in megabytes.

5. Double your estimate to allow for background traffic — you could measure this number, but given that most network operating systems are responsible for 25 to 50 percent of the network traffic, you can use this shortcut. At worst, you will err on the side of allowing more bandwidth, which is always a good thing.

6. Divide the number you calculated in Step 4 by 10 (working hours in a day — adjust as required). Now divide the number from Step 3 (amount of traffic the network can handle in one hour) by the number from Step 5 (amount of traffic one client will generate in one hour). This gives you the maximum number of hosts that you should put on one subnet in a perfect world.

Use Table 18-1 if you need to estimate the amount of traffic a user will generate in a single day.

Table 18-1
Calculating Station Traffic

E-Mail Traffic

A)	Number of e-mails per day
B)	Average size of e-mail bytes
C)	Percent of e-mails with attachments
D)	Average size of attachment bytes
E)	Message data per day (A*B)
F)	Attachment data per day (A*C*D)
G)	Mail traffic per day in megabytes ((E+F)/1024)

File Transfer Traffic (This only counts if the users will store files on the server.)

H)	Size of the average profile MB (if using network profiles)
I)	Average number of files worked on per day
J)	Average size of a file MB
K)	File transfer traffic per day MB (H+(I*J))

Browsing Traffic

L)	Number of pages visited per day
M)	Average size of page bytes (default: 10,240)
N)	Browser traffic per day (L*M/1024)
O)	Total traffic per station (G+K+N)

Total up the traffic from each of these estimates to get an idea of the amount of traffic that you will be generating. Application traffic will not be accounted for, because each separate network application will produce different amounts of network traffic, and it is that traffic that must be measured. Also, the calculation does not account for the traffic generated if you are running desktop applications from a server. When estimating the size of a Web page, remember that most pages these days are .ASP pages, which are built dynamically and are not normally cached on the client, so they will have to load on each visit.

As an example, consider a network that is using 100 Mbps cabling. Estimate the traffic for an average station using 100 as the number of messages per day, with 10 percent having attachments. The average message is 750 bytes (remember to include the header) and the average attachment is 35,000 bytes. Further profiles on this network will be stored locally, with an average of 75 files being used a day, each with an average size of .08MB (80 K). The users visit an average of 150 pages per day using the default size.

First, use Table 18-2 to calculate the per station traffic.

Table 18-2
Sample Traffic Calculation

E-Mail Traffic

A)	Number of e-mails per day	100
B)	Average size of e-mail bytes	750
C)	Percent of e-mails with attachments	10%
D)	Average size of attachment bytes	35,000
E)	Message data per day (A*B)	75,000
F)	Attachment data per day (A*C*D)	2,625,000
G)	Mail traffic per day MB ((E+F)/1024)	2,637

File Transfer Traffic (This only counts if the users will store files on the server.)

H)	Size of the average profile MB (if using network profiles)	N/A
I)	Average number of files worked on per day	75
J)	Average size of a file MB	.08
K)	File transfer traffic per day MB (H+(I*J))	6

Browsing Traffic

L)	Number of pages visited per day	150
M)	Average size of page bytes (default 10,240)	10,240
N)	Browser traffic per day (L*M/1024)	1,500
O)	Total traffic per station (G+K+N)	4,143

Now the maximum number of systems per subnet can be determined using the steps outlined above. The topology is 100 megabits per second Ethernet; dividing by ten gives us approximately 10 megabytes per second. If we then take the 10 megabytes per second and multiply it by 3,600 (seconds in an hour), we find that 36,000 megabytes of data can be moved in one hour.

If we take the 4,143 MB we calculated in Table 18-2 and multiply it by two (to cover server traffic) we get 8,286 megabytes per day, or 828.6 megabytes per hour.

Now we can take the amount of traffic the network can handle in an hour — 36,000 megabytes — and divide it by the 828.6 megabytes we calculated as the per station traffic. This gives us the number of stations that the topology will support — in this case, a little over 43 stations.

Now, we can calculate the number of subnets that we should have by taking the number of systems that we will have in the location and dividing it by 43. If, for example, you will have 2,394 systems, you should plan for around 55 subnets.

Our next step is to figure out the number of bits that are required to create this number of subnets. This number will be added to the number of bits that are already in use for the location. Since we need 55 subnets, we can write the number 55 in binary and simply count the number of bits. 55 in binary is 110111, or 7 bits.

Using the same tactic that we just used for the subnet portion of the IP address, we can now figure out the number of bits we will need for the host ID portion. We determined that the number of hosts on each subnet should be 43 or less. If we write 43 in binary, we get 101011, or 7 bits.

At this point, we have calculated all the parts of the IP addressing we need. We calculated 4 bits for the location, 7 bits for the subnet ID, and 7 bits for the host. If we add these three numbers, we find that we need 18 bits available in the host portion of the IP address for our environment to work. This means we must use a Class A address, since it provides 24 bits in the host portion (a Class B only allows 16 and a Class C only 8).

We could use a different Class B address for each location. The location required 4 bits, and without this, only 14 are needed. This will fit in the 16 bits that are left by a Class B address; however, each location requires a different Class B address — otherwise, there's no way to route between the offices. If they all used the same Class B address, there would be no way to tell them apart.

The next step will be to create a Class A subnetting scheme or subnet mask(s) that will accommodate our network.

Subnetting

Subnetting is a topic that has confused and mystified many people over the years. The goal of this section is to explain subnetting in what will hopefully be simple terms. Be forewarned: if you are not familiar with binary, this may hurt a little.

As discussed in Chapter 5, the IP address and subnet mask are used to extract the network ID. You saw that the network ID that is extracted will be used to determine if the address you are attempting to reach is local or remote so that packets can be routed differently. You also saw that there were three standard subnet masks: 255.0.0.0, 255.255.0.0, and 255.255.255.0.

These standard subnet masks are used to mask off the host portion of an IP address so that the network portion can be determined and the packet can be routed to the correct network. And because these masks correspond to the use of 8, 16, or 24 bits of the IP address to identify the network, the entire octet was either on or off, giving us easy numbers to work with.

Calculating the location ID

In our example, we use 4 bits for the location, 7 for the subnet, and only 7 for the host. This means that our subnetting will not be done in octets (groups of 8 bits). So, we will need to determine a custom subnet mask that can be used in our organization; in fact, we need two — one between locations and one that can be used in each location.

Let's review the process that is used to determine if an address is local or remote. Table 18-3 shows the calculations for a host with an IP address 158.35.64.7, and a subnet mask of 255.255.0.0 (the standard class B subnet mask), trying to communicate with a host at IP address 158.35.80.4.

Table 18-3 Determining If a Station is Local or Remote		
Item	**Dotted Decimal Notation**	**Binary Representation**
Local IP	158.35.64.7	10011110 00100011 01000000 00000111
Subnet Mask	255.255.0.0	11111111 11111111 00000000 00000000
Network ID	158.35.0.0	10011110 00100011 00000000 00000000
Target IP	158.35.80.4	10011110 00100011 01010000 00000100
Subnet Mask	255.255.0.0	11111111 11111111 00000000 00000000
Network ID	158.35.0.0	10011110 00100011 00000000 00000000

In Table 18-3, the two network IDs that are extracted match, and the system is local. As you can see, the AND process very easily extracts the network ID. In our case, though, we need to be able to make many different networks, so using this standard subnet mask will not work.

Now let's move from this simple example to the example that uses 4 bits for location, 7 bits for subnet, and 7 bits for the host. The first choice we need to make is what private network address to use. If you look at the choices again, you will notice that there was a Class A, a Class B, and a group of Class C addresses that were available (10, 172, and 192 starting octets.)

In our case, we need 7 bits for host, plus 7 bits for subnet and 4 bits for location — or a total of 18 bits. Since we cannot change the bits in the given address without changing the address, we need to perform the subnetting in the host portion of the address. The Class B address space allows 16 bits for the host (two octets) and the Class C only allows 8. That means we need to use the Class A address, or the 10.0.0.0 private network address.

Note In the real world, most organizations use the Class A 10.0.0.0 network address, because it provides the most potential for growth. In most cases, the second octet is used for the location; the third octet is used for the subnet ID; and the last octet for the host. This means that any company that has 256 or fewer locations with 256 or fewer subnets in each location can generally use the 10.0.0.0 address.

In reality, each of the locations is a separate network, and within each location, each subnet is a separate network. This means that we need to keep more of the address in the network portion and use less for the host.

In the standard Class A subnet mask, the bits that represent the network address are turned on (1s) and the host bits are turned off (0s).

```
1111111     00000000     00000000     00000000
10      0      0      0
```

So, if more networks are needed, more of the bits in the subnet mask will need to be used for the network — that is, more of the bits will need to be turned on (1s). If we add the four bits that will be used to determine the location, the subnet mask looks like this:

```
11111111     11110000     00000000     00000000
```

When the binary value is converted back to decimal, the new subnet mask appears turns out to be 255.240.0.0. The next step is to find out the starting IP address for each location, which we can call the location ID. The location ID will start with "10.". Because the "10." is the assigned portion of the address, if you are using valid Internet IP addresses you can simply substitute the assigned IP address in place of "10.". In the example, the location ID is completely in the second octet; thus, we know that only the values in the second octet will change. The last two octets will be 0.0 for all the location IDs.

Many people have difficulty understanding that not every change to the number in the second octet will be a different subnet. In the example, the subnets 10.14.0.0 and 10.15.0.0 are both in the same location; however, 10.16.0.0 is not in the same location. The 10.16.0.0 is in a different location, since the pattern in the first four bits of the second octet changes from 0000 in the case of 10.14.0.0 and 10.15.0.0 to 0001 in the case of 10.16.0.0.

This means we need to figure out what numbers make changes to the pattern in those first four bits. Each value that changes the pattern of four bits will become a different location ID. Obviously, you could write down all the numbers from 0 to 255 in binary and then scan through the list to see where the first four bits change, but that would take a while! There is a faster method: Find out where the last 1 bit is in the subnet mask and then determine that column's value. With four bits being used, the last bit is in the fourth column of the octet. The column values reading across an octet are 128, 64, 32, 16, 8, 4, 2, and 1. Therefore, the value of the fourth column is 16. We can call this the increment.

With the increment, we can now quickly figure out all the location IDs. We start with 0 and increment repeatedly by 16. So, the location IDs are 10.0.0.0, 10.16.0.0, 10.32.0.0, 10.48.0.0, 10.64.0.0, and so on. The reason this shortcut works is simple. There are only a certain number of combinations of the four bits at the beginning of the second octet. In binary, they look like this:

```
0000
0001
0010
0011
0100
0101
0110
0111
1000
1001
1010
1011
1100
1101
1110
1111
```

In reality, this is a list of the numbers 0 to 15 written in binary. Each number is one more than the previous number — in other words, each number is incremented by 1. However, these 4 bits lie at the beginning of an octet, not at the end, where the 1s column is. So in reality, we are looking for these numbers:

```
0000 0000
0001 0000
0010 0000
0011 0000
0100 0000
0101 0000
```

```
0110 0000
0111 0000
1000 0000
1001 0000
1010 0000
1011 0000
1100 0000
1101 0000
1110 0000
1111 0000
```

Notice that the only thing that has changed is that we have added a pile of 0s at the end. The change to the first four bits is exactly the same. The only difference from the previous list of binary numbers is that we are not incrementing the 1s column. We are in fact incrementing the fourth column, which has a value of 16. If, instead of 4 bits, we needed to use 3 bits, we would look for these numbers:

```
000 00000
001 00000
010 00000
011 00000
100 00000
101 00000
110 00000
111 00000
```

When we use three bits, we are really just incrementing the third column by one. So for three bits, the increment is the third column, or 32, and the location IDs are 10.0.0.0, 10.32.0.0, 10.64.0.0, 10.96.0.0, and so on. The same shortcut works regardless of the number of bits you use.

Regardless of the number of bits that are used, we can use Table 18-4 to relate the subnet mask to the increment. This is good news, as it saves a lot of time mucking around in binary.

Table 18-4
Possible Subnet Masks and the Related Increment

Subnet Mask	Binary	Column Value (Increment)
255.0.0.0	11111111 00000000 00000000 00000000	N/A
255.128.0.0	11111111 10000000 00000000 00000000	128
255.192.0.0	11111111 11000000 00000000 00000000	64
255.224.0.0	11111111 11100000 00000000 00000000	32
255.240.0.0	11111111 11110000 00000000 00000000	16

Continued

Table 18-4 *(continued)*		
Subnet Mask	Binary	Column Value (Increment)
255.248.0.0	11111111 11111000 00000000 00000000	8
255.252.0.0	11111111 11111100 00000000 00000000	4
255.254.0.0	11111111 11111110 00000000 00000000	2
255.255.0.0	11111111 11111111 00000000 00000000	1

At this point, you should understand how the location IDs were calculated. Here is the complete list of location IDs for the example network that we are using:

```
10.0.0.0
10.16.0.0
10.32.0.0
10.48.0.0
10.64.0.0
10.80.0.0
10.96.0.0
10.112.0.0
10.128.0.0
10.144.0.0
10.160.0.0
10.176.0.0
10.192.0.0
10.208.0.0
10.224.0.0
10.240.0.0
```

Computing the subnet ID

Now that we have the various location IDs, we can add the other 7 bits that will break each location down into subnets. This will set the last four bits is the second octet to 1 and also set three of the bits in the third octet to 1. That means the new subnet mask is 11111111.11111111.11100000.00000000, or 255.255.224.0 in dotted decimal notation.

As an example, assume that the location network ID of 10.32.0.0 is assigned to our Athens, Greece office. The subnet addresses for each subnet will start with 10.32.0.0. We determine the subnet ID's by incrementing this number by 32 in the third octet. (You'll notice that the 224 increment is 32 in Table 18-4).

If we follow the same strategy as before, the first subnet is 0, then 32, then 64, and so on. This means that the first subnet in the Athens office is 10.32.0.0, which is confusing because 10.32.32.0 is also the location ID. Thus, we won't use 10.32.32.0

as a subnet ID; rather we start with 10.32.32.0. Using the increment, we will start adding to find the other subnet IDs. The next few are 10.32.64.0, 10.32.96.0, 10.32.128.0, and so on.

So, what comes after 10.32.224.0? To answer this question, you have to ignore the boundaries that are imposed by the dotted decimal notation. You simply continue to increment in binary, as you did before (refer to Table 18-5).

Table 18-5
Crossing Dotted Decimal Boundaries

Assigned Portion	Location ID	Subnet ID	Host ID
00001010	0010	0000 111	00000 00000000
00001010	0010	0001 000	00000 00000000
00001010	0010	0001 001	00000 00000000

The subnet IDs that follow 10.32.224.0 are 10.33.0.0. and 10.33.32.0. Remember that the next value that will change the pattern in the first four bits of the second octet — that will, in fact, change the location ID — is 48. Thus, we will end up using subnet IDs that have 32, 33, 34, 36, 37, 38, 39, 40, 41, 42, 43,44,45,46, and 47 in Athens. Only when the number in the second octet changes to 48 are we looking at a different location.

Notice in Table 18-5 that I have broken down the addressing to the four different pieces we are working with here: 8 bits, the first octet that is assigned; 4 bits in the second octet used for the location ID; and 7 bits that span the second and third octets that are used for the subnet ID. The remaining portion, 13 bits, is available for the host ID. This is far more hosts than we actually require, but you still have to use all 32 bits in the address.

For our example network, we could have simply used the second octet for the location, the third octet for the subnet ID, and the last octet for the host ID. This would have saved us time performing the calculations and would have made the addressing much simpler, since the boundaries for the different parts of the address would have lined up with the octet boundaries. It would also have allowed for more growth. Right now, the only portion of the IP address with room for growth is the host ID. It would be better to have room for growth in the location ID and the subnet ID, since the number of hosts we can have per subnet is a physical limitation.

There are now two subnet masks that can be used: one to connect the offices together, and a second used in each office, as shown in Figure 18-1.

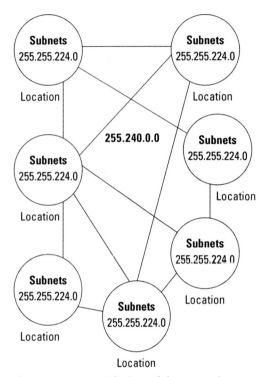

Figure 18-1: A quick view of the example network

As you can see, the subnet mask 255.255.224.0 is used within each location and 255.240.0.0 is used between locations. This ensures that any host on the network will see both of the other subnets in that location as a remote subnet. Furthermore, this scheme makes sure that each location will see other locations as remote networks.

Finding the host addresses

Now that we have calculated the location IDs and know how to calculate the subnet IDs in each location, we need to find the range of host addresses for each network. Looking again at the Athens office, let's use the 10.32.32.0 subnet as an example.

The address 10.32.32.0 is a full 32-bit address. However, we cannot use it for a host since it will be needed by the routers to build routing tables in our network. The address 10.32.32.0 is really the "name" of the entire subnet and is the address where the host portion is all 0s. Again, we will use an increment, however, it is finally a simple increment. Since the host ID always goes to the end of the IP address, it will always end in the last column, whose increment value is 1.

For the first host, we add 1 to the subnet ID of 10.32.32.0, which gives us 10.32.32.1. The next host will be 10.32.32.2, and so on. Just as before, when we reach the address 10.32.32.255, we cross the dotted decimal boundary. The next host will be 10.32.33.0, the next one will be 10.32.33.1, and so on.

The address where the host portion is all 0s is the subnet ID and can't be used for a host because it has a special meaning. There is another address in the host portion that cannot be used, and that is the address where the host portion is all 1s. This will be the broadcast address. In the example at hand, we would have:

```
00001010 00100001 00111111 11111111
```

In dotted decimal notation, the address is 10.32.63.255. Notice that if we add one more to this number, we would actually be at the next subnet ID, 10.32.64.0. This will always be the case, and is a shortcut to finding the broadcast address. Find the next subnet ID and subtract 1.

For the 10.32.32.0 subnet, we now have the subnet ID 10.32.32.0, the broadcast address 10.32.63.255, and the first valid host ID 10.32.32.1. Since only the first (all 0s) address and the last (all1s) address have special meaning, the last host is one back from the last or broadcast address. Here, that address is 10.32.63.254.

A quick look at supernetting

Supernetting, or *Classless Internet Domain Routing (CIDR),* is basically subnetting in reverse. With the limited number of Class A (126) and Class B (16,384) addresses, a problem arose with assigning IP addresses on the Internet to companies that had more than the 254 hosts allowed by a Class C address.

The problem has been addressed to a large degree by the use of the private network addresses and the use of proxy servers. These two functions have given companies all the internal addresses they need using valid Internet addresses. However, there are cases (for example, with ISPs and some large companies) that require large blocks of valid Internet addresses. The companies would have to settle for multiple Class C addresses without CIDR.

CIDR allows multiple small networks to be combined into a single large network. For example, if a company requires 620 valid Internet addresses, the company would require at least three Class C addresses.

In order to understand CIDR, we again have to abandon the artificial boundaries that are imposed by the dotted decimal notation and look at IP addresses for what they really are — 32-bit binary numbers. If we treat multiple Class C network addresses as a subnetted Class B address, the problem is simplified.

If a company needs 620 valid IP addresses, we can simply look at it as 620 hosts. In binary, the number becomes 10 01101100, or ten bits. In a Class B address, this would be simple: if you need 10 bits for the host IDs, you then have 6 bits for the subnet ID. Your subnet mask would be 255.255.252.0.

Since we need valid Internet addresses, you will have to work with an ISP provider who has been issued a large block of valid IPs from the Internet Assigned Numbers Authority (IANA). They will actually perform this calculation and find a range of Class C addresses that will act as the subnetted Class B.

If, for example, your provider was assigned the IP range 207.236.0.0 through 207.236.255.255, it would treat this as a Class B address of 207.236.0.0. From there, the process is similar to finding a subnet ID for this "Class B" network with a subnet mask of 255.255.252.0. The increment is 4 in this case. Therefore, they look at 207.236.48.0, 207.236.49.0, 207.236.50.0, and 207.236.51.0 as an example. If all the addresses in this range were free, they could assign you the address 207.236.48.0 with the subnet mask 255.255.252.0. This is actually 1,022 valid addresses. However, they would have to assign the whole block for routing purposes.

Now packets that are trying to find you will be sent to the 207.236.0.0 Class B network of your ISP, which will find that the address is part of 207.236.48.0 and forward it to your main router. From there, you will have subnetted the assigned address and your router will forward the address accordingly.

Essentially, CIDR allows us to use any address class as any other address class and break down — or group — addresses as best fits your needs.

Summary

This chapter discussed addressing schemes and looked at subnetting and supernetting. It will lead us into the discussion of routing that follows in the next chapter. As you now know, you cannot go very far into the design of your network without some legwork. You will need to have some idea of the number of physical locations you will deal with and the number of hosts that are likely to be in each location.

This chapter also covered the topic of subnetting. Unfortunately, this topic is one that you will probably need to review more than once before it clicks. The good news is that it does eventually click, so don't get frustrated — move on to the next chapter on routing, where the purpose of subnetting should become easier to understand.

✦   ✦   ✦

Designing Routing for Your Network

In Chapter 18, subnetting was examined, and you learned that you can extract the subnet ID from the IP address and the subnet mask. Now we see how these concepts can be applied. One point that has already been made several times is that you can't put an infinite number of systems onto a single network segment — therefore, you need to split your network into smaller, more manageable pieces.

This chapter discusses the basics of routing, and what happens as more and more segments are added to the network. Other topics that are examined include: classful and classless routing; variable length subnet masking; and various methods of sharing the routing information between the different routers on your network automatically rather than configuring the information manually.

Some Basics of Routing

Routing is the process of moving information from source to destination networks across any device that has two or more network interfaces and an IP stack. In other words, a computer will look at any packet it receives and determine if the packet is traveling to the network to which it is physically connected. If so, the packet will be sent out on that local interface. If not, the router will look for a route that it can use. In general, it will determine if one of the routers it is connected to can move the packet further along.

This is the cornerstone of routing and of routed networks: routers move the packets one "hop" at a time until they reach their destination. The router itself is a very simple device. In fact, any device that has two or more network interfaces and an IP layer can be made to route packets.

Suppose a network has been divided into two pieces. (For the purpose of this example, we will keep the subnetting simple.) The first network will be 10.10.2.0, and the other network will be 10.10.56.0. Both will use the subnet mask 255.255.255.0 (see Figure 19-1).

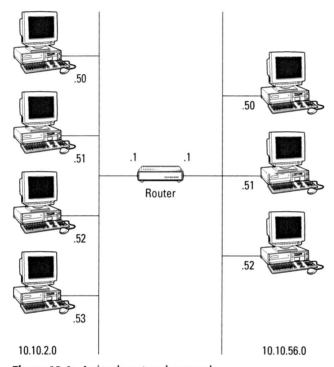

Figure 19-1: A simple network example

As you can see, the two networks are separated by a router, which has two network interfaces on each of the two networks: 10.10.2.1 and 10.10.56.1. When a host such as 10.10.2.51 tries to send to 10.10.2.53, the Internet layer will take the local host IP and subnet mask and extract the network ID 10.10.2.0. Since the target host could have a different subnet mask, it will then take the target IP and its own subnet mask (the only one it knows) and extract a possible network ID for the target host. In this example, it will come up with network ID 10.10.2.0, which matches its own network ID. Because both of the network IDs match, IP knows the target system is local and will now use Address Resolution Protocol (ARP) to find the Network Interface Card (NIC) address of the target and will send the packet directly to the host.

At this point, the router has not been involved and no routing has taken place. If the target IP were on the other side of the router, say 10.10.56.52, then the router will become involved. Again, the local host IP and subnet mask are used to extract the local subnet ID of 10.10.2.0. However, when the target IP address and the local subnet mask are used, the network ID 10.10.56.0 is extracted. This network ID does not match the local network ID of 10.10.2.0, and the packet will need to be routed. The routing process starts on the local station using the routing table.

The routing table

Routing actually starts on the local machine, which has a special table known as a *routing table*. The routing table is created every time the system is started and is used by IP to route packets. In the case of the local machine, the routing table normally contains the local entries and one entry that will send all other traffic to the local router. The following is a sample of the routing table you might find at host 10.10.2.51:

```
Network Destination           Netmask       Gateway    Interface  Metric
            0.0.0.0           0.0.0.0  10.10.2.1  10.10.2.51       1
          10.10.2.0   255.255.255.0  10.10.2.51  10.10.2.51       1
         10.10.2.51 255.255.255.255   127.0.0.1   127.0.0.1       1
    10.255.255.255 255.255.255.255  10.10.2.51  10.10.2.51       1
          127.0.0.0       255.0.0.0   127.0.0.1   127.0.0.1       1
          224.0.0.0       224.0.0.0  10.10.2.51  10.10.2.51       1
    255.255.255.255 255.255.255.255  10.10.2.51  10.10.2.51       1
```

At first glance, this table might look confusing, but it is actually not difficult to understand. The target IP will be combined with each netmask to extract a network ID. If the calculated network ID matches the network destination, then you found a route. You can then send the data using the NIC on the local system listed in the Interface column to the address in the Gateway column.

In the routing table, the first entry from the top shows 0.0.0.0 in both the netmask and network destination columns. Using this netmask with any IP address will always give you 0.0.0.0 as the network destination. Placing this entry first in the routing table might seem strange. However, the table is read backwards (bottom to top). In this case, the system will first check to see if the packet is being sent to the global broadcast address (255.255.255.255). Then it will check for multicasts (224.0.0.0), and finally, for the internal loop address (127.0.0.0).

After checking for these addresses, the system lists addresses for each local interface (if there were multiple network cards, it would repeat these lines for each interface). For each local interface, it first looks for a subnet broadcast (.255), then anything going to the local host, and finally anything going to the local subnet. It might seem redundant to check the local IP address, since the system has already checked if the packet is for the local network; however, a system with multiple network cards requires checking the local interfaces so that packets received on one interface (where they will be compared to that interface's IP and subnet mask) can be routed out a different interface.

The 0.0.0.0 entry is a catchall, known as the default route, and will only appear if the system has a configured default gateway. If no other route is found as the system compares the target IP address to each of the netmasks in the routing table, the default route will be used to send the packet to the configured router.

Returning to our example (where 10.10.2.51 is trying to communicate with 10.10.56.52), the local system will use the routing table shown above to determine the next hop. In this case, the default route will be used, and the system will use ARP to determine the NIC address for 10.10.2.1. The packet will then be sent to the host at IP address 10.10.2.1, which in this case is the router.

The router will receive the packet and will compare it with the IP address and the subnet mask of the local interface. In this case, the router will compare the packet that is targeted for 10.10.56.52 with the IP address 10.10.2.1, using the subnet mask 255.255.255.0. In the same way that the host did, the result of the comparison will signify that the host is remote (to this interface) and will cause the router to check its routing table.

```
Network Destination          Netmask      Gateway    Interface  Metric
           10.10.2.0    255.255.255.0    10.10.2.1    10.10.2.1       1
           10.10.2.1  255.255.255.255    127.0.0.1    127.0.0.1       1
      10.255.255.255  255.255.255.255    10.10.2.1    10.10.2.1       1
          10.10.56.0    255.255.255.0   10.10.56.1   10.10.56.1       1
          10.10.56.1  255.255.255.255    127.0.0.1    127.0.0.1       1
      10.255.255.255  255.255.255.255   10.10.56.1   10.10.56.1       1
           127.0.0.0        255.0.0.0    127.0.0.1    127.0.0.1       1
           224.0.0.0        224.0.0.0   10.10.2.51   10.10.2.51       1
     255.255.255.255  255.255.255.255   10.10.2.51   10.10.2.51       1
```

In this example, IP on the systems will find that the route 10.10.56.0 works with the netmask 255.255.255.0. The system will therefore pass the packet to gateway 10.10.56.1 (itself) for delivery to 10.10.56.52. ARP will be used to find the NIC address of the end host, and the packet will be delivered.

To review the process, the originating host uses its IP address and subnet mask and the target host's IP address to determine if the target is local. If so, the packet is sent directly to the host using its NIC address (determined by ARP). If the target is not local, then the originating host will check its routing table for a route to the host. If a route is found, the packet is sent to the configured gateway for that route using the NIC address (again, determined by ARP).

The gateway receives the packet and makes the same comparison with its IP address and subnet mask for the interface that received the packet. If the packet appears to be local (which means there's an error somewhere, since the host did the same comparison), the packet is sent to the target host using the NIC address. If the comparison shows that the target is remote, as it should be, then the routing table on the gateway is used to determine the next hop. If the next hop is local to any of the gateway's interfaces, the packet is sent to the queue for that interface and is sent directly to the target using the NIC address. If a route is found that isn't local, the gateway sends the packet to the next hop. If there is no route, the router returns the "request time out," "destination host not found," or "destination host unreachable" message to the originator using Internet Control Messaging Protocol (ICMP).

Building a routing table

You might be wondering where a routing table originates. Is the routing table loaded from a file? Is the routing table calculated? Do you have to do something to create the routing table? The answer to all these questions is yes.

But let's start slowly. In the example used throughout this section, routing has worked because the router was physically connected to each network and could therefore build its routing table based on these networks. In Figure 19-2, you see two routers and three networks, and neither router is directly connected to all three networks. This means that neither router can build a routing table that includes all three networks.

Figure 19-2 depicts two routers, Router A and Router B. Router A knows about networks 10.10.2.0 and 10.10.56.0 because it has a physical network connection to each of these networks. In the same way, Router B knows about 10.10.56.0 and 10.10.59.0.

If host 10.10.2.50 tries to communicate with host 10.10.59.51, there is a problem. The system checks the IP/subnet mask combination and determines that the system is remote. By virtue of the 0.0.0.0 (default gateway) entry in the routing table, it will send this packet to the configure router (Router A). Router A will also check the IP/subnet mask on the interface where it receives the packet and determine that the packet is to be delivered to a host that is remote to this interface. It will check its routing table, and because the routing table only contains information built from the local interfaces, it won't find a route. Router A doesn't know about 10.10.59.0, since there is no physical connection. Therefore, it returns a "destination host unreachable" message.

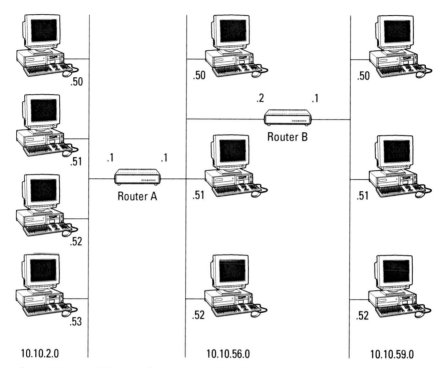

Figure 19-2: Building on the simple network example

Router A needs some method of passing the packet to Router B. The simplest method would be to configure Router A to send anything it doesn't know about to Router B — in other words, make Router B the default gateway for Router A. Router A would then use the default route to send the packet to Router B (since it couldn't find another route). Router B knows about the 10.10.59.0 network since it is physically connected to it. Consequently, Router B will deliver the packet.

However, a problem remains. Assume that host 10.10.2.50 is sending an echo request (PING). The packet is now at host 10.10.59.51, and that host is going to send an echo reply back to 10.10.2.50. It makes the comparison and discovers that the target is remote, finds its default gateway entry, and sends the packet to Router B. Router B checks the packet on the local interface and finds that it is remote; accordingly, it then checks the routing table and sends a "destination host unreachable" message to 10.10.59.51. The destination host cannot be reached because Router B doesn't know any more about network 10.10.2.0 than Router A knew about 10.10.59.0.Therefore, the best method for enabling Router A to pass the packet to Router B is to configure Router B to use Router A as the default gateway. This solution is easy to implement; however, it doesn't work if you add another network. Figure 19-3 illustrates the potential complications.

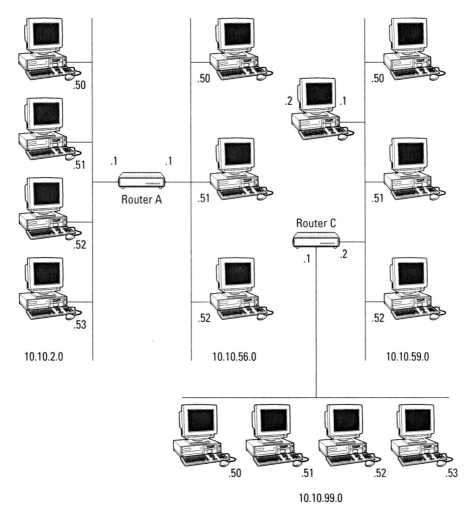

Figure 19-3: Adding another network

Static routing

As the network grows, the default gateway approach no longer works. Since only one default gateway entry will be significant, multiple entries are allowed — but only the first one the system comes across will be used unless it is down. In this case, you could fix the network by using a router with multiple interfaces (say four) so that all the networks are local to it; however, this might become difficult if there are 50 or 60 subnets that have to be connected.

What you need to do is tell the routers about the other networks, the networks that they are not physically connected to. You can do this by adding static routers to each router so they know where to send the packets intended for unknown networks. As seen in Figure 19-3, Router A knows about 10.10.2.0 and 10.10.56.0. We could add information about 10.10.59.0 and 10.10.99.0 that tells Router A to send those packets to Router B. Essentially, we need to add the following lines to the routing table:

```
Network Destination          Netmask              Gateway
Interface  Metric
       10.10.59.0    255.255.255.0          10.10.56.2
10.10.56.1          2
       10.10.99.0    255.255.255.0          10.10.56.2
10.10.56.1          3
```

If we add these lines to the routing table in Router A and add the correct routes for the other two routers, then information can flow across all the networks. In a small organization, this is the preferred method, since it doesn't involve any extra network traffic like dynamic routing does. The only concern is that if you change the way your network is configured, you have to redo all the static routes.

Adding a route is a simple operation on most operating systems. In general, all operating systems use the `route` command. The basic switches for the `route` command are:

✦ **Route Print** — Displays the routing table

✦ **Add** — Creates a static entry in the routing table

✦ **Delete** — Removes an entry from the routing table

✦ **Modify** — Changes an existing route

✦ **Flush** — Clears the routes in the table and reloads from file/registry

To add the routes we need for Router A to a Windows-based system, type:

```
route add 10.10.59.0 mask 255.255.255.0 10.10.56.2
route add 10.10.99.0 mask 255.255.255.0 10.10.56.2
```

On a Linux system, the command would look like this:

```
route -A inet add -net 10.10.59.0 netmask 255.255.255.0 gw
10.10.56.2
route -A inet add -net 10.10.99.0 netmask 255.255.255.0 gw
10.10.56.2
```

These commands will add the required route to the computer for the running configuration. However, the routes will be lost if the system crashes and needs to reload. Therefore, you will want to store the routes either in a file (in the UNIX world) or in the Registry (in the Windows world).

As the size of the network grows, so do the number of routers. Thus, you will eventually reach a point where you are no longer able to configure the routers manually and will need to find some method of automatically updating routing tables. This topic will be discussed in an upcoming section on dynamic routing.

Deploying Routing

Now that the routing basics have been covered, our discussion will turn to the physical layout of the network. The type of physical network that you use and the performance requirements that were examined in Chapter 18 also come into play during the layout of the network. In fact, these factors are closely intertwined.

The subnet mask that you looked at in Chapter 18 provides you with the basic mask that will be used on the client subnets. Now, all the client subnets need to be tied together with some sort of network hardware so they can communicate. This means planning the usage of your concentrators (or hubs) or switches to create a bus topology, or using your Multistation Access Units (MAUs) to create a ring.

Since most of you will use Ethernet, which is a bus topology, we will concentrate on that particular topology. For those using Token Ring, remember that you can normally exceed the number of hosts/segments that Ethernet will handle. The discussion in Chapter 18 gave you a basic formula to calculate the number of hosts you should have on a subnet.

Tying your subnets together

How do you tie the subnets together and still make routing work? The obvious method (the one used in previous examples) is to keep tacking the subnets on the end of the logical network (subnet – router – subnet) until you have sufficient subnets to accommodate the number of users you will have (see Figure 19-4).

This method is simple and easy to implement. However, if users need to communicate with other users several hops away, then the routers will be very busy. If any one router fails, the entire network can be easily impacted, since there is no redundancy and no concentration of servers.

Another obvious design is to set all the networks out in a circle around a central router. Again, this is simple to visualize, and all of the hosts should be able to communicate easily with one another (see Figure 19-5).

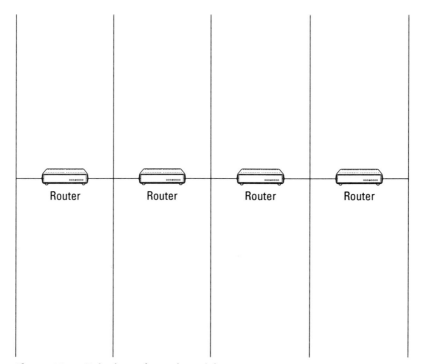

Figure 19-4: Stringing subnets in serial

Using a central router works fine for a small office. In addition, you could easily provide redundancy by adding a second router in the central position. The only concern is that a large amount of traffic will be flowing across a single router or pair of routers. Also, if you don't have a redundant router, your network will have a single point of failure to deal with.

The central router approach provides a building block that will allow you to grow your network. If you designate one of the subnets in Figure 19-5 as a "backbone," you would be looking at a router that connects three client subnets to the backbone. When you add more client subnets, you add another router to the backbone and then add the client subnet as spokes on that router (see Figure 19-6).

Figure 19-6 is a fairly normal design that is used in many networks. The corporate servers would typically be placed on the backbone (like the mail server) and the client servers (file/print) would be placed on the subnets with the clients. Here, the failure of a single router doesn't affect the entire network and there is room to grow. As you look at Figure 19-6, consider the calculations we made in Chapter 18, where each of those client subnets could contain either 30 or 126 computers. Across the twelve subnets, you might have 360 users, up to 1,512 users. Adding more users isn't difficult; drop in another router and add three more subnets, or maybe go to 4 or 8 subnets on each router.

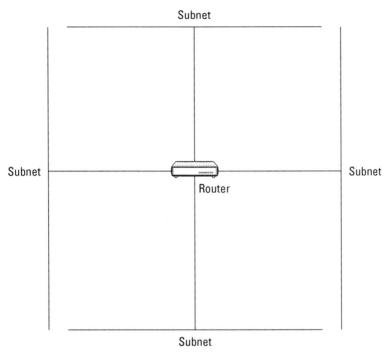

Figure 19-5: Subnets spread out around a central router

This design provides a great deal of flexibility; however, there is a limit to the amount of traffic the backbone can handle (even if the backbone is running FDDI). We can reduce this traffic by moving more servers down to the client subnets and ensuring that clients that will share data and communicate with each other are on the same subnet — or at least on the same router.

Eventually, though, you will need to expand beyond what a single backbone can handle. This can be done by simply splitting the backbone into different parts and configuring routing between the parts. You will probably already have multiple backbones, since networks typically encompass more than one location and each location will have its own backbone.

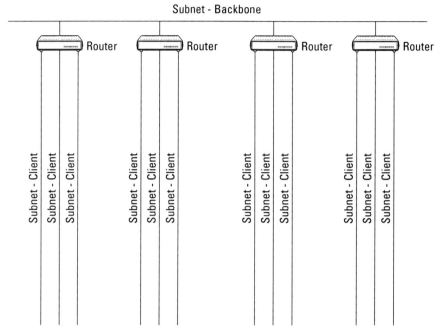

Figure 19-6: Using routers to connect client subnets to a backbone

Variable Length Subnet Masking

The problem with using a simple backbone strategy is traffic. If your servers are all on one backbone, or your users tend to work together a lot, you will end up with a great deal of traffic on your backbone. Variable Length Subnet Masking (VLSM, as defined in RFC 1817) is a solution that provides for multiple levels of backbone, and therefore, several different places where the traffic can cross from one network to another. Nevertheless, VLSM is hard to implement, because you now have to deal with different subnet masks in different parts of your network.

For the purpose of discussion, consider the subnet mask 255.255.255.224 as the optional subnet mask for our clients. This means that we want to limit each subnet to 30 IP addresses, which gives us room for 29 computers and the router interface. So, a 24-port switch might become the building block of the network. Let's also assume that we will use Linux systems as our low-level routers and that each will handle four network cards. This means that the subnets will be .0, .32, .64, and .96. The router interfaces will probably be .1, .33, .65, and .97, or the first IP address on each of the segments. One connection will need to be used for the connection to the large network, so let's use the .0 subnet. Figure 19-7 shows what this system might look like.

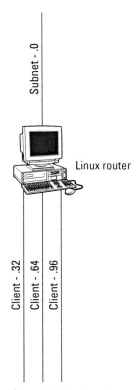

Figure 19-7: A router connecting four subnets

We now have a configuration where all the traffic for .0, .32, .64, or .96 networks will have to go into .1. Let's add some other octets to make this address look a little more normal. All the traffic for subnets 10.10.10.0, 10.10.10.32, 10.10.10.64, and 10.10.10.96 has to go to the interface 10.10.10.1. That router will then send the data for the other subnets to those subnets. However, this means that all the data for IP addresses 10.10.10.1 through 10.10.10.127 will go to this router. Although the netmask for the three client subnets has to be 255.255.255.224, we could use 255.255.255.128 (or fewer bits) in the netmask for the interface that will connect these clients to the larger network..

Note   Although we are using subnet masks in this chapter, you might also see a /*number of bits* notation that is easier to read once you're used to it. For example, 10.10.10.0, with a subnet mask of 255.255.254.0, would be written as 10.10.10.0/23.

Using this addressing scheme means that another router could have 10.10.10.129 as its address and handle routing for another three subnets. In fact, in Figure 19-8, you will see that if the subnet mask 255.255.254.0 is used, we can put even more routers together.

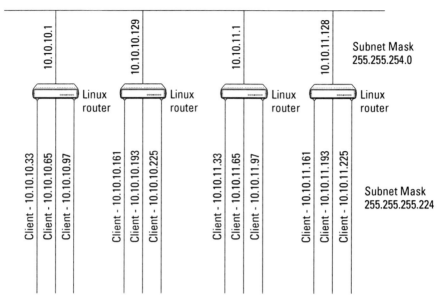

Figure 19-8: One group of four routers connecting 12 subnets

So, you've created a backbone scenario with custom subnet masks. Big deal, right? Well, if you carefully examine the addresses at the top of Figure 19-8, you will notice that *all twelve* of these networks can be described as 10.10.10.0 mask 255.255.254.0. This means that we can now view all of Figure 19-8 as a *single* node and replicate it several times to build a bigger network. Figure 19-9 shows the next level of hierarchy.

Obviously, using variable length subnet masks requires a little more planning, starting with your decision concerning the maximum number of hosts. However, using VLSM has some real advantages:

✦ You will be able to locate servers at any level of the hierarchy, meaning servers can be close to the users.

✦ You can assign different size blocks of addressing to a department or to a separate location, depending on their need.

✦ You will reduce the traffic that has to go all the way to the backbone.

Tip   If you are working in the Microsoft world, remember that Windows NT 4.0 and older operating systems cannot use VLSM. The reason these operating systems cannot use VLSM has to do with the way the operating systems ordered the entries in the routing table. Entries with long subnet masks must be checked first before VLSM will work.

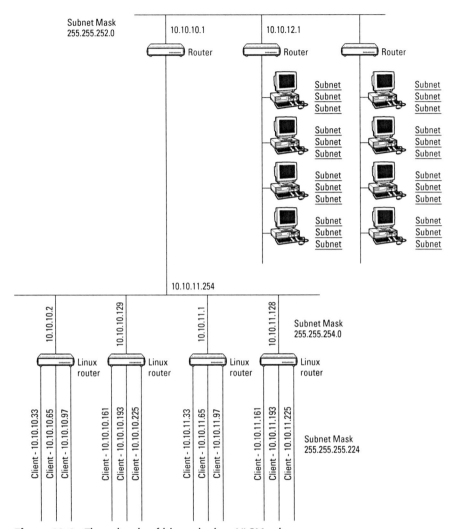

Figure 19-9: Three levels of hierarchy in a VLSM scheme

Connecting remote offices

How you connect remote offices will depend on the overall scheme you have used to build your network. Here are some key points to remember:

✦ You should give each office a contiguous block of addressing. This will make routing between offices easier.

✦ You will need to add static routes if the connection is using a demand dial interface.

✦ You will need to allow for a subnet between the routers on either end of the communications link. This can be a fake subnet if the link is point-to-point.

✦ You should have a back-up connection if the main connection goes down. For general traffic, this back-up connection could be an L2TP connection — or a PPTP connection for the Microsoft world.

In general, if you are using a central router in a small network, you will connect the outbound router to the spoke with the resources the remote users require, as shown in Figure 19-10.

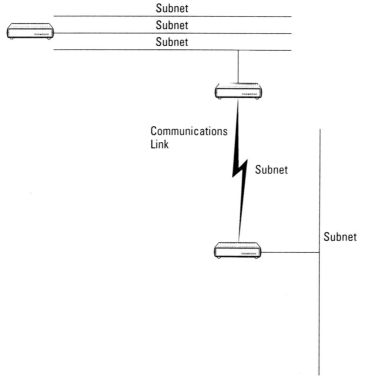

Figure 19-10: A router that links an office to another office in a simple network

If you are using backbones, then you should normally create a backbone in each office and connect the two routers for the link to the backbones in each office. For a VLSM implementation, you can break off a piece the size you need for the remote office and add a router at the appropriate level. Figure 19-11 provides an example of this.

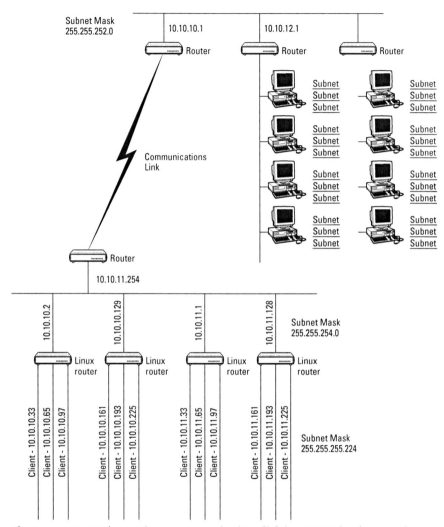

Figure 19-11: Implementing a communications link in a VLSM implementation

Dynamic Routing

As we saw earlier, routers use a routing table to determine where to send each packet that must be forwarded. This means that the routing table at each router needs to have all the required information to find the next hop to any system in the network. For a small network, you can do this by manually adding static routes to the router. For a larger network—or if the network changes frequently—manually configuring the routers is not necessarily an option.

In large or dynamic networks, you will normally use a *dynamic routing protocol,* which means the router will communicate its routing information with other routers on the network. There are several routing protocols that have been developed over the years. We will examine four of them:

✦ **IRD** — ICMP Router Discovery

✦ **RIP** — Routing Information Protocol

✦ **IGRP** — Internet Gateway Routing Protocol

✦ **OSPF** — Open Shortest Path First

One of the problems with large TCP/IP networks is that different groups within an organization (or even within different organizations) will manage different areas of a network. For simplicity's sake, large TCP/IP networks are usually broken down into Autonomous Systems (ASs). Each Autonomous System can use a different routing protocol to manage routes for interior gateways, known as the *Interior Gateway Protocol (IGP).* The IGP is responsible for ensuring that all of the gateways can find each other within the Autonomous System. However, IGP will not allow different Autonomous Systems to share routing information. RIP and IGRP are examples of IGPs, and serve to share routing information within an Autonomous System.

When you need to share information between different Autonomous Systems, you need to use an Exterior Gateway Protocol (a protocol used between different autonomous systems). IGRP can (to a degree) be used to do this. However, protocols like OSPF are better because they are designed specifically for that purpose.

ICMP Router Discovery

ICMP Router Discovery isn't really a routing protocol. It is a way for a host to find the local default gateway without the default gateway being manually configured. IRD uses two ICMP commands (Router Discovery and Router Advertisement) to let the client discover a router on their subnet.

Router advertisements

Routers that use IRD will periodically announce their presence on the network, either by using the multicasting address of 224.0.0.1 or by using the network broadcast of 255.255.255.255. When the time arrives (normally every 7 to 10 minutes), the router will announce on each local interface the IP address of that interface. In addition, there will be a preference number, so in case there are multiple routers, the client will take the one with the highest preference number. The preference number is included to give administrators control over which routers clients will normally use.

The announcement will also include a lifetime value (a Time to Live), which determines how long the client will be allowed to continue using the router. The lifetime should be set to a time that is longer than the announcement period — the default is 30 minutes.

Router Discovery

Typically, Router Discovery will occur if the host attempts to connect to a system outside its subnet within 7 to 10 minutes of starting up. If the host receives a Router Announcement, it will not need to perform Router Discovery. However, if the router on a subnet fails, or if the host immediately needs to connect to a remote network, then it can send a Router Discovery.

The router needs to be configured to allow discovery and will need to be configured to either use 255.255.255.255 as the destination address or 224.0.0.2 as the multicasting address. IRD-enabled routers will join the IP multicasting group on that address and will send a Router Announcement when they receive a Router Discovery request. Not all operating systems support IRD (even as a client). For example, older Microsoft clients cannot perform router discovery.

If you have a network that changes frequently *and* you do not plan to use DHCP, IRD is a useful protocol. In most cases, you should not have to use IRD within a corporate environment.

Routing Information Protocol

Routing Information Protocol (RIP defined in STD 34) is a good protocol that provides routers with the ability to share information about routes dynamically as network conditions change. There are two versions of RIP: version 1 and version 2. There are very few places that still implement RIP version 1; however, it is worth taking a moment to look at it, since it provides the basis for RIP version 2.

Version 1

As you should recall from the section on routing tables, there are several pieces that make up an entry:

- ✦ Destination network or host
- ✦ Netmask
- ✦ Interface
- ✦ Gateway
- ✦ Metric

Most of these pieces should now be familiar to you. If the result is the destination network or host, then the data is sent to the Interface for delivery to the gateway. You should understand that the target IP is combined with each netmask. Different routing protocols can use the metric to store different values. In RIP's case, the metric is the number of routers you need to go through.

The reason for a metric is constant — it will be used to determine the best path to a remote network, and therefore, to a remote host. Given the choice between a path that takes ten routers and a path that only takes four, we take the path that will only take 4. Figure 19-12 provides a simple example of a network.

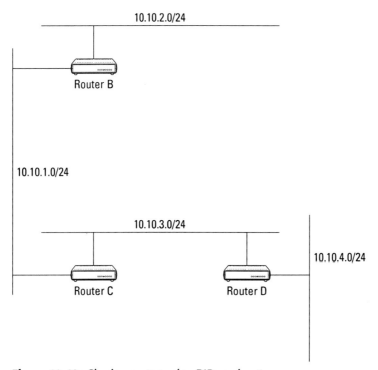

10.10.2.0/24

Router B

10.10.1.0/24

10.10.3.0/24

10.10.4.0/24

Router C   Router D

Figure 19-12: Sharing routes using RIP version 1

In Figure 19-12, four internal subnets are depicted with 24-bit subnet masks. There are three routers that are involved in routing. Clients on the 10.10.4.0 network might have a hard time contacting clients on the 10.10.2.0 network. Assuming the routers are RIP-enabled, and that we start with Router D, the process of sharing routes dynamically using RIP takes the following steps:

1. Router D knows about 10.10.4.0 and 10.10.3.0, so at the appropriate interval (30 seconds by default) Router D broadcasts its routing table.

2. Router C receives the broadcast and checks the routes that it contains.

3. Router C increases each metric in the broadcast by the metric for the interface it received the broadcast over (default 1).

4. Router C checks the routes. It finds a route to network 10.10.4.0 with a metric of two that it doesn't know about, so the route is added. It also finds a route to 10.10.3.0. However, a route to 10.10.3.0 already exists in Router C's routing table. Since there are two routes to the same network, the router compares the metrics. In the case of the route to 10.10.3.0, the router finds that the metric for its own route is less than the route in the broadcast. Since the metric for the routes in the broadcast are always increased by one before the routes are compared, routes to the local network will always win over the route advertised by a neighbor router.

5. Router C hits its broadcast time and broadcasts the routes it knows about, including the ones it learned.

6. Router B receives the broadcast and updates its information, adding routes for 10.10.4.0 and 10.10.3.0. The route for 10.10.1.0 is not added, since a local route already exists.

At this point, all the routers know about 10.10.4.0; Router B will also broadcast, updating Router C. In turn, Router C will broadcast and update Router D. Now all the routers will know about all the routes, and the network will be in a state of convergence. Unfortunately, RIP doesn't know that the network is in a state of convergence and will continue to broadcast every 30 seconds. These broadcasts can take up some bandwidth, especially if you have several routers.

In addition to continually broadcasting, there are other problems with RIP. One very serious problem is the sizes the broadcast packets can get to be. Suppose, for example, you were to use RIP on the Internet. If a router in San Diego, California broadcasts a RIP packet and the information is passed and added to from router to router, what will the broadcasts look like for the routers in Glasgow, Scotland? Obviously, the accumulated information from one side of the world to another would be tremendous. To stop RIP from destroying networks, the designers created a built-in safety feature. No route can have a metric of more than 15, which limits the effective network size that RIP can be used on.

Dealing with changing network conditions

One of the main reasons for implementing a dynamic protocol is that network conditions will change from time to time. Routers will crash, network cables will be cut, and communications links will fail. Therefore, any protocol that will be used must be able to deal with these changes.

RIP broadcasts its routing table every 30 seconds, and this allows new routes to propagate and old routes to be removed. There are, however, some conditions that will cause problems with RIP metrics that count to infinity.

Counting to infinity

When a route to a network goes down in RIP, the routers next to the point of failure will no longer receive updates from the neighboring router. If 180 seconds pass without receiving an update, the route is considered no longer reachable and the metric increases to 16. (You should recall that the largest allowable metric is 15, which makes the network unreachable). As these routers share their routing table with their neighbors, the metric continues to increase.

Some of you might see a problem here. In Figure 19-13, for example, you will notice that one of the networks has failed. Router C has a route through Router D to network 10.10.4.0 with a metric of 2; Router B has a route to network 10.10.4.0 through Router C with a metric of 3. The route metric for network 10.10.4.0 is set to 16 if Router C does not hear from Router D for a period of three announcements.

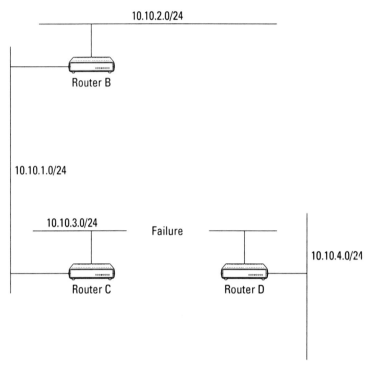

10.10.2.0/24

Router B

10.10.1.0/24

10.10.3.0/24   Failure

10.10.4.0/24

Router C   Router D

Figure 19-13: Counting to infinity

If Router C announces its routes first, there will be no problem. Router C will see a route to 10.10.4.0 with a metric of 3, which is better than 16, and will accept the route. Router C will now broadcast its routing information, including a route to 10.10.4.0 with a metric of 4. Router B will see that its route to 10.10.4.0 is through Router C and will update its table so the metric is now 5. This process will continue for a period of time until the route metric on both routers reaches 15. This is known as the *counting to infinity problem* and explains why the largest metric is 15.

Split horizons and poisoned reverse

Obviously, counting to infinity wastes time and bandwidth. However, two methods can be implemented that help reduce this problem. First, don't send routing updates to a neighbor you learned the route from. In the previous example, if Router B did not send the route back to Router C, there would be no problem. This method is known as *split horizons*.

The other method, called *poisoned reverse*, is very similar to split horizons, but handles the update differently. It will send the update back to the system it learned it from, but with a metric of 16. Note that both methods will stop a loop from occurring between two systems; however, if we look at Figure 19-14, we find that there is now another router on the network.

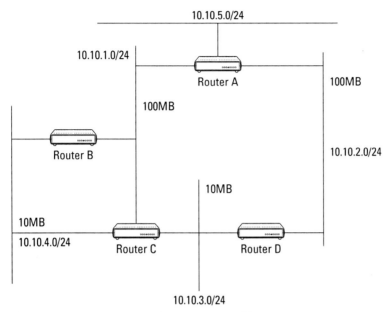

Figure 19-14: A more complex counting problem

Triggered updates

In this network, when the same failure occurs, Router C sends an update that is received by Router A but not by Router B, due to congestion or some other problem. Router A now has to mark the route to network 10.10.4.0 with a metric of 16. Router B updates and Router A finds that Router B has a route to 10.10.4.0 with a metric of 3. Router A sends its update. Since it learned about 10.10.4.0 from Router B, it shares this route with Router C.

At this point, Router A has a route through Router B, which has a route through Router C, which has a route through Router A. Again, we end up in a loop, increasing the metrics until they reach 15. Neither the split horizon nor the poisoned reverse methods were able to stop the counting to infinity problem from happening.

In order to stop this loop, we need to add another feature — called *triggered updates* — to the RIP protocol. This feature enables the router to send an immediate update to other routers when the route changes.

Garbage collection

After all the discussion about raising a metric to 16, you are probably wondering when these routes will be removed. The garbage collection process is actually quite simple. After 180 seconds, the route is set to a metric of 16 and the garbage collection timer is set to 120 seconds; when it reaches 0, the route is removed.

Version 2

Although it worked, there were some problems with RIP version 1. For example, it didn't send the netmask with the route. RIP version 2 (defined in RFC 2453) was an update to version 1, making changes to such areas as:

✦ Authentication

✦ Route tags

✦ Subnet masks

✦ Next hop router addresses

✦ Multicast support

Authentication

There was no form of authentication in version 1, which meant that any router placed on the network would be able to read the routes and get a picture of the network. This included silent RIP, a station that only listens for RIP broadcasts. In RIP version 2, the first RIP entry can be marked with an address type of 0xFFFF, which indicates this entry as the authentication information. The authentication was done this way so that more than one type of authentication could be used.

Currently, the only method that has been implemented is plain text. The plain text password can be up to 16 characters in length. This doesn't provide a great deal of security, but it is a step in the right direction.

Route Tags

Route Tags is a new attribute that has been added in RIP version 2 and that can be set on any route in the RIP packet. The purpose of Route Tags is to allow systems to set the route tag for routes that are learned from other protocols. For example, a system that runs OSPF might have learned about a route to another network that needs to be advertised internally within the Autonomous System. Routers that run both protocols would be expected to flag the route in RIP so that it is not treated like a regular RIP route.

Subnet masks

The inclusion of the subnet mask within RIP packets enables you to work with different types of subnetting schemes, including VLSM and supernetting. Some issues still exist—for example, if you mix routers using RIP version 1 and RIP version 2.

In VLSM, for example, a RIP version 1 router would not understand the difference between 10.10.10.0/23 and 10.10.10.0/27, and would therefore treat both as a route to the same network. RIP version 1 should not be used if you plan to use VLSM.

The same scenario comes into play with Classless Internet Domain Routing (CIDR). In this case, you might have combined 192.14.2.0 and 192.14.3.0—two Class C networks—into a single subnetted Class B of 192.14.2.0 mask 255.255.254.0. Because RIP version 1 does not send the subnet mask, this scenario will not work either.

Next hop router address

Entries in RIP version 2 packets should include a next hop field, which is the next router to which the packet will be sent. The next hop router address is intended to reduce the number of nonessential hops in networks where not all routers are running RIP. For a route to a network that a router is directly connected to, the field contains 0.0.0.0.

Multicasting

Multicasting has been added to reduce the load on systems on the network. Multicasting reduces the load on other systems, since the address 224.0.0.9 will only be of interest to systems that are listening for it. Other systems will discard the packet at the Physical layer, rather than the Internet layer.

RIP is a simple protocol that works. It is only limited by the size of the network that it will be able to handle. This limitation makes RIP a good choice for small networks. For larger networks, other protocols, such as Internet Gateway Routing Protocol (IGRP), should be used.

Internet Gateway Routing Protocol

Developed by Cisco as a replacement for RIP, IGRP is also a vector-based protocol. However, IGRP is superior to RIP because it:

✦ Provides stable routing, even in large or complex networks.

✦ Avoids routing loops, such as those found in RIP.

✦ Demonstrates fast response to changes in network topology.

✦ Has lower processing overhead than RIP.

✦ Can perform load balancing between routes of roughly equal desirability.

✦ Can account for line conditions and traffic levels.

✦ Can account for different types of service.

One of the advantages of IGRP over RIP is the recognition that there are different types of traffic and that the different types of traffic require different types of networks. For example, if you are moving 300 or 400MB files from location to location, you want to have the best maximum transmission unit (the largest size packet you can move on the route) that can deal with slight delays. If you are trying to do video conferencing, the amount of data is much less. However, any delays in transmission will be noticed.

To accommodate this, IGRP creates a metric that represents different values, including:

✦ Topology delay time

✦ Bandwidth of the narrowest segment of the path

✦ Channel occupancy of the path

✦ Reliability of the path

Topology delay time is the time it would take for the packet to reach the destination on an unloaded network. The Topology delay time allows the metric that is computed to accommodate links such as satellite, which can transfer large amounts of data but where there may be delays as the data travels between earth stations via the satellite. The fact that this value is based on the unloaded topology is accounted for by the *channel occupancy value,* which is essentially the percent of the bandwidth currently in use. The bandwidth is required to allow for paths that have to use slower links, such as a 56K line. The reliability is also important so that the number of retransmissions can be taken into account. The channel occupancy and reliability are both measured during the communications between routers.

The four values listed earlier are used to create a single metric that represents how good a particular path is — the metric is used to determine which information to keep in the router. The single metric is used to determine how to send data from the router. Along with this metric, the hop count (the number of gateways in the path) and the MTU (maximum transmission unit) are also passed between routers to enable the routers to make intelligent choices about routes.

As with RIP, each router using IGRP will periodically (90 seconds by default) broadcast its entire routing table to all neighboring routers. Here, the split horizon method seen in the discussion of RIP is also used to prevent looping. The routers that receive the broadcast will check the routes and add any new (or better) routes to their routing table.

The routers will use this information to determine the best path for any data they need to send. The calculation will be based on the values in the routing table and two weighting values. The first value is bandwidth weighting (BW), which is used to set the importance of bandwidth. The other is delay weighting (DW), which sets the importance of latency. The formula used to calculate the best path is as follows:

```
((BW / (PW * (1 - CO))) + (DW * TD)) X PR
```

In this formula, PW stands for minimum path bandwidth; CO for channel occupancy; TD for topology delay; and PR for path reliability.

The path with the smallest calculated value will be the path that is chosen. If multiple paths exist to the destination network and two or more tie for the lowest value, the router will use both paths, splitting the data over both. By using this formula, the router can now accommodate different types of service by using different weighting values. In addition, by storing the full path to any other network, load balancing can be achieved.

These enhancements make IGRP a better protocol than RIP. However, IGRP is also primarily an Internal Gateway Protocol. That is, it is used in a single Autonomous System. Next we examine OSPF, which functions as an External Gateway Protocol.

Open Shortest Path First

As networks grow, they eventually reach a point in which it is no longer possible to treat the entire network as a single Autonomous System. OSPF is designed to accommodate this dilemma by breaking the network into routing areas. OSPF also uses better metrics than RIP version 2 (defined in RFC 2328) and actually maintains information about the state of each interface on every router. Thus, each OSPF router can determine the optimum path for data from its perspective. Some of the features of OSPF include:

✦ No limitation on the number of hops

✦ Support for VLSM

✦ Use of multicasting for link state updates

✦ Faster convergence, since link state updates are sent instantly

✦ Metrics include information on link delays (not just hop count)

✦ Load balancing is supported

✦ Network is broken down into areas that can each support up to approximately 50 routers

✦ Authentication is enabled using clear text or message digest

✦ External route tags are enabled

As you may have guessed, there is a cost associated with these features — for example, the amount of overhead involved in using OSPF (because each link on each router has to be monitored by all routers in an area, there can be more traffic used in supporting the routing infrastructure). Another cost is the planning that is involved in configuring an OSPF implementation. Finally, since the routers will be calculating their own "best route," the routers themselves must have more resources (such as faster CPU and more memory).

Link states and costs

Each router will manage and propagate link state information, which means that for each logical connection, the router will collect several pieces of information (the IP address and subnet mask, the topology used on that link, other routers available using the link, and so on). This information will be propagated to all other routers in an area whenever the link state changes.

When a router is initialized or the state of one of its links changes, the router will create a link state advertisement that will be sent to all neighboring routers, such as RIP and IGRP. The neighboring routers will store a copy of this information and then forward the advertisement to all other networks it knows about — a process known as *flooding*. After the database is updated, each router will then recalculate its shortest path tree, which is a list of destination networks, the associated cost, and the next hop.

During the calculation of the shortest path tree, the cost of each link needs to be considered. Since each router actually knows about the type of connections the other routers in an area has, OSPF can calculate the cost of the entire path — not just the cost based on the value at the next router. The cost is based solely on the bandwidth of the link inverted. The fast link is assumed to be 100MB, so the cost for a 100MB connection is 1. The cost for a 10MB connection would be 100 divided by 10 (or 10), and the cost of a T1 connection at 1.544MB would be 100 divided by 1.544, or 64.

In building the shortest path tree, the router will assume it is the center of the network and will find the shortest path to any network through a neighbor. Consider the network shown in Figure 19-14.

In this figure, the router will build a tree to find every possible route and assign cost values to each link in the route. Local networks will receive a cost of 0, and all the other links will receive a cost based on the bandwidth, as discussed earlier. This process will lead to a tree for Router A that should look like Figure 19-15.

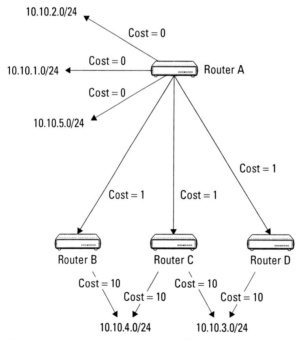

Figure 19-15: A diagram showing the shortest path tree for Router A

Using the shortest path tree, the router will now build its routing table. In this case, there will be two routes to 10.10.3.0 and 10.10.4.0, which will allow the router to load balance across the redundant routes.

In a stable network, OSPF works well and doesn't use excessive amounts of bandwidth. However, in an unstable network, OSPF can actually cause performance problems, due to flooding and the constant regeneration of the shortest path tree and routing tables.

Building areas into the network

As stated earlier, OSPF allows for the division of the Autonomous System into different areas, which means that the overall size of the network can grow to massive proportions. Depending on topology and stability, the "realistic" limit of the number of routers in any one area is around 50. After 50, the inherent instability of networks and the number of routers that must be kept up-to-date begins to seriously affect performance.

Although 50 routers may seem large, many networks greatly surpass this number. In these cases, you are forced to break the network into different areas. You might also break a network down for other reasons, such as different administrative areas.

In essence, an area acts as a boundary for flooding. Link state updates are *only* sent to routers within the same area, which makes it impossible to find a complete route to a host in another area. Instead, routers will calculate the best routes to the Area Border Router(s). These routers will be used not only to move data between areas but also routing information about the areas they connect. Routers that are within the area can be referred to as *Internal Routers* to distinguish them from Area Border Routers.

One area in an OSPF network will be designated Area 0 (the backbone), to which all Area Border Routers should be connected. This common area allows the Area Border Routers to create summary link information for the area they serve; this information can be shared with other Area Border Routers over Area 0. Figure 19-16 shows an example of how Area 0 might look conceptually.

In some cases, it may not be possible to physically connect all Area Border Routers to Area 0—perhaps because your network is geographically dispersed across many different regions with a few high-speed connections between groups of locations. In these cases, you can create a virtual link.

When a physical connection is not possible, virtual links can be used to connect remote portions of Area 0 together. However, the remote area will need to be physically connected to an area somewhere else, since the virtual link will happen through another area that is connected to all portions of Area 0. The area that is used to link the portions of Area 0 together will need to have an Area Border Router on each of the parts of Area 0. This virtual link is then created between these Area Border Routers.

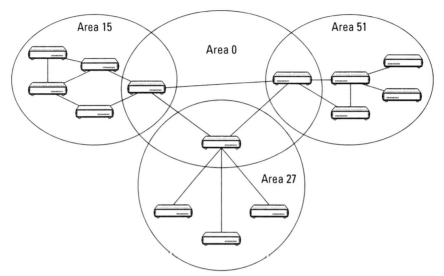

Figure 19-16: An OSPF network can be broken down into areas to reduce network load from flooding and to reduce the load on routers from recalculating routing tables.

The same process can be used to connect a remote area to Area 0. To do this, an ABR is placed between the remote area and an area connected to Area 0. The ABR between the two areas can then be used to create a virtual link with the ABR that connects directly to Area 0.

Other router's functions

At this point, you should have a handle on IRs and Area Border Routers. However, a router can take on some other roles that haven't yet been discussed. For example, it can act as an Autonomous System Border Router, or ASBR. ASBRs are used to connect your Autonomous System to other autonomous systems that are using other protocols.

The routes that ASBRs learn about will be passed through the network. The routes will be summarized by the ASBR since it could be connected to a very large network. The process of putting these known external links into the OSPF network is known as *redistribution*. The information is gathered from another protocol, such as RIP or IGRP, and then redistributed throughout the OSPF network.

Routers also need to find the other routers that they share connections with. In other words, a router should know about all the other routers on common physical segments. In OSPF, the process of finding other routers is called the *neighbor process*. The neighbor process is handled using Hello packets, which are simple packets that contain a list of known neighbors and other information about the sending router. Hello packets are sent out periodically using multicasting. When a Hello is received, any systems that are not on the neighbors list are added. To become neighbors, two routers must be in the same area so they can authenticate with each other. In addition, they need to agree on the Hello and Dead intervals. The Hello interval is the frequency at which the router will send the Hello packets. The *Dead interval* is the length of time a router will keep the neighbor listed if it hasn't heard from that neighbor.

The routers will use the neighbor process to identify each other and will then elect a "spokesperson," or Designated Router (DR), for that group of neighbors. The DR will coordinate information updates across the entire area. In other words, each router will pass updates to the DR, which will then send the updates to all other routers. The DR will be the router with the highest OSPF priority. There is also a Backup Designated Router (BDR) for that group of neighbors that will be used if the DR fails.

When the DR is elected, all other routers in the area will attempt to form an adjacency with that router. This goes beyond a simple Hello, and allows the routers to exchange databases. When the process starts, the adjacency is marked as down. As the neighboring process takes place, it is marked as Init — indicating that Hello packets have been seen — and then marked as Two-Way when neighbors are found. The neighboring process is really where the adjacency starts. The routers will then go into Exchange state, in which their databases are sent to each other. The two routers will enter the Loading stage as they load information from the other router. Finally, the adjacency is marked as Full, and each of the two databases will contain all the information from both routers.

Obviously, the neighboring process and building adjacencies requires that the media you are using carry broadcasts. Some mediums, such as frame relay and ATM, do not use broadcasts, which means that each router will have to be configured with its neighbors' IP address. Configuring a point-to-point sub-interface or a point-to-multipoint interface will also work, since these will provide the routers with the addresses of their neighbors. By configuring a point-to-point sub-interface between each router and the DR and BDR, you can ensure that all databases will be kept up-to-date. Using a point-to-multipoint interface reduces the number of sub-interfaces that need to be configured.

Summary

This chapter provided an overview of routing, starting with basic concepts — such as connecting to segments using a router — and then taking you through discussions on more advanced topics, such as OSPF. In essence, this chapter covered a few key decisions that need to be made when designing a network. The first decision is how to deploy routing. In other words, how will you physically structure your subnets so that users can pass information between each other? If you want to keep your network small and simple, using a central router will work fine. However, as the size of the network grows, you will need to go to a backbone at the very least. If you know the network will grow significantly, you might consider using VLSM.

The second decision is how to share information between routers. The answer to this question depends on the size of the network and how stable it is. If you have a small network with 15 or fewer routers, then manually configuring routes will probably work fine. You can then consider RIP or IGRP. RIP works better in small to medium-sized networks, and IGRP works better in medium-sized networks or networks where you will need to worry about quality of service. Finally, we looked at OSPF for use in very large networks.

✦   ✦   ✦

Planning Server Placement

✦   ✦   ✦   ✦

In This Chapter

Determining your
network service
needs

Planning load
balancing and
redundancy

✦   ✦   ✦   ✦

The last couple of chapters examined the building of the network — not the installation of the physical wires, but the TCP/IP addressing and routing concerns that make communications possible. In this chapter, we turn our attention to the servers that clients will use on the network.

We'll discuss the three types of servers that you find on a network and the performance issues for each. In addition, we'll look at different methods for load balancing and redundancy. But first, we'll look at how to determine what services you need to have running on your network.

Determining What Services Your Network Needs

In its most basic form, a network is a means for different users to access shared resources. For example, the shared resource could be a shared printer or a shared file server. In essence, a client program makes requests from another process, which is typically running on another system. In other words, a network allows two processes on two different computers to share the work.

As we look at some of the possible servers you will need on your network, you need to remember why you are placing them there. The servers will provide services to your users; thus, you want to ensure that you concentrate on the servers that the users will use. Most users are simply interested in being able to type a letter, print it, and handle their e-mail. In other words concentrating on the streaming media server so that you can broadcast video presentations across you network is probably not the best strategy if you want to keep the user community happy.

Therefore, you need to make a realistic assessment of the types of servers your network needs in order to service the client's needs. In addition to the basic user requirements such as printing and e-mail, some basic requirements for a network include the ability of computers to get an IP address and to resolve names (host or NetBIOS) to an IP address. You will decrease the number of help-desk requests by ensuring that the services required by both the users and the network are always available.

With basic connectivity, users can identify themselves to a *network authentication server* and then connect to servers that provide actual services. The servers that provide services to users fall into two main categories: *file servers* (including print servers) and *application servers*. This means that there are really three types of servers:

✦ **Network Infrastructure Servers**—This group includes DHCP, BOOTP, DNS, WINS, NIS, NDS, and Domain Controllers.

✦ **File and Print Servers**—This group is straightforward and includes both file and print servers.

✦ **Application Servers**—This group might include database servers, mail servers, groupware servers, and so on.

The particular combination of servers on your network depends primarily on two factors: the type of client operating systems that you have and the requirements of the users. In general, you need to have some basic services on nearly all networks, including:

✦ **DHCP**—The Dynamic Host Configuration Protocol is used to give out IP addresses and various configuration details, depending on the client's operating system. In general, all clients must at least take the IP address, and most will take the subnet mask, DNS server address, and gateway/router address. This provides the basic connectivity that all systems need and will save you the work of individually configuring each client.

✦ **DNS**—The Domain Name System provides host name or fully qualified domain names (FQDNs) to IP mapping. This means that clients can find servers using recognizable names easily, regardless of their location.

✦ **WINS**—You need Windows Internet Service to perform the NetBIOS name-to-IP address resolution.

Note   Although it is technically possible to have a network where there are no NetBIOS clients, this is fairly rare. In cases where you do not have NetBIOS servers, you will not need a WINS server.

✦ **File and Print servers**—Regardless of the network operating system you use, your users will want to share files with each other, or at least grab files they need from a server. Therefore, you need to provide file servers.

✦ **Mail** — The ability to send and receive mail has become "critical" for office environments. Employees expect to have the ability to exchange e-mail with employees in other offices and companies. Thus, creating an effective e-mail system is important.

These services provide a basic level of support for the operation of a successful network. We need to look at ways to ensure that these services can handle the client load. Thus, you need a good understanding of each service, including the protocols that it uses and the amount of network traffic that the protocols generate.

Now take a look at the services that are required for the network itself.

Deploying services on your network

As we start to look at the services that are required for the network to function, let's look at a basic example network. Figure 20-1 shows a simple network with nine client subnets and one backbone. In this case, assume that the network serves a typical small office of about 450 users. Thus, the average population on each client subnet is 50.

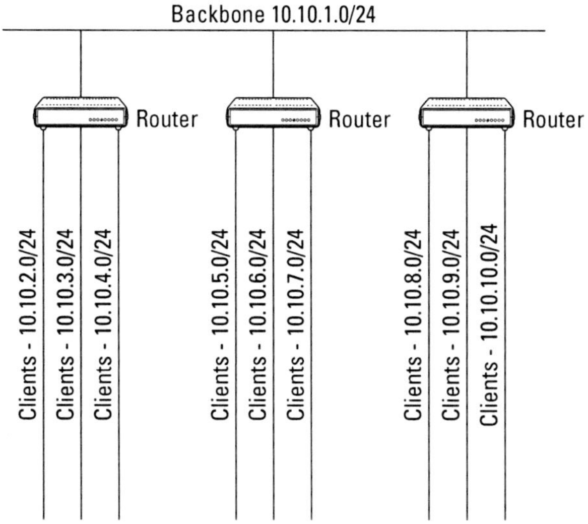

Backbone 10.10.1.0/24

Router   Router   Router

Clients - 10.10.2.0/24
Clients - 10.10.3.0/24
Clients - 10.10.4.0/24
Clients - 10.10.5.0/24
Clients - 10.10.6.0/24
Clients - 10.10.7.0/24
Clients - 10.10.8.0/24
Clients - 10.10.9.0/24
Clients - 10.10.10.0/24

Figure 20-1: Sample network that requires servers

We'll start by examining the DHCP requirements. DHCP, as you may recall, is a simple protocol that uses very little network bandwidth. In addition, few resources are needed to run DHCP, so the server doesn't need to be very large. In this case, only one DHCP server is required because one DHCP server can provide services to 450 clients. However, we need to make some provision for the fact that DHCP uses the broadcast address; otherwise, clients will not be able to get a DHCP address since there are routers present and routers do not forward broadcast traffic by default.

There are two methods will allow you to use DHCP in this routed environment. First, you can create DHCP relay agents to act as a go-between for the DHCP clients and the DHCP server. Because the relay agent would be able to direct the broadcast at the DHCP server, the server can be on another subnet without any problems. The second (and simpler method) is to enable BOOTP forwarding on the routers, which allows the routers to pass the request to the DHCP on another subnet.

In our case, we can enable BOOTP forwarding on the routers and place a single DHCP server on the backbone, as shown in Figure 20-2. Normally, you will have to enable this feature on your routers since it is off by default, since enabling BOOTP forwarding will increase the number of packets the router will need to deal with and can lead to congestion on the router.

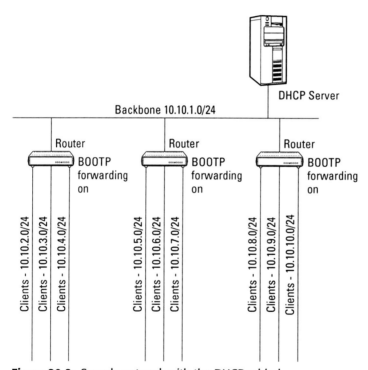

Figure 20-2: Sample network with the DHCP added

Now all the clients will be able to request a DHCP address, and the routers will pass these requests to the backbone where the DHCP (assuming it has a scope that is suitable for the client) will be able to service the request.

This is a simple case. However, you need to look at all the "what if" scenarios when you design your network. In this case, you might ask questions such as: What if the DHCP server fails? What if a router fails? What if another subnet is added locally?

What if another subnet is added remotely? Although the scenario in Figure 20-2 works, a more complicated network involving a remote location is depicted in Figure 20-3.

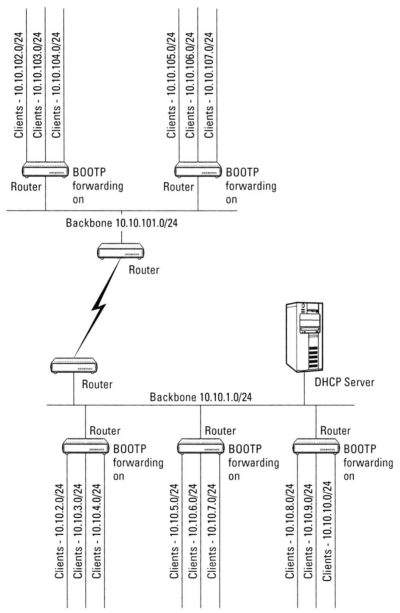

Figure 20-3: The sample network with added complexity

In Figure 20-3, the DHCP server is not able to provide addresses to the two remote networks, since the routers are not set to forward BOOTP packets. Even if they were, you need to consider whether you want to have the packets going back and forth over the communications link, which will increase the traffic on that link and slow the process down. These factors show a need for another DHCP server on the remote side of the connection that would deal with the clients on that side. However, if you think about the scenarios we looked at a moment ago, you can see that if one of five routers or two DHCP servers fail, some clients will not be able to get an IP address.

Thus, simply having the services on the network is *not* enough to ensure they will always be available regardless of any single point of failure. If you want your network to be tolerant of a single point of failure, you will need to plan redundancy for the network services. The difficulty of providing redundancy is only multiplied by the number of services you need to make your network run.

Combining services

In Figure 20-3, you would need to add another server on the remote network to handle DHCP. In addition we will need to do this for other network servers such as the DNS, WINS, and network authentication servers.

In the most basic network, you will have DHCP, DNS, and file and print servers. In order to provide redundancy for these three services, you would need to have six servers: two DHCP, two DNS, and two file/print. Further, as you add other remote networks such as the network in Figure 20-3 does, you will need to add three more servers to provide these basic services on the remote network.

Adding a server for each additional service you put on the network gets expensive, becomes increasingly difficult to manage, and increases the background traffic on the network. In order to reduce the number of servers that you will have on your network and therefore the number of servers that you must manage and that will be adding background traffic, you can combine multiple services on the same system. In the real world, this is a normal practice and in practice, you can run an entire network with only one server if the network is small enough. The only problem is that you are placing all your eggs in one basket. In other words, if the single server fails, all the services on that server are no longer available.

As you decide what services you can combine on a single system, you should consider what each of the services uses in the way of resources. To run services, a system needs four main resources:

- ✦ **CPU** — Services such as DHCP, DNS, and WINS; services that manage small lists don't need as much in the way of CPU power. Note that services that handle a large list (a database) such as Oracle or MS SQL server do actually need a good deal of CPU power.

- ✦ **Memory** — In all cases, memory will help a server. An often-overlooked fact is that the CPU doesn't talk to the disk or the keyboard or anything else — only to the memory. It is a quick and simple act for a system to move data in memory — for example, from a list of addresses in memory to buffer in memory where a packet is being built to respond to a DNS query.

Note
Remember that electrons moving down a wire are moving at roughly the speed of light, and that the read/write head of a hard disk cannot move at that speed without breaking the laws of physics. In theory, if the read/write head tried to do this, it would swell to the size of a planet and collapse in its own gravitational field, creating a black hole inside the system. My point is: in order to increase performance, you must add memory — and adding swap space (or virtual memory) is not the same thing as adding RAM.

✦ **Disk** — The performance of the disk sub-system is very important in some cases — primarily for application servers such as Oracle or MS SQL, which may have terabytes of data. For servers like DNS, WINS, and DHCP, the amount of data is so small that disk space is not as critical a factor.

✦ **Network** — The purpose of the network is to move data. Thus, the ability to move data between the server and the network will be very important. You will need to make sure that you use a decent network card, since this is where the server will be plugged into the network. If the server is connected to a port on a 10Mbps hub, then it has to compete with all the other systems on that hub for bandwidth. On the other hand, if it is plugged into a 100Mbps switch, there will be no other apparent traffic to compete with. So the connection, the type of card used, and the number of cards in the system will all affect the ability to move data and therefore the performance of the server.

When combining services, try to find those that won't compete for resources. In most instances, you can easily combine DNS, DHCP, WINS, and network authentication. In some cases, certain combinations of services make a lot of sense. For example, because Dynamic DNS works with the DHCP server to register the addresses to name mapping, if the services are on the same system, no network activity is generated. Likewise, DNS can be configured in the Microsoft world to check the WINS server if the address is not found and so combining these services would also make sense.

Once you have decided which services to combine, you simply need to determine the load characteristics of a system that will run them. You can use different tools to do this, depending on the platform you are using. In general, though, you should look at the four key resource areas previously discussed, first for a single client and then for increasingly larger groups of concurrent clients. At some point, one of the resources will reach its limit.

Note
Keep in mind that the number of concurrent users can exceed the maximum that the system will be able to handle. Since you will rarely, if ever, have all your users connected to a server at the same time, you can, to a certain extent, overutilize servers. You should look at the usage patterns — or at least consider them — as you plan the maximum number of users. Consider, for example, a file and print server; it is very unlikely that all the users will be saving a file to the network at the same time.

As an example, let's look at a DHCP server. In this network, systems tend to stay in one place, so we have extended the lease period to eight days. As you will recall from the discussions of DHCP in Chapter 9, setting a lease period of eight days means the clients will have to renew every four days. Next, we have to look at the server and determine the number of simultaneous connections it can handle. Assume that the servers we are going to use can handle 6,000 client requests at any time.

To calculate the number of DHCP server clients the server can handle, we next need to determine the length of time it will take to process a DHCP renewal request (we are looking at renewals primarily, as this will be the most frequent request). A DHCP renewal requires that a packet be received, the lease checked, and a new lease expiration date calculated; finally, a packet is sent to the client. You can use network packet analyzers or performance monitoring tools to find an exact figure. In practice, though, this process should never take more than one second. So, for the example, we will use this number.

Now that we have all the numbers, we need to combine them to determine the maximum number of clients one DHCP server can handle. The formula looks something like this:

```
processes/hour = 3,600 (seconds/hour) / time to perform the
process
clients/hour = processes/hour x simultaneous clients
total clients = renewal period in hours x clients/hour
```

If we take the numbers from the example and plug them into the formula, we get the following numbers:

```
processes/hour = 3,600 / 1
clients/hour= 3,600 x 6,000
total clients= 96 x 21,600,000
```

The total number of clients that the DHCP server will be able to handle in this case is 2,073,600,000. Obviously, you will never come near this number under real circumstances. However, if you take the number of clients that you hypothesize will use this DHCP server and divide it by the absolute total, you will have a rough idea of the percent of the total system resources the service (in this case DHCP) will be using. By working out the rough percentage for each of the services, you will be able to judge how loaded each of your servers is.

In Figure 20-4, all the basic network services — DHCP, DNS, WINS, and authentication — have been added to the sample network. At this point, if a router — or one of the network service's systems — goes down, some of the users on the network will not be able to access these services. Furthermore, if there were a power failure and the clients always checked with the DHCP server at startup and then registered with the WINS and DNS servers as well as authenticated with the network authentication server, these servers could be swamped when the power came back on. In other words, now that the basic services are on the network, you need to plan for load balancing and redundancy.

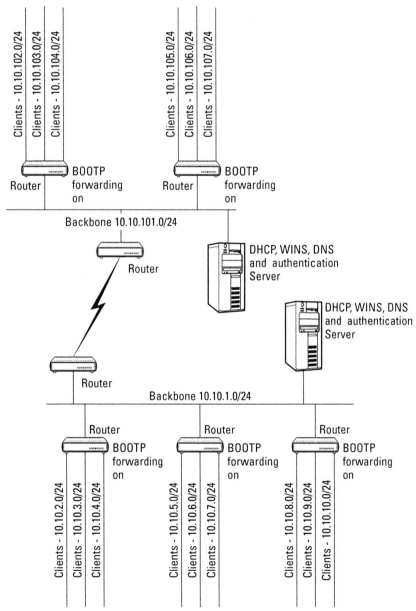

Figure 20-4: Sample network with sufficient network services in place

Planning Load Balancing and Redundancy

Although load balancing and redundancy are really two separate topics, you normally plan for them together — planning for one will usually provide for the other. Load balancing is the process of splitting client load across multiple servers so that the performance received by any client should be about the same. Redundancy ensures that a service is available regardless of the failure of a device or network segment.

For example, one of the simplest ways to provide redundancy is to add a second system that runs the service you are providing redundancy for. Since you will be able to configure half the clients to use one of the servers and the other half to use the other server, this also allows you to implement load balancing.

You can do four things to provide load balancing and/or redundancy:

✦ Add more systems

✦ Add multiple network cards to multihome a single system

✦ Create a server hierarchy

✦ Use clustered servers

In the next few sections, we look at each of these areas in detail.

Adding more systems

At the very least, any service that is needed to run your network should be on two different computers. This is just common sense — if your network depends entirely on a service and that service fails, then your network fails and your phone starts ringing. Adding more systems is beneficial and normally provides you with the redundancy that you require. However, adding an extra system means that you also need to provide methods that enable the two servers to synchronize with each other.

Imagine for a moment that your mail server is called Mercury and is at IP 10.10.1.58. You decide to move Mercury to a subnet closer to the users. It is now at 10.10.52.100. You have two DNS servers and only change the IP address in your main DNS server. All the clients find the new location and are able to send mail. What happens when the primary DNS goes offline? No mail equals unhappy users.

This situation could be avoided by configuring zone transfers. If you recall from the discussion of DNS in Chapter 11, you can configure the DNS service to transfer its zone files to a secondary server running on another system at a given period. However, keep in mind that this solution will add some network traffic. The same traffic condition applies to most services, since all of them need to be updated from time to time.

In the case of DNS, though, you can control the period of the zone transfers. If you expect frequent changes, set the time to a short period. If you expect only occasional changes, you can set it for a longer period. However, if the transfer will only occur every 24 hours, then when you move Mercury (the mail server discussed earlier) to a different IP address there could be a 24-hour period before the change is made in the secondary server. In addition, the entire zone file might have to be transferred, which would slow the process down a little more.

As some of you probably realize, the DNS zone transfer will probably take place in less than 24 hours, this is a worst-case scenario that has been planned for in the development of DNS. Most DNS services in use today will perform an incremental zone transfer, which removes the need to transfer the entire zone file. You can also configure a very long period between transfers and configure notification so that changes are immediately transferred. Thus, you can see how the protocols that you use have been adapting to the increasing size of networks. Most network authentication services follow the same logic, as does WINS. This means that these services *are* already trying to reduce the background traffic for you.

Services such as DHCP, however, are not quite so well configured. It is not part of their design to even consider other DHCP servers on the network, and therefore, it is more difficult to add another DHCP server to the network. Remember that DHCP is used to lease an address that is specific to a subnet from a pool or scope of addresses from that subnet. If you want to provide redundancy, the other DHCP servers would also need to have scope of address and information about which addresses have been leased or offered and which have not.

Even if this update protocol did exist, it would still be possible for two DHCP servers to offer the same address at approximately the same time. This would lead to the need for a resolution protocol so that one would be able to lease the address and the other would have to refuse to lease the address. Imagine the amount of confusion that could be caused in most offices as users turn their computers on and everyone is confirming addresses!

So, DHCP servers simply do not talk to each other. Thus, if you want to add a redundant system running DHCP, you will need to create two scopes (or more if you want more servers) and place one scope on each server. If the two scopes overlap, IP address conflicts will result; therefore, planning the scopes and ensuring that all the scope and server options are synchronized is important.

For WINS, DNS, and network authentication, adding multiple servers should be simple. But for DHCP, it is not. There is some method that can be configured for most other types of servers that will allow them to coordinate their data. The point is, you need to understand how the servers on your network function to effectively plan redundancy.

If you refer back to Figure 20-4, you can see that placing one more server will not provide redundancy. In this case, you need to provide at least two more servers — one on each backbone — to provide even a basic level of redundancy. When you do this, you prevent a single server failure from bringing down the network, or even a portion of it.

However, even if the servers are redundant, a router failure will affect some part of the network, either three client subnets or the connection between the two locations. Remember that a router is also a network service that you must consider when you look at redundancy. This means that you need to provide redundant routes from every segment to every other segment if you want the network to be tolerant of any single point of failure. In this case, we would need to double the number of routers or use routers that have built-in redundancy.

Multihoming systems

One thing to consider as a solution to load balancing is multihoming, which entails using multiple network cards in a server so users can access the system locally rather than through a router. Multihoming is a simple solution to load balancing — and increased performance — by adding *more* network cards. Although the speed of memory and CPUs and disks these days is considerable, you will still find "bottlenecks" at the network card. All client requests and all information provided to clients by the server have to pass through this *one* interface.

Maybe your problem is not the network card, but that the network segment is experiencing high traffic. In this case, putting two network cards in the same system on the same segment might not make much difference — especially with some of the network hardware we have today. But consider Figure 20-5.

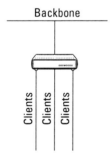

Figure 20-5: An example of a basic multihomed system

You may be thinking that what you see in Figure 20-5 is a router. Actually, it's a multihomed system. If you recall the discussion of routers in Chapter 19, you will remember that a router is a multihomed system that has at least the IP protocol. There is nothing that stops us from adding multiple network cards to any system. By adding multiple cards to a server, the server can be attached directly to the same subnet as the users.

In fact, there is nothing that prevents you from using a Windows or UNIX-based system as a router. In fact, many organizations use multihomed computers as routers internally because this is often less expensive than buying dedicated hardware routers. At the very least, using a computer that is multihomed can provide you with a backup router.

In fact, multihoming can be done with most servers, including application servers, where it can serve to greatly increase the number of clients the server can handle at one time. For example, Figure 20-6 depicts two SQL servers replicating data with each other over a private network while also servicing client requests over the main network. This scenario moves the replication traffic from the main backbone to an SQL backbone.

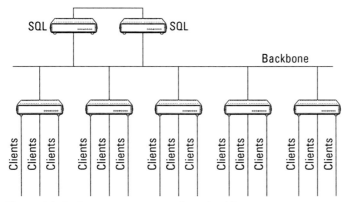

Figure 20-6: Servers can use a private backbone to communicate with each other.

Because the SQL servers can keep each other updated with frequent replication, changes can be nearly instantaneous (if not instant) using SQL server tools like replication and two-phase commit. Thus, clients can use either of the SQL servers, since they will mirror each other. Half the clients can be configured to use one of the SQL servers and the other half to use the other. If one of the servers happens to go down, the other server could pick up the slack (since it should be completely up-to-date). This type of scenario provides load balancing *and* some redundancy.

A separate backbone, as we see between the SQL servers in Figure 20-6, can be used effectively with any service that can replicate its data to another server. The downside is that there are more networks that need to be monitored. However, networks that have only a few systems tend to be more stable than networks with many clients.

In Figure 20-7, the basic structure seen in Figure 20-6 is extended to include many more clients and a proportional number of additional servers. Because of the reduced number of systems on the separate backbone, there is less traffic that the systems must compete with even when the number of clients increases dramatically. Another benefit of using a separate backbone is the ability to use native protocols on the separate backbone. For example, if the SQL servers were Microsoft SQL servers, the private backbone could run NetBEUI — a faster protocol for a single segment network.

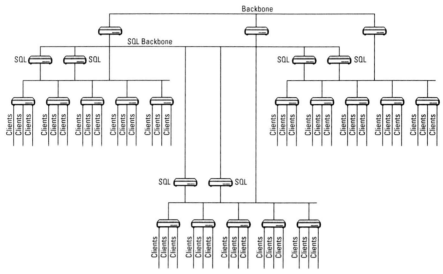

Figure 20-7: As network size increases, the number of hosts on the private backbone grows much more slowly than on the client backbone.

Multihoming and the use of separate backbones scales well in a case where you will have a service, such as SQL server, that can perform the type of replication or distributed queries that are required. It wouldn't work, however, for a service such as DNS, or something like a proxy server. In these cases, the changes people make on the server need to be made on the main server and then distributed to other servers. However, you can still use hierarchical servers to reduce overall network traffic.

Using hierarchical servers

In the case of SQL servers like those we looked at in Figures 20-6 and 20-7, the servers could use a separate backbone to improve communications between the servers, since the servers are peers to each other. In the case of DNS, however, this is not the case — there is a primary DNS server. Thus, you will need to find another solution to reduce overall network traffic. Consider Figure 20-8, which shows two DNS servers for an entire network. This setup makes the zone transfer very simple; however, all queries from clients have to go through two routers to get to a DNS server. Not only does this increase the delay in name resolution, but it also increases the amount of traffic that needs to move out of the local network segment.

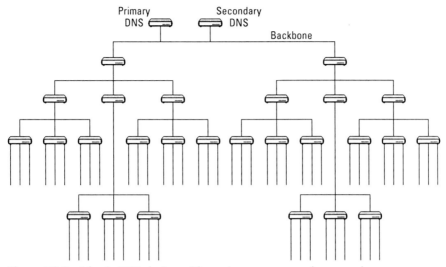

Figure 20-8: A basic DNS design with a primary server and a secondary server

Figure 20-9 shows how you could add more secondary DNS servers to the network to reduce the load on the two main servers and thus reduce the number of networks a query must cross. This could include adding DNS to the first level of routers as secondary DNS servers to the main server, which reduces the amount of resolution traffic coming from the clients to a minimum.

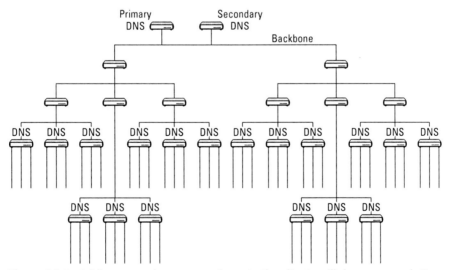

Figure 20-9: Adding secondary servers closer to the clients will decrease resolution traffic going through the network.

The downside of the scenario shown in Figure 20-9 is that all the changes made to the DNS will have to be replicated across a large number of DNS servers. In this network, there will probably be a fair number of servers, which means that update will be critical. The combination of a large number of servers that need to receive updates and the importance of the updates means that the time between zone transfers needs to be short, perhaps causing an unacceptable amount of traffic.

In this case, you could also configure the lower-level DNS servers as caching-only servers. That is, they won't hold a copy of the zone file. In order to ensure that the name can be resolved, they should be configured to forward requests for unknown names to the primary and secondary servers at the top level. These cache-only servers will query the main DNS server for name resolutions and then cache the answers locally for a period of time without having to transfer the entire zone. This reduces the number of servers that need to replicate the zone and the number of secondary servers that you need to manage. This works very well if we assume that users that use a particular DNS server are performing the same basic job function. In this case, the same server names would be resolved over and over and would normally be resolved from the local cache. Using caching-only servers in this case works well, especially if the Time to Live (TTL) of the DNS records is set to a high enough value.

> **Note**   If you set the Time to Live (TTL) to a high value to make this type of solution work, remember to decrease the TTL before changing DNS entries. For example, if you were going to move a mail server and your TTL for records is currently 8 hours, you might decrease the TTL to 15 minutes about 8 hours before the move. In some systems, you can change TTL on individual records, which makes setting the TTL for the one server possible.

If you intend to use a local caching-only server configured to forward requests "upstream" to the main DNS server, you might also consider configuring the slave option. This will prevent the DNS server from trying to go to the Internet or its configured root servers to resolve name queries. You could also configure the root zone on the local servers as the primary DNS server.

However you decide to use the local servers (as caching-only or secondary), you can add redundancy by simply adding a second DNS entry on the clients (using DHCP) that points to the main server. This scenario works well for DNS, as well as for WINS and proxy servers. In the case of a WINS server, an extra step would be required, where you would have the local WINS server push changes to one of the main WINS servers, and the main WINS server would pull the changes from the local server. This would implement one-way replication between the local WINS server and the main WINS server.

You can use additional servers, multihoming, and hierarchical servers — or a combination of all three — as a method to load balance user requests and provide redundancy. All three will work, but they all rely on the ability to spread the load across multiple servers. The good news is that most of the services you will need to use on the network allow for this type of solution. In cases where they won't (for example, certain databases or e-mail systems), you will need to find another solution, such as clustering.

Using clustering

If your company has money to burn and data that cannot be lost on a server that cannot go down, then clustering is the answer. Consider a large, national department store that allows customers to place orders by phone. It has a call center that manages calls from all over the country and takes thousands of orders an hour. Each order encapsulates hundreds of pieces of information. In this case, a server that crashes could cost the company literally hundreds of thousands of dollars. Between the crash itself and the time to locate, build, reload, and restore another system, hours or days could be lost.

Sometimes, a downed server is simply not an option and having multiple servers that have to replicate data with each other might not be fast enough to keep up with the data flow. The only option in this case is *clustering*.

Clustering (in its simplest form) involves two systems with a shared redundant disk system. Each system constantly checks the status of the other, and if the primary system fails, the secondary system uses information on the shared drives to pick up the slack. In Figure 20-10, you can see this simple form of clustering.

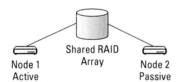

Shared RAID
Array

Node 1
Active

Node 2
Passive

Figure 20-10: A basic example of active/passive clustering

Figure 20-10 is an example of active/passive clustering. The second system does nothing until the primary node fails. When the primary node fails, the secondary node will take over the primary node's functions. This process will only work if *all* of the data for the services that "fail over" are on the shared drive set. In addition, the shared drive set needs to be redundant, or a drive failure will bring down the entire cluster.

The disk array is normally divided into different areas. In one of these areas, each system keeps information about the current connections. By tracking the connection information on disk, as well as keeping it in memory, the other system can pick up this information as part of the fail over. Typically, each service also has an area of its own so that the service can run on either system.

Each of the nodes in the cluster needs to be loaded with all the services that are to fail over, and the configuration of the services will need to also be kept synchronized on the nodes. The service itself will need a separate IP address from the systems so that the users will be able to connect to that service regardless of the system that is currently running the service.

Although clustering provides redundancy, it does *not* provide any form of load balancing. To provide load balancing, an active/active system must be configured in which both of the systems will be able to access the disk resource at the same time. For this to work, some form of locking must be supported so that data being modified by one system won't be modified at the same time by the other system. Locking allows one system to lock some or all of the resources so that resource contention — two processes trying to get to the same resource at the same time — doesn't occur. This means that the application and the clustering services must all work together and be designed specifically for that purpose. In cases where the service that is being clustered in an active/active fashion is something like a basic Web server, it is much simpler, since the clients are not updating any data.

In addition, another service is needed to spread the clients across the active nodes in the cluster. This can be done using DNS round robin or by using some other service, such as Microsoft's Network Load Balancing. In the TCP/IP world, *DNS round robin* is a simple and easy solution. When configuring DNS round robin, multiple host records are added to the zone file, each with the same name but with different IP addresses. The DNS server will then feed out the next IP address in sequence for each request it receives. In some implementations, the DNS server will also consider the IP address of the client — providing the IP address of a local interface if there is one.

Clustering can go beyond two systems and grow to a much greater number of nodes. As the number of nodes increases, the complexity and planning of the cluster gets more complicated. Clustering is an expensive solution and one that you would normally only consider for mission-critical servers or servers where you have no other choice because the service can operate in a distributed fashion.

There are different ways to achieve load balancing and redundancy. The methods vary greatly in complexity and cost; however, with key network services, some form of redundancy and load balancing should be considered. Figure 20-11 depicts a complete network with load balancing and redundancy in place.

In this case, the mail service is running on a cluster with three servers, and DNS round robin can be used to load balance across the servers. The primary DNS is on the backbone and would be configured to send changes to the two secondary servers. In turn, the routers closest to the clients that are also caching only DNS servers would be configured to use the two secondary servers as forwarders. The SQL servers would replicate the information to each other, and the clients would be configured to connect to their closest SQL Server. Each of the local routers also provides network authentication and would replicate with a main authentication server for that portion of the network. The main authentication server for each portion would then replicate all of its information to the other authentication servers. The alternate authentication servers would be configured for the clients as required by the authentication system used on the network.

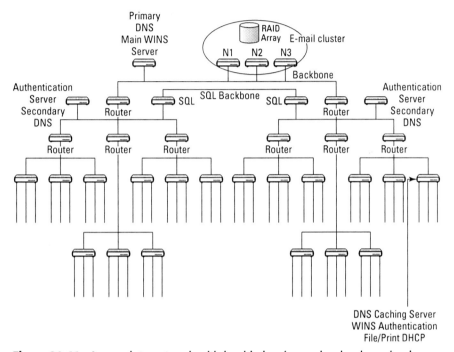

Figure 20-11: A complete network with load balancing and redundancy in place

Clients that need to will register with the local WINS server, which is running on the local router, and the local WINS server would replicate the client registrations up to the main WINS server. The clients would have the local WINS server and DNS server configured as their first choices, and the main name server configured as their second choice. This would be done using DHCP on the local network. The DHCP servers would contain a small portion of the addresses for the other two closest networks, and the local routers would be configured to relay BOOTP packets.

The *only* parts of the network that are not redundant are the routers and file and print servers. The routers could be made redundant using a second router or with clustering. The file and print services could also be made redundant using clustering, but is not typically done because of the cost. However, as the cost of clustering comes down, some organizations might even consider redundancy to this level.

Summary

You should now have a better idea about what can be done using server placement to provide redundancy and load balancing. You should also appreciate the fact that different types of servers need to be treated differently. Remember that the fewer hops a packet must go through, the faster the network will run. The network works best if the traffic can be kept within a segment — for example, users that will use the same servers should be placed on the same segment.

Advancements in computer technology make the network (the bandwidth) the most likely bottleneck in client server computing. You can plan for this bottleneck by using separate backbones for server-to-server communications and by planning client placement relative to the servers they need to use. By planning server placement and redundancy, you will be far ahead of the game.

As a final note, even if you do have a network that is completely redundant (completely tolerant of any single point of failure), you could still experience a double failure. Furthermore, providing triple redundancy would leave you open to triple failure. The truth is, trying to design a "failure-proof" network is impossible. You *still* need a good disaster-recovery plan that is enforced.

✦   ✦   ✦

Understanding Communications

Data communications is the ability to move data electronically over a physical medium. It can be as simple as running a fiber optic cable between two floors of a building, or it can involve constructing a large infrastructure that spans the entire globe.

If you are indeed spanning the globe, you will probably not be pulling your own fiber cables across that ocean. Instead, you will use a carrier that has fiber in place (or some other way to push data over the distance). In these cases you don't really need to know the details of how the whole network functions.

You are probably already familiar with the terms LAN and WAN, but their definitions follow:

- ✦ **LAN (local area network)** — A distinct, high-speed network that may contain multiple segments; however, all of the segments are within a single location.

- ✦ **CAN (campus area network)** — A network that connects local area networks (such as between several buildings). A communications link is used to channel data from one building to another. Typically, this type of network involves only short distance connections that you have put into place. For example, a municipality might have several buildings in a single area and run fiber optic cable between them.

- ✦ **MAN (metropolitan area network)** — A network that spans a larger area than a CAN and that normally involves a service provider of some sort. In general, a MAN is considered to be within a single city — thus, it's smaller than a WAN.

- ✦ **WAN (wide area network)** — A network that covers a large geographical distance, such as across a city or around the world. A WAN may have connections to the U.S., Canada, and England, for example. In general, any network that has connections to more than one city is considered a WAN.

Although you will occasionally hear about CANs or MANs, in the real world we normally refer to the LAN as the network within a building and a WAN as any network that has connections outside the building. The rest of this chapter will look at communications and the development of the technology that makes communications possible and then take a look at the choices you have to make when implementing these technologies.

Communications Background

Throughout this book, we have been discussing communications. We examined how a user's system will take data and encapsulate it into a TCP segment and how that data will then be sent to the IP layer. We have seen how IP uses ARP to find the next hosts, and then passes the data to the wire, where it will go to the remote host or to the router's network card.

But what happens when we are no longer on our network? Where does data go from the basic Ethernet or Token Ring network? Is the entire Internet really just a huge Ethernet network?

To really understand data communications, we need to jump back a few years — to 1878, when the first networks were being put into place. No, that isn't a typo. The *telephone* system was the first network to use switching, in particular circuit switching. Using manual or automatic switches, the telephone company provided a point-to-point connection between your phone and the phone of the person you were calling.

Connecting locations

The telephone system was the first system that used existing technology to enable communication between distant locations. In the early days, this communication was achieved with physical switches that created a physical wire between your location and the remote end. We use the same physical wires today to connect users on a LAN.

Obviously, some type of switch was needed, or a physical wire would have been required to connect all the phones to one another. (Picking up the phone would have connected you to all the other phones on the planet. Just imagine how big your cell phone would be!)

Switching technology

The first switches were simple devices involving an operator, who would push a jack into a hole on the switchboard to connect you to another phone. Essentially, the switch would physically connect the phones for the length of the call. The connection would be continuous only between those two phones. In other words, the connection was temporary, continuous, and exclusive.

Circuit switching works very well for voice communications, since voice is a real-time application. However, over long distances, this meant having to have many wires so that each phone call would have the two wires required for the connection. This meant running great quantities of cable, and to this day, makes long-distance calling expensive (since the cost of all the cabling and switches must be recovered). For a data connection that may have infrequent communications, the circuit had to be kept open, which was very expensive. Other methods had to be developed if data communications was going to thrive.

Packet switching

In looking at the data a computer would generate and send across a network, we can see two differences from voice communications. The primary difference is that *some* delay can be allowed in data communications, since the receiving systems can wait for the data — in voice communications, this would make the conversation choppy or unintelligible.

The other difference is that voice data is a continuous analog wave, whereas computer data is made up of bits that are packed into bytes (five, seven, or eight bits long). This means that a group of bytes can be further encapsulated into a packet that can be addressed. In fact, data communications (including byte stream communications) are frequently broken down into different units.

What the engineers back in the 1960's decided was to treat data as a series of packets rather than a stream of information. In doing so, they removed the need for a *continuous* connection, and thus paved the way for data communications. Now, when there was data that needed to be sent, it could go to a device on the edge of the network that would break it into appropriate sized chunks, address it, and then send it on the network. You could compare this process to that of a company mailroom.

TCP/IP is an example of a packet switching network. A switch which sit at the logical edge of each network segment, take data destined for other network segments, breaks the data into the appropriately sized packets (datagrams) for the next networks topology, and then sends it to another switch. This switch looks at the datagram and sends it on to the next switch until it gets to its final destination. As you've probably guessed, the switches in question here are actually routers. In fact, routers were first used to create the backbone of the ARPANet, the original incarnation of the Internet.

The problem with packet switching is that as traffic increases, the router has to work harder and harder to keep up. At some point, the router will become congested and will end up backing up datagrams, or possibly losing them. Eventually, other routers will be affected, causing the network to grind to a halt. Retransmissions will take place, in addition to new traffic exacerbating the problem.

This situation can make it nearly impossible to transmit data. Much of the problem was due to the nature of packet switching. There are no fixed routes that describe the path data will take as it moves across networks. Packets can take different routes from point A to point B as network conditions change, leading to packets that are received out of sequence or that time out on the network and are discarded. What was needed to resolve this basic problem with packet switching networks was the circuit base connections of circuit switching but without having to create a continuous connection. That's where frame switching, or frame relay, comes in.

Frame switching

In frame relay, a complete circuit is created for each transmission — like a phone call. A virtual private circuit can be programmed into the switch and as the connection is required, a Switched Virtual Circuit created on-the-fly. However, unlike with the circuit switches, the connections between the switches can be shared by data from several different customers. This makes it possible to run frame relay over shared connections. Frame relay also allows a Permanent Virtual Circuit to be established.

To better understand frame relay, take a look at Figure 21-1. It shows three locations — Houston, Chicago, and New York — that have a frame switch, which is connected to the physical high-speed backbone. In this case, the service provider has a physical wire from Houston to Chicago and New York, as well as a physical wire from Chicago to New York.

Now assume that Company B is paying for data to move between Chicago and Houston. In this case, the service provider creates a SVC between the two cities. The circuit tells the switch that any data coming from the equipment at the client's location in one city should go to the switch in the other city to be delivered to the equipment at the client location in the other city. Company A has locations in each city. In this case, each switch has two Switched Virtual Circuits to the equipment in each of the other locations.

The data for Company A and Company B that flows between Chicago and Houston will move over the same physical wire that exists between the two cities. The switch will ensure that the correct data gets to the correct clients. Of course, if the line becomes congested, all of the traffic between the two locations will slow down. This continues to be a problem with frame relay. The delay problem doesn't greatly affect data communications, but it does make it nearly impossible to pass uncompressed audio or video. In addition, there is no way to identify critical data.

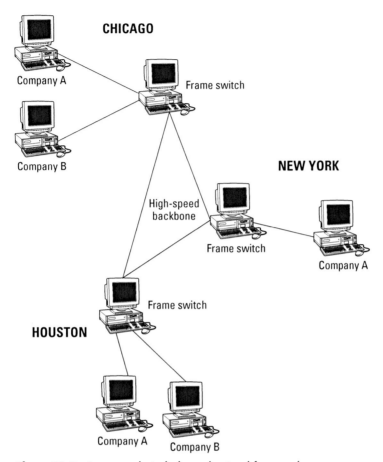

Figure 21-1: An example to help understand frame relay

Cell switching

Cell switching takes a more radical approach to the problem of moving data in an effort to create a single technology that can pass voice, data, video, and so on. Since phone companies were using their physical lines to move voice *and* data, the ability to share the physical lines effectively was a great concern for them.

In packet and frame switching, the data being passed has a variable length. However, most packet and frame relay systems are now configured to move packets or frames whose size is based on Ethernet, which is now the dominant network topology. One of the primary changes in cell switching was to move to a small fixed length packet, or cell. Whereas frames can vary in size (up to 4,096 octets), cells are always 53 octets (48 octets of data and 5 octets for overhead).

The fixed size of a cell means that switches no longer need to figure out the size of packets before performing any other operations on the data. There is no fragmentation and reassembly, buffers can hold a great number of cells, and the logic needed to deal with the small cells can be put into practice at the physical chip level.

Including the logic at the chip level increases the cost of the network cards, however. This is one of the main reasons, along with the development of gigabit Ethernet, that implementations such as Asynchronous Transfer Mode (ATM) do not typically go to the desktop. Since there are 5 octets of overhead to every 48 octets of data, cell switching also carries a tremendous amount of overhead.

Like frame relay, cell switching establishes a virtual circuit over the shared connections. In addition, cell switching can provide a guaranteed Quality of Service (QoS), which makes it useful for moving real-time data, such as voice and video, over the same shared lines that it uses to move data.

In many cases, your organization will not be in a position to lay the physical wires used to carry high-speed communications across the world. Therefore, you have to connect to a backbone or a public backbone (a.k.a., the Internet), which means you need to get a connection from your site to the larger networks. This can be done with a local ISP in the case of the Internet, or through a major ISP or the local telephone company if you wish to have a leased line.

Local ISP connections

Connecting to a local ISP is a simple method for providing access to the Internet; however, local ISPs usually don't have point-to-point facilities or leased lines. The local ISP will in turn be connected to a larger carrier that will provide access for the ISP to the Internet — essentially, the ISP resells bandwidth and should therefore provide some value-added feature.

You should take many factors into consideration when deciding which local ISP to use. First and foremost, ask yourself whether a particular ISP is likely to be in business six months from now. Many small ISPs have come and gone in the last few years. In some cases, they have disappeared quickly, leaving their clients stuck. Just remember, you get what you pay for — if a deal is too good to be true, it usually is. If the connection is going to be used solely for your clients to surf the Internet, then it doesn't matter. If, however, the connection will be your e-mail link to the outside world and will be used to connect offices using tunneling, then you probably don't want to skimp on the cost.

You also want to make sure that the ISP uses a reasonable client to bandwidth ratio — like airlines, ISPs will oversell their service. Normally, they can get away with this, because not everyone will be online at the same time. However, if the ISP is heavily oversold, your bandwidth may suffer. In addition, check out the ISP's want ads to get an idea how much they pay their employees, and thus, the quality of their workforce. Local ISPs, especially, can vary greatly in terms of experienced, professional support.

Finally, identify the sort of connection a local ISP has to its provider. If it has a T1, it may not be able to support many users; however, if it has multiple T3s and OC12s to multiple providers, you can be somewhat assured that the ISP is able to provide you with good service.

Major ISPs and voice carriers

If you want to be sure of your bandwidth, or you really need point-to-point connectivity without using a protocol such as L2TP or PPTP, then you should look for a major ISP/Voice Carrier. In most cases, voice carriers are the major ISP's, since the telephone companies have had time to string the wires across the country. Cable operators are getting into the fray with cable modems, which have helped keep the telephone companies relatively honest.

There are a couple of advantages to going with a major telephone company. First, they tend to have a lot of money invested in technology and people and plants and are therefore usually able to provide the best service. Second, they have the capability to provide point-to-point connections using dedicated lines, frame relay, and cell relay. They also tend to have the money to provide truly redundant systems meaning something as simple as a power outage or a simple line break shouldn't impact on your connectivity. I used the word *tend* for a reason — in some parts of the world, the local ISPs have better connections and better infrastructure than the telephone companies. So, it really pays to shop around.

On the down side, telephone companies are usually more expensive than local ISPs. You have to decide whether the ability to communicate between two points is worth paying the extra money.

How the pieces fit together

Some of you might be wondering how all of these pieces, the ISP's, the voice carriers, cell switching, circuit switching etc, fit together, and exactly what kind of interplay exists between the local ISPs and the telephone companies and your company. All of the pieces we've looked at in this chapter form a hierarchy, and you're on the bottom. You can connect to your local ISP, which will typically connect to the telephone company through a border router. From there, packets are moved up to the telephone company's local backbone and then routed to the backbone in the destination city, where it steps down to a border router and out to the target server.

In Figure 21-2 you can see the hierarchy. You are trying to connect from your desktop (located in Vancouver, B.C.) to a Web server (in St. John's, Newfoundland). As shown in the figure, the request sent from your system to the local router takes you to the local ISP. The link from your network to the ISP is point-to-point. At the ISP, there are many border routers, and your company comes in through one of them. The ISP then moves you to their backbone and passes your traffic up to the telephone company. Again, your traffic goes to a border router. From there, it is moved to the central area for your locale.

From the telco's local office, you are passed over an ATM backbone to the telco's remote locale, where the opposite happens. You are passed to a border router and then to the local ISP's main connection. From there, you go to the ISP's border router and on to the target's main router. Finally, you are on the remote network and will connect to the remote system.

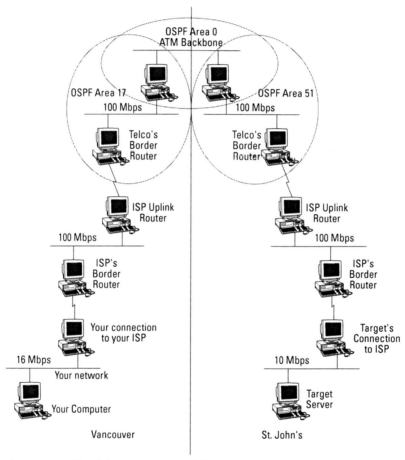

Figure 21-2: The full connection path between you and a target server

In the example given in the figure, the path is fairly short. However, consider what would happen if there were no direct connection from Vancouver to St. John's (if you know your geography, you'll realize there isn't). The packet might have to stop in Toronto, and possibly Halifax, adding more hops to the path. And of course, we're assuming that the two local ISPs are using the same backbone provider — although this would be an exception, rather than the norm. The following trace shows the route from a system in Montreal to a system in Winnipeg. In this case, both locations are connected to the Bell network.

```
 1    10 ms    <10 ms   <10 ms   207.236.145.33
 2     *       <10 ms    10 ms   10.30.235.1
 3   120 ms     91 ms    90 ms   mtlcorr01-fe0-0-0.in.bellnexxia.net
[206.108.105.129]
 4   <10 ms     10 ms    10 ms   core1-montreal02-pos11-0.in.bellnexxia.net
[206.108.97.145]
 5    10 ms     20 ms    20 ms   core2-toronto63-pos7-0.in.bellnexxia.net
[206.108.107.185]
 6   130 ms     10 ms    20 ms   core1-toronto63-pos2-0.in.bellnexxia.net
[206.108.107.153]
 7    40 ms     40 ms    40 ms   core1-winnipeg32-pos6-1.in.bellnexxia.net
[206.108.98.86]
 8    40 ms     40 ms    50 ms   dis4-winnipeg32-pos10-0.in.bellnexxia.net
[206.108.102.94]
 9    40 ms     40 ms    50 ms   mts-gw.dis1-winnipeg32-atm6-1-
0-1.in.bellnexxia.net [206.108.110.6]
10    40 ms     50 ms    40 ms   wnpgbr27-v102.mts.net [205.200.28.89]
11    41 ms     50 ms    50 ms   205.200.252.2
12    50 ms     40 ms    50 ms   WEBHOUSE [205.200.252.82]
```

In this case, the first couple of hops take us quickly into the border router, `mtlcorr01-fe0-0-0`. Because Bell is the provider, there is no local ISP to go through. From the local bell office, the data will travel to the inbound router in the Toronto core and out again, traveling to the core router in Winnipeg. From there, the data goes to a distribution router, passing the data through `mts-gw.dis1-winnipeg32-atm6-1-0-1` to the local ISP (the local telephone company in this case). From the local phone company, there is a connection to the local system, called *webhouse*.

This next trace (using `tracert` in the Windows world, or `traceroute` in the UNIX world) shows what happens when multiple telephone companies get involved.

```
 1   <10 ms     10 ms   <10 ms   207.236.145.33
 2   <10 ms     10 ms    10 ms   10.30.235.1
 3   <10 ms     10 ms    10 ms   mtlcorr01-fe0-0-0.in.bellnexxia.net
[206.108.105.129]
 4   <10 ms     10 ms    10 ms   core2-montreal02-pos11-0.in.bellnexxia.net
[206.108.97.205]
 5    10 ms     20 ms    10 ms   Ncore1-newyork83-pos4-0.in.bellnexxia.net
[206.108.99.190]
 6    10 ms     20 ms    10 ms   bx1-newyork83-pos3-0.in.bellnexxia.net
[206.108.103.186]
 7    10 ms     20 ms    10 ms   sl-gw9-nyc-7-3.sprintlink.net [160.81.43.13]
 8    10 ms     20 ms    10 ms   144.232.7.93
 9    10 ms     20 ms    10 ms   sl-bb22-nyc-14-0-2480M.sprintlink.net
[144.232.7.102]
10    30 ms     40 ms    30 ms   sl-bb20-rly-15-0.sprintlink.net [144.232.18.26]
11    30 ms     30 ms    20 ms   144.232.9.90
12    30 ms     30 ms    30 ms   gbr3-p50.wswdc.ip.att.net [12.123.9.50]
13    50 ms     50 ms    50 ms   gbr3-p80.sl9mo.ip.att.net [12.122.2.145]
14    91 ms    150 ms    90 ms   gbr3-p20.sffca.ip.att.net [12.122.2.74]
15   110 ms    181 ms   120 ms   12.122.255.222
16    90 ms     90 ms    90 ms   216.148.209.66
17    90 ms     90 ms    90 ms   www.redhat.com [216.148.218.195]
```

In this example, the packet has to cross the Bell network to New York, where it moves to the Sprint network. Sprint moves it to Washington D.C., where AT&T picks it up and moves it to somewhere in California. It finally goes to the target network. As you can see, moving data from point to point takes much work and cooperation.

Building your WAN

Now that we have looked at very types of switching and at how all the players, your company, the local ISP's and the voice carriers, work together you probably are eager to get started building the Internet mar II. However, in most cases, you will need to look at budget considerations closely and try to balance cost with usability.

You should thoroughly understand the traffic that will move between the different locations. As you do, you need to look at two factors: how much data you need to move between locations or between you and the Internet, and how much latency is allowed in the transmission of the data. Like the different routing protocols that were discussed in Chapter 19, these two factors will be very important when you decide what type of connection to use. The type of connection you choose will in turn affect the network operating system you decide on, and how you deploy it.

Once you have determined how much data you need to move between locations or between you and the Internet, and how much latency is allowed in the transmission of the data, you can begin to plan your connections. In some cases, you might also need to plan for redundancy or an alternate path between the points.

Point to point connection

The first part of designing your communications infrastructure is relatively easy — you need to determine what points in your network need to be connected. In other words, figure out the point-to-point paths through which your data will flow. In most cases, this involves a connection to an ISP or telephone company that provides you with a route through your network from point A to point B — a simple, though possibly expensive, solution.

Normally, the connection to an ISP or telephone company will be an ISDN connection or a leased line. In either case, you will be making a connection to the local office for the telephone company. In turn, the ISP or telephone company might use frame relay or cell relay to move the data to an office closer to your destination, and then use another point-to-point connection to that office. Typically, the slowest link in this configuration is the link from your office to the telephone company.

Tunneling

Rather than a simple point-to-point connection, you can use an option called tunneling. In this case, you get a link to the Internet from one or more providers, which provides a base level of connection between the two locations using the Internet. Once this base level of communication is established, you can create a virtual connection on top of it using a tunneling protocol. Figure 21-3 shows two systems connected to the Internet.

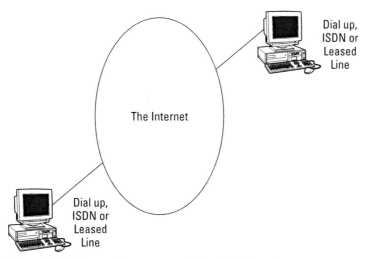

Figure 21-3: Two systems connected to the Internet

At this point, the two stations can communicate. The problem is that the network between them is not secure, so any data that is sent over the connection could be read on any of the intermediate networks. Obviously, this isn't a problem with a basic Web page. However, in many cases, you want to be able to secure the data. It is at this point that most organizations would use a tunnel connection as shown in Figure 21-4.

If we treat the Internet (the underlying network) as a physical-layer connection and then encapsulate information for transmission, we might be able to use the Internet as a connection. In essence, we need to run two network sessions — one to provide basic connectivity to the Internet and one that will act as a tunnel to send data. This means moving data through some layers of the network stack more than once; however, it does provide a simple solution for connectivity.

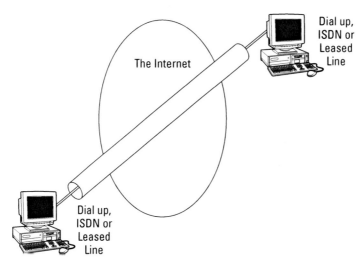

Figure 21-4: Two systems, both connected to the Internet, can create a virtual tunnel using the Internet as the physical connection only.

With tunneling, all data that is sent between the two systems can be encrypted. Various methods can be used for the encryption, depending on the tunneling protocol used to create the Virtual Private Network (VPN). L2TP and PPTP are two available protocols.

Point-to-Point tunneling protocol

Although point-to-point tunneling protocol, or PPTP, is primarily aimed at the dial-in user, it can be used to connect two offices over a TCP/IP network such as the Internet. Because Microsoft developed PPTP, the tunnel itself is not authenticated; rather, the logon passing through the tunnel is encrypted. The authentication of the remote user takes place in the normal manner.

When used for dial-in users, PPTP provides an easy-to-configure and relatively simple protocol that can be used to secure traffic. The client system will initiate a connection to the server over a TCP/IP network connection that already exists, which is encrypted across that connection only. This means that if the protocol is used to link two offices, only the point-to-point communications — that is, where the tunnel is between the two Windows systems acting as routers — will be encrypted.

For example, in Figure 21-5, the data on Network A and Network B is not encrypted—only the data that moves between the two routers through the tunnel. If a client on Network A sends data to a client on Network B, the data is not encrypted, since it would have to come down a PPTP stack first and then be encapsulated in a TCP/IP packet. Since the data from clients on Network A goes to the IP stack, it will not have been passed through the PPTP stack first, and thus, will not be encrypted.

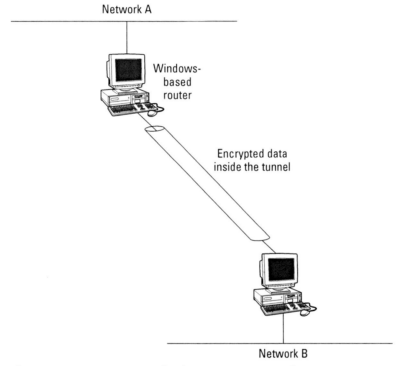

Figure 21-5: A PPTP connection between two networks

In Figure 21-6, the data from the application comes down the PPTP protocol stack and then passes through the TCP/IP stack. The first stack provides the encryption, and the second the actual transport. Since the packets from the network will not follow this same path, PPTP doesn't really work for connecting networks.

Application

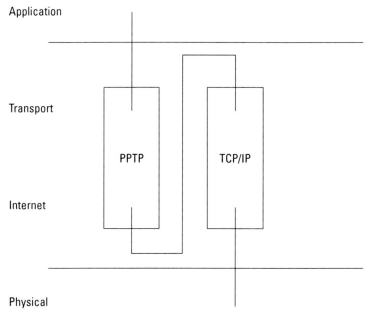

Transport

Internet

Physical

Figure 21-6: An architectural view of how PPTP works

Layer 2 tunneling protocol

Layer 2 tunneling protocol (L2TP) is a more common protocol among different platforms. Since there is support for this protocol from other vendors, L2TP provides a common protocol that can be used in networks where Microsoft systems are not used as routers. Together, Microsoft (for Windows 2000) and Cisco developed L2TP to provide a method of securing data transmissions on all types of media.

Another benefit over PPTP is the ability of L2TP to work in either tunneling mode or in end-to-end mode. End-to-end mode works like it does in PPTP — only the data from the local system will be encrypted and if the system acts as a router, there is no encryption. However, since L2TP is built into the TCP/IP protocol stack, you can enable tunneling mode, which enables L2TP to also encrypt data crossing between the routers.

If you plan to use the Internet as part of your backbone, you will want to use L2TP to send the data from point to point. But what about your leased line? As you learned earlier, there is no permanent point-to-point connection — frame relay and cell relay are used even for point-to-point connections from the telephone company, since this allows them to make better use of bandwidth. Thus, it would be nice to also encrypt the data that is going across these lines.

Encryption of data is a normal function for routers. Some form of encryption has been built into most routers for a while. L2TP is becoming the standard protocol used in routers.

Cross-Reference   A full discussion of security follows in Chapter 22.

Planning for Remote Access

The growing numbers of users that work at home, as well as the growing numbers of laptops, have made remote access a key issue in the last few years. Laptops, in particular, provide a challenge since they are sometimes on the network using an Ethernet card and sometimes dialing in using a modem and sometimes not connected at all. Using protocols like DHCP has simplified connectivity because the clients don't need to continually reconfigure IP addressing information.

Providing remote access used to be a matter of dropping a few modems and phone lines into an office and handing out phone numbers. This technique worked, but often at a significant cost, given the cost of the modems, the trunk charges for the phone lines to connect them to, and user support and long-distance charges. As we move forward, though, there are several available options for connecting remote users.

Choosing a dial-in strategy

There are several considerations to keep in mind when you evaluate your dial-in options. The first is security. If your organization does not think that encryption using L2TP or PPTP is sufficient to secure its data, then you will have to go with your own dial-in servers. If L2TP—with its triple DES encryption—is sufficient, you might be able to use it. Users can then dial into an ISP and create the connection across the Internet.

Hosting your own dial-in accounts

If you really need to host your own dial-in accounts because due to security issues, then you should be prepared for the expense. Setting up your own modem pool requires specialized equipment, and, to be honest, phone lines. In addition, you need to consider how to accommodate users that travel. Either they would have to dial in to a central number, or you would need to place modems in each branch that the user connects to. If the users are dialing into a central number, consider using an in-watts (1-800) number to keep the phone costs down. If this is not an option, you might consider having the system call the user back at the number the user gives. This could be done using an out-watts line to keep costs down. The only time you might have problems with this strategy is when users are calling from a hotel — the room phone might not be accessible from the outside.

Putting modems in each office can minimize costs, but you still have to deal with long distance charges if the traveling users are not near an office. You also need some way to control the authentication, since the user might be in Houston while his account is in Albany. In this case, the user's account information would have to be available to the server in Houston. Another issue arises if the user isn't able to dial in because he doesn't know the dial-in number for Houston. This information needs to be local to the laptop; otherwise, the users will need to call long distance to their support people to get the number.

Using tunneling

As an alternative to hosting your own modems, you could set your users up with accounts at a local, national, or international ISP. The ISP's local access numbers would provide a basic connection to the Internet, and the ISP's support numbers (usually 1-800 numbers that the ISP pays for) would provide the basic user support for connectivity issues. Thus, the expense of modems, phone lines, and long distance charges are removed from your operating budget — the amount of support calls looking for numbers might even be decreased.

Once users are connected to the Internet, they can "dial-in" to your PPTP or L2TP server. This also works for users at home who already have a cable modem or a DSL line. Even with the cost of the Internet connection and the dial-in accounts, this method is generally cheaper than hosting your own dial-in, notably when the next generation of modems comes out.

Working remotely

Now that some of the connectivity issues surrounding remote users have been discussed, it seems appropriate to look at some of the issues that arise from working remotely. Many users complain that working over the modem is extremely slow. They have a point. 56Kpbs is slower than a normal network speeds.

Unfortunately, there is very little that can be done to speed up simple file-based functions (for example, opening a file from the network or saving it back to the network). In a case where a modem user is trying to move a file from one location to another, the process will be slow because the file is being moved through the remote system. In other words, the entire file is moved to the local memory on the dialed-in system and then to the new location. There are, however, some options you can employ when the user is trying to work with an application on the remote network such as Telnet, Web-based tools, and terminal server.

Telnet

Telnet, or terminal emulation, is a tool that gives a remote user more speed. Telnet creates a session on a Telnet server and actually runs all the commands on that computer. It is primarily text-based; however, for moving or copying files or running text-based applications, it works very well. The client computer provides input and serves as an output device, meaning that only keystrokes and text responses have to cross the connection.

Web browsers

Since Telnet is text-based, users need to be able to type and work with simple text instructions. Obviously, this is not going to work for all users — so many organizations are now using Web-based applications in place of older text-based or traditional client-server applications. With the advent of technologies such as Java, the browser can even have client-side scripting and programs sent to it. This gives us a working client-server environment without a requirement for high-speed connections.

In a best-case scenario, if all code is kept on the server and the developers keep the design simple, you can run Web-based applications over the smallest of link speeds using a Web browser. The ability to use small link speeds and small clients is becoming a concern with the popularity of palm-top devices that can access the Internet — in many cases, these devices only transfer 19.2 Kbps and don't (normally) have a Java client built-in.

Terminal server

If you need to do all your work remotely, you might opt for a terminal server scenario. These servers are extensions of Telnet; they allow graphics, as well as text, to be used remotely. Citrix provides terminal servers for most platforms, and Microsoft has built terminal server into all of the Windows 2000 server operating systems.

Summary

This chapter looked at data communications, what is required to move data around, and some of the decisions that you will need to make concerning the provision of remote access. Hopefully, this chapter also brought up some questions about security, such as securing data that travels over the Internet or even the data that you let your ISP carry from point to point. In the next chapter, we will look at these security issues, which primarily involve the encryption of data and the authentication of users and servers.

✦   ✦   ✦

Planning for Network Security

Security is a key issue for anyone who works with computers. You hear horror stories about systems that are broken into and users that lose all their data — and frankly, most of these stories are true. What you need is a proactive strategy that will protect your data from any situation that arises. Planning ahead is essential, because when problems occur, you will be far too busy trying to recover information and get users back online to be wondering where you'll get a new computer or where you stored the backup from last month. However, this is a book on TCP/IP, not data recovery. So in this chapter, we will focus on the security weaknesses inherent to TCP/IP.

Assessing Your Risk

When it comes to planning your security strategy, the first step is to assess your risk. In other words, examine the data you have and the practices you use and then determine your vulnerabilities. In general, malicious attackers can target two main areas of your system: data or services. The impact of an attack will vary depending on what data or service is attacked. For example, if someone obtains a copy of your corporate phone list, you may be annoyed but you won't go bankrupt. On the other hand, if someone steals the plans for your prize widget, modifies them, and then sells the widget at a lower cost — well, to be blunt, that would be bad.

Another important step when planning your security policy is to identify different levels of security for different types of data. To set the different security levels, you need to identify the criteria for confidentiality — in other words, which company data can be shared with the public and which needs to be protected.

As an example of identifying different levels of security, we could look at marketing material. One of the main purposes of marketing material, including Web sites, is to establish the character of a company. Other companies will decide whether to do business with a company based on its image. Thus, people reading the information is a good thing; however, a person changing the information is a bad thing.

This brings up another point — when it comes to certain types of data, such as the chart of accounts in your financial system, many people will need the ability to read it; however, only a few will need to be able to change it. Table 22-1 may help illustrate this point — it lists some of the types of information that can exist in a company, who creates and uses it, and the effect on the company if the information is lost or corrupted.

Table 22-1
Some Types of Information and the Security Considerations Related to It

Type of Information	Used by	Created by	Effect
Web sites/marketing material	Everyone	Marketing	Company image, and therefore sales
Internal information, such as phone lists and vacation requests	Company employees	HR/Management	Day-to-day operations/social engineering attacks
Private information, such as financial projections	Management	Finance/Management	Company image and day-to-day operations
Secret information, such as design specs and plans	Production	Subject matter experts	Overall business

The types of information presented here are examples. The actual information you have to deal with will be different, but as you go about determining the different levels of security you require, you should look at the same details about the information in your company.

Attackers are motivated by a variety of reasons: to obtain information that will be used in other attacks or to compete against another company, to change the data in some way to make it useless, or to affect the processes that are using the information.

Typically, attacking your data means that someone has successfully attacked a server to gain access and then removed or changed the data on a server. One of the simplest ways to access the server is to get your username and password. There are different ways to do this. For example, every time you send or receive a file using FTP, your password and the data go across the network in clear text; every time you send mail over the Internet, it goes out in clear text; and every time you read your mail from an Internet mail account, it goes out in clear text. In other words, most of the protocols that are used on the Internet — indeed, most of the protocols that are traditionally used with TCP/IP — send data in clear text. So, anyone with a packet analyzer (which could be a piece of software running on a laptop) can grab all the information that is floating around on your network, including your username and password.

Even if an attacker hasn't got a username and password, your servers can still come under attack. Denial-of-service attacks, for example, send so much data to a server that it will never be able to keep up with the demand. In other cases, the attacker might send a malformed packet — perhaps continuous synchronization requests that the server will need to deal with. In the early days of Windows 95/NT 4.0, one popular attack was to send a malformed packet to port 135 (the Microsoft RPC port), which caused the system to hang, and in many cases, reboot — better known as WinNuke. In these types of attacks, the data isn't attacked; however, it will not be available.

After all this discussion about security attacks, you may feel like ripping your Internet connection out of the wall. However, if you are using a good firewall and following good security practices, the Internet is *not* your biggest threat. The truth is, internal (rather than external) attacks will comprise the majority of successful attacks on systems. For example, you've probably had a consultant, auditor, or at the very least a non-employee come into your office with a laptop. If you hooked them up to your network so they could print, you were probably unaware of the security risk you were taking. They could have very easily been running a packet sniffer or a package like L0phtCrack.

This means that you need to closely examine your system for possible internal threats. What types of people have access to your company's confidential information? In general, an internal attack can derive from an existing employee, an ex-employee, a consultant, a temporary employee, or even from a stranger. In all these cases, there is little that you can do to protect your information, outside of practicing good account management and good security policies. Some people are just curious and have no real malicious intent; in other cases, the attack is a serious attempt to access your confidential information.

Internal attacks can also use social engineering tactics, which play on the kindness of strangers. You've probably seen a movie or two where the hero simply walks into a building by pretending to be a worker or a pizza delivery person or an ambulance attendant. In a similar way, an attacker could pretend to be a computer repairperson and innocently ask a user for their password to fix their computer. Or the attacker could call the help desk from an internal telephone, pretending to be "so and so's" assistant, and saying that they needed to reset their password. You can combat this type of attack by ensuring that everyone knows the company's security policies and reports strange activities when they occur.

You can also defend against attacks by knowing what data is available to potential hackers. For example, on most Windows-based networks, a person will be able to capture the authentication packets as they go across the network, and then take the captured data and crack the passwords outside of your office. A file with literally thousands of passwords could be carried off on a floppy disk. Programs like LC3 (L0phtCrack) and PWDump make it easy for people to grab the packets as they cross the network, or even dump the Security Accounts Manager database with all the usernames and passwords.

So, do you have to give up your network and go back to a paper-based system? No, there are steps you can take, such as using IPSec to help secure your network. In addition, a good security policy will help if you enforce it evenly across the board.

Balancing Security and Usability

Before you even think about your specific security needs, you will have to consider how to balance the usability of the network and the security that you want to achieve. This ties in with our earlier discussion about different levels of security, since some data can be available to users, while other types of data should be tightly controlled.

Figure 22-1 shows the relationship between usability and security. On this chart, three different levels of data (public, internal, and secret) are indicated. Keep in mind that the names of these types of data may vary from one company to another.

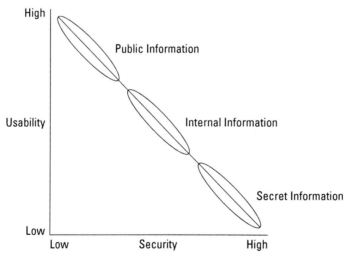

Figure 22-1: There is a strong relationship between usability and security.

In fact, when you start to plan the security on your network, determine how you are going to label the different levels of security and then determine what criteria will place data into each of the categories. As you develop your criteria, remember this rule of thumb: Keep It Simple. Unless you intend to categorize all the documents in the company yourself, the guidelines will need to be simple enough for others to understand and use. Another suggestion is to explain the threat as part of the security policy or possibly the new hire package for your company. In other words, explain why a particular document must be protected. This might be painfully obvious to you. However, someone with less experience may label the security policy as just another "stupid rule" — unless that policy is explained.

Understanding the types of attacks that can take place, the types of data that you have, and the level of security that each requires will allow you to move on to securing your network.

Securing Your Network

There are two aspects of securing a network — securing access to the data and securing the transmission of the data. Many organizations secure access to the data, but very few go the extra step to secure the transmission of the data. Specifically, most organizations require you to authenticate yourself before you access data, but most do not encrypt all data transmissions. Unfortunately, a network is not really protected unless both data access and data transmission is secured.

Encrypting data transmission

Encrypting the data that moves across your network will make authentication safer and will prevent people from capturing data that you send over the network. Data will be encrypted using any of several different standards that use some algorithm to scramble the bits of the message so that only the receiver of the data knows how to unscramble them. Most encryption methods rely on a shared key value that is used to scramble the data and then unscramble it at the other end. In general terms, this type of encryption is known as *PKI,* or *Public Key Infrastructure.*

In general, PKI performs two functions with which you are probably already familiar. You can place a signature on a message, or you can seal (encrypt) a message. The process will be slightly different for each function, and a different key pair will be used for each. A *key pair* is a pair of keys that can be used together — one is used to encrypt data and the other is used to decrypt it. Key pairs are created in such a way that only the other key in the pair will be able to decrypt the data that was encrypted by the first key. These are considered *asymmetric keys,* since the two keys are different.

Signing a message

Signing a message does not actually encrypt the message; rather, it places an electronic signature on the end of the message. This signature can be verified at the other end to ensure that the message was not changed during its transmission from one place to another.

To sign a message, a message digest is created using a hash function. A basic example of a hash would take the first 1,024 bits of a message and perform an XOR (see the Note below) with them on the next 1,024 bits. This result would then be XOR'd with the next 1,024 bits and so on until the end of the message. In the end, you have a string of 1,024 bits that is unique to that message. At least, the string is unique enough that if someone changed the message a little, the value would change.

Note   XOR stands for "exclusive OR" — a logical comparison where the two bits that are the same will yield a 0 bit and the two bits that are different will yield a 1 bit.

Though the hash process doesn't necessarily use XOR, it follows this process. The number of bits will depend on the exact algorithm used, but is generally at least 512. This message digest is then encrypted with the originator's private signing key, and the message is sent over the network.

When the message is received, the message digest is removed from the end of the message and the same algorithm is used to create the message digest on the receiving machine. Then the public signing key for the sender is used to decrypt the original message digest and the two are compared. If the two message digests are the same, the data was not tampered with in transit. If they differ, the message might have been tampered with. Obviously, this means that the public signing key must be known by the receiving system, or the message cannot be checked and there is little point in signing the message.

Sealing a message

To seal a message, the entire message is broken into pieces that are encrypted using the public key of the receiver. The message can then be sent over the network, and on the receiver's end, the receiver's private key is used to decrypt the message. Like signing, sealing relies on the ability to share the public keys and also leads to a problem if the message will be sent to multiple users.

For multiple destinations, a file key is generated and used to encrypt the message. This key will then be encrypted once for each recipient using his or her public signing key. When the message is sent, each recipient can decrypt the message using his or her private key. However, the problem of key distribution remains.

Symmetric key encryption

Obviously, it can be difficult to distribute keys across even a small network and ensure that all the users have all the public keys available. This makes it difficult to configure and set up asymmetric keys. In addition, if the data were to always use the same key, it would be easier for that key to be broken. Thus, PKI is generally used during the setup of a session so that a shared private key can be sent between the two systems. In other words, PKI is used to encrypt the session key that will be used by the two systems.

By using PKI for session setup only and then using a session key, it is relatively simple to handle the encryption and decryption of data and to change the key frequently.

Standard encryption algorithms

Now that we have looked at symmetric and asymmetric keys, it is worth taking a moment to look at some of the standard algorithms that are used for signing and for encrypting data. First, let's examine the following message authentication protocols:

✦ **Digital Signature Algorithm (DSA)** — This standard is used for signature generation and verification. It provides for a key size of up to 1,024 bits.

✦ **Secure Hash Algorithm (SHA-1)** — This is one of the hash algorithms that you may run across. It is slower than MD5, but provides for a longer message digest. SHA-1 can take a message of up to 2^{64} bits (2EB — exabytes) and return a 160-bit message hash.

✦ **Message Digest 5 (MD5)** — This is another common hash algorithm. It is faster than SHA-1, but only provides a 128-bit message digest.

✦ **Hash Message Authentication Code (HMAC)** — A Message Authentication Code (MAC) is created based on a key value and then included in the hash in such a way that the original data and the MAC are hashed into the same digest. HMAC is really an add-on to either SHA or MD5.

As you probably remember, authentication is only half the battle towards securing your network. In addition, you need to be able to provide encryption of the data. Some of the standards for encryption are:

✦ **Digital Encryption Standard (DES)** — DES is probably the most common standard, providing fast 56-bit encryption.

✦ **Digital Encryption Standard (DES) Cipher Block Chaining (CBC)** — In this scenario, the first block of plain text is encrypted using standard DES. All other blocks are then XOR'ed with the encrypted version of the previous block of text before being encrypted.

✦ **Triple Digital Encryption Standard (3DES)** — In general, this standard refers to the scenario where a single block will be encrypted three times with three separate 56-bit keys.

✦ **Digital Encryption Standard XOR (DESX)** — This is another variant of the DES standard, in which the unencrypted data will be XOR'ed with part of the key before it is encrypted. The encrypted block of data is then XOR'ed again with another part of the key.

✦ **Rivest's (Ron's) Cipher 2 (RC2)** — Developed by Ron Rivest of RSA (`www.rsa.com`), RC2 is a block cipher (encrypting groups of data) algorithm that uses a fixed block size of 64 bits. The key size is variable.

✦ **Rivest's (Ron's) Cipher 4 (RC4)** — Similar to RC2, except that streaming encryption is used. In other words, the length of data that is encrypted is not a fixed block size.

✦ **Rivest's (Ron's) Cipher 5 (RC5)** — The current version of the RC protocols, which uses a 32-, 64-, or 128-bit block ciphered with a key of 0 to 2,048 bits.

Authenticating users

The authentication process will normally be done using a user name and password. This standard has been around for a long time, and its limitations are fairly well known. However, the disadvantage of using passwords is that users forget where they wrote them down, or they simply forget them, or they use very simple passwords that can easily be guessed.

Most network operating systems now provide some way to force users to use strong passwords of a minimum length. It can be useful to force the minimum password length; however, it leads to more support calls to reset passwords and more little yellow Post-it notes with passwords written on them. In fact, you can sometimes tell how seriously someone takes security by the location of the Post-it note: on the monitor — low security; under the keyboard — medium security; under the pencil holder in the desk drawer — high security.

However, passwords will continue to be used for at least part of the user authentication process. How we get the password from the user to the server is also important.

Note   A strong password is one that contains characters from three or four different groups — uppercase letters, lowercase letters, numbers, and special symbols.

Clear text passwords

One basic method of security is to simply send the password in clear text from the client system to the server. This method was used extensively in the early days of computing, and is still used quite often. All of the UNIX-based (that is, TCP/IP-based) protocols started using this method. For example, SMTP, POP, FTP, Telnet, NNTP, and so on, all use clear text to send authentication.

Sending clear text passwords could be considered the apathy method of security, since you are counting on the apathy of others to keep them from getting your password. However, when clear text passwords are used these days, encryption is put onto the underlying connection, which makes it possible to use the clear text password without worrying that someone will grab it in transit. Two common methods for encrypting network communications are IPSec and SSL, discussed later in the chapter.

In general, you should try not to use clear text passwords without encryption on the connection.

NT/LAN Manager authentication

In the Windows world, NT/LAN Manager authentication is used for authenticating connections. The server will, over an encrypted connection, send an 8-byte challenge to the client computer. The client computer will use the user's password to create a 21-byte session key that it will then use to encrypt the challenge. The encrypted challenge will be returned to the server of the secure channel.

The server then decrypts the response from the client and extracts the session key. This is then compared to the session key that the server created using the user's password, and if the two match, the user will be allowed to log on. There is an obvious weakness here, in that the session key will also be the same and can be decrypted by breaking the 8-byte challenge that was originally set. The problem is exacerbated if the server still needs to provide logon services for Windows 95 or older clients, which used the LAN Manager key creation sequence.

Creating a LAN Manager key

In LAN Manager, passwords were 8 characters long and not case-sensitive. To generate the session's key, the system will use the password converted to uppercase. This is padded to 14 bytes, with spaces, and then the bits of each byte are reversed. The now 14-byte string is passed through a standard encryption algorithm (Digital Encryption Standard) to provide a 14-byte encrypted password.

At this point, the 8-byte challenge will be encrypted using the first 7 bytes of the encrypted, reversed password, and then the same challenge will be encrypted with the remaining 7 bytes. This results in a 16-byte session key that will be padded with 5 bytes of 0s to create the 21-byte response.

Although this type of key worked in the early days, today's systems have processing capabilities that make it possible to quickly reverse these steps and determine the original password. Programs such as L0phtCrack can do this easily.

Creating an NT key

This weakness of the LAN Manager Key, and the constant attempts to undermine the security in Microsoft operating systems, led to expanded password length and case sensitivity in Windows NT. In this case, the Unicode, case-sensitive version of the password is passed through Message Digest 4 encryption to create a 16-byte key that is then added with 5 bytes of 0s to create the key. This means that the 8-byte challenge can now be encrypted with a 16-byte key, which makes the logon in Windows NT more secure — but only if the clients can generate this key. By default, Windows NT asks for both keys, and both keys will be generated and sent. Windows NT/2000 can be configured not to request the LAN Manager key in the Registry; however, this must be configured on both the client and server.

Also note that once a user is authenticated and logged in to his or her workstation, this same authentication process will be repeated for each server that the user connects to. Each server will need to validate the user's logon to the server with a domain controller using a similar process.

X.509 certificates

Authentication can also be performed with a certificate. A certificate is the digital equivalent to your driver's license or passport. Like these documents, it is used to prove your identity. The current standard for digital certificates is the X.509 standard.

Certificates use PKI to provide a method of both authentication and to pass public keys. When passwords are used — either in clear text or using NT/LAN Manager — users have to be responsible for keeping the passwords safe. This may be a problem for some users. It also means that in all cases, a user must log on or the password must be stored on the system — probably in clear text.

In general, a certificate contains three main groups of information:

✦ The public key(s) of the subject

✦ Information about the subject

✦ Information about the issuer and their signature

As long as you trust the issuer of the certificate, you only need to verify that the identity of the server or user is the same as that in the certificate and that the certificate has not been revoked. Certificates are issued by a certificate authority, such as Verisign. The certificate authority should verify the details about the person to whom the certificate is issued and then issue the certificate only if everything checks out.

In reality, it is very easy to obtain a certificate for purposes such as e-mail, with little or no proof of identity. However, unlike using something like PGP certificates, X.509 certificates will normally cost you some amount of money. This is only necessary if you will use the certificate on the Internet for general use. If you will not use the certificates on the Internet, you can create your own internal certificate server by installing and configuring a certificate server.

A certificate server stores certificates and can simply host the certificates or be part of a PKI implementation. PKI includes not just the storage of certificates, but also the management tools that are required to issue, revoke, store, retrieve, and trust other organization certificates. The PKI infrastructure starts with the creation of a root certificate server. During this process, a certificate authority certificate will be created for the individual that will manage the security.

In some networks, there may be only one certificate server – in other networks, more certificate servers may be required. These certificate servers will be subordinate to the root certificate server and will need to be validated by the certificate authority. These servers can then be allowed to issue certificates for servers and individuals.

X.509 is probably the most widely accepted standard that has been set for certificates (you can also get a PGP certificate). X.509 is an ITU-T (International Telecommunications Union — Telecommunication Standardization Sector) standard, and in fact, is part of the X.500 specifications dealing with directory services. All X.509 certificates have the following data:

✦ **X.509 version number** — Identifies the version of the X.509 standard for this certificate, which determines what information can be specified in it.

✦ **Public key** — The public key of the certificate holder, together with an algorithm identifier that specifies which encryption algorithm the key uses.

✦ **Serial number** — Every certificate that is issued by a given authority will have a unique serial number.

✦ **Unique identifier** — The X.500 distinguished name (DN) of the subject of the certificate. This name is intended to be unique across the internal network or the Internet.

✦ **Validity period** — The certificate's valid from and to dates.

✦ **Name of the issuer** — The unique name of the certificate authority that signed the certificate. This is the certificate server that issued the certificate. This server must be trusted or the certificates are useless.

✦ **Digital signature** — The signature, using the private key of the certificate server, that ensures that the certificate has not been changed since it was issued.

✦ **Signature algorithm identifier** — Identifies the algorithm used to sign the certificate.

X.509 certificates are becoming very popular today, not only for use with the Internet but also for internal networks. Kerberos is another system that is becoming increasingly popular.

Kerberos

Kerberos was developed by MIT as an open network authentication protocol. It has proven to be a solid protocol and is thus widely accepted. Even Microsoft's Windows 2000 has incorporated Kerberos over the Windows NT/LAN Manager authentication scheme.

Kerberos uses strong cryptography so that a client can prove its identity to a server (and vice versa) across an insecure network connection. After a client and server have used Kerberos to prove their identity, they can also encrypt all of their communications to assure privacy and data integrity as they go about their business.

How Kerberos authentication works

Kerberos relies on messages between the client and server to provide security. These messages are encrypted using a variety of methods, including DES or 3DES encryption (depending on the implementation), the use of X.509 certificates, or even a shared secret password.

Communications for user authentication always take place between a client and an authentication server. Communications also take place between the various servers on a network and the authentication server. The user's password will be used to unlock a local copy of the encryption key or to generate the encryption key. In either case, the level of network security depends on whether users create and protect good passwords.

If the servers talk to the authentication server and the clients talk to the authentication server, it may seem like the clients and servers will never be able to encrypt data. However, once a client is authenticated by the authentication server, it will now go back to the authentication server any time it needs to communicate with another server. The authentication server will generate a session key for the communications between the client and the server and will use a ticket to give the key to the server.

It does this by giving the ticket to the client, which can then present the ticket to the server. The server can accept the ticket, which the authentication server will have signed just like a certificate once it verifies the signature. This could be a problem if the ticket was captured in transit. However, the ticket must be used within a given period of time or the session key will be invalid. Thus, setting the correct time on the servers is critical if you plan to implement Kerberos. A Kerberos ticket includes:

✦ The session key

✦ The user name

✦ An expiration time

✦ A digital signature

The signature from the authentication server is created using a key set that is only known to servers, not to clients. In this way, the server can be assured that the ticket originally came from the authentication server. The client sends an authenticator to the server along with the ticket it receives from the authentication server. This includes:

✦ The current time

✦ A checksum

✦ An optional encryption key

This ticket and authenticator are encrypted using the session key from the ticket received from the authentication server. When the data reaches the server, it will verify the ticket and extract the session key. It will then decrypt the authenticator and verify the information. If the checksum that was put into the authenticator matches, we can assume that the true client encrypted the authenticator, since only that client will have the session key. Next, the timestamp is checked to make sure the authenticator is fresh. Typically, the timestamp in the authenticator must be no more than five minutes off from the time of the server. If timestamp is fresh, the ticket is accepted and the client's identity is confirmed.

At this point, the server will generate a response, which includes the timestamp from the authenticator and additional information such as the server's name that it will encrypt and return to the client. The timestamp verifies that the server is the one with whom it was trying to communicate and the other information can be used to verify the name of the server. This option allows for mutual authentication of both client and server.

Obviously this whole process is a lot of work. It requires the user to enter the password each time he or she needs to connect to another server, or requires that the password is cached on the local system.

In order to avoid having the user enter the password for each connection or having the password cached locally, Kerberos uses a *ticket-granting ticket*. When a user initially logs for a session and is authenticated by the authentication server, a ticket and session key from the ticket-granting service is also returned by the authentication server. This ticket is the *ticket-granting ticket,* and it will be cached on the station for a short period of time, typically 8 hours. Since the ticket-granting ticket provides credentials for the user and is short-lived, the password can now be cleared from memory.

From that point on, the process is similar to the one outlined above, except that rather than having to go to the authentication server, the client computer can use a ticket-granting server. Even when the authentication server and ticket-granting server are one and the same, splitting the authentication process and the ticket granting process is a better approach, since the password is not sent over the network multiple times and is not stored on the client workstation.

How Kerberos authentication works

So far, we have looked at the authentication process in Kerberos; the other part of security is encryption. If you read along carefully, you probably noticed that part of the data included in every ticket is a session key. Applications that are aware of this session key, such as IPSec, can use it to secure the communications between systems.

As a final note on Kerberos, you should be aware that all the servers and clients that use a single authentication server in a Kerberos implementation are considered to be a Kerberos realm. Kerberos provides for cross-realm authentication using cross-realm keys (Kerberos version 4) or shared keys in a hierarchical structure (Kerberos version 5).

Using encryption and authentication together

If you want to completely secure your network, you will need to use authentication and encryption together. The last sections of this chapter examine some of the technologies that make use of both encryption and authentication methods.

Pretty Good Privacy

Pretty Good Privacy (PGP) is one implementation of PKI that has gained wide acceptance because it works — not to mention the fact that it's free. Another major benefit of PGP is that it is cross-platform. Essentially, it works the same way as PKI, with a couple of minor differences.

PGP will always create a session key that will be used to encrypt a file. The session key will then be encrypted using the recipient's public key, which may have been sent in clear text, or which you may have obtained from a public PGP key distribution center like the one at MIT (web.mit.edu/network/pgp.html). In addition, the file will normally be compressed. (Many of the methods used to crack encryption rely on finding the patterns in an encrypted message. By using compression, these patterns are reduced, making it harder for hackers to get at the information.)

In PGP, the keys are created by the user and, as noted, can be distributed in clear text or by using a public distribution service. The private key is protected on the user's machine with a pass phrase that needs to be entered every time the user wishes to encrypt or decrypt data. This can also lead to an attack known as *man-in-the middle*. In this type of attack, someone will generate a key that looks like it is another person's real key. The person with the fake key can then intercept the transmission using different means and decrypt the data on the local system using the private key that corresponds to the bogus public key. This problem can be circumvented using certificates such as the X.509 certificates discussed earlier.

You can find a wealth of information about PGP and the required software at The International PGP Home Page (www.pgpi.org).

Secure Sockets Layer

SSL has become a part of everyday life, as it is used to secure HTTP and other types of Internet servers. Basically SSL provides a method to encrypt data at the socket level — that is, between the application layer and the transport layer. SSL uses PKI to safely share a session key between a client and a server. In this case, the certificate will be used to both transfer the keys and to authenticate the server system.

The SSL process starts with the client connecting to a secure socket on the server — for example, port 443 for HTTPS. The server will send its X.509 certificate to the client, which contains the name of the server that the certificate was issued to and the public encryption key.

The client can then validate the certificate. When the certificate is issued, a certificate authority signs it. The client will either attempt to find that authority and obtain its public signing key or it will already have the certificate (all Web browsers include the certificate authority signing keys for most of the popular authorities, such as Verisign).

As discussed earlier, the message is hashed to generate the message digest — in this case, the certificate is the message. The signature — the original message digest of the certificate — is decrypted and then compared to the one created in the hash process that the system just did. If they are the same, the certificate can be trusted (assuming the signing authority is), and the name of the server in the certificate is compared to the name you connected to in the browser.

Assuming the names are the same, a session key is created for this connection and then encrypted with the public sealing key from the certificate. This session key is sent to the server, which will decrypt it with its private sealing key. Symmetric encryption will then be used to transfer data securely between the client and server.

In this case, session-key length will be dictated by the information in the certificate, which will provide information about the capabilities of the server. In some cases, the server and the client will not be able to communicate if one or the other requires a level of encryption the other doesn't provide.

IPSec

Developing secure communications depends on the ability of the programs at the application layer to handle the encryption and authentication. This means that in order to make protocols such as FTP or Telnet secure, both the standard clients and the standard servers would have to be rewritten. In fact, of all the services that run over TCP/IP, most would have to be rewritten to include some form of security. This leads to yet another problem — standards. Since some of these applications have to work together, it is important that the same secure mechanisms be used for all.

That's where IP Security (IPSec) comes in. If you recall the TCP/IP stack, all of the applications — client-side and server-side — sit at the Application layer. They use various ports in the sockets layer to communicate with either TCP (for connection-oriented communications) or UDP (for connectionless communications). TCP and UDP in turn use IP to package the data and direct it hither and yon, passing it through to the correct network interface.

In essence, IPSec takes the responsibility for encryption and authentication away from the application layer programs and moves it to the internetworking layer. By doing this all data that moves down the TCP/IP stack can be encrypted without the application layer programs being involved or even aware encryption is happening.

As you might have already guessed, IPSec ties in very nicely with Kerberos. Since it performs user authentication and passes session keys back and forth. The combination of IPSec and Kerberos provides a complete security solution — Kerberos managing the authentication of users and IPSec securing the traffic that passes over the network.

IPSec comprises two different protocols: Authentication Headers (AH) and Encapsulating Security Payload (ESP). These protocols provide the authentication of packets — not like Kerberos or an X.509 certificate, but by signing the packets that are sent and verifying them when they are received. The protocols can also encrypt the data that is passed in the packet so that it nearly impossible to read in transit. In the next few sections, we look at each of these protocols and then we will look at Security Associations (SA), which is the IPSec version of a session.

Authentication Headers

The AH protocol provides data integrity using a hashing algorithm and sequence numbers. Like a digital signature, a secure hashing algorithm is used to create an Integrity Check Value (ICV). This value can be created using Hash Message Authentication Code (HMAC), Message Digest 5 (MD5), or HMAC Secure Hash Algorithm (SHA).

The hash algorithm hashes parts of the IP header and the IP data portions of the IP packet. Only part of the IP header is used, because the hash is included in the header and is not known until it is calculated. Other fields that are excluded include the header checksum, the flags, the fragment offset, the time to live, and the type of service, since all of these can be changed in transit.

 Note   If the datagram must be fragmented at the source due to the underlying network topology, AH processing must take place before the datagram is fragmented. Therefore, fragments must be reassembled at the target host before AH processing.

The remaining information is hashed, and the value is placed into the IP header. This means that the header will now contain some extra information, including:

✦ **Length** — Indicates the length of the AH.

✦ **Security Parameters Index (SPI)** — Identifies the Security Association (SA) for the communication.

✦ **Sequence Number** — The sequence number is a simple count that is incremented for each packet sent over an SA. The number starts at 0, and is never allowed to cycle, and it indicates the packet number sent over the SA for the communication. The receiver checks this field to verify that a packet for the associated SA with this number has not been received already. If one has been received, the packet is rejected.

✦ **Authentication Data** — The authentication data contains the Integrity Check Value (ICV). The receiver will calculate the hash value and check it against this value to verify integrity of the data being transmitted. This is how the digital signature provides data integrity.

The sequence number provides a simple method of circumventing *replay attacks.* A replay attack is one in which a session is captured using a packet sniffer. Some of the data is then modified and the capture transmissions are then replayed to fool the receiver into thinking that a valid station is communicating.

When the session, or Security Association (SA), is negotiated, the sequence number is set to zero. The first packet that is sent will have a sequence number of 1, and the next will have a sequence number of 2 and so on. In addition, the sequence numbers must not be repeated during the life of a SA; therefore, once the sequence number has reached a maximum value of 2^{32}, a new SA must be established and the sequence number for the new SA will begin again at zero.

Authentication Headers can be used in either tunneling mode or transport mode. Both modes operate the same way. However, the data that is signed is different. In transport mode — that is, a direct connection between two machines – the AH header will follow the IP header, and the hash will cover the static fields of the IP header, the AH header, and the IP data. In tunnel mode, IPSec is used to create a tunnel between two end-points, such as routers. In this case, the AH header will follow the new tunneled IP header and will be calculated for the fields of the new IP header, the AH header, and the IP data.

Encapsulating Security Payload

ESP can be used to provide data integrity in a similar fashion to AH, but it also provides data encryption. However, ESP does not touch the IP header information. When ESP and AH are used together, ESP will first encrypt the data and then AH will sign the packet, which provides very strong security. In this case, there would be an IP header, an AH header, and an ESP header. When used for signing, ESP can use the same two signing protocols as AH. For encryption, it can use DES-CBC, DES 40-bit, and triple DES.

The fields included in the ESP header are similar to those in the AH header:

✦ **Security Parameters Index (SPI)** — Identifies the security association.

✦ **Sequence Number** — Used in the same manner as AH.

✦ **Payload Data** — The payload data varies, depending on the mode of operation. In transport mode, it has the TCP or UDP header and data; in tunnel mode, it also contains the original IP header.

In addition to the header, ESP also adds one or two trailers to the data. The first trailer contains the following fields:

✦ **Padding** — Used to round out the data to 32 bits or to a full block, depending on the encryption used.

✦ **Padding Length** — Indicates the length of the Padding field in bytes so it can be discarded by the receiver.

✦ **Next Header** — Tells the receiver what type of data has been encrypted. The IP protocol ID is used (IP = 0, TCP = 6, UDP = 17).

The second trailer is only used if ESP is configured to sign the data being transmitted as well. There is only one field in the second trailer, which is the Authentication Data. Like the AH protocol, this is the ICV that is calculated on the ESP header, the payload data, and the ESP trailer.

Like AH, ESP can work in two modes, although the difference lies in what is being signed or, in this case, encrypted. In transport mode, where two hosts are communicating directly, the ESP header, transport header and data, and ESP trailer are signed. The data is also encrypted. The following steps are used in transport mode to encrypt the data:

1. The transport (TCP or UDP) header and the data are encapsulated into the payload data.
2. The proper padding is appended, if needed. The padding requirements are based on the encrypting algorithm.
3. The payload data, padding, padding length, and next header fields are encrypted.

If encryption and authentication are both selected, then encryption is performed first.

In tunnel mode, ESP will sign the ESP header, the original IP header, the transport header and data, and the ESP trailer. The same three steps are used for encryption, the difference being that the entire original IP datagram will be encrypted.

Security Associations

In most cases, two stations have to create a session before they can communicate. In IPSec, this session is referred to as a *Security Association (SA)*. An SA defines the common security setting and keys used to protect the communication from end to end. Obviously, multiple associations may exist if a computer is communicating with more than one computer and using IPSec simultaneously. In these situations, the receiving computer uses the *Security Parameters Index (SPI)* to map the packet to the correct SA, and therefore, the correct encryption keys.

The *Internet Security Association and Key Management Protocol (ISAKMP)* will negotiate the security setting that will become the SA. On the sending computer, the IPSec SA is stored in a database that associates the SA, the user ID, and the destination address. On the receiving end, the same information is stored in a similar database. In addition, the receiving end will create a reciprocal SA. The Security Parameters Index (SPI) will be used to match inbound packets with the correct SA. During the negotiation, the target system creates the SPI and passes it to the sending system. The system includes the SPI in every AH or ESP Header. The receiver uses a hash of the SPI and the destination address to quickly look up the appropriate SA in its SA database.

To build the SA between the two computers, the Internet Engineering Task Force (IETF) has established a standard method of security association and key exchange, which combines the ISAKMP and the Oakley key generation. ISAKMP defines the general procedures and message formats that need to be used during Security Association creation, maintenance, modification, and deletion.

The specific protocol ISAKMP used to perform these duties is the Oakley Key Determination Protocol. Two negotiations must take place before IPSec can start processing IP packets. Oakley generates and manages the authenticated keys used to encrypt and decrypt the information for both negotiations. Oakley uses the Diffie-Hellman key exchange protocol.

Note that Oakley has two modes that it will operate in. The Oakley Main Mode provides for new key generation material and a new encryption key. The Oakley Quick Mode is used when each party already has key generation material, but a new encryption key needs to be generated. Oakley Quick Mode can only be used after Main Mode has been used to provide key generation material.

To ensure successful, secure communication, ISAKMP/Oakley performs a two-phase operation. Confidentiality and authentication during each phase is assured by the use of negotiated encryption and authentication algorithms, agreed on by the two ISAKMP peers. These algorithms are configurable.

The first negotiation includes user-identity authentication for the two hosts that wish to communicate and the exchange of session keys for securing data. ISAKMP manages this first negotiation.

The second negotiation follows the key exchange. The two hosts must agree on what security settings they will use to secure their IP communication. The policy defining the rules for this negotiation (for example, what algorithms are allowable) is called the *IPSec policy*.

The first negotiation establishes a secure channel between the two computers for the communication. This is known as the *ISAKMP SA*. To create the secure channel, ISAKMP authenticates computer identities and exchanges information to establish the shared secret key. The Oakley Main Mode provides the necessary identity protection during this exchange, which ensures total privacy because no identity information is sent without encryption between the communicating hosts.

In the second negotiation, a security association is established between the two computers. The information about the association is passed to the IPSec driver — along with the shared key — on both the sending and receiving computers. During this negotiation, keying material is refreshed or new keys are generated if necessary.

Summary

In this chapter, you gained an understanding of issues related to network security. Security is one of the most important areas to plan for — and certainly the most difficult to enforce.

There are two main aspects of security: encryption and authentication. Encryption keeps your data safe as it passes over the network, and authentication ensures that only the right people gain access to the network resources. In this chapter, we discussed some of the protocols that can be used to handle encryption and authentication.

This chapter didn't delve into user accounts or groups, nor did it discuss access control lists; however, these and other facets of account management are equally important in ensuring that your data remains safe. How these functions take place, though, will depend on the network operating system that you are using and are outside the scope of this book.

✦   ✦   ✦

Troubleshooting Network and Connectivity Problems

◆ ◆ ◆ ◆

In This Chapter

Understanding the troubleshooting process

Checking the IP configuration

Checking connectivity

Checking name resolution

Checking the client and server

◆ ◆ ◆ ◆

In a perfect world, everything would work all the time. However, we live in the real world, where machines break down and human error causes accidents. In the face of such imperfections, our only alternative is to locate the source of our problems and find ways to remedy them.

In simple terms, troubleshooting is the process of determining why some procedure or product doesn't work. There are two ways to troubleshoot: one, identifying the problem with a *new* product or process that won't work, and two, figuring out why something that was working has *stopped* working. The type of work you do — as an installer, network administrator, or programmer — will determine your method of troubleshooting. In most cases, making something work for the first time may simply involve following the instructions in the manual. Surprisingly, only about 4 percent of people working in a technical occupation read a manual before trying to install a new product.

In general, successful troubleshooting requires a thorough understanding of the system you are troubleshooting — whether it is as simple as a computer that won't connect or as complicated as the new seven-tier application that fails during a particular function. If you know what steps the application(s) have to take and how they interrelate, then troubleshooting becomes a simple matter of tracing through the set of steps that should take place and identifying (typically by observation) where the steps break down.

With regards to TCP/IP, the process of troubleshooting is the same. TCP/IP is a system of software and hardware components, and each of these components must be in working order to ensure the success of the entire process. First, this chapter examines the basic troubleshooting process.

The Troubleshooting Process

Connecting two computers may seem like a simple matter, but many steps are taken to ensure this connectivity. For example, if you are trying to connect to another company's Web site, your computer must have an IP address, which means that your DHCP server must be running. For DHCP packets to get to your computer, your routers must be forwarding BOOTP packets, your DHCP relay agent must be working, or you must be on the same subnet as the DHCP server. When you have an IP address, you then need to be able to get from your local subnet to the external gateway, which means that your local router and all the routers in between must be working and that the routing protocol you use on your network must be functioning. When you are at the external gateway, you might be going through a proxy server that needs to be operational and probably a firewall. The firewall might be tied into your authentication systems, which must then also be working.

As your request leaves your network through the firewall, you are now at the mercy of the Internet. This part of the journey involves the router that connects your company to its ISP, the ISP's internal network, and destination systems' ISP's internal network and routers working. The link between the ISPs relies on the fact that the upstream ISP or voice carrier has lines or satellites that are working, in addition to routers and internal networks. It also requires that all of these systems have a functioning routing protocol that will allow them to find a router from point A to point D. On the network, where the Web server you're trying to connect to is located, the following must be working: the firewall, the internal routing, the hub or switch, the remote computer that runs the Web site, and the software for that Web site. Since many sites are now data-driven, the database server on the remote end also needs to be working.

Taking the scenario from the previous two paragraphs a step further, all of the systems must be able to communicate at a basic level, which means that all the layers of the TCP/IP stack of each system needs to be functioning correctly. The Application layer must be talking to the ports correctly, which need to be able to pass data to TCP or UDP without corruption. These protocols rely on IP, which relies on ARP and needs to be able to work with ICMP and IGMP. And, of course, the network cards must be working.

The last three paragraphs provide an overview of the process that occurs every time you read a Web page. As you've probably guessed, communication over TCP/IP is not simple or terribly efficient. However, it seems to work fairly well.

Just as "a journey of a thousand miles starts with a single step," so does the process of troubleshooting. In our case, the first step is the local system. We begin there.

Checking the IP Configuration

One of the most obvious places to start troubleshooting is with the TCP/IP configuration. The IP configuration provides the IP address and subnet mask that determine the system's identity. The configuration also provides the gateway address that is needed to take packets to other networks. The configuration provides pointers to the DNS and WINS servers that will be required to find names. The configuration provides the port addresses that are needed to connect to the services on the remote system. Remember, a system that is working tends to remain so until acted upon by a user, and sometimes users will change the configuration.

Checking the IP configuration for Microsoft Windows

The way you check the IP configuration will depend on the particular operating system (Microsoft or UNIX and its derivatives) that you are using. Because more desktop clients run Microsoft operating systems, our discussion starts there.

Using ipconfig

Windows 95 and 98 include a graphical utility — called WINIPCFG — that allows you to check the IP configuration. This utility can be run from the Start menu's Run command. In the resource kit for both Windows 95 and 98, you can also find a copy of ipconfig, which is a command line utility that gives the same information as WINIPCFG. Since ipconfig covers all of the Windows platforms, we will look at ipconfig in detail.

The ipconfig utility lets you view the configuration of the system. The output of ipconfig includes:

```
Windows IP Configuration

0 Ethernet adapter :

        IP Address. . . . . . . . . : 192.168.0.1
        Subnet Mask . . . . . . . . : 255.255.255.0
        Default Gateway . . . . . . :

1 Ethernet adapter :

        IP Address. . . . . . . . . : 48.53.66.7
        Subnet Mask . . . . . . . . : 255.255.192.0
        Default Gateway . . . . . . : 48.53.64.1
```

With this utility, we can quickly check the IP address, subnet mask, and default gateway. In this case, the IP address and subnet mask are correct and the system is, in fact, configured with a default gateway.

There are a couple of specific addresses to look out for with the newer releases of Windows. First, look for any system with an address in the range 169.145.x.x. This address range is used for automatic IP addressing in DHCP clients. Thus, if the client tries to get an IP address from a DHCP server and cannot, Windows 2000 and Windows ME will assign them one from this range. Obviously, this could lead to duplicate IP addressing, so Microsoft is very careful to check the address before it is used by pinging to avoid duplicate IP addresses. If a system goes to automatic IP addressing, it does not inform the user. Typically, the user will first become aware of the problem when they discover that they can't log on, resulting in a call to the help desk.

You should also look out for the address 192.168.0.1. One of the new features of Windows 2000 is connection sharing, which allows you to have a connection (for example, to the Internet) through your provider and another connection to a local area network; thus, with the click of a button, you act as a basic router between the connection to your provider and the internal 192.168.0.0 network. A user who is playing around might try connection sharing and ignore the large pop-up warning. And suddenly one of the network cards has the wrong address and the system can't communicate.

Both automatic IP addressing and connection sharing are part of Microsoft's plan to make networking easier for the home user and for small offices by reducing the need for technical knowledge. Nevertheless, the off switch for these features is difficult to find and work with.

Using ipconfig to resolve DHCP address problems

Microsoft has been pushing the use of Dynamic Host Configuration Protocol (DHCP) for many years. However, DHCP is not infallible and there are several items you can fix with the `ipconfig` command.

The automatic IP addressing that we just discussed represents the basic issue — the host either received wrong information or didn't receive any information at all. To check the DHCP status of the adapter, you can use the `ipconfig /all` command, which provides the output seen here.

```
Windows IP Configuration

        Host Name . . . . . . . . . : hydra.scrimtech.com
        DNS Servers . . . . . . . . : 207.236.145.41
                                      207.236.145.40
        Node Type . . . . . . . . . : Broadcast
        NetBIOS Scope ID. . . . . . :
        IP Routing Enabled. . . . . : No
```

```
          WINS Proxy Enabled. . . . . : No
          NetBIOS Resolution Uses DNS : Yes

0 Ethernet adapter :

          Description . . . . . . . . : NDIS 5.0 driver
          Physical Address. . . . . . : 00-E0-18-C4-1A-56
          DHCP Enabled. . . . . . . . : No
          IP Address. . . . . . . . . : 192.168.0.1
          Subnet Mask . . . . . . . . : 255.255.255.0
          Default Gateway . . . . . . :
          Primary WINS Server . . . . :
          Secondary WINS Server . . . :
          Lease Obtained. . . . . . . :
          Lease Expires . . . . . . . :

1 Ethernet adapter :

          Description . . . . . . . . : Realtek RTL8029(AS)
          Physical Address. . . . . . : 00-40-05-5B-C6-A5
          DHCP Enabled. . . . . . . . : No
          IP Address. . . . . . . . . : 24.112.92.45
          Subnet Mask . . . . . . . . : 255.255.252.0
          Default Gateway . . . . . . : 24.112.92.1
          Primary WINS Server . . . . :
          Secondary WINS Server . . . :
          Lease Obtained. . . . . . . :
          Lease Expires . . . . . . . :
```

In this case, we want to look at the DHCP-enabled entry and make sure it's correct. If the host is supposed to be DHCP-enabled and it's not, then the IP configuration is probably wrong. Even if the client is correctly configured, the operating system may not be working correctly, so you may have to get rid of the existing information and try again.

You can use the `ipconfig /release` command to clear the information and then the `ipconfig /renew` command to have the system attempt to get a new address. Assuming these actions are successful, you should now be able to communicate. If not, manually check the IP configuration, since any locally configured values will block the values from the DHCP server. If you are not able to get a DHCP address when you try to renew, then the problem is not the configuration but the basic connectivity.

Checking the IP configuration for UNIX systems

As with the Windows environment, the UNIX environment includes graphical interfaces. Some of these utilities allow you to check the IP configuration and some don't. This section examines the `ifconfig` command, which is similar to — but more powerful than — `ipconfig`.

The basic `ifconfig` command will provide you with most of the configuration information you need. For example,

```
[root@www3 /etc]# ifconfig
eth0      Link encap:Ethernet HWaddr 00:00:E8:88:23:80
          inet addr: 48.53.66.9  Bcast:24.255.255.255  Mask:255.255.192.0
          UP BROADCAST RUNNING MULTICAST  MTU:1500  Metric:1
          RX packets:36215554 errors:6 dropped:0 overruns:0 frame:0
          TX packets:44883929 errors:7 dropped:0 overruns:0 carrier:0
          collisions:0 txqueuelen:100
          Interupt:11 Base address:0xd000
```

Again, we want to check the basic IP address and subnet mask. We also want to make sure the interface is UP. As you can see, we can't check the default gateway from here. Instead, we need to use the `route` command.

```
[root@www3 /etc]# route
Kernel IP routing table
Destination     Gateway         Genmask         Flags Metric Ref    Use Iface
48.53.64.0      *               255.255.192.0   U     0      0        0 eth0
127.0.0.0       *               255.0.0.0       U     0      0        0 lo
default         48.53.64.1      0.0.0.0         UG    0      0        0 eth0
```

We need to find the entry for the default (notice the G in the Flags column, which indicates the gateway). In this case, the default entry is the last line and points to the correct address. In some versions and derivatives, the default might be shown as 0.0.0.0 with a netmask of 0.0.0.0, or you might be required to use the `route print` command instead of just `route`. If these values are not correct, you will need to correct them.

Assuming that the configuration is okay, you move to the next step — checking connectivity. Start by making sure that the network cable is plugged into both the wall and the computer.

Testing Connectivity

When you are checking connectivity, you are simply trying to determine if the computer is able to talk on the network. Make sure the lights are illuminated on the back of the NIC. Most network cards have been given lights for just that purpose. You should also check that the collision light is not constantly on. If it is, you may have more serious problems, such as network saturation.

Let's break down the required functions that need to occur within a local system so that the system can effectively communicate with other hosts:

✦ The subnet mask, IP address, and configured gateway must be correct for the network segment.

✦ Your application needs to know the correct port and needs to be able to communicate with the sockets layer.

✦ The sockets layer must be able to pass data to the transport protocols TCP and UDP.

✦ TCP and UDP need to be able to package the information and communicate with IP.

✦ IP needs to be able to determine if the packet is for a local or remote network; if the packet is for a remote network, IP must have a route to that network.

✦ IP needs to be able to use ARP to determine the network card address of the next hop.

✦ IP needs to be able to pass the data to the network interface layer; in turn, the network interface layer must be able to use the physical layer to send the data on the wire.

✦ The physical layer must be connected to the network.

The best and fastest way to test nearly all of the problems listed above is ping. *Ping* is a simple utility that will send a packet from one system to another system and wait for a reply. In most cases, you test base connectivity using ping before you even check the IP address. Table 23-1 lists destinations that you can ping. Each eliminates a different problem (assume the local system is 48.53.66.7 netmask 255.255.192.0).

Table 23-1
Using Ping to Test TCP/IP

Destination	*Checks. . . .*
Ping 127.0.0.1 (the loop back address)	That the sockets layer is working and can talk to the transport layer. Makes sure that TCP/UDP can communicate with the IP layer and checks that the IP layer is able to read its routing table.
Ping 48.53.66.7 (the address of the local system)	That the IP layer is able to read the routing table. It also checks that the network interface layer properly registered the local IP address with the IP layer.
Ping 48.53.66.9 (the address of a nearby system on the same subnet)	That IP can use ARP to resolve addresses and ensures that the IP layer can send and receive data through the network interface and physical layers. It also makes sure the IP address is correct for the subnet.
Ping 48.53.120.1 (the address of a distant system on the same subnet)	That the subnet mask is not too restrictive and causing IP to see local hosts as remote hosts.
Ping 48.53.180.22 (the address of a remote system)	That the subnet mask is not too general, causing IP to see remote hosts as local. Also checks that the routing table is being used and that you are able to connect to your local gateway, thereby checking that the gateway address is correct.

Most of the possible problems that were listed earlier can be easily checked using ping. The exception is whether the services are using the right ports. You can check this easily enough by examining the services file (in the Windows directory for Windows 9x and ME, the Winnt\system32\drivers\etc directory for Windows NT/2000 and the /etc directory in most UNIX implementations).

If you are having a problem with a particular service that people are trying to connect to, you might check the services file (in addition to other basics, such as whether or not the service is running). The following listing is a quick look at the beginning of a service's file.

```
echo            7/tcp
echo            7/udp
discard         9/tcp     sink null
discard         9/udp     sink null
systat         11/tcp
systat         11/tcp     users
daytime        13/tcp
daytime        13/udp
netstat        15/tcp
qotd           17/tcp     quote
qotd           17/udp     quote
chargen        19/tcp     ttytst source
chargen        19/udp     ttytst source
ftp-data       20/tcp
ftp            21/tcp
telnet         23/tcp
smtp           25/tcp     mail
time           37/tcp     timserver
time           37/udp     timserver
rlp            39/udp     resource       # resource location
name           42/tcp     nameserver
name           42/udp     nameserver
whois          43/tcp     nicname        # usually to sri-nic
domain         53/tcp     nameserver     # name-domain server
domain         53/udp     nameserver
nameserver     53/tcp     domain         # name-domain server
nameserver     53/udp     domain
mtp            57/tcp                    # deprecated
bootp          67/udp                    # boot program server
tftp           69/udp
rje            77/tcp     netrjs
finger         79/tcp
link           87/tcp     ttylink
supdup         95/tcp
hostnames     101/tcp     hostname       # usually from sri-nic
iso-tsap      102/tcp
dictionary    103/tcp     webster
x400          103/tcp                    # ISO Mail
x400-snd      104/tcp
csnet-ns      105/tcp
```

```
pop                     109/tcp    postoffice
pop2                    109/tcp                       # Post Office
pop3                    110/tcp    postoffice
```

The format of the services file is very simple — protocol followed by port and transport protocol, and then an alias in some cases, and possibly a comment (after the # — as in "# ISO Mail"). The first 1,024 ports (from 0 to 1,023) are under the control of the Internet Assigned Numbers Authority (IANA) and are common to all platforms. After these first 1,024 ports, the port numbers used are specific to the application that you are trying to make work.

You should also be aware that the ports above 1,023 can also be used by clients that are connecting to the server. Typically, client software simply grabs a dynamic port above 1,023. You can use the netstat command to see the active connections. The output will look similar to this:

```
Active Connections

   Proto  Local Address          Foreign Address         State
   TCP    MEDUSA:1034            cyclops:ms-sql-s        ESTABLISHED
   TCP    MEDUSA:ftp             nic-31-c26-199.mn.mediaone.net:3161  CLOSE_WAIT
   TCP    MEDUSA:ftp             as2-5-7.dro.hs.bonet.se:1414  CLOSE_WAIT
   TCP    MEDUSA:ftp             pD953868C.dip.t-dialin.net:3704  CLOSE_WAIT
   TCP    MEDUSA:3389            cr32507-b.rchrd1.on.wave.home.com:2766
ESTABLISHED
   TCP    MEDUSA:ftp             h24-70-96-200.cg.shawcable.net:61186
ESTABLISHED
   TCP    MEDUSA:http            proxy1-external.hnsn1.on.home.com:3105
ESTABLISHED
   TCP    MEDUSA:http            proxy1-external.hnsn1.on.home.com:11891
ESTABLISHED
   TCP    MEDUSA:http            1Cust247.tnt4.krk1.da.uu.net:1789  ESTABLISHED
   TCP    MEDUSA:http            1Cust247.tnt4.krk1.da.uu.net:1790  ESTABLISHED
   TCP    MEDUSA:http            1Cust247.tnt4.krk1.da.uu.net:1791  ESTABLISHED
   TCP    MEDUSA:http            1Cust247.tnt4.krk1.da.uu.net:1792  ESTABLISHED
   TCP    MEDUSA:http            frasier.ford.com:25643  ESTABLISHED
   TCP    MEDUSA:http            frasier.ford.com:26175  ESTABLISHED
   TCP    MEDUSA:http            161.184.2.194:2284      ESTABLISHED
   TCP    MEDUSA:http            161.184.2.194:2285      ESTABLISHED
   TCP    MEDUSA:http            206.191.84.251:1843     ESTABLISHED
   TCP    MEDUSA:http            206.191.84.251:2295     ESTABLISHED
   TCP    MEDUSA:http            ppp-207-193-12-179.hstntx.swbell.net:1843
ESTABLISHED
```

You can check the ports that are open on a system using netstat -a, which is used to view all ports including listening ports. This will look more like the following:

```
Active Connections

   Proto  Local Address          Foreign Address         State
   TCP    MEDUSA:ftp             MEDUSA:0                LISTENING
   TCP    MEDUSA:smtp            MEDUSA:0                LISTENING
```

```
TCP    MEDUSA:domain          MEDUSA:0                LISTENING
TCP    MEDUSA:http            MEDUSA:0                LISTENING
TCP    MEDUSA:epmap           MEDUSA:0                LISTENING
TCP    MEDUSA:https           MEDUSA:0                LISTENING
TCP    MEDUSA:microsoft-ds    MEDUSA:0                LISTENING
TCP    MEDUSA:1025            MEDUSA:0                LISTENING
TCP    MEDUSA:1026            MEDUSA:0                LISTENING
TCP    MEDUSA:1029            MEDUSA:0                LISTENING
TCP    MEDUSA:1030            MEDUSA:0                LISTENING
TCP    MEDUSA:1032            MEDUSA:0                LISTENING
TCP    MEDUSA:1033            MEDUSA:0                LISTENING
TCP    MEDUSA:1034            MEDUSA:0                LISTENING
TCP    MEDUSA:3372            MEDUSA:0                LISTENING
TCP    MEDUSA:3389            MEDUSA:0                LISTENING
TCP    MEDUSA:netbios-ssn     MEDUSA:0                LISTENING
TCP    MEDUSA:1034            cyclops:ms-sql-s        ESTABLISHED
TCP    MEDUSA:ftp             nic-31-c26-199.mn.mediaone.net:3161  CLOSE_WAIT
TCP    MEDUSA:ftp             as2-5-7.dro.hs.bonet.se:1414  CLOSE_WAIT
TCP    MEDUSA:ftp             pD953868C.dip.t-dialin.net:3704  CLOSE_WAIT
TCP    MEDUSA:netbios-ssn     MEDUSA:0                LISTENING
TCP    MEDUSA:3389            cr32507-b.rchrd1.on.wave.home.com:2766
ESTABLISHED
TCP    MEDUSA:ftp             h24-70-96-200.cg.shawcable.net:61186
ESTABLISHED
TCP    MEDUSA:http            1Cust247.tnt4.krk1.da.uu.net:1789  ESTABLISHED
TCP    MEDUSA:http            1Cust247.tnt4.krk1.da.uu.net:1790  ESTABLISHED
TCP    MEDUSA:http            1Cust247.tnt4.krk1.da.uu.net:1791  ESTABLISHED
TCP    MEDUSA:http            1Cust247.tnt4.krk1.da.uu.net:1792  ESTABLISHED
TCP    MEDUSA:http            frasier.ford.com:25643  ESTABLISHED
TCP    MEDUSA:http            frasier.ford.com:26175  ESTABLISHED
TCP    MEDUSA:http            aigb35sqy1ue.ab.hsia.telus.net:2041  ESTABLISHED
TCP    MEDUSA:http            aigb35sqy1ue.ab.hsia.telus.net:2043  ESTABLISHED
TCP    MEDUSA:http            aigb35sqy1ue.ab.hsia.telus.net:2047  ESTABLISHED
TCP    MEDUSA:http            aigb35sqy1ue.ab.hsia.telus.net:2048  ESTABLISHED
TCP    MEDUSA:http            aigb35sqy1ue.ab.hsia.telus.net:2049  ESTABLISHED
TCP    MEDUSA:http            aigb35sqy1ue.ab.hsia.telus.net:knetd
ESTABLISHED
TCP    MEDUSA:http            161.184.2.194:2284      ESTABLISHED
TCP    MEDUSA:http            161.184.2.194:2285      ESTABLISHED
TCP    MEDUSA:http            ppp-207-193-12-179.hstntx.swbell.net:1843
ESTABLISHED
UDP    MEDUSA:epmap           *:*
UDP    MEDUSA:microsoft-ds    *:*
UDP    MEDUSA:1028            *:*
UDP    MEDUSA:1031            *:*
UDP    MEDUSA:3456            *:*
UDP    MEDUSA:domain          *:*
UDP    MEDUSA:1027            *:*
UDP    MEDUSA:domain          *:*
UDP    MEDUSA:netbios-ns      *:*
UDP    MEDUSA:netbios-dgm     *:*
```

```
UDP     MEDUSA:domain           *:*
UDP     MEDUSA:netbios-ns       *:*
UDP     MEDUSA:netbios-dgm      *:*
UDP     MEDUSA:domain           *:*
UDP     MEDUSA:domain           *:*
UDP     MEDUSA:domain           *:*
UDP     MEDUSA:domain           *:*
```

If you do find a problem using the `ping` command, the next step in troubleshooting is to determine what exactly is wrong. First, verify the configuration of the host you are working on and verify the information that it is receiving from the DHCP (if it uses one). If the configuration of the local system is correct, then you need to move to other possible solutions.

The first solution to a problem on systems that use a graphical interface such as Windows is to reboot the computer. Graphical operating systems tend to tie the base level functionality of the operating system into the graphical environment. These operating systems are all notorious for having memory management problems and occasionally a poorly written application running on one of these operating systems will affect the memory used by the OS for configuration or some important piece of code. To a large degree, this has been fixed in Windows NT, which is generally an exception to this rule.

Assuming the local station is okay, you need to test the connection to the remote host. You can use the `traceroute` utility to test the route that packets take from the local system through the routers and to the destination host. The `traceroute` command uses the same ICMP Echo Request command that ping uses; however, it starts with a Time to Live on the packet of 1. This forces the packet to time out on the first router, and it will return an ICMP message, telling the system it timed out. By sending packet after packet, incrementing the Time to Live for each, `traceroute` (`tracert` on Windows) builds a list of the routers the packets are passing through. `Traceroute` shows you the path as it goes along. The `traceroute` output looks like this:

```
Tracing route to hungryminds.com [168.215.86.100]
over a maximum of 30 hops:

  1    <10 ms    <10 ms    10 ms    207.236.145.33
  2     *        <10 ms    10 ms    10.30.235.1
  3    <10 ms     10 ms    10 ms    mtlcorr02-fe0-0-0.in.bellnexxia.net
[206.108.105.130]
  4    <10 ms     10 ms    10 ms    core1-montreal02-pos11-1.in.bellnexxia.net
[206.108.97.149]
  5     10 ms     20 ms    20 ms    Ncore2-newyork83-pos2-0.in.bellnexxia.net
[206.108.103.214]
  6     10 ms     20 ms    10 ms    bx2-newyork83-pos4-0.in.bellnexxia.net
[206.108.103.198]
  7     10 ms     20 ms    10 ms    jfk1-core1-s3-1.atlas.icix.net [165.117.50.253]
```

```
 8    10 ms    20 ms    10 ms   jfk3-core2-pos7-0.atlas.icix.net
[165.117.48.165]
 9    50 ms    50 ms    50 ms   ord2-core2-pos5-0.atlas.icix.net [165.117.48.38]
10    40 ms    50 ms    50 ms   ord2-core3-pos7-0.atlas.icix.net [165.117.48.94]
11    40 ms    40 ms    50 ms   ord2-core4-pos7-0.atlas.icix.net [165.117.48.98]
12    70 ms    70 ms    70 ms   dfw3-core1-pos5-0.atlas.icix.net [165.117.48.69]
13    70 ms    70 ms    70 ms   dfw3-core2-pos6-0.atlas.icix.net
[165.117.48.122]
14    70 ms    70 ms    70 ms   dfw3-core3-pos6-0.atlas.icix.net
[165.117.48.126]
15    70 ms    81 ms    70 ms   iah2-core1-pos6-3.atlas.icix.net [165.117.50.86]
16    70 ms    80 ms    70 ms   iah1-core2-s3-0-0.atlas.icix.net
[165.117.63.221]
17    70 ms    80 ms    80 ms   iah1-core1-fa10-1-0.atlas.icix.net
[165.117.57.81]
18   280 ms    80 ms    80 ms   206.181.103.170
19    90 ms    90 ms   221 ms   jr-01-at-0-1-0-4-155m.dlfw.twtelecom.net
[207.67.50.49]
20   100 ms   101 ms   100 ms   jr-01-so-0-0-2-155m.chrl.twtelecom.net
[207.67.84.53]
21   130 ms   140 ms   150 ms   jr-01-so-0-0-0-155m.iplt.twtelecom.net
[207.67.84.50]
22   140 ms   140 ms   230 ms   pa1-atm0-10-bbr01.iplt.twtelecom.net
[207.67.50.14]
23   140 ms   170 ms   140 ms   168-215-52-186.twtelecom.net [207.67.94.186]
24   140 ms   150 ms   141 ms   websrv.hungryminds.com [168.215.86.100]

Trace complete.
```

In this trace from a server in Montreal, Canada, to the Hungry Minds Web server in Indiana, the shortest path is not necessarily the one your packets are going to take. An * in the second line indicates a timeout. In fact, you occasionally get a hop where all three entries are timeouts. If all three tries time out, it indicates that the router timed out altogether. If the router times out time after time, you have found the problem — the router is down.

Another problem occurs when two systems on the network share the same IP address. This is not supposed to happen, but if it does, your system may resolve the MAC address to one system at first and to the other the next time.

If the address resolution protocol is not functioning properly, you will not be able to resolve an IP address to a MAC address. The Address Resolution Protocol utility, ARP.EXE, allows you to verify the ability to resolve addresses. ARP, as discussed in Chapters 4 and 5, resolves IP addresses to MAC addresses.

The only time you should have a problem with the ARP is if a static resolution is added to the ARP cache, which may be done for performance purposes. However, if the network adapter is changed in the system for which the IP address was entered, the mapping will cause problems. You can check for this problem by using the ARP utility to check the ARP table for static entries.

The ARP table contains the remote IP-to-MAC address mappings. Some clients or servers will have static entries in their ARP tables. If there are static entries, the address resolutions should be checked (and if the mapping is no longer valid, it should be discarded). On nearly all operating systems, you can check the ARP table with the `arp -a` command. The output looks like this:

```
Interface: 24.112.92.45 on Interface 0x3
  Internet Address       Physical Address       Type
  24.112.92.1            00-01-97-d5-25-00      dynamic
  24.112.92.10           00-80-c6-ea-e6-67      dynamic
  24.112.92.11           00-80-c6-ea-ef-1a      dynamic
  24.112.92.12           00-e0-29-1e-3f-a8      dynamic
  24.112.92.14           00-80-c6-f8-14-0f      dynamic
  24.112.92.16           00-a0-0c-c0-ff-ff      dynamic
  24.112.92.17           00-05-02-b7-3a-80      dynamic
  24.112.92.18           00-50-ba-1f-8e-ec      dynamic
  24.112.92.19           00-e0-29-10-fa-d3      dynamic
  24.112.92.20           00-80-c8-c1-f6-72      dynamic
  24.112.92.21           00-80-c6-f0-90-d7      dynamic
  24.112.92.23           00-80-c8-c1-e0-e5      dynamic
  24.112.92.26           00-00-21-d5-4c-e2      dynamic
  24.112.92.28           00-60-08-05-69-c1      dynamic
  24.112.92.31           00-80-c6-f0-1f-88      dynamic
  24.112.92.32           00-20-78-dc-16-fe      dynamic
  24.112.92.34           00-80-c6-f8-26-58      dynamic
  24.112.92.35           00-80-c8-de-78-1f      dynamic
  24.112.92.36           00-00-c0-0a-ce-f9      dynamic
  24.112.92.38           00-50-18-01-1a-f5      dynamic
  24.112.92.42           00-e0-29-63-a7-ba      dynamic
  24.112.92.47           00-80-c8-dd-55-18      dynamic
  24.112.92.49           00-80-c6-f1-72-85      dynamic
  24.112.92.50           00-50-18-01-76-6f      dynamic
  24.112.92.51           00-e0-29-33-1a-ff      dynamic
  24.112.92.53           00-e0-29-3a-8a-04      dynamic
  24.112.92.54           00-e0-29-0e-f6-67      dynamic
  24.112.92.56           00-50-ba-56-dd-4a      dynamic
  24.112.92.58           00-03-6d-00-78-22      dynamic
  24.112.92.59           00-04-5a-92-48-82      dynamic
  24.112.92.61           00-80-c6-ea-22-79      dynamic
  24.112.92.62           00-05-02-51-fb-5d      dynamic
  24.112.92.64           00-50-04-9b-7b-f0      dynamic
  24.112.92.65           00-e0-29-05-07-14      dynamic
```

In the output shown above, all of the systems are showing up as dynamic addresses. All you need to do to clear them is wait a few minutes. Typically, the ARP cache times out quickly to ensure that the correct address is always used.

Now that we've looked at basic connectivity, let's take a look at another major issue that you will face — name resolution.

Troubleshooting Name Resolution

A key area when it comes to troubleshooting is name resolution. In fact, one of the most common service calls is to reset a forgotten password.

Basically, there are two names that you will have to deal with and each is resolved in a different manner. The first, of course, is the host name — either in the form of a simple host name or in the form of a Fully Qualified Domain Name (FQDN) — and the second is the NetBIOS name for Microsoft networks or networks that use Samba.

Troubleshooting host name resolution

Host name resolution is surprisingly simple. In fact, most errors are due to typos, either at the station that is trying to connect or in the database files in the DNS server. The quickest way to determine if you are having a name resolution problem is to try pinging the name. If you can ping the server by the server's name, all of the underlying network pieces are functioning. Normally, this will be the first step you take in troubleshooting. If you cannot ping the server by name, you then perform the steps outlined in the previous section. A simple ping of a server might look like this:

```
Pinging www.dilbert.com [209.67.27.69] with 32 bytes of data:

Reply from 209.67.27.69: bytes=32 time=28ms TTL=241
Reply from 209.67.27.69: bytes=32 time=41ms TTL=241
Reply from 209.67.27.69: bytes=32 time=28ms TTL=241
Reply from 209.67.27.69: bytes=32 time=13ms TTL=241

Ping statistics for 209.67.27.69:
    Packets: Sent = 4, Received = 4, Lost = 0 (0% loss),
Approximate round trip times in milli-seconds:
    Minimum = 13ms, Maximum =  41ms, Average =  27ms
```

In this case, the server is up and running. You may have a name resolution problem if the system comes back with something like the following:

```
Unknown host fred.flintstone.com.
```

In this case, the system is trying to tell you that the server name could not be found; therefore, you will not be able to ping the server. Another problem you might encounter is one where the address resolves, but to the wrong address. Here is an example.

```
Pinging www7.AlzheimerCalgary.com [207.236.154.14] with 32 bytes of data:

Request timed out.
Request timed out.
```

```
Request timed out.
Request timed out.

Ping statistics for 207.236.154.14:
    Packets: Sent = 4, Received = 0, Lost = 4 (100% loss),
Approximate round trip times in milli-seconds:
    Minimum = 0ms, Maximum =  0ms, Average =  0ms
```

There are a couple of simple steps that you can take to determine if the problem is local or at the DNS server. First, check the hosts file and make sure it doesn't contain an entry for the item that you are trying to locate. Normally, the hosts file will be checked first to reduce traffic on the network. It is found in the Windows directory for Windows 9x and ME, in the Winnt\system32\drivers\etc directory for Windows NT/2000, and in the /etc directory for most UNIX implementations.

If the host is listed in the hosts file, ensure that the spelling is correct and that the IP address is correct. If so — and you can still ping the IP — then the problem is likely to be at the Application layer, or the server may have been moved and another server taken over the IP address.

Assuming that the name you're trying to reach is not in the hosts file, the next step is to ensure that the correct DNS server address is being used and that you can reach the DNS server. This is simply a matter of checking the IP address of the DNS server and trying to ping it. In the case of Windows operating systems, you can again use `ipconfig /all`. The DNS server information will be in the system-wide configuration for non-Windows 2000 systems and under the adapters in Windows 2000. For UNIX and derivatives, it's best to consult your documentation (some will store the name server address in a file and others in memory).

Assuming the name server address is correct, you need to check the address of the server you are trying to connect with on a DNS server. If the name server you are using should have the address (in other words, is authoritative for the zone), then you will next want to check the name server and ensure the name is in correctly and that the IP address for the name is also correct. If this is the case — and you can ping the server by the IP address — you need to look at the Application layer. If you can't ping the address, the server or part of the network is probably down.

Note
In Windows 2000 and some variants of UNIX, the DNS service has become dynamic. In other words, the servers and clients will register with the DNS server rather than make it necessary for an administrator to enter the information. You might have to force the server to reregister its name to IP making it the DNS server.

If the DNS server is not authoritative for the zone, then it is acting for the resolution as a caching-only server. This means that it will need to get the address for the server from another DNS server, either in your network or on the Internet. In this case, the problem could be with the remote DNS server or with the network in between. Here, you want to quickly check and make sure that all parts of your network are functioning up to the point where the resolution request is timing out. If you can ping the host (you must know the IP) and only the name resolution isn't working, you can temporarily add the name-to-IP resolution to the hosts file.

> **Note**   Since a static mapping can lead to other problems if the remote system changes locations, and therefore IP addresses, the name-to-IP address mapping should be removed as soon as possible.

If you still haven't found the problem, you can use a tool called the nslookup utility, which allows you to see what resolution the name server will give for different names. This tool is available on Microsoft Windows NT/2000 and on most UNIX implementations. There are two operating modes for nslookup: query mode, where you send the server a simple query, and interactive mode, where you can use the standard `ls` command to list information about the contents of the server. The following is an example of the standard query mode:

```
nslookup www.GolfCanada.com

Server:   localhost
Address:  127.0.0.1

Name:     www.GolfCanada.com
Address:  48.53.66.7
```

Standard queries cover both forward and reverse lookups. The interactive mode will allow you to get a little more specific about the type of record that you are looking up. For example, a lookup for a mail exchanger (mx) record looks like this:

```
> ls -t mx Scrimger.org
[cyclops.scrimtech.com]
 Scrimger.org.              MX    10   mail.Scrimger.org
>
```

In most cases, if the host name is not resolving but you have the IP address, you can simply use the IP address and not be concerned with the name at all. This is *not* the case with NetBIOS names. In the TCP/IP world, a combination of the IP address and the socket number or port is used to identify the service that you want to use. Together, the IP address and port number form a *socket*, which is one end of a connection (the other being the IP address and port number of the client). Imagine trying to deliver a package to a building in downtown New York City with only a street address — as you pull up to the skyscraper, you quickly realize that without a suite number, you have a serious problem. The same is true of data going to a host that has twenty or thirty services running.

The host name really isn't important (as long as you have the IP address and port number or the socket) because TCP/IP was developed to handle networking in a large dispersed network. NetBIOS, however, was developed for use on a single segment network, and therefore doesn't work this way — for NetBIOS, the name is the network identity of the computer.

Troubleshooting NetBIOS name resolution

When NetBIOS was developed, no one saw a real need for wide area networks beyond the existing mainframe solutions. Therefore, NetBIOS was developed to use the friendly name of the computer as the address rather than something like an IP address or IPX node number. Thus, in order to get to the right server, you need to know the correct name.

The 15-character NetBIOS name is the network identity of a NetBIOS system. In the early 1980s, these systems were intended to use NetBEUI (which was designed specifically to work with NetBIOS names) as their transport protocol. There is a 16th character to the NetBIOS name, which is the service number. The service number identifies the service that you are connecting to on the computer, just like the port number in TCP/IP. For any NetBIOS name, there can only be 256 service numbers; however, more than one NetBIOS name can be registered on a computer. Therefore, we come to a simple truth, as shown in Table 23-2.

Table 23-2
Comparing TCP/IP and NetBIOS

	Native TCP/IP	NetBIOS
Network Identifier	TCP/IP Address	NetBIOS Name
Service Identifier	Port Number	Service Number

At this point, you must connect to the station with the correct IP using the right port to communicate using native TCP/IP. Therefore, you need to connect to the correct computer name and the correct service number when using NetBIOS networking.

There is a further problem. NetBIOS is not intended for use outside a single network segment and performs all name resolution functions using broadcasts. Since these broadcasts would flood the networks if routers ever passed them, routers don't forward broadcasts. Therefore, all the name functions of native NetBIOS are restricted to a single segment, which defeats the purpose of TCP/IP.

Because NetBIOS name functions are restricted to a single segment, it has had to be retrofitted to work in a multi-segment network. A couple of approaches were used to solve this problem. The first was to use a simple file — similar to the hosts file — named lmhosts (the lm stands for LAN Manager). This simple file would list the servers and their IP addresses. It included the ability to point out which of these servers were authentication servers (domain controllers). The other solution was to create a server that would manage the NetBIOS name functions.

In the early days, when TCP/IP and NetBIOS were used together, there were usually a small enough number of servers that it wasn't a problem to maintain the file. However, this started to change — the number of updates to the file became difficult to maintain and administration became a problem, primarily because the file, like the hosts file, had to be located on each client machine.

This leads to the centralized lmhosts file. In this scenario, the local lmhosts file on each system would list authentication servers and the address of a central server (or servers) that had the full copy of the lmhosts file. In this way, the client could grab the resolutions from the central server as needed; it didn't have to constantly update its local copy of the lmhosts file.

Finally, when Microsoft released Window NT, it put out a service that was similar to DNS but that dealt specifically with NetBIOS names. Technically known as a *NetBIOS Name Server (NBNS),* the service in Windows NT was named *Windows Internet Naming Service (WINS).* WINS allowed for the dynamic registration of names, as well as name renewal, resolution, and release.

When it comes to fixing a problem with name resolution, many of the same steps that were used for DNS can also be followed. Again, check the configuration of the workstation and verify that the IP address of the NBNS or WINS server is correct. Try pinging the server to ensure that (at the very least) the server itself is running. And check the server to ensure that the name you are looking for is actually there.

One of the problems with troubleshooting NetBIOS name problems is that the way the tools the client will use to resolve the name is not fixed. There are, in fact, four different ways a NetBIOS client can work with the tools that are available for name resolution. The particular method a client will use is set by the node type and can be viewed using the `ipconfig /all` command. In the output, you will see a line that tells you the node type: Broadcast, Peer-to-Peer, Mixed, or Hybrid. Typically, the node type will either be Broadcast (for stations with no WINS server address configured) or Hybrid (for those that have a WINS server address). The node type is probably the first thing you should check if the basic information seems accurate.

Next, check the NetBIOS name cache for any preloaded entries. In some cases, preloaded entries are used to speed up the connection to a particular server; however, if the IP address of a server changes, the lmhosts file (from which the information is loaded) needs to be changed as well. You can check the name cache using the `nbtstat -c` command, which displays the cache. The output might look like this:

```
C:\WINNT\system32\drivers\etc>nbtstat -c

External:
Node IpAddress: [207.236.145.40] Scope Id: []
```

```
                    NetBIOS Remote Cache Name Table

        Name              Type        Host Address    Life [sec]
        -------------------------------------------------------------
        WEB          <1C>  GROUP        192.168.7.8        -1
        MINOTAUR     <03>  UNIQUE       192.168.7.8        -1
        MINOTAUR     <00>  UNIQUE       192.168.7.8        -1
        MINOTAUR     <20>  UNIQUE       192.168.7.8        -1

Internal:
Node IpAddress: [192.168.1.2] Scope Id: []

                    NetBIOS Remote Cache Name Table

        Name              Type        Host Address    Life [sec]
        -------------------------------------------------------------
        WEB          <1C>  GROUP        192.168.7.8        -1
        CYCLOPS      <03>  UNIQUE       192.168.1.1        -1
        CYCLOPS      <00>  UNIQUE       192.168.1.1        -1
        CYCLOPS      <20>  UNIQUE       192.168.1.1        -1
```

In this case, the Life columns are all set to –1, which indicates that the names are all preloaded. We might try removing the #PRE directive in the lmhosts file and reloading the cache using `nbtstat -R`. The client will use the WINS server to locate the server it is looking for, and the problem might be resolved. Microsoft operating systems come with a file called lmhosts.sam, which explains all the options you can put into the lmhosts file.

Assuming that all of the configuration you've already looked at is fine, there are now some new problems to contend with. In DNS, the name space is arranged in a hierarchical way. That is, different levels exist. When you try to resolve a name, you can also go to the root level using the FQDN and work your way back to the system you're trying to find. This is *not* the case with WINS or NBNS servers. By its very design, the NetBIOS name space is a flat name space. Thus, there may be literally tens of thousands of names in the WINS database for an organization (especially since all of the systems, including client-only computers, will register their names).

DNS uses the hierarchical name space because the number of hosts that it has to deal with would swamp a single server. WINS must face the same challenge. The solution in the case of WINS, however, was to add several servers as peers and configure the servers to replicate. This means that part of troubleshooting WINS is being able to troubleshoot problems with replication.

Troubleshooting replication means checking the IP addresses in the WINS manager for the two servers involved and ensuring that at least one is a push partner and one is a pull partner. In reality, they should be both — unless you have designed your WINS infrastructure specifically to work in a hub-and-spoke configuration.

If all else fails, you can try to add the resolution to the lmhosts file. If this resolves the problem, you should take a serious look at the WINS servers, since they may have a corrupt database or may not be replicating properly.

Verifying the Client and Server

The last part of troubleshooting you will really need to check internally is the actual client and server. Technically, the *client* is a software package that runs on a computer, and the *server* is a package that runs on a server, which might be the same computer or a different computer. As with all software, there is the possibility that a server to which you are trying to connect isn't running, isn't running right, or isn't configured for connections right now.

In general, a quick test to see if the service is running in the native TCP/IP world is to try talking to another service on the system. If you can connect to Telnet but not to FTP, the problem lies with the FTP server or client. You can try connecting to the FTP service from another station or to a different FTP server from the local station, which will help you determine on which end the trouble lies.

The same test can be used with NetBIOS. If you can't connect to the server service, try using `net send` to send a message to the system. You can also use the `net view` command to read the shares on other systems and determine whether the client is working. One of the most common NetBIOS world problems is permission, and you can test to see if this is the problem by trying to map the drive at the command line where you will see the error message.

Remember, the problem isn't necessarily the client — it could be the server. You should also remember that you probably have more permissions than the user. So try the permissions once you've successfully connected.

Summary

Troubleshooting systems can be a difficult process. Some may even say it's more of an art than a science. Hopefully, this chapter has simplified the troubleshooting process by breaking it down into a set of easy-to-follow steps. Remember, computers are devices that follow a certain logic. If you understand the logic, you should be able to easily identify the source of the problem.

✦   ✦   ✦

Monitoring TCP/IP Networks

Y ou should now be at a point where your network is
installed, all services are running correctly, and
your users are happy. Unfortunately, your work as a system
administrator doesn't end there. Maintenance begins — the
actions you must take to ensure that the network continues
to run within its design parameters.

There are two approaches to maintaining a network. First, you
can assume that the network will continue to run the way it is
supposed to and respond to problems as they occur. Because
administrators are often overtaxed, this approach is common.
Second, you can *constantly* monitor your network, ensuring
that the servers continue to run at optimum levels. If you
have the resources, constant monitoring is a better approach
and will often let you deal with issues proactively.

Administrators who take this approach will also use information
from the monitoring process to plan server upgrades and
replacements and continue to tune the network until every
last piece of it is working close to 100 percent. However, this
approach entails time and patience, and many companies don't
see the value in it. As stated earlier, most organizations deal
with problems only when they arise.

In many cases, a small amount of monitoring will yield
tremendous results. In this chapter, we discuss various
monitoring tools. We start by looking at the steps you should
take to monitor a server and then those you should take to
monitor traffic that's actually on the network. We will limit
our discussion to the tools that accompany the different
operating systems; because there are literally thousands of
third-party utilities for UNIX and the Windows platform, it
would be impossible to include all of them.

We continue by examining the function of the Simple Network Management Protocol (SNMP). The chapter concludes with a discussion of TCP window size (the majority of TCP/IP tuning) and the Maximum Transmission Unit (MTU).

Monitoring the Physical Hardware

When it comes to monitoring a server, you first need to know exactly what type of server you have. There are different hardware requirements — and slightly different configurations — for different servers. Server resources can be broken down into four main areas that affect performance. It is the combination of the resources in these four areas that will determine how well a server will perform a given task, and therefore, your monitoring should concentrate on these:

  ✦ **Processor** — The number and speed of CPUs in the system

  ✦ **Memory** — The amount and speed of physical RAM in the system

  ✦ **Disk** — The type of disks (SCIS or IDE), their speed, access time, and configuration (RAID or not)

  ✦ **Network** — The number of network cards, their speed, and how they connect to the network (gigabit switch, hub, and so on)

The combination of the resources in the four hardware areas determines how well the computer will perform in a given role (for example, authentication server versus application server). If you are running Windows 2000 and you have less that 256MB of RAM, then the other factors — disk, network, and CPU — don't matter. You could, in fact, have 0 + 1 RAID (mirrored stripe sets) configured and eight network connections to each of your network segments and eight 900 MHz Xeon processors. The system won't run well, since the memory will become a bottleneck. On the other hand, 2GB of RAM in a system that is running a Duron 600 won't really make it much faster than if it had 512MB of RAM.

A balance has to be achieved between the resources on the system. Our discussion now turns to the different roles that a server can perform. Remember that in some cases, a server performs simultaneous roles; thus, special attention needs to be given to ensuring that the system has sufficient resources to perform all its tasks.

Considerations for authentication servers

The process of authentication might include sending and receiving information to and from the user, possibly encrypting messages, hashing messages to check signatures, decrypting messages, and checking users against a list of users and passwords. There is also a requirement to share users' information with other servers on the network (especially in the case of Microsoft networks).

The requirements for authentication dictate that some CPU ability is required — notably the ability to perform math (since the encryption/decryption is algorithm based). In addition, the ability to deal with network traffic for the actual authentication and for sharing information with other authentication servers is important. The account information about a user will be relatively small; thus, account databases won't be large in size compared to other databases. So there won't necessarily be a great deal of disk activity. Since there aren't likely to be many updates after the initial configuration, most of the information can be cached.

You should make sure that an authentication server has good network I/O and a reasonably powerful processor. In addition, sufficient RAM is required, enough to cache account information. The disk is less important that the other three hardware areas since there aren't likely to be thousands of updates every day.

Considerations for file and print servers

A file or print server transfers files of various sizes across the network. File transfers are aided greatly by both read-ahead and write-behind caching. The disk subsystem comes into play here — especially on a file server, since the files will actually reside on the server. The CPU, on the other hand, is not overly active, since moving files is handled primarily by the BIOS. There will be some security issues to deal with, but certainly not to the extent that there are with the authentication servers.

When it comes to the four hardware areas, the network is important, as is the disk subsystem. The memory will come into play, since we certainly don't want the system to have to start swapping memory to disk. In addition, using the memory for caching will help balance the performance of the network and disk systems when one or the other gets temporarily overloaded. The CPU is still important; however in this case, it is the least important area.

Considerations for application servers

When it comes to application servers, you must consider the type of application that the server will be running. For example, if you are running a file-based mail system, you are really running a file server, not a mail server. On the other hand, an active mail system such as Microsoft Exchange or Lotus Notes requires a great deal more CPU and memory (since both of CPU and memory are essentially databases).

Typically, most application servers fall into one of two categories. The server application will essentially be a file server (such as a mail server or a Web server without extensions, like ASP or Orbs) or a database server (such as Microsoft Exchange or a news server). Since we have already discussed file servers, let's look at the requirements for a database server, bearing in mind that the required resources depend on the exact server.

In general, a database server has large — perhaps even enormous — files. The database server may frequently be called on to run through the file, find a specific piece of information, and return this to the user. Therefore, the database server needs to have a strong disk subsystem. Since all of the data will need to get into RAM before the CPU can perform any work on the data, memory again comes into play. Whether RAM is more or less important than CPU depends on the amount of work that the server performs with the data. If every single piece of data needs to be encrypted on disk, the CPU will be more important than the RAM; otherwise, RAM is probably more important than CPU. In this case, the queries that are sent to the server are typically small, and the responses are also small relative to the data set. Therefore, the network component on the system is less important than the other hardware areas.

Again, there are no absolutes. You need to examine the specific requirements for your application server and for your network and how you have configured the users to interact with the application server. As an example, consider an office where desktop applications are kept on the server rather than on the desktop. In this case, the main hardware resource for file and print servers will be the network, not the disk. Memory will also be more important than disk, since you want as much as possible to answer requests from RAM and not have to touch the disk. However, you can *never* assume this based on the last time you set a similar application server — you need to monitor the systems and see specifically how the current system works.

Monitoring tools

During the design phase of your network, perform some testing to determine what hard resources you need. Then, after implementation, test again to ensure that the real world lives up to this testing. The requirement for testing means you need tools to help you monitor the services that you are putting on a server. These tools will vary, depending on your operating system. First, we examine a tool called Microsoft Performance Monitor (known simply as Performance in Windows 2000). We then look at a few common UNIX tools that do about the same job as Performance Monitor.

Microsoft's Performance Monitor

As its name suggests, the Performance Monitor that appeared in Windows NT is a useful tool for monitoring performance of a computer or service. The tool is built to interact with any service that you install on a system and can be used directly on the system. You can also use Performance Monitor from a remote system, which will reduce the impact of monitoring on the results.

The information that you look at in the Performance Monitor can come from a captured log file or from live data. Because you can view data from a log file, you can capture performance information over a period of time and then view and analyze the information later. In Windows NT, scheduling the system to capture performance data meant using the AT command and some fancy settings; in Windows 2000, scheduling the system to capture performance data is easily set up in the Performance Logs, and can even be started using a performance condition. Furthermore, the information can be gathered from more than one computer so different computers can be compared to each other. The information that you can monitor is broken down in a logical fashion:

- ✦ **Computer** — You can choose the computer that you want to monitor.

- ✦ **Object** — This is the area or application that you want to monitor on the computer.

- ✦ **Counter** — After you choose the object that you want to monitor, a list of aspects of that object are listed for you.

- ✦ **Instance** — In some cases, you will have a service or application running on the computer more than once. Each running copy of the service or application is considered a separate instance. You can choose to monitor all instances collectively, or a single instance of an object. For example, if a computer has four drives, you could choose to monitor just the drive that stores the print files for a print server.

When working with Performance, or any monitoring tool, remember that the load a single client station will put on a system will be different in many cases from the load that two or five or twenty will add. In other words, you can't monitor the load that a single client places on the system. The first client station may load up the cache, or start the service, or wake up the service, and so on. When monitoring, it is important to test what a single client does to a server — as well as what two or five or twenty do — so you get a real feel for the load.

Also, remember that not every client will use resources at the same time. For example, if you have a call center where 150 users take service calls from across the country, they do not all request or send information to the server at the same time — they will be talking part of the time, typing part of the time, and so on. In the case of a file server, the number of likely simultaneous clients is even less, since it is unlikely that everyone will try to save a file at exactly the same moment.

Monitoring performance on UNIX systems

While the Microsoft world has a single tool — Performance Monitor — that does close to everything, the UNIX world has many different tools, including add-in tools that can be found on such places as the Internet. Given that fact, this section discusses the basic tools that should be included with all (or at least close to all) versions of UNIX. Keep in mind that differences between versions may exist, so check the `man` pages if you get "strange" results (`man` is a UNIX command that will help on whatever topic you enter. For example, `man ifconfig` brings up help — the manual page — on the `ifconfig` command).

The following list covers most of the common commands that can be used to check the performance of a UNIX server:

✦ **uptime** — The `uptime` command returns one line of text displaying the current time, how long the system has been running, how many users are currently logged on, and the system load averages for the past one, five, and fifteen minutes. The load averages are the average number of processes ready to run during the last one, five, and fifteen minutes.

✦ **w** — The `w` command displays information about users that are currently on the machine and their processes. First, it shows the information from the `uptime` command and usage information per logged-on user. The Information includes the login name, the tty name, the remote host, the login time, the idle time, JCPU, PCPU, and the command line of their current process. The JCPU is the amount of time for any process the user is currently running through this connection including background processes. The PCPU is the process time for the current interactive process only.

✦ **top** — The `top` command gives you a real-time view of processor activity. It displays a listing of the most CPU-intensive tasks on the system, and has an interactive interface mode where you can manipulate the processes. You can sort the tasks by CPU usage, memory usage, and runtime. The output from this command includes the following:

  • **uptime** — Displays the same information as the `uptime` command.

  • **processes** — The total number of processes running at the time of the last update, and a breakdown of the running processes into the number of processes that are running, sleeping, stopped, or undead.

  • **CPU states** — Shows the percentage of CPU time in user mode, system mode, niced tasks, and idle. Time spent in niced tasks will also be counted in system and user time, so the total will be more than 100 percent.

  • **mem** — Memory usage statistics, including available total memory, free memory, used memory, shared memory, and memory used for buffers.

  • **swap** — Swap space statistics, including total swap space, available swap space, and used swap space.

✦ **ps** — The `ps` command provides information similar to the `top` command; however, if you use different options with the `ps` command, you can get more information on a single process.

✦ **pstree** — The `pstree` command provides a view of the running procedures in a tree format so that parent-child relationships can easily be seen.

✦ **/proc** — Like everything else in UNIX, running processes are also treated as files so that permissions can be set (instead of treating them like objects, as in Windows NT/2000). /proc is the pseudo directory structure where the processes live. Here, you can find several files that provide you with detailed information about running processes.

✦ **vmstat** — The `vmstat` command provides information on processes, memory, paging, block IO, traps, and CPU activity. The first time you run `vmstat`, the report that is produced gives averages since the last reboot. Additional reports give information on a sampling period of a given length of delay.

✦ **df** — The `df`, or disk free, command displays information about the amount of disk space available.

✦ **free** — Using `free` displays the total amount of free and used physical and swap memory in the system, as well as the shared memory and buffers used by the kernel.

There are many different commands that can be used as tools to measure performance in UNIX systems. In addition to these, there are quite literally hundreds of others.

The important thing to keep in mind, though, is that you want to balance system resources and provide enough hardware resources for the server to successfully perform its different roles. It doesn't make sense to have 1GB of RAM in a system that will be used for word processing. Now that we have discussed the tools that are used to monitor server performance, let's take a look at the different tools that are used to monitor the network.

Tools for Monitoring the Network

As you might have guessed, the best server in the world won't do you the least bit of good if the network is so busy that no one can access it — or if the network is so error-prone that systems have to retransmit constantly. In this section, we take a look at some of the tools you can use to check the network's performance.

To start, think back to the beginning of Chapter 23, where we discussed connecting to a remote Web server "from the 10,000-foot perspective." This is the same perspective we need to have when monitoring the network. Consider a network that has five subnets that contain the users, the subnets each connected to the backbone where the servers are located through a router. In this case, ensuring that any single server can push data straight to a gigabit Ethernet switch at full speed won't make a difference if the network on the other side of the switch is bogged down, or if one or more of the networks on the other side of the routers are saturated.

Many of the tools that are used for troubleshooting are also going to be useful for ensuring successful network performance. We start with the simplest of the tools — ping. So far, we have used ping to determine connectivity and to identify the source of the problem in the local stack. However, we can also use it to identify the source of network problems.

Using ping to monitor the network

Ping is the most popular tool in the TCP/IP world. However, many people don't make use of its full capabilities. Besides simply checking basic connectivity, ping can be used to determine Maximum Transmit Segment Size (MTSS), which indicates how large a packet you can send along a path without fragmentation. We will use this information later when we talk about tuning the TCP/IP window size. Determining the MTSS is accomplished using the –l (length) and –f (don't fragment) switches and changing the length of the packet until it no longer gets through without fragmenting.

You can also use ping when you are setting up the routing environment in your network. This is especially important if you plan to use static routing in your network. With the –j (loose source route) and/or –k (strict source route) switches, you can try passing packets through different sets of routers and using different paths so you can determine the best set of routers to go from point to point. Ping and these switches can also be used to ensure that your routing protocol is giving you the best possible route; if it's not, you can change the cost of going through some routers to ensure that the best path is, in fact, used.

Note   The –j switch (loose source route) is also available for the traceroute (tracert) utility.

The –r switch (record route) can be used with the `ping` command to give you a quick look at the route packets are taking. This switch is also useful for monitoring and optimizing your routing topology.

Using netstat to monitor the network

We've already seen that the `netstat` command can be used to determine what network connections you have with other systems and what ports you have that are listening (services). There are two switches that can change the way the `netstat` command works. The –n switch stops `netstat` from resolving IP addresses and port numbers and displays the information in numeric-only format. This reduces the time it takes to display the information. If you set an interval value so that the information is refreshed periodically, the –n switch is useful since the system won't have to resolve the IP addresses to names.

The –p switch lets you choose to only view one protocol: TCP, UDP, or IP. It can also speed up the display and remove the extraneous data from the screen. For example, the following output uses the –a, –n, and –p switches together to look quickly at some specific information.

```
C:\>netstat -a -n -p TCP

Active Connections

    Proto  Local Address         Foreign Address          State
    TCP    0.0.0.0:21            0.0.0.0:0                LISTENING
    TCP    0.0.0.0:25            0.0.0.0:0                LISTENING
    TCP    0.0.0.0:53            0.0.0.0:0                LISTENING
    TCP    0.0.0.0:80            0.0.0.0:0                LISTENING
    TCP    0.0.0.0:135           0.0.0.0:0                LISTENING
    TCP    0.0.0.0:443           0.0.0.0:0                LISTENING
    TCP    0.0.0.0:445           0.0.0.0:0                LISTENING
    TCP    0.0.0.0:1025          0.0.0.0:0                LISTENING
    TCP    0.0.0.0:1026           0.0.0.0:0               LISTENING
    TCP    0.0.0.0:1029           0.0.0.0:0               LISTENING
    TCP    0.0.0.0:1030           0.0.0.0:0               LISTENING
    TCP    0.0.0.0:1032           0.0.0.0:0               LISTENING
    TCP    0.0.0.0:1033           0.0.0.0:0               LISTENING
    TCP    0.0.0.0:1034           0.0.0.0:0               LISTENING
    TCP    0.0.0.0:3372           0.0.0.0:0               LISTENING
    TCP    0.0.0.0:3389           0.0.0.0:0               LISTENING
    TCP    192.168.1.2:20        192.168.1.1:4509         TIME_WAIT
    TCP    192.168.1.2:20        192.168.1.1:4511         TIME_WAIT
    TCP    192.168.1.2:21        192.168.1.1:4512         ESTABLISHED
    TCP    192.168.1.2:139       0.0.0.0:0                LISTENING
    TCP    192.168.1.2:1034      192.168.1.1:1433         ESTABLISHED
    TCP    217.236.145.40:21     24.31.26.199:3161        CLOSE_WAIT
    TCP    217.236.145.40:21     62.155.219.72:1612       CLOSE_WAIT
    TCP    217.236.145.40:21     194.236.217.102:1414     CLOSE_WAIT
    TCP    217.236.145.40:21     212.179.232.173:3984     CLOSE_WAIT
    TCP    217.236.145.40:21     217.83.134.140:3704      CLOSE_WAIT
    TCP    217.236.145.40:139    0.0.0.0:0                LISTENING
    TCP    217.236.145.40:3389   24.112.92.45:3704        ESTABLISHED
    TCP    217.236.145.42:21     24.70.96.200:61186       ESTABLISHED
    TCP    217.236.145.42:80     206.98.210.9:42221       ESTABLISHED
    TCP    217.236.145.42:80     206.98.210.9:42423       ESTABLISHED
    TCP    217.236.145.42:80     216.154.50.72:1191       ESTABLISHED
    TCP    217.236.145.42:80     216.154.50.72:1192       ESTABLISHED
    TCP    217.236.145.44:80     24.42.182.247:3656       ESTABLISHED
    TCP    217.236.145.44:80     24.42.182.247:3662       ESTABLISHED
    TCP    217.236.145.44:80     24.69.255.202:43919      ESTABLISHED
    TCP    217.236.145.44:80     24.69.255.203:29360      ESTABLISHED
    TCP    217.236.145.44:80     24.69.255.203:29394      ESTABLISHED
    TCP    217.236.145.44:80     24.69.255.204:20832      ESTABLISHED
    TCP    217.236.145.44:80     24.69.255.204:20835      ESTABLISHED
    TCP    217.236.145.44:80     24.69.255.205:7256       ESTABLISHED
    TCP    217.236.145.44:80     24.71.223.140:43896      ESTABLISHED
    TCP    217.236.145.44:80     205.200.178.107:3160     ESTABLISHED
    TCP    217.236.145.44:80     205.200.178.107:3162     ESTABLISHED
    TCP    217.236.145.44:80     205.200.178.107:3167     ESTABLISHED
```

In the code listing above, the output uses a numerical format and is focused on the TCP protocol. The entries with 0.0.0.0:0 as the foreign address are listening ports — that is, a service has opened the port and is listening for clients that want to connect. By adding a number (*x*) at the end of the command line, you could have the data refresh every *x* number of seconds. Having the information refresh can be useful to watch a connection from a remote system if you know the IP address. The information at the end of the line lets you follow through all the connection states. The following list describes the states that netstat will report:

✦ **CLOSED** — The TCP session has been closed.

✦ **FIN_WAIT_1** — The connection is being closed.

✦ **SYN_RECEIVED** — A session request has been received.

✦ **CLOSE_WAIT** — The connection is being closed.

✦ **FIN_WAIT_2** — The connection is being closed.

✦ **SYN_SEND** — A session is being requested.

✦ **ESTABLISHED** — A session currently exists between the systems.

✦ **LISTEN** — A service has performed a passive open on a port.

✦ **TIMED_WAIT** — The session is currently waiting for activity from the other computer.

✦ **LAST_ACK** — Your system has made a last acknowledgement.

You can also use netstat -r to show the routing table, and to show the current Ethernet statistics using netstat -e. The output will look like the following:

```
C:\>netstat -e
Interface Statistics

                          Received            Sent

Bytes                   4081977305        3955519850
Unicast packets           18629760          21377538
Non-unicast packets          51740             11234
Discards                         0                 0
Errors                           0                 0
Unknown protocols          2349364

C:\>
```

The Ethernet statistics give you a quick breakdown of the traffic that is present on the network—how much traffic there is and (by looking at the Discards and Errors) how much of that traffic is bad traffic. To obtain more detailed information about the TCP/IP protocols, you can use the –s switch to get per protocol statistics, as seen in the following output:

```
C:\>netstat -s

IP Statistics

    Packets Received                     = 18647515
    Received Header Errors               = 0
    Received Address Errors              = 0
    Datagrams Forwarded                  = 0
    Unknown Protocols Received           = 0
    Received Packets Discarded           = 0
    Received Packets Delivered           = 18647487
    Output Requests                      = 21404452
    Routing Discards                     = 0
    Discarded Output Packets             = 0
    Output Packet No Route               = 0
    Reassembly Required                  = 31
    Reassembly Successful                = 3
    Reassembly Failures                  = 23
    Datagrams Successfully Fragmented    = 0
    Datagrams Failing Fragmentation      = 0
    Fragments Created                    = 0

ICMP Statistics

                              Received      Sent
    Messages                  4172          4066
    Errors                    10            0
    Destination Unreachable   2776          3228
    Time Exceeded             488           20
    Parameter Problems        0             0
    Source Quenches           90            0
    Redirects                 15            0
    Echos                     742           76
    Echo Replies              6             742
    Timestamps                0             0
    Timestamp Replies         0             0
    Address Masks             0             0
    Address Mask Replies      0             0
```

```
TCP Statistics

    Active Opens                    = 56720
    Passive Opens                   = 400635
    Failed Connection Attempts      = 4056
    Reset Connections               = 118408
    Current Connections             = 16
    Segments Received               = 18218773
    Segments Sent                   = 20675882
    Segments Retransmitted          = 301091

UDP Statistics

    Datagrams Received   = 421972
    No Ports             = 48378
    Receive Errors       = 0
    Datagrams Sent       = 418751
```

There is a lot of information shown in the code listing, so we'll look at the sections individually.

IP statistics

This first section to look at is IP Statistics. In the example output, we see a fairly good set of statistics. Even if a few errors exist, the ratio of errors to packets received and delivered is so small as to be insignificant (less than a few percent). For example, the total number of errors is 23 (all reassembly failures). If we compare that number to the 18.6 million packets that were received without error, we realize the percentage of errors is inconsequential. In reality, the errors in the output could be seen as either intentionally or unintentionally malformed packets — an attempt to hack the server (this happens to be a Web server). If the ratio of bad to good data were much higher, we'd be concerned.

ICMP statistics

In the ICMP Statistics section, we like to see the total of all types of ICMP packets stay fairly low. In general, these values will indicate whether there is a problem of some sort. In this case, the number of ICMP messages is fairly low compared to the total number of packets sent using IP.

For the sake of completeness, let's look at the important individual values. The first item, Errors, is just that, an error. This is normally a bad packet where the IP information was okay but the ICMP header info was corrupted. The Destination Unreachable line could be of concern if the number were larger. This means the server, or one of the routers between the server and the host, could not find a route to the destination host.

The Time Exceeded line gives you the number of packets that could not be delivered because they timed out on the network. If this number is high on your internal network, then you probably have one or more segments that are swamped and the routers on that network segment cannot keep up with the load. If the connection is external, then the network at your ISP or the Internet is congested. The Parameter Problems lines listed the number of packets that requested an unsupported function or in which some of the data had been corrupted.

If the Source Quench messages were significant, it would indicate a problem with the upstream router. A router sends a source quench when it can't handle the traffic it's receiving and wants the sender to "shut up." An ICMP Redirect tells the sender (the server, in this case) to use a different gateway. If you see a significant number in the Redirects line — over 50 percent — you would want to consider changing the default gateway for this server.

Echo and Echo Reply are better known as ping, which uses these functions. If you see a very high number of these messages, you might consider logging some network traffic, as a ping attack is the simplest type of denial-of-service attack. Timestamps and Address Masks messages are normally seen in the UNIX world; these are requests for information (the time from a server or its subnet mask) — again, if the number is significant, you will want to find out who is sending this type of ICMP message.

TCP statistics

In the TCP Statistics section, the number of active and passive opens is listed. An active open is the server making a connection (in this case, to the SQL server), and a passive open is a service that is waiting (listening) for connections. Hopefully, the number of failed connection attempts (caused by network errors or malformed packets) is as low as possible. Reset Connections refers to the number of sessions the server has closed, normally because the connection has timed out. Current Connections is useful if you are performing load testing to see how many people can be connected to the system at the same time.

Typically, the number of segments sent and received should be close to the number of IP packets sent and received. The Segments Sent and Segments Received values are a measure of TCP traffic or session-oriented traffic, so if the server is a media server which multicasts on a continuous basis, these numbers will be much smaller than the IP numbers. The last value, Segments Retransmitted, is also an important indicator of overall network performance. If this number is high, a larger number of packets are not reaching their destination. This could mean a problem with router delay or router error, and should be looked at. In the sample output, the Segments Retransmitted value is 301,091. If you divide this by the Segments Sent, 20,675,882, you find that only 1.46 percent of traffic has to be retransmitted, which is fine for the Internet.

UDP statistics

The last section in the sample output is UDP Statistics. The values you find here depend on the type of server. In this case, the server is also a DNS server; therefore, high numbers are not a problem. The fact that some 10 percent (No Ports divided by Datagrams Received) is going to No Port would be a concern on an internal network. On the Internet, it just represents hackers trying to see what ports are open on the server.

As you can see, netstat allows us to quickly check the status of a server. Of course, this check won't be comprehensive, especially if the server is using NetBIOS. However, as we discovered in Chapter 23, there is a NetBIOS version of the netstat command, called nbtstat.

Using nbtstat to monitor NetBIOS sessions

nbtstat will give us information about the NetBIOS sessions on a system, including information on names and name resolution.

The –c switch, which we talked about in Chapter 23, provides the names from the NetBIOS name cache. In addition, several switches enable you to see the names that are registered on your system or another system on the network. For example, the –n switch provides a list of names that are registered on the local machine. The output looks like this:

```
C:\>nbtstat -n

HomeNet:
Node IpAddress: [192.168.0.1] Scope Id: []

             NetBIOS Local Name Table

        Name              Type         Status
    ---------------------------------------------
    HYDRA          <00>  UNIQUE      Registered
    SCRIMGER       <00>  GROUP       Registered
    HYDRA          <20>  UNIQUE      Registered
    HYDRA          <03>  UNIQUE      Registered
    SCRIMGER       <1E>  GROUP       Registered
    INet~Services  <1C>  GROUP       Registered
    SCRIM          <03>  UNIQUE      Registered
    IS~HYDRA.......<00>  UNIQUE      Registered
    SCRIMGER       <1D>  UNIQUE      Registered
    .._MSBROWSE__.<01>  GROUP       Registered
    HYDRA          <01>  UNIQUE      Registered
```

```
Internet:
Node IpAddress: [48.53.66.7] Scope Id: []

                  NetBIOS Local Name Table

         Name                 Type          Status
      ---------------------------------------------------
      HYDRA            <03>  UNIQUE      Registered
      INet~Services    <1C>  GROUP       Registered
      SCRIM            <03>  UNIQUE      Registered
      IS~HYDRA.......<00>  UNIQUE      Registered
      HYDRA            <01>  UNIQUE      Registered
```

Using `nbtstat -n` will help ensure that the name people will try to connect with has been registered by the system on the network. With the –a and –A options, you can look at the names registered on a remote machine. The –a specifies the remote machine name, and the –A lets you specify the remote machine by IP address. The results are similar to those for –n.

The –r switch allows us to see the names that were found either by broadcast or by using WINS. However, it does not display the names that are preloaded using the lmhosts file.

The switch used for monitoring is the –s or –S switch, which displays a list of NetBIOS sessions that are currently active. The –s or –S switches let you monitor when a session passes through the various stages. The Status column indicates the current state of the NetBIOS connection. In fact, the connection can be in many different states, as seen in the following list:

✦ **Connected** — A NetBIOS session has been established between the two hosts.

✦ **Associated** — Your system has requested a connection and has resolved the remote name to an IP address. This is an active open.

✦ **Listening** — This is a service on your computer that is currently not being used. This is a passive open.

✦ **Idle** — The service that opened the port has since paused or hung. No activity will be possible until the service resumes.

✦ **Connecting** — At this point, your system is attempting to create a NetBIOS session. The system is currently attempting to resolve the name of the remote host to an IP address.

✦ **Accepting** — A service on your system has been asked to open a session and is in the process of negotiating the session with the remote host.

+ **Reconnecting** — After a session has dropped (often due to timing out), your system tries to reconnect.

+ **Outbound** — A TCP three-way handshake is in process, which will establish the Transport layer session that will be used to establish the NetBIOS session.

+ **Inbound** — This is the same as outbound, except that a connection is being made *to* a service on your system.

+ **Disconnecting** — The remote system has requested that a session be terminated, so the session is being shut down.

+ **Disconnected** — Your system is requesting that a session be terminated.

The –s and –S switches can be useful if you're trying to monitor a NetBIOS application and want to watch it through all the session states. However, at this point we are still looking at the network from the server's point of view. To really understand the traffic that you are dealing with, it is useful to see the actual data on the network itself.

Working with sniffers to capture network traffic

The basics of a packet analyzer (or packet sniffer) are simple. Since the media, Ethernet or Token Ring, is broadcast based, every system on the network receives every packet that is sent on the network. In most cases, the Media Access Control (MAC) address is of no interest, so the packet is silently discarded. However, suppose that instead of being choosy, the network card accepted any packets that came along and put them in a file?

The result would be a file containing all the traffic circulating on your network. You could then look at the packets and analyze the information. To do this, packet analyzers need to put the network card in a mode called Promiscuous — a mode in which all traffic is accepted and passed up the stack. This data can then be read from the file as text or interpreted using a tool such as Network Monitor. In the following sections, we will look at two different tools: the relatively simple snoop command from Solaris, and more complex Network Monitor from Microsoft.

Using snoop

Snoop is a program that puts your network card into Promiscuous mode and captures all packets on your network, in either real time or capture file format. First, you need to decide whether you want real-time data to flash across your screen or whether you want to capture packets to a file. Realistically, the data would move across the screen too quickly to be useful. Therefore, you will normally have to capture the data to a file, since you won't be able to read the data flashing across your screen. To start the capture process, use the snoop command like this:

```
#snoop -o filename
```

All data will be saved in binary format to a file called `filename`. In this case, all traffic will be captured until you stop the program, so it might be handy to tell Snoop how many packets to capture (using the –c switch). You can also control the amount of information that is gathered using snoop by choosing the Operation mode. By default, snoop is in Summary mode, which provides only basic information. Here is an example of the Summary mode output:

```
85 0.01548 hydra -> TEST.FODDER.COM TELNET C port=5633
```

You can also choose to be in the Verbose Summary mode or the Full Verbose mode. To use the Verbose Summary mode, add –V to the command line. The output will now look like this:

```
85 0.01548 hydra -> TEST.FODDER.COM ETHER Type=0800 (IP), size
= 58 bytes
85 0.01548 hydra -> TEST.FODDER.COM IP D=217.53.64.1
S=48.53.66.7 LEN=44, ID=5232
85 0.01548 hydra -> TEST.FODDER.COM TCP D=23 S=5633 Syn
Seq=82349322 Len=0 Win=8760
85 0.01548 hydra -> TEST.FODDER.COM TELNET C port=5633
```

In this case, we can see what's happening at each of the layers and can, in fact, tell that the output packet shown in the code is the first step in the TCP three-way handshake. Finally, if you want (or need to), you can obtain detailed information about the packet that is crossing the network by using the –v switch. The output will look like this:

```
ETHER:  ----- Ether Header -----
ETHER:
ETHER: Packet 85 arrived at 15:26:11.47
ETHER: Packet size = 58 bytes
ETHER: Destination = 8:0:20:3d:dc:a1, Sun
ETHER: Source = 8:0:20:ec:8f:7a, Sun
ETHER: Ethertype = 0800 (IP)
ETHER:
IP:  ----- IP Header -----
IP:
IP: Version = 4
IP: Header length = 20 bytes
IP: Type of service = 0x00
IP: xxx. .... = 0 (precedence)
IP: ...0 .... = normal delay
IP: .... 0... = normal throughput
IP: .... .0.. = normal reliability
IP: Total length = 44 bytes
IP: Identification = 6082
IP: Flags = 0x4
IP: .1.. .... = do not fragment
IP: ..0. .... = last fragment
IP: Fragment offset = 0 bytes
IP: Time to live = 255 seconds/hops
IP: Protocol = 6 (TCP)
```

```
IP: Header checksum = 6045
IP: Source address = 48.53.66.7, hydra
IP: Destination address = 217.53.64.1, test.fodder.com
IP: No options
IP:
TCP: ----- TCP Header -----
TCP:
TCP: Source port = 5633
TCP: Destination port = 23 (TELNET)
TCP: Sequence number = 82349322
TCP: Acknowledgement number = 0
TCP: Data offset = 24 bytes
TCP: Flags = 0x02
TCP: ..0. .... = No urgent pointer
TCP: ...0 .... = No acknowledgement
TCP: .... 0... = No push
TCP: .... .0.. = No reset
TCP: .... ..1. = Syn
TCP: .... ...0 = No Fin
TCP: Window = 8760
TCP: Checksum = 0x6de1
TCP: Urgent pointer = 0
TCP: Options: (4 bytes)
TCP: - Maximum segment size = 1460 bytes
TCP:
TELNET: ----- TELNET: -----
TELNET:
TELNET: ""
TELNET:
```

In the real world, you normally start with the Summary or Verbose Summary modes to get a feel for what's happening on your network and then use the Verbose mode to look at specific problems. Keep in mind that the more data you capture, the more load will be placed on the system that is performing the capture. It is possible to overload the system, which will force it to drop packets.

The next question, of course, is how to read the information. Again, you use the snoop command but with the –i switch (input) and the filename. This lets you display the information. You can even use –p to tell the system which packets you want to see. This brings up an interesting point. If capturing data in Verbose mode may potentially overload the system, isn't there some way to capture only the data we need?

The answer is yes. You can use snoop's filtering capabilities to capture only specific packets of data from the network. Some possible options include filtering by the hostname or the IP address or by the MAC address. The traffic direction can also be filtered using "to" and "from." In addition, more than one condition can be placed using the "and" and "or" operators and you can filter out traffic using the "!" or "not" operators. You can also filter by the transport protocol, using "tcp," "udp," or "icmp," and you can filter data based on the port number.

As you can see, Snoop is a powerful packet analyzer that allows you to capture and filter traffic and analyze traffic one packet at a time if you wish. It doesn't, however, run on Microsoft platforms. In that case, you are required to use Network Monitor.

Using Network Monitor

Both snoop and Network Monitor are packet analyzers. Both will capture and save traffic and allow you to analyze it afterwards. Both also provide you with a real-time mode. The function of Network Monitor is the same as snoop; however, the form is very different, and for those who are not familiar with packets and their structure, the Network Monitor is easier to use. Network Monitor comes with several different protocol parsers and will actually do much of the interpretation of the captured packets for you — displaying the captured information in an easy-to-read format.

Be aware that there are different versions of the network monitor. One version comes with Systems Management Server (SMS). Another version shipped with Windows NT, but it can only capture data to or from the local system and has no replay or editing capabilities The version that comes with SMS does allow you to put the network card in Promiscuous mode and to capture all the data on the network.

The Network Monitor comes in two pieces: the Network Monitor Driver (Agent in Windows NT), which is used to actually capture the data that will be analyzed. The other part is the Network Monitor itself, which is a tool that enables you to work with the information that is captured.

Working with Network Monitor is simple. Open the Network Monitor tool and, if requested, tell it which network card you want to capture from. It will list the cards using the MAC address, so you might have to use `ipconfig /all` to determine the MAC address of the card you want to monitor on. Once the tool is open, you can either set up the filtering to reduce the packets you will capture, or you can simply start capturing using Capture ➪ Start from the menu.

While you are capturing, you will see four information panes, providing real-time information about the data being captured. These panes, and the information they include, are:

✦ **Graph** — This pane includes bar charts that dynamically display current activity on the network. There are five bars, including % Network Utilization, Frames Per Second, Bytes Per Second, Broadcasts Per Second, and Multicasts Per Second. A small line will appear in each of the bars, giving you the maximum capture level for that bar.

✦ **Total Statistics** — This pane displays cumulative network statistics summarizing network traffic in five areas: Network Statistics, Capture Statistics, Per Second Statistics, Network Card (MAC) Statistics, and Network Card (MAC) Error Statistics.

✦ **Session Statistics** — This pane displays statistics about sessions that are currently operating on the network.

✦ **Station Statistics**—This pane displays statistics about sessions in which this computer is participating.

Unlike snoop, the data is being captured to a memory buffer, which means that Network Monitor is less likely to drop packets. You can change the size of the buffer under Capture; Buffer Settings let you control how much information you want to keep. If the buffer is filled, older data is discarded to make room for new entries. When you are finished capturing, you can either use Capture ➪ Stop to stop the capture, or Capture ➪ Stop and View to jump right into viewing the data. You can also save the data to a file for later analysis.

At first glance, the capture will look like the summary mode from snoop — a list of all the packets that were captured. When you choose any frame and double-click on it, you can zoom into the frame to get more detail. The original summary pane will still be displayed at the top; however, a detail window and a hex window will also appear. The detail window initially looks like the Verbose Summary mode shown for snoop, and the hex window is just that — raw data in hexadecimal. As you click on different parts of the frame, the related data will be highlighted in the hex pane.

What's nice is that you can now double-click on the information shown in the details pane and drill down to the part of the packet that you want to see. Once the information that you want to see has been opened up, you can click through a series of entries in the summary pane and watch the series of events unfold.

Showing you the captured data is the basic function of Network Monitor. There are many different ways to filter data: by editing the data and retransmitting it; by using the "experts" to determine the protocol distribution on your network; and so on. You can even configure Network Monitor to use a monitor driver on another computer to capture data remotely.

Of course, there are countless other network sniffers — some with more features and some with less. However, you need to find the one that works best on your platform.. The information from a network packet analyzer can be a little overwhelming at first, but it can be very useful for tuning, troubleshooting, and security. Another tool you might need on your network to perform monitoring is Simple Network Management Protocol (SNMP).

Simple Network Management Protocol

Simple Network Management Protocol (SNMP) enables you to remotely troubleshoot and monitor hubs, routers, and other devices. Using SNMP, you can glean information about remote devices without having to be physically present at the device itself and without the device having a user interface. Many of the hardware devices you will use have some form of built-in SNMP so that you can remotely administer them.

SNMP consists of three different parts: the agent, which is part of the hardware device or software that will be managed; the management station, which enables you to monitor these devices and software; and the Management Information Bases (MIBs), which provide a common naming scheme between agents and management stations.

Using SNMP, monitoring the network can be centralized in almost any size network. SNMP uses UDP on ports 161 and 162 for all of its functions, meaning that the network traffic is small and that a session is not required between the hosts for communications. On the other hand, security is a concern with SNMP. Allowing just anyone to read your SNMP information, intentionally or unintentionally, can be a problem since SNMP can give out a lot of information — notably from Microsoft operating systems.

The Internet Engineering Task Force (IETF) is currently trying to find a more secure management protocol that will work with as many different types of devices as SNMP does. In the meantime, the security for SNMP is handled by setting the community name.

Community names

A community is really a management group for a set of hosts running the SNMP service. A community will consist of at least one management station and one or more agents. Communities are given a community name, which is like a group name you would create for security. In most implementations, the default community name is public — this name should generally be changed, so that if someone is trying to get at the information, they won't know the community name.

Other than using community names, no established security exists for SNMP. The data is not encrypted. No specific setup will stop someone from accessing the network, discovering the community names and addresses used using a sniffer, and then sending fake requests to agents to read your data. This is why most of the information available through SNMP is read-only, preventing unauthorized changes. Most implementations will allow you to specify which stations the agent can respond to and will allow you to configure a station to which the SNMP agent will send authentication errors (called traps).

The SNMP management system

The management system is the main component in SNMP. Generally, it is a piece of software that will run on a system and allow you to query the different agents and read values from them. In addition, management stations will generally let you set up watch values and automatic queries, essentially allowing the management software to watch the network and alert you if there is a problem.

Again, SNMP is a simple protocol, and SNMP allows the management station to send only a few commands. The management station will send the query to the agent on port 161 UDP. If the community names are the same, and the agent hasn't been configured to not respond to the station, it will return the information to the management station on the same port. The commands that are available to all systems are:

✦ **get** — This is a request for a specific value.

✦ **get-next** — This requests the next object's value, which is useful in cases where you may have several instances of the same object (for example, several IP addresses on the same NIC).

✦ **set** — This command is supposed to change the value of the object. In general, objects are read-only because of the lack of security in SNMP.

In each case, an OID or object ID would be given to tell the agent what value you want to see or set. The object ID relates to the MIB.

The SNMP agent

The SNMP agent is primarily responsible for answering the queries of the management station. The agent could, however, send a trap, which is an exception or error, to the management station. The management station could then take action on the condition normally logging the information. There are options that you can usually configure on the SNMP agent:

✦ **Contact** — The contact name of the person you want to alert about conditions on this station.

✦ **Location** — A descriptive field for the computer to help find the system sending the alert.

In addition, there is normally a place in the agent configuration to set the services the agent manages. This is a list of the type of items that the agent can be monitoring:

✦ **Physical** — The agent is managing physical devices, such as repeaters or hubs.

✦ **Applications** — The agent uses or provides an application that uses TCP/IP.

✦ **Datalink/Subnetwork** — The agent is managing a bridge.

✦ **Internet** — The agent is an IP router.

✦ **End-to-End** — The agent uses TCP/IP to communicate.

As you can see, the agent is a very basic tool, which allows it to be built in to firmware that can go in many different devices.

Management Information Base

A Management Information Base (MIB) is really just a set of variables that describe the objects that can be managed on an agent. An object identifier is used to reference the variables. The management station can query the value of the variable and, in some cases, set it. However, if every manufacturer was allowed to simply make up object identifiers, there would be a problem — what's called number 8 by one manufacturer might be called something entirely different by another manufacturer.

To prevent this type of inconsistency, the numbering of MIB variables (or object identifiers) is managed by the International Standards Organization (ISO). A manufacturer can apply to the ISO for a MIB and receive the starting point for their object identifiers, which is like an assigned IP address. They can then add to the assigned object identifier, and can even create a hierarchy for different product lines, and within that, different products, and so on.

Each object then has a completely unique object identifier and object name. For example, the TCP/IP or Internet MIB II is `Iso.org.dod.internet.mangement.mibii`, and its object identifier is 1.3.6.2.1. Obviously, numbers, rather than names, are used by the SNMP protocol for purposes of communication, although the name is displayed in the management software for us. In most cases, you can add MIBs as you add objects that will be managed — as long as you add them to both the agent and the management station.

SNMP is a useful tool for managing large networks and is one of the few tools that works over great distances. The only issue with SNMP is security. Now that we have taken a look at the tools that you use to monitor your network, lets take a quick look at the TCP Window Size. This parameter is the only universal tuning parameter in TCP/IP and will affect the speed at which data can be transmitted.

Tuning TCP Window Size

TCP uses a system of sliding windows for transferring data between machines. Each machine has both a send and receive window that it uses to buffer data and make the communication process more efficient. Communications are more efficient because the window can "slide" across the data, meaning that the data does not have to be broken down into messages. Instead, the data inside the window is sent and acknowledged and then the window moves on.

A receive window allows a machine to receive packets out of order and reorganize them while it waits for more packets. This reorganization may be necessary, since IP cannot guarantee the orderly delivery of packets. Changes in network conditions, congestion at routers, or other problems may cause some of the packets to arrive late or to be lost altogether. Since the size of the transmit window will be set to the size of the receive window during session establishment, the sizing of the receive window can affect the network performance of the system.

The sliding window process is relatively simple. During the session setup, the size of the transmit window is set to the same size as the receive window, and the two stations will exchange and synchronize sequence numbers. The transmit window is placed at the beginning of the data that is in buffer waiting to be sent. The data in the window is taken in sequence and packed into TCP segments as the data and each segment is sent with the appropriate sequence number.

The receiving system will receive the segments from the IP layer and place them in the receive window in the order of sequence numbers contained in the packets. When the receive window contains a series of packets that are in order, an acknowledgement is sent, indicating the next sequence number that is expected. As the receive window fills, it slides past the received data; as the acknowledgements are received at the transmitting station, the transmit windows slide past the acknowledged data and more data is sent.

Following this logic, the window size really determines the amount of data that can be on the network at a single time. The window size should be set as an even multiple of the Maximum Transmit Segment Size that was mentioned during our discussion of ping to ensure that only full segments will be on the network. However, setting the size can lead to some serious problems with communications.

If you set the window size too small, you can never place much data on the network. This would be fine if data really did move from point A to point B instantly. However, what will happen is that you will get the small amount of data on the network and then have to wait until it is acknowledged before you transmit the next piece of data. If the window size is too large, you will have problems jamming it through the network and will end up with fragmentation, which will slow down the process. You also run the risk of running out the retransmit timer and resending the packet just because the receiver has not got it all yet. Like most things, you should work with this in a lab before considering making changes in the production environment.

For most operating systems, the window size is already set correctly for Ethernet. There will be cases where you will need to determine the best window size. As was pointed out earlier, you will use the `ping` command with the –f and –l switches to do this. The –f switch sets the "do not fragment" flag on the packet and the –l sets the packet size.

Using the `ping` command with these switches, you will start trying to ping the remote sever with large packets. You will get a message that the packet needs to be fragmented but the do not fragment switch was set. Eventually, you will get a response from the remote server. You now need to work between the last value that didn't work and the value that did to narrow down the exact value of the maximum transmit segment size.

In the following code listing, you can see the start of this process. In the end, the maximum transmit segment size ended up being 1,472 bytes.

```
C:\>ping 24.42.96.14 -n 1 -f -l 3000
Pinging 24.42.96.14 with 3000 bytes of data:
Packet needs to be fragmented but DF set.

C:\>ping 24.42.96.14 -n 1 -f -l 2000
Pinging 24.42.96.14 with 2000 bytes of data:
Packet needs to be fragmented but DF set.

C:\>ping 24.42.96.14 -n 1 -f -l 1000
Pinging 24.42.96.14 with 1000 bytes of data:
Reply from 24.42.96.14: bytes=1000 time=201ms TTL=122

C:\>ping 24.42.96.14 -n 1 -f -l 1500
Pinging 24.42.96.14 with 1500 bytes of data:
Packet needs to be fragmented but DF set.

C:\>ping 24.42.96.14 -n 1 -f -l 1250
Pinging 24.42.96.14 with 1250 bytes of data:
Reply from 24.42.96.14: bytes=1250 time=221ms TTL=122

C:\>ping 24.42.96.14 -n 1 -f -l 1325
Pinging 24.42.96.14 with 1325 bytes of data:
Reply from 24.42.96.14: bytes=1325 time=210ms TTL=122

C:\>ping 24.42.96.14 -n 1 -f -l 1400
Pinging 24.42.96.14 with 1400 bytes of data:
Reply from 24.42.96.14: bytes=1400 time=241ms TTL=122

C:\>ping 24.42.96.14 -n 1 -f -l 1450
Pinging 24.42.96.14 with 1450 bytes of data:
Reply from 24.42.96.14: bytes=1450 time=241ms TTL=122

C:\>ping 24.42.96.14 -n 1 -f -l 1475
Pinging 24.42.96.14 with 1475 bytes of data:
Packet needs to be fragmented but DF set.
```

The next factors you need to consider when setting the TCP window size are network reliability and speed. If you allow your system to place a large number of packets in the send window, the network must be able to reliably transport them to the remote station. Your network also has to be able to get all of the transmitted packets to the remote for it to respond before the retransmit timer expires. If you place a large number of packets in the send window, all the data can be sent quickly. If the network cannot handle this, you will end up retransmitting, which will not increase performance.

The number of packets in the send window is determined by trial and error. A good starting point is eight packets in the window. Take the number of packets and multiply it by the maximum transmit segment size. The value is the receive window size that you want to use. Set this value using ifconfig in UNIX or in the Registry for Windows. Once it is set and any required reboots are made, try transmitting data between two hosts.

Use netstat to determine the number of re-transmissions that take place. If there are none, try increasing the number of packets in the window. If there are many and the transfer is slow, reduce the number of packets in the window. Continue this process until you are transferring data as fast as possible without re-transmissions. As a quick note, you should use the same file for all tests, and for the most accurate results, you should use two systems when testing and configure them both with the same window size.

Remember, though, that this will only optimize traffic between two hosts. When you communicate with another host using a system where you have set the window size, the results may vary. Always note the original size so you can change the value back.

Summary

This chapter focused on monitoring the network, and discussed some of the common tools that are used to perform this task. To truly understand monitoring, you will need to work with these tools to gain firsthand experience of their capabilities. Remember, however, that different servers have different hardware resource requirements and these are usually a combination of memory, CPU, disk subsystem, and network. Network monitoring and the TCP/IP sizes are really just a part of the larger whole.

✦ ✦ ✦

Planning for the Future

It's time to take a look at the latest technological trends and how they will affect our work and home environments in the future. We start by discussing IPv6, which was first recommended as a replacement for IPv4 in 1994. Over the next few years, we should see IPv6 taking hold. It won't replace IPv4 in our lifetime, but it will become the predominant protocol for certain devices that are coming to market in the near future. We will then take a brief look at the world of wireless Internet. As more and more users become mobile and as the traditional workplace changes, new communication technologies will be developed, just as the pager and the cell phone were developed in the 1980s. Many of today's cell phone manufacturers and Personal Digital Assistant/Personal Information Manager (PDA/PIM) makers are fighting to combine these two products into a single device. Already, devices such as the Neopoint phone and the Nokia Communicator have been developed. In addition, other devices, such as Blackberry from Research in Motion, can help you stay connected "24/7." These devices and smart appliances will probably be the first to use the IPv6 address space.

TCP/IP will also be invading the household (for better or worse) in the area of appliances that connect to the Internet. This goes far beyond Web TV, which is actually showing up on Web server hit counters. NCR, an appliance manufacturer, has already developed a Microwave Bank that allows you to check your bank balance on a touch screen built into the door of the microwave. Various manufacturers are in the process of developing refrigerators that allow you to surf the Internet from a built-in screen on the door. It seems that there is a market for this kind of technology — especially since manufacturers are willing to spending millions of dollars to develop it. These devices will probably be using the IPv6 stack.

Towards the end of the chapter, we'll discuss how to cope with the technological changes that are taking place. We start now with a discussion of IPv6, since most of the new technology will depend on a sufficient amount of address space.

Looking at IPv6

As stated earlier, the current standard for the IP protocol is IPv4. Work on IPv6 (or IPng) began in 1991, but the protocol wasn't officially recommended as a replacement for IPv4 until an IETF meeting in Toronto in 1994. One of the main reasons for the development of IPv6 was the growth in the number of hosts that were connected to the Internet. This growth threatened to consume all of the address space from the Internet and also made the resulting routing architecture difficult to manage. At the time, these were serious issues that needed to be addressed.

Obviously, IPv6 was not the only solution that was offered. Other solutions were developed, namely the Network Address Translation (NAT) protocol, and the proxy server (which is based on NAT). The NAT protocol and the proxy server allowed companies to use private network addresses internally and still be able to access the Internet. This greatly reduced the number of IP addresses to a few addresses for items (such as the proxy server, the mail server, and the Web server) that any one company needed to have for each connected system.

Still more reduction in IP address use was required, since the system of address classes in IPv4 required that a company be assigned a complete class "C" address block — at least 254 addresses. Thankfully, it was discovered that subnetting could be done at the ISP level, as well as the company level, which allowed the ISPs to split the class "C" addresses so that each company could be given the approximate number of addresses they required.

The concept of Classless Internet Domain Routing (CIDR), or supernetting, could also be used to combine several small addresses — for example, a group of class "C" addresses into something that looked and acted like a class "B", or part of one. This allowed companies that needed more than 254 addresses to have those addresses as a single block. As a result, the *entire* company could be viewed as a single address for routing purposes.

The routing problem on the Internet was helped to a large degree by Variable Length Subnet Masking (VLSM), which allowed a hierarchy to develop in Internet routing and made routing more efficient.

Given these additions to the IPv4 world, the necessity for IPv6 seemed to slip. However, as was pointed out earlier, IPv6 will probably become more common — not on the Internet proper, but in wireless Internet and smart appliances. This will lead to large, almost separate networks, that will connect to the Internet proper using dual stack routers (routers that provide both IPv4 and IPv6 capabilities).

The size of the Internet today makes it *highly* unlikely that we will see IPv6 on the Internet proper — especially since all the routers would have to be replaced in the entire world at the same time. There might be a long transition period, during which compatibility would be managed with tools like dual stack routers. This would (in essence) start to build the Internet mark II. As companies that need the capabilities of IPv6 work with each other, they will create their own connectivity. In the end, we are likely to end up with two Internets: the one we know today and another using IPv6 that handles wireless Internet and smart appliances.

Changes from IPv4

IPv6 introduces several changes to the IPv4 protocol. These changes make the protocol much more flexible and reliable and provide almost unlimited address space. The following is a list of the major changes:

- ✦ **Expanded routing and addressing capabilities** — IPv6 increases the IP address size from 32 bits to 128 bits. This supports more levels of the addressing hierarchy and a much greater number of addressable nodes.

- ✦ **IPv6 adds a scope field to multicast addresses** — This creates a new type of address, called an *anycast address*. It can be used to identify sets of nodes where a packet sent to an anycast address is delivered to one of the nodes.

- ✦ **Header format simplification** — Some IPv4 header fields have been dropped or made optional. This reduces the cost of packet handling and keeps the bandwidth overhead as low as possible (despite the increased size of the addresses).

- ✦ **Improved support for options** — The new IP header encodes options in such a way as to allow for more efficient forwarding and fewer limits on the length of options, resulting in the flexibility to introduce new options in the future.

- ✦ **Quality-of-service capabilities** — A new capability is added to enable the labeling of packets belonging to particular traffic "flows" for which the sender requests special handling, such as non-default quality of service or "real-time" service.

- ✦ **Authentication and privacy capabilities** — IPv6 includes the definition of extensions, which provide support for authentication, data integrity, and confidentiality.

In addition to the basic parts of the IPv6 header, IPv6 has the ability to include a header extension. By using the header extension, designers have made future extensions to the protocol possible without having to redefine the entire protocol.

These extension headers are located between the actual header and the transport layer protocol. Therefore, any device that is not aware of the extension headers can ignore them. In this way, routers will typically not need to look at the extensions reducing the overhead on the router. Extension headers are also no longer limited to 40 bytes; the fact that headers are separate from the IP header means they can be essentially any length; in addition, multiple headers are possible. Some of the headers that have already been defined include those listed here:

✦ Routing

✦ Extended Routing (like loose source route)

✦ Fragmentation

✦ Fragmentation and Reassembly

✦ Authentication

✦ Integrity and Authentication Security

✦ Encapsulation

✦ Confidentiality

✦ Hop-by-Hop Options

✦ Destination Options

Obviously, more special headers will be developed over time to enable wireless Internet and smart appliances to communicate.

IPv6 addressing

In IPv6, the address has changed dramatically. When you first look at an IPv6 implementation, you notice that there are now 128 bits in the address, instead of 32. This provides an incredibly large number of addresses: 340,282,366,920,938,463,463,374,607,431,768,211,456 to be exact.

There are still unicast addresses (direct transmission to another computer), as well as multicast addresses (sending information to multiple computers that are tuned in). In addition, a new type of address (the anycast address) allows a packet to be directed at an IPv6 address. Any number of hosts that are configured with the anycast address will be able to respond — it is like a NetBIOS group name and can be used to identify systems that are running a service.

You can use three different formats to express an IPv6 address.

✦ The preferred format represents the address in eight fields of 16 bits. The 16 bits are represented as a string of four hex digits. For example: 1079:0005:AB45:5F4C:0010:BA97:0043:34AB.

✦ You can suppress leading zeros in any of the eight fields. There must, however, be at least one digit in each of the eight fields. For example: 1079:5:AB45:5F4C:10:BA97:43:34AB.

✦ Many assigned IPv6 addresses contain long strings of zeros. There is a special syntax for these addresses. In place of the zeros, you can use "::". For example, the address 1090:0:0:0:0:876:AABC: 1234 can be written as 1090::876:AABC: 1234.

Wireless Internet

It's almost impossible to go anywhere these days without running into someone talking on a cell phone. Cell phones have become a part of everyday life to such an extent that some people we know don't have a home phone; rather, everyone in the family has a cell phone. There is an incredible push for the cell phone to do more and more and to be our connection to the rest of the world.

Most of the phones that are being sold today come with a utility called a *mobile browser* — a Web browser built directly into the phone. The digital cell phone is a really a node on a digital network. This means that the phone itself is converting analog (voice) to digital signals and then transmitting the data in a digital fashion using a radio transceiver. The signals then go into the carrier's digital network and are routed to the person you called. At some point, the digital information is converted back to analog and your voice can be heard.

Computers are digital (meaning simply that they use 0s and 1s to store and process information). So, it makes sense that if you have a digital network, a digital cell, and a digital laptop, you should be able to communicate over the cell phone connection. If you have a PDA (such as a Blackberry) with a built-in modem, you don't even need the cell phone. Data is sent using circuit switching with runs at 9,600 bps or by using Short Message Service (SMS) for messaging.

The latest addition to circuit switching and SMS, General Packet Radio Service (GPRS), is being introduced. GPRS promises to take us into the third generation of wireless systems. GPRS is being introduced to efficiently transport high-speed data over the current wireless network infrastructures. GPRS signaling and data traffic do not travel through the cellular network. The cellular network is *only* used to look up GPRS user profile data. Depending on the implementation, GPRS can use between 1 and 8 radio channel timeslots, which can be shared.

In GPRS, the user's data is broken into packets and transported over separate Public Land Mobile Networks (PLMNs) using an IP backbone. Once on the IP backbone (IPv4 or IPv6), it can be routed anywhere. Thus, GPRS provides much greater speeds than the existing technology (14,400 bps to 115,000 bps, compared to 9,600 bps). It makes the mobile phone or device a *practical* way to access the Internet. Because of the ability to use a range of bandwidths, GPRS allows for both shortburst traffic, such as e-mail and Web browsing, and large transfers that will make cellular laptop use practical. Additionally, GPRS supports Quality of Service, so service providers can offer priority services to users. In the near future, you should be able to get better graphics and be able to do more with the mobile browser that you have in your phone. However, you might want to upgrade that phone (since surfing on a 2×40 character display is annoying, to say the least). It would, of course, be great if you could connect to the Internet directly from your PDA. Although it is possible to connect from a PDA with a built-in modem such as the Palm VIIx or the RIM Blackberry, you can get an add-on modem that will allow you to connect to the Internet for other cases.

The current challenge is to integrate the functions of a PDA and the connectivity of a cell phone into a usable package. Several manufacturers have already achieved this, to a greater or lesser degree. As with all first-generation products, look for them to improve and rapidly come down in price.

Wireless Application Protocol (WAP) is the general term applied to a set of protocols that were defined in an initiative driven by Unwired Planet, Motorola, Nokia, and Ericsson. In the near future, there will be a great many advances made in WAP for the growing army of mobile workers.

With the current bandwidth limitations and graphics restrictions, you can't just jump onto a Web package and start surfing. The information that goes to your cell phone or radio-enabled PDA should be a little different than normal content. Having said that, in most cases, you can hit a regular Web page; however, you do this through a WAP gateway. The gateway will act like a proxy server, getting the page you requested and then sending it to you. Keep in mind that it will also strip the graphics and other features on the Web page that your phone doesn't support.

As with TCP/IP and nearly every other networking technology, there are multiple layers in the WAP protocol:

> ✦ **Transport layer** — Wireless Datagram Protocol (WDP)
>
> ✦ **Security layer** — Wireless Transport Layer Security (WTLS)
>
> ✦ **Transaction layer** — Wireless Transaction Protocol (WTP)
>
> ✦ **Session layer** — Wireless Session Protocol (WSP)
>
> ✦ **Application layer** — Wireless Application Environment (WAE)

Wireless Datagram Protocol

Like the Physical layer in the TCP/IP stack, the Wireless Datagram Protocol (WDP) layer operates above the data carrier services — which, like the Network Access layer, manage the movement of the 0s and 1s that make up the data. This serves to isolate the upper-layer protocols from the details of the underlying network.

Wireless Transport Layer Security

Based on Secure Sockets Layer or Transport Layer Security (which is an emerging new definition of SSL), the Wireless Transport Layer Security (WTLS) protocol is intended for use with the WAP transport protocols and is optimized for use over narrow-band communication channels. WTLS provides the following features:

> ✦ **Data integrity and privacy** — WTLS provides data encryption so that data transmitted between the server and the device is secured. It also ensures that data is not changed in transit.

✦ **Authentication** — As we saw in Chapter 22, it is possible to use SSL to authenticate both the server and client. These functions are included in WTLS.

✦ **Denial-of-service protection** — Since a session key is used, relay attacks can be detected and rejected.

This layer of the protocol stack is optional and under the control of the application being used. In addition, this layer can be used between devices and between the server and the device.

Wireless Transaction Protocol

The Wireless Transaction Protocol (WTP) is essentially a combination of TCP and UDP. In fact, it can provide similar levels of service. Data can be sent one way in either reliable or unreliable forms, which are like TCP and UDP, with an acknowledgement for the single packet. Also, a reliable form of communication is possible (which is like the TCP protocol). By combining the functions of TCP and UDP, the need to load an extra protocol is reduced.

With WTP, data that is to be transmitted can be concentrated. Thus, rather than sending five segments, only one would be needed — the amount of concentration depends on the underlying network. In addition, asynchronous transactions and delayed acknowledgements are possible.

Wireless Session Protocol

Wireless Session Protocol (WSP) is the equivalent of the Session layer in the TCP/IP stack. It provides an interface for the Application layer to the lower-level protocols. WSP can use either the connection-oriented Transaction layer or it can communicate directly with the Transport layer. At this point in time, WSP provides mainly services, which are suited to browsing applications; however, this limitation will change as the protocols mature and evolve.

Wireless Application Environment

At the time of writing, the Application layer essentially provides a framework for future development. The developers are hoping to provide a single cross-platform environment or Wireless Application Environment (WAE) that can be easily supported by all vendors. Thus, developers will be able to deploy applications that will work on many different platforms. At this point, there is really only a micro-browser with the following components:

✦ **Wireless Markup Language (WML)** — A lightweight markup language that is, in fact, an XML application. It has been optimized for use in hand-held mobile devices.

✦ **WMLScript** — A lightweight scripting language that is similar to JavaScript.

✦ **Wireless Telephony Application (WTA, WTAI)** — Telephony services and programming interfaces.

✦ **Content Formats** — A set of data formats that are well defined and include images, phonebook records, and calendar information.

Of course, these protocols are just what the phones come with now. As we move forward, the PDA and phone will becomes one device and more options will be available, which will lead to the use of larger operating systems. A battle for the dominant operating system in the smart appliances world is already being waged between different manufacturers.

Smart Appliances

What is a smart appliance? To be honest, most appliances sold over the last few years are smart - in the sense that they have on-board computers and some form of operating environment. However, the trend over the last few years has been to build more and more complex operating environments into *all* types of devices. And this trend is starting to include connectivity — in other words, devices are being developed that can communicate with each other and with vendors and suppliers.

The goal of developers seems to be to give you connectivity from anywhere. They want you to have "information at your fingertips" (Bill Gates's philosophy), although some would claim that this goes to extremes. For example, do we really want a refrigerator that can order groceries, an oven that can turn on based on the location provided by the GPS attached to your car, or a stereo that can tune into the Internet? Maybe we'll even get to the point when a toothbrush can notify your dentist that you have a cavity.

There are Orwellian overtones to this discussion, but the reality is, these devices are on their way. Many people can already surf the Internet from their television set, or listen to music piped in from the Internet. You can already buy a refrigerator or microwave oven that has a browser built into the door. Obviously, the development of these kinds of devices raises a host of privacy issues. We have to trust manufacturers not to gather personal information about us. We can almost guarantee that you will soon see advertising coming to a toaster near you.

Now we turn to a more practical concern. What operating system will run these devices? What will the capabilities of that operating system be? There are three main contenders in the battle for the device market: Microsoft's Windows CE operating system; the JavaOS for Appliances operating system from Sun; and an operating system from Lucent called Inferno. None of these operating systems have appeared to win the battle yet. The market (just think about the number of devices you have in your house) may end up being split among the operating systems. Let's take a look at Windows CE as an example of these operating systems, since it appears to have an early lead.

Microsoft had to jump into the embedded systems market, and they did so with not one — but three — different embedded operating systems. In all cases, they have brought a fairly full version of Windows to the embedded world. An obvious question is: why do they need more than one embedded operating system?

Windows CE is a version of Windows 98 that has been adapted fully to the embedded marketplace, providing some key design features needed to operate and still be stored on a ROM chip. This includes modularity — in other words, the operating system has been broken down into some 200 different modules that can be combined to provide the exact environment that the manufacturer needs. The modularization of the operating system allows the manufacturer to take out those parts that are not needed, which allows the operating system to be stripped down to as little as 400K. This means that it is possible to actually remove the interface or adapt it if required.

The other two choices from Microsoft for an embedded operating system are Embedded NT and Windows 2000 with the Server Appliance Kit, although these operating systems are intended more for small mobile PCs and dedicated servers, where the OS is built directly into the computer hardware.

In general, Embedded NT and Windows 2000 with the Server Appliance Kit are robust — in other words, you won't have to reboot your fridge as often. There is a price to pay though — each of these operating systems has a much larger footprint (memory requirement) than Windows CE.

This section focuses on Windows CE, because it is the embedded OS that will be used for smart appliances. In a nutshell, Windows CE is a version of Windows that was designed to run on embedded devices. Its main features include:

✦ **Componentization** — The operating system is made up of 200-odd components, allowing the device manufacturer to choose the components they need. This also allows for a memory footprint of as little as 400 kilobits.

✦ **Processor-independent** — Microsoft provides broad hardware support for 180 CPUs and hundreds of Board Service Packages (BSPs), buses, storage media, and device drivers. In addition, manufacturers can build their hardware support with Platform Builder tools.

✦ **Real-time operation** — The operating system supports real-time operation, with features like bounded deterministic response times, reduced interrupt latencies, 256 priority levels, nested interrupt support, and virtual memory protection.

However, the real advantage of Windows CE is that developers will have a familiar "playground" to work in. Microsoft has invested many resources into making sure that developers will be able to move to the Windows CE world quickly (since one of the keys to winning the OS battle is to have the developers and the applications available when the manufacturers need them). Windows CE provides developers with these additional features:

✦ **Development environment** — Windows CE has a comprehensive development environment with integrated development and testing tools. These tools provide the same visual environment as Visual Studio and the common Win32 programming model.

✦ **Extensibility** — The componentization of the operating system includes the ability for manufacturers and third parties to develop drop-in operating system components.

✦ **Microsoft support** — Microsoft's developer support provides worldwide support and a partner network spanning 200 system integrators, more than 60 third-party application developers, and 28 silicon vendors.

✦ **Standard services** — Windows CE includes many of the standard services developers are used to in Windows programming, including DCOM, ADO, and Microsoft Message Queue Service (MSMQ).

✦ **Internet services** — Windows CE includes a customizable version of Internet Explorer and a Web server, as well as Extensible Markup Language (XML) support.

✦ **ActiveX Data Objects (ADO)** — ADO provides the developer with the ability to connect to data services, as well as work with data locally.

✦ **Internet Connection Sharing (ICS)** — ICS allows for the development of Windows CE 3.0–based devices that can share Internet access.

✦ **TCP/IP services** — Windows CE provides support for Domain Name System and Windows Internet Name Service, Telephony API (TAPI), and Simple Network Management Protocol.

With all these tools available for developers, many CE applications are likely to appear in the current handheld devices. In this arena, Microsoft has a great advantage, since many users and developers are already used to the Windows environment.

Planning for the Future

The best way to plan for the future is to build a solid network that allows for the growth that you predict for your company over the next few years. As you build your network, keep in mind the discussions in this book. They will help you expand your network and incorporate new protocols and services. Just as important, monitor your network servers to ensure that they continue to function properly; upgrade or replace them as required.

Also, keep informed about changes that are occurring in the market. If you are aware that changes are coming, and you have already looked at the new technologies, you can start developing a strategy to implement them in your own network.

Build a lab that you and your staff can use to test new services that will be introduced on a network. The lab should mimic your actual network as much as possible.

Changing parts of your network can be stressful. However, it's a certainty that the computer industry is never going to stand still, so you might as well deal with the changes. Plan your network so that it can adapt to change, test protocols under real network conditions, and implement new services and protocols in a measured and controlled way — doing so will ensure that your network continues to function.

Summary

This chapter has presented an overview of some of the new technologies that you will likely deal with in the near future. First, we looked at IPv6, which is now starting to build the Internet mark II. Then we discussed the wireless Internet, which will provide us with connectivity anytime from anywhere. You were introduced to "Big Brother," who will soon be coming to a fridge or microwave near you. With embedded operating systems such as Windows CE, you can expect to see more and more devices that talk and display information on a screen.

In the last part of the chapter, we looked at the real issues surrounding planning for these types of technological changes. In the end, strong testing and managed implementations of the protocols will be necessary. There are, of course, hundreds of new developments we could have discussed — enough to fill books — but what we have looked at in this chapter are key developments that will affect TCP/IP.

✦　　✦　　✦

DNS Top-Level Domains

DNS top-level domains are grouped into three categories: generic, special, and country code. Generic and special TLDs are used by U.S. industries and government with the exception of the .com domain, which everyone seems to be using. The country code TLDs are used for industry and government based outside the United States. This appendix lists the contents of these categories as of June 2001. Note that many countries have chosen to implement gTLDs and sTLDs as subdomains to their own ccTLDs. An updated listing of top-level domains may be found at www.alldomains.com.

Generic Top-Level Domains

Generic top-level domains (gTLDs) are used in the United States and abroad for commercial for-profit companies, networking firms, and non-profit organizations. gTLDs are:

- ◆ **Com** — Commercial organizations
- ◆ **Net** — Networking organizations
- ◆ **Org** — Non-profit organizations

Special Top-Level Domains

Special top-level domains (sTLDs) are used in the United States for government departments, and the U.S. military. sTLDs are:

- ◆ **Gov** — U.S. government departments
- ◆ **Int** — International organizations
- ◆ **Mil** — U.S. military

Country Code Top-Level Domains and Subdomains

Countries, other than the United States, have their own top-level domains and subdomains. The following is a current list of ccTLDs, followed by their country and subdomains:

- ✦ **Ac — Ascension Island**
  - Com.ac
  - Edu.ac
  - Gov.ac
  - Mil.ac
  - Net.ac
  - Org.a
- ✦ **Ad — Andorra**
- ✦ **Ae — United Arab Emirates**
  - Com.ae
  - Net.ae
  - Org.ae
- ✦ **Af — Afghanistan**
- ✦ **Ag — Antigua**
- ✦ **Ai — Anquilla**
- ✦ **Al — Albania**
- ✦ **Am — Armenia**
- ✦ **An — Antilles**
- ✦ **Ao — Angola**
- ✦ **Aq — Antarctica**
- ✦ **Ar — Argentina**
  - Com.ar
  - Net.ar
  - Org.ar
- ✦ **As — American Samoa**

✦ **At — Austria**
- Ac.at
- Co.at

✦ **Au — Australia**
- Asn.au
- Com.au
- Conf.au
- Csiro.au
- Gov.au
- Id.au
- Info.au
- Net.au
- Org.au
- Org.au
- Oz.au
- Telememo.au

✦ **Aw — Aruba**

✦ **Az — Azerbaijan**
- Com.az
- Net.az
- Org.az

✦ **Ba — Bosnia**

✦ **Bb — Barbados**
- Com.bb
- Net.bb
- Org.bb

✦ **Bd — Bangladesh**

✦ **Be — Belgium**

✦ **Bf — Burkina Faso**

✦ **Bg — Bulgaria**

✦ **Bh — Bahrain**

- ✦ **Bi — Burundi**
- ✦ **Bj — Benin**
- ✦ **Bm — Bermuda**
  - Com.bm
  - Edu.bm
  - Gov.bm
  - Net.bm
  - Org.bm
- ✦ **Bn — Brunei**
- ✦ **Bo — Bolivia**
- ✦ **Br — Brazil**
  - Art.br
  - Com.br
  - Esp.br
  - Etc.br
  - G12.br
  - Gov.br
  - Ind.br
  - Inf.br
  - Mil.br
  - Net.br
  - Org.br
  - Psi.br
  - Rec.br
  - Tmp.br
- ✦ **Bs — The Bahamas**
  - Com.bs
  - Net.bs
  - Org.bs
- ✦ **Bt — Bhutan**
- ✦ **Bv — Bouvet Island**
- ✦ **Bw — Botswana**
- ✦ **By — Belarus**

◆ **Bz—Belize**

◆ **Ca—Canada**

  • Ab.ca

  • Bc.ca

  • Mb.ca

  • Nb.ca

  • Nf.ca

  • Ns.ca

  • Nt.ca

  • On.ca

  • Pe.ca

  • Qc.ca

  • Sk.ca

  • Yk.ca

◆ **Cc—Cocos Island.**

◆ **Cf—Central African Republic.**

◆ **Cg—Congo**

◆ **Ch—Switzerland**

◆ **Ci—Cote d'Ivoire**

◆ **Ck—Cook Island**

  • Co.ck

◆ **Cl—Chile**

◆ **Cm—Cameroon**

◆ **Cn—China**

  • Ac.cn

  • Ah.cn

  • Bj.cn

  • Com.cn

  • Cq.cn

  • Edu.cn

  • Gd.cn

  • Gov.cn

  • Gs.cn

- Gx.cn
- Gz.cn
- Hb.cn
- He.cn
- Hi.cn
- Hk.cn
- Hl.cn
- Hn.cn
- Jl.cn
- Js.cn
- Ln.cn
- Mo.cn
- Net.cn
- Nm.cn
- Nx.cn
- Org.cn
- Qh.cn
- Sc.cn
- Sh.cn
- Sn.cn
- Sx.cn
- Tj.cn
- Tw.cn
- Xj.cn
- Xz.cn
- Yn.cn
- Zj.cn

✦ **Co — Colombia**

- Arts.co
- Com.co
- Edu.co
- Firm.co
- Gov.co

- Info.co
- Int.co
- Mil.co
- Nom.co
- Org.co
- Rec.co
- Store.co
- Web.co

✦ **Cr — Costa Rica**

- Ac.cr
- Co.cr
- Ed.cr
- Fi.cr
- Go.cr
- Or.cr
- Sa.cr

✦ **Cu — Cuba**

- Com.cu
- Net.cu
- Org.cu

✦ **Cv — Cape Verde**

✦ **Cx — Christmas Island**

✦ **Cy — Cyprus**

- Ac.cy
- Com.cy
- Gov.cy
- Net.cy
- Org.cy

✦ **Cz — Czech Republic**

✦ **De — Germany**

✦ **Dj — Djibouti**

✦ **Dk — Denmark**

✦ **Dm — Dominica**

- ✦ **Do — Dominican Republic**
  - Art.do
  - Com.do
  - Edu.do
  - Gov.do
  - Mil.do
  - Net.do
  - Org.do
  - Web.do
- ✦ **Dz — Algeria**
- ✦ **Ec — Ecuador**
  - Com.ec
  - K12.ec
  - Edu.ec
  - Fin.ec
  - Med.ec
  - Gov.ec
  - Mil.ec
  - Org.ec
  - Net.ec
- ✦ **Ee — Estonia**
- ✦ **Eg — Egypt**
  - Com.eg
  - Edu.eg
  - Eun.eg
  - Gov.eg
  - Net.eg
  - Org.eg
  - Sci.eg
- ✦ **Eh — Western Sahara**
- ✦ **Er — Eritrea**
- ✦ **Es — Spain**

✦ **Et — Ethiopia**

✦ **Fi — Finland**

✦ **Fj — Fiji**

- Ac.fj
- Com.fj
- Gov.fj
- Id.fj
- Org.fj
- School.fj

✦ **Fk — Falkland Islands**

✦ **Fm — Micronesia**

✦ **Fo — Faroe Island**

✦ **Fr — France**

✦ **Fx — France, Metropolitan**

✦ **Ga — Gabon**

✦ **Gb — United Kingdom**

✦ **Gd — Grenada**

✦ **Ge — Georgia**

- Com.ge
- Edu.ge
- Gov.ge
- Mil.ge
- Net.ge
- Org.ge
- Pvt.ge

✦ **Gf — French Guiana**

✦ **Gg — Channel Islands, Guernsey**

- Ac.gg
- Alderney.gg
- Co.gg
- Gov.gg
- Guernsey.gg

- Ind.gg
- Ltd.gg
- Net.gg
- Org.gg
- Sark.gg
- Sch.gg

✦ **Gh — Ghana**

✦ **Gi — Gibraltar**

✦ **Gl — Greenland**

✦ **Gm — Gambia**

✦ **Gn — Guinea**

✦ **Gp — Guadeloupe**

✦ **Gq — Equatorial Guinea**

✦ **Gr — Greece**

✦ **Gs — South Georgia and the South Sandwich Islands**

✦ **Gt — Guatemala**

✦ **Gu — Guam**

- Com.gu
- Edu.gu
- Gov.gu
- Mil.gu
- Net.gu
- Org.gu

✦ **Gw — Guinea Bissau**

✦ **Gy — Guyana**

✦ **Hk — Hong Kong**

- Com.hk
- Net.hk
- Org.hk

✦ **Hm — Heard Island**

✦ **Hn — Honduras**

✦ **Hr — Croatia**

✦ **Ht — Haiti**

✦ **Hu — Hungary**

- Co.hu
- Info.hu
- Nui.hu
- Org.hu
- Priv.hu
- Tm.hu

✦ **Id — Indonesia**

- Ac.id
- Co.id
- Go.id
- Mil.id
- Net.id
- Or.id

✦ **Ie — Ireland**

✦ **Il — Israel**

- Ac.il
- Co.il
- Gov.il
- K12.il
- Muni.il
- Net.il
- Org.il

✦ **Im — Isle of Man**

- Ac.im
- Co.im
- Gov.im
- Lkd.co.im
- Net.im

- Nic.im
- Org.im
- Plc.co.im

✦ **In — India**

- Ac.in
- Co.in
- Ernet.in
- Gov.in
- Net.in
- Nic.in
- Res.in

✦ **Io — British Indian Ocean Territory**

✦ **Iq — Iraq**

✦ **Ir — Iran**

✦ **Is — Iceland**

✦ **It — Italy**

✦ **Je — Channel Islands, Jersey**

- Ac.je
- Co.je
- Gov.je
- Ind.je
- Jersey.je
- Ltd.je
- Net.je
- Org.je
- Sch.je

✦ **Jm — Jamaica**

✦ **Jo — Jordan**

- Com.jo
- Gov.jo
- Edu.jo
- Net.jo

✦ **Jp — Japan**

- Ac.jp
- Ad.jp
- Co.jp
- Gov.jp
- Net.jp
- Org.jp

✦ **Ke — Kenya**

✦ **Kg — Kyrgyzstan**

✦ **Kh — Cambodia**

- Com.kh
- Net.kh
- Org.kh

✦ **Ki — Kiribati**

✦ **Km — Comoros**

✦ **Kn — St. Kitts & Nevis**

✦ **Kp — North Korea**

✦ **Kr — South Korea**

- Ac.kr
- Co.kr
- Go.kr
- Nm.kr
- Or.kr
- Re.kr

✦ **Kw — Kuwait**

✦ **Ky — Cayman Islands**

✦ **Kz — Kazakhstan**

✦ **La — Laos**

- Com.la
- Net.la
- Org.la

- ✦ **Lb — Lebanon**
  - Com.lb
  - Gov.lb
  - Mil.lb
  - Net.lb
  - Org.lb
- ✦ **Lc — Saint Lucia**
  - Com.lc
  - Edu.lc
  - Gov.lc
  - Net.lc
  - Org.lc
- ✦ **Li — Liechtenstein**
- ✦ **Lk — Sri Lanka**
- ✦ **Lr — Liberia**
- ✦ **Ls — Lesotho**
- ✦ **Lt — Lithuania**
- ✦ **Lu — Luxembourg**
- ✦ **Lv — Latvia**
  - Asn.lv
  - Com.lv
  - Conf.lv
  - Edu.lv
  - Gov.lv
  - Id.lv
  - Mil.lv
  - Net.lv
  - Org.lv
- ✦ **Ly — Libya**
  - Com.ly
  - Net.ly
  - Org.ly

- ✦ Ma — Morocco
- ✦ Mc — Monaco
- ✦ Md — Moldova
- ✦ Mg — Madagascar
- ✦ Mh — Marshall Island
- ✦ Mk — Macedonia
- ✦ Ml — Mali
- ✦ Mm — Myanmar
  - Edu.mm
  - Com.mm
  - Gov.mm
  - Net.mm
  - Org.mm
- ✦ Mn — Mongolia
- ✦ Mo — Macao
  - Com.mo
  - Edu.mo
  - Gov.mo
  - Net.mo
  - Org.mo
- ✦ Mp — Northern Mariana Islands
- ✦ Mq — Martinique
- ✦ Mr — Mauritania
- ✦ Ms — Montserrat
- ✦ Mt — Malta
  - Com.mt
  - Net.mt
  - Org.mt
- ✦ Mu — Mauritius
- ✦ Mv — Maldives
- ✦ Mw — Malawi

- ✦ **Mx — Mexico**
    - Com.mx
    - Net.mx
    - Org.mx
- ✦ **My — Malaysia**
    - Com.my
    - Edu.my
    - Gov.my
    - Net.my
    - Org.my
- ✦ **Mz — Mozambique**
- ✦ **Na — Namibia**
    - Com.na
    - Net.na
    - Org.na
- ✦ **Nc — New Caledonia**
    - Com.nc
    - Net.nc
    - Org.nc
- ✦ **Ne — Niger**
- ✦ **Nf — Norfolk Island**
- ✦ **Ng — Nigeria**
- ✦ **Ni — Nicaragua**
    - Com.ni
- ✦ **Nl — Netherlands**
- ✦ **No — Norway**
- ✦ **Np — Nepal**
    - Com.np
    - Net.np
    - Ort.np
- ✦ **Nr — Nauru**

- ✦ **Nu — Niue**
- ✦ **Nz — New Zealand**
  - Ac.nz
  - Co.nz
  - Gen.nz
  - Govt.nz
  - Net.nz
  - Org.nz
- ✦ **Om — Oman**
- ✦ **Pa — Panama**
  - Ac.pa
  - Com.pa
  - Edu.pa
  - Gob.pa
  - Net.pa
  - Org.pa
  - Sld.pa
- ✦ **Pe — Peru**
  - Com.pe
  - Net.pe
  - Org.pe
- ✦ **Pf — Polynesia**
- ✦ **Pg — Papua New Guinea**
- ✦ **Ph — Philippines**
  - Com.ph
  - Mil.ph
  - Net.ph
  - Ngo.ph
  - Org.ph
- ✦ **Pk — Pakistan**

- **Pl — Poland**
  - Com.pl
  - Net.pl
  - Rg.pl
- **Pm — St. Pierre**
- **Pn — Pitcairn**
- **Pr — Puerto Rico**
- **Pt — Portugal**
- **Pw — Palau**
- **Py — Paraguay**
  - Com.py
  - Edu.py
  - Net.py
  - Org.py
- **Qa — Qatar**
- **Re — Reunion**
- **Ro — Romania**
- **Ru — Russia**
  - Com.ru
  - Net.ru
  - Org.ru
- **Rw — Rwanda**
- **Sa — Saudi Arabia**
- **Sb — Solomon Island**
- **Sc — Seychelles**
- **Sd — Sudan**
- **Se — Sweden**
- **Sg — Singapore**
  - Com.sg
  - Edu.sg
  - Gov.sg
  - Net.sg
  - Org.sg

✦ **Sh — St. Helena**
- Com.sh
- Edu.sh
- Gov.sh
- Mil.sh
- Net.sh
- Org.sh

✦ **Si — Slovenia**

✦ **Sj — Svalbard**

✦ **Sk — Slovakia**

✦ **Sl — Sierra Leone**

✦ **Sm — San Marino**

✦ **Sn — Senegal**

✦ **So — Somalia**

✦ **Sr — Suriname**

✦ **St — Sao Tome**

✦ **Sv — Salvador**
- Co.sv

✦ **Sy — Syria**
- Com.sy
- Net.sy
- Org.sy

✦ **Sz — Swaziland**

✦ **Tc — Turks & Caicos Island**

✦ **Td — Chad**

✦ **Tf — French Southern Territories**

✦ **Tg — Togo**

✦ **Th — Thailand**
- Ac.th
- Co.th
- Go.th
- Net.th
- Or.th

+ **Tj — Tajikistan**
+ **Tk — Tokelau**
+ **Tm — Turkmenistan**
+ **Tn — Tunisia**
  - Com.tn
  - Edunet.tn
  - Ens.tn
  - Fin.tn
  - Gov.tn
  - Ind.tn
  - Info.tn
  - Intl.tn
  - Nat.tn
  - Net.tn
  - Org.tn
  - Rnrt.tn
  - Rns.tn
  - Rnu.tn
  - Tourism.tn
+ **To — Tonga**
+ **Tp — East Timor**
+ **Tr — Turkey**
  - Bbs.tr
  - Com.tr
  - Edu.tr
  - Gov.tr
  - K12.tr
  - Mil.tr
  - Net.tr
  - Org.tr
+ **Tt — Trinidad**

- ✦ **Tv — Tuvalu**
- ✦ **Tw — Taiwan**
  - Com.tw
  - Edu.tw
  - Gove.tw
  - Net.tw
  - Org.tw
- ✦ **Tz — Tanzania**
- ✦ **Ua — Ukraine**
  - Com.ua
  - Gov.ua
  - Net.ua
- ✦ **Ug — Uganda**
  - Ac.ug
  - Co.ug
  - Go.ug
  - Or.ug
- ✦ **Uk — United Kingdom**
  - Ac.uk
  - Co.uk
  - Gov.uk
  - Ltd.uk
  - Mod.uk
  - Net.uk
  - Nhs.uk
  - Org.uk
  - Plc.uk
  - Police.uk
  - Sch.uk
- ✦ **Um — U.S. Minor Island**
- ✦ **Us — United States**

- ✦ **Uy — Uruguay**
  - Com.uy
  - Edu.uy
  - Net.uy
  - Org.uy
- ✦ **Uz — Uzbekistan**
- ✦ **Va — Vatican City**
- ✦ **Vc — St. Vincent**
- ✦ **Ve — Venezuela**
  - Arts.ve
  - Bib.ve
  - Co.ve
  - Com.ve
  - Edu.ve
  - Firm.ve
  - Gov.ve
  - Info.ve
  - Int.ve
  - Mil.ve
  - Net.ve
  - Nom.ve
  - Org.ve
  - Rec.ve
  - Store.ve
  - Tec.ve
  - Web.ve
- ✦ **Vg — Virgin Islands (British)**
- ✦ **Vi — Virgin Islands (U.S.)**
  - Co.vi
  - Net.vi
  - Org.vi

✦ **Vn — Vietnam**

✦ **Vu — Vanuatu**

✦ **Wf — Wallis & Futuna Islands**

✦ **Ws — Samoa**

✦ **Ye — Yemen**

✦ **Yt — Mayotte**

✦ **Yu — Yugoslavia**

- Ac.yu

- Co.yu

- Edu.yu

- Org.yu

✦ **Za — South Africa**

- Ac.za

- Alt.za

- Co.za

- Edu.za

- Gov.za

- Mil.za

- Net.za

- Ngo.za

- Nom.za

- Org.za

- School.za

- Tm.za

- Web.za

✦ **Zm — Zambia**

✦ **Zr — Zaire**

✦ **Zw — Zimbabwe**

✦   ✦   ✦

Index

Printed in the United States
69510LVS00006B/49